Readers and Reviewers Praise the Previous Edition

The authors extract the most useful features, tips, and shortcuts —things that you would never discover without lots of time spent in forums and mailing lists....I own every book, manual, video, and interactive CD-ROM ever written or produced about GoLive and CyberStudio. I've long since packed them away in boxes. Except for two: *Real World Adobe GoLive 4* and *Real World Adobe GoLive 5*. For now at least, they have no peer. Not even close. — *Steve J., GoLive consultant, San Francisco*

The smarter I get with GoLive, the more help your book offers. I refer to it a lot. — *Iain J., Spain*

I've read a lot of good books on computers, graphics, etc., in order to learn what the heck I'm doing. But none of them have been indispensable, and I would readily loan the others to friends. This one, however, is **mine, mine, mine**! — *Gay W., San Diego*

This book digs deep and delivers nuggets of pure gold. — *Ralph S., Milwaukie*

Real World Adobe GoLive 5 is an important asset and reference book for the GoLive user. — *Amazon.com editorial review*

This book isn't a quick start guide on how to use each tool, …[rather], it is a production oriented book with tons of advice and tips. This is an exhaustive and comprehensive work. — *Joyce Evans, The Internet Eye Magazine*

Your book is dynamite; it has cleared up mysteries that have been plaguing me since day one, using the old German version of GoLive CyberStudio. One of the best computer books I've ever encountered. Needless to say, I am planning to order your next book. — *Lito T.-J.*

It's my website production "Bible" and I wouldn't be without it. — *Lindsay B.*

Real World
Adobe
GoLive 6

by

Jeff Carlson

Glenn Fleishman

For Lynn D. and Kimberly

Real World Adobe GoLive 6

By Jeff Carlson and Glenn Fleishman

Copyright © 2002 by Jeff Carlson and Glenn Fleishman

Peachpit Press

1249 Eighth Street
Berkeley, CA 94710
510/524-2178 or 800/283-9444 (voice)
510/524-2221 (fax)

Find us on the World Wide Web at: http://www.peachpit.com.
To report errors, please send a note to errata@peachpit.com.
Peachpit Press is a division of Pearson Education.

Real World Adobe GoLive 6 is published in association with Adobe Press.

For resources mentioned in this book, see: http://www.realworldgolive.com/six/

Editor: Serena Herr
Production Coordinator: Connie-Jeung Mills
Copy Editor: Don Sellers
Proofreaders: Charles Fleishman, Helen Meyers, Liane Thomas
Interior design: Jeff Carlson
Interior illustration: Jeff Tolbert
Book production: Don Sellers, Jeff Tolbert
Cover design: Gee + Chung Design
Cover illustration: Jeff Brice
Indexer: Caroline Parks
Space images throughout: NASA (www.nasa.gov)

Colophon

This book was written in Microsoft Word v. X, and created using Adobe Photoshop 6 and 7, Adobe Illustrator 10, Adobe LiveMotion 2, Adobe GoLive 6 (of course), SnapzProX (Mac), HyperSnapX (Windows), and QuarkXPress 4.11—with a liberal use of Qualcomm Eudora, Entourage v. X, Timbuktu Pro, and Linux boxes running Red Hat 7—on a variety of computers, including a generic Pentium II, Connectix Virtual PC 5, a Macintosh G4 Cube, some iBooks, a Titanium PowerBook G4, and several others. The fonts used are Adobe Minion and Formata.

ISBN 0-201-88298-1

9 8 7 6 5 4 3 2 1

Printed and bound in the United States of America

Foreword

By John Kranz, senior product manager, Adobe GoLive

Programs are shaped by users, not engineers. Glenn and Jeff asked me to share some insights into the influences that shaped GoLive 6 into the product they so masterfully cover in these pages.

As with any Adobe software product, we conduct research to find which elements customers consider most critical as we move from release to release. GoLive 6 represents not only the efforts of the Adobe employees who designed and programmed this product, but, more importantly, the countless customers who we've heard from on an informal or formal basis.

Special thanks are due to our GoLive Advisory Council members, beta customers, and particularly to Jeff and Glenn who have an incredible knowledge not only about our product, but about Web publishing in general. The amount of feedback and data received is truly staggering, but it all came together to tell us which elements were crucial for this release.

At times, we feel like Martha Stewart, concocting what we hope will be received as the perfect Web publishing recipe. Initial press coverage of GoLive 6 and customer testimonials help us feel that we've listened and responded well.

A few key areas proved most important to users. I'd like to walk through these in the same divisions Jeff and Glenn used for sections in the book.

Building Pages

Usability research—watching customers actually work with the program itself—played an important role here. We refined the user interface to ensure a simpler workflow for creating and working with pages.

Managing screen real estate. GoLive 6 introduces custom workspaces and palette stashing. You no longer need to continuously move and adjust palette positions; their locations can be saved and defined as a set—a top customer feature request. Stashing palettes was enthusiastically received during the early testing cycle as another way to help manage screen real estate.

Table layout. Customer interviews and workflow studies confirmed that working with HTML tables, particularly nested tables, can be a great challenge. We added nested table navigation to the Table palette to allow for easy zooming in and out of nested tables.

Table correction. GoLive uses a visual indicator (red numbers) to point out any table sizes that are incorrectly put together. An auto-correct feature, clicking the red number in the Table palette, rewrites the code to be browser legal.

Product integration. The Smart Object concept introduced in GoLive 5 goes much further in 6. The biggest improvement lies in including support for Variables in native Adobe source files. You can modify elements of a Photoshop, Illustrator, or LiveMotion file directly within GoLive without affecting the original file.

Code and Servers

When all is said and done, it's the code that matters most to many customers, particularly HTML purists. In this new release, we knew that three areas were critical: DTD validation of source code (think of it as syntax-checking on steroids), Section 508 compliance for accessible pages, and Dynamic Content and server-side scripting/database integration.

DTD validation. The integrity of the HTML source code is always at the forefront of our customers' minds. GoLive 6 introduces a robust treatment for source syntax checking, by relying on the Document Type Definition (DTD) for each major HTML specification as defined by the World Wide Web Consortium (W3C, www.w3c.org). The result is a comprehensive diagnostic check of markup language, including visual feedback for errors uncovered in the source code syntax.

Section 508 compliance. Section 508 is a U.S. Federal code that requires governmental agencies' electronic resources and information technology be fully accessible to people with disabilities. This has had a ripple effect on corporate and privately-run Web sites as well—adobe.com itself being one. GoLive 6 adds accessibility validation through the Site Reports feature. An entire Web site can be checked for common requirements, and GoLive indicates which problems appear.

Dynamic Content and server-side scripting/database integration. More and more pages created for the Web are dynamic in nature, whether through a simple server-side include, or a complex Web-based application. GoLive extended its 5.0 support for ASP (Active Server Pages) to now include the commonly used server scripting languages JSP (JavaServer Pages) and PHP (PHP: Hypertext Preprocessor) in GoLive 6.

Customer feedback and usability results showed that Web designers require more assistance in creating and configuring a dynamic Web site; the process of setting up a proper server environment was often found more difficult than creating the pages itself! (When you read Chapter 23 of this book, *Building Dynamic Content*, you'll see why.)

The streamlined user interface in GoLive 6—including a new Dynamic Site Wizard, a new tab in the Objects palette for Dynamic Content, and pre-configured servers—help the designer set up database and scripting with simple installers. These services should allow the relative novice a simple route to use server-side scripting to create a dynamic Web site.

Sites

The greatest advance in GoLive 6 is the Adobe Web Workgroup Server (AWWS) that ships as part of the product package. As the authors point out, the workgroup server may very well transform the way people collaborate and do their own work. The server is extremely simple to install and administer, yet it's an extremely powerful tool collaboration and centralized site manager.

The workgroup server allows simple file check in and out, which prevents overwriting existing files. But there's much more: centralized link management lets the server correct files even while they're checked out, ensuring the structure of the Web site doesn't break even with multiple designers editing pages simultaneously. The added ability to revert to any previous version of a source document represents one of the key customer requests we gathered when conducting customer interviews.

The workgroup server has incredible power hidden beneath a simple interface. You don't need to learn a new workflow; rather, the workgroup features have been largely integrated directly into GoLive itself, with a new toolbar and enhancements to the Site window.

Initial results of collaboration delivered with the Adobe Web Workgroup Server, which any WebDAV-enabled client can take advantage of, has been extremely positive.

Advanced

Advanced features, like Actions and Cascading Style Sheets, have been refined and improved, but the GoLive SDK (Software Developer Kit) is actually what I call the "silent killer app" of the product. The SDK now allows outside programmers to add a tremendous amount of additional functionality to Go-Live, as well as to tap into its existing features and combine or extend them in new ways. Examples of the benefits the SDK can provide can be found by visiting the Adobe Xchange (xchange.studio.adobe.com), and checking out the many great GoLive extensions already created.

New Release, New Power

Adobe GoLive 6 is no longer just a single application: it's now several applications in one, and several applications bundled in one package. When you look at competing products, you would need to invest in several different packages to achieve the same results, requiring a more complex workflow with less integration and seamlessness. All the features in GoLive 6, including workgroup collaboration, site design, dynamic server-side scripting, wireless-device authoring, and more, are designed from the ground up to be unified and streamlined under one roof to keep the learning curve at a reasonable angle of ascent.

As we continue to make advances in the product, which many of you are helping us define, Adobe invites you to voice your opinion on which features are most important to you, including which new features you would like to see addressed in a future release. Visit our Adobe User-to-User forum (www.adobe.com/support/forums/main.html) or simply send us an e-mail at golivewishlist@adobe.com.

Sit back and read these pages as Glenn and Jeff take you through a journey on how to take full advantage of this product to craft your Web design efforts.

On behalf of the entire GoLive Product Team, we thank you for your continued support!

—*April 2002*

Preface

GoLive has come a long way from our first look at it when it was called GoLive CyberStudio 3. Even back then, we had a lot of affection for the program, as it transformed the way we worked, turning us from HTML hand-coders tediously typing every character to graphical wizards, dragging and dropping with great delight.

After Adobe purchased GoLive, Inc., and changed the product name itself to GoLive, we watched it mature through version 4 (mostly useful) to version 5 (pretty much there). With GoLive 6, we see the pinnacle of this process, with a powerful program that does pretty much everything it needs to. Coupled with the Workgroup Server for collaboration and revision management, and the vastly improved database integration support, we're pretty much content.

In the previous version of this book covering GoLive 5, we complained that Adobe had fixed so many problems and extended so many features from GoLive 4 to 5 that we sounded like broken records noting each fix. From GoLive 5 to 6, there's more extension than correction: in this edition, we document not only new features, but the additional richness brought to parts of the program we've been working with for three years.

In this edition, we offer sidebars in nearly every chapter on the added features, as well as "New in 6" tips to help identify new items you might find useful in making the transition from 5 to 6.

Real World Means Real World

Our focus is and always has been on production: taking design ideas and turning them into practical expressions of page structure and HTML code. This book tries to advise you on using GoLive for that kind of production work, whether you're modifying a few pages every couple of days, or running a 10,000-page site with shared navigational elements.

If you want to know how to use GoLive from the ground up and create world-class pages that work across all browsers, and make best use of the built-in features of GoLive, buy this book (if you're just browsing), or read it from cover to cover (if you've already purchased it).

If you're looking for a book on graphic design or designing on the Web, this isn't it. This also isn't an HTML introduction that advises you on the content and values of each tag (though you'll find that we do cover many tags in detail as they relate to GoLive features). We eschew general discussions of aesthetic principles and encyclopedic coverage of coding in favor of production-oriented advice and tips. For instance, we explain how to get around some limitations in the underlying HTML to achieve a purpose; we also explain why certain design ideas may work better as expressed in HTML than others. (See our Web site at realworldgolive.com/six/books.html for recommendations on complementary books that are intended for both HTML and Web design beginners, or those interested in that approach to GoLive or other subjects.)

Who's This Book For?

We wrote this book with two types of users in mind:

The intermediate user. Before starting on the first edition of this book, we categorized ourselves between intermediate and advanced GoLive users; by the time we had finished, after months of hard work pushing and pulling the program, we called ourselves "advanced." To paraphrase Keanu Reeves's eloquence in *The Matrix,* "We know kung-fu." (Your reply should be: "Show me.") We want to transfer that acquisition of knowledge to the intermediate user who needs to get more out of the program, but has reached a plateau in the learning curve.

We've ferreted out all the day-to-day, real-world tricks and techniques you need to accomplish your specific tasks in the first three parts of the book. We also cover all the options, basics, and extras of tools to visually edit and manage pages and sites.

Part 4, *Advanced,* is where you, an intermediate user, can really leap ahead. You might be interested, for example, in writing Cascading Style Sheet definitions and applying Actions: we offer a chapter on each, among other topics.

The advanced user. For a program as vast and deep as GoLive, we find ourselves often wishing for a reference that tells us everything about the program, even the fiddly little bits like editing XML-based settings files.

The *Building Pages* and *Sites and Groups* sections might be more of a review than a primer for an advanced user, but we've tried to include as much detail and advice as possible for achieving the best results, or for learning new tips to improve your workflow. A review of selected chapters might help you eke out even more efficiency.

The *Code and Servers* and *Advanced* parts of the book are aimed at helping those users who already know the basics of a protocol GoLive supports, like HTML, SMIL, DHTML, or XML, to quickly use those features with GoLive's tools; or to bypass GoLive's tools with knowledge of how GoLive interacts with hand coding.

Starting Out? Wait!

If you've never touched the underlying HTML of a Web page, never used a graphical page editor, and never worked on a Web site in any capacity, our book will frustrate you and leave you weak with rage. How's that for honesty? Don't start reading this Real World title until you're up to speed on the basics. We recommend a number of books for getting started on our Web site (see realworldgolive.com/six/books.html). We don't recommend diving in feet-first without getting acclimated to the water first.

How This Book Is Structured

Real World Adobe GoLive 6 is broken into four parts:

Building Pages. GoLive has a fully integrated visual page editor that allows you to drag and drop elements onto a page, format text, add colors, and control tables, frames, and other structured elements. This part of the book fully delves into each area in turn. We start with an overview, and then proceed through the Layout Editor, the Head section, text and fonts, images, color, tables, layout grids, frames, and floating boxes, and forms.

Code and Servers. The section pushes under the covers of the program, looking at editing HTML source code and working with database-driven dynamic content. We also deal with parts of a page that need to work with a server, such as forms. We then finish with a sampling of other Web publishing formats such as XHTML and designing for mobile Web-enabled devices.

Sites and Groups. GoLive shines at site management, which includes tracking content across a site—such as images, links, and colors—and correctly uploading new files to a remote Web server. This part walks through the overall organization of the Site window, in which site management is focused in GoLive, and then into individual tabs and subjects. We cover prototyping and building new sites and site sections using the site diagram feature; uploading, downloading, and synchronizing content through built-in FTP (File Transfer Protocol) and WebDAV support; and working in groups collaboratively via the new Workgroup Server (WGS).

Advanced. This section handles advanced scripting and definitions that GoLive assists with or builds for. This includes the JavaScript scripting language; animation via DHTML (Dynamic HTML); prefabricated GoLive Actions that allow complicated combinations of behavior; Cascading Style Sheets for controlling text ranges and text blocks; setting up Dynamic Content sources to hook GoLive into databases and feed live content out on Web pages; and Web Settings, which is a many-tabbed dialog box acting as a kind of GoLive command and control center for all the assumptions about global HTML behavior, HTML tags and attributes, browser simulations, CSS, and file mapping.

Appendixes. But wait, there's more! In Appendix A, we offer up Macintosh-specific issues and extras: a few things that are found only in the Macintosh version of GoLive, including AppleScript support and Apple ColorSync color management. Ditto, we cover Windows issues and special features in Appendix B.

How to Read This Book

No, this isn't a trick headline: we really do have recommendations. There's too much structured content in this book for a straight-through reading; many features aren't relevant to all users. Our recommendations for getting the most of this book:

- **Scan it first.** Glance through the whole thing to find out where we've put everything and why. The structure we've laid out so far helps, and you can, of course, use the table of contents and index. But it's a big book, and we want you to know the lay of the land.

- **Answer your pressing questions.** Are there subjects you just don't understand? Features that drive you nuts? Parts of the program you adore and want to know more about? Check out the index, and look up those parts of the book.

- **Find the right chapter.** We've tried to structure this real-world book around themes and subjects that we focus on in our professional work on the Web, and that people have told us they use in their working methods.

- **Read the whole thing.** If you can't restrain yourself, stay up 'til 5 a.m. and read the book cover-to-cover. Once you're done, pop it in the shredder and fill a pillowcase with it. You'll sleep like a baby.

More Knowledge than Fits in Print

We've created a Web site at realworldgolive.com/six/ that's more than marketing (though we admit to a little of that; it *is* the Web, after all). Use it as a real resource for getting answers to your pressing questions and sharing information with other users, as well as the authors and contributors to this book.

The site contains updates to the book, fixes to errata (we freely admit that we lack infallibility), references to online resources, excerpts or the entire text of articles written by us on GoLive specifics, advanced advice on using the program, and news about GoLive developments.

You can also participate in an active, moderated, archived forum on GoLive that will provide a way for you to get some real answers to some real stumpers. The forum has been up and running for almost three years, and hundreds of readers continue to interact daily on it.

Many of the examples used in the book can be found at the site, as well; this is especially useful with some of the tutorial material in the *Advanced* part of the book.

Of course, you can also buy the book from the site—but, wait…you've already bought the book, haven't you? (If not, support your authors and booksellers by spending your hard-earned money to share our hard-earned knowledge.)

What's Different in the Third Edition

This third edition of *Real World Adobe GoLive* covers GoLive 6 from start to finish, but we do mention important new features or differences in the program from GoLive 5 to 6. If you've used previous versions of GoLive, look for the section at the start of many chapters that summarizes all the new features in GoLive 6 for that subject, if any.

Generally, we fixed errors, rewrote sections that needed revision, wrote entirely new chapters about subjects that didn't exist in GoLive 5 or that we felt needed more coverage than we originally provided.

We also eliminated the GoLive Basics part of the book. Our readers told us they could find that material in a more how-to fashion in other books and wanted us to devote our space to more nitty-gritty detail. We listened and expanded the rest of the book to fill that role.

Conventions Used in This Book

We believe in making text contextually self-explanatory, and have tried to keep fonts, formatting, and special dingbats to a minimum. However, a few conventions are worth highlighting.

Because this book covers both Mac OS and Windows versions of Adobe GoLive, as well as multiple versions of both operating systems, we've made a lot of effort to be as inclusive as possible. The screen captures you see throughout the book were made fairly arbitrarily on either platform to emphasize how similar they are. However, whenever something is significantly different between the display in the two platforms, we've included platform-specific screen captures.

Similarly, whenever a key command or menu item is specific to a platform, in the text you see a note such as, "To bring up the contextual menu, Control-click on the Mac or right-click under Windows." At the same time, we didn't go overboard. GoLive is full of keyboard shortcuts and contextual menus that speed up access to its controls, but we don't note every one. In general, if it took longer to mention all the alternate methods of accessing a feature than to actually describe it, we opted for brevity.

Tip: This is a Tip!

Tips appear called-out using a bold black bar (as this one is), and generally contain real-world advice, ideas on tweaking settings, or slightly extraneous bits of knowledge that you might enjoy.

New in 6: This Head

Items marked with this tag have attention brought to them particularly for users of GoLive 5 who might find the change noteworthy or perplexing.

Code samples are marked in the Courier font to indicate something you can type in:

```
.foobar { text-size: 1000 px }
```

Humor is not specially marked throughout, and you need to apply a special irony filter to your optical input in order to recognize it. (Sarcasm is strictly avoided.)

Our Team

We couldn't have written this book without the help of some very fine people who shaped the book with their work and advice.

Our crack copy editor Don Sellers, a man who we admire and occasionally worship, a man described in print as "cheap but not mean," read every word we wrote and helped us make the prose better and better. Liane Thomas and Helen Meyers had the thankless task of proofreading the book, cross-checking every last little detail.

Glenn's dad, Charles Fleishman, was our technical double-checker, making sure that keystrokes, menus, and dialog boxes did what we said they did.

Caroline Parks indexed the book, accepting with aplomb hundreds of pages at one go, and deciphering our strange, secret jokes. Her in-depth index makes good reading on its own.

Jeff Tolbert, in addition to putting up with our strange humor and 10 a.m. lunch cravings, designed the section title pages and created the site that we use for examples throughout the book (and which is available for download from our Web site to follow along with how-tos in the book). We also roped him into doing quite a bit of last-minute layout and figure creation, and he's even still speaking to us.

Our friends and colleagues Agen Schmitz and Neil Robertson wrote large swaths of the first edition of this book and helped us revise the second. Their day jobs are demanding, however, and we took on the task of revising their contributions all by our lonesomes (much more approachable with GoLive 6, but giving rise to the question: if you have a coauthor, are you really lonesome?).

Acknowledgements

The Peachpit team as always helped get us in gear for a new edition. Despite a lousy economy, our collective depression over events on 9/11/01, and the loss of jobs by many of our readers, Peachpit believed in this book and in us, and encouraged us to go for the gusto with a third go-round. Thanks so much to Nancy Aldrich-Ruenzel, Peachpit's publisher, our editor Serena Herr, and production coordinator Connie Jeung-Mills.

Our heartfelt thanks also extend to Adobe's remarkable GoLive product marketing and engineering team, including John Kranz, Lynn Grillo (not Lisa, a name we decided to bestow on her in the previous edition), and Adam Pratt, as well as Jens, Lance, Philip, Erik, Bernard, Veronika, and many others. We also loved the beta list for the GoLive 6 release: a group of hardy souls found from Brazil to Australia to the remotest part of Ireland who were unstinting in offering troubleshooing advice and solace.

Jeff and Glenn (that's us) share a small and tidy office in a lovely part of Seattle with a bunch of fellow procrastinators and caffeine imbibers. The aforementioned Jeff Tolbert knows when to drag us away from our computers for some fresh air, but more important never hesitated when we needed last-minute help. We're always admiringly amazed at the elusive David Blatner, Man of Ten Thousand Projects. And Steve Roth simultaneously provides the foundation for most of our book-making knowledge and helps us remember that there's much more to the world than pixels and PowerBooks.

From Glenn: "I receive unending support from those I love who also miraculously and consistently love me back, even in the throes of the several-week writing binge that recurs with each edition of this book. My sweetheart and mate, Lynn D. Warner, manned the home front during difficult times to allow me the freedom to work day and night. My folks, grandparents, cousins, and siblings alternately support, poke fun at, and ease the writing game. (I thank my dad particularly for his reality check as an intermediate GoLive user.) I had an incredibly fun time writing this edition, and my co-author continues to be bearded (but not for very long). Jeff's good humor even after many nights of little sleep makes him a perfect collaborator on these large projects."

From Jeff: "We start each *Real World Adobe GoLive* revision with the same mantra: *it's going to be easier this time around.* The cruel joke is that it's both easier and terribly difficult, no matter what you do. There are people in my life who understand this obsession with the book-writing process, and still love me nonetheless, make it possible to veer between extremes and come out sane at the end of the project. It would take another 900 pages to explain how my wife Kimberly supports me in this crazy endeavor. My family has somehow acquired the sense of when it's time to ask me how the book is going and when to distract me with other topics. And my comrade Glenn not only knows how to get the best work out of me (which I hope I repay in kind), but is a great friend and officemate."

Overview

Table of Contents

CHAPTER 3

Head Section. 85

CHAPTER 4

Text and Fonts. 95

CHAPTER 6
Color 189

CHAPTER 7
Tables 209

CHAPTER 8
Layout Grids **251**

CHAPTER 9
Frames **265**

CHAPTER 10
Floating Boxes **287**

CHAPTER 11

Templates 299

CHAPTER 12

Rich Media. 309

PART 2

Code and Servers. 323

CHAPTER 13

Forms 325

CHAPTER 16
Languages and Scripting.................................415

PART 3
Sites and Groups....................................431

CHAPTER 17
Managing Sites.......................................433

CHAPTER 18

Diagramming and Mapping **455**

CHAPTER 19

Managing Files, Folders, and Links 513

CHAPTER 27
Defining Cascading Style Sheets. 769

CHAPTER 28
Controlling Web Settings 801

CHAPTER 1

Going Live

Picking a program in any field, whether it's Web publishing, illustration, page layout, or even accounting is akin to joining a political party. People have strong feelings about products that often can't be explained through an objective review of the component parts. And that's just fine with us.

You spend a lot of time with a program mediating between your abilities and the desired outcome. It's not bad to have a deep relationship with an application as you learn to mold it to your ends. GoLive has matured over the years through many versions into a consistent and powerful tool that should encompass virtually all of your Web page design, database integration, and site management needs. In this chapter, we walk through installing GoLive, working with its metaphors for production and management, customizing your settings and workspace, and understanding the palettes and editors used in different parts of the program. We also tell you where else in the book to look for each of the parts of the program by task and nature.

Tip: Skip It!

Already know how GoLive works and want to get to the meat? Skip this chapter. We're providing a friendly and sensible introduction to our first-time GoLive users, but if you're on top of your game, charge on down the court.

Installing GoLive

This isn't a book where we hold your hand by telling you how to turn on your computer, use a mouse, or install software. However, a few particulars are worth mentioning when it comes to introducing GoLive to your computer.

Tip: Help!

The online help in GoLive 6 is truly wonderful; be sure to install it if you choose a Custom install (it's installed automatically in the Typical configuration). You can search by keywords on the most obscure topics in the program and get detailed help plus clickable cross-references. We don't see any reason to crack the print manual.

Mac OS X and All Windows Versions

Run the installer, follow directions, and you're done! How's that for simple?

If you choose a Custom installation, you can install additional dictionaries and the software SDK extension, required for using third-party extensions.

Tip: SSI Include

The SDK is also where the SSI Include module is hidden if you use server-side includes.

Tip: Memory (Windows only)

Some Windows users found earlier versions of GoLive eating up their memory. Even though you can't specifically assign memory to individual applications under Windows, you can increase the overall system virtual memory allotment.

In Windows XP, for instance, open the Control Panel folder, open the System control panel, select the Advanced tab, then click the Settings button in the Performance area, and select the Advanced tab. Click the Change button in the Virtual Memory area. You can then reset the Custom Size values to something larger. Reboot and this should take care of the problem if you're experiencing it.

Tip: Dual OS (Mac only)

If you install GoLive under OS X, it automatically puts all the pieces in the right places to run under OS 9, should you choose to run in the older environment.

Mac OS 9

The installer under Mac OS 9 works simply as well, but you've got one extra variable: GoLive 6 likes memory. Lots of memory. After installing the program, select the application, choose Get Info from the File menu, and select Memory from the popup menu. Set this number as high as you can: 80 megabytes (enter 80000 in the field, since OS 9 still insanely refers to memory here in kilobytes), 120 megabytes, whatever you can spare.

Tip: Install in OS X First (Mac only)

If you install GoLive 6 under OS 9, all the pieces needed for OS X are installed, but not in the right place. The reverse isn't true: installing under OS X works by default on both versions of the operating system.

Workgroup Server

The Workgroup Server (WGS) allows you to remotely store, archive, and upload files in a site. It's best used for collaborating with other designers or production people, but because it stores multiple backup copies of every file you upload, it's a handy tool for ensuring you don't make permanent, accidental changes to a site.

The WGS runs only under Windows XP, Windows 2000, and Mac OS X 10.1 or later, although you don't need these systems to access it once it's installed. These more robust systems are required to handle the underlying support for the WGS. The CD-ROM for the WGS is hidden in the back of the Adobe Web Workgroup Server User Guide.

To install the WGS, first quit any Adobe programs, and then run the installer. At one point during the installation, you are asked for port numbers and a server name, which you should typically leave set as is. The WGS might require a static IP (instead of a dynamic, local network address) and changes in local and network firewalls.

It can take several minutes for the WGS to fully set itself up and finish. This is because Adobe relies on a Java engine that must compile components on its first run; after that point, the speed should be more than adequate. The installation and setup process is described in greater depth in Chapter 21, *Working in Groups*.

The GoLive Way

GoLive takes a slightly different approach from other graphical design programs that use icons and visual metaphors for creating layouts and manipulating objects.

In many programs, you select a tool from a toolbar and then proceed to use that tool to act on objects on a page. For instance, in QuarkXPress, you select a Text Box tool to draw a text box on the page. You then select that box and fill it with text or just start typing.

GoLive, on the other hand, has a somewhat different approach for each kind of object you might work with. GoLive splits activities and objects into the following four categories, more or less.

- **Page elements,** such as tables, forms, and images, appear in the Layout Editor much like in a browser window; a separate preview mode is even closer. The objects are fully editable, and can be moved, resized, deleted, or otherwise inserted or restructured.

- **Source code,** typically HTML, but also including that from other markup languages, can be edited by hand and then previewed in various locations in GoLive.

- **Site elements,** such as files and directories, appear just as they do on the Windows Desktop or Macintosh Finder as icons in hierarchical folders. Files and folders can be moved, deleted, and created. The same is true for remote files on FTP or WebDAV file servers, or files stored on a Workgroup Server. Everything on a page has a corresponding Inspector. Single items and groups can often be edited or set via palettes.

- **Complex activities and features,** such as JavaScript, Cascading Style Sheets (CSS), Dynamic Content, and Dynamic HTML (DHTML) are controlled through a combination of technical code and graphical previews. Each advanced activity has its own special editor or similar window.

These four categories naturally divide this book as well into the *Pages, Code and Servers, Sites and Groups,* and *Advanced* sections.

Pages

The basic element in GoLive is the page, where everything is built. Create a new page by choosing New Page from the File menu. From here you can populate your page with all sorts of items. Let's look at text (plain typing) and page elements.

Tip: New on Open

When you first start up GoLive, it displays a dialog box asking you whether you want to create a New Page or other objects. We typically turn this off by checking the box labeled Don't Show Again. You can also set this preference in the General pane; see "Detailing the Work Area," later in this chapter.

Text

Just start typing on the page. Text starts at the upper left on a blank page, but with objects already on a page, you can move the cursor, click to change the insertion point, and start typing.

Tip: Inserting Text in a Layout Grid

Layout grids, used for setting the exact placement of items on a page using table cells, can only have text added when you drag in a Layout Text Box or click on a grid element and select paste. See Chapter 8, *Layout Grids*.

To format text, choose options from the Toolbar, the contextual menu (Control-click on the Mac, right-click under Windows), or the Type menu.

With text selected, choosing options like Heading 1 from the Type menu's Paragraph Format submenu changes the selected text to a preset heading style. With just an insertion point, changing text formatting affects any text typed in after that point.

Page Elements

Many users are confused when first faced with GoLive's approach to adding page elements such as tables, images, and form elements, because it involves three discrete steps:

1. Find the kind of object you need in the Objects palette.

2. Drag that object onto the page.

3. Use the Inspector to link to the object and/or set its parameters.

For instance, if you wanted to create a form with a couple of text fields and a submit button—a routine, almost daily task for maintaining most Web sites—you go back to the Objects palette again and again for the "supplies" you need to build the form, much like a contractor making trips to a stack of lumber, nails, and tools at the job site (see Figure 1-1).

In the *Building Pages* part of the book, Chapters 2 to 12, we cover the use of all the page elements including tables, images, color, and layout grids, as well as the various parts of a page, like the head section, plus rich media, such as QuickTime and Real media.

Figure 1-1
Assortment
of Objects
palettes

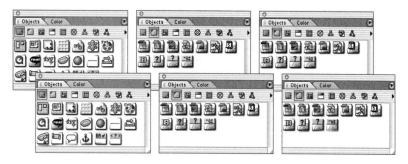

Source

GoLive lets users get under the hood pretty easily through three basic and several more advanced views into the underlying markup code that is the beating heart of the Web.

The Source Code palette, the Source Code Editor in the Document window, and the Split Source view all allow viewing and modifying source code directly (see Figure 1-3). Changing the source code is often a way to bypass missing pieces in GoLive or to satisfy one's inner geek. It's also just plain efficient to make a small change.

In the *Code and Servers* part of the book, Chapters 13 to 16, we deal with a variety of more advanced coding and features that require a server on the other end, from source editing to forms to working with advanced media and browsers as fun as those built into cellular phones.

Our Protean Friend, the Inspector

The Inspector palette is the single most used part of GoLive. It's a protean palette, one that changes contextually based on whatever is selected (see Figure 1-2). Inspectors have names in their lower-left corner that correspond to the currently selected object or text.

The Inspector is truly remarkable because it works whether you have an object selected in the Layout Editor, the Outline Editor, the JavaScript Editor, the CSS Editor, the Site window, or numerous other places in the program.

In previous versions, the Inspector was modal in part: it required you to press return for GoLive to accept values after you had typed something in. Starting with GoLive 5, the Inspector became completely interactive. Now, whenever you modify a setting, it's immediately applied to the page. Many changes in the Inspector palette—virtually all of them, in fact—can be undone using the Undo command in the Edit menu, or via the History palette, which allows you to walk back to a specific change.

Figure 1-2
Inspector examples

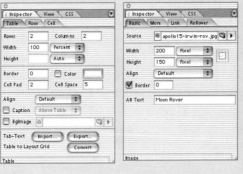

Figure 1-3
Source code
views

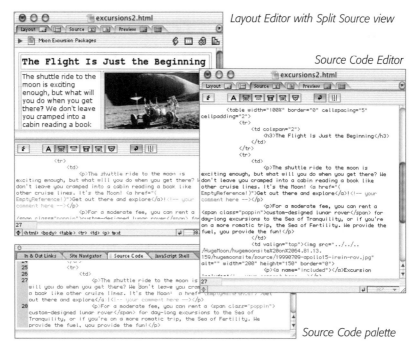

Layout Editor with Split Source view

Source Code Editor

Source Code palette

Two Approaches to Building Web Pages

We try not to get overly metaphysical when it comes to our work (though sometimes we're up late pondering questions such as, "If a designer is camping in the woods, does the Web cease to exist?"), but sometimes it's impossible to avoid. Understanding one of the main philosophies behind working in GoLive applies to the work you carry out from now on.

GoLive offers two approaches to building pages: direct application and layout grids. In direct application, you type text and insert images and other elements using the basic structure of a Web page: content is read from left to right, top to bottom. Even when you're adding elements such as tables, you're bound by that structure, much the way you'd perform the same tasks in a word processor. (See Chapter 2, *Layout*.)

The alternative is to use layout grids, which, in a sense, circumvents the standard Web page structure. You first add a layout grid to your page, and then build everything else onto the grid, akin to using a page-layout application such as QuarkXPress or InDesign. (See Chapter 8, *Layout Grids*.)

Both approaches are legitimate, just as both approaches have their own advantages and disadvantages. We began designing for the Web in the days before graphical editing tools existed, so we tend to favor the direct application approach (and also because a layout grid is, at heart, just a complex table). However, we've run into lots of designers who find the layout grid approach more closely parallels their experience using page-layout programs.

Building a Page, Step by Step

Despite the advanced features and multitude of options available in GoLive, the program is based on a simple premise: adding items to a page and editing them.

The following steps illustrate how to create a simple page depicting a recent vacation, which contains some text, an image, and a couple of hyperlinks.

1. Choose New Page from the File menu. A new Document window appears, with the Layout Editor visible.

2. Give the page a name, which appears in the title bar of a Web browser window. To add the title, click the text just above the editing area next to the Page icon, which reads, "Welcome to Adobe GoLive 6", and enter a title, such as "Moon Trip". Hit Enter

to accept the change, or click anywhere in the editing area.

3. Save the page by choosing Save As from the File menu. Give the file a name that doesn't include spaces and is all lowercase, such as "moonwalk.html".

4. In the editing area, where your cursor is located, type some descriptive text: "I thought I'd bring a pebble home!" Hit Return or Enter to create a new paragraph (see Figure 1-4).

5. Now let's add a photo. Go to the Objects palette, which displays the Basic tab by default. Locate the Image icon, and drag it to the Layout Editor (see Figure 1-5).

6. In the Inspector, which displays Image-specific options, click the Browse button

Figure 1-4
Starting a basic page

Figure 1-5
Adding an image

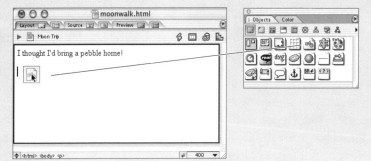

next to the Source field. Use the Open dialog box that appears to locate an image, then click the Open button. The image appears on your page (see Figure 1-6).

7. Since there are probably more photos from the trip, let's create a link to another page. Click somewhere below the image to deselect it, then hit Return or Enter to create a new paragraph. Then type, "Go to shuttle photos."

8. Highlight the words "shuttle photos" and click the New Link button on the Toolbar

or in the Inspector. The text turns blue and underlined; in the Inspector, the address field now reads "(EmptyReference!)".

9. Highlight "(EmptyReference!)" and type the name of the file you wish to link to, in this case "shuttle.html" (see Figure 1-7). If you were linking to another Web site, you would enter the full URL, such as "http://www.hugemoonexpeditions.com/shuttle.html".

Save the file. Your new Web page is ready to be viewed in a Web browser.

Figure 1-6
Image added

Browse button

Figure 1-7
Creating a new link

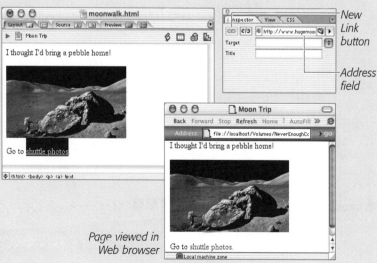

New Link button

Address field

Page viewed in Web browser

Site Elements

The site management features in GoLive make it the fine and powerful program it's become today. With a separate file containing pointers to all the elements in a site—the site file—and the Site window showing a graphical representation of all the objects and relationships, a single click can have far reaching implications. Although you can certainly start desiging by building individual pages, these days we almost always begin by creating a new site.

In the Site window, you work with features that span the whole site, such as links from one file to another, links to external resources, site maps that paint a picture of relationships, and moving files from the local copy on your hard drive to remote places like your Web server.

The site metaphor is less abstract than the page metaphor. Select items in the Site window's Files, External, Diagrams, or other tabs, and the appropriate Inspector items appear, allowing modification.

Drag an item in the Files tab into a folder, for example, and GoLive—watching your every move—asks you if it should rewrite all pointers to that link wherever they occur in a site.

The third part of the book, *Sites and Groups* (Chapters 17 to 21), encompasses managing files and sites.

Advanced Features

GoLive isn't just a graphical pretty face. No! Nestled into every crevice are advanced features including support for Cascading Style Sheets (CSS), Dynamic HTML (DHTML), database integration via Dynamic Content, JavaScript, and prefabricated sequences known as Actions.

Each of these advanced features typically has its own unique editor, palette, or window. For instance, DHTML animations are edited via the DHTML Timeline Editor, and JavaScript is developed in the JavaScript Editor (see Figure 1-8).

Because these features are so varied, there's no generic advice that helps you work with them. We devote the fourth part of the book, Chapters 22 to 28, to working with each of these advanced features.

Detailing the Work Area

To the first-time GoLive user, the program probably seems like an explosion of palettes and windows. We prefer to think of it in terms of a workshop: all your tools are hung on the wall in plain sight, ready to be used. Once you're familiar with the locations and purposes of the tools, you'll be reaching for them without looking.

Figure 1-8
JavaScript
Editor

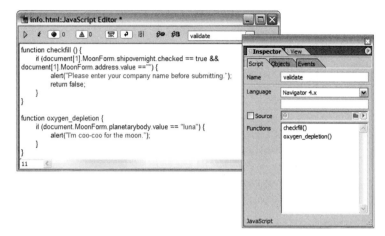

Desktop Management

GoLive lets you control and reset the palettes, editors, and other items that can litter your screen. It also lets you fool around with open windows to make the display more legible.

Tip: Multiple Monitors

If ever there was justification for using multiple monitors, GoLive is it. If you own a Mac and can afford multiple monitors (we'd each love to use a pair of Apple 23-inch Cinema HD displays if we could afford them), the extra real estate can be used effectively to display and expand several key GoLive palettes. (Unfortunately, Windows still does not support spanned display using multiple monitors.)

Workspace

Choose the Workspace submenu from the Window menu to manage floating items, such as palettes (see Figure 1-9, next page).

Select Default Workspace to reset your desktop to the GoLive default: the Objects palette, the Inspector, and the main Toolbar, plus the Workgroup Toolbar.

If you reconfigure your GoLive workspace area, you can choose Save Workspace to create a custom template that can be reloaded later. If multiple

Figure 1-9
Changing
workspace

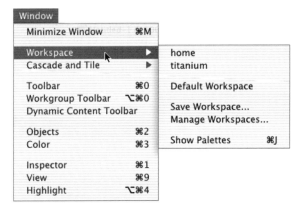

people use the same copy of GoLive on the same machine, this is a nice way to customize it for each person's attitude on palettes and floating items.

Manage Workspaces lets you add and delete items. Clicking New and naming a workspace sets the currently active Workspace to that name.

Hide Palettes is a simple way to remove everything floating all at once.

Cascade and Tile

This submenu of the Window menu controls open documents and site windows. Choose Cascade to put windows on top of each other, slightly offset from the upper left (see Figure 1-10). Choose Tile Horizontally or Tile Vertically to rearrange the windows so that their maximum dimensions allow all windows to be shown simultaneously (see Figure 1-11).

Tip: Disarray

Arrange Icons appears on the Windows version of the GoLive menu, but seems to have no function associated with it.

Figure 1-10
Cascaded
windows

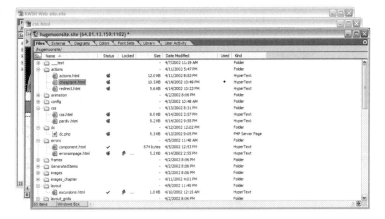

Figure 1-11
Tiled windows

Palettes

Palettes multiply like rabbits in GoLive: each successive version adds several more. This section helps review the wide variety of palettes and points you to the chapters in which you can find more information.

Docking and Positioning

Palettes help minimize screen space through docking, in which multiple palettes can overlap through tabs in the same window.

To view a palette on its own, tear it away from its group by clicking the palette's title tab and dragging it out of the group. To dock it with its default group (or add it to another group), click and drag the title tab and drop it onto a group palette; on the Mac, an outline appears within the group palette to show that it's ready to accept visitors.

Tip: Repositioning

If you click and drag the bar at the top of the palette, you only move the palette's position and can't drop it onto another palette group.

Tip: Reordering Tabs

When one palette is dropped onto another, its title tab appears at the end of the list. You can't change the order of tabs unless you drag all tabs out of the group, then drag and drop palettes in the order you desire.

Yes, it *is* possible to make one gigantic super palette—but this isn't recommended for the claustrophobic (see Figure 1-12). We couldn't resist trying, though.

Figure 1-12
Super palette!

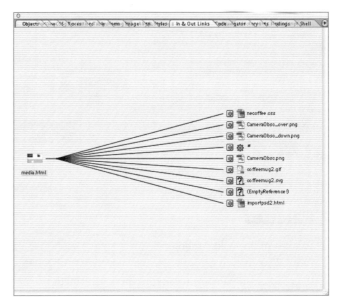

When a palette is selected, a checkmark appears next to it in the Window menu. If you drag a palette out of its original grouping, the grouped list does not change in the Window menu; it's possible to have all members of a group selected and checked in the menu.

To hide a palette that's included in a group, click one of the other tabs in the group. To close a palette (either individual or group), click the close box in the upper left (Mac) or upper right (Windows) corner of the palette bar. Pressing Command-W (Mac) or Control-W (Windows) closes open files and does not affect palettes.

Tip: Palette Keyboard Shortcuts

Speaking of the Window menu, both Windows and Mac versions include handy references to the various palette keyboard shortcuts.

Tip: Hiding All

Sometimes you want to temporarily hide all palettes to view a large Web page: type Control-J (Windows) or Command-J (Mac) to hide them, and the same combination to make them reappear.

Popout Menu. A button at the top right corner of a palette is active when there's a popout menu with extra controls (see Figure 1-13). For instance, the Objects and Color palettes list their individual tabs, while the Tracing Image palette lets you position an image or crop a section.

Figure 1-13
Popout menu

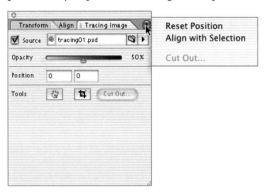

Resizing. To change the size of a palette, click and hold its bottom right corner and drag to the new size. Under Windows, you can also use any of the palette's outside edges to resize it. If you click on another palette tab within a group, that palette loses the dimensions you just dragged; GoLive forgets the last display size of the selected palette.

Docking. To keep everything in order, overlapped palettes snap to the border of another palette or other objects on the page, like the Dock in OS X or the Toolbar.

You can overlap palettes if you want (just continue dragging to a desired point), but GoLive's first inclination is to dock palettes into a larger entity.

Objects

The Objects palette is the WYSIWYG heart of GoLive (see Figure 1-14). While seeming a little cumbersome at first—especially for those of us who pine for keyboard shortcuts—dragging and dropping tag icons onto a page quickly becomes second nature.

Figure 1-14
Objects palette

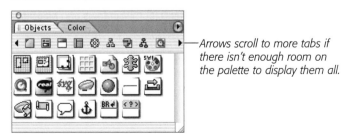

Arrows scroll to more tabs if there isn't enough room on the palette to display them all.

You can access each tab of the Objects palette by clicking on each tab. (The tabs look more like buttons, but work like tabs, which they were in the previous versions of the product. So we call them tabs for clarity.) If the palette is in its default width, you can click the left or right arrows on either side to scroll through more tabs. Or, you can click the popout menu at the top right and select a tab name.

The popout menu also has a Configure submenu from which you can select a filter that only shows HTML or HTML-like objects that are legal in various specifications, like the strict version of HTML 4.0 or one of the cell phones that GoLive can preview. (See Chapter 14, *Source Editing*, for more on sets and syntax.)

The Undo and Redo items in the popout menu work in conjunction with HTML objects dragged into the Library tab (or the Library section of the Object palette's Site Extras tab).

Color

Select Color from the Window menu to activate the Color palette, from which you can select colors and shades of gray to add to items on your page, including text, table cells, and page backgrounds (see Figure 1-15).

Figure 1-15
Color palette

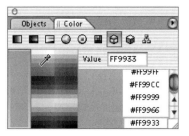

To add color to an item, select a color from one of the Color palette's tabs and drag a color swatch from the Preview pane to the desired location, such as highlighted text on a page, a color field on an Inspector, or the Text Color field on the Text toolbar.

You have nine tabs to choose colors from, each of which allows you to manipulate, select, and store colors just a little differently. For more information, see Chapter 6, *Color*.

Inspector

See earlier in this chapter for the sidebar: "Our Protean Friend, the Inspector."

View

The View palette allows you to change settings associated with the current document view. If you're looking at the Source Code Editor, for instance, the View palette shows checkboxes that correspond to several of the display options, such as Word Wrap (see Figure 1-16). The View palette is discussed in each part of the interface with which it is paired.

Figure 1-16
View palette

Two views of the View palette

Highlight

The Highlight palette, new to GoLive 6, lets you color-code and identify items on a page by syntax, including CSS styles, errors on the page, or other tags and features (see Figure 1-17). You can also click the lighting bolt to bring up the Check Syntax option. Highlight and checking syntax are discussed in Chapter 14, *Source Editing*.

Transform and Align

These two palettes take objects on a page or grid and distribute, align, or center them. Transform and Align commands are available for items on layout

Figure 1-17
Highlight palette

grids (see Chapter 8, *Layout Grids*) and for diagrams (see Chapter 18, *Diagramming and Mapping*).

Tracing Image

Using the Tracing Image palette, you can create a page layout based on a schematic saved as an image file. See Chapter 5, *Images*.

Dynamic Bindings

When working with Dynamic Content, the Dynamic Bindings palette lets you connect objects on a page (text, tables, containers, and form elements) to fields in a database or XML data source. We talk about these elements and the palette's functions in Chapter 15, *Dynamic Content and Databases*.

Floating Boxes

Floating boxes, those positioned rectangles you can place and stack on a page, are managed via the Floating Boxes palette. You can rearrange their order, convert boxes to layout grids, and change the visibility or editability of floating boxes. We cover floating boxes in, naturally, Chapter 10, *Floating Boxes*.

Table

The Table palette enables you to easily make selections (from individual cells to entire rows and columns), as well as sort content and apply preformatted and saved styles. In GoLive 6, the palette shows precise measurements of cells, and allows you to fix errors by clicking a red number (which indicates a mismatch in overall table and cell widths).

The Table palette also lets you set color schemes for a table and sort entries by field. For more information, see Chapter 7, *Tables*.

Actions

GoLive Actions are prefabricated sets of code that you can combine to set up complex sets of behaviors attached to text, buttons, and animations. Actions can preload images, add sounds, dynamically change the content of images, open links in new browser windows, and other functionality.

This palette lets you attach Actions to specific triggers, and configure the Actions behavior. For more information, see Chapter 26, *Applying Actions*.

HTML Styles

HTML Styles let you define characteristics for hard-coded font and color parameters. This palette, new to GoLive 6, is discussed in Chapter 4, *Text and Fonts*.

CSS

Cascading Style Sheets (CSS) can be set once and used to control text through a page or site. CSS can make paragraphs dance, and put borders around objects, as well as create more interesting backgrounds and let you set custom images for list bullets.

The CSS palette works differently depending on whether you have a page or a site in the foreground. With a site as the front-most window, the CSS palette allows you to link external CSS style sheets to one or more HTML files simultaneously and to rearrange the cascade order of precedence. With a page selected, the palette shows any class definitions, which you can apply to items or swaths of a page.

The basics of CSS formatting are discussed further in Chapter 4, *Text and Fonts*; advanced configurations are covered in Chapter 27, *Defining Cascading Style Sheets*.

Template Regions

GoLive Templates are plain Web pages marked up with areas that cannot be edited by default. This allows a designer to create a pattern that a user can follow in creating new pages. The Template Regions palette displays editable regions and allows those to be added to and changed. Chapter 11, *Templates*, offers the full skinny on this new GoLive 6 feature.

Source Code

If you like to see what's happening in the background of your HTML page as you add objects, open the Source Code palette. It displays every addition, every added attribute and value pair, and all the text you type as it happens. (The Split Source view also offers this display in the same window as the document you're working.) Visit Chapter 14, *Source Editing*, for the ins and outs of this valuable floating item.

In & Out Links

The In & Out Links palette reveals the relationship among a selected page, incoming links (all the media and pages that point to the selected page), and outgoing links (graphics, URLs, email addresses, and other pages the selected page includes or points to).

It can also show which font sets, colors, external links (URLs), and email addresses are used on which pages (see Figure 1-18, next page). If the item is a Web page—or an Acrobat PDF, QuickTime movie, or Flash animation with embedded URLs—the In & Out Links palette shows all outbound links. You can select any page or item in any of the Site window's tabs, including any item in a design or in the Navigation or Links Views.

Chapter 19, *Managing Files, Folders, and Links,* devotes extensive coverage to using this interactive palette to examine and fix links.

Figure 1-18
In & Out Links
palette

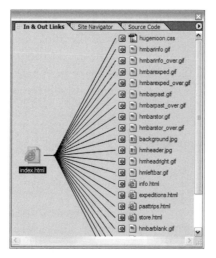

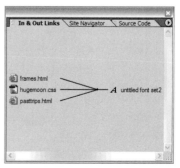

The In & Out Links palette can display links within a page (left), as well as pages linked to a font set or color set (top).

Pending Links

If you prototype a site using the Diagram feature, you can create relationships between pages that simulate links. Any of these putative links can then be linked into actual content on a page. The Pending Links palette shows the status of outstanding links as well as links already connected on a page. Various icons help sort out navigational directions as well (parent, child, sibling, or just a plain link).

See Chapter 18, *Diagramming and Mapping,* for insight on creating new parts of sites and pages in conjunction with Pending Links.

Site Navigator

The Site Navigator palette works with diagram windows and Navigation and Links Views. It controls the view of a large, unwieldy collection of files much like the Navigator palette in Photoshop (see Figure 1-19). See Chapter 18, *Diagramming and Mapping,* for more on working with this feature.

JavaScript Shell

The JavaScript Shell is a debugging tool designed to work with GoLive's Software Developer's Kit (SDK). Only programmers will be able to get something out of this palette. See the documentation on the CD-ROM that comes with GoLive 6 for more on developing extensions and palettes with the SDK.

Figure 1-19
Site Navigator
palette

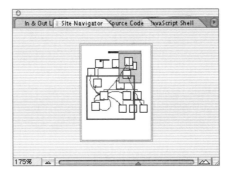

History

The History palette records actions taken in GoLive and allows you to revert to many previous states. It's really a multiple-level Undo/Redo with more information about the steps that were taken; it's almost identical to Photoshop's History palette.

The History palette works with almost every part of the program, maintaining separate "undo" lists for each. In GoLive 6, Adobe added history options for the site window and various editors, allowing you to step backwards, whether moving files or editing CSS styles. The amount of history can vary depending on context.

You can see up to 20 history steps unless you change the default from the History Options item in the palette's popout menu. Selecting Clear History erases the stored steps currently displayed.

The most recent modification is found at the bottom of the list, and the active state is indicated with a tab arrow on the left side of the list.

Tip: Undo and Redo

Command-Z (Mac) or Control-Z (Windows) removes changes made to a page, and takes you step-by-step back through the History palette. Command-Shift-Z (Mac) or Control-Shift-Z (Windows) recreates your changes and steps you forward through the list.

Tip: Revert to Saved

To return to the state of the document as of your last save, choose Revert to Saved from the File menu.

Click a level in the history above your current state to revert to that previous state. All levels below a selected state become inactive, and the page displays the state it was in at that point in the editing process (see Figure 1-20).

If you select a previous state in the history, then make a modification to the page, the inactive items below are wiped out and replaced by the new changes. Click the top-most level (marked with the ellipsis) to return to the original state of the document if less than 20 modifications (by default) have been made; if more than 20 modifications have been made, clicking this item brings you back to the document's state 20 changes from the most recent edit.

Figure 1-20
History palette

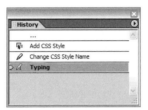

Those who forget history are doomed to repeat it, but GoLive 6 now remembers its history contextually as you switch between site windows, editors, and document windows.

Tip: Forgetting History

GoLive does, however, clear the History palette if you switch between modes on a page, like from Layout Editor to HTML Source Editor.

Hints

Adobe built several hundred tips into the Hints palette, which are contextually delivered based on items you've selected (see Figure 1-21). Hint: Bring up the Hints palette for hints about the Hints palette.

Figure 1-21
Hints palette

The Toolbar

Like the Inspector, GoLive's Toolbar contextually changes to fit the task at hand (see Figure 1-22).

Figure 1-22
GoLive
Toolbars

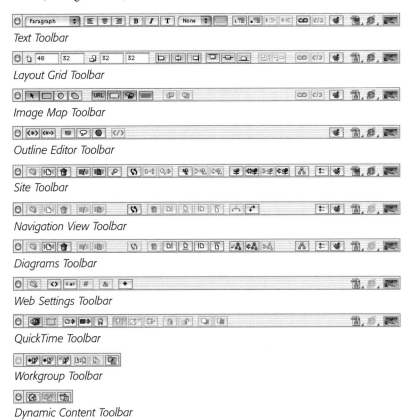

Text Toolbar

Layout Grid Toolbar

Image Map Toolbar

Outline Editor Toolbar

Site Toolbar

Navigation View Toolbar

Diagrams Toolbar

Web Settings Toolbar

QuickTime Toolbar

Workgroup Toolbar

Dynamic Content Toolbar

Text Toolbar

If you work at all with creating or editing pages in GoLive, you see a lot of the Text toolbar. Through it, you can control both the way text looks and the way paragraphs containing text and objects act. For more information, see Chapter 4, *Text and Fonts*.

Layout Grid Toolbar

If you add a layout grid to a page while in the Layout Editor, GoLive brings up the Layout Grid toolbar once you click in the grid. However, everything within the Toolbar is inactive until you add either a Layout Text Box or an object to the grid. For details on using layout grids, see Chapter 8, *Layout Grids*.

Image Map Toolbar

To create an image map and bring up the Image Map toolbar, check Use Map on the More tab of the Image Inspector. See Chapter 5, *Images*, for how to work with image maps.

Outline Editor Toolbar

In the Document window, clicking the Outline Editor tab opens the Outline Editor, which in turn brings up the Outline toolbar. The Outline toolbar isn't essential for working in the Outline Editor (as you can drag in tag icons from the Palette), but it can be helpful. The Outline Editor is discussed in Chapter 14, *Source Editing*.

Site Toolbar

The Site toolbar allows you to do basic maintenance, like adding folders to and deleting items from your site, displaying Mac file information or Windows properties, and opening GoLive's Find dialog box. For more information, see Chapter 17, *Managing Sites*.

Navigation View Toolbar

The Navigation view changes the Site toolbar only slightly. The first six buttons remain, though the New Folder button is inactive. The new buttons that follow allow you to add new blank pages when in the Navigation tab, including new next and previous pages, and new child and parent pages. These buttons are not active in the Links tab. For more information, see Chapter 18, *Diagramming and Mapping*.

Diagrams Toolbar

Opening a diagram window in the Diagrams tab brings up the Diagrams toolbar, from which you can add pages to sections and make a design go live—that is, move the placeholder sections and pages into a real site document. For more information, see Chapter 18, *Diagramming and Mapping*.

Web Settings Toolbar

Open Web Settings (Command-Shift-K on the Mac or Control-Shift-K under Windows) and click the Markup or Characters tab to bring up the Web Settings toolbar. (An inactive Text toolbar appears when the Global tab is selected.) For more information, see Chapter 28, *Controlling Web Settings*.

QuickTime Toolbar

When you open a QuickTime file (by double-clicking the file in the Site window or double-clicking a plug-in icon where the file is placed within an individual page), the file is opened in the QuickTime Movie Editor and its attending QuickTime toolbar appears. See Chapter 12, *Rich Media*, for a brief introduction to QuickTime, and a full chapter devoted to editing QuickTime movies within GoLive at realworldgolive.com/six/quicktime.html.

Workgroup Toolbar

The Workgroup toolbar has a few shortcuts for working with workgroup sites, including checking files in and out. This toolbar is displayed by default, and is activated when the frontmost site window is a workgroup site, or any pages in the front are part of a workgroup site. The Workgroup Server is fully dissected in Chapter 21, *Working in Groups*.

Dynamic Content Toolbar

When you have a page or site window containing Dynamic Content frontmost, the Dynamic Content offers a few, limited options: toggle on or offline status, toggle page item highlighting, and bring up the Dynamic Content pane of Site Settings. The Toolbar is discussed alongside Dynamic Content in Chapter 15, *Dynamic Content and Databases*.

Advanced Feature Editors

Four of GoLive's advanced features—Cascading Style Sheets, Dynamic HTML (DHTML) animation, Content Sources, and JavaScript—are handled largely through four separate windows (with the help, of course, of several different Inspectors). The JavaScript, DHTML Timeline, Content Source, and CSS Editors are opened by clicking their respective buttons in the top-right corner of a Document window set to Layout Editor, (see Figure 1-23).

Figure 1-23
Advanced
feature editor
buttons

Click to access
advanced
feature editors.

JavaScript Editor

The JavaScript Editor allows a combination of drag-and-drop for triggers and page properties and simple typing to code and format JavaScript. Click the script icon in the Document window, and then click New Head Script or New Body Script to start coding. See Chapter 24, *Authoring JavaScript*, for the full details.

DHTML Timeline Editor

To add DHTML animations to your page, you first must add a Floating Box placeholder, then place any kind of HTML content in it. Click the film strip icon in the top right of the Layout Editor to open the DHTML Timeline Editor. This displays a single animation track (denoted by the number 1 and an arrow showing the active track) within a scene and a single keyframe (denoted by the small box surrounding a dot) within the track, placed at the timeline's starting point.

See Chapter 25, *Creating Animation with DHTML*, for information about configuring DHTML animations. See Chapter 10, *Floating Boxes*, for more on configuring individual floating boxes.

Content Sources

The conduits that connect GoLive's scripting language support to individual databases are called data sources. The sets of records retrieved from these data sources and linked into individual pages are Content Sources. To work with records from any supported database, the ecommerce solutions bundled with GoLive (through Adobe partners), or XML data, you create a Content Source on a dynamically enabled page, and use the Content Source Inspector to link and configure which records it contains.

See Chapter 15, *Dynamic Content and Databases*, on configuring Content Sources and linking them to containers, text placeholders, form elements, and tables on a page.

CSS Editor

To configure Cascading Style Sheets (CSS) for a particular page, click the CSS Editor icon in the Layout Editor. This is a collection point for the classes, tags, and IDs that you add to your page. Buttons at the bottom of the Editor allow you to add items. The CSS Style Inspector configures individual styles (see Figure 1-24). For more information, see Chapter 27, *Defining Cascading Style Sheets*.

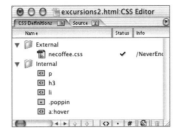

Figure 1-24
CSS Editor

Preferences

The GoLive workspace comprises piles upon piles of preferences that control the display of both page previews and the entire workspace.

This section tries to make some sense of how you control all of these interactions before you get deep into creating pages and sites. Most of these settings and windows need only be configured once when you first use the program.

Global Preferences

These options are all global, affecting program behavior or HTML, pages, or sites created or modified after the options are changed.

To change Preferences, press Command-K (Mac) or Control-K (Windows), or select Preferences from the Edit menu. Preferences shows a list of panes for each major setting area on the left side of the window. Those with a toggle triangle (Mac) or plus sign (Windows) to their left have additional preference sections. To reveal and hide those items, simply click the triangle or plus/minus signs.

On the Mac, your preference settings are written to a file named "Adobe GoLive 6.0 Prefs." In OS 9.1 or later, this file is in the System Folder's Preferences folder. Under OS X 10.1 or later, the file is in your individual folder in the Users directory, nested within Library and then Preferences. In Windows, the preferences file (GoLive.RData) is placed in the GoLive application folder (which, in turn, is buried in the Program Files folder).

Tip: Delete Prefs for a Clean Tomorrow

If you are having problems with GoLive crashing, or if you just want to start from scratch, quit GoLive and delete the preferences file. When you start GoLive again, your preferences are restored to the program's default settings.

General

When you open Preferences for the first time, GoLive deposits you at the top in the General pane, which sets a variety of standard program behaviors.

When you launch the program, GoLive opens an introductory dialog box with options for creating a new page, new site, or opening an existing file. If you want to change this, click the Don't Show Again box at the bottom of the screen. To change this setting in Preferences, from the At Launch popup menu select Create New Page, Show Intro Screen (allowing you to select from several screens), or Do Nothing.

If you want the Document window to open in a mode other than the Layout Editor (such as the Outline Editor), select that item in the Default Mode popup menu (see Figure 1-25).

Figure 1-25
Default Mode
popup menu

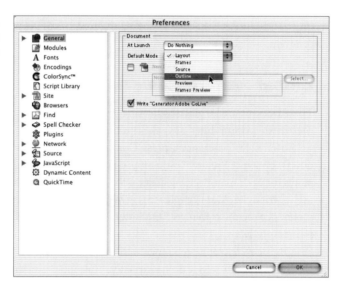

To open a specific file each time you create a new HTML document in GoLive (by selecting New from the File menu), check the New Document box, then click the Select button and navigate to the desired file. If you uncheck this option later, then decide that wasn't such a good idea, GoLive retains the location of the file as an inactive entry in the file field.

Tip: Open Stationery

If you work with a specific design structure for new pages in your site, designate a Stationery file or Template as your default new file. See Chapter 19, *Managing Files, Folders, and Links*, for more on Stationery and Template files.

GoLive also defaults to inserting a Meta tag into a page's Head section that tells the world GoLive 6 created the page; here's the code:

```
<meta name="generator" content="Adobe GoLive 6">
```

If you don't want to add this to your page, simply uncheck Write "Generator Adobe GoLive".

Reveal the other General preference items by clicking the expansion triangle (Mac) or the plus sign (Windows) to the left of the General pane.

URL Handling. Click URL Handling to configure a couple of basic URLisms. Select the Check URLs Case-Sensitive option to allow GoLive to treat internal URLs as if capitalization counts. We recommend this because several platforms care about case.

Tip: Change Case

You cannot change case sensitivity after a site is created.

If you're working with a site that uses Unicode multi-byte language encoding, check UTF 8. You can also choose whether to use "%HH" Escaping, in which special characters in URLs are automatically encoded in a format that allows those characters to work without error as links.

If you want GoLive to add "mailto:" automatically in front of email addresses typed in a URL field, check Auto Add "mailto:" to Addresses.

Tip: Auto Mail

Be sure to select this option, as it's best to always have mailto in front of an address; there's no reason we can think of not to, and this option saves a step in typing.

To change all links to absolute URLs (in reference to the base URL of the site) rather than relative (which uses the current site's root location as the reference point), check Make New Links Absolute. (See Chapter 19, *Managing Files, Folders, and Links,* for how to find, change, or use a site's root location.)

Checking Cut URLs After This [sic] Characters (a grammatical whoops left uncorrected over two versions of the software) allows you to trim the way URLs with arguments attached to them are displayed. A URL can include information that gets passed to a server, generally after a question mark to mark the start of the data part of the URL; GoLive distinguishes URLs from one another by the entire URL unless you check this box.

The URL Filter area allows you to set patterns, such as file extensions or directory paths, that GoLive treats as special files; these are ignored when the program creates a list of missing linked files and other errors. The filter allows you to keep GoLive from wanting to find CGI scripts, for instance, that aren't stored on your local hard drive; we typically add "/cgi-bin/" to the list.

To change which files GoLive considers to be missing, click the New Item button and type a file extension or directory pattern (like .pdf or /pdfs/) in the URL Filter text field. Any file or folder that matches this pattern has its own icon replaced with a gear icon to indicate that it's a special file (see Figure 1-26).

To get rid of filters, select one or more and click the Remove Selected Items button.

Figure 1-26
URL Handling
preferences

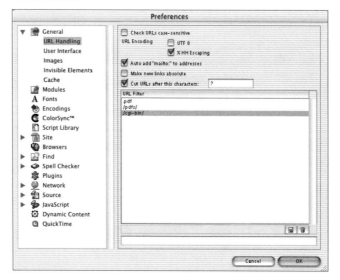

User Interface. Check the Launch Other Applications to Edit Media Files box to automatically open the parent media application when double-clicking an item in a GoLive page or site document (such as opening RealPlayer to access a RealAudio file).

Under Sizeknobs, you can choose the size of resizing items from the popup menu, pick a color using the Color Picker or Color dialog box, and set buttons to 2D or 3D.

Images. Click Images to set GoLive's image drag and drop support and low-source image creation preferences (see Figure 1-27).

When you drag images into an open window, GoLive displays the Save for Web dialog, giving you the ability to control the image's compression settings

Figure 1-27
Images
preferences

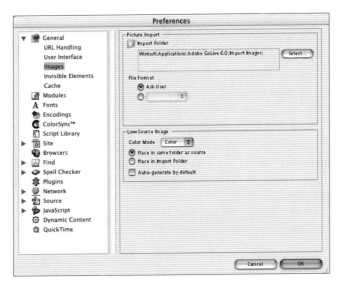

and saving it as a GIF, JPEG, or PNG formatted file. For more on the Save for Web options, see Chapter 5, *Images*.

You can turn off Save for Web by disabling the Smart Links in the Modules pane, in which case the Picture Import settings are used. If you're building lots of comps on the fly, Save for Web can be a speed bump to your productivity. Letting GoLive create temporary files of images you're not going to keep anyway is much faster.

If the Save for Web option is disabled, the image preview GoLive creates is saved as a temporary browser-compatible image file (with a generic numerical name, such as "image7106732.jpg"). Under Picture Import, you can select a folder where these collected images reside. GoLive defaults to placing these images in the Import Images folder.

Under File Format, select the browser-compatible file format to use when saving dragged and dropped images—GIF or JPEG.

With GIF chosen, you can check Interlaced to have the image load gradually, which increases the file's size slightly. With JPEG, you can check Progressive (which acts like Interlaced), as well as your desired compression level from the popup menu. On the Mac, you can also check Use QuickTime, which uses QuickTime's JPEG encoding algorithm instead of Adobe's (see Figure 1-28, next page).

If you check the Ask User option, the Import Image dialog box appears when you import an image, which allows you to navigate to a desired directory folder and choose the format of the file. This is handy, as it lets you give the file a coherent name (instead of something like "image-1276465113.jpg");

Figure 1-28
Image File
Format
preferences

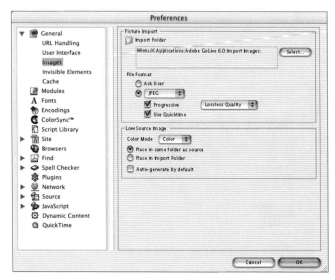

Figure 1-28
Image File
Format
preferences

however it does take away a bit of control over the formatting of the file. For instance, if you choose JPEG, GoLive automatically saves the file as a progressive JPEG, and you don't know which level of compression is selected. In addition, this import/save dialog doesn't contain the nifty GoLive Save button that lets you choose to go directly to the site's Root, Stationery, or Components folders (see Figure 1-29).

If you want to generate low-source versions of images placed into GoLive pages, you can choose to store those either in the same folder as the original image or into the folder designated as the Picture Import location. Choose B/W (black and white) or Color from the popup menu. If you want GoLive to

Figure 1-29
Saving to open
site folders

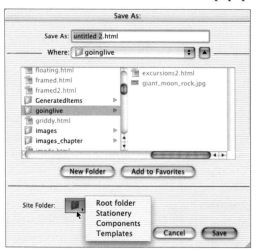

generate these low-resolution images automatically, check that option. Remember you can also create low-source images via the Image Inspector's More tab (See Figure 1-30).

Figure 1-30
Specifying a
low-source
image

Invisible Elements. GoLive can be awfully crowded in its Document window with placeholders for objects and errors. The default set shows all of the invisible objects (which aren't, in fact, invisible, given that they're all checked, but we'll let that pass). You can create custom sets and check different options to hide or show various items.

Cache. We were glad to see the return of this feature, which made a faux show in version 4 and a no-show in version 5. It allows GoLive to store elements in a cache folder that you can select to store temporary copies of files used for previewing. Set the size if you think 32 MB is too little or too much, and click Clear Cache Now to erase the currently stored files.

GoLive Modules

You can control several aspects of GoLive's functionality via the Modules pane. We broke out the detail of which Modules control which features—because it's quite, quite long—at the end of this chapter in "Modules."

Fonts

In the Fonts pane, you can set the default fonts that GoLive uses to display text within your documents for all of the different languages and writing scripts supported. Remember that these are not font set preferences, which determine how your audience views your published Web pages; they apply to GoLive's internal rendering only.

Click a toggle triangle (Mac) or plus sign (Windows) to the left of a language group, like Western, to reveal the types of fonts you can set (Proportional, Monospaced, Serif, Sans Serif, Cursive, and Fantasy).

Select a font to activate the Font popup menu at the bottom of the window, then choose from the list of available system fonts and point sizes using the Font and Size popup menus. On the Mac, GoLive also provides a preview pane when you click the Font Sample toggle triangle (see Figure 1-31).

Figure 1-31
Viewing a
font sample

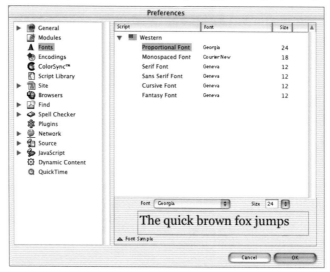

Encodings

If you leave the Encodings module turned off, you only see the Western encodings (for ISO-8859-1 and X-MAC-ROMAN). However, with the Encodings module turned on and the appropriate items installed, you see the full range of non-Roman-alphabet characters from outside this Western European group, and are able to add those characters to your GoLive pages.

In the Encodings pane, go through the list and select all language encodings you want to make available to GoLive (see Figure 1-32). Checking an encoding as the Default Encoding at the bottom of the pane grays and disables its checkbox. You can select all encoding subsets for a group (revealed by clicking the group's toggle triangle or plus sign) by checking the group.

The Use Charset Info option is checked by default, which tells GoLive to place character set information in the Head section's Meta content tag. If this is unchecked, the Scanning Limit X Characters field becomes inactive; the value in this field tells GoLive how many bytes to search to find encoding and character set information when it opens.

Figure 1-32
Encodings
preferences

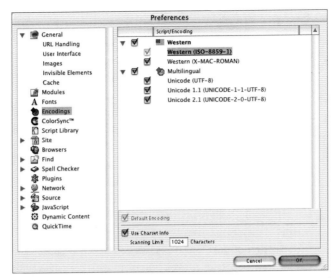

The selected default encoding used when a file was created appears in the File menu's Document Encoding submenu.

ColorSync (Mac Only)

On the Mac, you can use Apple's ColorSync color management system to display colors within images consistently. This can be done either globally (for all images within GoLive via Preferences), regionally (for all images on a single page via the Page Inspector), or locally (for an individual image via the Image Inspector).

With Display Images Using ColorSync checked, you can also check Use Default RGB Profile If Not Specified, which then uses a color profile built into GoLive when ColorSync is activated but no RGB profile is embedded into an image. If Display Images Using ColorSync is unchecked, the Use Default RGB Profile becomes inactive (see Figure 1-33). For more information, consult Chapter 5, *Images*.

Figure 1-33
ColorSync
preferences

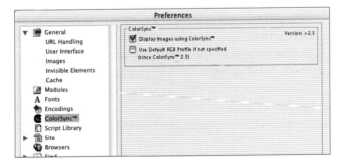

Script Library

When you use DHTML animations or certain smart objects on a page, GoLive writes the JavaScript for the object in the page's source code by default. If you want to handle code in this way, keep the Write Code in Page option selected in the Script Library pane.

But if you use Components in your pages, you need to choose Import GoLive Script Library to write the code for all Actions and other JavaScript features into a script library named CSScriptLib.js; it places a reference to this common file in the Head section of each new page.

If you have a site document open, GoLive creates this library file at the root level of the site in a new folder called "GeneratedItems". You can modify both the folder and file names in the Folder for Script Library and Name of Script Library, respectively.

Selecting Import GoLive Script Library only shifts this code to the library file for new pages. To move code from existing pages with dynamic components to the library file, you must go into an individual page, open the Page Inspector to the HTML tab, select the Import GoLive Script Library radio button, then save the page.

Click the Rebuild button whenever you change the Actions you have loaded into GoLive; this forces the program to rebuild the external JavaScript library to reflect the new set of Actions.

This preference can be set in the Site Settings of an individual site as well, a new option in GoLive 6. For more information, see Chapter 24, *Authoring JavaScript* and Chapter 26, *Applying Actions*.

Site and Its Subpanes

The Site pane and its subsidiaries allow you to configure some of the minute elements of GoLive's site management features, from folder names and the way files are deleted to defining page status and export parameters. We explain these options in great, great detail in Chapter 17, *Managing Sites*.

Browsers

With a page open in GoLive or selected in the Site window, clicking the Show in Browser button from the Toolbar opens that page in a browser or set of browsers designated in the Browsers pane.

If you click the Show in Browser button without first having chosen browsers, you receive an error dialog box reminding you of this fact. Click the Specify button to open up the Browsers preferences.

To gather a list of all browsers found on your system, click the Find All button. After GoLive searches your hard drive, a list appears in the pane above (see Figure 1-34). To remove a browser from the list, select it and click the Remove button. To add a new browser, click the Add button and navigate to that browser application.

Check the box next to one or more browsers that you want to set as your default. After exiting Preferences by clicking OK, clicking the Show in Browser button opens all of the checked browsers to preview your selected page.

If you didn't check a default browser and you click the Show in Browser button, GoLive reminds you that you didn't set this option.

Figure 1-34
Browser
preferences

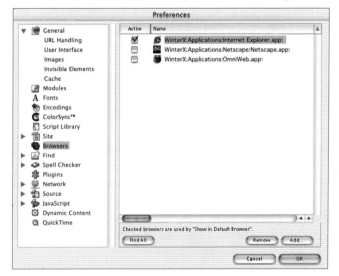

Find and Regular Expressions

The When Match Is Found popup sets how the Find dialog behaves. Activate Document brings the Document window to the front when a search term is located, while Keep Find Window in Front keeps the Find dialog active. Choosing Close Find Window closes the Find dialog as soon as your search item is located, though if nothing is returned the Find dialog remains open.

You can search across a site for items in a file's HTML source code by selecting Source Mode from the Treat Files In popup menu. When an item is found, GoLive opens the page to the highlighted item in the Source Code Editor. In Preferences, you can choose to search only Web pages (Use Only HTML Files) or all Web pages and associated style sheets (Use HTML and Text Files).

The Regular Expressions settings beneath the Find pane let you set up a list of wildcard search options for GoLive to use as prefabricated searches when using regular-expression pattern matching (see Figure 1-35).

Figure 1-35
Regular
Expressions to
use with the
Find feature

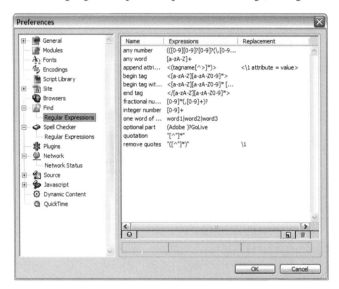

GoLive comes with several built-in patterns. To create a new pattern, click the New Item button and type a descriptive name for this item in the highlighted Name field. In the Regular Expression field, type what you want to search for, such as any number that follows the word "GoLive" or a common change you make across your site.

If you plan on using the Replace feature as well, enter the word or string that replaces the found text in the Replacement field. After exiting Preferences, open up the Find dialog, click the popup menu button to the right of the Find field, and select the item you just created from the list.

To learn more about GoLive's Find feature, see Chapter 14, *Source Editing* (basic Find on page and the Find by Element feature), and Chapter 22, *Advanced Features* (site-wide searches and regular expressions).

Spell Checker and Regular Expressions

When checking spelling on GoLive pages, you can store unrecognized words in a personal dictionary by pressing the Learn button. To edit this customized collection, go to the Spell Checker pane of the Preferences, select a word from the list, and make your edit in the text field below the list pane (see Figure 1-36). Choose a particular language from the popup menu to see the personal dictionary associated with that language.

Figure 1-36
Spell Checker
personal
dictionary

As with the Find feature, GoLive also provides a Regular Expressions section for spelling where you can create a list of wildcard spelling strings for GoLive to ignore (see Figure 1-37). GoLive's built-in list includes a pattern for normal URLs (like ftp and http) to keep them from popping up left and right while you attempt to check spelling.

To learn more about using GoLive's Spell Checking feature, see Chapter 2, *Layout*.

Figure 1-37
Spell Checker
regular
expressions

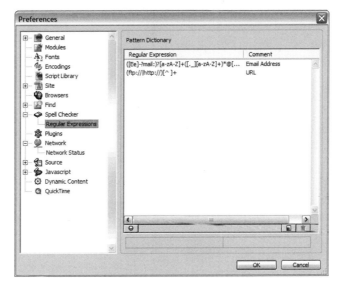

Plugins

GoLive works with media files (like QuickTime, Flash, etc.) in much the same way that Web browsers do, with plug-ins that handle the media's playback stored in the Plugins folder within the GoLive application folder. If you place a media file onto a page without including the plug-in, you can't preview the file directly in GoLive.

Under the Plugins pane, you find a collection of media players placed into the Plugins folder listed with the MIME type, the player that handles this type, and the file name extension that triggers GoLive to use this plug-in player. Below the list pane, you can make modifications to these fields, as well as choose another plug-in player that can handle that file type (if one is available). You can also designate whether GoLive should or should not play the file when previewed.

To add a new item, click the New Item button and enter a valid MIME type. If an appropriate plug-in player already resides within the Plugins folder, GoLive assigns that in the popup menu. Type the file suffix in the Extensions field, then any comments in the Info field (see Figure 1-38).

For more information, see Chapter 12, *Rich Media*.

Network

In the Network pane, you can set up basic connectivity. If your ISP or network requires that you connect via a proxy server (for filtering or security reasons), check either the Use FTP Proxy or Use HTTP Proxy options and fill in the server address and Port number below.

Figure 1-38
Plugins
preferences

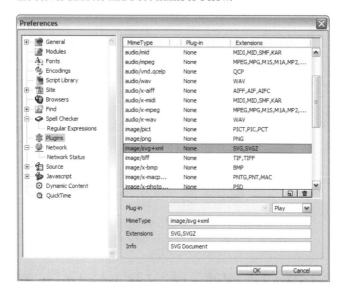

Check Keep Connections Alive to continue to ping the Web via your Internet connection so it doesn't close down due to lack of activity.

Checking Resolve Links follows aliases and shortcuts and symbolic links on the remote file server to find out what they point to. You can uncheck this option to prevent GoLive from looking up the link destinations. (The feature should be called resolve alias/shortcuts, as the term *link* is only used in Unix environments.)

Mac-specific options. Keep the Use ISO 8859-1 Translation option checked to use the Latin1 character encoding set, which covers the majority of Western European languages. This option exists because the Mac can use an alternate character set.

You can choose to extract network settings from the Internet control panel in OS 9 or Network System Preferences pane in OS X; see Appendix A, *Macintosh Issues & Extras,* for details.

Checking Use System Keychain for Passwords allows users of Mac OS 9 or later to store passwords for FTP and WebDAV sites in the system Keychain feature, which encrypts passwords using a passphrase. Check Ask Before Adding Passwords to avoid adding passwords without being aware of it.

Network Status. Network Status works in conjunction with all of the network operations of the program, showing any errors or just plain system messages, depending on the options you've chosen (see Figure 1-39). Checking Warnings and Status Messages increases the amount of feedback that GoLive offers, which can help debug problems with connections or file transfers—if

Figure 1-39
Network Status
preferences

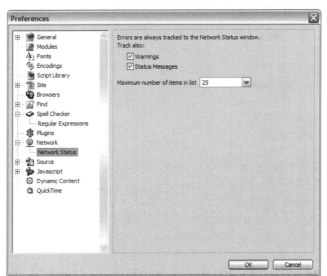

not for you, then for the person from whom you ask for help. Use the popup menu to choose the maximum number of items in the list, which ranges from five to unlimited.

To learn more about the features referenced in the Network pane, see Chapter 20, *Synchronizing Sites*.

Source and JavaScript

Click Source to set the general source code appearance and preferences or the JavaScript pane for that language's display in the JavaScript Editor (see Figure 1-40). Because these settings are almost identical, we're collapsing them into one spot to avoid repetition.

General preferences. The preview below the checkboxes in the Source and JavaScript pane shows the results of your code display choices.

- **Drag and drop (Source).** To turn off drag and drop support, uncheck Enable Dragging of Marked Text.

- **Bold for Tags (Source).** Set or unset Bold for Tags to control whether source code displays tags in bold.

- **Line Numbers, Word Wrap (both).** Check or uncheck Line Numbers and Word Wrap to display numbers next to each line item (helpful for debugging), or whether lines should run to the end off the edge of the screen, or be soft wrapped to fit. Word Wrap doesn't affect line numbering.

Figure 1-40
General
JavaScript
preferences

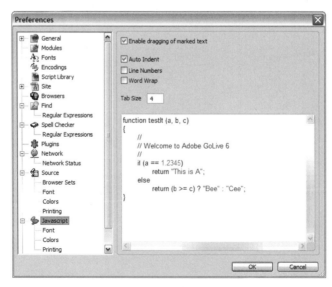

- **Auto Indent, Tab Size (both).** Auto Indent is checked by default. Change Tab Size to control how much indent is used.

Browser Sets (Source only). Browser Sets controls code specifications that the Source Code Editor's Check Syntax feature can use as one of a number of options to find problems in the HTML (see Figure 1-41).

Figure 1-41
Browser Sets
preferences

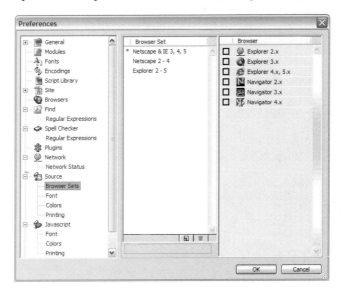

To modify an existing set, select it in the list, then check the browsers you want to include in that set. To create a new set, click the New Set button, type a name in the text field, then check the browsers you want to include in the set. You can delete sets by choosing them and clicking Remove Selected Sets.

For more information, see Chapter 14, *Source Editing*, and Chapter 28, *Controlling Web Settings*.

Font (Source, JavaScript). Choose a font found on your system to format code in any of the places source code or JavaScript are displayed (see Figure 1-42, next page). Use the Name, Size, and Style popup menus on the Mac or the Font, Style, and Size lists under Windows to set your font formatting. On the Mac, checking Condense shortens the space between letters, while Extend adds space.

Colors (Source, JavaScript). Colors sets the display of various elements and various kinds of code (see Figure 1-43, next page).

Figure 1-42
JavaScript font
preferences

Figure 1-42
JavaScript font
preferences

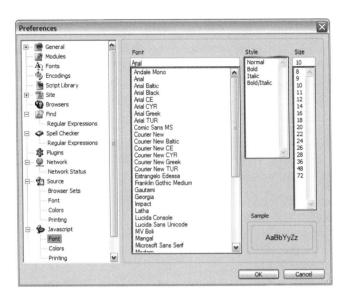

Figure 1-43
Source colors
preferences

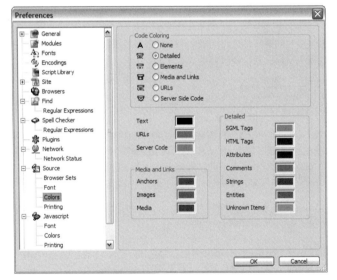

- **Code Coloring (Source).** Source code can be colored depending on which items you want highlighted. None uses the default text color; Detailed sets off each kind of code and syntax as a different color, set in the bottom half of the pane; Elements shows just the stuff in tag brackets; Media and Links spotlight entire tags for images, plug-in files, and links; URLs colorizes only the link reference and image tags; and Server Side Code highlights generic code from Dynamic Content and scripting languages.

- **Color swatches (Source).** You can set the colors for the various items that correspond to Code Coloring. The color you choose in the Text color field is displayed for all page content; or, it's the color used if no syntax highlighting is selected.

- **Code Coloring (JavaScript).** JavaScript has fewer options, but you can turn code coloring on or off, and set the color for various bits of JavaScript syntax. Operators, for instance, are the symbols used for equals, less than, string comparisons, and so on.

Printing (Source and JavaScript). Check Printer Specific Settings to have the options below take effect, such as the different colored syntax highlighting, bold typeface for tags, and line numbers along the left side of the page (see Figure 1-44). (Some of these options are only effective on a color printer, but black-and-white printers simulate colors as grays.)

Check Use Special Font for Printing to use a specific font style with your printed pages. Here you can set an available font, its size, and whether it's printed as bold, condensed, or extended.

Figure 1-44
JavaScript printing preferences

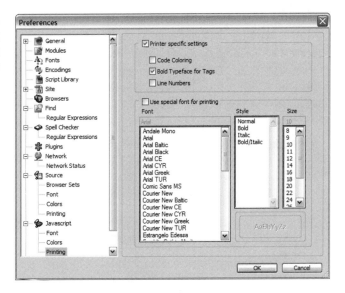

Dynamic Content

Enter a value in the HTTP Timeout field to set how long GoLive waits before reporting an error when it can't access a content source from an open page. Keep the Use Cached Responses When Online option checked to keep a broad category of responses in memory to reduce queries. You can also check Use

Cached Responses When Offline to still work with some information from the scripting server even when not connected to it. Click the Clear Cache Now button to flush cached valucs.

For much, much more on adding dynamic content in GoLive, see Chapter 15, *Dynamic Content and Databases*, and Chapter 23, *Building Dynamic Content.*

QuickTime

The QuickTime section of Preferences allows you to set a scratch disk, where GoLive saves temporary movie files (much like Photoshop and Premiere).

Additionally, you can configure the color, style, frequency, and subdivision of layout grids when you're editing QuickTime movies in the Layout tab of GoLive's built-in QuickTime editor.

Adding QuickTime movies to a page is covered in chapter 12, *Rich Media*. Editing QuickTime movies in GoLive is detailed our interactive chapter devoted to QuickTime controls at realworldgolive.com/six/quicktime.html.

Servers

GoLive requires that you configure the settings for any FTP or WebDAV servers you want to connect to in the Servers dialog box, reached via the Edit menu (see Figure 1-45). Anywhere you can choose an FTP or WebDAV server also offers an Edit Servers menu item that accesses the options found in this dialog box as well.

Click the New Item button, and then enter the following details:

- **Nickname.** Type a shorthand name for the server; this name appears in all the popup and submenus from which you can select an FTP or WebDAV server. Make it descriptive.

- **Server.** Enter ftp:// followed by the server name for FTP servers, or http:// for WebDAV servers. You can include the path to your directory, if you like, and GoLive copies that to the Directory field.

- **Directory.** Enter the path through subfolders to your directory where you store the files for the site. You can browse by clicking the Browse button if you've entered the Username and Password already. GoLive offers up a window into the server at the Directory level you've already specified or the root of your login area (see Figure 1-46).

- **Username and Password.** Enter your user name and password for this server. Check Save to enable the Password field.

Figure 1-45
Servers

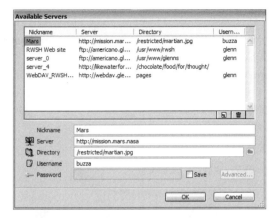

Figure 1-46
Server
directory

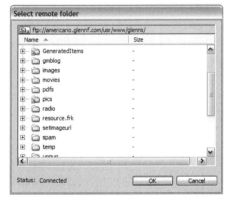

- **Advanced.** Click Advanced to set three options: Use Passive Mode (a way of working with firewalls that may restrict the more active default FTP method), Keep Connections Alive (which tries to keep an FTP connection open for as long as you have it active in your site), and Resolve Links (which turns aliases and shortcuts into their actual paths on the server).

Remove a server by selecting it in the list and clicking Remove Selected Items. Edit a server by selecting it and changing the values below the list.

Adobe Online Settings

Adobe offers updates and other information through the Adobe Online system that can (with your permission) send details about your configuration and determine what files or software you need to be up to date.

To set up your connection settings, select Adobe Online Settings from the Edit menu (which brings up a box labeled Adobe Online Preferences, of course).

Under Update Options, select how frequently you'd like your machine to connect with Adobe Online. You can choose Never for manual connections or Once a Day, Week, or Month.

Clicking Updates, selecting Updates from the Help menu, or clicking the Adobe Online button (the long one) on the Toolbar sends details of your configuration to Adobe and then brings up the Adobe Product Updates dialog box in which you can view available software.

Keyboard Shortcuts

Ever get into a rut where you've learned the keystrokes for a program and just don't want to change them for a new revision? Keyboard Shortcuts offers a way out. You can define or modify the keys you press for any menu or option in GoLive by selecting Keyboard Shortcuts from the Edit menu.

You can create different sets and assign different keyboard shortcuts for different users or different functions (see Figure 1-47). You can also pass these around among many users to standardize for training.

Keyboard Shortcuts comes with two settings—GoLive Factory Defaults, and GoLive 5 Set. The GoLive Factory Defaults cannot be modified, so you edit shortcuts by creating a new set (see Figure 1-48).

Figure 1-47
Assigning keyboard shortcuts

Figure 1-48
Creating a new keyboard shortcut set

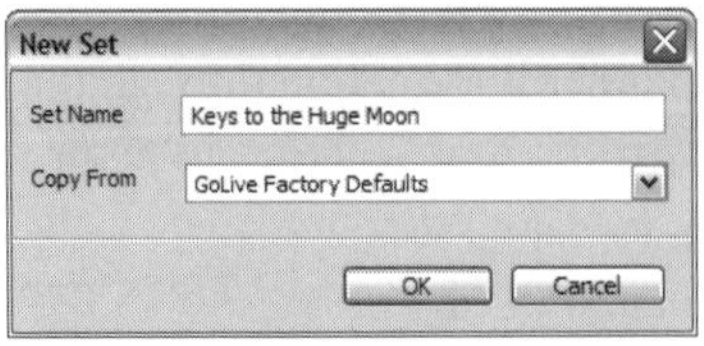

Tip: Blast from the Recent Past

The GoLive 5 Set preserves all of the keyboard shortcuts that were present in the previous release of the program.

To create a new set, click the New Set button, which opens up the New Set dialog box. A copy of the name of the currently viewed set is placed into the Set Name field, preceded by "Copy of". Keep this name or enter a new one. You can choose another set to copy settings from via the popup menu below the name. Click OK to make the set.

To add a shortcut to a menu item that has no existing shortcut, or to edit a menu item's existing shortcut, select the item from the list. For example, expand the Edit section and select Group. In the Press New Shortcut field, type a new keyboard combination. If you choose a command that's already in use, such as Command-G, the Currently Assigned field notes that the shortcut is already paired with the Edit menu's Find Next item.

You could simply choose another keyboard combination, or you could be stubborn and click the Assign button to switch shortcut assignments from the original menu item to the newly selected item.

Tip: Printing Keystrokes (Mac only)

With Keyboard Shortcuts open, press Command P or select Print from the File menu. The trick is to expand all items that you want to be printed; items that aren't expanded don't have their underlying items printed.

Modules

You can control several aspects of GoLive's functionality via the Modules pane in Preferences. You can turn modules on and off to increase responsiveness and memory requirements for GoLive. If you make a change to the Modules list, you must quit and then restart GoLive to make the changes take effect.

To learn more about each Module, click the Show Item Information toggle triangle below the list. With a Module selected, this pane reveals the size of the module, as well as its version number and when it was last modified. You can also read a brief description of the point of the Module.

Tip: And Now the Name's Not the Same

Adobe still has a problem harmonizing the names of things between the Mac and Windows version. Some of the names below appear in one version under Macintosh (typically with Module stuck on the end) and another under Windows.

AdobeOnlineModule. Adobe integrates all of its programs with the Internet for updates and special notices; this Module handles that interaction. The Adobe Online features are available through the button at far right in the main Toolbar, or the bottom several items in the Help menu.

ARM Module. For workgroup sites, the ARM Module lets GoLive hand files off to Photoshop, Illustrator, and LiveMotion when they're checked out, and then checks them back in when modified and saved from those applications. The module is off by default.

Color Palette. Displays GoLive's integrated Color Palette and allows for dragging and dropping color swatches. If unchecked, the Color Palette isn't available and you have to rely on the Color Picker (Mac) or the Colors dialog box (Windows) for choosing colors.

DynamicContent Module. Checking this item allows you to use GoLive's database integration features, including linking to databases sources. It adds menus, objects, and a toolbar.

Encodings. Accesses a plethora of international text encodings, from Japanese to Chinese (Traditional and Simplified) to Greek to Devanagari. This option is off by default.

Extend Script. Enables the customization of GoLive via JavaScript using a Software Developer's Kit (SDK). You can add dialog boxes, tabs in the Objects palette, and other controls.

Tip: Latest Version

Extend Script is periodically upgraded as Adobe improves its SDK; check their site or use Adobe Online to ensure you have the latest version when you install third-party plug-ins.

Find by Element. Adds the Element tab to the Find dialog, which enables you to search for specific tags and attributes.

Modules Manager. In theory this would allow you to enable or disable GoLive's collection of modules. However, since it is checked by default and appears in the module list as inactive, you can't turn it off. But you can still admire it, nonetheless.

Network. Network is set to support a File Transfer Protocol (FTP) connection. If unchecked, the FTP tab in the Site window's Extras tab isn't available, and all FTP fields in the Site Settings dialog box (accessed via the Site toolbar) are inactive.

Network Status. Helps you troubleshoot network problems through the display of FTP and WebDAV log information.

Open Recent Files (Mac). Provides access to documents (pages, site documents, and media files) most recently opened. If unchecked, the Open Recent menu item doesn't appear in the Mac's File menu.

Outline Mode. Allows you to view and edit HTML source code in the Outline Editor's graphical format. If unchecked, the Outline Editor tab isn't available.

Preview Mode. Allows you to preview the layout of pages and frame sets. If unchecked, the Document window's Layout Preview tab is not available (nor is the Frame Preview tab on the Mac).

QuickTime Module. Activates GoLive's QuickTime editing features (such as the Movie Viewer and Timeline Editor).

Scripting Module. Contains GoLive's JavaScript features, including the JavaScript Editor. If this is unchecked, the JavaScript Editor icon doesn't appear in the Layout Editor, and other JavaScript features are removed. (It does not stop you from using JavaScript in pages, however.)

Site Module. Manages Web sites via the GoLive site file, including all links, images, external URLs, colors, font sets, etc. If unchecked, GoLive doesn't allow you to create or open site documents.

Site Planning. Activates the Diagrams tab in the Site document, which enables you to prototype new pages or structures in a site, or map existing pages by navigation hierarchy or links. It also includes the Site Reports feature for finding errors or other parameters in pages throughout a site.

Smart Links. Enables you to synchronize original Photoshop, Illustrator, and LiveMotion image files (TIFF, EPS, PSD, etc.) with their Web-friendly cousins (GIF, PNG, JPEG). Adds the Smart Photoshop, Smart Illustrator, Smart

LiveMotion, and Smart Generic items to the Objects palette's Smart tab, and activates the Save for Web feature for images that are dragged into GoLive.

Smart Objects. Activates the DHTML/JavaScript items in the Objects palette's Smart tab (such as Rollover and URL Popup).

Spell Checker. Allows you to check spelling within an individual document or an entire site. If unchecked, the Check Spelling option is removed from the Edit menu.

SWF Module (Mac), SWF (Windows). Manages links embedded within Shockwave/Flash files.

WebDAV. Allows you to connect to and exchange files with WebDAV servers.

WebDownload. Allows you to download the entire contents of a Web page or site, including embedded images and style sheets. It can follow links from page to page and suck the contents of those pages as well. For details on this feature, see Chapter 2, *Layout.*

XMP. XMP allows rich XML data to be embedded inside native file formats, like those used for Photoshop or InDesign. For more information about this standard and its uses, see www.adobe.com/products/xmp/main.html.

Extend Scripts folder. Any third-party scripts are referenced in this folder, allowing you to turn them on or off. GoLive ships with several items in this folder for special cases.

- **i-mode Emoji:** support for special characters used in i-mode phones.
- **LayoutGrid:** allows conversion of layout grids to tables.
- **PageGenerator:** takes a list of queries to a dynamic site and generates static pages (see Chapter 15, *Dynamic Content and Databases*).
- **SetTitle:** warns you if a page is saved without the Title being set (to avoid "Welcome to Adobe GoLive 6" on all your untitled pages).
- **WML:** more support for this markup language via an Objects palette tab.
- **Workflow:** allows you to set values attached to a field via a Workflow palette for the next editor and percentage of a file completed in workgroup sites.

Andalay La Vida

With the background of interface and approach in hand, you're ready to set foot into the deep recesses of GoLive. Part 1 covers the basics of objects on a page; Part 2, the more complicated issues of working with code and servers; Part 3, site building and working in groups; and Part 4, advanced features that you may wind up using every day.

Off you go, now!

Building Pages
PART 1

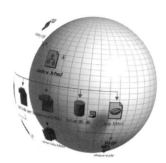

CHAPTER 2
Layout

GoLive exists to create and edit the basic unit of the Web: the *page*, a set of text, images, and other items that comprise the contents of a browser window; some parts you see, others are hidden beneath the surface. You add these elements by typing or dragging them to GoLive's Layout Editor, much as you would edit a page in a desktop-publishing program like InDesign or QuarkXPress.

However, when you take a closer look at it, the Web page is quite different from its bound-for-paper cousins. The structure of HTML presents several advantages and limitations for designers; understanding them will help you avoid unexpected problems and unnecessary work.

Page Structure

The whole point of using a graphical program like GoLive is to avoid hand-coding HTML. It's easier to drag an image file from the Desktop onto a GoLive page, for example, than it is to write the HTML that describes the file's location and dimensions. (Even if you've been hand-coding Web pages for years, it's usually faster to drag and drop elements—and it's better for your hands and fingers in the long run.) But unlike print page-layout programs, which allow you to place elements anywhere within the workspace, Web pages are more dependent upon how browsers read and display the underlying HTML.

Understanding the fundamental structure of the Web can go a long way toward creating page designs that load clean on multiple platforms.

Top-Down Design

Building pages for the Web is more akin to working in a word processor than a desktop-publishing program. Everything on a page is inline, treated like just another text character. When a Web browser builds a page, it reads the HTML from the first character to the last, placing elements based on the order they appear in the code.

When you place an image, GoLive doesn't calculate its position based on the number of pixels between the image's border and the edge of the page. Instead, GoLive recognizes that the image appears as a character within a paragraph (see Figure 2-1).

Designers employ many techniques to give the illusion that objects aren't tied to this structure, such as wrapping text around images, or using tables or layout grids to position elements. But underneath, every element exists as an inline object within the page's text—even in cases where no text is to be seen.

For a practical example, let's look again at positioning an image. We want a photograph to appear against the right side of the page, with text wrapping around its left side. In a typical desktop-publishing program, you'd position

What's New in 6

The conundrum of writing a book about a program like GoLive is that dozens of major and minor things are new in each version (and no doubt hundreds of little things most people wouldn't notice). Since this book isn't meant to be a litany of revision notes, we're going to stick with mentioning the really important stuff.

In terms of everyday work, we're happy to see the new Split Source view, which uses part of the Layout Editor to display your page graphically and the rest to display the underlying HTML code.

An important, but easily overlooked, addition is the Document window popout menu, located in the upper-right corner of the window. From here you can set the page's document type (Doctype), which instructs Web browsers how to render the page's contents, as well as apply a Template to the page.

Once it's visible, you can't miss the new Highlight palette, which provides a way to locate specific elements on a page by pointing them out like a highlighter pen.

If you're developing material that gets fed from online databases, the Open Content Source Editor icon in the Document window provides a quick way to manipulate objects within GoLive's extensive Dynamic Content features.

And lest we forget an item that we use almost more than any other in GoLive, the URL Getter now includes a Link popout menu to the right of the URL field in Inspectors, which lists recently-used URLs and page names stored elsewhere within your site.

Figure 2-1
Inline image
placement

Image at start of paragraph   Image at end of paragraph

the image on the page, then drop a text block alongside it. (You could also put the text behind the image and enable the program's text-wrapping features, but in this case we'll keep things simple.) However, in standard HTML, the image is treated as just another character: placing it at the beginning or end of the paragraph produces different results. For now, put the image at the beginning of the paragraph.

To wrap the text, set the image's alignment to Right in the Image Inspector. The image shifts to the right edge of the screen, and its top edge is aligned with the height of the first line of text. Now, drag and drop the image so it follows the last character in the paragraph. Although the photograph is still aligned against the right edge of the screen, the text of the next paragraph is wrapped (see Figure 2-2).

Quirks like this can sometimes drive traditional designers crazy, and illustrates the importance of understanding the limitations of one's medium.

Tip: Pushing Pixel Positioning

If you're familiar with Cascading Style Sheets, you're probably thinking that we've gone out of our heads (and so early in the book, too). In fact, CSS does

Figure 2-2
Right
alignment

Right align at start of paragraph   Right align at end of paragraph

allow you to position elements with pixel-level control (one of its coolest features). But as you'll see, even the code required to accomplish this feat still appears inline within the HTML. See Chapter 27, *Defining Cascading Style Sheets*, and Chapter 10, *Floating Boxes*, for more on precise positioning.

Anatomy of a Web Page

No matter the length or complexity, a Web page is divided into two parts: the Head section and the Body section. The other chapters in this part of the book are devoted to what you can do in these two sections.

Head Section

Like the rounded (and attractive, we might add) protuberance supported by your shoulders, a Web page's Head is vital to the operation of the whole organism. At its simplest, the Head section defines the title of the page (which appears in the browser window's title bar); getting more complex, the Head can contain each of the following elements. See Chapter 3, *Head Section*, for more on how to keep a smart Head on your shoulders.

- **Encoding tag.** This bit of code tells a browser which character set to use to display the page. Although Western (ISO-8859-1) is what most people are probably familiar with, modern browsers can correctly display pages in other non-Roman alphabets if the operating system is set up to handle it.

- **Base tag.** You can identify a URL to act as the basis of all links on the page.

- **Meta tags**. Search engines and other archival systems read Meta tags to gain overview information about your page, including a brief description and relevant keywords.

- **Link tags**. You can define special relationships between the Web page and other pages on the Web.

- **Scripts.** Code that's used for effects, like image rollovers or advanced functionality, is stored in the Head section and referenced from commands in the rest of the page. Examples include JavaScript, Jscript, and VBScript.

- **Cascading Style Sheets (CSS).** You can gain advanced typographic control and precise positioning using CSS. The code either appears directly in the Head section, or exists in an external file that is specified in the Head.

Body Section

The Body section contains everything else in a Web page. Separate chapters cover each aspect of the following elements and tools.

- **Layout:** the basics of building pages (this chapter)
- **Text and Fonts:** everything about specifying typographic characteristics, using typefaces, and structuring paragraphs—including working with the typographic features of Cascading Style Sheets (Chapter 4)
- **Images:** inserting and manipulating images, creating image maps, using the Tracing Image feature; sharing pixels and code with Photoshop, Illustrator, LiveMotion, and other tools (Chapter 5)
- **Color:** managing the options in the voluminous Color palette (Chapter 6)
- **Tables:** the ins and outs of creating tables (Chapter 7)
- **Layout Grids:** GoLive's near-exact positioning tools (Chapter 8)
- **Frames:** how to use GoLive's Frame icons, Frame Editor, and Layout Preview or Frame Preview to create frames that work (Chapter 9)
- **Floating Boxes:** break out of inline constraints by building boxes that use CSS for positioning and manipulation (Chapter 10)
- **Templates:** set which areas of a page can be edited by others (Chapter 11)
- **Rich Media:** adding QuickTime, Real media, plug-ins, and other media (Chapter 12)
- **Forms:** an explanation of form elements, structuring forms, and integrating with a server (Chapter 13)
- **Source Editing:** editing the underlying HTML code (Chapter 14)
- **Dynamic Content and Databases:** building Web pages that contain ever-changing information pulled from databases (Chapter 15)
- **Languages and Scripting:** other Web technologies, such as creating pages for wireless devices and using server-side scripting languages (Chapter 16)

The Document Window

We all have our favorite places, the spots where we tend to gravitate. You could own a house with a hundred rooms, but we bet you'd spend most of your time in only one or two. The same idea applies to GoLive. Although it has a wide variety of editing and preview screens, the bulk of your time is spent in its main rooms: the Document window, and specifically, the Layout Editor.

Tabs line the top of each Document window. They correspond to GoLive's different modes of editing and previewing. Each mode allows you to view your page in a different manner. The tabs are Layout Editor, Frame Editor, Source Code Editor, Outline Editor, Layout Preview, and the Mac-only Frame Preview (see Figure 2-3). When you first launch GoLive, the Document window is set to show the Layout Editor by default.

Tip: Change Your First View

If you'd rather have another editing mode—such as Frame Editor—as your default when creating a new document, you can set your preference through the General pane's Document settings in the Preferences dialog box. Select a view from the Default Mode menu (see Figure 2-4).

If you collapse the Document window on the Mac to a width of 279 pixels or fewer, the Layout, Source, and Preview tabs are represented only by icons (the Frame Editor and Frame Preview tabs are normally represented only by icons). In Windows, the tabs do not collapse when minimizing the Document window.

Figure 2-3
Page modes

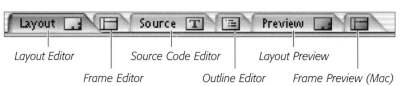

Layout Editor   Source Code Editor   Layout Preview

        Frame Editor   Outline Editor   Frame Preview (Mac)

Figure 2-4
Setting the
Default Mode

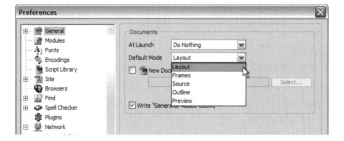

Status Bar

The area running along the bottom of the Document window is the Status Bar, a convenient place to display four different features (see Figure 2-5): the Split Source view control, the Markup Tree, the Line Break Mode popup menu, and the Window Size popup menu (which is identified as the Window Resolution popup menu by GoLive's Tooltips).

Split Source view. New in GoLive 6, you can view your page's layout and its source code in the same window (this feature works with each editor except the Source Code Editor). Click the Split Source view control—an up/down arrow icon in the lower-left corner of the screen—to dedicate the lower portion of your window to an editable peek at your source code (see Figure 2-5). You can resize the pane by clicking and dragging the divider between panes, or return to an all-Layout-Editor window by clicking the control again. For more on the Split Source view, see Chapter 14, *Source Editing*.

Figure 2-5
Status Bar and
Split Source
view

Split Source view

Split Source view control

Markup Tree

Status Bar

Markup Tree. As you're working in the Document window, the Markup Tree indicates which HTML tag is in use at the text-insertion point, and lists the hierarchy of tags leading back to the beginning of the page. For example, a blank page with a few words typed onto it displays the following line in the Markup Tree:

`<html><body><p>text`

Reading from right to left, this line simply means that some text appears within a paragraph (<p>), which is part of the page's body section (<body>), which is contained in an HTML page (<html>). Clicking any of these tags selects the range of material on the page—handy when you're working with complex tables or multiple floating boxes. See Chapter 14, *Source Editing*, for more information.

Line Break Mode. Don't you wish kids could just play nice and get along? We have similar thoughts when the subject of line endings comes up. Different operating systems use different code to indicate a line break within a text file, which is why the Switch Line Break Mode popup menu exists at all. If you need to change the platform for which line breaks are targeted, select one of the options that appears when you click the popup menu (see Figure 2-6).

This popup menu isn't turned on by default: you don't see it displayed when you run your copy of GoLive out of the box. Control-click (Mac) or right-click (Windows) on the Status Bar to bring up the contextual menu, and choose Line Break Mode from the Status Bar popup menu.

Figure 2-6
Line Break
Mode

Window Size/Resolution popup menu. Like most windows, the Document window's size can be adjusted by dragging the lower-right corner on the Mac, or dragging any outer edge under Windows. The value at the bottom-right edge of the window is its current width. Click the number to bring up the Window Size/Resolution popup menu, which includes six preset widths, from 50 to 780 pixels (you can't type in another value, unfortunately).

What if your Web pages need to be targeted to a different size? You can set up a new default window size by resizing it to your desired width and height, then selecting Settings from the popup menu. Make sure Markup Document Windows is checked in the Window Settings dialog box. Then click OK. From here on, every document opened—new and old—appears at both this pixel width and height. To return to GoLive's default width, return to the Window Settings dialog box and click the Use Default Settings button. Note that the Window Size popup menu is not available in source or outline editors, nor is it available in the Preview tab in Windows.

If you have a tracing image specified (see Chapter 5, *Images*), select Tracing Image from the Window Resolution popup menu to collapse the window's size to the image's dimensions.

Document Window Popout Menu

In the upper-right corner of the Document window, Adobe nestled an unobtrusive popout menu that turns out to be quite handy and important. From here you can specify how a Web browser should interpret your page, save the page in other formats, convert between HTML and XHTML, apply templates, or configure the Status Bar.

Doctype. A page's document type seems, at first glance, to be superfluous code. Essentially, selecting a type from the Doctype submenu adds some text at the beginning of your page's HTML source that tells browsers what type of page it is (see Figure 2-7). In many cases this doesn't matter, since today's Web browsers are remarkably flexible when translating code to screen. At the same time, however, we've fixed pages created with perfectly valid code that appear out of whack in some browsers by simply tweaking the Doctype.

In terms of GoLive, the Doctype setting is important when you use the Syntax Checker tool (see Chapter 14, *Source Editing*), since the Doctype determines which rules GoLive checks your code against.

By default, the HTML 4 Transitional option is selected; if you're using frames, GoLive automatically selects the HTML 4 Frameset doctype. You can also choose HTML 4 Strict, which is a more rigorous approach to coding. If you're creating pages for wireless devices, choose one of the i-mode settings. The same rules apply if you're working with an XHTML (extensible HTML) page, only with the XHTML doctype settings—again, see Chapter 14 for more details.

Figure 2-7
Layout Editor
popout menu

Markup. The Markup option in the popout menu lets you convert an HTML page to an XHTML page, and vice-versa. See Chapter 16, *Languages and Scripting*.

Save As. This submenu provides an easy way to save your page as a stationery item, template, or Component. See Chapter 19, *Managing Files, Folders, and Links* (for Stationery and Components), and Chapter 11, *Templates.*

Template (Layout Editor only). The Layout Editor takes advantage of GoLive's Templates feature, where you can assign editable areas of a page. From this submenu, you can apply an existing template to your page, or lock the page so it can't be editable except in the designated areas. See Chapter 11, *Templates*, for details.

Status Bar. The Status Bar submenu contains the same options we discussed earlier in the "Status Bar" section of this chapter.

Layout Editor

The Layout Editor is where you will likely spend the most time when developing content for individual pages. (Of course, if you're an old-school hand-coder who can't "see" a page without a panoply of tags and attributes, there's the Source Code Editor, which is detailed in Chapter 14, *Source Editing.*) The Layout Editor has a number of icons on the bar below the Document window's tabs that activate editing tools; you can also select the following options from the View menu (see Figure 2-8).

Head section. If you click the arrow at the far left of the bar, the Head section opens up below it, which is where you can configure items that contain information about the page, such as keywords and a page refresh rate. You find icons for these tags under the Head tab of the Objects palette.

Figure 2-8
Layout Editor

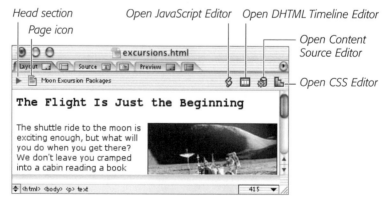

Head section   *Open JavaScript Editor*   *Open DHTML Timeline Editor*

Page icon

Open Content Source Editor

Open CSS Editor

Tip: Opening the Head Section

If you don't have the Head section already open, you can drag an icon from the Object palette's Head tab and place it over the toggle arrow for a second. The Head section then opens for you to place the tag. Or, simply drag a Head icon to the Layout Editor, which puts the tag in the Head section for you.

Moving to the right, clicking the Page icon calls up the Page Inspector, which allows you to configure a page's basic attributes, including page title, background and link colors, and a designated ColorSync profile. You could also click the default "Welcome to Adobe GoLive 6" to the right of the Page icon to rename your page's title, bypassing the Page Inspector. When done typing, press Return, Enter, or Tab, or click elsewhere, to accept the change.

Tip: Welcome to the GoLive California

A whole lotta pages have the words Welcome to Adobe GoLive emabarassingly emblazoned across their titlebar. Adobe wonderfully added a nifty option to ensure you aren't one of those loozers. In a site, you can choose the Site Reports tab in the Find feature, click the Errors tab, and mark the Pages with Inaccurate Titles option and the Default Title (see Figure 2-9) option. This lets you avoid the heartbreak of other designers pointing and laughing.

Figure 2-9
Retracting
a warm
"Welcome to
Adobe GoLive"

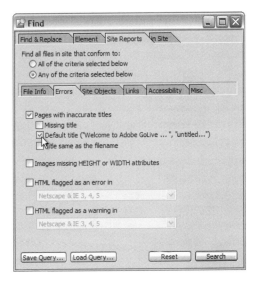

Open JavaScript Editor. Clicking the script icon opens the JavaScript Editor and displays the JavaScript Inspector. If you prefer to enter a script from scratch, click the New Script Item button (labeled Create Script under

Windows) and start typing (or paste in) the script's code in the main window area. Scripts can be stored in either the Head section or the body of your HTML document. (See Chapter 24, *Authoring JavaScript*, for more information on using JavaScript in GoLive.)

Open DHTML Timeline Editor. Clicking the filmstrip icon brings up the DHTML Timeline Editor, where you can configure DHTML-based animations. (If you're looking to take advantage of GoLive's QuickTime editing features, the movies are edited with a similar-looking, but not identical, interface; we cover QuickTime editing on our Web site at realworldgolive. com/six/quicktime.html.) The DHTML Timeline Editor allows you to position and move objects in sequences over periods of time using Dynamic HTML (see Chapter 25, *Creating Animation with DHTML*).

Open Content Source Editor. If you're using Dynamic Content on your site, you rely on the Content Source Editor, which lets you create sets of records derived from databases and other sources (see Chapter 15, *Dynamic Content and Databases*, and Chapter 23, *Building Dynamic Content*).

Open CSS Editor. Clicking the stairstepped icon opens the CSS Editor, from which you can add text and paragraph styles to a page using the CSS specification (see Chapter 27, *Defining Cascading Style Sheets*).

Rulers. Although no longer present as a button in GoLive 6, you can display horizontal and vertical rulers to measure your layout against: select Show Rulers from the View menu (see Figure 2-10). If you are editing a table cell, the ruler recalculates its horizontal and vertical zero settings to match the cell. To get rid of the rulers, simply choose Hide Rulers from the View menu.

Figure 2-10
Layout rulers

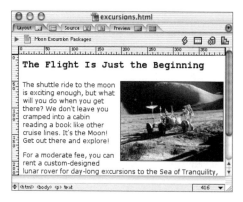

Frame Editor

At the top of the Document window, click the Frame Editor tab. GoLive displays a window chock full of nothing but a reminder in the middle that there are "No Frames." To add a frame configuration to your page, click the Object palette's Frames tab and select one of the many pre-designed frame sets. (The icons give you an idea of the basic layout of the frame set.) Double-click or drag the icon of your desired set into the Document window (see Figure 2-11).

Figure 2-11
Dragging a
Frame Set
icon to
Frame Editor

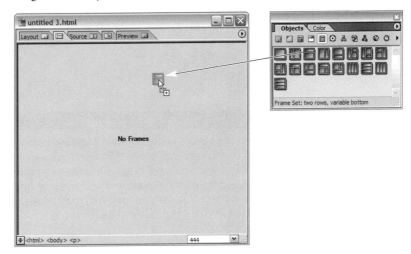

The Document window is then filled with the layout of the frame set, with an "(EmptyReference!)" icon in each frame indicating that it needs to be linked to an HTML page. The Frame Set Inspector also pops up and allows you to configure orientation (either horizontal or vertical) and borders (size, color, and framing).

Click within one of the individual frames, and the Frame Set Inspector changes to the Frame Inspector (see Figure 2-12, next page). (If you want to return to the Frame Set Inspector, click a frame border.) Here you can specify the frame's size—choosing either Pixel or Percent from the popup menu to the right of the Size field—as well as the frame's name.

To specify a content file for the frame, type the name and directory location of the file in the URL field, or click the Browse button and navigate to the file. If you are adding a content file from a site file, you can use the URL field's controls or drag and drop a file from the Site window. If you want to add another frame to the mix, choose an icon from the Frames tab of the Objects palette and drag it into the Document window. The layout is modified according to the frame that was added. See Chapter 9, *Frames*.

Figure 2-12
Selecting a
frame after
frame set
is added

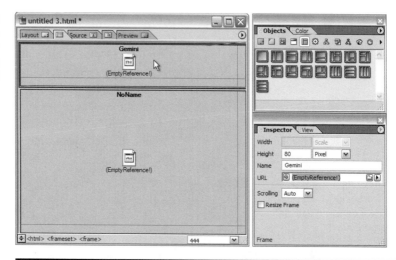

If you return to the Layout Editor after placing your frame set, notice that the Page icon has changed to indicate that frames have indeed been added (see Figure 2-13). Clicking the icon still calls up the Page Inspector for you to configure link colors, etc. You can type text and add material into the Layout Editor, but if you have content files selected for the frames, whatever you add is placed into a Noframes tag and is not visible in the browser.

Figure 2-13
Frameset icon

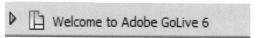

Layout Preview and Frame Preview

To see how your work previews in a browser and to test your links, click the Layout Preview tab (which is the only preview tab in Windows). GoLive's previewing capabilities give you a close approximation of how your page's layout behaves when viewed by your audience (see Figure 2-14).

GoLive doesn't preview most JavaScript effects coded into a page, though it displays image rollovers, which are based on JavaScript. However, if you've placed plug-in players into the Plug-ins folder found in the GoLive application folder, you can preview a page's plug-in files, such as Real media movies. If not, preview the page in an external browser that uses the plug-in.

If you aren't seeing the Layout Preview tab, it's probably because the module isn't loaded. Go to the Modules pane in Preferences and make sure that the Preview Mode Module is checked. Then quit and relaunch the program.

Figure 2-14
Layout Preview

Layout Editor   *Layout Preview*

Moving the mouse over a link turns your cursor into a pointing hand, denoting that the link is indeed hot. Click a link to an internal page (one that is stored on your hard drive) to open that page. However, if you click a link to an external URL, GoLive opens the link in your default browser or browsers (defined in the Browsers pane of GoLive's Preferences).

Since GoLive's previewing feature is limited, it's best to use the actual external browsers your audience might use to preview your pages. After setting up a list of available browsers found on your hard drive in Preferences, click and hold the arrow just to the right of the Toolbar's Show in Browser button (available in just about every contextual toolbar) to reveal the list. If you just click the button, your page opens in the default browser(s). You can also preview a page in your default browser(s) by pressing Command-T on the Mac or Control-T under Windows (or accessing this item, as well as your browser list, from the Preview In submenu of the File menu).

Frame Preview. If you're designing a page with frames and using a Mac, click the Frame Preview tab to preview the page. If you haven't built frames and click the Frame Preview tab, GoLive reminds you that you have no frames. Windows users need not worry about this, as the Preview tab handles both non-framed and framed pages.

The Inspector

In the real world, Inspectors are often investigators with an uncanny eye for detail; in GoLive, the Inspector is the tool used to narrow your focus on whatever item is currently selected. With the item's Inspector visible, you can control nearly all its settings. Whenever you click something, select something, or type something, the Inspector comes into play (see Figure 2-15). It changes to adapt to whatever you're doing: there are different Inspector configurations for pages, tables, forms, frames, images, layout grids…you get the idea.

We're covering the Page Inspector in detail in this chapter to give you an idea of how the Inspector works, and also to familiarize you with essential components, such as the URL Getter, below. Throughout the rest of the book, we simply refer to the commands found in the Inspector in context.

Figure 2-15
The Inspector

URL Getter

When you need to define the path to a reference page or the source file for an image file, multimedia plug-in, or Java applet, GoLive provides the URL Getter. This is the name for the set of fields and buttons that allow you to choose or type in a URL or path. The default on creating a new link is a text-input field with "(EmptyReference!)" placed into it to remind you to grab the necessary file (see Figure 2-16). If you don't replace this text, "(Empty-Reference!)" is literally inserted into the HTML of your page.

You have six choices for entering or selecting the reference in the URL Getter:

• Type the file name and directory location directly into the text field.

• Use the Point & Shoot button's lasso to rope that dogie…er, file—click and hold the button, then drag the line it creates to the file you want.

Figure 2-16
The Inspector's
URL Getter

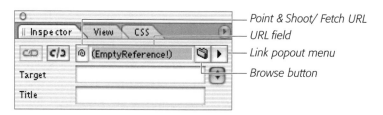

— Point & Shoot/ Fetch URL
— URL field
— Link popout menu
— Browse button

Remember, Point & Shoot works only in conjunction with files placed into site documents, or other open windows.

Tip: Fetch, GoLive, Fetch!

The draggable at-sign that is Point & Shoot file selection is technically called Fetch URL in the tool tip that appears when you hover above the icon. We like Point & Shoot, an earlier name of the feature that's descriptive and everyone's used to. So we ain't changing!

- Click the Browse button to navigate through your hard drive's file directory to the source file.

- Option-click (Mac) or Alt-click (Windows) the Browse button to access the Edit URL dialog box, in which you can enter or edit longer URLs.

- Click the Link popout menu to the far right of the URL Getter to view a list of recent files and miscellaneous related URLs.

- Either Control-click (Mac) or right-click (Windows) anywhere in the URL field to bring up the contextual menu, which includes the options found in the Link popout menu.

To use a full directory path from the root of the directory to the individual file, instead of GoLive's relative default, deselect Relative in the Link popout menu or contextual menu.

For more information on manipulating URLs, see Chapter 19, *Managing Files, Folders, and Links.*

Tip: Best Keyboard Shortcut Ever (Mac)

GoLive really, really wants you to use its Point & Shoot feature, which certainly isn't a bad desire. On the Mac, though, you can bypass all that mousing in favor of a keyboard shortcut. Press Command-comma to jump your text-insertion point from a linked text selection to the Text Inspector's URL field. Press Command-semicolon to return the insertion point back to the text selection in the Document window.

Page Inspector

The Page Inspector is used to set up the basic attributes of an individual page, from page title and link colors to whether a color profile is used. While in the Layout Editor, click the Page icon in the upper-left corner of the Document window.

Page Tab

In the Title field, you can type a descriptive title that appears in a browser's top title bar. GoLive defaults to "Welcome to Adobe GoLive 6", so be sure to remember to change the title to reflect your page (see Figure 2-17).

Figure 2-17
The Inspector's
Page tab

Tip: Templates for Titles

You can avoid the default page title problem by creating a simple template that GoLive opens as a default whenever it creates a new, blank page. Open the Preferences dialog box, and make this selection under the General pane, where you can choose a page to open each time.

Tip: Adding Descriptions to Page Titles

According to friends who specialize in promoting Web sites and understanding search engines, the text that appears in a page's title (in the Title tag set by GoLive's Page Title field) appears to be the most heavily weighted information that most search engines index. To get your site noticed, consider adding a longer description of your site in addition to the name of the individual page. GoLive doesn't seem to limit the number of characters within the Page Title field, so you can write as long a description as you want. However, long page titles don't always fit within a Web browser's title bar, and could look a little messy.

The Text Colors section allows you to set colors for body text, standard link text, active links, and visited links. To change one of these settings, select the Color palette from the Window menu, or click a color field. Choose a color from the Color palette and drag a swatch from the Preview pane to the desired color field. You can also set a background color or image to appear behind your page's text and images. For the full explanation of background images, consult "Blending into the Background," a sidebar in Chapter 5, *Images*.

GoLive also includes fields for Margin Width and Height, which allow you to add space from the top and left edges of a page. But because of differences in attributes for this feature prior to Netscape 6, GoLive cleverly includes four terms in the body tag.

Here's an example of placing 20 pixels of width from the left and 40 pixels from the top:

```
<body leftmargin="20" marginwidth="20" topmargin="40"
marginheight="40">
```

Tip: Count Zero Increment

Internet Explorer always used the attribute names Leftmargin and Topmargin, while Netscape only adopted those terms in version 6. In older Netscape releases, the browser required attributes named Marginwidth and Marginheight.

However, technically, you shouldn't use either! CSS allows you to specify the offset from the top and left as a page-wide property, and it's the recommended way to do it in the future. See Chapter 27, *Defining Cascading Style Sheets*, for more on this.

HTML Tab

If you don't want your page to automatically include such basic tags as Html, Head, Title, or Body—for instance, if you were planning to bring in customized HTML fragments later—you can uncheck these options on the Page Inspector's HTML tab (see Figure 2-18).

Figure 2-18
The Inspector's
HTML tab

If one or more of the tags are unchecked, you can reset them all to be checked by clicking the Select All button.

The JavaScript Functions options correspond to GoLive's Actions—prefabricated JavaScript code that allows you to accomplish sophisticated tasks without hand coding. GoLive defaults to Import GoLive Script Library, which constructs a separate file containing all the necessary code for all Actions; your HTML page refers to this file, and a browser loads it separately. The other option, Write Code into Page, includes all necessary JavaScript code in the individual HTML page. For the full details, see Chapter 26, *Applying Actions*.

If you choose Import GoLive Script Library, the Component button becomes inactive—GoLive's way of denoting that this file is ready for use as a Component file, which requires any scripting (your own or from GoLive's built-in actions) to be written to the script library file. To learn more about using Components, see Chapter 19, *Managing Files, Folders, and Links*.

ColorSync Tab (Mac)

On the Macintosh, GoLive applies Apple's ColorSync color-matching capabilities by default to all JPEG images collected on a page. The ColorSync tab lets you change GoLive's default settings (see Figure 2-19). You can select an external color profile by clicking the Profile radio button and either using the Point & Shoot button or clicking the Browse button to select the profile. You can also choose not to use any color profile; this is wise, as the integration of ColorSync color-management into browsers is currently limited to Explorer 4.0 and later on the Mac.

If you choose an external color profile, be sure to check that it gets uploaded to your Web site, as GoLive's link parser does not monitor color profiles. See Chapter 5, *Images*, for more on ColorSync.

Figure 2-19
The Inspector's
ColorSync tab

Viewing Options

If you're spending most of your time in the Document window anyway, shouldn't you be able to control what gets displayed? Using the controls in the View palette, you can configure how GoLive looks and acts as you work in the Layout Editor, Outline Editor, and Preview windows (see Figure 2-20).

You can also highlight items, such as HTML elements and areas where Cascading Style Sheet definitions have been applied, using GoLive's new Highlight palette.

New in 6: No More View Controller

The View palette replaces (and improves upon) the View Controller found in earlier versions of GoLive.

View Palette

We really want to believe that what we see in the Document window is what users will see when the page is viewed on the Web. But because there are so many variations in how browsers interpret HTML code, it's almost impossible to maintain that belief. Using the View palette's controls, you can make GoLive approximate how your page will display on a number of different browsers, plus show alternate views of page elements such as link colors.

Tip: Contextual View Palette

The View palette changes to suit which editor you're working in. With the Outline Editor active, you're only given the option to display images or not. With the Source Code Editor active, the View palette contains options for syntax coloring (see Chapter 14, *Source Editing*).

Profile. The Profile popup menu adjusts the formatting of the display based on the browser you choose from the list (see Figure 2-20). This is primarily useful when you're designing pages for cell phones or other handheld devices that don't support the full range of HTML (see Chapter 16, *Languages and Scripting*). The Allow Overlapping Paragraphs box controls the display of text with negative margin values, which can be accomplished using CSS. (See Chapter 27, *Defining Cascading Style Sheets*.)

Figure 2-20
View palette

Visibility. GoLive draws a number of things onscreen that will never appear in a Web browser: form containers, placeholder icons for comments, etc. The Visibility option in the View palette lets you create sets that control what is displayed and what is hidden. Choose Edit Set from the popup menu to bring up the Invisible Elements portion of GoLive's preferences (you can also get there by choosing Preferences from the Edit menu, then selecting Invisible Elements from the General category).

In the default set, all of the items are enabled. To selectively decide which elements appear, first create a new set by clicking the New Set button, and then click the elements' checkboxes in the list: boxes that are marked remain invisible when the set is active, while unmarked boxes are displayed. (We know, it seems backwards that enabling something makes it go away, but the logic makes some sense if you stare at it long enough.)

With a set created, exit the Preferences dialog box and select the set in the View palette's Visibility popup menu (see Figure 2-21). You can also press Command-I (Mac) or Shift-Control-I (Windows) to hide and show all invisible items, or select the corresponding option under the View menu.

Figure 2-21
Visibility
preferences

All elements displayed

Custom set (at left) applied

Images. If you uncheck the Images box, images disappear from your page, leaving only the border, a generic image icon, and any Alt text. The Background box hides or displays a page's background image. If you've specified low-source previews of your images, checking the Low Source box displays them instead of the original ones.

Fonts. GoLive can display text in any font you choose, but that doesn't guarantee people viewing your page will have those fonts installed on their computers. The Fonts popup menu lets you view text only in Times, or using any font except for Web fonts such as Georgia or Verdana. (See Chapter 4, *Text and Fonts*, for more on applying different type styles.)

States. You can define colors for linked text, including colors for active links (when you click on them) and visited links. To easily see how your links will look in your selected colors, choose Normal, Active, or Visited from the States popup menu.

If you're using CSS to define a hover style for links (where the appearance changes just by positioning your mouse cursor over the link), choose Hover from the popup menu to see how the links appear (see Figure 2-22). Similarly, if you've set up a separate style for when a link has focus (such as when you tab among links and fields on the page without using the mouse), choose Focus from the popup menu to preview the style.

Figure 2-22
Previewing
hover style

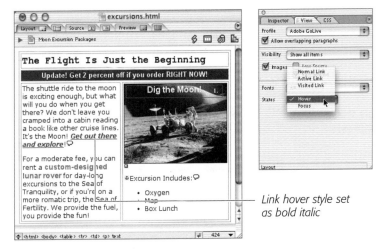

*Link hover style set
as bold italic*

Highlight Palette

One of the cooler (we think) new features in GoLive 6 is the Highlight palette, which has three functions. It's used to identify bad links on your page; it can identify specific elements on the page, such as all Heading 1 text or all forms; and it also reports on HTML code problems using GoLive's Syntax Checker (this last function is detailed in Chapter 14, *Source Editing*). Choose Highlight from the Window menu to display the palette.

Selecting an element or link warning highlights all occurrences of it on the page, as if you had taken a highlighter pen and marked it on paper. The column to the right of the popup menus indicates how many occurrences were found on the page. You can move through the occurrences by clicking the Select Previous and Select Next Highlighted Object arrow buttons. The Rescan button searches the page again using the selections you made in the popup menus, and the Clear button resets the selections to none.

Tip: Multiple Selections

Choosing more than one successive item from the popup menus adds them to the search. For example, selecting the Form tag from the Elements menu and then selecting a style name from the CSS menu results in a page that displays all instances of both tags. Click the Clear button before making a new selection if you want just one option shown.

Link Warnings. Few things are more embarassing to a Web designer than publishing a site that has incorrect links. We've come to the conclusion that it's a rite of passage for designers, but that doesn't mean you can't do something about it. Click the Link Warnings button (the green bug) on the Highlight palette to see which links don't resolve correctly (see Figure 2-23). A Link Warnings button also appears on the Toolbar, or you can choose Show Link Warnings from the View menu.

Figure 2-23
Link Warnings

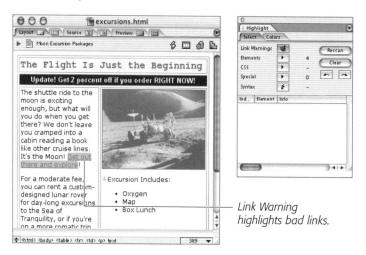

Link Warning highlights bad links.

Elements. To view an instance of a particular HTML tag, choose it from the Elements popup menu. Only elements that appear in your page are shown in the menu.

CSS. It's easy to see which CSS definitions are applied to the objects on your page using the CSS popup menu. As with elements, only styles currently in use within your page are shown (even if you've specified multiple styles in the CSS Editor).

Tip: Highlight in CSS Palette

When you select a CSS style in the Highlight palette, the name of the style is also highlighted in the CSS palette if that is visible (see Figure 2-24).

Special. The Special popup menu includes items that would be awkward to locate if you were looking for just an element or style name, such as JavaScript Actions and Comment items. The Special Items option highlights generic, non-HTML tags.

Figure 2-24
Highlighting
CSS elements

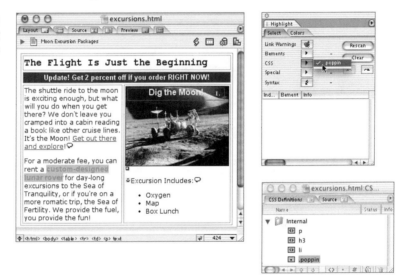

Saving and Loading Highlighting Sets

When you find a magical combination of highlighted items that you need on a regular basis, you can save a highlighting set that remembers which tags and options are selected.

After you've made your selections, choose Save Highlighting Set from the palette's popout menu and save the file to your hard disk.

To apply the set later, choose Load Highlighting Set from the popout menu and locate the file you saved.

Setting Highlight Coloring

If your background color is close enough to the default highlighting colors that they're hard to distinguish, switch to the Colors tab of the Highlight palette to redefine the colors (see Figure 2-25).

To change one, drag a new color from the Colors palette to the color field to the right of the option you'd like to change. The horizontal slider controls the opacity of the color you choose. You can also choose to display highlighting as an outline instead of a color overlay by clicking the Show Border Only On/Off button.

Figure 2-25
Setting highlight coloring

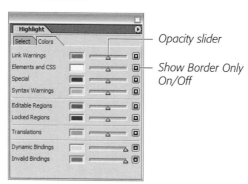

— Opacity slider

— Show Border Only On/Off

Document Statistics

You usually have to wait until a page is fully designed and created to test how long it might take for an average user to download, images and all. Fortunately, GoLive offers the Document Statistics feature, which can provide a total size for all the content on the page, a word and character count, and an estimate for download time at different speeds (see Figure 2-26). With a document open, choose Document Statistics from the Special menu.

GoLive doesn't take into account real-world issues like latency in its estimates, however. Latency is the amount of time it takes to move data from point A to point B, not how fast the data is moving. An analogy would be a stream of cars that gets stopped on a slow stretch of road between two exits on a highway: they might travel 60 mph before and after the slow stretch, but it still takes each car a while to get through the bottleneck.

Go Live also doesn't account for Internet slowdowns and platform and browser overhead (how long they take to deal with content once it has arrived). For instance, a page with eight images that's only 20K total would take 21 seconds to download at 9,600 bits per second (bps) according to GoLive. However, most browsers are configured to download only four to eight items

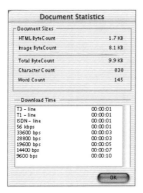

Figure 2-26
Document
Statistics

at a time (four is typically the default). Plus, a 9,600-bps modem has high latency, meaning that it takes a while to get data gushing through the pipe. The slower the connection, generally the higher the latency, slowing down the whole process.

So for up to 28,800 bps, we'd multiply GoLive's estimate by three for real-world purposes; up to ISDN, we'd multiply by two. For T1 (about 1.5 megabits per second or Mbps) and T3 (about 45 Mbps), the estimates are useful for pages with lots of multimedia, but the mechanisms by which data gets sent across the Net seem to limit all Web transfers to an effective throttle of about 400 kilobits per second (kbps) maximum, or one-fourth of a T1 line. (FTP can be much faster, but the Web seems to max out lower.)

Tip: Missing Bandwidth Options

Oddly, this feature doesn't note any DSL or cable modem speeds, despite the large numbers of people adopting that technology over the last couple of years. DSL and cable modem speeds fall between ISDN and T1.

Download Page

Download Page is a special, standalone feature that lets you type in any Web page location starting with http://, causing GoLive to download the page, as well as any images or other objects that appear on the page (see Figure 2-27, next page). (The exception is anything referenced in JavaScript or other scripting languages; it only downloads media mentioned in HTML tags.) Select Download Page from the File menu, type the Web page's address, then click the Save As button to specify a destination for the files.

GoLive opens a page with the same title, but all the images are stored in the same folder as the HTML page; so, you cannot retain the original page's

file structure (such as having images in a separate folder). You can edit and save this page with its new image references, and then upload it back to the server. However, doing so usually breaks all of the links on the page, as they have been rewritten to reflect the local storage location of the downloaded images.

If you use the FTP or WebDAV Browser features described in Chapter 20, *Synchronizing Sites*, double-clicking a page in those windows brings up a page in the exact manner as using Download Page. The difference is that with the Browsers, you must have access to a server; with Web Download, you need merely enter a URL.

Tip: Download Site

You can download an entire site, if you want, or part of a site, by using the New Site item in the File menu. Select Single User and then Import from Server. You can then specify a URL and a number of parameters, including whether to retrieve files from sites not referenced in that URL, and how many link levels to follow. We analyze that feature in Chapter 17, *Managing Sites*.

Tip: URL Getter Download

If you have an external URL specified as one of your links, you can easily download that page to your hard disk. Control-click (Mac) or right-click (Windows) the URL Getter and select Download from the contextual menu that appears. You can also bring up the contextual menu on the link in your page, then select Download Page from the Hyperlink submenu.

Turn the Page

No doubt at some point you've woken up in the middle of the night and made your way through your house without turning on the lights. How is it you can make it all the way to the kitchen in the dark? Your familiarity with the locations of walls and doors, and your memory of where furniture is placed, keeps you from stumbling around blind.

After you've used GoLive a dozen or so times, you gain the same sense of familiarity. Moving through its layout editors and around the document quickly becomes second nature, so you can focus on the task of creating great Web pages.

CHAPTER 3

Head Section

Okay class, don your lab coats and grab your scalpels, because it's time to delve into one of the most important—and most overlooked—portions of a Web page's anatomy: the Head section. Like the control centers of the human brain that regulate your breathing and heart rate, the Head section provides fundamental information required to display a Web page. Without it, your hard-won designs appear as nothing more than plain text.

When used successfully, the Head section directs JavaScript scripts and CSS styles, and also describes the meta information—information about the rest of the information, like a précis or summary—for search-engine placement and easier archiving.

A browser reads and interprets the Head section of a page before it moves on down to the body, so things that affect the rest of the page—like scripts—need to be stored in the Head section unless there's a highly specific reason not to. Don't worry; although this section is important, it's not overly oblongata. In fact, you may come to lobe it.

Tip: What's in Your Head?

The Head section, as GoLive calls it, is really just the part of the page that starts with <HEAD> and ends with </HEAD>. The rest of an HTML page is the body part, which is—you guessed it—surrounded by Body tags.

To view the Head section in the Layout Editor, click the expansion triangle to the left of the page icon (see Figure 3-1).

Several kinds of objects wind up in the Head section in HTML and in GoLive. You can find corresponding icons for most of these items in the Head

Figure 3-1
Head section

tab of the Objects palette (see Figure 3-2). To add icons to your page, double-click them, or drag them into the Layout Editor's Head section. You can also bring up the contextual menu within the section, select the Insert Object item, and choose one from the Head submenu.

Figure 3-2
Head tab in
the Objects
palette

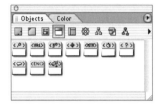

Tip: Drag and Expand

If the Head section of the Layout Editor isn't expanded, but you've already grabbed an icon, don't drop what you're doing. Drag the icon directly onto the expansion triangle to automatically show the section.

Tip: Body Double

If you drop a Head section icon onto the Body part of the page, GoLive automatically plops it into the Head section for you and opens the Head section if it was closed.

• **Title.** Title contains the name that appears in the browser window's title bar. (This object is inserted automatically in new pages.)

What's New in 6

If you're familiar with the way previous versions of GoLive used this section of the Layout Editor, then you've got your Head screwed on straight. A couple of small changes are worth noting, however.

The Keyword Inspector now includes a few more options for managing lists of words. You can now sort the keywords alphabetically, as well as remove duplicate words.

GoLive 6 also adds a new Encoding head element, which defines which character set a Web browser should use when displaying the page.

- **Base.** The Base tag identifies a static URL that gets used as the basis of any relative link on the page. This tag overrides the current location of the page within its site, which typically gets used to determine relative links.

- **Meta tags.** Meta tags contain information about the contents of the document, including a description of the content, keywords derived from the page, and so on.

- **Link tags.** Links are a special kind of tag that create a relationship between the page they appear on and other pages or objects. For instance, you can embed fonts in a Web page via a Link tag to connect to the font file elsewhere on your site or on the Internet. (Note how this kind of link differs from hypertext links, which don't contain information about the kind of link they are, but simply point to another location.)

- **Scripts.** JavaScript, Jscript, VBScript, and other scripting languages generally—though not exclusively—put their code into the Head section. (See Chapter 25, *Authoring JavaScript*, for more on where to locate JavaScript code and when to use the Head Script icon versus the Body Script icon.)

It's All Relative

HTML pages use two different ways of linking to other resources: fully qualified "absolute" links and relative links. We explain this distinction in great depth in the "Absolute versus Relative" sidebar in Chapter 19, *Managing Files, Folders, and Links*, but here's a sneak preview.

Fully qualified absolute links require a resource type, a server name, and a file location. For instance, a file link might look like:

```
http://www.necoffee.com/flavor/syrup
/doubletall.html
```

The "http" is the resource type (Web protocol), the server is www.necoffee.com, and the file location includes the whole path after the server: /flavor/syrup/doubletall.html.

A relative link uses the location of the page on which it appears to navigate to the resource, which has to be stored locally. So if you're view-

ing a page that's located at

```
http://www.necoffee.com/flavor/syrup
/doubletall.html
```

and you put a relative reference to the page of

```
snickerdoodle.html
```

a Web browser constructs a full reference of

```
http://www.necoffee.com/flavor/syrup
/snickerdoodle.html
```

If you need to navigate to a higher folder, use two dots plus a slash to signify "up one folder level." So a relative link up two levels from doubletall.html of

```
../../decaf/notenough/whybother.
html
```

causes a browser to construct a link of

```
http://www.necoffee.com/decaf/note-
nough/whybother.html
```

- **Cascading Style Sheets (CSS).** CSS enables advanced typographic control and the ability to position elements precisely on a page (see Chapter 28, *Defining Cascading Style Sheets*).

- **Comments and other code.** The Head tab of the Objects palette also includes icons for adding comments to the Head section, as well as specialized code that you don't want GoLive to touch.

IsIndex

Long ago, the IsIndex tag in a Head section alerted search engines that they could perform a keyword search on the page and optionally display a search text box when the page was loaded into a Web browser. However, IsIndex hasn't been recommended for use for several years and is included just for compatibility with older pages.

Base

The Base tag lets you change the local context in which relative links are interpreted (see the sidebar, "It's All Relative"). Drag the Base tag into the Head section, and the Base Inspector lets you set the reference (see Figure 3-3). Check the Base box and choose a location to which relative links are appended.

To ensure that all references are written back to the root of the site (or the starting slash after the server name for your site), uncheck the Relative option from the URL Getter's Link popout menu.

Using the Target field, you can direct all your page's links to a specific window; for example, a target of "_blank" causes every link destination to open in a new browser window.

Meta

Meta tags allow you to specify information about the page on which the tag appears, such as a description of its content or keywords that describe the

Figure 3-3
Setting Base
URL via the
Base Inspector

content. You can code numerous Meta tags by hand; GoLive provides the HTML framework. However, GoLive also prefabricates four kinds of commonly used Meta tags.

Plain Meta Tag

Drag the Meta icon from the Head tab into the Head section; GoLive brings up the Meta Inspector (see Figure 3-4). You can set the Meta tag through the popup menu to either Name or HTTP-Equivalent. Names are used for information about the page; HTTP-Equivalent is used for simulating header information that accompanies a Web page when it's sent by a server to a browser.

Figure 3-4
Meta tags in Layout Editor with Split Source View and Meta Inspector

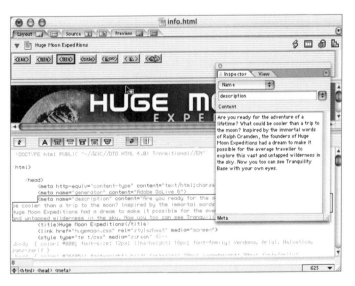

In the field beneath the first popup menu, enter the Meta tag's title, such as "description", or choose from the list available in the popup menu to the right of the field. In the Content text area below that, enter the contents of the tag, such as a description of the page.

A great explanation of a variety of available Meta tags and their specifications can be found at www.webdeveloper.com/html/html_metatags.html.

Encoding

The Encoding element helps to facilitate the "worldwide" aspect of the World Wide Web. GoLive automatically inserts this tag into the Head section by default, specifying the ISO-8859-1 character set. When you select the Encoding icon in the Head section, the Encoding Inspector lets you choose from Western, Unicode, and foreign language sets (see Figure 3-5). Click a radio button next to the character set you want to activate.

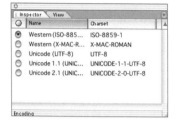

Refresh

The Refresh tag lets you set an amount of time before the browser automatically loads another page. You can even choose to reload the same page if you're providing updated information that changes every few seconds or minutes while the page stays open, like a traffic status page. Typically, Refresh is used with a setting of zero seconds to redirect a browser to another page when a page has moved and the Web designer doesn't have direct access to server settings to create an automatic redirection.

The Refresh Inspector sports only a few settings (see Figure 3-6). Set a number of seconds in the Delay field before the page reloads. Then, either choose Target this Document or select Target URL to specify another page to load through the URL Getter.

Keywords

A well-produced page includes keywords in a Meta tag. Internet search engines consult Meta tags, in part, to construct their indexes and place those pages in order of precedence on their results pages.

There are two ways to add keywords in GoLive: by selecting words on a page and using the contextual menu's or the Special menu's Add to Keywords item; or, by typing them in via the Keywords Inspector.

Using the Add to Keywords item automatically creates a Keywords icon in the Head section if it isn't already present. You can also drag the icon from the Head tab of the Objects palette. Selecting it brings up the Keywords Inspector where you can type in words and hit Return or Enter to add them to the Keywords list (see Figure 3-7).

Figure 3-6
Refresh
Inspector

Figure 3-7
Keywords
Inspector

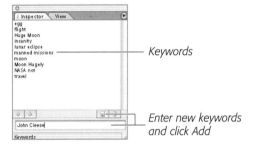

Keywords

Enter new keywords
and click Add

Clicking the New Keyword button creates an entry labeled New Keyword, which is fairly useless as you might as well just enter something from scratch. To delete one or more keywords, select them and click the Remove Selected Keywords button.

Tip: Duplicating Keywords

Where the New Keyword button comes in handy is if you want to duplicate keywords. With a word selected, click the button to create a clone of the original. If you're using longer keywords (a keyword isn't limited to just one word, after all), this can be a quicker way to modify phrases slightly.

To edit a keyword, select it and make any changes in the editable field at the bottom of the palette; hit return or click outside the field to apply the change.

Some search engines use the order of keywords to affect the ranking in their results pages (though results vary among different engines). If you want to re-order the keywords, select a word or group of words and click the Move Item Upwards or Move Item Downwards buttons in the lower-left corner of the Inspector.

You can also sort the list alphabetically using the first two options on the Inspector's popout menu. Ascending order sorts from A to Z; descending sorts from Z to A.

The Remove Duplicates command on the popout menu is a quick way to weed out multiple copies of the same keyword. However, words spelled the same with different capitalization aren't removed.

Tip: Search Secrets

We recommend consulting Danny Sullivan's Search Engine Watch (www.searchenginewatch.com) for the best information on the subject of improving your search engine placement chances using keywords.

Link

The Link tag lets you create relationships between the current document and other documents on a site or on the Internet. Typically, you use this tag for two purposes:

- To connect the contents of external CSS style sheets, as described in Chapter 28, *Defining Cascading Style Sheets*. There's no reason to code this kind of Link tag by hand, as GoLive includes a built-in linking feature that automatically creates the right Link tag code. (If you create one of these by hand, GoLive shows the file in the CSS Editor's External folder.)

- To reference fonts that are retrieved by a 4.0 or later Netscape browser or Internet Explorer running an ActiveX object rendered to display type in a browser window. (Internet Explorer uses a different method to link in fonts as part of the CSS specification; see Chapter 28 for more on that, as well.)

The Link Inspector lets you enter the appropriate attributes depending on the kind of link. However, few common uses for this tag currently exist.

If you'd like more information on what values you can use with the Link tag, see www.w3.org/TR/html401/struct/links.html#edef-LINK. It's a little dense, but it's the best resource available.

Element

You may want to add tags that aren't offered by GoLive. In this case, double-click or drag the Element icon to the Head section. GoLive initially creates a Noedit tag, which is a proprietary tag that gets ignored by browsers. In the Tag Inspector, replace "noedit" in the Element field with the name of your new tag (see Figure 3-8). If there are attributes and values associated with the tag, click the New Attribute (Mac) or New Item (Windows) button in the lower right, then fill in the corresponding fields at the bottom of the window. Like the Keywords Inspector, you can re-order the attributes using the arrow buttons at the lower-left.

Switch to the Content tab and type whatever appears between the beginning and end sections of the tag you've just created.

Figure 3-8
Element
Inspector

Comment

Good Web designers tend to talk to themselves—and not just in a crazy way. It's helpful to jot notes within the code of a Web page as references, but you don't want that code displayed in a browser. The Comment icon in the Head section is just like the Comment icon in the Basic portion of the Objects palette: it creates the following code, which you can edit between the dashes and brackets.

```
<!-- comment content -->
```

Double-click or drag the icon to the Head section to add a comment, then edit the comment text in the Comment Inspector (see Figure 3-9).

Figure 3-9
Comment
Inspector

Head and Shoulders

On the Web, having a good Head section not only can affect how your page displays in a Web browser, but also how your page is displayed by search engines and other tools that use Meta tag information. In the real world, we compliment people's intelligence by saying they have "a good head on their shoulders." Employing a good Head section in your Web pages complements the wisdom of the head on *your* shoulders.

CHAPTER 4
Text and Fonts

Despite the flash and glitter of images on the Web, text forms the majority of what you peruse on a page. But text has received the least amount of hype and attention. While advances in sound, animation, and image compression have transformed the look and experience of the online world, most of the Web's words are still viewed in browsers' default fonts. Like the flashing "12:00" displayed on millions of VCRs, 12-point Times is the modern user option that never gets changed. (Many people don't know they can change it.)

In GoLive, you can specify a broad range of fonts as well as type styles: bold, italic, underline, strikethrough (which GoLive calls strikeout), paragraph alignment, bulleted lists, variable type sizes, colors, and more. In addition to this visual formatting, you can also assign structural definitions like Code, Pre, and heading styles, whose appearance is determined by each Web browser.

More significant is that you can use Cascading Style Sheets (CSS) to set styles. CSS isn't new to GoLive by any means, but only recently—as larger numbers of CSS-compatible browsers have come into use—has it become a preferred approach to formatting. Not only can you define the way text appears, you can store that information in a single file, enabling you to make a style change once and have it apply to every occurrence throughout your site. (See "CSS Formatting," later in this chapter, for an overview of styling text using CSS, and Chapter 27, *Defining Cascading Style Sheets*, for more depth on the topic.) At this point, we don't even begin a Web project without building a collection of style sheets.

GoLive also goes beyond formatting issues into the area of sitewide font management and organization using font sets, which broaden compatibility among browsers.

Entering Text

Before we get ahead of ourselves and launch into transmogrifying text appearance, we need to be able to enter and modify some text to work with. You can type directly into the Layout Editor as if it were a dedicated word processor, copy and paste text from another program, or drag text from an open application directly into GoLive.

New in 6: Pasting Text

When you pasted text into GoLive 5, it would automatically put a full paragraph after the pasted selection. In GoLive 6, it minds the pasted content, removing a major editing irritancy.

Paragraphs and Line Breaks

As you type or edit text, two types of line breaks are available: paragraphs and line breaks. Following word processing convention, GoLive formats text in paragraphs by default. Pressing Return (Mac) or Enter (Windows) inserts a

What's New in 6

We usually use this space to talk about how GoLive has added new features, which are often implemented to address changes in the Web design world. In the case of text and fonts, however, we're pleasantly surprised to note that in this area the Web design world is actually finally catching up to GoLive. As browsers adopted real Web standards, using Cascading Style Sheets has become our preferred method of formatting text in most situations—a capability GoLive has long possessed.

However, that doesn't mean Adobe skimped on improving GoLive. Version 6 makes using sitewide font sets much more powerful by being able to change a set's definition and have the change apply to every occurrence in your site.

GoLive 6 also introduces HTML Styles, a method of creating CSS-like definitions using traditional HTML formatting code. Also, in the "small but significant" department, the default paragraph formatting on a page is no longer None, replaced by the more accurate Paragraph to indicate that even the first line of a blank page is enclosed in <P> tags.

paragraph break, which on the Web signals that extra vertical space is added following the end of the paragraph.

If you'd rather not let Web browsers determine how much space belongs after each paragraph, you can insert line breaks, which move the successive text to the next line without adding extra vertical space: press Shift-Return (Mac) or Shift-Enter (Windows) to insert a line break. If you're feeling particularly mouse-happy, you can also double-click the Line Break icon in the Basic tab of the Objects palette, or drag it to the desired location in your document. Some designers use multiple line breaks to separate paragraphs in order to maintain more control over how much space appears before and after their paragraphs (see Figure 4-1).

Tip: Oh, Bad Break!

The BR tag, which creates a line break, keeps the current spacing between lines and other paragraph properties while moving the text following it to the margin. If you need to control spacing between paragraphs more precisely, you may want to opt for CSS (see Chapter 27, *Defining Cascading Style Sheets*).

Figure 4-1
Paragraph and
line breaks

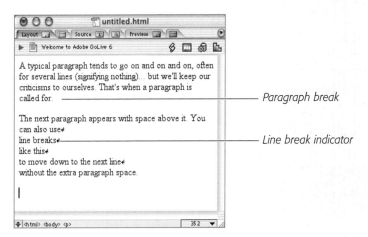

Tip: Pasting Text Corrects HTML Entities

If you copy and paste text from an outside source into the Layout Editor, GoLive automatically converts some nonstandard text elements into their HTML entities. For example, an ampersand (&) becomes "&" in the page's HTML code, the copyright symbol (©) turns into "©", and an accented letter like the "e" in "café" is transformed into "é". This helps ensure that readers don't see strange characters when their browsers hit those elements in the HTML source code. (See "Characters Tab" in Chapter 28, *Controlling Web Settings*, for a discussion of HTML entities.)

Navigating Text

With so many words on the Web, you need effective ways of navigating them all, whether you're traversing a couple paragraphs or several screens' worth of text. This may seem like a basic point, but, like designing a Web page, you'd be surprised at the difference good navigation makes.

Navigating with the Mouse

The easiest way to move around is to use your mouse to place the text-insertion point where you want to type or edit. Double-clicking selects a single word; triple-clicking selects a line, and quadruple-clicking selects an entire paragraph. If you right-click in Windows, or Control-click on a Macintosh, the contextual menu offers the option to Select All. (Typing Command-A on a Mac or Control-A in Windows also selects all text and objects on a page.)

GoLive supports drag-and-drop editing, so you can select a block of text, then drag the selection to a new location—even onto another open page window. To make a quick copy of a text range, hold down Option (Mac) or Control (Windows) while you move it (see Figure 4-2).

Figure 4-2
Drag-copying
text selections

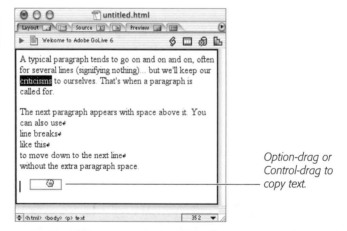

Option-drag or
Control-drag to
copy text.

Tip: Make Text Clippings (Mac)

Not only can you drag text blocks to other documents within GoLive or other open applications, you can also create a text clipping on the Macintosh by dragging text to the Desktop. This can be handy if you need to use a block of text frequently, but don't want to set up a GoLive Component. Dragging text from the Source Code Editor works the same way.

Navigating with the Keyboard

You may not always want to reach for the mouse when you're typing, so it's important to know how to get around via the keyboard using the arrow keys and modifiers. Table 4-1 lists the results of the possible key combinations. Holding down Shift when performing any of the following actions selects the text range from the cursor's starting position.

Table 4-1 The keys to success	**Arrow Key**	**Macintosh**	**Windows**	**Result**
	Up/Down			moves cursor up/down one line
	Left/Right			moves cursor one character to the left/right
	Left	Option	Control	moves cursor one word* to the left
	Left	Command	Alt	moves cursor to beginning of line
	Right	Option	Control	moves cursor one word* to the right
	Right	Command	Control-Alt	moves cursor to end of line**

* The cursor jumps between the beginnings and ends of words when using Option, rather than just the beginnings.

** The exception is when a line ends with a line break, rather than a full paragraph character, in which case the cursor is placed at the beginning of the next line.

Tip: Navigating Without Moving

Pressing the Home, End, Page Up, and Page Down keys changes what's displayed in the Layout Editor, but doesn't move your cursor to those locations. If you want your cursor to appear at the end of the document, for instance, you must either move it with the arrow keys, or scroll to the end and click where the cursor should appear.

On the other hand, this method of navigation makes it easier to locate your cursor if you've scrolled elsewhere on the page: just press one of the arrow keys to force GoLive to display the cursor. If the page structure makes it difficult to see the cursor by itself, press Shift plus an arrow key to spot the newly-highlighted text.

Formatting Text

Before launching into the specifics of styling text on a Web page, we need to explain the differences between structural formatting, styled-text formatting, and Cascading Style Sheets.

Structural formatting. In the early days of the Web, there was no guarantee that someone reading your document had the same typefaces or support for styled text, such as offered in a word processor. HTML was devised as a set of tags defining a document's structure rather than the specifics of its appearance. Structuring tags circumvented the need to support several proprietary file formats; HTML files are plain text, readable by nearly every computer system from Palm handheld to Unix workstation to IBM mainframe.

So, for example, instead of creating a headline in 36-point Franklin Gothic type, the relevant text was simply tagged as a headline, letting the browser format it to the program's settings for what a headline should be—in most cases, this meant bold type set two to three times larger than the body text. This structural approach provided more flexibility when sharing information because it identified sections of a document—such as headlines, quotations, and code examples—as objects, not as text with local formatting applied.

Styled-text formatting. Unfortunately, structure tended to drive designers nuts in early implementations of HTML, because designers are accustomed to specifying exactly how something will look. That's why HTML also allows styled-text formatting, letting you display text in italics, or underlined, or in a monospaced font (as just a few examples) without assigning a structural classification to it. This is the method used most often on the Web, especially for one-off instances of bold or italic to denote emphasis.

Cascading Style Sheets. CSS defines typographic specifications for ranges of HTML, including color, size, character and line spacing, and font face; and absolute positioning, borders, margins, and other spacing controls for chunks of HTML that display text, images, and other objects.

CSS also defines the interaction between adjacent blocks of HTML to control overlap or text wrapping. You can package these specifications into a style sheet which is applied via generic or special HTML tags and attributes to different types of text and HTML selections.

You can also base one CSS on another, inheriting all its definitions and adding or changing selected ones. This is where the *cascading* part of CSS comes in, as you can modify style sheets that underlie many other style sheets. The display of the text is based on specifications that cascade through the style sheets, from the first parent style down to the last child, which is actually applied to the text.

Not only does CSS give you much more control over text appearance, it retains structural formatting—you can still create a line of Heading 1 text, but specify its exact size, font, and color. This capability is good not only for us visual control freaks, but also for maintaining a markup structure that provides your pages with the highest level of accessibility.

Since CSS has become our preferred method of formatting, and because we devote an entire chapter to defining style sheets, let's first take a quick overview of how to apply styles using CSS.

CSS Formatting

The first step in using CSS is to define styles, which can reside within a page or in an external file that's referenced by a page. In the Layout Editor, click the Open CSS Editor button, or select CSS Editor from the View menu.

CSS styles come in three varieties: elements, classes, and IDs. Since IDs aren't used for text formatting, we limit our discussion here to elements and classes.

Tip: Styles and Selectors

Technically, CSS styles are called selectors: they select tags or objects or text ranges on a page. But we like GoLive's approach of calling them styles, as it's closer to how we, as designers, think of their task: they style type or paragraphs.

Tip: Internal and External

In the real world, we almost always create an external style sheet file that all the pages in our site reference. In this section, however, we're using internal styles to avoid complexity and not repeat the more advanced advice in Chapter 27. Fortunately, creating and editing styles is the same whether you're defining internal or external style sheets. GoLive even uses the same interface and approach to editing styles wherever they appear.

Elements. To redefine the formatting of an existing HTML tag, such as headings, click the New Element Style button in the CSS Editor. A new element appears in the CSS Editor; rename it to the tag you'd like to edit (for example, "h1" to change the Heading 1 formatting). In the CSS Style Inspector, use the assorted sections to apply changes to the color, size, font family, weight, and other options (see Figure 4-3). Thereafter, any text with that element applied shows up with your new formatting.

Figure 4-3
Default style
versus CSS
defined style

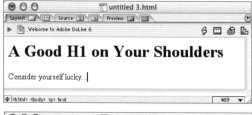

*Heading 1 style in its
default incarnation
(top) and after an
H1 CSS definition is
created (bottom)*

Tip: Preview Styles

Add some text to your page and apply the CSS style you're editing. As you make changes in the CSS Style Inspector, the text is updated so you can see exactly what your style looks like.

Classes. Whereas elements are typically used to redefine formatting for existing HTML tags, classes can be given any name and applied to discrete sections of text. Think of a class as a jeweler's hammer, compared to an element's sledgehammer. Click the New Class Style button in the CSS Editor, rename it (for example, "sidebartext"), and define its formatting in the CSS Style Inspector.

Unlike elements, classes must be manually applied to text on your page. Select a range of text, switch to the CSS palette, and mark one of the following boxes to the right of your class name, depending on which text should display in the style (see Figure 4-4). You can also apply styles by bringing up the contextual menu, selecting Apply CSS Style, and choosing a style name from the Span, Paragraph, or Div submenus.

Figure 4-4
Types of
CSS styles

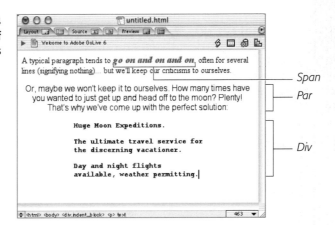

- **Span.** Selecting Span applies the style only to the text that's selected. This is good for highlighting a single word or sentence.

- **Par.** If you want to apply the style to an entire paragraph, select Par. If there's no selection, Par applies to the paragraph in which the text-insertion point is located. In a selection that crosses multiple paragraphs, Par applies separately to each paragraph in the selection.

- **Div.** Use Div to apply the style to a larger block of paragraphs. Div is especially useful if you wish to create a border around a section; if you were to use Par, it would make borders around each paragraph instead of the whole group.

Tip: Multiple Styles

It's possible to combine the way styles are applied: for example, a class can be set with both Par and Div marked in the CSS palette (see Figure 4-5). You might set the font separately for different paragraphs, but want the leading to be the same for an entire section, as one example. For more information on why you'd do this, see Chapter 27.

Figure 4-5
Mixing
CSS styles

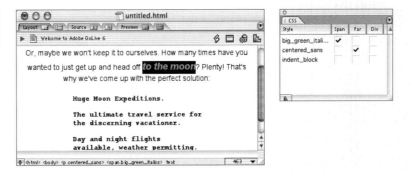

Basic CSS Formatting Walk-Through: Internal Styles

CSS can be a bit daunting due to the large number of variables you can set when building styles. However, once you get the basic gist of how styles work, the rest of it wraps neatly into place around your headspace. Here's a quick step-by-step introduction to creating a simple set of style sheets. For more depth, see Chapter 27, *Defining Cascading Style Sheets*.

For this example, we want to redefine a heading element.

1. In the Layout Editor, type a sample headline and use the Paragraph Formatting popup menu in the Toolbar to apply a Header 2 style. We use this as a reference when editing the CSS style.
2. Click the Open CSS Editor button, or choose the same option from the View menu.

3. Click the New Element Style button in the CSS Editor.
4. Rename the new element to H2 in the CSS Editor (see Figure 4-6).
5. In the CSS Style Inspector, make sure the Font tab is active. Select Maroon from the Color popup menu.
6. We want the size to be consistent in every browser, so enter "30px" (which is short for 30 pixels) in the Size field.
7. This is a heading, after all, so select Bold from the Weight popup menu.
8. To make the heading pop a little more, in the Font Family section click the New Font Family button; choose "Arial, Helvetica, Geneva, Swiss, SunSans-Regular" from the popup menu that appears (see Figure 4-7).

Figure 4-6
Defining a new internal element style

Figure 4-7
Changing the style's font

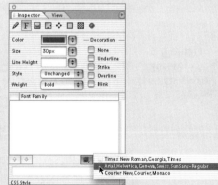

Now, we also want to create a class style that can be applied to any range of text. (This example has less formatting to save space.)

1. In the CSS Editor, click the New Class Style button and rename the new class to "sidebartext" (of course, you can choose any name you wish). Since you've already defined it as a class style, GoLive automatically adds a period at the beginning of the name to define it as a class for Web browsers.

2. Go back to the CSS Style Inspector and change the color. This time, pick any color from the Color palette and drag it onto the field instead of selecting a color from the popup list.

3. From the Style popup menu, choose Italic (see Figure 4-8).

4. Now, return to the Layout Editor and type a couple of paragraphs of text. Leave your cursor in the middle of the first paragraph.

5. Display the CSS palette by choosing CSS from the Window menu. You should see "sidebartext" in the list.

6. Click the Par box to apply the style to the entire paragraph.

7. To see the difference between Par and Span, uncheck the Par box, then highlight a few words of text in the Layout Editor.

8. Now click the Span box in the CSS palette. Only the text you highlighted shows up in the "sidebartext" style (see Figure 4-9).

Figure 4-8
Specifying a
class style

Figure 4-9
Applying class
style to a
range of text

Basic CSS Formatting Walk-Through: External Styles

One of the true advantages of CSS is the ability to define a style once, then use it on multiple pages throughout a site. External style sheets save you from having to define the same style for every page where it appears.

For practical purposes, we more often create an external style sheet, which makes editing the style infinitely easier.

1. From the File menu, choose Cascading Style Sheet from the New Special submenu. A new window appears with the name "untitled.css".

2. Save the file as "coolstyles.css". You can choose something else, but retain the ".css" extension. The file appears as a CSS Editor window (see Figure 4-10).

3. Create styles as you did when you built the internal styles. When you're finished, save and close the file.

4. Open one of your site's pages, or create a new page, and then bring up the CSS Editor. Click the New Link to External CSS button; a new folder titled "External" appears with an "(EmptyReference!)" placeholder (see Figure 4-11).

5. Click the placeholder and switch to the External Style Sheet Inspector. In the Reference field, specify the "coolstyles.css" file (also see Figure 4-11).

6. The styles you created in the external file appear in the CSS palette. Click the Span, Par, or Div boxes as you did earlier to apply the style.

Figure 4-10
External style sheet window

Figure 4-11
Referencing the external style sheet file

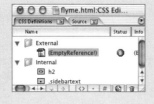

HTML Text Formatting

Although CSS represents the future, HTML text formatting is still frequently used to style text on Web pages. Although we strongly recommend switching entirely to CSS, there's no ignoring reality.

GoLive currently supports many ways to style text, available either from the Toolbar or the Type menu. Styles may be applied to any highlighted text in the Layout Editor, and overlaid, one on top of another (bold + italic + underline). Table 4-2 displays the basic styled text options.

Table 4-2
Text styles

Text Style	Example
Plain Text	Typefaces by Josef Stylin'
Bold	**Typefaces by Josef Stylin'**
Italic	*Typefaces by Josef Stylin'*
Underline	<u>Typefaces by Josef Stylin'</u>
Strikeout	~~Typefaces by Josef Stylin'~~
Superscript	Typefaces by $^{Josef Stylin'}$
Subscript	Typefaces by $_{Josef Stylin'}$
Teletype*	`Typefaces by Josef Stylin'`
Blink	(see next tip)
Nobreak**	

* Teletype is a method of applying local formatting to display text in a monospaced font.

** Nobreak lets you specify that the highlighted text not wrap to the next line if it's being displayed in a narrow browser window, a table cell, or beside an aligned image.

Tip: Don't Blink

The Blink tag was introduced by Netscape and quickly became one of the most derided tags ever, since not everyone wants to be repeatedly flashed by text. GoLive does not display the blink effect in either the Layout Editor or the Layout Preview; you have to open the page in a Netscape browser to see it in action. Although we have seen an occasional clever use of Blink (it convincingly reproduces a word processor's flashing cursor), we don't recommend its use.

Tip: Can't Blink?

So, you're persistent and really want to use Blink—but in the Type menu's Style submenu, the option is grayed-out and inaccessible. Is this a hint from GoLive's engineers that you should reconsider? Although we're sure the Adobe folks have plenty of opinions about Web design, in this case the bug actually is a feature. By default, new pages include the Doctype information for Transitional HTML specification (see Chapter 2, *Layout*, for more on Doctype). Since Blink is a Netscape-only tag, the option to use it is disabled because it doesn't fit the page's defined spec. If you go to the Layout Editor's popout menu and choose None from the Doctype submenu, the Blink option returns.

Tip: Contextual Text Formatting

Tired of reaching for the menus whenever you want to apply text formatting? GoLive includes extensive contextual menu support for applying all of the formatting found under the Type menu. With text selected, simply Control-click (Mac) or right-click (Windows) to access the contextual menu (see Figure 4-12).

Figure 4-12
Contextual
choices

Tip: Mix and Match Styles

You don't have to pick just one text style or text structure tag; feel free to mix and match them as you wish. If your style soup gets to be too murky, simply go to the Type menu and select Plain Text from the Style submenu, or Plain Structure from the Structure submenu, or both.

Text Structure

The Structure submenu of GoLive's Type menu lists the structural formatting options, which are also applied to any highlighted text. Unlike the text styles, the appearance of text formatted with these tags depends on how a browser is configured to display them. Structural definitions tend to identify the *kind* of content rather than the formatting that should be applied to them; for instance, "quotation" instead of "italic."

Structural definitions are helpful when using Cascading Style Sheets as well; for example, you could specify that text marked as Emphasis appear not only in italics, but colored red and slightly larger than the rest of the text. The descriptions in Table 4-3 note GoLive's display as well as the common appearance in Web browsers (though they may differ among products, platforms, and versions).

Table 4-3
Structural
styles

Structure	Appearance
Plain Structure	The default style offers no frills.
Emphasis	Text appears in italics.
Strong	Text appears in bold.
Quotation	Text appears in italics.
Sample	Text appears in a monospaced font.
Definition	A truly structural tag, the text doesn't change its appearance in GoLive.
Variable	Text appears in italics.
Code	Text appears in a monospaced font.
Keyboard	Text appears in a monospaced font.

Paragraph Formatting

In addition to formatting snippets of highlighted text, HTML includes the ability to choose a format that gets applied to an entire paragraph. Unlike text styles and structure, you cannot mix and match paragraph formats.

Paragraph and None. In previous versions of GoLive, every paragraph on your page was enclosed in <P> tags, so the paragraph formatting option was set to None. However, paragraphs defined as such in HTML aren't the same as text with no formatting—each browser adds some space following a <P> defined paragraph. So, GoLive 6 adds Paragraph to the paragraph format menu to denote that the <P> tags are in use. To get rid of that extra space, set the option to None.

Headings. Web browsers include built-in definitions for six heading levels. Structurally, headings act as classifications whose appearances can be easily manipulated with Cascading Style Sheets; stylistically, headings often pack an obvious "this is clearly a headline" punch to your text. You can apply headings from the Type menu's Paragraph Format submenu or the Paragraph Format popup menu on the Toolbar (see Figure 4-13).

Figure 4-13
Heading
formats

Preformatted. Preformatted text disobeys a few laws of HTML for the sake of making things easier for Web authors. Normally, Web browsers ignore line breaks and multiple spaces in an HTML file, relying on paragraph and other vertical markers—like the end of a list—to identify paragraphs and other blocks of text that should be separated vertically. Preformatted text instead reproduces the text exactly as it appears in the HTML, in a monospaced font including any hard returns, even without paragraph or line break tags (see Figure 4-14). Preformatted text works well when showing longer code samples or content, like bracketed text, that would normally require HTML entities to display properly.

Tip: Exporting and Uploading with Pre

In Part 3, *Sites and Groups*, we discuss using features like Export and Upload to Server to strip unwanted white space and other useless HTML from Web pages. If you use Preformatted text, which uses the Pre tag in HTML, some of this superfluous spacing may be useful for page formatting. We recommend not stripping HTML on pages that use the Pre tag.

Address. This format is used for addresses or other contact information that Internet search-engine indexers look for when scanning your Web site. GoLive and most browsers display the text in italics.

Figure 4-14
Preformatted
text

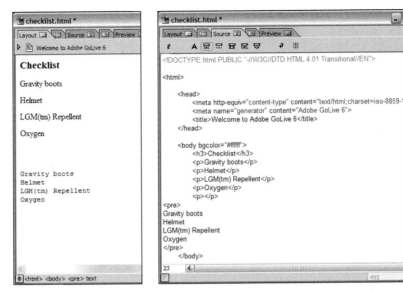

The line breaks of the preformatted section (at right, within the Pre tags in the Source Code Editor) are applied without requiring HTML tags, as in the top list.

Text Alignment

Most of the text we read in Western European languages is aligned to the left edge of a page or column, but that doesn't mean there isn't room for a little nonconformity here and there. Since GoLive handles all kinds of text encodings, multiple alignment styles can be handy for that purpose.

In addition to left-side alignment, GoLive can center or right-align paragraphs: click the desired alignment button on the Toolbar or choose from the Alignment submenu of the Type or contextual menu. To return to the paragraph's default alignment, either select Default from the Alignment submenu or click a highlighted alignment button to deactivate it (see Figure 4-15).

Figure 4-15
Text alignment
using the
Toolbar

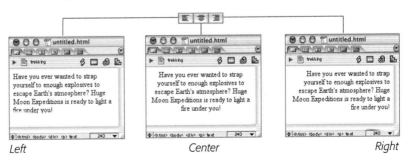

Left   Center   Right

Alignment overrides. Paragraph alignment is only one of several methods GoLive offers for aligning elements. Paragraph alignment is much different than image alignment, which wraps text around the image (see Chapter 5, *Images*). You can also align text within a table cell by setting the cell's alignment attribute (see Chapter 7, *Tables*). And, as you might expect, the various alignments can be combined depending on the layout you're aiming for. In this case, it's good to know how the alignments interact with each other, and which ones override the others.

In general, paragraph alignment dominates. If you enter text within a table cell and set its paragraph alignment to Right, the text remains aligned right even if the table cell's horizontal alignment is set to Left or Center. When setting image or table alignment for purposes of wrapping text, however, you can get both effects simultaneously. An image with Alignment set to Left, but placed in a paragraph that's been aligned right, sticks to the left of the screen while the wrapped text appears beside it aligned right (see Figure 4-16).

Figure 4-16
Alignment overrides

Text aligned right

Image aligned left

Block indent. Although not technically an alignment attribute, GoLive supports block indentation of paragraphs, which simply indents the paragraph using HTML's Blockquote tag. From the Alignment submenu of the Type menu, choose Increase Block Indent or Decrease Block Indent, depending on how far you want to indent the text. Unlike using an unnumbered list (see "Unnumbered List" later in this chapter), Block Indent brings the paragraph's margins in from both the left and right sides (see Figure 4-17).

Figure 4-17
Block indent

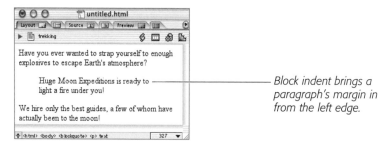

Block indent brings a paragraph's margin in from the left edge.

Text Size

Text size in HTML isn't expressed in points, as it is most everywhere else on your computer, because HTML doesn't understand descriptions like 10-point Times. In order to make the Web more accessible, text size is expressed structurally, not stylistically, based on the text-size settings in most Web browsers. This way, it doesn't matter how large your monitor is, or whether you're viewing it at its maximum resolution—the text on a Web page is almost guaranteed to be readable. To further complicate the issue, text sizes in HTML are relational, so trying to emulate 10-point Times, for example, might mean setting the type size at 3, -1, +1, or others depending on the user's browser settings. Don't be daunted, however: you still have plenty of control over the appearance of your text.

Choose from 22 size options by using the Font Size popup menu on the Toolbar, or the Size submenu under the Type menu; the default text size is None (see Figure 4-18).

Figure 4-18
Text sizes

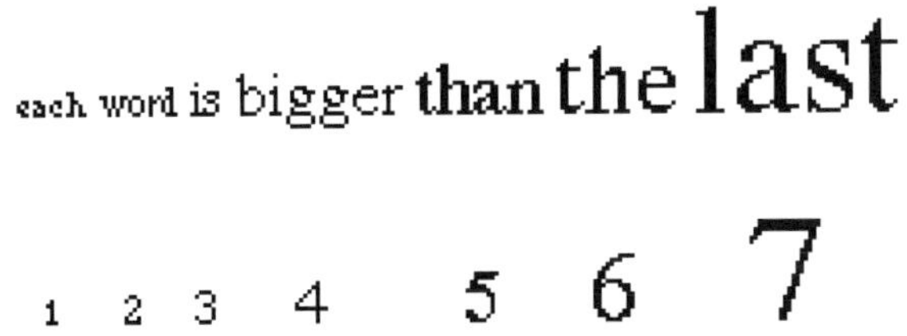

each word is bigger than the last

1   2   3   4   5   6   7

Tip: How Big Is None?

How nitpicky do you want to get? GoLive 4 and earlier versions tracked text size solely on a scale of 1 to 7, with 3 being the default size. With the addition of relative text sizes, it was harder to convince Web designers that 3 was the default, so the None option was introduced in GoLive 5.

One could argue that "none" represents nothing, or zero, which would mean that the text wouldn't even exist, and therefore theoretically all of your hard work would be obliterated when you chose the None option. But we're sure you have much better uses for your time than theorizing about nonexistent numbers.

Absolute versus relative text sizes in HTML. There are two ways to express font size within HTML. Absolute sizing specifies a number on a 1 to 7 scale; relative sizing tells the browser to use a size that's equal to a number more or less than the browser's default font size, ranging from -7 to +7.

In reality, each method is somewhat relative, since there's no way outside of using CSS to define a specific point size. And, in fact, modern Web browsers no longer use the 1 to 7 range to establish their default text sizes; in most cases, the type is assigned a point size (such as 16 point Times). To enlarge text onscreen, Internet Explorer and Netscape use a "Text Zoom" or "Text Size" option, which magnifies all sizes by a certain percentage.

Tip: Text Sizes on the Web

Ever wondered why some Web pages viewed on a Macintosh have unusually small text? It's not your eyes—our colleague Geoff Duncan published a thorough explanation in the online journal *TidBITS*. You can find a link to the article at www.realworldgolive.com/six/.

Lists and Indents

Without the margin and indent features of a word processor, formatting list material would be a frustrating endeavor. Fortunately, GoLive supports and previews HTML's list features, not only making it easy to create typical lists of items, but also lists for presentation purposes.

Numbered List. To create a list that includes numbers before each paragraph, highlight the text and click the Numbered List button on the Toolbar, or select Default Numbered List from the List submenu of the Type menu. You can choose which style of numbering you want displayed by choosing the other options from the same menu (see Figure 4-19).

Figure 4-19
List types

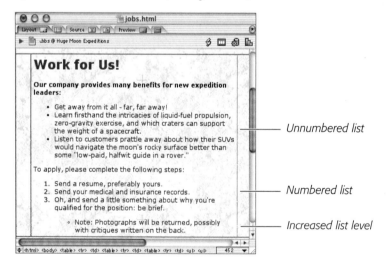

Unnumbered list

Numbered list

Increased list level

Tip: No Need to Select All Text

Since lists are a paragraph (or block) setting, you don't need to select every character in a paragraph before applying the list-level commands. As long as a portion of the paragraph is selected, the entire block between returns is formatted in the list style.

Unnumbered List. If your list isn't dependent on numbering, create an unnumbered list by clicking the Unnumbered List button on the Toolbar or selecting Default Unnumbered List from the List submenu of the Type menu. The menu also includes the option to use bullets, circles, or squares at the beginning of list items.

Tip: CSS Bullets

With CSS, you can specify a wider variety of bullets for unnumbered lists, including images you specify yourself. Browsers starting with Internet Explorer 4.0 and Netscape 6 support this very cool design feature. Other browsers just use the default shapes.

Increasing and decreasing list levels. One advantage to using lists is that you don't have to precede each item with a number or bullet; a list can just as easily serve as an indented margin for the selected range of text. Click the Increase List Level button on the Toolbar or select it from the Type menu's List submenu to push the text horizontally to the right. The Decrease List Level button and menu item move the text back toward the left margin.

If you decrease the list beyond the first level, the text reverts to normal paragraph text; clicking the Numbered List or Unnumbered List buttons with an active list selected also removes the list formatting.

Term and Definition. Harking back to its academic origins, HTML includes the capability to define terms and definitions (structural formatting). Select part of a paragraph and choose Term from the List submenu of the Type menu to tag it as a term; the appearance doesn't change in the Layout Editor. To create a definition for the term, select the text and choose Definition from the same submenu. This action formats the text indented from the left margin without the vertical space imposed by normal paragraphs (see Figure 4-20, next page).

Indenting using horizontal spacers. Another method of indenting text is the use of HTML-defined spacers called Horizontal Spacers in GoLive. Despite their name, these spacers are not limited to horizontal.

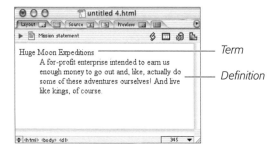

Figure 4-20
Term and
definition

Double-click the Horizontal Spacer icon from the Objects palette's Basic tab, or drag it to the Layout Editor to add a spacer. You can specify its width in the Spacer Inspector to create a single line indent by changing the value in the Width field or stretching the spacer element by its object handle. A spacer also can be set to Vertical, which fills the length of the text and offers a variable height value; or Block, which creates a rectangular space that can be aligned like an image. The Block style can be aligned similar to an image (where text wraps around it) by choosing an option from the Alignment popup menu.

Tip: Spacers Are Pre-Netscape 6 Only

The downside to spacers is that they're only recognized by Netscape browsers prior to version 6.0, which limits their usefulness.

Text Color

A page's default text color can be set in the Page Inspector, but there are times when you may want to apply local color formatting within the body text.

Applying text color. To color a range of text, first select it in the Layout Editor, and then choose a color from the Color palette. Drag the color swatch from the Preview pane and drop it anywhere on the selected text to apply the new color (see Figure 4-21).

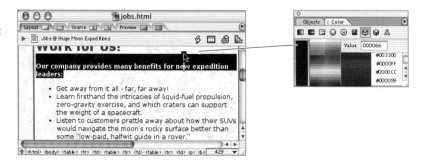

Figure 4-21
Coloring text

You can also take advantage of the Text Color field, located on the Toolbar. Drag a color swatch from the Color palette to the Text Color field to define a color. If a range of text is selected, the color is applied to the text; if no text is selected, any text you type beginning at the insertion point's location assumes that color.

Tip: Many Unhappy Returns

GoLive likes to keep its text formatting orderly within the underlying HTML, which means that the style you're typing with in one paragraph won't carry over to the next when you hit Return or Enter. To test, specify a color in the Text Color field and apply bold formatting; type a few words, then hit Return to make a new paragraph. The text now shows up in the default formatting. The only attributes that get carried into the next paragraph are structural ones: header, alignment, and list items. Applying other text formatting after you've entered the text will likely save you time and frustration.

If that's too much dragging and dropping for you, select a text range and then click once on the Text Color field to use it in active mode. The highlighted text dynamically changes colors as you click on colors in the Color palette.

Tip: Popup Text Color

To quickly choose a Web-safe color, Control-click (Mac) or right-click (Windows) the Text Color field to display a popup grid of the Web Color List. Hold down Option (Mac) or Alt (Windows) to view a grid of the Web Name List.

If you're editing text in the Source Code Editor and don't know the hex value of a specific color, dropping a color swatch in your text inserts the following code (the value in quotes changes depending on the color; in this case, the color is black), which you can use in a FONT tag:

```
COLOR="#000000"
```

Removing text color. If you decide that colors just aren't working visually within your text, highlight the colored area and select Remove Color from the Type menu to return to the page's default text color.

Using Fonts

A welcome change in modern Web browsers is the ability to specify typefaces other than the limited selection used in a browser's preferences. Just as color and text formatting can affect the tone and presentation of your text, using different fonts adds to the character of Web pages. Font support also allows you to employ faces such as Verdana or Georgia that were created specifically for onscreen reading.

Unfortunately, there's no guarantee that all the viewers of your page have your specified fonts installed on their systems. However, this doesn't turn out to be too much of a downside (Maybe it's more of a slightly-vertically-declined plane?) because of the flexible way HTML handles font selection.

Specifying Fonts

Before leaping into how GoLive handles font selection, we quickly need to explain how Web browsers treat fonts. As with text size, typefaces are defined using either the Font tag, which tells the browser which font to use for the text that follows it, or by assigning CSS styles. But if the viewer's computer doesn't have that font installed, he sees only the default text—still acceptable, but it misses the mark on communicating the designer's vision. To improve the chances of using a font that's installed on someone's machine, fonts are usually defined in groups, called "font sets," and separated by commas.

A Web browser looks at the first font listed, and uses it if it's installed. If it's not available, the browser moves on to the next font, then the next, and the next, until either a match is found or the list ends, at which point the default font comes back into play. For greater compatibility, designers choose fonts that are more likely to be installed on users' machines, such as the fonts used by the operating system. In HTML, the code looks something like this:

```
<FONT face="Arial, Helvetica, Geneva, Swiss, SunSans-Regular">
```

When using a CSS definition, the code appears as:

```
.fonttest  { font-family: Arial, Helvetica, Geneva, Swiss, SunSans-Regular }
```

In these examples, most browsers and platforms are accounted for: Arial is a default Windows font, Helvetica ships with the Mac OS, and the other fonts are variations of typical sans-serif fonts.

Tip: Specifying Fonts Using CSS

As we mentioned earlier, we prefer to use Cascading Style Sheets to handle text formatting, and nowhere is that more appropriate than when specifying fonts. It's easier to define them once and have the setting applied throughout a page or site than to name a font every time a paragraph appears (see the "Basic CSS Formatting Walk-Through" sidebars, earlier). Also, CSS dramatically reduces the amount of code required to display your pages (see Figure 4-22).

Figure 4-22
Font styling
versus
CSS styling

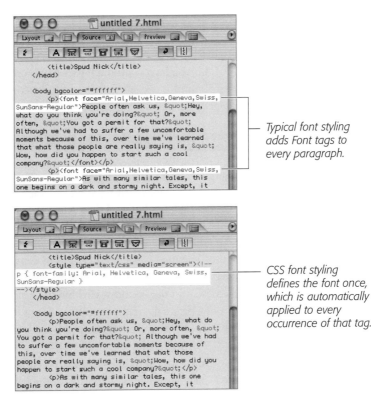

Typical font styling
adds Font tags to
every paragraph.

CSS font styling
defines the font once,
which is automatically
applied to every
occurrence of that tag.

Applying font sets. Styling text using a particular font set is an easy task: go to the Type menu, then navigate to the Font submenu. The font sets are noted only by the name of the first font in the set, but the backup font options get applied as well (see Figure 4-23).

If you're using CSS, select the style name you want to edit in the CSS Editor. Then, in the Font tab of the CSS Style Inspector, click the New Font Family button and choose a set from the popup menu that appears.

Figure 4-23
Applying
a font set

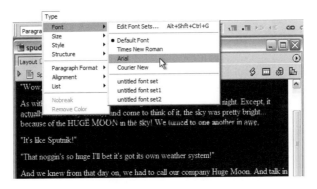

Editing Font Sets

GoLive is preconfigured with three common font sets that all but ensure that any viewer sees the fonts displayed. Although they work well, we have enough typographical sense behind our eyeballs to want to customize the font sets and use other typefaces (see the sidebar, "Seen Onscreen").

Tip: Font Set, Fontset

You're not cracking up—GoLive sometimes calls font sets "fontsets," "font sets," or "fonts," depending on where in the program you are. Whenever you're selecting a range of text and applying a type choice, you're using a font set, whether the set has one member in it or a dozen.

Font Set Editor. To edit or create font sets, choose Edit Font Sets from the Font submenu of the Type menu. The Font Set Editor contains the list of default font sets, which appear in every GoLive document. If you have any pages open, these are also listed in the window; clicking the expansion triangle or plus sign to the left of a page's file name reveals the font sets available to that page. Each page contains at least the sets present in the Default Font Sets list (Figure 4-24).

To create a new, empty font set, click the Create a New Fontset button. A new font set (called "New Font Name") appears in the list belonging to the frontmost page, or the Default Font Sets list if no pages are open. Since the set takes its name from the first font in the new set, click that first font (not the set's bolded title), and choose a font from the popup menu at the bottom of the dialog box. If your intended font isn't installed, select the contents of the

Figure 4-24
Font Set Editor

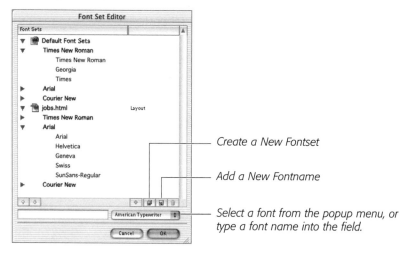

Create a New Fontset

Add a New Fontname

Select a font from the popup menu, or type a font name into the field.

text field and type the name of the font you want to use. With either method, the set takes the name of the font you specify. If you want to add more fonts, simply click the Add a New Fontname button and repeat this process.

Tip: Creating New Default Sets

If you want to create a new default font set when other pages are open, first highlight the Default Font Sets title and then click the Create New Fontset button. If you have no files open, the Edit Font Sets dialog box shows only the Default Font Sets list.

To remove a font or font set, highlight it and click what may be GoLive's smallest button with the second-longest name: Delete the Selected Fontnames and Fontsets (the one with the trash can icon). The honor of longest name must surely go to the button with the plus-sign icon: Duplicate the Selected Fontnames and Fontsets, which makes a copy of the selected font.

Tip: Redundant Duplicate

If you highlight a font name, its name appears in the text field at the bottom of the window. Clicking the Add a New Fontname button acts just like the Duplicate button. In fact, once you've added a font name in the Edit Font Sets window, the last-selected or last-created font name appears the next time you start to make a new font set. The exception here is when you select a font set

Seen Onscreen

Most of the fonts installed on your computer herald from a long history of printed typography. Being able to view on your computer screen close approximations of what a typeface would look like when printed was one of the strengths behind early desktop publishing. The problem is, those fonts were designed with print in mind, and aren't necessarily designed to be read on-screen.

With the popularity of the Web and CD-ROM-based multimedia, typographers are devoting more efforts to making fonts that read better onscreen—some of which may never see the printed page. After a bit of trial and error, we've become partial to a handful of faces that we use when designing for (and browsing) the Web, reading email every day, and using word processors. Favorite faces include Microsoft's free fonts Verdana and Georgia; Adobe's Minion Web and Myriad Web; and Apple's venerable New York and occasionally even Geneva.

Each of these fonts features, on average, a taller x-height (the vertical measurement of a lower-case letter x), roomier letterspacing, and a pixel-level attention to detail that avoids mis-shapen or overly jagged letters. If you've been suffering with Times all this time, try a font that's been designed expressly for onscreen reading; the difference is an eye-opener (and an eye-saver).

name: the Duplicate button creates a duplicate set with all of the original's font names intact. When you're finished, click OK. As far as we can tell, you can enter as many fonts as you like, or stick with only one. With your font sets created, apply them as normal from the Font menu or the CSS Style Inspector if you're using CSS.

Tip: Careful Typing Produces Better Typography

When you type the names in the Font Names field, it doesn't matter whether you have these fonts installed on your system, or whether the fonts exist at all. GoLive assumes that you know what you're typing, and accepts it. If you make a spelling mistake or typo, such as "New Yurk" instead of "New York," a Web browser looks for New Yurk, then moves on to the next font in the list.

Tip: Make Your Fonts Available

If you're worried someone may not possess the font you have in mind for your page, consider using one that is freely accessible. Microsoft has made several fonts, such as Verdana, Georgia, and Trebuchet, available as free downloads from its Web site at www.microsoft.com/typography/. The fonts are also now added when you install a recent version of any Microsoft product. The downloads are fairly small, so your viewers can install them easily and return to your site later to get the full effect of what you've designed.

Using Sitewide Font Sets

So far we've been dealing with defining fonts either on specific pages or globally throughout GoLive. That takes care of most of your font interaction, but the program isn't content to limit itself to just those two approaches. You can also manage and apply fonts on a sitewide basis as well using site-specific font sets. In a site window, click the Font Sets tab to display the list of sitewide font sets (see Figure 4-25).

When you're working with lots of pages, it's easy to create a number of different font sets that may not all match; perhaps in your experimentation

Figure 4-25
Sitewide font
sets list

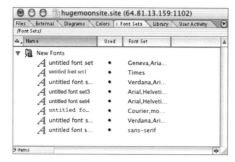

you included Verdana but not Arial on one page, instead of applying an existing set. We use the Font Sets tab as a place to organize a core group of fonts to ensure consistency throughout a site.

Creating New Entries

To create a new font set, first make sure the Font Sets tab of your site window is visible. Go to the Site tab of the Objects palette and double-click or drag the Font Set icon to the site window, which creates a new entry called "untitled font set." Clicking the set brings up the Font Set Inspector, which is almost identical to the Font Set Editor described earlier. Although you don't have to give your new set a name, we highly recommend it; type a descriptive name in the Name field.

A "New Font" placeholder appears highlighted in the font list—type a new name in the text field at the bottom of the Inspector, or choose a font from the popup menu. To add more fonts to the set, click the New Item button and specify their names. The Move Item Upwards and Move Item Downwards buttons rearrange the preferred order of the list. As you'd expect, the Remove Selected Items button deletes entries.

Creating New Folders

For more organizational finesse, you can create folders to categorize your sets. For example, you could create slightly different sets for different areas of your site, and group them in the Font Sets tab using folders (see Figure 4-26). To make new folders, double-click or drag the Font Set Group icon from the Site tab of the Objects palette. Since these folders are just containers, you can only rename them, either by typing in the Font Set Group Inspector, or clicking the folder name in the list and typing when the name becomes editable.

With your folder created, simply populate it by dragging in font sets.

Figure 4-26
New font
set group

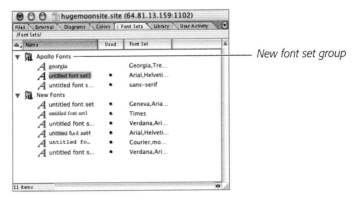

New font set group

Extracting

Of course, you don't have to start a site project by creating new font sets from scratch. Most likely, you've been tinkering with pages and fonts already, and want to just discover what sets are already "out there." With the Font Sets tab visible, select Get Fonts Sets Used from the Site menu or the contextual menu. GoLive creates a folder called New Fonts and deposits a list of untitled font sets that correspond to the sets used on all your pages (see Figure 4-27).

Later, when you've cleaned up the mess a bit, use the Remove Unused Font Sets command (also found in the Site menu or contextual menu) to delete the unwanted stragglers.

Figure 4-27
Getting font
sets used
in a site

Tip: Where Is It?

To see which font sets are used on which pages, bring up the In & Out Links palette and click a font set name.

Tip: Used Indicator Applies to Closed Pages

The Font Sets tab only keeps track of pages in your site that are closed. We discovered this when we had a page open that included the only instance of a font set: the Used indicator in the Font Sets window disappeared when the page was open, but reappeared when it was closed, even though that font set was always present in the page.

Editing

Having a list of font sets is exciting and all, but what can you do with it? Impose your will, of course! When you select a font set, you can employ the same controls you used to create a new set to add or delete font names or rearrange their order. If a set is being used somewhere in your site, editing the set automatically updates the pages where it appears.

Applying

When you create new sets in the Font Set tab, their names appear at the bottom of the Type menu's Font submenu (or in the contextual menu), enabling you to highlight text on a page and apply a sitewide set. Or, if you prefer, you can highlight some text, bring the site window forward, and drag sets from the Font Set tab directly onto the text selection.

Tip: Sitewide Sets Not Available to CSS

Managing sitewide font sets is a feature exclusive to GoLive, so any sets you create in the Font Sets tab aren't recognized in the CSS Style Inspector. To make sets appear there, you need to use the Font Set Editor, described earlier.

HTML Styles

If you want to use predefined styles in your pages, but don't want to apply them via CSS, GoLive 6 offers a new HTML Styles feature. The main advantage to this approach is backward compatibility: if you know your audience is likely to be using pre-4.0 browsers, which don't support CSS well, then HTML Styles gives you a way to apply multiple formatting attributes to your text with a click of the mouse.

However, this *is* a Real World book, and we honestly don't see much use for HTML Styles. Although an HTML style makes it easier to apply more than one type of formatting to text, changing the style later *does not* update the occurrences you've previously made in your pages. So any time or effort you saved by setting up HTML styles is liable to be expended (with interest) later if you need to go back and edit the formatting wherever it appears.

Nonetheless, even if we don't recommend using HTML Styles, we'd be remiss if we didn't cover how it works.

Applying HTML Styles

There are two types of HTML styles you can apply: inline styles, which change only selected text, and paragraph styles, which change an entire paragraph regardless of which text is selected. To help you get started, GoLive includes four preset HTML styles to give you an idea of what's possible; choose HTML Styles from the Window menu to view its palette.

Simply position your cursor within the text you want to change and either drag or double-click the style name. If you're adding an inline style, which is identified by an "I" icon to the left of the style name, you need to first select the text on your page before applying the style (see Figure 4-28). You can also select a style name and click the Apply Style button.

Figure 4-28
Applying
an inline
HTML style

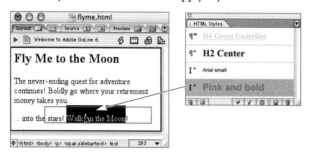

Tip: Cursor Needs Positioning

Before dragging a paragraph style to your page, make sure your cursor is placed within the paragraph you want to format. Although dragging an HTML style to a page displays a cursor beneath your mouse pointer, when you drop the style on the page, the style is only applied to the paragraph where your original cursor resides.

The way the style behaves depends on its Apply Mode, which can be set to either replace the text's existing formatting, or just add to it. You can easily tell which mode is in use by examining the icon to the left of the style name: a double-arrow line indicates the style replaces formatting, while a plus sign denotes the style will be added.

Creating New HTML Styles

Of course, your pages would start looking less-than-inspired if you stick with GoLive's four preset styles. You can either create a new style from scratch or define a style based on how some text is already formatted.

Tip: Popout Menu

Most of the style commands are also available from the popout menu located at the top right of the HTML Styles palette.

Defining a new style. In the HTML Styles palette, click the New Style button to bring up the New Style dialog box (see Figure 4-29). Use the Name field to give the style a new title.

Most of the controls in the Basic tab are familiar: choose font, size, color, alignment, paragraph formatting, and appearance (both HTML and structural

Figure 4-29
Creating a new
HTML style

formatting) using the collection of buttons and popup menus. A preview area at the bottom of the dialog box previews approximately what the style will look like. Just above the preview area are two options specific to HTML Styles:

- **Apply As.** Click either the Apply As Paragraph or Apply As Inline buttons to specify whether the style affects an entire paragraph or just the text that is selected.

- **Apply Mode.** This popup menu determines whether the style overrides existing formatting (Replace) or adds to it (Add).

Tip: Color Field

Unlike every other Color field in GoLive, the one in the Edit Style dialog box doesn't interact with the Color palette. Instead, click it to display the operating system's color picker options. However, it does recognize a great shortcut: Control-click (Mac) or right-click (Windows) the field to see the palette of Web-safe colors. (See Chapter 6, *Color*, for more on working with color in GoLive.)

You're not limited to the standard text styling options under the Basic tab, however. Clicking the Advanced tab reveals the HTML tags and attributes that you chose in the Basic tab, and offers the capability to add more.

Click the New Tag button to create a new entry in the list. Using the text field below the list, type the tag's name, plus an attribute and value if needed. For example, suppose you want your style to make a paragraph appear as an entry in an unnumbered list, where each item uses square bullets instead of the default. To do this, you'd create two new tags: enter "LI" (the HTML tag for a list item) in the Name column, "type" in the Attribute column, and "square" in the Value column; then, you'd enter "UL" (HTML for unnumbered list) as a separate tag. When you apply the style to your paragraph, it shows up in a list (see Figure 4-30, next page).

Figure 4-30
Advanced
HTML style
options

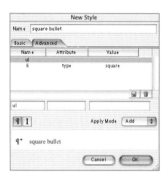

HTML style applied

When you're finished setting up the different options, click OK to go back to the Layout Editor, where you can apply your new style. If you later want to edit the style, select it in the HTML Styles palette and click the Edit Style button to return to the Edit Style dialog box. (But remember that changing the style doesn't affect any text where the style was previously applied; you'll have to reapply the edited style manually.)

Tip: Tag List Order

The list order in the Advanced tab is the same order that tags are written in the page's source code. When you create a new tag, it appears at the top of the list, so it would appear first in the HTML. However, in our unnumbered list above, the <UL> tag must appear before the <LI> tag in the code for the list to work. So, in the Style Editor, you must create the <LI> tag first, even though in the code it appears second. Unfortunately, there's no way to re-order the list, so if you need a tag to appear at the bottom of the list, you may have to manually re-enter all of the tags you set up in the Basic tab.

Tip: Tab Switching Bug

If you add a new tag in the Advanced tab, then switch to the Basic tab and make a change, the tag you added is gone when you switch back to the Advanced tab. Hopefully, Adobe will address this in a future release.

Defining a style based on existing formatting. When you're experimenting with design options, you probably don't have the time or inclination to set up HTML styles before entering any of your text. Instead, easily create new styles that take on the formatting of existing text. Position your cursor amid your formatted text and bring up the HTML Styles palette. Then click the New Style button—its attributes are already entered in the Edit Style dialog box.

You can also redefine an existing style with the formatting of your sample text. In this case, select a style in the HTML Styles palette and click the Capture Style button.

Removing Styles

If your HTML style just isn't working in your text, getting rid of it is fairly straightforward. Highlight the text you wish to neutralize and select Clear Inline Styles or Clear Paragraph Styles from the HTML Styles palette's popout menu (see Figure 4-31). Most likely, you need to invoke both commands to completely clear your text.

Figure 4-31
Removing
HTML styles
from a page

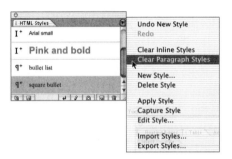

Exporting and Importing HTML Styles

With a set of styles created, you may find yourself in the enviable position of sparking jealousy in the other members of your Web team. Go ahead and share your styles—not only will you endear yourself to them, you may even discover a practical need to have everyone working from the same set of styles to maintain consistency in your site.

In the HTML Styles palette, click the Export Style button. Despite its name, this command actually exports *all* of the styles into a single XML file. In the Save dialog box that appears, give the file a descriptive name (instead of the generic "styles.xml") and choose a location.

If someone else on your team exported styles for you, import them into your copy of GoLive by clicking the Import Style button and locating the XML file.

Tip: All for One

Since you're actually exporting and importing the full list of styles, make sure you know what you're passing around. Any styles you created are overwritten when you import a new XML file. For this reason, it's a good idea to export your styles (and name the backup file something like "jeff-html-styles-4.xml") before importing any new ones.

Spellchecking

Spellchecking is the best thing ever to hit comptures. Computres. Computers. But it requires human intelligence to operate successfully. GoLive's spellchecking offers most of the standard features found in Microsoft Word and other applications.

You can spellcheck a single page or an entire site; the controls are identical. Bring the page you want checked to the forefront and select Check Spelling from the Edit menu (see Figure 4-32).

If you want to spellcheck a site, you need to have its Site window open when you bring up the Check Spelling dialog box. Click the Check in Files option at the bottom of the window and expand its triangle to reveal the files list. Choose your site name from the Files From popup menu, or use the Add Files button to add individual files. When you check spelling, each page is opened and checked in turn.

Language. Select a language from your installed dictionaries if the default doesn't match the language of the page.

Tip: Worldwide Spellchecking

Because GoLive was designed for an international audience, you can spellcheck for any of the languages you have installed. GoLive includes dictionaries for almost all Western European languages and all their "Americas" versions (French Canadian, US English, and Brazilian Portuguese).

Figure 4-32
Check Spelling

From Top. Check this option to examine the entire page; otherwise, the spellchecking starts at the text-insertion point.

More Options. Sometimes a spellchecker will flag words that you know aren't in its dictionary, but are correct anyway. The More Options section (click the triangle at the bottom of the screen to display) provides the following features, which can be activated by clicking their checkboxes:

- Find uncapitalized begin [sic] of sentences

- Find repeated words

- Ignore single characters

- Ignore words with only uppercase

- Ignore words with numbers

- Ignore numbers

- Ignore roman numerals

Tip: Ignoring Patterns

Spellchecking can also ignore patterns of text using regular expressions. If you reveal the Regular Expressions settings under the Spell Checker pane in Preferences, you can add patterns that GoLive excludes when it spellchecks. It has two built-in patterns to avoid flagging URLs and email addresses. See Chapter 22, *Advanced Features*, for details on using this feature.

Checking

Click the Start button to begin spellchecking. GoLive displays each word it finds misspelled at the top of the dialog box, along with a brief description of the problem (such as "Unknown word" or "Space missing"). If it suggests a replacement, it places it in the field below the misspelling. This field can be edited, or you can enter a word when GoLive offers no suggestions. Other choices appear in the Suggestions list; select a word to have it automatically inserted in the replacement field.

The other options are controlled via the buttons along the right edge of the window.

Stop. During a spellchecking operation, the Start button becomes the Stop button, which predictably stops the process. Closing the Check Spelling dialog box also ends the operation.

Delete. GoLive deletes the word from the page where the misspelling was found.

Change. Click Change to apply the word suggested by GoLive's dictionary, or your own replacement if you typed it in.

Ignore. This skips just the current instance of the word.

Ignore All. GoLive remembers this word during the spellchecking "session" and skips all subsequent instances of it.

Learn. GoLive adds the word to its exception dictionary, which you can edit via the Preferences dialog box's Spell Checker pane.

Next File. This option is only available when you're spellchecking a site, and it allows you to force GoLive to move to the next file, even if the current file has not been completely checked.

Tip: Switching to Document

You can click the Layout Editor to make changes at any time while spellchecking. If you position your text-insertion point elsewhere in the document, though, the Spellchecker continues its search where it left off, not from the new position of the cursor.

You Look Simply...Fontastic

Text on the Web used to be about as exciting as the endless columns of copy on old-time newspapers: it seemed to go on and on and on, without offering any pizzazz. What most people don't realize is that a lot of hard work went into making those newspaper columns as readable as possible—legibility was not sacrificed, just a bit of excitement. The Web, finally, is reaching the point where legibility and control can co-exist, and the presentation of type can be just as interesting as the snazziest graphics.

CHAPTER 5

Images

The Web existed before it could handle images, but it wasn't as exciting. To make it more useful, the early browser engineers threw in support for poor-resolution, limited-color-range images that displayed at excruciatingly slow speeds and—presto!—the commercial Web was suddenly a hot property. Folks began banging down the doors to be let in, no matter how pokey it was.

Combining images with text on a page also marked the beginning of wide-scale online publishing and opened the field for graphic designers to make an impact.

Before visual editors existed, adding images to a page by hand coding HTML tags was a laborious process. GoLive, in contrast, lets you add images by dragging them into a document window from the Desktop or Site window, or by browsing local drives and other networked resources.

Once an image is on a page, you can assign attributes, like alignment and spacing, via the Image Inspector, which let you immediately preview how the settings look on a page. You can also easily add interactivity to a page by setting up rollovers, or images that change when you move your mouse cursor over them.

Image Formats

Before the Web, bigger seemed better: larger images had more resolution, and image formats that were lossless—that is, preserved all the data and color variation in an image—were the ideal choice. But the Web shook things up. The relatively small amount of bandwidth available to most Web users got overwhelmed by the size of most uncompressed, full-resolution, high-fidelity color images. Obviously, some kind of accommodation had to be made.

To that end, two image formats, GIF and JPEG, rose to the top. GIF was the first format that the earliest graphical Web browser supported (that's Mosaic, for you history buffs). And, for better or for worse, we're stuck with it. JPEG, on the other hand, offers some superior tradeoffs in image quality versus image size. As most users' systems can now handle displaying thousands or millions of colors on their monitors at once, its use has really taken off.

PNG, a third format designed from the ground up to meet the needs of Web users, offers a variety of tradeoffs among compression, color palette, and image quality.

GoLive doesn't have the ability to edit images directly, but it's helpful to know the advantages and limitations of each format to get the best performance out of your pages.

GIF. Images saved as GIF (Graphics Interchange Format, pronounced "jiff") files are the universal language of the Web, with all browsers in all versions displaying almost all kinds of GIFs. The GIF format compresses data in two ways: first, by reducing the number of colors in the image to a palette of no more than 256 different colors; and second, by analyzing patterns of repeated color and replacing them with tokens that take up much less space (see Figure 5-1). Line art, such as logos or simple drawings, work best saved as GIF files.

GIFs also support two extra features useful for Web page design. You can set a transparent color in a GIF so that the background shows through, allowing you to simulate the layering of images over other images or a background.

What's New in 6

Image support has changed only slightly in GoLive 6.

The Smart Generic object allows you to connect any kind of image that GoLive knows the file format for. This is a laundry list of well-known and obscure types long supported in Photoshop.

The Rollover tab of the Image Inspector adds lean rollovers, very compact code for creating an image change when the user's mouse passes over and/or clicks the image. Before this, you had to use the special Smart Rollover Action, or attach multiple Actions to a linked image.

The biggest change in GoLive 6 is the addition of support for Photoshop, LiveMotion, and Illustrator Variables. Variables allow GoLive to change the contents of certain layers in native files from those applications. For instance, a Photoshop file with a text layer imported via a Smart Photoshop object can have the text replaced and re-rendered within GoLive to create an entirely new image.

Figure 5-1
GIF image

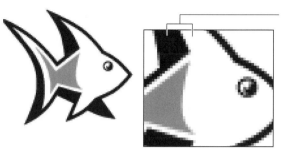

Large areas of solid color, combined with a low number of colors in the image, make logos and line art excellent candidates for the GIF format.

And, you can include multiple frames in a single GIF to provide simple animation; many Web ad banners use GIFs to cycle through a message.

JPEG. For images that are more "photographic" in nature, turn to JPEG (Joint Photographic Experts Group, the body that came up with the specification). JPEG is a lossy compression format, meaning that the algorithm that creates the JPEG throws away information when assembling the compressed image file. The JPEG algorithm can provide more or less faithful color and image quality on a sliding scale from most faithful (in which the most accurate representation of the image is created at about a 2 to 1 ratio), to least faithful—in which visible artifacts in the image show, including pixelization, but the ratio can be as high as 100 to 1. JPEG uses a perceptual system so that the least important color distinctions are removed first; it also has built-in compression to further reduce the amount of space the final data takes up.

Although it sounds like the end result would resemble a patchwork of pixels, JPEGs can be surprisingly accurate to the original image while drastically reducing file size (see Figure 5-2). JPEG images don't support transparency or animation, however.

Figure 5-2
JPEG image

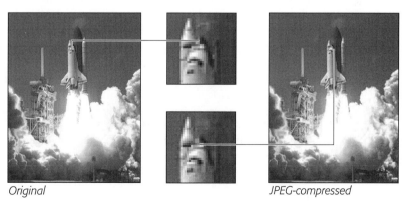

Original   *JPEG-compressed*

PNG. The newcomer to the graphics world is PNG (Portable Network Graphics), pronounced "ping." PNG images compress slightly better than GIF images (anywhere from five to 25 percent improvement), and feature alpha-channel transparency like Photoshop's (providing more options than GIF's one-bit transparency), gamma correction, and improved interlacing for faster perceived downloading (see Figure 5-3). PNG offers completely faithful image reproduction in which no color or quality is lost; or, you can use a GIF-like palette to reduce the number of colors to 256 or fewer.

Figure 5-3
PNG transparency

Inserting Images

Like most page elements in GoLive, inserting an image is a simple drag-and-drop operation. Drag the Image icon from the Basic tab of the Objects palette to a location on the Layout Editor; you can also double-click the Image icon to insert an image placeholder, or use the Insert Object option found in the contextual menu.

If you're in the Source Code Editor, you can drag or double-click the Image icon to insert the appropriate HTML code into the document. Similarly, dragging the icon to the Outline Editor inserts an image object (though double-clicking does nothing). Each of these actions inserts a blank image placeholder sized to match the icon's dimensions (32 pixels square).

Enter the path to the image you want to use in the Source field of the Image Inspector's Basic tab, click the Browse button to locate the file, or use the Point & Shoot tool to specify a source image (see Figure 5-4).

Tip: Faster File Choosing

You can use the previous steps to specify a different image for the placeholder, but two contextual menu items may be quicker. Bring up the contextual menu on the image and from the Source Link submenu, choose either Browse Link, which is the same as clicking the Inspector's Browse button, or Edit Link, which brings up the Edit URL dialog. Don't confuse this with the New Link item, a few items down the list, which creates a new hyperlink (see Figure 5-5).

Figure 5-4
Specifying an image file

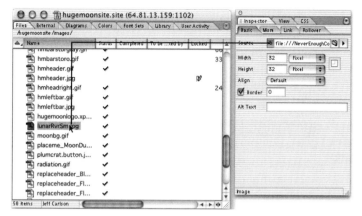

Figure 5-5
Specifying an image using the contextual menu

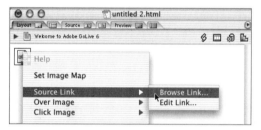

If you already know which graphic file you want to use, drag it from the Desktop or the Site window to the Layout Editor. You can also drag images between open files. Unlike inserting an image placeholder, however, dragging an image file directly to the Source Code Editor creates a link to the file, not the code required to display the image.

Working with Images

An image isn't just a picture on the screen. Although a Web browser can figure out how to display an image based solely on the name of the graphic file, HTML provides several attributes for defining images and how they relate to surrounding material.

Image Attributes

Control over the display of images has become a factor that sets newer browsers apart. The latest HTML specifications and extra browser features offer a number of settings that let you better control an image's appearance. A few features are dedicated to improving how quickly or crisply browsers display images.

Width and height. It's our shared opinion that every Web page should include the height and width tags for every image; fortunately, GoLive offers this feature by default when an image is placed or imported. Providing width and height measurements to browsers helps speed up page loading because the browser doesn't have to retrieve images to know their size.

Tip: Dimensions in Files

GIF, JPEG, and PNG image file formats all list their dimensions in the first few characters of the data that comprises the file. But the browser still has to retrieve part or all of the file before it grabs that information if you don't specify width and height.

GoLive automatically pulls the height and width values from each image when placed on the page and displays the information in the Basic tab of the Image Inspector. If you really don't want the values to appear in the HTML, select Image from the Height and Width popup menus, and GoLive leaves the fields blank.

Tip: Other Dimensions

If you edit the height and width that GoLive fills in for the image, a browser resizes the image to fit the dimensions you specified—though with degraded results. See "Resizing Images," later in this chapter.

Border. HTML provides a method for drawing borders around images, but we guess that 90 percent of border usage is to apply a setting of "0" to help suppress the ugly blue line that shows up around linked graphics by default when no border is specified (see "Linking Images" later in this chapter). If you want a border of greater than zero (GoLive's default, thankfully) to appear, enter a number in the Border field to specify the border's width in pixels (see Figure 5-6). If the image is linked, the border displays as the page's link color; otherwise, it shows up as the page's text color.

If you turn the Border setting off, GoLive's Layout Editor and Preview mode show a standard browser default border of two pixels for linked images (though it doesn't appear for unlinked images).

Alt Text. The Alt Text attribute holds text that gets displayed before images load on a page or when the user doesn't want to or can't load images. In GoLive, type the text in the Alt Text field, located on the Basic tab of the Image Inspector.

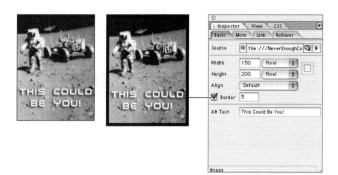

Figure 5-6
Setting border
width in
the Image
Inspector

The Alt Text is usually a description of the image that should load in its place, giving the viewer a quick preview of what's to appear while waiting for the rest of the graphics and text to load.

Tip: Accessibility Through Text

Adding Alt tags to your images also makes your pages more accessible for those text-only Web warriors who surf with images turned off or in the pure text lynx browser for Unix. It's also a great aid to the visually impaired who require non-graphical elements to navigate a page.

The Site Reports tab of the Find feature lets you search through a site for accessibility-related problems, including the missing Alt attribute (see Figure 5-7).

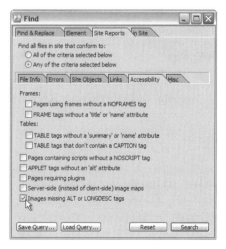

Figure 5-7
Finding
missing Alt
attributes

HSpace and VSpace. These attributes define the space, in pixels, that pads the image from surrounding text or other items; HSpace adds space both to the left and right of an image, while VSpace adds it to the top and bottom. The two corresponding fields are found in the More tab. Padding an image comes in handy when wrapping text around it, so the text and the picture aren't crammed against each other (see Figure 5-8).

Because the HSpace and VSpace options add space to both directions of an image, not just either side, we prefer using a transparent GIF to the right of a flush-left image, or to the left of a flush-right one. This allows us to space just in one direction and leave the other flush with the margin.

The Shimmer Action from Oliver Michalak is a free tool that inserts a transparent GIF at the dimensions you specify and copies it to your local site file. You can find it at www.omich.de/golive/Shimmer/.

Figure 5-8
HSpace and
VSpace

Resizing Images

As you should expect from a visual editor, GoLive supports resizing any images you place on a page. You can stretch, squash, or proportionally resize them to your heart's content.

However, we suggest thinking twice before publishing a page with images that have been resized in GoLive. Web browsers generally don't display a resized image very well, because they're trying to compensate for the graphic's new size based on the limited amount of information available in the original. Also, a browser is not Photoshop; it doesn't have the algorithms and tools to provide the kind of resampling and smoothing that a photo-editing program can.

The information here refers to just changing an image's dimensions in the HTML for a standard Web graphic format (GIF, JPEG, PNG). If you're using smart objects, such as native Photoshop files, you're actually causing GoLive to resample or recreate the image itself, retaining a higher degree of quality. See "Smart Objects," later in this chapter.

Resized images, though not horrible, do tend to appear blocky or have misplaced pixels—a trained Web designer can usually spot immediately if the height and width values in the HTML don't match the intrinsic dimensions of the graphic. Plus, you're asking the browser to do extra work, which can slow its rendering time, making viewers wait a bit longer to see a full page. For finished pages, it's always better to resize the original in a true image editor, then save it as a new file (like "doggy_sm.gif").

Tip: Resize While Designing

We don't want to make a blanket statement that resizing in GoLive is a bad tool. Resizing images is good for mocking up pages during development; it allows you to experiment with different image sizes and placement on the page without having to create multiple resized versions. Just remember to create a final image that matches the final specifications you choose.

Resizing in the Image Inspector. To change the dimensions of an image, enter new values in the Width and Height fields in the Basic tab. When the values don't match the graphic's actual measurements, a resize warning icon appears in a corner of the image (see Figure 5-9). Clicking the Set to Original Size button to the right of the Width and Height fields returns the image to its original dimensions and proportion.

You can also choose to express the dimensions in percentages by selecting Percent from the popup menus to the right of the Height and Width fields. Be aware, however, that you're not specifying a percentage of the original image size, but a percentage of the page. So, an image with a width set to 100 percent would fill the width of the entire window when viewed in a Web browser (see Figure 5-10, next page).

If you'd rather not include the size values at all, select Image from the popup menus to remove the values and restore the image's actual dimensions.

Figure 5-9
Resizing
images

*Resize warning icon
appears in image...*

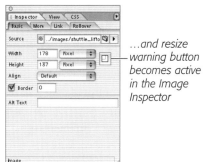

*...and resize
warning button
becomes active
in the Image
Inspector*

Figure 5-10
Choosing
percent
for width

*Percentage resize in relation
to size of the browser window*

Resizing using object handles. Dragging an image's object handles also re-sizes the image, allowing you to change the size manually without using the Image Inspector's numeric values. To resize the image proportionally, press the Shift key while dragging the corner handle (see Figure 5-11).

If you've opted to resize the image using percentage values, you can't use object handles to manipulate the graphic.

Figure 5-11
Dynamically
resizing
images

*Shift-drag to maintain original
image proportions*

Aligning Images

As with text, you can specify how an image is aligned on the page. However, image alignment offers more than just the ability to push a picture to one side of the screen or the other; text can wrap around aligned images.

Unlike placing images in a page-layout program, images on the Web are treated as if they were just another character or element. (They were original-ly called "inline images," which fell out of fashion some time ago.) So when you're specifying an image's alignment, you're telling a Web browser how the image should display in relation to the line of text in which it's contained.

Tip: Place Images at the Front of the Line

You can put an image anywhere you like, but we prefer to position them at the beginning of a line or paragraph of text. If you're using left or right alignment, text wrapping is much more consistent than if the image appears at the end of a paragraph. Keep in mind that a Web browser reads the page the same as you read text—left to right, top to bottom—and formats it accordingly.

With an image selected, choose one of the following options from the Basic tab's Align menu.

Left, Right. These are the most commonly used alignment settings, and it's plain to see why: text and other elements wrap around an image, making the best use of space and generally presenting a more professional look to the page (see Figure 5-12). Unlike the rest of the alignment options, left and right alignment can change the location of the image itself. Depending on the size of your image, the wrapping can be unflattering, so watch out for odd results. If several pictures are left-aligned without much text between them, an awkward stairstepping effect happens (see Figure 5-13, next page).

Figure 5-12
Aligning
images

Top, Middle, Bottom. Not surprisingly, these settings place text at the top, in the middle, or at the bottom of the image. That's fine for single lines of text, but if your graphic appears at the beginning of a paragraph, only the first line is affected; the rest of the paragraph in that case falls below the image (see Figure 5-14, next page).

Figure 5-13
Stairstepping
effect

Depending on the height of the line, however, these settings can position an image above or below the text surrounding it. For example, if the line of text includes a large image that increases the line height, placing a smaller image on the same line and setting its alignment to Top would align the tops of both images, lifting the second image high above the text (see Figure 5-14).

Tip: Easy Margin Control

If you don't like the various ways HTML indents text (such as block indent or unnumbered lists as described in Chapter 4, *Text and Fonts*), you can control the size of a text margin by placing an aligned image to the left of it. Insert a transparent GIF at the beginning of the text section, and specify its height to be large enough to span the depth of the text; make its width the distance you want from the edge of the page's true margin. (You can use the Shimmer Action, noted in an earlier tip.)

Figure 5-14
Top, Middle,
and Bottom
alignment

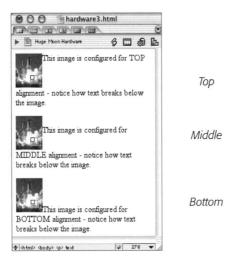

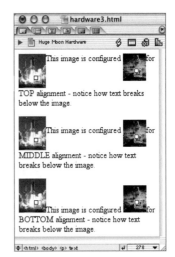

Then, set the image's alignment to Left or Right and watch the text snap into place. This won't work in all circumstances, since text sizes can vary widely among browsers and platforms, but it's often a simpler method than building tables or using other means.

Text Top, Baseline. Images aligned to Text Top or Baseline stick to the height of the text, regardless of the text's line height (see Figure 5-15).

Abs Middle, Abs Bottom. This pair of alignment settings positions text and other elements at the absolute middle or bottom in relation to the aligned image, which may not necessarily be based on the midpoint of the text's height. This is often useful when centering images used as bullets to text lines (see Figure 5-15).

Figure 5-15
Text Top,
Abs Middle,
Baseline,
and Abs
Bottom
alignment

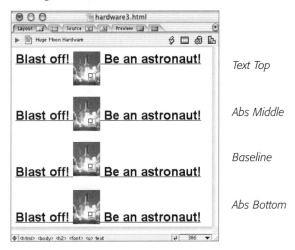

Low-source Images

Speed is everything when it comes to Web graphics. You want your viewer to see the page as fast as possible, but not everyone has a fast connection to the Internet (yet). And although you can optimize most graphics down to a small number of bytes, some images end up large enough that it's going to take time for most users to download and display them.

One perceptual trick to get around this dilemma is to offer sneak-peek versions of your graphics that are small enough to download quickly, but take up the same space and contain the same image as the higher resolution graphic. Typically, these low-source images (defined in HTML as "lowsrc") are black and white to keep the file size smaller; sometimes the low source is a 1-bit GIF, while the full-resolution image is a 24-bit color JPG. The browser shows the smaller image first, and then displays the higher-resolution image on top of it when the low-source image has finished loading (or, if it's a progressively saved image, as it starts to load).

If you've created your own low-source image, click the Low box in the Image Inspector's More tab to specify the file (see Figure 5-16).

Tip: Use Any Image as Low Source

Although the purpose of using low-source images is to load a preview version of a graphic quickly, you can actually specify any graphic as a low-source image. Some designers have used this to create some surprising effects.

Generating low-source images. GoLive can generate a low-source image for you when you click the Generate button.

By default, the low-source image GoLive creates is a color GIF that exists in the same directory as the original image. Check the Auto Update box to make GoLive update the low-source version whenever the referenced image changes.

In GoLive's preferences, you can choose to save low-source files in the Import Images folder. You can also set whether the preview image is rendered in black and white or color. If you check the Auto-Generate by Default box, GoLive creates low-source images for every graphic you place on your pages.

Tip: Clever Color Previews

GoLive features a clever way to create its color low-source images. GoLive reduces the color palette and also shrinks the image down to half the size of the original, thereby reducing the number of pixels in the file. When displayed at the same size as the original, you get a rough preview that's still in color, but also loads quickly.

Figure 5-16
Low-source
image

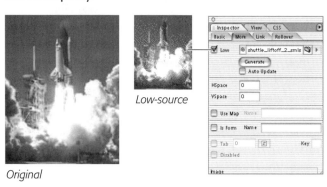

Low-source

Original

Tip: Animated GIFs

GoLive can generate a low-source GIF of any image you throw at it, even ani-mated GIFs. However, only the first frame of the animation is rendered as the low source, not the full series of frames.

Linking Images

Images can stand out from their surroundings in more effective ways than text. Also, most navigation systems tend to use images as buttons or other ele-ments. So you frequently find yourself turning an image into a hypertext but-ton, which, when clicked, works just like a text link. Any image can be turned into a link with a minimum of fuss.

With an image selected, choose one of the following: select New Link from the Special menu; click the New Link button on the Toolbar; click the New Link button in the Link tab of the Image Inspector; or select New Link from the contextual menu. Then specify the link's destination using Point & Shoot navigation, clicking Browse and locating the file, or by entering the path to the file in the URL field. If you want, enter the link's title text and a target for the link. You can also use the contextual menu's Apply Link option to select a link you've used before, or select a destination from the Image Inspector's Link popout menu in the Link tab.

Rollovers

Taking linked images one step further, rollovers allow you to automatically change an image's appearance based on whether your mouse pointer is above it ("rolling" over it, hence the name) or if it's being clicked, such as a button. Previously, rollovers were a luxury afforded to designers who dared to delve into JavaScript, which is what makes the effect work.

GoLive can create two types of rollovers, *smart* and *lean*, which both achieve the same effect. The difference is in how their code is written.

Smart rollovers are object-oriented, and rely on JavaScript code that's stored in a page's Head section, or in an external file that GoLive writes auto-matically (CSScriptLib.js, in your site's GeneratedItems folder). The benefits to this approach are that several rollovers can use the same JavaScript source, but more importantly, that you can apply Actions to rollovers (see Chapters 24, *Authoring JavaScript*, and 26, *Applying Actions*, for more information).

Lean rollovers, on the other hand, use less code and are easier to hand off to someone else on your team who needs to hand-code extra functionality. By default, the JavaScript code is still written to the external CSScriptLib.js file, though; if you're going to pass along your page, go to the HTML tab of the Page Inspector (in the Layout Editor, click the page icon to bring up this Inspector), and select the Write Code Into Page radio button. (You can set this as the default behavior for new pages in the Script Library portion of GoLive's preferences.)

Tip: Lean *and* smart?

If your page contains more than about 10 rollovers, using smart rollovers ends up writing less code in the long run.

Tip: Rollovers and Site Window

If you're building rollovers that use the external CSScriptLib.js file, make sure your site window is open. Otherwise, GoLive references its master copy of that file, which exists in GoLive's application folder and isn't available to anyone but you. With a site file open, the rollover correctly points to the CSScriptLib.js file in the GeneratedItems folder.

Creating Lean Rollovers

Lean rollovers can be created from any image on your page. Select an image and switch to the Image Inspector's Rollover tab. In addition to a Name field that lets you title the rollover (highly recommended), and the Normal field that represents the original image, there are two fields for the rollover states.

Over. Specify a separate image that displays when the mouse pointer passes above the original image. Filling in the field automatically selects the Preload checkbox—when the page is loaded, the image is stored in the browser's memory, even if it doesn't initially appear on the page. If you want, enter some descriptive text in the Message field that gets displayed at the bottom of the browser window (see Figure 5-17).

Down. The Down option displays a different image when you click your mouse button on the original or Over image. The options here are the same as the Over option.

Tip: Rollover Image Sizes

The main restriction when using rollovers is that each image must share the same dimensions as the original; if not, the Over and Down images appear stretched or compressed. To get around this, format your off-size image in a space that's the same size as the original image, but with a transparent background (see Figure 5-18).

Tip: Automatic Linking

Rollovers don't work unless the original image is linked, even if the link doesn't go anywhere. If you don't specify one in the Link tab, GoLive creates a blank link for you and sets it to "#" when you use the Rollover tab's options.

Tip: More Ways to Roll a Cat

Because rollovers have become so popular on the Web, there are numerous methods of implementing them in HTML. See Chapter 24, *Authoring JavaScript* for information on creating more compact rollover code.

Detect Rollover Images

You can build images with multiple rollover states individually if you want, but designers are increasingly using products like ImageReady to automatically generate the pieces required to put together a rollover. Fortunately, you often end up with a set of files with names like "aboutbox_over" and "about-

Figure 5-17
Lean rollover

Normal

Over

Figure 5-18
Off-size
image used
for rollover

Normal

Over (off-size photo)

— *Transparent area makes up for odd size of image.*

box_down". To save you some time, GoLive can search for these file name variations and build rollovers from them. From the Image Inspector's popout menu, choose Detect Rollover Images. GoLive looks through the directory where the original image is located, and fills in the other rollover fields if matches are found.

If your image-editing program uses different file name modifiers, choose Rollover Settings from the popout menu, where you can define up to three sets of name variations (see Figure 5-19).

Figure 5-19
Rollover
Settings

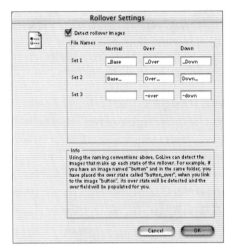

Clear Rollover

If you want to get rid of the rollover and start fresh, you can uncheck the various boxes to remove the code from your page. Or, since you're clearly a more sensible type of person, choose Clear Rollover from the popout menu.

Creating Smart Rollovers

From the Smart tab of the Objects palette, drag the Rollover icon to your page; the placeholder includes a small green triangle in the upper-left corner to indicate it's a smart rollover.

In the Rollover Inspector, identify the rollover in the Name field, then specify the Normal image using the URL getter in the Image section. The other fields in the Inspector correspond to standard image attributes.

Next, click the Over icon and specify which image appears when a person's mouse pointer is rolled over the image (see Figure 5-20). If you want a third image to appear when the user clicks on the rollover, specify it using the Down icon.

Figure 5-20
Creating a
Smart Rollover

Tip: Take the Fat Out

You can easily convert a smart rollover to a lean rollover: select the smart rollover and choose Convert to Lean Rollover from the contextual menu or the Rollover Inspector's popout menu, which gives you the option to apply to the selected image or all rollovers on the page. This option is also available from the Rollover Inspector's popout menu.

Tip: Smart Rollovers

You can't directly create a lean rollover from a smart object such as a Smart Photoshop image (see "Smart Objects" for more on these). But that doesn't mean you can't get smart rollovers. Instead, create the rollover in Adobe ImageReady. When you add the file as a Smart Photoshop object, GoLive senses that it's a rollover and configures the settings in the Rollover tab appropriately.

Tip: Not Just for Buttons

Rollovers are most commonly used to create buttons, which can appear pressed when clicked, or highlight when they're rolled over. However, don't let convention restrict your imagination: a rollover can replace any image, making it easy to swap loosely-related things (such as a portrait that's replaced by a person's baby picture when rolled over, for example).

Smart Objects

It's a rare day when GoLive is the only application running on our computers. Typically, we switch between GoLive and a host of graphics programs in order to create the hundreds of prototype pages and images required to test our ideas and their iterations. This used to mean spending lots of time in Photoshop converting all our graphics—even the scrap ones we knew weren't going to be to final production images—to GIF or JPEG format just to view them in a Web browser.

GoLive's smart objects have significantly changed our Web workflow. Using what Adobe calls Smart Links technology, we can drag and drop native Photoshop, Illustrator, and LiveMotion files onto your Web pages. Adding Photoshop or Illustrator files activates the Save for Web feature, which creates an optimized GIF, JPEG, or PNG version of the original; LiveMotion files are simply added to the page, and don't use Save for Web; rather, GoLive launches LiveMotion and instructs it to update files as needed. Editing the original file automatically updates the Web version, and making changes to the Web version (such as resizing the image) prompts GoLive to re-render it using data from the original.

In short, you can add an image to your page once, then edit it innumerable times without pointing to new versions of the file. Even better, the source application can remain closed.

To add a smart object, select the Smart tab of the Objects palette and drag a Smart Photoshop, Smart Illustrator, Smart LiveMotion, or Smart Generic icon to your page. You can also drag and drop a native file from the Site window or the Desktop (see Figure 5-21).

Figure 5-21
Smart objects
icons and
placeholders

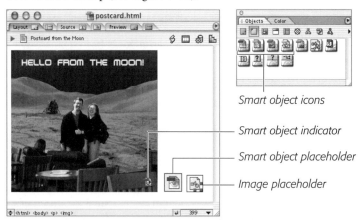

Smart object icons

Smart object indicator

Smart object placeholder

Image placeholder

Tip: Smart Illustrator Options

In addition to the standard Web formats, Smart Illustrator objects also give you the opportunity to convert Illustrator files into SVG (Scalable Vector Graphics), SVG Compressed, and SWF (Shockwave Flash) formats. In each case, the appropriate plug-in is used to display and handle the file.

Tip: Smart Sign

Smart objects include an icon in the lower-right corner of the image to indicate they're not regular images.

Tip: Missing a Smart Object Icon?

If you don't see an icon for the smart module you want, be sure you have the appropriate application installed. If you own Photoshop and Illustrator, but still don't see the icons, you may have to upgrade to a more recent version of those applications. Photoshop 5.5, Illustrator 9, and LiveMotion 1.0 are the minimum requirements to use smart objects.

Save for Web

Adding a Smart Photoshop or Smart Illustrator object to your page activates the Save for Web feature, a surprisingly sophisticated dialog box that optimizes your images for the Web. LiveMotion files contain vector-based data, and are converted directly to the Shockwave Flash (SWF) format; therefore, the Save for Web dialog doesn't appear (see "Smart LiveMotion Objects" later in this chapter).

Tip: Drag and Drop from Photoshop

You can also drag and drop a Photoshop layer to your GoLive page to add an image. Save for Web intercepts the drop and handles the optimization duties from there.

Save for Web offers four views of your source image, accessible by clicking the tabs at the top of the dialog box:

- **Original** displays the unchanged image.

- **Optimized** previews the image based on the values in the Settings area.

- **2-Up** shows the original image and its optimized preview. You can view any preview in the panes by clicking one and selecting new settings values.

- **4-Up** shows the original, its optimized preview, and two alternate optimizations. Like the 2-Up view, you can use the four panes to preview any settings, not just the ones displayed by default.

Suppose you've come up with a good combination of settings, but want to compare your configuration with others. In the 4-Up view, select Repopulate Views from the Optimize popout menu to use the selected pane as the baseline for the other panes.

Additionally, you can zoom in on any of the versions using the Zoom tool or by changing the Zoom Level popup menu (see Figure 5-22, next page).

As you're working, if you don't like what you've done to the poor image, holding down Option (Mac) or Alt (Windows) changes the Cancel button

Figure 5-22
Save for Web
view controls

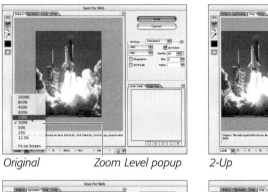

Original   Zoom Level popup   2-Up

Optimized

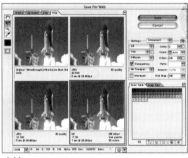

4-Up

into a Reset button, which reverts to the initial Save for Web settings. Conversely, if you do like what you've done and want to save the same settings for later, choose Save Settings from the Optimize popout menu.

After you've added the smart object to your page, you can return to the Save for Web dialog by clicking the Settings button in the Inspector's Basic tab.

Image Settings

With Save for Web, you almost don't need Photoshop or other image editors. Use the controls in the Settings area of the dialog box to compress and optimize images for the Web (see Figure 5-23). The Settings popup menu provides a number of saved sets that load the most common settings, but you can also save your own custom settings by selecting Save Settings from the Optimize popout menu.

Tip: Wireless Imaging

The Settings popup menu now includes two options geared for generating images to be used on wireless devices: GIF i-mode 1-bit and GIF i-mode 256. These prefabricated settings help to reduce the image's file size, but remember that these devices tend to have tiny screens: you need to reduce the image's dimensions using the Image Size tab, too (more on that later).

Figure 5-23
Settings
overview

Optimized File Format ————

Color Reduction Algorithm ———

Diffusion Algorithm —————

Transparency Dither —————

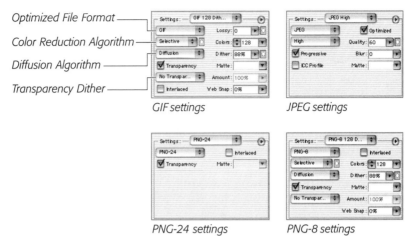

GIF settings   *JPEG settings*

PNG-24 settings   *PNG-8 settings*

Optimized File Format. Choose which type of file you're creating: GIF, JPEG, PNG-8 (8-bit), PNG-24 (24-bit), or WBMP, a format used on PDAs and some cellular phones.

Color Reduction Algorithm (GIF and PNG-8). Save for Web can compress the image data using a handful of different methods of determining the image's color table.

- **Perceptual** uses an algorithm based on colors that are commonly perceived by the human eye.

- **Selective** is similar to perceptual, but with an eye (ahem) toward favoring Web-safe colors.

- **Adaptive** builds a color table based on the colors most frequently appearing in the image.

- **Web** uses the strict Web-safe color table, which comprises 216 colors shared by the Mac OS and Windows color palettes.

- **Custom** effectively freezes the current color table, so that any further changes to the image retain the same set of colors.

- **Black and White** uses only those two colors of pixels. This creates very small files, but at an obvious loss of quality.

- **Grayscale** converts the image's colors into their gray counterparts.

- **Mac OS** and **Windows** use the 8-bit color palette used by the two operating systems. It can be helpful to target an OS palette if you know your audience will be using just one or the other; otherwise, the differences between the two mean the image quality will suffer when viewed under the system not chosen.

- Other color tables are listed if you load them into the Color Table panel (see "Color Table," later in this chapter).

Compression Quality (JPEG). The default compression qualities—Low, Medium, High, and Maximum—are general shortcuts for assigning Quality values (see next).

Quality (JPEG). The Quality value determines how much JPEG compression is applied to the image. Since JPEG is a lossy algorithm, a lower Quality setting means more image data is being thrown away. Type a new number or use the slider activated by the popup menu button to change the value.

Blur (JPEG). One strength of JPEG compression is that it can remove redundant image data based on how the eye perceives color. When an image is more blurry, more data can be extracted, diminishing the file size. The Blur setting applies a Photoshop-style Gaussian Blur effect on the image, smoothing compression artifacts. Of course, unless you're trying to convince users that they need to buy a new computer display, a lower Blur setting is recommended.

Optimized (JPEG). Checking the Optimized checkbox can produce smaller JPEG files, but some older Web browsers can't display optimized JPEGs. However, in this day and age when more people are using modern browsers, we recommend checking this option to squeeze every last pixel out of your files.

Dithering Algorithm (GIF, PNG-8, and WBMP). Dithering is a method of simulating colors by positioning similar colors near one another. For example, you could create a green image without using any green pixels by making a pattern of alternating blue and yellow pixels. Fortunately, you don't have to go to that much trouble to employ dithering in your Web images. From the Dithering popup menu, select No Dither, Diffusion, Pattern, or Noise. Each one combines pixels in its own way (except for No Dither, of course), so try each one to arrive at the best result. In the case of WBMP images, dithering has less to do with colors (since there are only two, black and white), and everything to do with the pattern of using black pixels to approximate the image's tones.

Dither (GIF, PNG-8, and WBMP). Choosing the Diffusion dithering algorithm gives you an additional control: the amount of dithering applied. Higher percentages produce images that are more grainy, while low percentages create larger areas of flat color.

Transparency (GIF, PNG-8, and PNG-24). If image formats didn't have a method for specifying transparent colors, the Web would be an ugly stack of rectangular image blocks. Fortunately, each format except for JPEG allows you to set one color (or more, in the case of PNG) as transparent. Save for Web gets its cue from the source application to designate a transparent color. Empty pixels in Photoshop (indicated by the presence of the workspace's white and gray grid pattern) become transparent when you click the Transparent box (see Figure 5-24).

Transparency Dither (GIF and PNG-8) Transparency doesn't always work well for objects that need to blend into their environments, such as drop shadows. One workaround is to use a Transparency Dither option, which applies transparency to selected pixels around an object. Choose from Diffusion, Pattern, or Noise dithering options from the Transparency Dither popup menu; if you choose Diffusion, the Amount field gives you control over how much of the effect to apply.

Figure 5-24
Transparency

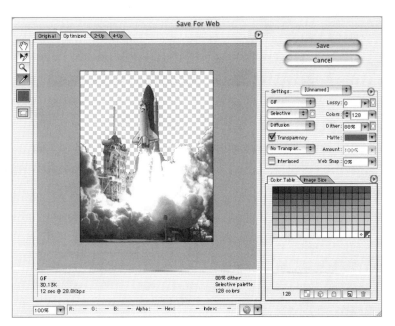

Matte. Instead of transparency, you can choose to matte unused portions of an image, filling them with a solid color. In most cases, the matte color is the same as the page's background color, but you have some control over this setting. The Matte popup menu lets you select None, the Eyedropper Color, White, or Black. Choosing Other opens the operating system's color picker in order to select any color; you can also just click the Matte color field.

Interlaced (GIF, PNG-8, and PNG-24). Check the Interlaced box if you want your images to incrementally display as they load, creating a perceptual decrease in the time it takes to draw the page in a browser.

Progressive (JPEG). Like the Interlaced option, checking the Progressive box causes JPEG files to be partially viewed as they load.

ICC Profile (JPEG). Check this box if you want to use Photoshop images that contain embedded ICC Profiles, which some browsers can use to color-correct images.

Lossy (GIF). Save for Web attempts to create an optimized image that's as true to the original as possible. However, this can result in larger-than-ideal file sizes (and, therefore, longer download times). The Lossy field gives you a scale of 1 to 100 that determines how much information can be thrown out of the image ("lost") in order to achieve better compression (see Figure 5-25). The lossier an image is, the better it compresses, but the lower its quality.

Tip: Lost Lace

Checking the Interlaced option disables the Lossy setting for GIF images. Depending on how high the Lossy setting, this can significantly increase the size of your file.

Colors (GIF and PNG-8). Another way of controlling image compression is to limit the maximum number of colors used by the image. To change that number, click the up or down arrow buttons in the Colors field, type a new value into the field directly, or select a number from the popup menu to the right of the field. Save for Web calculates which colors to use by analyzing the ones used most in the image. The file size is smaller with less colors, but also of lower quality.

Web Snap (GIF and PNG-8). Unless you've set the Color Reduction algorithm to Web, the colors in your image aren't likely to be Web safe. (See

Figure 5-25
Lossy setting

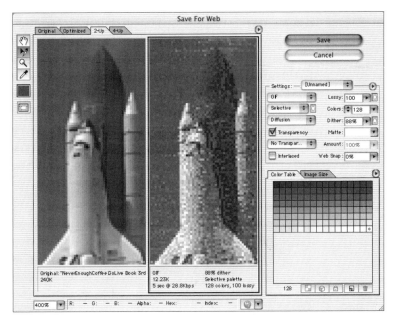

Chapter 6, *Color*, for more on Web-safe colors.) The Web Snap setting determines a percentage of tolerance for automatically switching colors to the Web-safe palette. A higher Web Snap setting means more colors are Web-safe, which improves compatibility but can often degrade quality.

Optimize to File Size. Kilobytes are the reigning currencies in some production environments, where strict quotas are established to ensure that Web page sizes don't expand to infinity (and beyond!). If you know that an image needs to be a certain size, Save for Web can apply the settings required to hit that goal.

From the Optimize popout menu, select Optimize to File Size and enter a number in the KB field (see Figure 5-26). The Start With option can build on settings you've already applied, or use its built-in guesses for GIF and JPEG settings. If slices have been defined in the original image, you can apply the

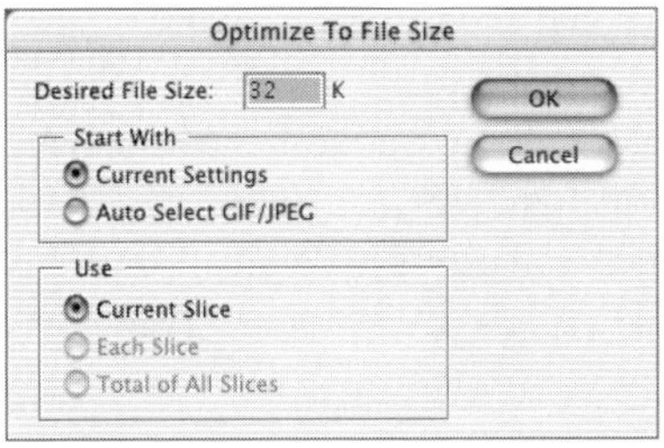

Figure 5-26
Optimimize
to File Size

optimization to each one separately, all of them together, or just the current slice (see "Working with Sliced Images," later in this chapter).

Color Table (GIF and PNG-8 Only)

The Color Table tab is a handy guide to which colors appear in your image, but it's not just there for show. You can edit your colors as well as see which ones are being used (see Figure 5-27).

Color values corresponding to the cursor's position are also displayed numerically along the bottom of the Save for Web dialog; you don't have to click a color to see its numbers.

Figure 5-27
Save for Web
Color Table

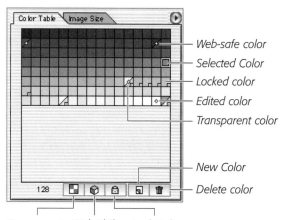

Selecting colors. Click a color square to select it, represented by a white outline. To select multiple squares, hold down Shift for a contiguous selection or Control to grab non-contiguous colors.

The Color Palette popout menu (not to be confused with the Color palette) to the right of the table lets you select all colors, all Web-safe colors, and all non-Web-safe colors; you can also deselect all colors.

Changing colors. Double-click a color square to bring up your operating system's default color dialog and choose a new color.

Sorting colors. The Color Palette popout menu also includes commands for sorting the table's colors. Choose from Unsorted, Sort by Hue, Sort by Luminance, and Sort by Popularity. This type of control is helpful when you want to isolate or change a single color or a small range of colors.

For example, to easily change the background color of an image (without using the Matte feature), select Sort by Popularity from the popout menu, then click the first image square. In many cases, the background color appears the most, so it becomes the first square. You can then change the color value by double-clicking the square and choosing a replacement color.

Locking colors. Select a color square, or a range of squares, and click the Lock Color button, or choose Lock/Unlock Selected Colors from the Color Palette popout menu. Locking a color ensures the color doesn't change as you apply more settings to the image.

Snapping to Web colors. Although you could easily set the Color Algorithm popup menu to Web in order to work with just Web colors, the colors chosen by Save for Web occasionally aren't the ones you want to use. An orange might get switched to a Web color that's more yellow than red, for example.

To gain some control over the decision, select a color square and then click the Web Shift button, or choose Web Shift/Unshift Selected Colors from the Color Palette popout menu. If the Web-safe color chosen by Save for Web isn't what you had in mind, click the button or choose the popout menu item again to unshift the color, then choose a different color closer to what you expect and try again.

Mapping transparent colors. For color-by-color control over transparency, select one or more color squares and click the Transparent button, or choose Map/Unmap Selected Colors to/from Transparent option from the popout menu. To undo your transparent selections, choose Unmap All Transparent Colors from the popout menu.

Deleting colors. To selectively remove colors from the image, highlight them and click the Delete Color button or choose Delete Color from the Color Palette popout menu.

Saving and loading color palettes. Of course, you don't have to rely on what Save for Web throws at you. Some Web sites use a strict color palette to maintain consistency throughout all pages. To bring in an outside color palette, choose Load Color Table from the popout menu. Similarly, you can save a color palette by selecting Save Color Table.

Image Size Tab

Even if your image is an actual-size photo of a Cray supercomputer, you can add it to your Web page at any size you like. The Image Size tab allows you to numerically change the dimensions of your image and control the way Save for Web recalculates how the image is resized.

In the New Size area, enter new measurements in the Width and Height fields. If the Constrain Proportions box is checked, you only need to change one of the fields. Alternately, specify a percentage of change in the Percent field.

The Quality popup menu determines the type of calculation that's performed: Smooth (Bicubic) results in better, but sometimes blurry, images; Jagged (Nearest Neighbor) doesn't try to compensate for quality and stays closer to the image's pattern of pixels (see Figure 5-28).

Figure 5-28
Quality settings for resized images

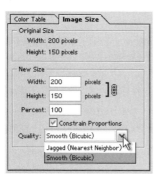

Original

Smooth (Bicubic)

Jagged (Nearest Neighbor)

Browser Preview

Lest you think that Save for Web doesn't offer enough options for previewing your final image, you can click the Browser button at the bottom of the dialog box. Not only will you see the optimized version of the image, but Save for Web also writes a summary box containing the image's optimization settings and HTML required to view the image.

The Browser button works the same as the Show in Browser button located on the Toolbar, and is based on the browser settings in GoLive's Preferences. Use the popup menu to choose among multiple installed browsers, or select Other to locate a browser not listed.

Smart LiveMotion Objects

In our discussion of smart objects so far we've largely avoided talking about files created in LiveMotion. While Photoshop and Illustrator images are processed through the Save for Web feature, LiveMotion files are simply added to the page. Their data is vector-based, which means that the browser draws (and animates) images based on mathematical commands instead of noting colors for each individual pixel. The advantage of this approach is that LiveMotion files tend to be smaller in size, and therefore load faster. They can also be scaled to any size without a loss of resolution; smooth curves stay smooth and type stays crisp.

As with other smart objects, add LiveMotion files to your page by dragging them from the Desktop or Site window; or, drag the Smart LiveMotion icon from the Smart tab of the Objects palette and specify a file in the Source field of the Live Plugin Inspector (see Figure 5-29). GoLive converts the file into a Flash movie and prompts you to name and save the SWF file.

With the exception of providing a Smart Link to the original LiveMotion file, GoLive treats Smart LiveMotion objects no differently than SWF (Flash) plug-in objects. (See Chapter 12, *Rich Media*, for more on working with plug-ins and their Inspector settings).

Figure 5-29
Smart
LiveMotion
object

Smart Generic Objects

Naturally, the folks at Adobe want to showcase how Photoshop, Illustrator, and LiveMotion work together with GoLive. But they're not bullies about it: the Save for Web features can be applied to nearly any image, removing the need to do basic Web optimization in an outside program.

Drag the Smart Generic icon from the Smart tab of the Objects palette, then point it at an image file. The feature supports BMP, PCX, Pixar, Amiga IFF, TIFF, TARGA, PDF, EPS, JPEG, PNG, and PICT (Mac OS only) formats. With the exception of JPEG and PNG files (which GoLive understands as normal images), dragging any of the other types of files onto your page from the Desktop automatically assigns them as Smart Generic objects. Using Smart Generic objects gives you the same advantages as the other smart tools, such as having the image re-optimized if you resize it on the page.

Tip: Quick Rasterize

Need to rasterize a PDF or EPS file, and already have GoLive open? Drag the file onto a GoLive page, which creates a Smart Generic object and processes it using Save for Web. With multi-page PDF files, choose which page to convert.

Working with Smart Objects

Using the Save for Web feature to process your images on their way into GoLive is powerful stuff, but the real utility of smart objects happens within the Layout Editor.

Re-Optimizing Smart Objects. Once you've run Save for Web, you're not stuck with the optimization settings you chose. Simply select the smart object and click the Settings button in the Inspector to jump back into Save for Web.

Scale. The Scale menu in the Inspector controls how a smart object is resized on a template page. See Chapter 11, *Templates*, for more information.

Resizing Smart Objects. So you've optimized your image and placed it on a page, only to realize that its width should be 275 pixels instead of 300. Previously, you'd have to go back into Photoshop or Illustrator, resize the image, then resave it in its optimized form.

Now, simply resize the image on your page by either dragging the image's control handles or entering new values in the Width and Height fields of the Inspector. GoLive temporarily displays a resize warning icon, then recreates the optimized image using data from the source application (see Figure 5-30).

Tip: Resizing Multiple Copies of the Same Image

If you have two or more instances of the same smart object on your page, re-sizing one doesn't resize them all. Although the Web image file gets optimized for the new dimensions, only the active object has its Width and Height values changed; the others display the resize warning icon. You can manually select each one and click the Resize button on the Inspector, or better yet, use the Find feature's Element tab to quickly update the dimensions in one pass (see Chapter 14, *Source Editing*, for more on GoLive's search-and-replace features).

Tip: Resize Button Shifts to Original

Clicking the Resize button on a smart object Inspector resets the dimensions of the image to those of the original source file, not the size of the first generated Web version.

Figure 5-30
Resizing
smart object

Original smart object

For a normal image, this would be the end result after resizing. Note the chunky edges.

Image is smoother after being automatically processed in Photoshop

In the case of Smart LiveMotion objects, changing their dimensions in the Layout Editor doesn't prompt GoLive to get new data from LiveMotion. There is no resizing calculation because vector art has to be rendered from scratch to display on screen. The Flash plug-in installed in a user's browser renders the LiveMotion content.

Tip: LiveMotion Resizing

When you resize a Smart LiveMotion object proportionally (hold down Shift when dragging the lower-right corner's handle), the image is similarly resized in a browser. However, if you resize in one direction, or disproportionally, the image doesn't appear stretched as you would expect (despite the fact that GoLive shows a stretched preview in the Layout Editor). Instead, the image resizes proportionally, but based on the narrowest dimension, height or width. Any extra defined area just fills with blank space (see Figure 5-31).

Figure 5-31
Resizing Smart
LiveMotion
object

Resized in GoLive

Appearance in Web browser

Tip: Dumbing Down Smart Objects

From an HTML point of view, the only thing that distinguishes a smart object from a regular image is the Smart Link that points to the original source file, implemented using the Livesrc attribute.

```
<img src="images/coffeegood.gif" livesrc="graphics/
coffeegood.psd" width="201" height="70">
```

To strip out the Livesrc attribute in your page or site, use GoLive's Find by Element feature. Select Find from the Edit menu and click the Element tab. Enter "img" in the Name Is field, and choose Keep Element from the first popup menu in the Action area. Click the New Action button, select Delete from the Action popup menu, and type "livesrc" into the Attribute field. Finally, specify the files you wish to process, and hit the Start button. This operation can't be undone; make sure you have backups handy.

Tip: Adding Smarts to Dumb Images

Did you place your images already, but now want to link them to their Photoshop or Illustrator originals? Simply go into the Source Code Editor, locate the Img tag, and add the following to the tag's attributes.

```
livesrc="fluctuating/self/images/weird.liv"
```

When you switch back to the Layout Editor, your formerly dumb image has become a smart object.

Smart Object Variables

If intelligently resizing images was the only feature of smart objects, we'd be tempted to just call them "bright," or maybe even "precocious for their age." But to be viewed as truly smart, we expect more, and GoLive delivers. Using Variables, you can specify custom text to appear styled within an image, make objects visible or invisible, and more without changing the original file.

Smart Photoshop Variables

Of the three Adobe programs that use Variables, Photoshop is the most limited. Still, you can still save hours that would otherwise be spent fiddling with numerous Photoshop files. Essentially, you can take a text layer in Photoshop and assign custom text for it in GoLive. GoLive retains any styling (such as colors, drop shadows, etc.), since the text ends up as an image, but you specify the actual text in GoLive. Follow the following steps to use Photoshop Variables.

1. In Photoshop, create a file that contains a text field, and style the text (see Figure 5-32). GoLive uses the topmost text layer of a Photoshop file as its variable.

Figure 5-32
Styling text
in Photoshop

2. On your page, add the Photoshop file using the Smart Photoshop icon; you're greeted with the Variable Settings dialog box (see Figure 5-33).

3. Highlight Topmost Textlayer and click the Use box to activate it.

4. In the field below, type the text you want to in place of the text in the Photoshop file. Press OK.

5. GoLive takes you through the Save for Web dialog box. Configure your compression settings, click Save, and then, after a short bit of processing, the image with your custom text is displayed (see Figure 5-33).

If you want to change the variable text, click the Variables button in the Smart Photoshop Image Inspector, which takes you back to the Variable Settings dialog box.

Figure 5-33
Changing the
variable text

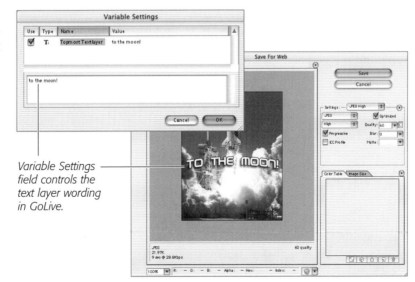

*Variable Settings
field controls the
text layer wording
in GoLive.*

Smart Illustrator Variables

Illustrator 10 provides more options when using Variables, which require a bit more preparation in Illustrator. In addition to customizing text, you can control the visibility of objects within the image. However, Variables only work with Illustrator files saved in SVG format.

Setting up the Illustrator file. In Illustrator, you need to define which objects are to be used as Variables, and specify what type of Variables they are. Illustrator offers four Variable types, but GoLive recognizes only two: text and visibility Variables.

1. Create a few objects and at least one block of text. Unlike Photoshop, you can use more than one text block as variables.

2. From the Window menu, choose Variables to display the Variables palette.

3. Click the New Variable button, then double-click the Variable that appears in the list.

4. In the Variable Options dialog box, name the Variable, and select Text String from the Type popup menu (see Figure 5-34). Click OK.

5. Select the text block in your document, and make sure your Variable is highlighted in the Variables palette.

6. Click the Make Text Dynamic button. The text's contents appear in the Objects column (see Figure 5-35).

Figure 5-34
Creating a text
Variable in
Illustrator

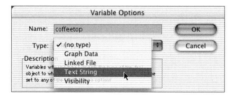

Figure 5-35
Making text
layer into a
dynamic
variable in
Illustrator

To specify an object whose visibility will be a variable, follow the same steps, but with the following changes: in the Variable Options dialog box, choose Visibility instead of Text String from the Type popup menu; and, after you've selected an object, click the Make Visibility Dynamic button instead of the Make Text Dynamic button.

When you're finished with the file, remember to save it in SVG format. In the SVG Options dialog box that appears, click the Advanced button and make sure that Include Extended Syntax for Variable Data is checked.

Tip: Text Visibility

You can choose to make a text block visible or invisible, in addition to having dynamic text. After selecting the block, click the Make Visibility Dynamic button. If it was previously set to Make Text Dynamic, a new variable is created so you can take advantage of both types of variables.

Controlling Illustrator variables in GoLive. With the prep work out of the way in Illustrator, taking advantage of the variables in GoLive is a snap.

1. Add the Smart Illustrator object to your page, either by dragging its icon from the Smart tab of the Objects palette and specifying the file, or just dragging the SVG file into the Layout Editor.

2. In the Variable Options dialog box, mark the Use boxes for the ones you want to use, and enter any text you want to appear in the Text String variables (see Figure 5-36). Click OK.

3. The Save for Web dialog box appears. Choose your optimization settings, and then click OK.

If you want to adjust the variables later, click the Variables button in the Smart Illustrator Image Inspector.

Figure 5-36
Setting text and visibility Variable options in GoLive

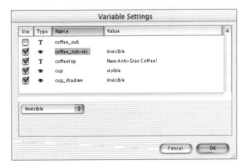

Smart LiveMotion Variables

As with Smart Illustrator objects, it takes a bit of preparation to activate Variables in a LiveMotion 2.0 file.

Setting up the LiveMotion file. Unfortunately, LiveMotion doesn't include a handy Variables palette, so defining objects as Variables isn't as obvious.

1. Create an object or text block in LiveMotion.

2. With the item selected, bring up the Web palette by choosing Web from the Window menu.

3. Name the item by typing in the Replace field (see Figure 5-37). This identifies the object or text box as a variable.

4. Save the file.

Figure 5-37
Setting up
Variables in
LiveMotion

Controlling LiveMotion Variables in GoLive. With your Variables defined in LiveMotion, you have several options for controlling them in GoLive.

1. Add your file using the Smart LiveMotion icon, or drag the file directly to your page from the Site window or the Desktop.

2. In the Variable Settings dialog box, click the name of a variable object to edit it (see Figure 5-38). If it's a text box, the text-related attributes such as Set Text, Set Font, and Set Font Size become editable. Click their boxes and apply a value in the associated fields or popup menus. If the Variable is an object, other options such as Set Link and Set Style are activated; the Set Style and Set Texture popup menus correspond to the style and texture options in LiveMotion.

3. When you're done with the Variable settings, click OK.

4. In the Matte Color dialog box, choose a color that fills the unused portions of your image. Click OK to add the smart object to your page.

Figure 5-38
Setting
LiveMotion
Variable
options in
GoLive

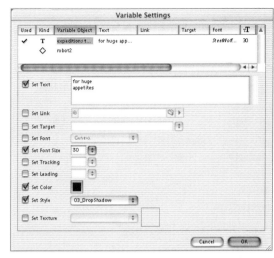

Convert Text to Banner

A somewhat faster method of specifying Variable text is the Convert Text to Banner feature. Highlight some text on your page, and then choose Convert Text to Banner from the Special menu or the contextual menu. GoLive prompts you to locate a smart objects file to use, then takes you through the Variable Settings and Save for Web dialog boxes as explained earlier. The result is a new smart image containing the text, which no longer appears as text on the page (see Figure 5-39).

Figure 5-39
Convert Text
to Banner

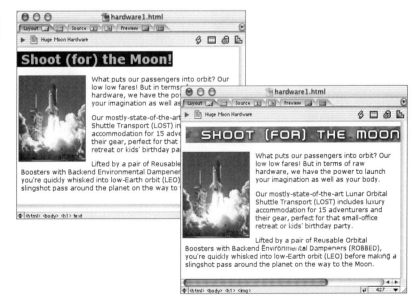

Variables in the Real World

We can see a lot of potential in using Variables, but it was a common Web element that made us initially excited about Variables: the humble navigation button. Using Variables to create a series of buttons immediately trimmed a lot of time spent adding different button titles in Photoshop or Illustrator. We're using the Smart Photoshop object in this example, but you can use Illustrator or LiveMotion files, as well (see Figure 5-40).

1. In Photoshop, create a single button image.

2. Add some text to the button—it doesn't matter what the text reads.

3. Save the file and switch to GoLive.

4. Add the file as a Smart Photoshop object to your page.

5. In the Variable Settings dialog box, click the Use checkbox for the text layer and type the name of your first button.

6. Click OK, and then apply your optimization settings in the Save for Web dialog box. When GoLive saves the Target file, the text you set is included in the file name (such as "button_About.gif"), minus any spaces. If you change the text at a later point in time, however, the file name remains the same as when it was first saved.

7. Repeat the same procedure for the next button, making sure to create a new Smart Photoshop object for it. If you duplicate one you created, it shares the same target file, which means that changing the variable updates both images.

If you need to change any aspect of the button, such as its font or background color, edit the master file in Photoshop. The changes apply to all instances on your page, while retaining the custom text for each button.

Figure 5-40
Creating buttons using Variables

Start with a single button image with a text layer created in Photoshop.

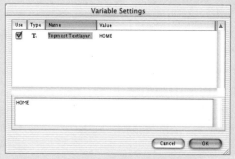

In GoLive, add the button as a Smart Photoshop image, and define Variable text for the button's label.

Repeat to add more buttons. Be sure to start with a new Smart Photoshop object each time.

Import Photoshop Layers to Floating Boxes

It's not uncommon to find designers who "think Photoshop." For them, illustrations aren't made up of different graphics; instead, they're different Photoshop layers, and anything can be fixed with a few Curves and Levels tweaks. Using GoLive's Import Photoshop Layers to Floating Boxes feature, you can bring in any Photoshop file containing multiple layers, each of which is converted to a floating box. This allows you to do much of the prep work for animations or other special effects in Photoshop, and then get right to work by moving items around in GoLive.

Select Photoshop Layers to Floating Boxes from the File menu's Import submenu and then choose the Photoshop file to add. After selecting the file, specify a folder as the root for the images that are created. GoLive uses Save for Web to process each layer, giving you the chance to save each image in its own format.

When Save for Web is finished, your page includes a series of floating boxes, each of which contains the image corresponding to one of the Photoshop layers. (See Chapter 10, *Floating Boxes*, for more information.) GoLive also assigns a depth setting to each box in order to replicate the layer order (see Figure 5-41).

Import Photoshop Layers to Floating Boxes doesn't function like a Smart Photoshop object. Changes made to the original file do not update the referenced file on the GoLive page. On the other hand, if changes are warranted, it's easy enough to re-import the changed file in place of the older version.

Figure 5-41
Import
Photoshop
Layers to
Floating Boxes

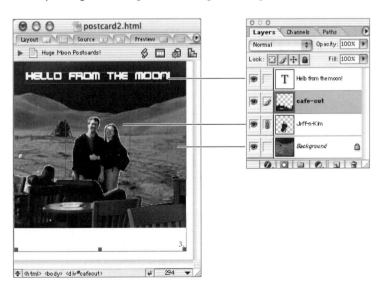

Tip: Bypass Save for Web

You can bypass the Save for Web dialog for each layer by Control-clicking the OK button. This takes the image settings of the first layer and applies them to the remaining ones.

Tip: Name Your Photoshop Layers

If you're not already in the habit of naming layers in Photoshop, we encourage you to do so. GoLive automatically uses the layer name as the name of its corresponding floating box. However, because of how some browsers interpret the code needed to work with floating box information, be sure that none of your layer names begins with a number.

Tip: Background Image Layer

If you hold down the Option (Mac) or Alt (Windows) key when selecting Photoshop Layers to Floating Boxes, the lowest layer of an imported Photoshop layer becomes the background layer for your Web page.

Imagemaps

One of the differences between the Web and full-screen multimedia development tools is that you can't define any area on the screen as a link with the Web, where most multimedia programs use the whole screen as an interface. However, the Web does let you turn images (which could take up an entire screen) into an analogue of multimedia by letting you define one, several, or dozens of areas on an image that each have separate links and other image properties.

These images with definable areas are called imagemaps; they've been around since near the dawn of the Web, and they're one of the most common tools to use with a site navigation strip or graphical interface on the Web.

You can define the regions in an imagemap using a variety of shapes, including rectangles, circles, and polygons. Each region's exact pixel coordinates at each point on the shape (or the oval's center point and width and height) are stored in the HTML file. When a Web browser is told that an image is acting as an imagemap, the browser examines the pixel location where a user clicks, and loads the corresponding URL for that region.

Tip: Client- and Server-Side

In the olden days, imagemaps required a server to process the user's clicks—the imagemap's region file resided on a server, and a special program there, often called htimage, handled the translation. These were called server-side imagemaps, as opposed to in-the-HTML client-side imagemaps. No page on the planet should be using server-side imagemaps, but some still are.

Before GoLive and other visual editors, building imagemaps required a third-party mapping program—or a great deal of patience and graph paper—to calculate each region's coordinates by hand. Now, creating an imagemap is a matter of switching tabs in the Image Inspector. With an image selected, click the More tab and check the Use Map box. GoLive creates a name for the map based on the filename, but you may want to change the name to something that doesn't look like the name of a future android's serial number.

To link a portion of an imagemap, use the region tools located in the Toolbar to highlight an area for the link, and enter the destination address using the URL Getter in the Map Area Inspector. The other fields for that region (Title, Target, Alt, etc.) act the same as if you were defining a single image link (see Figure 5-42).

Figure 5-42
Imagemap
controls

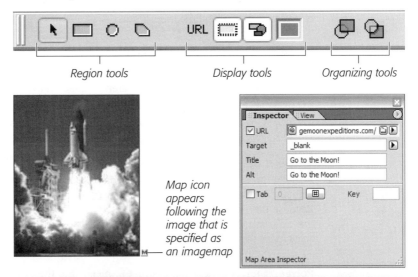

Region tools   Display tools   Organizing tools

Map icon
appears
following the
image that is
specified as
an imagemap

Inspector   View

☑ URL   gemoonexpeditions.com/
Target   _blank
Title   Go to the Moon!
Alt   Go to the Moon!

☐ Tab   0   ⊞   Key

Map Area Inspector

Tip: Map Icon

A small M icon, similar to the one used for floating boxes, represents the block of text used to define the map coordinates, and appears after the imagemap image. If you want, you can move it anywhere on your layout without adverse effects; some designers prefer to store all their imagemap code at the beginning or end of the page. The only problem you may run into with the M icon is when you disable an imagemap; unchecking the Use Map box on the Image Inspector turns the imagemap off, but leaves the icon, which you have to delete manually.

Tip: Grabbing Imagemaps

If the Use Map box is checked, GoLive won't let you grab or move the image as you normally would. The internal area is reserved for the imagemap tools, which take over when your cursor is in that region. So, to select the image, click on its edge (the cursor changes into an object-select cursor), then move or resize the image as usual.

Tip: Smart Imagemaps

You can build imagemaps out of Smart Photoshop and Smart Illustrator objects as well as normal images. If you resize the image, GoLive even adjusts the map sizes accordingly.

Region Tools

The region tools are used to define and select areas in your image that lead to other URLs.

Selection tool. An all-purpose pointer, the Selection tool is used to select, move, and resize imagemap regions.

Rectangle and circle tools. Use these tools to create simple rectangular or circular regions (see Figure 5-43). Don't worry if the shapes you create aren't pixel-perfect; since imagemap areas aren't visible on the Web, they only need to cover the approximate area where you want the viewer to click to follow a link. The Circle tool creates only proportional circles, not ovals.

Tip: Imagemap Browser Highlights

Actually, the only time you might see imagemaps appear on the Web is when you tab through a page using recent versions of Internet Explorer or Netscape. Because the browsers can use the Tab key to move from each link or field to the next, even the shapes on an imagemap can show up. We've seen some scary maps on occasion, but it's not quite like letting your slip show.

Polygon tool. For regions that don't fit nicely into the rectangular or circular molds, the polygon tool provides a highly flexible way to build custom-shaped link fields. With the Polygon tool selected, click to create a series of points connected by straight line segments around the area; GoLive automatically closes the selection, so you won't have any open-ended polygon fields (see Figure 5-43).

When you're finished defining the region, select one of the other region tools to deselect the polygon. If you then click the polygon with the Selection

Figure 5-43
Mapping tools

Rectangle   Polygon   Circle

tool, the object is selected as a grouped object, which you can resize. If you re-size the image, the regions scale in proportion.

If you want to edit the shape's individual points, double-click the region with the selection tool to activate the polygon's defining points. After modifying them, click outside the shape or select another region tool to deselect it again. Once you've created a polygon, you cannot add new points or remove existing points.

Tip: Adding Points in HTML

If you're really desperate not to start from scratch, you can insert extra point co-ordinates in the HTML. A point in a polygon requires two values: the x and y co-ordinates, which are listed in the code that defines the shape, as in this example:

```
<area href="poly_gone.html"
coords="102,189,64,160,115,103,150,179" shape="polygon">
```

Each pair of numbers represents one point, which means there are four points to this polygon. To add another point, get the location values of the new point (open the image in Photoshop and use the Info palette to indicate where your cursor is), then add them to the list, x before y.

Tip: Complex Polygons Increase File Size

If you're fanatical about keeping your HTML files as small as possible so they load quickly, try not to use too many complex polygons in an imagemap. Unlike rectangles and circles, which require only a few pixel coordinates, each point of a polygon must be defined in the HTML (see Figure 5-44, next page). Granted, we're talking about text, which loads much faster compared to almost every-thing else on the Web; but the less work the browser has to do, the faster the page loads and responds.

Figure 5-44
Polygon code

Polygon code

Region Display Tools

GoLive makes it easy to identify and control the appearance of imagemap regions while you're working in the Layout Editor (see Figure 5-45).

Display URLs. For a quick reference of where the region's link takes viewers, the Display URLs button writes the HTML link on top of the appropriate area of the mapped image.

Frame regions. Clicking this button displays a dotted line around region edges.

Color regions. With this button selected, regions are filled with a color to make them even easier to find. Colored regions are semi-transparent so you can still see the images beneath them.

Select color. Everyone has his or her own color favorites. If a hot pink region color clashes too much with your page's ochre-colored background, feel free

Figure 5-45
Region
display tools

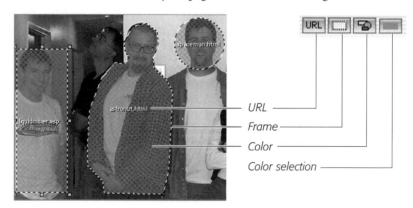

URL
Frame
Color
Color selection

to select a new color for the region highlight. The color you select applies to all regions; you can't color-code different regions with different colors (though that would be a neat feature in a future version of GoLive).

Organizing Regions

GoLive also includes two buttons for changing the layer order of imagemap regions. If you wind up with overlapping regions and you don't want to re-draw boundaries, you can use the Bring Region to Front or Send Region to Back buttons to bring the right one to the top.

Tip: Reordering Directives

Although layered regions aren't really a function of HTML imagemaps, Web browsers do read the imagemap directives (the lists of shapes and coordinates) in the order they appear in the file. So a directive coming earlier than another is the equivalent of being a higher layer. When you use Bring Region to Front or Send Region to Back, GoLive shuffles the HTML; very neat.

Tip: Storing Other Links

Another use of imagemap layers in GoLive would be as a quick method of ro-tating links for the same image that change often. You could set them up all at once, then bring an inactive link region to the front when the need arises. It does bulk up your HTML and it does slow down an imagemap's processing time in a browser when a user clicks, so don't go hog wild.

Working with Sliced Images

A common technique when designing images for the Web is to take a larger composition and slice it into several smaller images. Perhaps you want to ani-mate just a portion of an illustration with an animated GIF, or you've created a navigation bar with elements that change on a regular basis. Designers were forced to create the image in Photoshop, then manually split up the pieces and place them onto a Web page. ImageReady and other applications put an end to that in the last few years. These programs have included methods of automatically slicing images into regular pieces, and building an HTML structure (typically using tables) which holds the pieces together.

Smart Sliced Images

Using options found in the Save for Web feature, GoLive handles sliced im-ages with ease. In Photoshop, or ImageReady, set up the slices for your image.

Then, bring the native file into GoLive using the Smart Photoshop icon (which also works with ImageReady files) or the Smart Illustrator icon. Or, you can drag the file into the Layout Editor. GoLive prompts you to specify the location of the data folder it creates to store the image slices, then brings up the Save for Web dialog box (see Figure 5-46). After you define your settings, the sliced image appears in the Layout Editor like any other image, but you can click directly on the slices.

How does GoLive accomplish this magic? Underneath that image is a bit of GoLive trickery called a Smart Photoshop Table, which resembles a layout grid, which in turn is just a table (see Chapters 7 and 8 for more information)

To return to Save for Web, select the entire object (click at the edge of the sliced image when the cursor turns into an object select cursor). In the Smart Photoshop Table Inspector, click the Settings button.

Using Save for Web with Slices

At this point, most of the typical Save for Web settings are inactive, because your image has become a set of multiple images. Use the Slice Select Tool and choose a slice to work with. Shift-click multiple slices to select them, or click and drag with the Slice Select Tool; any slices within the selection marquee are highlighted.

Figure 5-46
Slices in
Save for Web

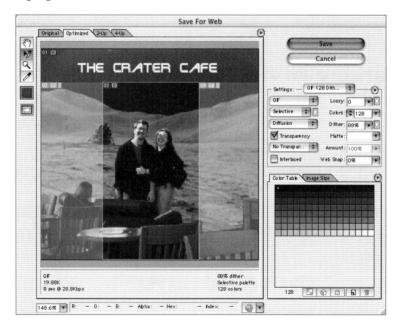

To preview the image without the overlay indicating where slices occur, click the Toggle Slices Visibility button; clicking a sliced area with the Slice Select Tool automatically displays the overlay again.

Applying properties to slices. While in the Save for Web dialog box, double-click a slice to bring up the Slice Options dialog box. Although the settings here can also be applied in the Layout Editor, doing it in Save for Web means they are retained in the event that the original image changes. Slices show up with dark blue outlines if they have attributes applied.

You can modify a slice in several ways: change its name, add a link to it, set a target for it, specify its Alt text, and compose a message that can be shown when a user rolls his or her cursor over the slice in some browsers (see Figure 5-47). If transparency is applied, you can also set a slice's background color.

Figure 5-47
Setting slice options

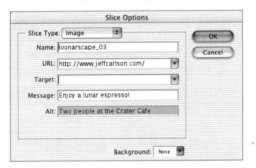

In addition to Image, the popup menu at the top of the dialog offers a No Image option. Frequently, designers use sliced images in order to create areas within the image to swap text or other images into. Type some text into the Text Displayed in Cell field, or leave it blank for none. In the Layout Editor, GoLive uses a Layout Text Box to hold the text.

Tip: Text Styling, No Image

The Text Displayed in Cell field only lets you type in unformatted text...or does it? Although you can't access any of GoLive's text formatting features within the Save for Web dialog box, feel free to type HTML tags to customize the display of the text. When the image appears in the Layout Editor, however, you can apply styles to the text as you normally would.

Tip: Slices Return

Images with slices set to No Image aren't permanently stricken. Switching the popup menu back to Image restores the image data from the original file.

Save for Web Output Settings. Taking an original image and creating slices involves managing not only several files, but also the HTML code used to display them. As you would expect, GoLive includes settings for controlling every last tag and filename involved. (We swear, Save for Web is the most Swiss-Army-knife-like software feature we've seen in a long time.)

With the Save for Web dialog box open, select Edit Output Settings from the popout menu. The Output Settings dialog box includes two categories of options, which you can access using the popup menu below Settings, or using the Prev and Next buttons (see Figure 5-48).

- **Saving Files.** Use the popup menus in the File Naming section to specify how files are named when working with rollover images. The Filename Compatibility area ensures that the files will be recognized on Windows, Mac, and Unix systems. The Optimized Files options let you define a folder for the generated images, copy the page's background image, and embed an optional copyright notice.

- **Slices.** The Default Slice Naming option in this section determines how slices are named when the image is converted. As with the previous section, use the popup menus to set which information (including date stamps) is incorporated into the title.

Importing Other Sliced Images

Although not as convenient as working with smart sliced images, it's easy to take a sliced composition created in an application like Fireworks and add it to your GoLive page.

In GoLive, open the HTML file created by the other program containing the composition. In most cases, the slices are built into a table structure, so simply select the table and drag it to your Web page or copy and paste it.

Tracing Image

It would be nice if Web pages could leap in final form from our brains to the computer screen. There are even some late nights when it feels like we've stared at a monitor long enough to accomplish that feat. But unlike Mozart, who had the annoying tendency to compose his symphonies in completed first drafts, we find ourselves creating Web pages in several stages.

Many designers work up dummy pages in Photoshop or Illustrator as sketches, and then use those roughs as the basis for building pages with more refinement. To support this common tactic, Adobe added the Tracing Image

Figure 5-48
Output
Settings
for slices

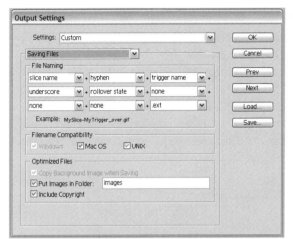

Saving Files settings

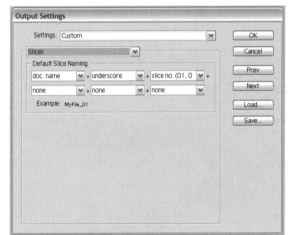

Slices settings

feature to GoLive. Simply put, it lets you display an image in the Layout Editor as a point of reference. Unlike other images, a tracing image can't be selected directly, which means you can build objects on top of it.

But a tracing image can be more than just a background template or guide. You can cut out portions of the image to be used on your page, rather than grab them from their original source file (or rebuild them).

Tip: There Can Be Only One

Only one tracing image can be active at a time. However, any portions that have been cut out remain on the page, so once you're done with one tracing image, feel free to load another and work on another section of the design.

Before you can begin tracing, you need to specify your source image. If it's not already visible, select Tracing Image from the Window menu to bring up the Tracing Image palette (see Figure 5-49).

Click the Source box and choose the image you want to use. GoLive can handle the following formats: 8-bit RGB Photoshop, JPEG, GIF, PNG, BMP, TARGA, PCX, PICT, PIXAR, TIFF, and Amiga IFF. The image appears aligned to the upper-left corner of the Layout Editor, and has a 50-percent opacity. The Opacity slider controls how see-through the image is (see Figure 5-50).

Figure 5-49
Tracing Image
palette

Figure 5-50
Tracing image
on a page

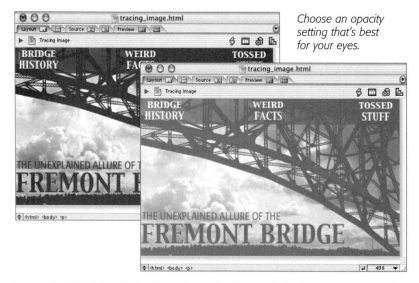

Choose an opacity setting that's best for your eyes.

Tip: Resize to Tracing Image

To collapse or expand the Document window to the size of your tracing image, select Tracing Image from the Change Window Size popup menu at the lower-right corner of the window.

To remove a tracing image, just deselect the Source box. GoLive remembers your last tracing image if you haven't closed the file, so if you enable the image again later, you won't have to go in search of the image file.

Positioning a Tracing Image

A tracing image can appear anywhere within the Layout Editor. Four controls let you easily position the image (see Figure 5-51).

- **Position fields.** Enter values into the two Position fields on the Tracing Image palette. The left field controls horizontal position, while the right field controls the vertical, both measured from the upper-left corner of the image. Entering negative numbers moves the image off the window.

- **Move Image Tool.** As its icon suggests, the Move Image Tool lets you grab the image and reposition it freely. It's possible to place the image beyond the visible area of the page; use the Position fields to bring it back.

- **Reset Position command.** To quickly restore the image's position to the upper-left corner of the window, select Reset Position from the Tracing Image palette's popout menu.

- **Align with Selection command.** Also available on the palette's popout menu, the Align with Selection command sets the tracing image's top-left corner to match the position of an object selected on the page. Any object works, including text selections.

Figure 5-51
Positioning a
tracing image

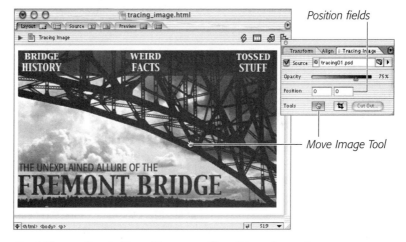

Cutting Out Sections of a Tracing Image

Click the Cut Out Tool and drag a selection on the tracing image corresponding to the area to be cut out. You can use the resize handles on the selection box to resize it, or move it by clicking and dragging within the box.

When you've determined the area to be extracted, either click the Cut Out button on the Tracing Image palette, or select Cut Out from the popout menu. In the Save for Web dialog, set the optimization settings for the image, then click OK. Cut out portions appear as floating boxes in the Layout Editor, and can be placed anywhere on the page (see Figure 5-52). (Also see Chapter 10, *Floating Boxes.*)

Tip: Cut Section Retains Dimensions

When you cut out subsequent areas of the same tracing image, the last selection is activated when you choose the Cut Out Tool. This is helpful when breaking out a navigation bar or similar element where each button or link needs to be the same size and shape as the last.

Figure 5-52
Cutting out
sections of a
tracing image

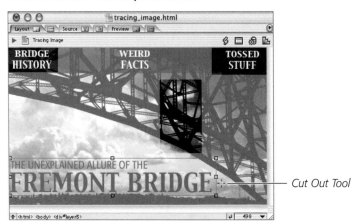

Cut Out Tool

ColorSync (Macintosh Only)

If you work with more than one computer system, you can see that what you view on one screen may not be exactly the same as what you view on another. Monitor brands and hardware differ, and software treats images differently depending on the company and the platform. Apple's answer to this is ColorSync, a system that attempts to make images appear as the designer intended no matter which combination of hardware and software is being used.

For ColorSync to work in GoLive, make sure the Display Images Using ColorSync box is checked in the ColorSync section of GoLive's preferences.

Tip: ColorSync Installation

You need to have ColorSync installed on your Macintosh; some versions of Mac OS didn't install it by default (or you might have chosen not to install it). You can usually install it off the latest CD-ROM you have with your system, but we recommend getting the most up-to-date version. Go to Apple's ColorSync Web site at www.apple.com/colorsync/, to find the latest version.

Tip: Great Idea, Minimal Support

We like the possibilities that ColorSync offers, but currently there's very little support for it on the Web; at this writing, only Internet Explorer 4.5 and higher for Macintosh can display an image with a ColorSync profile applied.

ColorSync Profiles. This feat of color management magic is accomplished through the use of ColorSync Profiles, sets of data that describe how your monitor, scanner, digital camera, or other device "sees" color. These characterizations generally rely on feeding color into them and using a colorimeter to measure their output values so that their subjective notion of color can be compared to an absolute, physical property of color.

Tip: Roll Your Own Profiles

If you don't have a profile set up for your monitor, you can use either the Monitors or Adobe Gamma control panel to use your eyeballs to create a rough profile. Click the Colors button in Monitors, then the Calibrate button, and follow the instructions. With Adobe Gamma, select the control panel, and it walks you through a calibration process. Remember to name your custom profile something intelligible, like "Glenn's 420GS monitor." This process can take you a surprisingly high degree closer to what images should objectively look like on your screen.

In GoLive, you can apply a ColorSync profile to an image by switching to the Link tab of the Image Inspector, and clicking the Profile button in the ColorSync section. Use the URL Getter to locate the profile that represents your hardware configuration.

From here you can also choose to use GoLive's built-in profile or not use it at all by selecting Default or None, respectively.

Tip: Embedded Profiles

Photoshop 5.0 and later support the ability to embed a ColorSync profile into an image when saving it. If a profile already exists within the image file, its name appears in the Embedded field.

Page-wide implementation. You can specify profiles for every image on your page, but since it's more likely you'll set the same profile each time, GoLive has a way to apply a single profile to an entire page. Click the Page icon in the Layout Editor, then switch to the ColorSync tab of the Page Inspector to link to a profile.

Tip: Copy Profiles to Site Folder

To make an externally-referenced profile work, you need to upload it to your Web site along with the HTML and image files that use it. So although you can link to a profile located in the ColorSync Profiles folder within the System Folder, it doesn't get automatically uploaded to the site, and therefore isn't referenced.

Imagine Great Images

It's not an understatement to say that inline images turned the Web from an interesting way to share information into a new designers' medium. GoLive makes it easy to add images to your Web pages, freeing you to spend your time making great images.

CHAPTER 6
Color

We've each taken our fair share of art and design courses throughout school and beyond. Littered amid that history of paper, canvas, brushes, and charcoal lie dozens, even hundreds, of mostly-squeezed paint tubes covering the full visible-color spectrum (and maybe even some ultraviolet and infrared colors too). Although we were taught that color is actually the perception of light interacting with a surface, our stained–hands-on experience told us that color was usually a combination of pigments that eventually swirled into a brownish muck at the center of our palettes.

Today, most of our color usage has returned to the realm of light, with trillions of photons projected daily to ignite pixels with specific hues on our screens. Coming up with a certain color on the Web is a matter of combining numerical values, not watercolors or oils. But that doesn't mean you have to suppress your inner fingerpainter. GoLive's color capabilities let you easily choose the tone you want, or experiment with several different ones.

In fact, the robustness of GoLive's color features continues to surprise us: not only does it offer a palette of the 216 "Web safe" colors, it includes resources for defining colors in RGB, CMYK, and HLS color spaces, long the bastions of print publishing.

Tip: The Slightly Misleading ColorSync Name

GoLive supports Apple's ColorSync technology on the Macintosh, which is an effort to make the colors viewed on one computer appear the same on other, dissimilar machines. However, ColorSync deals with synchronizing the color of images, not HTML-based color found in objects like table cells or text. See Chapter 5, *Images*, for more information about this unique approach to providing a consistent viewing experience.

Color on the Web

Color is a subjective thing; for example, the paint in Jeff's living room is perceived as cream by some people and slightly pink by others (cream is the intended perception). Depending on the lighting, the time of day, the colors of objects in the same field of vision, and dozens of other factors, one color can take on multiple appearances. The same is true on the Web, where we must deal with hundreds of different monitor types and calibration settings, plus the default color values of different browsers and operating systems.

We also have to deal with color in a historical context. Although these days you can buy a fully-loaded PC system for less than $500, it was only a few years ago when even moderate-quality hardware was expensive. We didn't have 17-inch monitors that displayed millions of colors, because the horsepower and memory requirements to drive them were affordable only to very wealthy corporations. As a result, many of today's Web standards are based on the state of computing when those standards were first created.

The field of color management has slowly evolved with the technology in order to work toward color's holy grail: everyone seeing the same color. We're not there yet, but we are getting closer.

Color Between Platforms

One of the frustrations of Web designers is that Macintosh and Windows operating systems use different bases for displaying color. This is especially evident in images, but carries over to background and text colors as well because the two systems feature different gamma defaults. Gamma is a representation of how the same input value, like a specific percentage of black defined in software, gets displayed as the output in a given physical system, like a monitor or printer. Due to the ways in which the two operating systems translate

What's New in 6

There are only a few changes of note when it comes to color. The Color palette's popout menu now features an Only Web Colors option which, when checked, limits the color palette to Web-safe colors no matter which color picker you're using. A more significant change has been made to sitewide color sets. In earlier versions of GoLive, the Colors tab of the Site window was a glorified reference for seeing which colors were used throughout your site. In GoLive 6, you can now change the color value of an entry in the Colors tab and have the change applied to every instance of that color in your site.

color values for display at the software level, colors tend to be lighter on a Macintosh, or darker under Windows, depending on your point of view.

Tip: Adjusting and Simulating Gamma

You can tweak gamma settings on both platforms to varying degrees by using the Adobe Gamma control panel that ships with Photoshop 5 and later for both platforms (see Figure 6-1). This control panel allows you to simulate Windows gamma on a Mac more effectively than the reverse. Also, Adobe ImageReady (Mac and Windows), which ships with Photoshop 5.5 and later, features a gamma simulator for the opposite platform when previewing images (see Figure 6-2).

Figure 6-1
Adobe Gamma
control panel

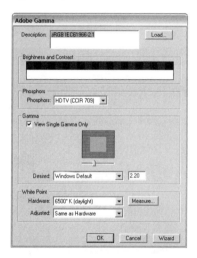

Figure 6-2
Simulated
gamma using
ImageReady

An image viewed on a Mac...   ...appears darker under Windows.

The Web-safe color palette. Color also differs among platforms because the engineers who built color into the operating systems chose slightly different values to use for each default color palette. Of the 256 colors available in a basic color system, 216 of them match up across all platforms, including Mac, Windows, and typical Unix interfaces. This group is commonly called the Web-safe, or sometimes browser-safe, color palette. Using colors from this palette makes it more likely that what you see on your screen looks the same on another computer system, even if that system has old equipment or is set to display fewer colors.

Keeping this information in mind can help prevent problems later on, and underscores the point that you should be sure to test your pages on as many platforms as possible.

Tip: Quick Web-Safe Color Palette

Be careful: after reading this tip you may not want to read the rest of this chapter! No matter which color space you have selected in the Color palette, you can always access the Web-safe palette by Control-clicking (Mac) or right-clicking (Windows) the Preview pane or any color field. This brings up a table of the 216 "safe" colors, plus their hexadecimal equivalents (see Figure 6-3). If you also hold down the Option (Mac) or Alt (Windows) key, the grid displays the Web Name List colors instead. Release the mouse button over the color you want to load. If you Control-click a color field in the Inspector, the new color is applied immediately to your selected object. You may never need the Color palette again—but stick around, there's more valuable information in this chapter.

Tip: Macintosh Color Palette Easter Egg

With the popup Web-safe palette visible, press and hold the Command and Shift keys to view the text of a song in Spanish at the bottom of the palette.

Figure 6-3
Quick Web-safe color list

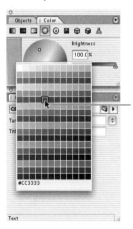

Roll the mouse pointer over the Web-safe colors, then click to select the one you want.

Tip: Technicolor Sunrise

The general consensus about color on the Web is beginning to veer away from the limited Web-safe spectrum. Even the least expensive Windows-based clone these days is capable of displaying thousands or millions of colors, so designers are starting to open up their palettes. Although as a general rule we still advocate sticking with the Web-safe palette, it's a good bet that most of your viewers will probably be able to view your colors (taking gamma issues into account).

Applying Colors

Normally, we would make a point of explaining all the options available before telling you how to implement a feature. But in this case, applying colors is so easy we want to give away the how-to first. The section following this one, "Selecting Colors," offers the skinny on how best to find the color you're looking for.

To bring up the Color palette—if it's not visible—select Color from the Window menu. You can also click any color field in an Inspector or the Text Color field on the Toolbar.

Drag & Drop Color

GoLive lets you apply colors to text, tables, layout text boxes, floating boxes, frame borders, and just about anything else that contains a color field in its Inspector. From one of the color tabs, select a color to load into the Preview pane, then drag a color swatch from that pane to an object's color field (see Figure 6-4). If you're using the Web Color List, Web Name List, or Site Color List, you can drag the swatch directly from the color list in each tab.

Some items allow color to be applied directly, rather than through the Inspector palette. You can drop a color swatch onto a highlighted selection of text, for example, or drop directly onto a floating box or layout text box. If you

Figure 6-4
Applying color

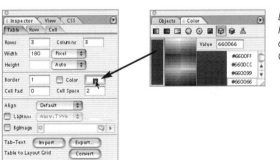

Drag from the Preview pane to an Inspector's Color field.

try to drop a color onto an area of text that isn't highlighted, the text you type from that point will be that color.

Tip: Color Field Dragging

Typically, when you click a Color field, its color appears in the Color palette's Preview pane. If you want to apply a color to an object directly from the Color field (instead of making a trip to the Color palette), hold down Command (Mac) or Control (Windows) and click to grab the color swatch and drag it out.

Tip: Drag to Select a Background Color

To change the background color of a page, you normally must drag a color swatch onto the appropriate field in the Page Inspector. However, a shortcut is to drag a color swatch directly onto the Page icon in the Document window's Layout Editor.

Tip: Applying Text Color Without the Text

Ever the inquisitive types, we tried dropping color swatches on everything to see what would happen, including images and table borders. Unfortunately, we weren't able to apply table background colors without using the color field in the Table Inspector, nor turn photos of pets and family members hot pink. We did discover that dropping a swatch onto an object that doesn't directly react to the color actually adds a font color to that area. So, any text typed immediately following an image appears in that color.

Active Color

Sometimes, especially if you're experimenting with a number of color combinations, you don't want to drag and drop swatches like they've been ripped out of some torn-up Pantone guide. GoLive's active color mode enables you to apply colors to an object as you highlight it.

First, select an object whose color can change, such as a table cell. To switch modes, click once on the Color field in the Inspector; a dark border surrounds it to indicate the mode shift (see Figure 6-5). As you click on different colors in the Color palette, the object's color changes too.

Applying Colors in Other Editors

Although setting colors in the Layout Editor is the easiest and most visual approach, GoLive offers a couple of interesting color uses in the Source Code Editor and the HTML Outline Editor.

Figure 6-5
Active color
mode

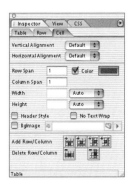

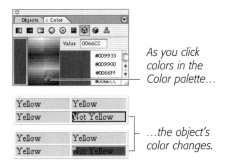

*As you click
colors in the
Color palette...*

*...the object's
color changes.*

Source Code Editor. You can't apply a color to objects while editing their HTML code, but you can use the Color palette to help you grab the right hexadecimal values that define colors. If you drag a color swatch anywhere in the Source Code Editor or the Source Code window, GoLive inserts

```
color="[color value]"
```

at the point where you dropped the swatch. This way, you can set up a tag (like a font definition or table cell), then insert the color you want without having to look up the hex value.

HTML Outline Editor. Drop a color swatch onto the color attribute of a tag to change it. This can be especially useful for setting attributes that aren't directly supported in the Layout Editor.

Selecting Colors

It's great to select color by eye in a visual editor rather than imagining color while looking up, and then typing in, hexadecimal values; it's another reason we like working in a WYSIWYG editor. Now all we have to do is click the Color palette and we don't even have to worry about what the color's numeric values are.

But which color palette to click? GoLive includes nine different palettes on the Color palette that each offer a different way of selecting colors.

Tip: The Color Palette's Color Palette?

Before you begin to think we're repeating ourselves, we just wanted to point out the difference between Color palette (capitalized) and color palette (not capitalized). The Color palette is the floating window where GoLive's color controls are located. A color palette is the portion of a tab on the Color palette where the actual colors are located. This is a good example of how real-world metaphors can get confusing in the computer world. A physical palette is what we use to hold and mix colors on, but the notion of a digital palette that can hold other things (like commands, text fields, etc.) works well when describing the floating windows. Now, before you begin to think we're repeating ourselves, we just wanted to point out....

The Value of Color Values

If the Web were a box of crayons, there would be a lot of confused kids. Although we would look at a color and call it "red," computers need a numeric definition of what constitutes red. With the exception of the Web Name List, the values in the different palettes are expressed either as digits, percentages, or in hexadecimal notation.

Digits. Values range from 0 (none of the color) to 255 (all of the color), for a total of 256 colors. (This total is the practical minimum number of colors available. We say "practical" because it's possible to work with just 16, 4, or even 2 colors on some older systems, but modern operating systems typically offer only three options: 256, thousands, or millions of colors). Mixing different colors this way gives you a full spectrum of color (see Figure 6-6).

Figure 6-6
Color notation

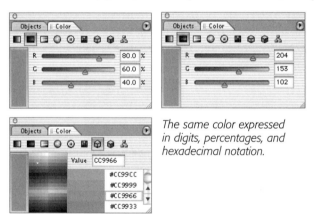

The same color expressed in digits, percentages, and hexadecimal notation.

Percentages. Choosing Percent Values from the Color palette's popout menu switches the value display to percentages in the RGB, CMYK, Grayscale, and Web-safe palettes. Offset printers mix percentage amounts of inks to arrive at a desired color, and the technique has migrated to the digital realm as well.

Hexadecimal notation. When it comes down to adding color to HTML code, the values end up in hexadecimal notation, which is just a more compact and neat way to specify the color value (for example, the hex notation for yellow is "#FFFF00"). GoLive's great color strength is that you don't need to mess with hexadecimal; choose a color visually, and GoLive supplies the correct hex value. Then again, if you know the hex value but not its color, type the code into the Value field (if it appears) to see its match.

Only Web Colors. A new option in GoLive 6 is the Only Web Colors item in the Color palette's popout menu. When this is selected, each color palette displays only the corresponding Web-safe colors (see Figure 6-7). This lets you use the different methods of selecting colors while still sticking with the Web-safe spectrum.

Figure 6-7
Only Web
Colors

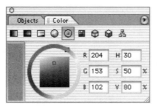 

Full color spectrum   *Only Web Colors enabled*

GoLive's Color Palettes

With the Color palette displayed, clicking the buttons brings up the following palettes; you can also select them from the popout menu's list. To display or hide the buttons, choose Show Buttons from the popout menu.

Gray Slider. Classic like old movies and early television, the grayscale palette displays up to 256 levels of gray.

Tip: Switching to Gray

When you click the Gray Slider button, the color in the Preview pane doesn't automatically change to its gray equivalent—but the slider is positioned to the correct value. Simply click the slider without moving it to load the gray value into the Preview pane.

RGB Sliders. The RGB Sliders palette selects colors using mixtures of red, green, and blue, which is the combination that monitors use to display color. Technically, everything you're looking at onscreen is represented in RGB.

CMYK Sliders. If you're trying to match a color from a printed color swatch, enter its values in the CMYK Sliders palette. Cyan, magenta, yellow, and black (represented by K, since B already stands for blue) are the four ink colors used in process-color printing.

HSB Wheel. The HSB Wheel palette displays the full range of colors compatible with your existing monitor and screen depth; choose your color, then use the Brightness slider to achieve just the right shade. HSB is short for Hue (or sometimes Hue Angle), Saturation, and Brightness. Hue is calculated based on a 360-degree scale—hence the circular representation—and saturation is measured from the middle of the wheel to the edge. For example, if your screen is set to display 256 colors, you see more dithering (where the computer pairs different-colored pixels in an attempt to approximate the original color if it's not available) than if you were viewing at a resolution of thousands of colors (see Figure 6-8).

Figure 6-8
Dithering

Fewer colors are displayed on 8-bit screens.

16-bit and higher screens display more colors.

Tip: Slider Slickness

The grayscale, RGB, CMYK, and Web color palettes feature sliders as well as numeric fields for defining a color. Click and hold the slider knob while dragging to change the color amounts. If you click along a slider's path, the knob jumps to the mouse arrow's location.

HSV Picker. The HSV Picker displays colors based on their hue, saturation, and value. Hue is represented as a number between 0 and 360 (creating the circle); saturation and value are expressed in percentages. Some people find this to be a quicker and more visual way to nab the color they're looking for. Note that the RGB values are also shown here.

Palettes palette. This oddly-named palette presents the built-in 256-color system palettes. From the popup menu, you can also choose to display a reduced palette of 16 colors or 16 grays, desktop colors (the ones the system reserves for its own use), or a custom palette of colors you can drag from the Preview pane.

Tip: Access System Colors

To access the full range of colors on your system, Command-Option-click (Mac) or Control-Shift-click (Windows) the Preview pane; use Option-Click (Mac) or Shift-click (Windows) within a Color field. The operating system's color options window appears, enabling you to choose colors, for example, from Apple's Crayon Color Picker (see Figure 6-9).

Figure 6-9
Apple's Crayon
Color Picker

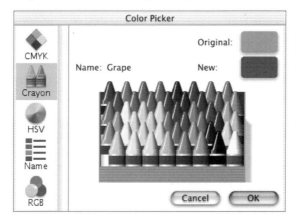

Web Color List. Honestly, this is the palette we keep open 90 percent of the time. It offers an overview of the colors available as well as a scrolling list (with hex labels) showing larger swatches of the colors. But the main reason is that the Web Color List displays only the Web-safe color palette. Sticking to this ensures that our colors are viewable on any system; there's nothing worse than spending a lot of effort choosing the perfect color, only to realize it looks like garbage on other computers.

Web Name List. Some days, we'd like to give it all up and become the people who name colors—did they hire these folks away from mail-order catalogs (PapayaWhip? Lavenderblush? MistyRose?). The Web Name List displays a list of colors that Web browsers recognize by name (so in the HTML, "#FFDAB9" is actually substituted with "PeachPuff"). If you know the name of a color, you can type it, or even part of its name, into the Name field and hit Return to get a match. Despite the often-creative naming schemes, the downside is that not all the colors in this palette display the same on all browsers.

Site Color List. The Site Color List simply reflects the contents of whatever colors are present in the Colors tab of the Site window when a site file is open. You cannot add colors to this tab, only use it as a quick reference to select colors that you already have in a site. The name of the current site reflected in the palette is displayed in the lower-left corner of the Color palette. See the next section for information on how to create and store site colors.

Tip: Select a Color from Anywhere on the Screen

Frequently, we have an image or other element that contains the exact color we want to use on our page. Instead of trying to match it to a value in one of the Color palette tabs, you can grab the value directly. Switch to the Palettes palette or Web Color List, then click within the color proxy to the left of the tab, but keep the mouse button pressed. Now, feel free to roam the eyedropper cursor over any part of your screen, even the menu bar or applications that are visible behind GoLive. When you release the mouse button, the color beneath the eyedropper is loaded into the Preview pane.

Tip: The Quicker Color Picker-Upper

GoLive's active color mode can be especially handy if you want to quickly pick up a color that appears elsewhere on the page. For example, if you want a table cell to match the color of another cell, but don't know the latter's color, simply select the first cell, click the Color field to enter active mode, then use the eyedropper tool to point at the second cell's background color.

Why So Much Color?

As we mentioned at the beginning of this chapter, there are only 216 Web-safe colors. In most cases, you want your site to be available to the most possible viewers, which is why most designers stick to the Web-safe color palette. So why does GoLive include support for color spaces that don't necessarily show up on the Web, like CMYK?

We can think of a few reasons. There will come a day (soon, we believe) when we're not limited by the number of colors that can be displayed safely, so GoLive has the functionality required to scale up when needed. Virtually all the tens of millions of machines shipping in the last few years include video display cards that show thousands or millions of colors on a monitor. However, many millions of older machines are still being phased out and upgraded.

Second, if you're working with a group that you can identify as having more modern equipment or if you're designing for a corporate intranet in which you know that everyone's machine is capable of more than the lowest common denominator, you can use the full breadth of color.

Third, having access to these other color spaces is helpful when you're building a site that ties into, or is based upon, printed materials. If a client has decided that a principal color for his or her ad campaign is a mixture of 118C/121M/22Y/48K, you can plug that value into the CMYK Slider and grab a corresponding RGB or Web-safe color. The last thing you want to do on a deadline is stare at your monitor trying to match a sample color swatch.

Sitewide Color Sets

Each appearance of a color throughout a site stands on its own as a separate occurrence. We used to keep several pieces of paper nearby with scrawled hex color values to make sure the colors were consistent throughout a site. Updating these elements occupied vast amounts of time, and often required innumerable manual search-and-replace routines to maintain consistency.

Thankfully, those days are waning. GoLive provides a central location in the Site window for structuring and viewing the colors used throughout your site: with a site open, click the Colors tab in the left pane of the Site window to display color sets. This tool is especially useful for staying within a designated color palette, particularly when there are several members of a group working on the same site. But it's also useful in a new way in GoLive 6: changing a color value in the Colors tab can change that color on each page it appears.

Creating Color Sets

Let's start with the basics: making new entries in the Colors tab, which can also be grouped into folders representing subcategories or hierarchies.

New Entries

GoLive offers several ways to create new colors. Whichever method you select creates a new entry called "untitled color". If you create several new entries, GoLive adds a number to the subsequent items, as in "untitled color 2".

You can create new colors in one of seven ways.

- From the Site menu, select Color from the New submenu.

- From the Site tab of the Objects palette, drag a Color icon into the Colors tab in the Site window.

- From the Site tab of the Objects palette, double-click the Color icon.

- Drag a color swatch from the Color palette directly into the Colors tab (see Figure 6-10, next page).

- Control-click (Mac) or right-click (Windows) and select New Color from the contextual menu.

- On any page in the site, return to the Colors tab in the Site window, and select Get Colors Used from the Site menu or the contextual menu (see "Extracting Colors," later in this chapter).

- Drag colors from the Colors tab of one Site window to another.

Figure 6-10
Dragging color
swatch into
Colors tab

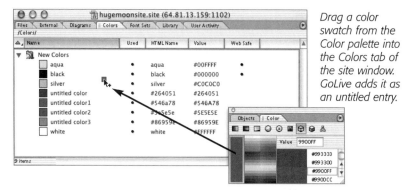

*Drag a color
swatch from the
Color palette into
the Colors tab of
the site window.
GoLive adds it as
an untitled entry.*

You might create a set of colors from scratch in the Colors tab that you're going to use throughout a site, name it distinctly, and then apply it as needed. This is easier than specifying a color each time, or letting GoLive name a color generically—with "untitled"—after you create it (see "Applying Colors," later in this chapter).

GoLive displays the color's name, whether it's used in the site, the HTML code for the color, the hexadecimal value, and whether it's Web safe or not.

Tip: In & Out Links Palette

You can use the In & Out Links palette to display the pages where colors are used. Selecting a color with the In & Out Links palette displayed shows all HTML files that contain that color (see Figure 6-11).

Figure 6-11
Using the
In & Out Links
palette to view
a color's usage

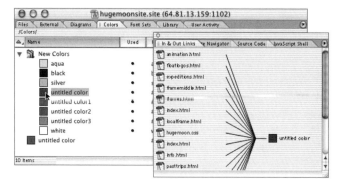

New Folders

A folder in the Colors tab is simply a way to name a group of colors. You can nest folders as deep as you like, putting folder inside folder inside folder. Creating folders can be useful when you're trying to map out where colors are used in different parts of the site, but this is not a feature we commonly find ourselves using.

GoLive automatically creates a folder called New Colors if you've manipulated or deleted entries and then selected Get Colors Used. You can create new folders in five ways.

- Under the Site menu, select Folder from the New submenu.

- From the Site tab of the Objects palette, drag the Color Group icon into the tab.

- From the Site tab of the Objects palette, double-click the Color Group icon. (If you don't deselect the first color group, double-clicking the icon again creates a nested group.)

- Click the New Folder icon on the Toolbar.

- Select New Folder from the contextual menu.

Once you've created a new folder, you can drag any other colors into it. If you try to drag a color into a folder that already contains an item with the same name, GoLive asks you if you want to replace the existing one.

Tip: Inconsistent Group Naming

GoLive names groups inconsistently, sometimes calling them folders (as in the Site menu and contextual menu) or groups (in the Objects palette's Site tab). Don't worry; it's always the same thing.

Color and CSS

Color is an attribute that many HTML tags like to attach to themselves, like Font and TR (table row). But the way of the present, not the future, is to not attach colors throughout a site in individual HTML tags, but rather to centralize colors and other text and structural attributes in Cascading Style Sheets (CSS). CSS lets you specify a variety of formatting and spacing settings and apply them to any ranges, paragraphs, table cells, or other tags or chunks on a page.

CSS works in the browser rather than being hardcoded in pages. The advantage is simple: if you define a CSS for Heading 3, changing the color of that Heading 3 throughout an entire site could require a single edit and no page updates. Rather, the next time the browser loads that central style sheet, it displays Heading 3s in the new color.

It may take a while to wrap your head around centralized management, but it's definitely the way to go, rather than using GoLive's color management tool that we describe in this section. (All other color tips are equally useful for CSS, which uses the Color palette.)

For more on CSS, read Chapter 27, *Defining Cascading Style Sheets.*

Extracting Colors

GoLive maintains an internal list of colors in the site file, in the same way it tracks external references and internal links. However, it doesn't automatically update the Colors tab to display all those items.

When you've made changes to any pages in a site and want to view the current list of active colors, select Get Colors Used from the Site menu or the contextual menu. GoLive updates the list to add any colors not already present. If you're starting from scratch with no colors listed, GoLive adds them all, and names them just as if you were creating them from scratch: "untitled color", "untitled color 1", and so on.

If you import a site into GoLive, the program automatically scans the site for colors, font sets, links, and external references, and populates all of the tabs in the Site window with "untitled" entries.

GoLive uses the contents of a color—its stored value, like "#FFFF33"—to determine whether or not every color in the site is already listed.

You can also use the Clear Site item in the Site menu, which bundles together a number of site-maintenance features in one fell swoop; we discuss Clear Site in depth in Chapter 19, *Managing Files, Folders, and Links*.

Editing Colors

Editing colors is simple; select one in the list and rename it in the Color Inspector, or click the title again to highlight and type a new name within the Colors tab. To change the color value, drag a new color from the Colors palette into the Color field of the Color Inspector.

Tip: Renaming Color Sets

We recommend that you rename colors to be more descriptive and mnemonic (like "main table cell background color") instead of generic ("untitled color 17"). It's a good way to identify the color's purpose, as well as the name of its color.

If a color is currently being used by pages in your site, changing the color value applies the change to each occurrence, so be careful about which ones you change. You could easily inadvertently turn your beige backgrounds on every page to lime green! When a page does need to be updated after you make a change, GoLive displays a dialog box listing the affected files and giving you the option to continue or cancel (see Figure 6-12).

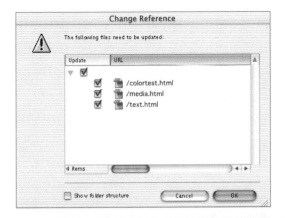

Figure 6-12
Updating a
color definition
throughout
a site

Tip: Changes Apply to Closed Files

Making color changes to color entries only works on pages that aren't currently open in GoLive. Save and close any open page to ensure that new colors stick.

Tip: Copying Confusion

You can select a color and duplicate or copy-and-paste it to create an identical entry, which you can then move to a different folder if you want to. However, changing its color value can lead to some interesting results.

GoLive uses either the hexadecimal code or the name of the color as reference; if you have two or twelve copies of that color in your Colors list, they all share the same value. However, changing the value in the Color Inspector does not automatically adjust each occurrence in the list. What's more, any pages where that color appears (look in the In & Out Links palette) get changed only for the most-recently-created duplicate—the other copies of the color in the list lose their links to pages.

Our advice? Don't hassle with creating copies of colors in the Colors tab.

Applying Colors

The Colors tab isn't just useful for seeing what's going on in a site; it can also be used as a source for applying colors to items on a page. Carefully drag an object from the background without releasing the mouse button, hover over the selected text or the color swatch in an Inspector, and then release (see Figure 6-13, next page). GoLive doesn't bring windows to the front when you're dragging these items onto selections, so you have to play windows gymnastics to display the tab in the background and the HTML page's selection in the foreground. However, you can switch windows by first dragging the color onto the Select Window button on the Toolbar.

Figure 6-13
Applying a
color from
the Colors tab

Colors may be applied through many methods. You can:

- Drag a color from the Colors tab onto the Color field in any Inspector.

- Drag a color onto a selection on an HTML page, and GoLive sets the selection to that color.

- Click the Color palette's Site Colors button, select a color, and apply it as you would any other color; the name of the current site file appears in the lower left corner (see Figure 6-14).

Figure 6-14
Site Colors
palette

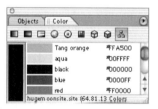

Deleting and Removing Unused Colors

If you want to delete a color, highlight it and click the Delete button in the Toolbar. If you want to clean out a cluttered Colors tab after completing a site, select Remove Unused Colors from the Site menu or contextual menu.

If a color you created from scratch has not yet been applied to text or to another object somewhere in the site, don't use this command. Remove Unused Colors deletes every color that isn't applied. If you created those elements to use later, you would have to recreate them.

You can also use the Clean Up Site command, described in depth in Chapter 19, *Managing Files, Folders, and Links,* to remove unused colors, font sets, links, and other doodads, all at the same time. This option can be set as a default for workgroup sites, too; sites are cleaned up every time you publish files to a Publish Server (see Chapter 21, *Working in Groups*).

The Art of Color

In some respects, GoLive has made color a more complex issue than in other Web design applications. With nine color palettes available, selecting the right hue or background shade can be almost overwhelming. Almost. In reality, the simplicity of applying colors to Web objects overcomes the number of methods for selecting those colors. It's almost enough to make us hang up our paints and brushes for good. Almost.

CHAPTER 7
Tables

The Web hasn't always been a designer's medium. As we mentioned in Chapter 4, *Text and Fonts*, HTML is a *structural* formatting language, which means anyone with a browser sees the same information regardless of his or her choice of font, type style, or screen size. However, this flexibility became a problem when representing tabular information like spreadsheet results. Netscape introduced HTML tables in one of their very early browser upgrades, and tables became the tool of choice to display structurally defined rows and columns.

We've spent enough time around graphic designers (and each other) to know that designers not only appreciate useful tools, they also like to discover new uses for those tools that the tool makers never dreamed about. It wasn't long before the Web's first designers turned the tables on tables. Now the unassuming HTML table has become one of the most reliable and flexible tools used by Web designers. With tables, you can build a framework that controls where elements appear, paint in colors without using images, and add variety to your pages.

The "traditional" cost of wielding this tool has been complexity. Even veteran HTML coders can be found glued to their monitors deciphering which tags belong to which table cell (and trying to find the one errant tag that's preventing the table from being drawn at all in some browsers). Fortunately, GoLive's table tools make it easy to create, edit, and bend tables to your will in ways that barely resemble a standard table—and with a minimum amount of direct code wrangling.

Creating a Table

If you've ever used a spreadsheet application like Microsoft Excel, tables are a familiar sight. No matter how you stretch, shift, or align them, tables always remain rectangular blocks of cells (see Figure 7-1). Because of this structure, cells naturally fall into rows (horizontal, left-to-right) and columns (vertical, top-to-bottom). As you'll see, tables are highly configurable. They can contain column headings and captions, can be nested within other tables, and be manipulated in a variety of ways. You can specify the size and number of cells, the amount of space between their internal edges and contents, the width of their border, their alignment, and, as they say, much, much more.

Figure 7-1
A basic table
in GoLive

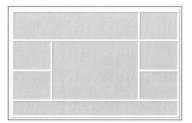

Building a New Table

To take advantage of these features, you first need to create a table, a quick and painless process. From the Basic tab of the Objects palette, drag and drop the

What's New in 6

Since tables themselves haven't changed much over the years, we weren't expecting much difference in how GoLive 6 handled them—but were we in for a surprise.

The Table palette (which can be displayed by selecting its name from the Window menu) now displays the pixel or percentage measurements of every row, column, and cell. If you're sometimes math-challenged under a deadline, as Jeff can be, you'll love this new capability to troubleshoot your cell widths at a glance. Clicking an error in measurement shown in the

Table palette even automatically fixes your mistake!

Also new in GoLive 6 is a set of small but welcome additions: the Table Inspector now includes buttons for adding rows and columns to any side of a cell. In previous versions, you could only use the buttons to add columns to the left of, or rows just above, a selected cell.

You can also access these table-editing commands from a new Table submenu, located under the Special menu, as well as from contextual menus.

Table icon on your page; you can also double-click the icon to insert a table at your current text insertion point. Alternately, bring up the contextual menu and select the Insert Object menu, then the Basic submenu, and finally the Table item. A perfectly useful three-column by three-row table appears (see Figure 7-2).

Figure 7-2
Building a
new table

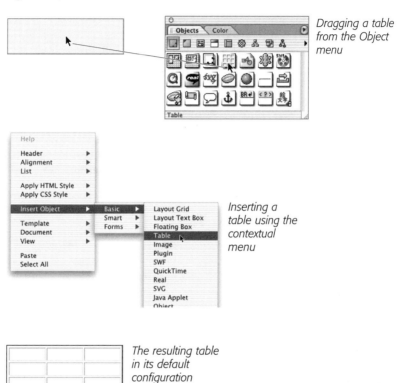

Dragging a table
from the Object
menu

Inserting a
table using the
contextual
menu

The resulting table
in its default
configuration

Tip: Cool Table Creation Shortcut

Hold down Command (Mac) or Ctrl (Windows), click the Table icon, and drag. A table preview appears underneath your pointer, enabling you to specify the number of rows and columns you want your table to have. When you release the mouse button, the new table appears on your page (Figure 7-3, next page).

To start entering information, click inside a cell—not on its border—and begin typing. Or, drag in page elements from the Objects palette, such as images or forms, or items from tabs in the Site window; consider each cell to be a microcosmic Web page. You've just accomplished in a few seconds what formerly took hand coders several minutes to set up.

Figure 7-3
Command/
Ctrl -drag to
specify the
number of
rows and
columns

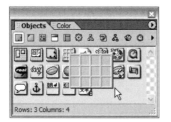

With a basic table in place, you can now begin to modify most of its attributes from within GoLive's Table Inspector tabs. Virtually all of these attributes display correctly in all current Web browsers.

Tip: HTML 4.0 and Tables

The HTML 4.0 specification offers additional table attributes, but GoLive doesn't support all of them visually. See Elizabeth Castro's book, *HTML 4 for the World Wide Web*, for descriptions of the available attributes.

Where's the Column Tab?

It's like one of those "What's missing from this scene?" tests. The Table Inspector contains tabs for Table, Row, and Cell. Why not a tab for Column?

The reason hearkens back to ye olde days of code: HTML allows you to specify the settings for a row because cells are defined as elements that exist within rows. Tables are built sequentially left-to-right, then top-to-bottom.

As a browser reads HTML that constructs a table, it's working much like an old-fashioned typewriter. It reads an enclosing Table tag followed by a row tag, followed by individual cell tags. It puts each new cell to the right of the previous cell until it reaches an end-of-row tag. It then moves down to the next row starting at the same left margin, and builds cell-by-cell across. (See Figure 7-4, built from the following HTML.)

```
<TABLE>
<TR>
   <TD>Left Cell, Row 1</TD>
   <TD>Right Cell, Row 1</TD>
</TR>
<TR>
   <TD>Left Cell, Row 2</TD>
   <TD>Right Cell, Row 2</TD>
</TR>
</TABLE>
```

Since all the settings for formatting the cells are contained either in the row (TR) or cell (TD) tags, there's no need for a separate column tag.

Figure 7-4
No column tab

Left Cell, Row 1	Right Cell, Row 1
Left Cell, Row 2	Right Cell, Row 2

Tip: Tables with Style

The attributes mentioned here are all applied using elements of the Table tag in HTML. However, you can also apply many table attributes via style sheet definitions as well. First, define a CSS class selector with the attributes you want, such as a background color, typeface, or background image. Then, with a cell or table selected, choose Apply CSS Style to <tag> from the contextual menu (<tag> varies based on your selection), and choose the selector. This gives you the advantage, for example, of changing the color of a table that appears on every page with one change, instead of manually making the change at each occurrence. Alternatively, you can create a tag selector that applies to all table cells or tables. See Chapter 28 for more on CSS.

Border. You can specify a table's border thickness in pixels by changing the value in the Border field of the Table Inspector's Table tab; GoLive's default border setting is one pixel. The higher the border setting, the larger the "picture frame" appears (see Figure 7-5).

If you don't want borders to appear at all, set the border value to zero. GoLive displays invisible borders using gray lines. (If you don't see them, make sure you have Show Invisible Items active in the View menu.) Note that the

Figure 7-5
Setting the border thickness

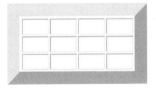 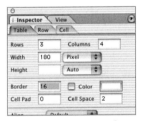

value you assign in the Border field applies only to the border surrounding the table, not to the borders of the cells inside, unless the value is set to zero.

Width and Height. The Width and Height fields control the size of tables, rows, and cells in their respective tabs in the Table Inspector. Rows, however, can only have their height set, not their width.

There are three ways of controlling width and height, all of which are found in the popup menus that accompany the fields.

- **Auto.** The default setting tells the Web browser to take the current window's width and height, add in the contents of the cells, and figure out how wide and tall to make each cell and the entire table. In the Table palette, cells with Auto measurements show up as gray numbers. Auto is often good for tables that don't require specific dimensions, as the browser tries to ensure that everything fits.

- **Pixel.** Enter a number to specify the number of pixels wide or tall a table or cell should be. When you enter a pixel value, the corresponding number in the Table palette appears in black. If your table is part of a page's structure, you most likely want to use pixels (see "Tables as Structure," later in the chapter).

- **Percent.** Because not all Web browser windows share the same dimensions, you can set a table to take up a percentage of the space in a browser window, or set a cell to use a certain percentage of the table's dimensions.

Provide the Numbers—the Correct Numbers

When a Web browser encounters table code that's missing width values, it has to read and examine the HTML code for the entire table to determine its dimensions before drawing it. For large tables, that can take a long time.

To help make your pages load faster, be sure to include table and cell widths when you specify your table settings.

But even those specifications can introduce problems if your math happens to be more art than science. For example, create a new table that's 400 pixels wide. Now select the top cells in each row and specify widths for each so that the

numbers don't add up to 400 (let's say 75, 10, and 35). The table retains its width, but also retains the values you assigned, which only add up to 120 pixels (see Figure 7-6).

In GoLive 6, you're less likely to make this mistake thanks to the improved Table palette. In the example above, the last cell width of 35 appears in red to indicate that the math is wrong. (Click the red number, and GoLive fixes your math by adjusting cell dimensions.)

Most browsers are forgiving enough to approximate the widths. But we've seen unexpected results when the numbers don't add up.

Figure 7-6
The importance of using the correct numbers for table widths

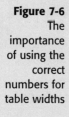
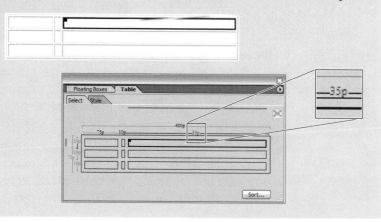

You can choose numbers higher than 100 to force a table off the edge of the screen, if you want, but why?

Tip: Specifying Column Widths

It's a good idea to include table and cell widths to help speed up the display of your Web pages, but you don't have to get carried away. A table column always stretches to fit the width of the widest cell, pulling the other cells in the column with it. So don't feel obliged to set the width for every cell in your table. Specifying the width of just one cell in a column saves you a little time, and streamlines your code. When you click another cell in that column, GoLive displays the correct value in the Width field.

Cell padding and cell spacing. The Cell Pad field in the Table tab (called cell-padding in HTML) controls the indent on all four sides of a cell from the cell and table borders. The Cell Space field (called cellspacing in HTML) controls the thickness in pixels of a table's internal cell borders (see Figure 7-7).

Figure 7-7
Cell padding
(dark gray)
and cell
spacing
(white)

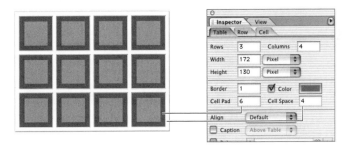

Cell padding and cell spacing accomplish similar tasks: they both add breathing room to the cells' contents. However, in the case of colored backgrounds in table cells, the difference can be drastic (see "Adding Color to Tables," later in this chapter). Suppose you're using different colors for different cells, and have applied a separate color to the entire table. If you set the Cell Pad amount to zero, your text gets crammed right against the cell's edges; by contrast, a larger value adds space around the cell's contents to better offset the text (see Figure 7-8).

Figure 7-8
Offsetting text
with cell
padding

Trip	Length	Cost
Tranquility	2 weeks	$1.5 million
Fra Mauro	3 weeks	$2.8 million

Trip	Length	Cost
Tranquility	2 weeks	$1.5 million
Fra Mauro	3 weeks	$2.8 million

Cell padding set to 0 (left) and 4 (right)

Using a higher Cell Space value increases space between cells, but has its own pitfalls. In the example table above, the background color of the table shows through the wider cell borders in Internet Explorer; the same is true for Netscape 6.x (see Figure 7-9). Under Netscape 4.x and its predecesors, however, the larger cell borders become transparent, leaving you with multiple cell islands separated by the Web page's background color or image (see Figure 7-10).

Figure 7-9
Cell spacing
border colors

Internet Explorer

Netscape

Figure 7-10
Cell spacing
becomes
invisible in
Netscape 4.x

Since cell spacing and cell padding are table-wide values—you can't set them for individual cells—it's easy to experiment with different combinations and view the results immediately.

Header style. With a cell selected, check Header Style in the Cell tab to center the cell's contents and apply bold formatting to its text (see Figure 7-11). Although you could just as easily apply bold to the text and specify the cell's alignment to get the same effect, the table header style is treated as a unique element in HTML—another example of structural formatting versus visual formatting.

You generally use table headers for column or row headings at the top or left of a table, but you can apply the style to any cell. You can also apply local formatting on top of the table header style.

Figure 7-11
Applying
Header Style
to a table cell

Tip: Sometimes Math Is Hard

Cell spacing and cell padding have a tendency to confuse a table's Width value. When you increase cell spacing or cell padding, you're adding pixels that increase the overall width and height of the table (see Figure 7-12). However, the table Width field remains the same, and doesn't reflect the increased width. Fortunately, the Table palette comes through again: click the angry red number for overall table width, and GoLive fixes the table's width to include the extra space for your padding and spacing.

If you really want to keep the table the same width to avoid swelling out other elements on your page, factor the cell padding and cell spacing amounts into the table width value. For example, if your 200-pixel table with a border set to 0 (zero) contains two columns that are both 100 pixels wide, but you want a cell spacing of 10 pixels, you would need to reduce cell widths by a cumulative total of 30 pixels to maintain the table width: 10 each for the left and right edges, plus 10 for the border separating the two cells (see Figure 7-13, next page).

Figure 7-12
No added
width with cell
padding and
cell spacing

Trip	Length	Cost
Tranquility	2 weeks	$1.5 million
Fra Mauro	3 weeks	$2.8 million

2

Trip	Length	Cost
Tranquility	2 weeks	$1.5 million
Fra Mauro	3 weeks	$2.8 million

Trip	Length	Cost
Tranquility	2 weeks	$1.5 million
Fra Mauro	3 weeks	$2.8 million

4

Trip	Length	Cost
Tranquility	2 weeks	$1.5 million
Fra Mauro	3 weeks	$2.8 million

Trip	Length	Cost
Tranquility	2 weeks	$1.5 million
Fra Mauro	3 weeks	$2.8 million

6

Trip	Length	Cost
Tranquility	2 weeks	$1.5 million
Fra Mauro	3 weeks	$2.8 million

Cell padding

Cell spacing

Note that only the interior spacing changes, not the overall width of the table, when configuring these two attributes.

Figure 7-13
Adjusting cell
width to
compensate
for cell spacing

*Subtract the amount of
Cell Spacing (10 pixels
here) for the left and
right edges and for the
border separating the
table's columns (in this
case, adding up to 30
extra pixels).*

No Text Wrap. A table column always stretches to accommodate the widest cell, as we pointed out earlier. But in most cases, that stretching applies only to the width of the longest word in a cell. By default, text within cells wraps to the next line. If you want a cell's text to remain on one line, check the No Text Wrap box in the Cell tab.

Background color. Applying colored backgrounds within tables adds color to a page without having to download images, speeding up a page's load time. You can apply color to entire tables, rows in a table, individual cells, or all three, by checking the Color box located on the Table, Row, or Cell tabs in the Table Inspector.

Clicking the color field beside the checkbox displays the Color palette (if it's not already visible). Select a color from the Color palette and drag it to the color field in the Table Inspector to apply the color.

A table color is applied to the entire table. In the Layout Editor, cell colors stop at the edges of their cells, so in a table with wide border sizes, the page's background color shows through the borders.

Cell colors override row colors, which override table colors, so you can specify all three and use that hierarchy to determine which color a cell will ultimately be. For instance, you might want to use an overall table background to contrast with the page's background color, and alternate colors in every other row to make the contents easier to read. Specific cells might be in yet another color to highlight certain facts or figures (see Figure 7-14).

Tip: CSS Color

To make it even more complicated, you can use CSS and entirely bypass setting colors through the Table Inspector. However, this can become problematic if you want to apply table styles, which don't recognize CSS formatting; see "Table Styles" later in this chapter.

Figure 7-14
Coloring parts
of a table

Site	Year Est.	Cost	Children Allowed
Ocean of Storms	2000	$3M	no
Sea of Snakes	2002	$2M	no
Lunar Alps	2001	$6M	no

Setting color for the entire table

Site	Year Est.	Cost	Children Allowed
Ocean of Storms	2000	$3M	no
Sea of Snakes	2002	$2M	no
Lunar Alps	2001	$6M	no

Setting color for different rows

Site	Year Est.	Cost	Children Allowed
Ocean of Storms	2000	$3M	no
Sea of Snakes	2002	$2M	no
Lunar Alps	2001	$6M	no

Setting color for a specific cell

Tip: Fill Cells to Show Their Colors

Even if you've applied a color to a table cell, you don't see the color unless the cell has something in it. In otherwise empty cells, insert a non-breaking space to solve the problem: Option-spacebar on the Macintosh, or Shift-spacebar under Windows.

You can also insert non-breaking spaces into multiple cells at once. Select the cells, then choose Insert Nonbreaking Space from the contextual menu.

BgImage. Alternately, you can apply a background image to the table, which is tiled like a page's background image. Check the BgImage box and choose an image file via the URL Getter. Be aware that background images display differently in various Web browsers.

In Internet Explorer (4.0+) and Netscape 6.2 and later, the image appears behind the entire table, even the borders; set a higher Cell Space value to see this at work. If you have a cell color selected, the color supercedes the background image (see Figure 7-15).

Figure 7-15
Table
background
image in
newer
browsers

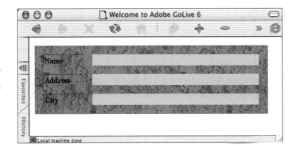

Tip: Background Images in Netscape

Netscape's older browsers (4.x, and the initial releases of 6.0 and 6.1) take a different approach (see Figure 7-16). Only the cells themselves include the background image, not the borders, and the cell color shows up behind the image (if the image contains transparency; otherwise, you don't see the cell color at all). If the cell is empty, the background doesn't appear at all.

Figure 7-16
Table background image in older versions of Netscape

Tip: CSS Background Images

CSS selectors can also incorporate background images with a greater degree of control than via the Table Inspector, such as the offset from which an image starts repeating.

Alignment. Tables support two types of alignment: the alignment of the table itself, which forces other elements to wrap around it, and alignment of the contents of table cells.

With the table selected, select Left, Right, or Center from the Align popup menu in the Table tab. Just as with images, the text that follows wraps around the table. Unlike images, however, you can't control how much space appears between the edge of the table and its surrounding items.

Controlling the alignment within cells offers much more flexibility (see Figure 7-17). When you select a cell, you can access both Vertical and Horizontal alignment menus on the Cell tab. Contents can be set vertically to Top, Middle, or Bottom, while the horizontal options include the expected Left, Right, and Center.

Tip: Fast Cell Application

You can select many cells at once and apply horizontal and vertical alignment options to them via the Cell tab.

You can also apply the same settings to the contents of a row by switching to the Row tab and making your choices. This is a quicker method of applying

Figure 7-17
Vertical and
horizontal
alignment

*Selecting a cell makes the Vertical and Horizontal
Alignment popup menus on the Cell tab active.*

the settings across multiple cells. If the Row and Cell alignment settings contradict each other, Cell settings override Row settings.

All the alignment popup menus also include Default as an option, which applies the settings found in Table 7-1.

Table 7-1
Default
alignment
settings for
various table
attributes

Attribute	Setting
Table	Left*
Row, vertical	Middle
Row, horizontal	Left
Cell, vertical	Middle
Cell, horizontal	Left

* Naturally, alignment can vary depending on your Web browser's settings, providing yet another reason why testing on a variety of platforms and browsers is essential.

Tip: Check Paragraph Alignment

Paragraph formatting surrounding a table also affects the table's alignment on the page. If the paragraph is set to be right-aligned, for example, the table hugs the right side of the page, even though you haven't specified any table alignment within the Table tab.

This applies even if your table isn't embedded in a paragraph. If you had set text alignment, then delete the text and replace it with the table, it's likely that the alignment settings could still exist.

Select the table by highlighting it as you would a character, and check the alignment buttons on GoLive's Toolbar. The table alignment settings are as much about controlling how elements wrap around the table as they are about pushing elements to the left or right sides of the pages.

Caption. A table can also optionally contain a caption. With the table selected, check the Caption box on the Table tab, then choose whether the caption appears above or below the table (see Figure 7-18, next page). A space appears

Figure 7-18
Table caption

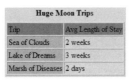

*Checking Caption places
a text field above or below
the table.*

where you can place your cursor and begin typing. Just as with regular text,
you can apply local formatting (font face, size, color, etc.), but it appears centered by default in GoLive.

Tip: Accessibility

Typical guidelines for making Web pages accessible to visually impaired visitors
and others with accessibility issues require assigning a caption to a table.

Tip: Aligning Captions

Here's yet another example of how different browsers choose to interpret
HTML. When you choose Below from the Caption popup menu, GoLive places
an Align="bottom" attribute in the Caption tag. (It adds nothing if Above is chosen, since that's the default.) If you don't want your caption to be aligned in the
center of your table, and you're using Internet Explorer or a version of Netscape
beyond version 6, you can use the alignment buttons in the Text Toolbar to substitute Left or Right in the Align attribute. If you're using an earlier version of
Netscape, the point is moot, since the browser only supports top and bottom
alignment.

When you select the table, the caption is selected as well. This symbiosis is
great if you need to reposition the table, but it can be dangerous if you decide
to detach the caption. Be sure to copy and paste the text in the body of your
page, because the text gets deleted if you uncheck the Caption box.

The Fine Art of Table Selection

Despite the painstaking care taken to develop any software program, there are
always bits—even in a 6.0 software release—that make you feel more like a

Swiss watchmaker instead of a designer: some task that requires intense concentration and focus to get just right. A little slip and that watch don't tell time too well no more. In GoLive, selecting tables takes a good eye and a steady hand too, especially in a complicated or nested table.

Working around the Table Default

Having tables spring full-formed into the world is a wonderful thing, especially if you've ever spent time writing them by hand. (We explain how the underlying code works later in this chapter.) But sometimes you don't want to apply GoLive's default table attributes, which have these specifications every time: three columns, three rows, a width of 180 pixels, border set to 1, cell padding set to zero, and cell spacing set to 2.

Why would you want to change GoLive's table defaults? Perhaps you know that every table in your site will have five columns, or you need a white background color every time. Whatever the reason, you'll be happy to know that you have choices beyond a 3-by-3 default table.

The secret is in GoLive's Web Settings. Open the Web Settings window, then click the Markup tab. In the left column, expand the Web option, then click HTML. In the right column, locate and expand the Table option. From here, click the attribute you wish to change. For example, you can give new tables a width of 500 by selecting the "width" attribute. In the Web Settings Attribute Inspector, click the box labeled Create this Attribute, and enter the number in the Value field. For more on how to use this powerful yet terrifying portion of GoLive, see Chapter 28, *Controlling Web Settings.*

If you'd rather just keep a template of the table handy, you can also use the Library tab in the Objects palette or the Library tab of a Site window, either of which can hold any object you create on an HTML page. Create a new table and apply your settings. Highlight it by positioning your cursor to the right or left of the table and selecting it as you would select any other character or image. Grab the selection and drag it to the appropriate Library tab (see Figure 7-19). Double-click your new icon to give it a descriptive name. You can then drag and drop the icon onto any page, instead of dropping the standard Table icon.

Figure 7-19
Dragging a table to the Library

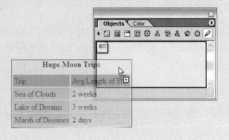

Select the table using the cursor (above) and drag it into the Library (right).

Every good lesson has a fundamental key idea, and here's the one that transforms table selection from random guesswork to precision selecting: it's not how you use your mouse, but *where* you use it. Being a visual Web editor, GoLive takes a spatial approach to table selection, so the position of your cursor on the table determines what's going to happen when you click the mouse button. The cursor also changes shape depending on the table region it's pointing at.

Selecting the Contents of a Cell

It's likely you want to start entering information into your table first thing, so click in the middle of a cell to place your text cursor within it. The cursor becomes an I-beam or text-insertion cursor (see Figure 7-20), which you can use to type text or provide a target for placing other elements such as graphics.

Figure 7-20
Selection and
insertion
cursors

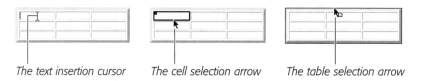

The text insertion cursor   *The cell selection arrow*   *The table selection arrow*

Tip: Can't Get a Cursor to Appear

You may find yourself unable to get a text-insertion tool to appear when you click at the top of a large cell (see Figure 7-21). That's because the default setting for a newly created cell is to center text top to bottom within the cell. When you click at the top, GoLive doesn't associate that action with text because no text is supposed to appear at the top.

You can solve this dilemma in one of two ways: set the table cell's vertical alignment to Top (see later in this chapter); or, click in the middle of the field.

Figure 7-21
Accessing text
tool in large
cells

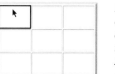

If at first you don't succeed, click within the middle area of a larger cell to acquire the text-insertion tool, or select a Top vertical alignment for the cell.

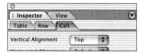

Tip: Selecting All Contents Within a Cell

Typically, choosing Select All would seem to select everything on your page. But the engineers at Adobe get extra credit for making GoLive smart about selecting items within a cell. With your text cursor active within a cell, choose Select All from the Edit menu, or type Command-A (Mac) or Control-A (Windows), to highlight objects and text within that cell only.

We use Select All within cells constantly, especially when we want to copy the contents of one cell (including font, color, and size attributes) and paste them into another.

Tip: Use Tab to Move Between Cells

Tables can be particularly mouse-intensive items in GoLive. Give your wrists a break by using the Tab key to move among cells, left to right, then down to the next row. Pressing Shift-Tab reverses the direction. (Tabbing at the end of a table inserts a new row, though, just like in Microsoft Word's table feature.)

Selecting an Entire Table

Move the cursor to either the top or left side of a table and you notice that the arrow becomes an object selection cursor. Clicking the table in this state selects the table and displays the Table tab in the Table Inspector. If you continue to hold on, you can drag and drop the entire table to another location on the page, in another open window, or into the Library tab of the Objects palette or any open Site window.

You can also place the cursor at the right edge of the table to select it. However, if the table's width is set in pixels, the cursor becomes an icon with arrows pointing left and right. The cursor remains an arrow if the Table's width is set to Auto or Percent.

You can also select a table by highlighting it as you would a block of text, or by placing the text cursor at the left or right side of the table and pressing Shift with either the left arrow or right arrow key. Unfortunately, this only selects the table as an object on the page, like text or an image. You need to click the top or left edges of a table to be able to bring up the Table Inspector and access GoLive's table-editing features.

Selecting a Cell

You'll probably spend more time selecting individual cells than other table elements, because cells are where most of the formatting happens. Position your cursor over a cell's bottom border or its right border (making sure the pointer is not an I-beam), and click.

If the table's width is set in pixels and the cursor turns into the resizing cursor when you're attempting to select the rightmost cell, you've moved too far to the right, and clicking here selects the entire table instead.

Another option is to click a cell's corresponding proxy in the Select tab of the Table palette (see Figure 7-22).

Figure 7-22
Selecting a cell
in the Table
pallette

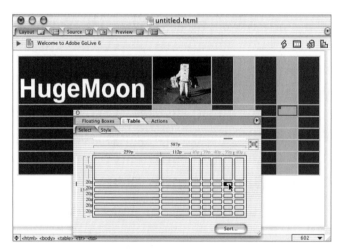

With a cell selected, you can return to editing its contents by pressing the Return or Enter key. This can come in handy if a cell is so small that you can't get the mouse's I-beam cursor to appear; simply select the cell and hit Return or Enter.

Tip: Increase Cell Spacing for Easier Cell Selection

If you're having trouble positioning your cursor to select cells, it's okay to cheat a little. Increase the Cell Space value in the Table tab while you're editing, which gives you larger borders between cells; anything higher than 10 works nicely. GoLive considers the border between cells part of the cell, so your pointer does not even have to be touching the edge of the cell to select it. When you're finished editing, just restore the previous Cell Space value. (Since it's a table-wide setting, you only have to change it once.)

Tip: Table Editing Through Cell Selection

When you select a cell, the Cell tab automatically comes up in the Table Inspector. But it can be helpful to remember that although the cell is the primary item selected, you can also make changes to values that affect the whole table. If you switch to the Table tab or the Row tab, you don't need to deselect the cell and reselect the table or row to edit those attributes.

Selecting Multiple Cells

The ability to select more than one cell and apply settings to them all is one of the great benefits of using GoLive instead of hand-coding HTML table tags. Hold down the Shift key when selecting cells to select multiple, non-contiguous cells. This also applies to clicking areas of the table's proxy in the Table palette.

Tip: Contiguous

Contiguous means adjoining. Contiguous ranges are cells that butt up against each other top, bottom, left, or right. Non-contiguous ranges are arbitrary selections made without regard for adjacency.

To choose a contiguous range of cells, click to select a cell, then drag without releasing the mouse button. Or, simply click and drag on the Table palette's proxy. If any cells in that range were previously selected, they become deselected. Blue horizontal and vertical indicator lines make it easier to see the range selection.

Tip: Resize Proxy

The Table palette can be made much larger to increase the size of the proxy when you're trying to select proportionately tiny cells. In fact, the Table palette is an excellent example of why you might want to use a multiple-monitor setup when working with GoLive: put the Table palette on a secondary screen, resized as large as space allows.

With one or more cells selected, you can also choose Select All to choose all the cells.

With multiple cells selected, you can't add or delete rows or columns using the buttons in the Cell tab of the Table Inspector (see "Editing Tables," later in this chapter). However, you can change the values for the Width and Height fields, and change whether selected cells' dimensions are specified as Pixel, Percent, or Auto.

If some settings conflict, such as cell alignment, the affected popup menus become blank. If you then choose an option from the same affected menu, it resets all cells selected to that popup choice. Leaving it alone preserves the original settings.

Selecting a Row or Column

At the left or top edge of a table, position your cursor so that it's just barely between the edge and the interior of the nearest cell: the cursor changes to an arrow pointing right or down. Clicking the left edge selects all the cells in the adjacent row; clicking the top edge selects all the cells in the nearest column.

To select an entire row using the Table palette, click to the left of the table proxy; click at the top of the table proxy to select a column. The cursor changes to an arrow, as with the table itself, when you're in the right position. Holding down the Shift key allows you to select multiple, non-contiguous rows or columns.

Nesting Tables

You can place whole tables within the cells of a surrounding table, commonly referred to as nesting. This is often done when a page's overall structure is defined by a table, and a standard table needs to be displayed on the page (see "Tables as Structure," later in this chapter). The problem sometimes is that selecting individual cells from within nested tables can be difficult if the tables' borders run against each other.

Fortunately, GoLive has implemented two nice capabilities to get around the problem. Select a cell and then press Control-Return (Mac) or Control-Enter (Windows) to select the cell's parent table. If that table is nested within another table cell, then that (grandparent?) cell is selected (see Figure 7-23). You can repeat this process for as many levels as it takes to get to the top of the table hierarchy. Or, with a cell selected in a nested table, click the Select Parent Table button in the Table palette (the outward pointing button in its upper right), which jumps you out a whole table level, not just a cell level (Figure 7-24).

Tip: Quick Cell Selection without Leaving the Keyboard

If your text cursor is within a cell, you can use Control-Return/Enter to select the cell and bring up the Table Inspector. If we're typing with both hands on the keyboard, it can be a pain to grab the mouse, locate the cursor's position, maneuver the pointer to an edge of the cell, and finally click to select it. This way, one Control-Return/Enter keyboard action saves us four steps, some unnecessary hand-flailing, and a bit of brainpower, too!

Figure 7-23
Nested tables

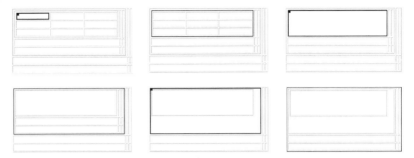

Starting with a single selected cell, press Control-Return (Control-Enter in Windows) to select the cell's table, again to select the cell where that table is nested, again to select that cell's entire table, and so on....

Figure 7-24
The Select
Parent Table
button

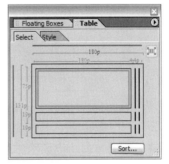

Click the Select Parent Table button...   *...to jump out one table level*

Editing Tables

It's highly unlikely that every table you create needs to look like GoLive's default. Using the flexible table editing tools in GoLive, you can resize a table's dimensions, add and remove cells, and "span" cells over others to customize the table's appearance.

Resizing Cells and Tables

There are two methods of resizing table elements. With the table or a cell highlighted, you can input pixel or percentage values into the Width or Height fields in the Table, Row, or Cell tabs of the Table Inspector. If you already know the table's dimensions, this is the best way to set specific values.

Sometimes, though, you don't have the math worked out, or you just want to begin with a boring old table and see how you can mold and stretch it into a close approximation of the masterpiece in your head. This is where the second method comes in: manipulating table dimensions by dragging the table's borders. In some cases, you can resize elements by simply clicking and dragging; other capabilities require the use of a modifier key, like Command or Control, as you click and drag.

As we mentioned earlier, the results from manually resizing tables and cells depend on whether the Width and Height values are set to Pixel, Percent, or Auto. If the cells' width attributes are set to Auto, you can squish and stretch as much as you want. Also, remember that cells never shrink narrower than their contents, so the longest word or object in a cell defines that cell's (and column's) minimum width.

The following rules apply when manually resizing (see Figure 7-25).

Figure 7-25
Dragging to
resize tables
and cells

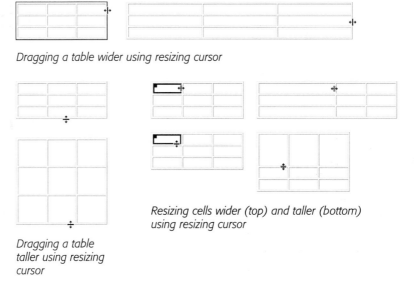

Dragging a table wider using resizing cursor

Dragging a table
taller using resizing
cursor

Resizing cells wider (top) and taller (bottom)
using resizing cursor

Table width. Position your cursor at the table's far right edge until it becomes a resize cursor (a left-and-right arrow icon) to change the width of an entire table. Clicking and dragging lets you expand or compress the width; GoLive automatically adjusts the internal cell widths to maintain their individual settings if possible.

If your table and cells are set to Auto widths, however, the resize cursor doesn't appear. Hold down the Option (Mac) or Alt (Windows) key when the pointer is in the right edge region to invoke the resizing control. When you click and drag, your table's Width setting automatically switches to Pixel.

Table height. Similar to setting table width, position the cursor at the lowest edge of the table until it becomes a resize cursor (in this case an up-down arrow), then click and drag to adjust the height. Also, as with table width, you may need to hold down the Option or Alt key to invoke the resize control if the table's height is set to Auto, which changes the setting to Pixel.

Cell width. Follow the same basic procedure when resizing table cells. If a cell is set up to be measured in pixels, you see a resize cursor appear; if not, press Option or Alt when you drag. You can only adjust cell widths from the right border.

Cell height. Position your cursor at the bottom of a cell. If you don't see the resize cursor, press Option or Alt and then drag to change the height.

Adding and Deleting Cell Rows and Columns

You can attack the problem of adding and deleting cells in five ways:

- using the Table Inspector
- dragging table borders with command keys held down (adding cells only)
- using keyboard shortcuts
- using the contextual menu
- selecting menu commands

However, these methods don't all produce the same results. Knowing what to expect saves you time and hopefully prevents you from unintentionally deleting table data, as GoLive happily dispenses with the contents of deleted rows or columns without warning you.

Tip: Add and Delete Apply to Rows and Columns

It's important to mention here that these add and delete functions only apply to rows and columns. If you're trying to remove a single cell within a table so that another cell expands to take its place, what you really want to do is hide that cell using the spanning techniques mentioned later in "Merging Cells."

Adding and deleting using the Table Inspector. If you've just created a new table and know the number of rows and columns it needs, enter those numbers in the Rows and Columns fields of the Table tab. New columns are added to the right of existing columns, while new rows are appended to the bottom of the table. Enter a number smaller than the current number of rows or columns to remove cells from the right side or bottom of the table. You can change these figures at any time.

At the bottom of the Cell tab in the Table Inspector are six buttons for adding and deleting rows. They are only active when a single cell is selected, even if you're removing a column and have only cells in that column selected. Clicking the Delete Row or Delete Column button deletes whichever row or column contains the selected cell. Clicking the Add Row/Column buttons adds a row or column (see Figure 7-26).

Figure 7-26
Using the
Add/Delete
Rows/Columns
buttons

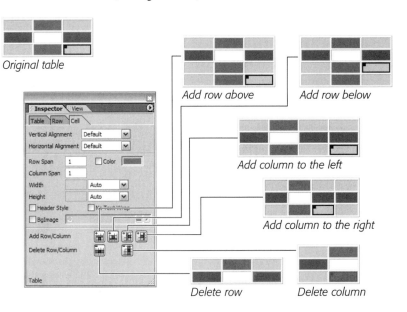

Original table

Add row above   Add row below

Add column to the left

Add column to the right

Delete row   Delete column

Adding by dragging table borders. As a rule, we like to avoid making frequent trips to the Table Inspector, which is why we like the capability of adding rows and columns by dragging their borders. This only works on the table as a whole (you can't drag a cell border in the middle of the table and expect a new column to appear there), but it's a great way to expand a table quickly and easily. (Unfortunately, you can't delete rows or columns using this method, though it's a feature we'd like to see.)

Position your cursor on the table's right edge (for adding columns) or the bottom edge (for adding rows), just as if you're going to resize the table. With the Command key (Macintosh) or the Control-Shift keys (Windows) held down, click and drag the table's border. A plus sign (+) appears on the arrow cursor, and dotted outlines representing new cells appear. Continue to drag until you've added as many columns or rows as you'd like, then release the mouse button. These columns and rows often appear awfully thin; GoLive uses the absolute minimum defaults when previewing what will be added.

Adding and deleting using keyboard shortcuts. As you've no doubt guessed, we love keyboard shortcuts. Select a single cell and quickly add or delete rows and columns using the keys described in Table 7-2.

Table 7-2
Keyboard shortcuts for adding and deleting rows and columns

Action	Numeric Keypad or Standalone Key	Standard Keyboard
Add a row	* (asterisk)	* (asterisk)
Add a column	+ (plus sign)	+ (plus sign)
Delete a row	Shift-Del	Shift-Delete (Mac) or Control-Shift-Delete (Windows)
Delete a column	Del	Delete (Mac) or Control-Delete (Windows)

Tip: Copying and Pasting Cells

To copy the contents and attributes of a cell, simply select the cell and use the Edit menu's Copy command, then paste it into another cell. If you select a contiguous range of cells, like a two-by-two square, you can paste it into a similar range of cells. Using the Cut command works the same, but clears the contents of the original cell or cells.

Adding and deleting using the contextual menu or GoLive's menus. With a cell, row, or column selected, the contextual menu shows options for adding and deleting rows and columns (see Figure 7-27, next page). The contextual menu also offers another way to delete rows or columns, with an interesting twist. Select an entire row or column, then choose Clear or Delete from the contextual menu to delete the selected cells. If you have multiple cells selected that don't belong to the same row or column, applying Clear or Delete erases the contents of the cells (including text formatting), not the cells themselves.

Figure 7-27
Adding and
deleting using
the contextual
menu

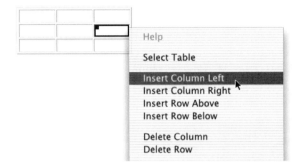

Figure 7-27
Adding and
deleting using
the contextual
menu

Merging Cells

Even if you're really using a table to display tabular information instead of as a formatting element, it's rare that you want to maintain an even grid of cells. There are times when a cell's contents need to fit across the two cells below it, for example, or you want an image to run down the length of the table. Merging cells, also called cell spanning, enables you to instruct one cell to extend or span, like a bridge, across other cells (see Figure 7-28).

Figure 7-28
Cell spanning

Location	Attractions		
Sea of Tranquility	picnic area	swimming	hiking
Ocean of Storms	sailing (very dangerous)		beaches
Lake of Dreams	canoeing	hiking	fishing
Marsh of Disease	none		

Cell spanning follows the same directional principle as table cells, operating from left to right, top to bottom. So, select a cell that is either to the left or the top of the cell that's going to be overtaken by the span. With the cell highlighted, go to the Table Inspector and enter the number of cells it covers in the Row Span or Column Span field of the Cell tab. Alternately, you can hold down the Shift key and press the right arrow or down arrow key to apply the span; pressing Shift and the left or up arrow removes the span.

When dealing with cells that are part of a column or row span, think of that area as a single cell—the upper left one in the spanned section—that has simply grown to hide the other spanned cells. The cells that are "hidden" behind the spanned cell aren't affected by changes applied to them, such as when you select a column by clicking at the top of the column. There is no way to select a cell that is "hidden" by a span.

The contextual menu and the Special menu's Table submenu offer an extra cell-spanning goodie. With contiguous cells selected, bring up the menu and choose Merge Cells.

Tip: Inserting Oversized Contents into Spanned Cells

A cell resizes to fit its contents; a graphic or text too large to fit into a cell's existing dimensions causes it to grow. If you plan to use cell spanning to accommodate a

A Bad Idea Made Worse

We mentioned at the outset of this chapter that you can use tables to paint without images—clearly a catchy overstatement used to grab your interest, right? Well, you'd be surprised. Most table and cell coloring is used as a backdrop to text or other elements on a page. But an April Fool's joke proved that you can also use tables to reproduce images, pixel-for-pixel.

Every Web image is made up of rows and columns of colored pixels, aligned in a rectangular grid. Sound familiar? For the April 1, 1998 issue of the electronic journal *TidBITS*, Jeff wondered if it would be possible to reproduce an image by substituting colored pixels with colored table cells, thereby eliminating the need to load an image at all.

Travis Anton of utility developer BoxTop Software (www.boxtopsoft.com) took the idea one step further and created PhotoHTML, a fully-functional Photoshop plug-in that con-

verts images into HTML tables (see Figure 7-29). The only graphic used is an invisible spacer GIF to make sure that each cell is populated to make the background color display in all browsers.

As with too many brilliant ideas, alas, PhotoHTML has one major flaw: the code required to reproduce even a small image in table format winds up being larger than the graphic it replaced! And if the pseudo-image is large, most browsers either tend to take a long time to parse and render the code, or choke on it entirely. Designers, please don't try this at home! (Unless you really want to, in which case it can be downloaded from realworldgolive.com/example.html.)

Warning: a really good way to crash GoLive is to open a PhotoHTML file larger than about 50K; GoLive really tries to open it, but it *kinna handle it, Cap'n!*

Figure 7-29
A handsome lad blown to smithereens

large graphic or text, it might be easier to apply the dimensions before inserting the element to avoid throwing off any preset values in the surrounding cells.

Adding Color to Tables

Originally, the only method for adding color to a Web page was by specifying its background color or image, or by adding other images to the layout. When you start adding colorful images, as we're all too aware, your download times begin to crawl under the weight of all those pixels. The emergence of colored table cells offered a refreshing change: visual variety without loading a single image! Even better, applying colors to tables in GoLive is a simple matter of dragging and dropping swatches from the Color palette—with only a few oddities to watch out for.

The Table, Row, and Cell tabs in the Table Inspector each contain a Color field, plus a checkbox for activating or deactivating the color. If the Color palette is not visible, clicking the Color field displays it, and, if there's a color in the field, drops that color into the preview pane. Clicking the field once also switches to active color mode, where you can apply colors by clicking swatches in the Color palette. (See Chapter 6, *Color*, for more about color in GoLive.)

Applying a cell or row color. With a cell or group of cells selected, choose a color from the Color palette and drag it to the Color field in the Row or Cell tab. Dropping the color in the field automatically checks the Color box if it wasn't already selected, and applies the color. Once a color has been loaded into the Color field, you can check or uncheck the Color box to apply or remove the color without erasing it.

Cell colors override row colors, so if you apply a different color to a cell within that row, the cell's color is displayed (see Figure 7-30). Unchecking the Color box in the Cell tab reverts the cell's color to the row color.

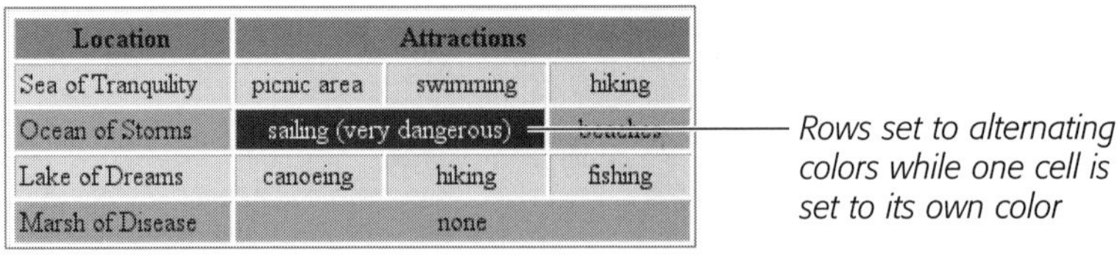

Figure 7-30
Cell color
overrides row
color which
overrides
background
color

Location	Attractions		
Sea of Tranquility	picnic area	swimming	hiking
Ocean of Storms	sailing (very dangerous)		beaches
Lake of Dreams	canoeing	hiking	fishing
Marsh of Disease	none		

Rows set to alternating colors while one cell is set to its own color

Tip: Adding Non-Breaking Spaces

In order for cells to display a background color, they need to be populated. If they're completely empty, then the Web page's background color or image shows through. The traditional solution to color empty cells has been to insert a non-breaking space by typing Option-spacebar on the Mac or Shift-spacebar under Windows. However, doing that in a complex table can be a time-consuming, and annoying, process. Instead, select the cells and choose Insert Nonbreaking Spaces from the contextual menu or the Special menu's Table submenu to automatically insert the non-breaking space tag. GoLive is even smart enough to ignore cells that already contain content. You can also select Remove Nonbreaking Spaces to reverse the effect.

Applying a table color. Like setting a background color for your page, you can specify a background color for an entire table. Follow the same procedure for applying a color as above, but drop it onto the Color field in the Table tab.

As we mentioned in "Merging Cells," earlier in the chapter, Web browsers don't display table colors consistently. GoLive's Layout Editor displays only the table's cells filled with the background color, not the space occupied by its borders (increase the Cell Pad and Cell Space values to see a vivid example of this). When you view the table in many versions of Netscape before 6.2, the borders are transparent and reveal bits of a page's background color or image; but if you look at it in Internet Explorer or Netscape 6.2 or later, the table color is applied to the entire table, borders included (see Figure 7-31). Also remember that the color doesn't show up at all in cells which are completely empty. Also, individual cell colors, as well as row colors, override the table color.

Figure 7-31
Background
show-through

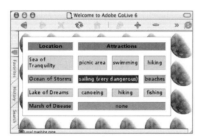 

In a table with exaggerated cell spacing, it's clear how Internet Explorer and Netscape 6.2 and later show the table's background color, while earlier versions of Netscape Navigator show the background image through the interstices.

Tip: Nest Tables to Create Colored Borders

Build a table containing only one cell, set the Border value to zero, and apply your desired border color to the entire table. Then, create a new table within the cell, sized smaller than the first depending on how thick you want the colored border to be. Set this table's background color so that the back table does not show through (Figure 7-32). Not only do you have more control over the border effect, the result is consistent in browsers as old as 4.0, as well as later browsers (especially in terms of border size and line weight).

Figure 7-32
The nested-table border trick

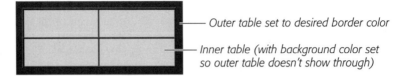

Outer table set to desired border color

Inner table (with background color set so outer table doesn't show through)

Tip: Don't Drag Colors to the Cell Itself

You can only apply a cell color using the Color field in one of the Table Inspector's tabs. If you drag a swatch from the Color palette to the table itself, GoLive thinks you're specifying a text color.

Table Styles

Tables are complicated elements, especially now that designers often rely on them for adding visual punch to otherwise basic pages. In many cases, such as coloring table cells, making changes throughout a site can be a time-consuming process. GoLive's table styles feature lets you set up formatting options such as cell color, padding, and spacing to automate repetitive table making.

Applying a table style. GoLive ships with several prefabricated styles to get you started. With a table selected in the Layout Editor, click the Style tab in the Table palette and choose a style from the popup menu. Click the Apply button to activate that style (see Figure 7-33).

Tip: Stylin' Selections

You don't have to select the whole table to apply a style. If your cursor is within any cell, the style applies to the entire table. If you have a cell selected, however, that cell becomes the top-left corner of the table style; any cells above or to the left of the selected one aren't affected.

Creating and editing new styles. Of course, you're not limited to using just GoLive's built-in styles; one big advantage of table styles is the ability to create your own. Start by building a table in the Layout Editor. The following elements can be stored in a style definition.

Figure 7-33
Applying a
table style

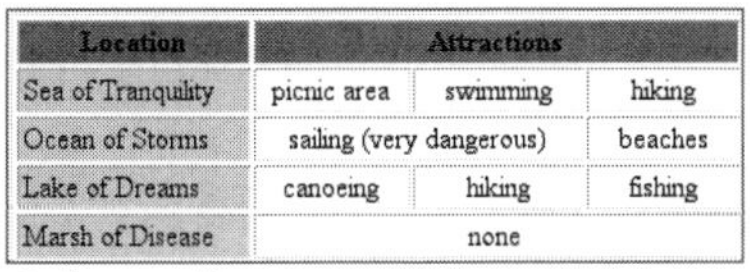

Before styling

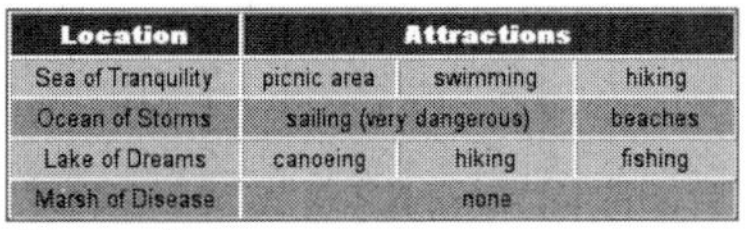

After styling

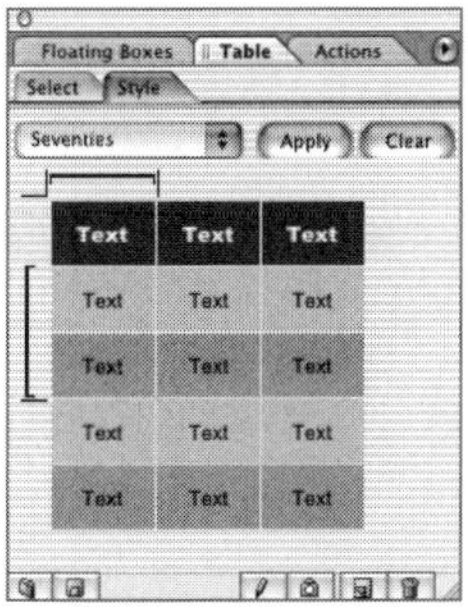

- **Cell padding**
- **Cell spacing**
- **Border size**
- **Cell, row, and table color**
- **Font face**
- **Font size**
- **Type style (bold, italic, etc.)**
- **Text structure (strong, quotation, etc.)**
- **Text color**

Once your table appears the way you like, go to the Style tab of the Table palette and click the New Table Style button, which creates a style based on the table you have selected (Figure 7-34, next page). (If no cell or table is selected, the New Table Style button makes a copy of the style listed in the popup menu.) To change the style's settings, simply edit the table in the Layout Editor, then click the Capture Table Style button. There are also buttons for renaming and deleting styles.

Tip: Popout Menu Styles

The table styles commands are also available in the Table palette's popout menu. But personally, we prefer the buttons (it is said that we like to push other people's buttons, after all).

The blue bars appearing above and to the left of the style preview on the Table palette control how cell styles repeat throughout the table. Cells falling in the range of the bars repeat horizontally or vertically, depending on the bar (see Figure 7-35). To change the definitions, click and drag the edge of a bar: the portions appearing within the thicker blue bars are the repeated portions.

Figure 7-34
Creating a new
table style

New Style button

Figure 7-35
Changing the
way a style
repeats

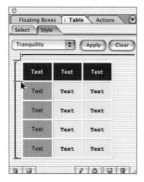

Tip: Define Styles with Small Tables

When you're creating a new style, GoLive uses the entire table as reference; the thin blue lines along the top and left-side edges of the table proxy indicate the original size of the table. (If you can't see the thin blue lines, resize the Table palette as large as you can.) If you base your style on a large table, the style you expect may only be repeated for a few rows or columns, after which the original style goes into effect. Creating a new style based on a smaller table ensures a consistent pattern.

Tip: Style Power

Are you switching to a different table style, but a few cells refuse to change? Check the cell styles in your style definition. When you apply styles, cell attributes overpower row attributes. If the new style specifies a row color of green, for example, but the existing style calls for a cell color of white, that lone cell remains white unless you change it by hand.

Tip: CSS Selectors Not Saved

The table styles feature grabs its definitions from table tag attributes, so if you're using CSS class selectors assigned to table elements to define characteristics like cell color, that information isn't saved in a table style definition.

Importing and exporting table styles. If you've spent time setting up several table styles, share them with your group by exporting them. Simply click the Export Table Style button in the Table palette and choose a destination for the file (Figure 7-36). This saves all your styles, including the GoLive defaults (unless you've deleted or changed them), into an XML document.

Figure 7-36
Exporting a
style

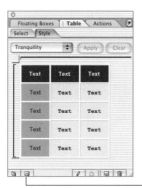

—— *Export Style button*

To import your styles on another machine, click the Import Table Style button and choose the file you created. Be careful: any styles that existed before importing will be erased in favor of the new set.

Tip: Restore Default Table Styles

We anticipate that nearly everyone will make this mistake at first: you bring up the Table palette's Style tab, then click the Capture button to create a new style from your table. Unfortunately, this changes the currently selected style (Gray, in most cases) instead of making a new style. Don't worry, there's an easy fix.

Click the Import Table Style button. Navigate to the folder where the GoLive application resides, open the Settings folder, then open the Styles folder and choose the tables.xml file.

Tip: Export Table Styles to GoLive 5

If some members of your group are still using GoLive 5, you can still share your table styles. Simply create the table style you want, and save the table in its own HTML file. Send that page to your coworkers, who can then open the page, click the table, and capture a new style based on yours.

Sorting Table Cells

Web tables have always been just for show: they can approximate the type of tables found in spreadsheets, databases, and some word processors, but once the table has been created, you might think you'd tediously have to copy and paste an enormous amount to get the order just right.

Fortunately, GoLive has a sort feature like the one in Excel and Word that makes it a snap to reorder rows by the contents of columns.

Click the Sort button at the bottom of the Table palette's Select tab to bring up the Sort Table dialog box (Figure 7-37). Choose whether to sort by rows or columns from the Sort popup menu near the bottom. Then, select which column or row will be the basis of the sort by choosing from the Sort By popup menu. The menu to the right specifies ascending order (1, 2, 3…x) or descending order (x…3, 2, 1). You can apply up to three search criteria using the Then by popup menus.

If you select the Sort Without Header options from the bottom popup menu, GoLive ignores the first row or column and applies the sort based on the remaining cells.

Turning Layout Grids into Tables

Although there's no built-in support for converting layout grids into tables, that doesn't mean it's impossible. Grids don't exist in HTML, which means GoLive is performing a clever hack to create a complex table at the source code level that responds according to its grid features.

Click a layout grid to select it, and uncheck the Visible checkboxes in the Layout Grid Inspector. Switch to the HTML Source Editor and locate the beginning of the grid, which looks something like this:

```
<table border="0" cellspacing="0"
cellpadding="0" cool gridx="16"
gridy="16" width="394"
height="305" bgcolor="#ffffcc">
```

Looks familiar, doesn't it? To turn the grid into a genuine table, remove the attribute "cool". When you switch back to the Layout Editor, you see a standard table, which you can edit and clean up using GoLive's table tools. It's not exactly beautiful, but it could mean a lot less work required to manipulate the information.

Once you've done this change, it's unlikely you can switch the table back to a grid without performing major surgery. Make sure to save the page (or back it up) before trying. Also, if you use any of the Strip Options to exclude GoLive-specific code when uploading or exporting files, those resulting pages can't be brought back into grid management either.

Figure 7-37
Sorting
table cells

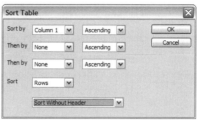

...brings up the Sort Table dialog box.

Clicking the Sort button...

To sort only a few rows or columns, first select them before hitting the Sort button. Or, you can always choose Sort Whole Table to apply a sort no matter what is currently selected.

For example, a table of college donors can be sorted to group all donors by their state of residence, then listed by the amount donated (see Figure 7-38).

Figure 7-38
Sorting
multiple rows
by multiple
criteria

Huge Moon Donors

Donor	Birthplace	Amount
Wally Schirra	New Jersey	$10,000
Neil Armstrong	Ohio	$60,000
Alan B. Shepard	New Hampshire	$30,000
John Glenn	Ohio	$80,000

Table before sorting

Huge Moon Donors

Donor	Birthplace	Amount
Alan B. Shepard	New Hampshire	$30,000
Wally Schirra	New Jersey	$10,000
Neil Armstrong	Ohio	$60,000
John Glenn	Ohio	$80,000

Table after sorting

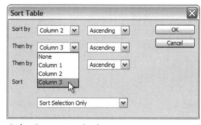

Selecting sort criteria

Tip: Don't Mix Symbols

GoLive is good about sorting, performing numerical and alphabetical sorts depending on the cells' contents, including those preceded by a currency symbol. However, it doesn't know how to handle mixed situations in which, say, you've included a dollar ($) and a euro (€). If you need to do more complicated sorts, you're better off doing them in a spreadsheet program before bringing them into GoLive (see next section).

Importing and Exporting Table Content

So far, we've been concentrating on building and editing tables from the ground up. Often, however, we need to build a table from preexisting data, such as a spreadsheet. Although it's possible to create a table and then type the values into the cells, GoLive's features are much more efficient.

The easiest method by far is to use Copy and Paste. In Excel, copy the desired cells. Switch to GoLive, create a blank table, and select a cell; the table's number of rows and columns don't have to match the number in the spreadsheet. Choose Paste from the Edit menu and watch GoLive fill out the table with all of your data in the right places (Figure 7-39).

Figure 7-39 Copying and Pasting table data

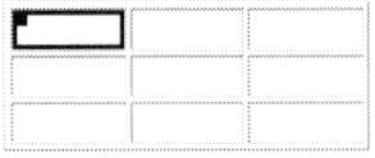

New table before pasting data

Location	Attractions		
Sea of Tranquility	picnic area	swimming	hiking
Ocean of Storms	sailing (very dangerous)		beaches
Lake of Dreams	canoeing	hiking	fishing
Marsh of Disease	none		
Bay of Rainbows	surfing	swimming	sailing
Lunar Alps	hiking	rock climbing	

The same table after pasting data

Another method is to use the Tab-Text Import button on the Table Inspector. GoLive reads and parses delimited text files, which simply means that each cell of spreadsheet information is separated by a specific character. You can import files delimited by tabs, spaces, semicolons, or commas into GoLive. If you haven't done so already, open your spreadsheet and save it as a text-only delimited file.

Tabular data almost always come from a spreadsheet program, but that doesn't mean you have to buy Microsoft Excel for this purpose. The delimited format can be created in any word processor or text editor, and can be easily exported from most database programs, like Microsoft Access and FileMaker Pro. What's important is that the data live in a text-only file.

Tip: Choosing the Right Delimiter

The point of a delimiter is to pick a character that doesn't get used for any other purpose in the file in question unless it's enclosed with two sets of quotation marks. The quotation marks denote that everything between them is data.

So if you use tabs, spaces, semicolons, and commas throughout your data, make sure to set up your output so quotation marks surround all cell data. (Some programs do this by default, like FileMaker Pro.)

We often use tabs as delimiters because most spreadsheet and database programs don't let you enter tab characters as data; we can be sure they're unique.

Now, switch to GoLive and create a new table. Don't worry about specifying the number of rows or columns; GoLive automatically generates the cells it needs. Select the table and click the Tab-Text Import button in the Table tab, or choose Import Tab-Delimited Text from the contextual menu (Figure 7-40). When prompted for the file, be sure to specify the type of delimiter from the Col. Separator popup menu before clicking OK or Open.

Figure 7-40
Importing
using the
contextual
menu

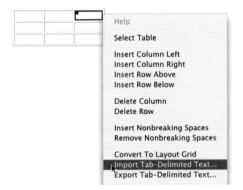

| Help |
| Select Table |
| Insert Column Left |
| Insert Column Right |
| Insert Row Above |
| Insert Row Below |
| Delete Column |
| Delete Row |
| Insert Nonbreaking Spaces |
| Remove Nonbreaking Spaces |
| Convert To Layout Grid |
| Import Tab–Delimited Text... |
| Export Tab–Delimited Text... |

Tip: Importing with a Cell Selected

It's quicker to select the table as a whole, which displays the Table tab in the Table Inspector, then click the Import Tab-Text button. However, the process also works if you have one or more cells in the table selected. Switch from the Cell tab to the Table tab and click the Import button; the incoming data automatically begins at the cell that was selected.

Tip: Don't Merge Cells Before Importing

GoLive's table import feature lets you start with a default 3-by-3 table and change its dimensions to accommodate the imported information. However, if you've merged cells within the table before importing, those cells remain merged, possibly throwing off the cell order of your incoming data.

Tip: Importing Into a Populated Table

If you want to merge two sets of tabular data into one table, you're better off using your spreadsheet or a word-processing program to paste the text of the second table after the first. You can import delimited data into a table that already contains data, but the results are less than desirable. GoLive starts filling the table from the upper-left cell, even if it's occupied. You don't actually lose your original data, but it is forced to coexist with the new information, resulting in cells containing both.

Importing into nested tables. Earlier in the chapter we mentioned that you could nest tables within tables, and you can do the same with nested tables based on imported data. After you build a table, simply create a new table within one of the parent table's cells and click the Import button on the Table tab.

Exporting table content. To pull tabular data out of GoLive as a tab-delimited file, select the table and click the Export button on the Table tab. You don't have the choice of which delimeter to use, but any spreadsheet or database program can easily open the file you create.

Applying Text Formatting to Multiple Cells

Since we can select multiple cells, it makes sense that we should be able to set formatting on those selected cells. Unfortunately, some attributes work across multiple selections while others don't. Table 7-3 lists how much control you have with more than one cell selected.

	Can Change	Cannot Change
Table 7-3 Multiple formatting hits and misses	Font color	List formatting
	Cell color	
	Font set	
	Cell alignment	
	No text wrap	
	Font style (bold, italic, etc.)	
	Header style	
	Remove font color	
	Nobreak style	

Tip: Apply Formatting to Cells

Most formatting is applied at the cell level, so if you want to change the text font throughout your table, you need to select all the cells and make the change, instead of selecting the table as a whole.

Tables as Structure

Web browsers were created to suit the user, who could specify his or her own fonts and sizes and expect that the text would wrap to fit any browser window size. Unfortunately, this had the side effect of driving some graphic designers completely insane, because they had such limited control over the visual presentation. From a graphic design standpoint, the original approach was akin to making every printed brochure a letter-size sheet of white paper with Courier text.

But when HTML tables appeared, designers realized they didn't have to be restricted to traditional tabular data. Instead, tables can provide the framework necessary to invite all sorts of design flexibility. We know designers who start every page by creating a table enclosing its contents. With a table as the structure of your page, you can specify columns or sidebars or special areas for navigation graphics.

Fixed Versus Percentage Measurements

If you know the dimensions of your design, you can specify fixed pixel widths to establish—and retain—the design's measurements, regardless of the size of the browser window. This enables you to control where images and other elements are placed. Instead of working on a sliding, unpredictable layout, you've created a framework which has predictable results.

Using tables doesn't mean you lose the ability to create a page that adapts to the viewer's screen, however. A fixed-width table that occupies the first 500 pixels of a window may look fine in most browsers, but can get lost amid the expanse of a window opened to its fullest on a large monitor. (Similarly, the right edge of your layout gets cut out of smaller windows.) In times like this, consider tailoring your design to use percentage widths instead; you still maintain control over where objects load, but the cells expand or contract to make the best use of the available space (see "Width and Height" earlier in the chapter).

Tip: Fill the Window

Make your tables fill an entire browser window using percentage width and height values. You can still use pixel measurements to constrain columns and rows within the table (such as a navigation bar that needs to remain 125 pixels wide), but the rest of the table expands to occupy the entire window.

Tip: Create Structural Templates

If you've created a design that relies on the same underlying table structure, or frequently-used structures like navigation bars, speed up your work by using the Library tab of the Objects palette or the site-specific Library tab in any Site window. Create a blank table with the dimensions you need (including any static elements such as logos, etc.), then drag it to the Library tab. When you create a new GoLive document, simply drag that table template to your page to start building its contents.

Tip: Stitching Together Split Images

If you're using a larger image that's been split into smaller ones, placing these smaller sections into a table ensures that they don't drift apart in some layouts. Create a table cell for each section, setting each cell's alignment so that the images get pushed together; for example, in a 2-by-2 table, the upper-left corner's horizontal alignment would be set to Right while its vertical alignment would be set to Bottom. Make sure that the cell padding, cell spacing, and border values are set to zero to remove spaces introduced by those attributes. (Programs that slice-and-dice for you, like Adobe ImageReady, Photoshop, or Macromedia Fireworks automatically create a table structure like this.)

Building Forms Using Tables

Forms are notoriously tricky to lay out on a page, since the size of text fields and other form elements vary widely among browsers and platforms. Building your form with table cells, however, imposes a structure that helps keep your forms visually consistent (see Figure 7-41).

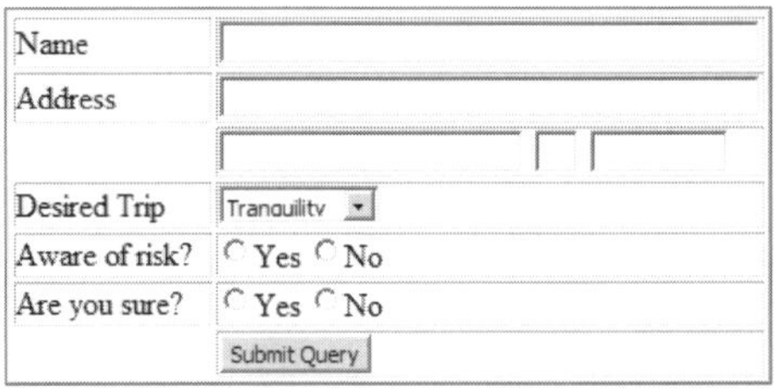

Figure 7-41
Using tables to
structure forms

Place item labels in the first cell in a row, and then put form elements like text fields or checkboxes into their own cells to the right on the same row. This lines up the left edges of all your fields, making the form easier to follow and enter data into.

Tip: Nest Table in Form Object

Forms in GoLive comprise a form object as a container holding the form elements. To properly let GoLive work with a form and to create the right underlying HTML, first drag a form object onto the page, and then put the table entirely inside it (see Figure 7-42). Any elements you place in the table are nested correctly inside the form.

Figure 7-42
Form embedded in a table

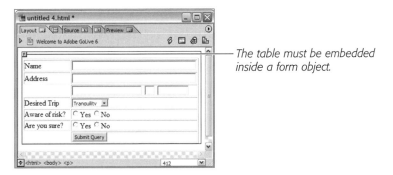

The table must be embedded inside a form object.

You can use cell-alignment settings to balance descriptive text naming a field or set of fields and the form-entry fields themselves. We often set vertical alignment to Middle to offset font size and automatic leading discrepancies, especially when placing checkboxes or radio buttons alongside text.

Converting Tables to Layout Grids

Perhaps you're using GoLive to edit an existing site with a table-based structure, or maybe you've decided that the extra elements your client wants added to a site would be better off created with one of GoLive's layout grids. Whatever the reason, you don't have to throw away your previous tables and start over.

Select a table, then click the Table to Layout Grid button (labeled Convert); or, select Convert to Layout Grid from the contextual menu or the Table submenu under the Special menu. The dimensions of the table change to a layout grid. Images and other objects in the table remain in the same places; cells containing text become layout textboxes (see Figure 7-43, next page). Unfortunately, GoLive offers no easy method of converting a grid back into a table. It's unfortunate because in the underlying HTML, grids are tables—just highly complicated ones. (For more on working with layout grids, see Chapter 8, *Layout Grids*.)

Figure 7-43
Table turned
into layout grid

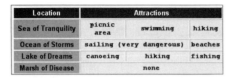

This simple form was turned into a layout grid, transforming each cell into a layout text box, each of which can hold any kind of HTML content, not just text.

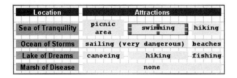

Ubiquitous Tables

Whether they're displaying complex tabular data or providing the skeletal structure of an entire page, tables have evolved into a tool that few designers can live without. It might take you a little time to learn the subtleties of creating and modifying tables in GoLive, especially to get the hang of selecting individual cells. But the time you save later is well worth suffering that initial burst of feature-shock.

CHAPTER 8
Layout Grids

From the dawn of time—1994—designers have had one ambition: to place an object precisely where they want it on a Web page. GoLive supports two major solutions to this goal, layout grids and floating boxes. However, each has its own set of drawbacks and considerations.

GoLive's layout grids are actually complex arrays of table cells carefully spaced and controlled so that they force objects to appear in specific positions based on the table formatting. Floating boxes, which are covered in more detail in Chapter 11, employ Cascading Style Sheets (CSS) to specify the absolute position of a block of HTML on a page (see Table 8-1).

Creating Layout Grids

Layout grids use a graph-paper metaphor for locating items on a page (see Figure 8-1). You can set a grid to rigidly lock all items dragged onto it to the defined grid lines, or you can disable that control for horizontal and/or vertical directions to freely drag objects around.

Figure 8-1
Text and objects on a layout grid

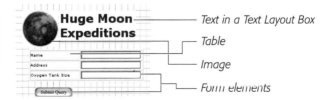

	Feature	Grids	Floating Boxes
Table 8-1 Grids versus floating boxes	HTML structure	Table cells and special tags	Standard CSS
	Browser support	Complexity requires 3.0 or higher browser	Any 4.0 and higher browser, including Opera
	Positioning units	In units as small as one pixel (only available measurement unit)	In any increment of any absolute units, such as whole pixels, fractions of an inch, etc.
	Arbitrary positioning anywhere on page	No, grids are inserted into normal HTML flow; objects on grids can be placed precisely	Yes, floating boxes can be positioned precisely anywhere on a page
	Animation	No	Yes, used with JavaScript as the basis of DHTML animation
	HTML beauty	Pretty dense, difficult to hand edit, proprietary GoLive tags	Compact and straightforward, but all coordinate-based, so still quite difficult to hand edit
	Overlapping objects	No, each grid is its own object on the page in the HTML flow	Yes, each floating box has its own layer setting which allows transparency and overlap between any number of boxes
	Contain the other	Grids can't contain floating boxes except inside Layout Text Boxes	Floating boxes can contain grids (as well as any HTML)
	What can be put on or in them	Every kind of HTML object except text, which requires a special Layout Text Box (which can hold floating boxes and other HTML, including other grids)	No limitations; like a mini-HTML page

Getting started couldn't be simpler. From the Basic tab of the Objects palette, drag the Layout Grid icon onto an HTML page (see Figure 8-2). GoLive inserts a 201-by-201 pixel grid with 16-pixels-square grid spacing. This also brings up the Layout Grid Inspector and adds layout controls to the Toolbar when the grid is clicked.

Figure 8-2
Dragging in a
layout grid

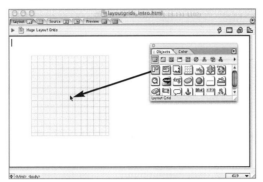

Editing the Grid

Grids have a set of properties including dimensions, color, and alignment that can be set or edited through dragging or through the Layout Grid Inspector.

Location. Like nearly everything else in HTML, layout grids are inline objects. You can move a grid to a new location within the text on a page by dragging or copying and pasting it, but you can't give it an arbitrary location.

Tip: Put the Grid Where You Want It

We hate to contradict ourselves like this, but in reality you can specify an arbitrary location for a layout grid. However, it's not always a pretty sight. Create a floating box (which uses CSS to achieve absolute positioning), then place a layout grid inside the box. Chapter 10, *Floating Boxes*, explains more about using floating boxes.

Grid units. Grid units are preset at 16 pixels in both directions, but you can modify these through the Horizontal and Vertical fields in the Layout Grid Inspector. If you uncheck Snap for either or both directions, objects can be dragged to any spot on a grid regardless of the grid lines. Unchecking Visible

What's New in 6

Layout grids haven't received much work in GoLive 6, probably because they were greatly improved in GoLive 5. However, they weren't completely ignored. Grids and Layout Text Boxes can now display a background image, and you can now convert the grid to a table without manually editing the HTML code. Also, even though you could copy and paste text into a grid to create a Layout Text Box, GoLive 6 lets you specify a point where the box appears.

for either or both directions removes the grid lines display. Note that if the Snap box is checked for a direction, but the Visible box is not checked, objects will still snap to the invisible guides.

Resizing. The Layout Grid Inspector includes fields for changing the height and width of the grid, but often it's easier to drag the grid into shape using its resizing handles. To make them appear, click the edge of the grid (your mouse pointer adds a small gray box to indicate you've hit the spot). The grid always grows or shrinks on the right and bottom edges.

Holding down the Shift key while dragging keeps the grid proportionate. You can't resize a grid smaller than the object occupying the right or bottom edge.

Optimizing. When the grid is populated by other objects, clicking the Optimize button in the Layout Grid Inspector resizes the box to the farthest right and bottom edges of the objects (see Figure 8-3). To optimize only the grid's width, Shift-click the Optimize button; holding down Option (Mac) or Alt (Windows) when clicking Optimize affects just the grid's height.

Figure 8-3
Optimizing the
layout grid

After optimization

Before optimization

Alignment. Like an image, a grid can be aligned by default (to the uppermost and leftmost location available), to the left or right, or centered. Text and other objects wrap around the grid when the Align setting is set to Left or Right. When centered, the grid appears in the middle of the screen, with text and other surrounding objects appearing above and below it.

Background color. Drag a color swatch onto the Color field to set the background of the entire grid. Or, click the field once to enable its active color mode, so you can apply colors by clicking values in the Color palette's tabs.

Tip: Color My Table

Remember that a layout grid is actually a table, deep inside. If you set the background color via this option, you're using the Color attribute. You can define a CSS style and apply it, instead (see Figure 8-4).

Figure 8-4
Setting
background
via CSS style

Background image. A layout grid can also accommodate a background image. Check the Image box in the Layout Grid Inspector, then use the URL Getter to specify an image file. The image tiles to fill the size of the grid; however, you can ensure that the background appears only once by clicking the Use Image Size button (see Figure 8-5).

Figure 8-5
Setting
background via
CSS style

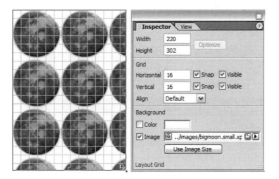

Tip: Use Image Size Disabled?

If the objects you've placed on your grid occupy a larger area than the size of your background image, the Use Image Size button is unavailable.

Grid Objects

Nearly any HTML object from the Objects palette can be dragged directly onto a layout grid. GoLive displays a bounding box of the item as you drag it around the grid, so you can see its size and to which grid lines it adheres if Snap is set for either direction. You can also drag image files from a Site window or the desktop, though the bounding box does not appear.

Tip: Stacking Multiple Objects

You can select and drag multiple objects from the desktop at once and drop them onto a layout grid. They arrive overlapped, and colored red to indicate a warning (see Figure 8-6). When you drag them to new locations, GoLive removes the warning. This only applies when dropping files from a Site window or the desktop; GoLive won't allow you to stack objects once they're on the grid.

Figure 8-6
Stacking multiple objects

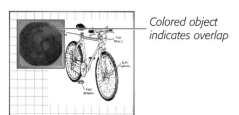

Colored object
indicates overlap

Layout Text Box

When adding text, you can't simply drag it in from any source. Instead, you create a Layout Text Box, which can contain any kind of HTML object itself, including layout grids and floating boxes.

Tip: Indecent Enclosure

You can nest a floating box with a layout grid inside a Layout Text Box inside a layout grid (see Figure 8-7). Only a higher power knows exactly how any given browser would react to this abomination, however.

Figure 8-7
Nesting layout grids inside floating boxes ad infinitum

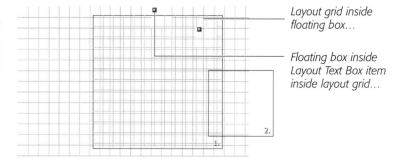

Layout grid inside
floating box...

Floating box inside
Layout Text Box item
inside layout grid...

Drag the Layout Text Box icon from the Basic tab of the Objects Palette to create a new 32-by-32 pixel box. Then, simply click to insert your cursor and begin typing. As you add more text, the box's height automatically increases (see Figure 8-8).

Figure 8-8
Typing in a
Layout Text Box

Use the handles along the Layout Text Box's border to resize the box. As with the grid, holding down Shift resizes proportionally. (If you don't see the resizing handles, click the box's border.)

GoLive is smart about text boxes: by default you can't resize the box to be smaller than its contents. To get around this limitation, check the Allow Content Overflow option in the Layout Text Box inspector to change the box's dimensions (see Figure 8-9). GoLive uses a small plus sign to indicate that a box contains overflow.

Figure 8-9
Allow Content
Overflow

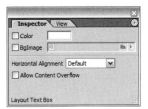 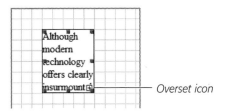

Overset icon

Also in the Layout Text Box inspector, choose a background color for the box using the Color field, or choose an image by marking the BgImage checkbox and specifying an image file. (Applying color to the text itself is the same as in the rest of the Layout Editor; see Chapter 5, *Text and Fonts*.) The text within can be aligned left, right, or center by choosing an option from the Horizontal Alignment popup menu in the Layout Text Box Inspector.

Behind the Grid

Layout grids are just tables at heart, which is why they can be displayed in any Web browser. However, to take advantage of their special editing features in GoLive, grids make use of non-standard HTML, which is ignored by browsers when displaying the page. Here's what the code used to define a grid looks like:

```
<TABLE width="201" border="0"
cellspacing="0" cellpadding="0"
bgcolor="#ffff99" cool gridx="16"
gridy="16" height="201" showgridx
showgridy usegridx usegridy>
```

By removing these attributes, you can end up with a normal—though more confusing—table. The following custom HTML tags control aspects of the grid.

- **Cool** identifies the table as a layout grid. We can only guess that the early GoLive engineers thought the feature was so great as to give it the moniker "cool."

- **Gridx** and **Gridy** both specify the grid size increments.

- **Usegridx** makes objects on the grid snap to the horizontal grid lines.

- **Usegridy** enables objects to snap to vertical grid lines.

- **Showgridx** displays the horizontal grid lines.

- **Showgridy** displays the vertical grid lines.

Other grid-specific tags appear throughout the rest of the table:

- **Xpos** indicates a Layout Text Box's origin from the left side of the grid.

- **Csheight** tells GoLive how tall the Layout Text Box appears, even if its text occupies part of that space.

- **Cntrlrow** appears at the end of the table's code, and indicates a row that's used as a guide for sizing the table's columns. A control column is also added to the right-most edge of the table, though it isn't identified as such.

- **Csgroup** identifies a group of objects; each object then gets its own Csgroup attribute to specify to which group it belongs.

The last non-standard HTML element that appears frequently throughout a grid is the Spacer tag, which GoLive uses to make sure empty table cells display properly in Netscape. See Chapter 5, *Text and Fonts*, for more on the Spacer tag.

Remember, HTML attributes that are not part of the underlying HTML specification may break certain corporate, accessibility, or standard validator systems that check on an HTML page's content. To bypass this situation, use the option to remove GoLive-specific tags when you upload, export, or publish a site found in the Strip Options dialog box (see Figure 8-10).

Figure 8-10
Strip
Options

Tip: Visual Text Buffers

Being able to fill a Layout Text Box with color makes it easy to display text as a separate entity from the grid or page background. Unfortunately, a Layout Text Box offers no way to add a margin to keep the text from butting up against the box's edge. Instead, create an empty Layout Text Box, sized to approximately the grid width, and run it alongside the main text box. It's not a pretty solution, but it works.

Working with Grid Objects

The whole point of layout grids is to put objects where you want them to appear, not where HTML tells you they belong. The grid gives you a canvas to do just that.

Moving. After an object is placed, it can be dragged around and positioned almost anywhere on a layout grid, provided that the object doesn't overlap other objects. If you drag it near the edge, the bounding box for the item stops previewing if its left or top edge goes too far to the right or down (see Figure 8-11).

You can also move an object using the keyboard by selecting it and pressing the arrow keys; it will move in grid increments if Snap is checked in the Layout Grid Inspector, or one-pixel increments if Snap is turned off. Pressing Control (Windows) or Option (Mac) plus an arrow key moves an object using the opposite method to the one that's selected.

Figure 8-11
Dragging an object off the layout grid

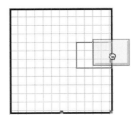
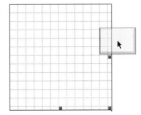

The bounding box displays only while the object is on the grid (left); the layout grid's highlight and the object's bounding box disappear when it leaves the grid (right).

To reposition an object numerically, use the Toolbar or Transform palette's Horizontal Position and Vertical Position fields (see Figure 8-12).

Figure 8-12
An object's coordinates in the Toolbar

Horizontal and Vertical Position fields

Tip: Snapped Off

Moving an object using the arrow keys with Snap off can result in odd behavior if you then turn Snap back on. Suppose you moved your Layout Text Box three pixels to the right and three pixels down with Snap off. When you re-enable Snap and use the arrow keys again, the box doesn't jump back to the layout grid's visible lines, as one might expect, but instead moves the box according to the size of the horizontal and vertical grid settings in the Layout Grid Inspector—16 pixels is the default increment (see Figure 8-13). So, the Snap setting is really just snapping to a pixel value, instead of the grid lines you see.

Figure 8-13
Grid increments and snap

With Snap turned off, the object is moved off the grid increment.

With Snap back on, a right arrow press moves the object a whole grid increment.

Resizing. Objects on a layout grid can be resized by grabbing their control handles and dragging (see Figure 8-14). You can also enter values into the Width and Height fields in the Toolbar and the Transform palette.

Objects can also be resized using the keyboard. Hold the Shift key and press an arrow key to resize by a grid increment; add Control (Windows) or Option (Mac) to modify in pixel increments. If Snap is disabled, the results are reversed: pressing Shift-arrow key resizes in pixel increments, while Control- or Option-Shift-arrow key modifies in grid increments.

Figure 8-14
Resizing an object in a layout grid

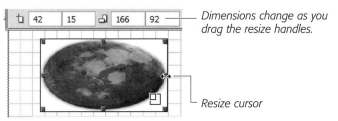

Dimensions change as you drag the resize handles.

Resize cursor

Aligning. With two or more objects selected, you can use the alignment features in the Toolbar or in the Align palette (see Figure 8-15).

Tip: Align Design

All the features described here work identically with objects in the Design tab of a diagram window.

Figure 8-15
Alignment
options

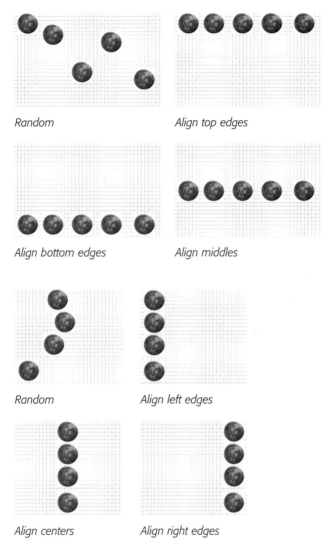

Random

Align top edges

Align bottom edges

Align middles

Random

Align left edges

Align centers

Align right edges

The horizontal and vertical alignment buttons in the toolbar use the layout grid as a base, so clicking the Align Top button, for example, shifts the selected objects as a group and aligns the highest object with the top of the layout grid. These are the same buttons labeled Align to Parent on the Align palette. To align objects with each other, use that palette's Align Objects buttons (see Figure 8-16, next page).

Figure 8-16
Align to Parent
versus Align
Objects

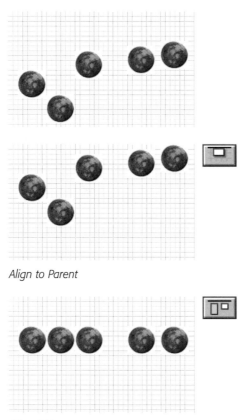

Align to Parent

Align Objects

Distributing. With three or more objects selected, the Distribute Objects and Distribute Spacing portions of the Align palette provide options for scattering or reshuffling the objects in relation to each other (see Figure 8-17).

Tip: Align Your Thinking with GoLive

Like a chess champion, GoLive tries to stay a few moves ahead of you to antici-pate your actions. Depending on the positions of the objects you've selected, only the alignment and distribution buttons that would work successfully are active. If you think you're in the clear but GoLive won't let you perform an align-ment or distribution, double-check that a piece of an object isn't jutting into an-other item's horizontal or vertical space.

Grouping. To work with multiple objects as a united whole, click the Group button in the Toolbar or on the Transform palette (see Figure 8-18). The

Figure 8-17
Distribute

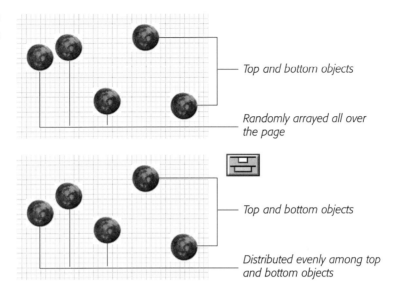

— Top and bottom objects

— Randomly arrayed all over the page

— Top and bottom objects

— Distributed evenly among top and bottom objects

Group Inspector includes either a Protection button marked with a lock icon (Mac), or a checkbox labeled Group is locked (Windows). When the lock is active, clicking an object within a group selects the entire group. When the lock is off, you can select individual items—though you can't move or resize them while they're part of the group.

Select the group and click the Ungroup button on the Toolbar to turn them back into individual objects.

Figure 8-18
Grouped
objects

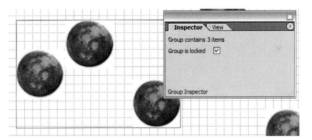

Converting Layout Grids to Tables

Since layout grids are tables at heart, GoLive 6 offers the capability to easily convert a grid to a table, just as you can convert a table to a layout grid (see Chapter 5, *Tables*). With your layout grid selected, choose Layout Grid to Table from the Special menu.

Tip: No Conversion Option?

If you don't see Layout Grid to Table in the Special menu, don't fret. Instead, open GoLive's preferences and click the Modules option in the left column. In the right portion of the window, scroll down to the Extend Scripts folder, and expand it. Mark the LayoutGrid checkbox, then click OK to exit the preferences dialog box. Quit the program and run GoLive again, and the Layout Grid to Table option should now be available.

A Convert dialog box appears with two options. Marking Strip Control Row and Column removes the one-pixel row and column that GoLive uses to make sure the grid is displayed properly; we like this option, because those extra pixels of width and height can knock an otherwise tight design out of whack.

If you uncheck that box, the Replace Spacers by Image option becomes active; since layout grids use the Netscape-invented Spacer tag to fill otherwise blank table cells, the table may not display properly. Instead, use the URL Getter here to specify a spacer.gif image (see Chapter 5, *Images*, for more on spacer GIFs) as a substitute. Clicking OK then converts the grid to a normal table.

You Control the Vertical, You Control the Horizontal

Designers want more control over their Web designs, and layout grids offer some means of control. Although they're not a perfect implementation, they can be great for mocking up quick design ideas or simple layouts which contain frequently changed elements.

CHAPTER 9
Frames

In the physical world, windows serve a specific purpose: the clear glass allows us to enjoy the sunshine and look outside without actually having to go out there (an important distinction if you've ever lived in a sunny, cold, climate). The window's frame usually acts as a border for the stuff that's happening outside—the window's "content." You can change the size and shape of the window, but the content remains the same.

Now picture a church or cathedral—preferably something gothic, European. There are lots of windows, all made of glass, but the multicolored panes stretching to the ceiling take on a completely different purpose. Each window is something to look at, not through, and its different panes tell their own stories—content spanning the ages.

In the digital world, we usually employ one window through which to view a section of the Internet. That Web browser window frequently changes shape and position on our screens, and occasionally joins other similar browser windows when we're "multitasking." But essentially, the window is a single pane of clear glass looking outside at the Web.

At least it was, until Netscape introduced the concept of frames. Like the stained-glass cathedral windows, frames allow you to split a browser window into multiple sections. They can simultaneously display different parts of the Web, different parts of your site, or even act as graphical interface elements.

Frames versus Frame Sets

Looking at a framed page in a Web browser, it's easy to see what's happening on the surface: within your browser's window, the separate panes display different pieces of information, including other Web sites that weren't necessarily built with frames in mind (see Figure 9-1). The structure beneath the surface, though, can be a bit confusing at first, especially if you're accustomed to building non-framed Web pages (see Figure 9-2).

Figure 9-1
Framed page
in browser

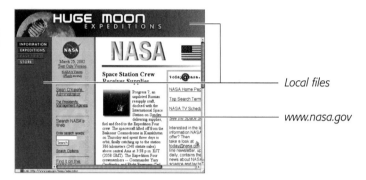

Local files

www.nasa.gov

Figure 9-2
GoLive's Frame
Editor

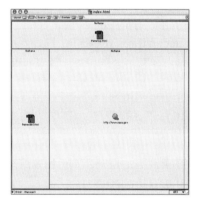

The same page as above, viewed in the Frame Editor

What's New in 6

At this point, frames are a well-established aspect of HTML, so most of the frame features in GoLive 6 mirror GoLive 5, with a few exceptions. For example, moving a frame within your layout requires that you Shift-drag it into place, instead of simply dragging.

Also, Adobe's engineers have added something to help make the process of creating frame sets a little easier: the Frame Set Inspector now includes Orientation controls. If you want to take a frame set whose frames are side-by-side and turn them into a set of frames stacked top-to-bottom, a simple click makes the change. This can be a time saver when you're experimenting with layouts and the look of your framed pages.

Frame Set. To create a framed collection of pages, first create an HTML document with one or more frame sets: HTML code that contains the geometry of the frames in the browser window, including their absolute locations and dimensions of each frame. Each frame set references individual HTML files that make up the contents of the framed page. Frame sets also contain any properties specific to each frame, such as its border width and border color.

In GoLive, the document you create and save in the Frame Editor contains one or more frame sets. In fact, when GoLive creates a frame set that contains both horizontal and vertical frames, it's actually placing a pair of nested frame sets (see "Creating Nested Frame Sets" later in this chapter for more information).

Frame. The window panes created by the frame set are the frames themselves, and contain the external HTML files referenced by the frame set. In GoLive, you can specify each frame's size and name, whether or not its scrollbars are visible, and whether the user can resize the frame borders manually by dragging them. These attributes are all defined within the frame set file, not the HTML files that make up the frames' contents (see "Creating Frames," below, to configure these settings). With Web frames, you're pointing at separate HTML files that comprise the frame's content. At first, this may seem like an awkward solution, what with having to pull together several files to create one Web page, but it's clean and it works.

Tip: Self-Reference Framing

If you start building a normal page and realize later that it should be a framed page instead, start over from scratch. In a moment of ineptitude, Jeff once switched to the Frame Editor, added a frame set, then referenced the same file as the source of one of the frames. Crashing ensued.

Creating Frames

GoLive's frame-creation tools make setting up frames no more difficult than the steps we've covered so far to build basic pages.

Building and Populating a Frame Set

GoLive includes 16 preset frame set layouts, plus one Frame icon for adding individual frames to existing frame sets. To create a new frame set, click the Frame Editor tab in the document window, choose a layout icon from the

Frames tab of the Objects palette, then drag it to the Frame Editor (see Figure 9-3). Don't worry if the layout doesn't initially reflect the structure you're trying to build; you can easily manipulate the frames later.

Tip: Single Frame Icon versus Other Frame Set Icons

Think of the single Frame icon, in the upper-left corner, as a paintbrush included in a set of paint-by-numbers pages: you can start by coloring the numbered regions, but the paintbrush gives you the freedom to paint wherever you want. While the Frame Set icons easily create prefabricated framed layouts, the single Frame icon is used to create individual frames in the Frame Editor; wherever you drop it on a framed page, GoLive automatically edits frame sets to accommodate the new frame.

Keep Your Framesets and Frames Separate

Indulge us if we repeat an important point: the contents of a Web page can be displayed within a frame, but the Web page must be a separate entity from the frameset. Fortunately (or unfortunately, if you don't like crashing programs), a self-reference problem in GoLive illustrates this point beautifully.

Suppose you've been working on a page in GoLive's Layout Editor, and realize midway into editing it that the page would work better in frames.

The *right* thing to do would be to save and close the existing file, create a new GoLive document, and start over by building your frameset. The current file would then be referenced by this new frameset.

However, the logical, intuitive action—if you hadn't worked much with frames in GoLive—would be to click on the Frame Editor, drag over a frame icon, and start creating a frameset.

The next logical act would be to reference the page you were just working on in the Layout Editor by using Point & Shoot to select it from the Site window's Files tab, as the source of one of the frames.

If you now were to switch to Frame Preview, you'd instigate a self-referencing loop that can't be broken without forcibly quitting GoLive (press Command-Option-Esc on the Mac and click Force Quit); in Windows, it's sometimes possible to click on another view to break out of the loop, though you may have to resort to hitting Control-Alt-Delete to end the task...ouch!

GoLive is helpful in one important respect in this situation: the content you added in the Layout Editor is still there, surrounded by Noframe tags which separate it from the frameset-specific code. This way, people using Web browsers that can't (or won't) display frames can still see the material you've created in the Layout Editor. See "Using the Noframe Version of a Frameset," later in this chapter.

Remember: create framed pages from scratch, not by starting in the Layout Editor and switching to the Frame Editor.

Figure 9-3
Dragging
frame layout
icons

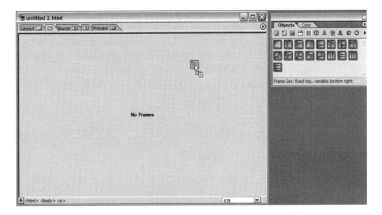

New in 6: Single Frame Icon Can't Create Frame Sets

In GoLive 5, you could drag the single Frame icon to a blank Frame Editor and automatically create a new frame set. However, GoLive 6 doesn't allow this, because single-frame pages don't work reliably in Netscape prior to version 6.

Clicking anywhere within a frame selects that frame and displays the Frame Inspector, which controls settings for individual frames. To select a frame set instead, click a border separating the frames. Alternately, you can bring up the contextual menu and choose Select Frame Set from the Frameset submenu. This displays the Frame Set Inspector, which handles global frame options and values.

Do You Really Need Frames?

Before you start going frame-happy, determine if you really need to use frames on your site. Most of the frame examples we've seen while cruising the Web really don't require frames; a much simpler Web page can do just as well. Frames tend to introduce a layer of complexity to a site that, in many cases, is completely unnecessary. This isn't to say that frames should be avoided; we just don't like seeing people struggle through unnecessary amounts of work when a simpler solution is at hand.

One test for whether or not to use frames is to think about how complex the site's or section's navigation would be if it were flat pages: would you need to build new and extensive navigations bars or path indicators? Maybe using frames is a good idea, then.

Another good use of frames is linking to external sites. A simple frame set with a thin left column full of URLs and a fat right frame in which the destination page appears can save a user lots of time spent clicking the Back button. Use the site's content and your own design sense to determine if frames are appropriate.

Tip: Frame Set or Empty GoLive Document?

If you view an existing HTML file in GoLive through the Layout Editor and discover no content on the page, don't be alarmed. It could be just a frame set. To make a quick determination, look at the document's Page icon (see Figure 9-4). A frame set file displays a frame icon; regular HTML files feature a regular page icon design with horizontal lines.

Figure 9-4
Two flavors of
the Page icon

Page icon as seen in the Layout Editor   Page icon indicating a framed page

Tip: Identifying the Frame Set Icons

The Frame Set icons have been designed to easily depict the relative size and frame border placements you're likely to end up with when you drag them into the Frame Editor. However, the last four icons seem redundant; the only differences among the two vertical frames and the two horizontal frames are their color schemes. Or are they? Figure 9-5 illustrates what you should expect when you drag them to your document.

Figure 9-5
Identifying
the four
"redundant"
frame icons

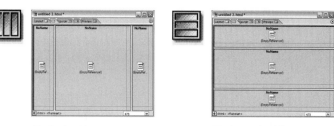

Vertical, wide center   Horizontal, wide center

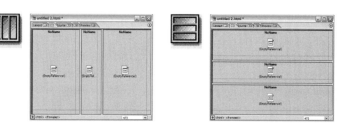

Vertical, narrow center   Horizontal, narrow center

New in 6: Descriptions

GoLive 6 includes a brief description in the Objects palette when you roll over an icon. These summaries describe which frames have fixed widths and which have variable widths.

Adding and deleting frames. If you want to create a framed page with a different look or a different number of frames than the prefabricated icons in the Frames tab of the Objects palette, drag the single Frame icon to the location you want to insert a new frame.

Dragging this icon onto an existing horizontal frame usually splits it into two vertical frames. Likewise, dragging it onto a vertical frame usually splits it into two horizontal ones (see Figure 9-6).

Figure 9-6
Adding frames
with the single
Frame icon

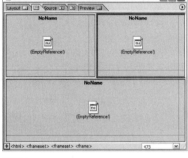

 Original frameset layout dragged in from the Palette…

 …and after adding single frame icon to top frame

If you make too many new frames, delete them one by one by clicking within each frame's borders to select it, and then pressing the Delete key. You can't select multiple frames and delete them at once.

Creating Nested Frame Sets

Like tables, frame sets can be nested within frames. As mentioned earlier, when GoLive creates a frame set that contains both horizontal and vertical frames, it's actually creating a pair of nested frame sets (see Figure 9-7). Simply drag a new Frame Set icon from the Objects palette into an existing frame. The existing frame doesn't act as a container, the way a table cell holds a nested table; instead, the frame resizes to accommodate the new incoming frame set. For example, suppose you have a frame set containing two horizontal frames. If you drag one of the two-frame Frame Set icons from the palette, you end up with four separate frames, not three as you'd expect with tables. You can select a nested frame set by clicking one of its frame borders; a dark outline indicates the current selection. To select a nested frame set's enclosing frame set, choose Select Parent Frameset from the contextual menu.

Figure 9-7
Nested frame
sets

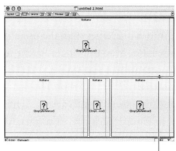 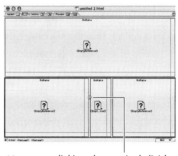

Clicking the horizontal divider
highlights the page's master frame
set, indicated by a bold box
surrounding the frame set.

However, clicking the vertical divider
reveals that the bottom panes belong
to their own frame set, which is
nested within the master frame set.

Using the Noframe Version of a Frame Set

Frames aren't for everyone nor everyone's browsers. Some browsers have the option to not view frames, while truly ancient browsers don't recognize frame coding at all. Text-based browsers and browsers used by people with accessibility issues (sight impaired, for instance) may not handle frames, either. Users in these situations typically would see a blank page when encountering a frame set, and such pages may not conform to necessary guidelines when creating pages for government or non-profit organizations.

Fortunately, GoLive automatically adds the simple Noframe tag to every framed document. With Noframe in the HTML, the browsers mentioned above ignore the frame set code and display the content included within the Body tags.

Use the Layout Editor to build the Noframe page, just as you would a normal document, without worrying about it interfering with your frames (see Figure 9-8). To preview the page in GoLive for Macintosh, switch to the Layout Preview.

Figure 9-8
Noframe page

People who
can't view
frames see the
Noframe page,
which you build
in GoLive's
Layout Editor.

If you're running the Windows version, you can't preview the Noframe page because Windows uses an embedded version of Microsoft Internet Explorer to preview pages. Internet Explorer supports frames, which is why

Adobe doesn't provide a non-framed preview tab. You just have to rely on the Layout Editor's view as the preview of your Noframe content.

In most cases you can add a line or two of text explaining that the viewer has happened upon a framed page. But you can also build a full page that echoes the contents of the frames and leads the user either to the pages that load within the frames (see below), or to alternate pages set up specifically for folks who can't or won't view frames. This way, your pages' content is available to everyone in one form or another.

Tip: Frames and Search Engines

Frames can often confuse search engines, because the content of your frame set file doesn't actually include the content of the framed page. If you've put a lot of time and effort into including descriptive Meta tags in your files, your work may be ignored by search engine robots which look only at the frame set information. So, be sure to put your Meta tag information in the frame set file as well.

Specifying the Contents of a Frame

With a basic frame set built, it's time to populate the frames within it. There are four methods for linking frames in a framed page to HTML files (see Figure 9-9).

Drag and drop existing files. From either the Desktop or an open Site window, drag an HTML file's icon to the desired frame. You can also grab the Page icon from an open document and drop it onto a frame.

Point & Shoot. Here's another area where GoLive's Point & Shoot tool comes in handy. With your mouse pointer placed anywhere within a frame, hold down the Command key (Mac) or Alt key (Windows) and drag from the frame to the file you want to use in the Files tab of the Site window. You can also "shoot" at the Page icon of an open file. The Frame Inspector's Fetch URL button works too.

Tip: Point & Shoot for Anchored Links

You can display a specific section of an HTML file, other than its beginning, within a frame. With the destination page open, use Point & Shoot from your frame and aim for an anchor within that page. Similarly, you can direct your cursor to an anchored link within a file being displayed in the Site window (indicated by a gray anchor icon beside the link). If an anchor doesn't currently exist in the destination page, using Point & Shoot will create a new anchor in an open file at the point where you release the mouse button.

Figure 9-9
Methods of
populating
frames

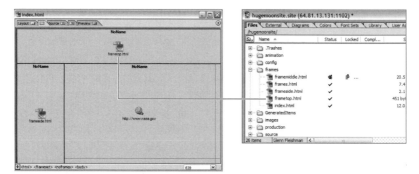

Point & Shoot from a frame to the Site window…

*…drag and drop a file from the
Site window…*

*…or type the filename in the
Frame Inspector's URL field.*

Direct entry. When a frame is selected, type the path name of the frame's
source file into the Frame Inspector's URL Getter, or click the Browse button
to search for the file. On the Mac, Option-clicking the Browse button brings
up the Edit URL dialog box where you can see more text as you type; under
Windows, right-click the Browse button and select Edit Link. This path can be
a pointer to a file on your hard disk, or a page that exists elsewhere on the
Web, in which case a globe icon appears within the frame.

Link menu. The Link popup menu that appears as part of every URL Getter
has a partial list of internal pages and external URLs, typically representing
the most recently added or used items. You can select a page or link from this
menu as well.

Previewing Framed Content
The Frame Editor makes it easy to see which files appear in each frame, but
displaying just the file icons is contrary to the whole idea of creating Web
pages visually. Two options are available for seeing what your frame set looks
like in a real browser.

Frame Preview and Preview windows. If you're running the Macintosh version of GoLive, click the Frame Preview tab in the Document window to get a fairly accurate representation of what the framed page will look like in a Web browser (see Figure 9-10).

The Windows version uses only one Preview window. If the document contains frame sets, the frames are previewed there. On the Mac, only local files are displayed, so any external URLs referenced in the Frame Inspector's URL field remain blank, even if you have an active Internet connection; GoLive for Windows doesn't have this limitation. You cannot edit the frames in the Frame Preview window.

Figure 9-10
Previewing a
framed page

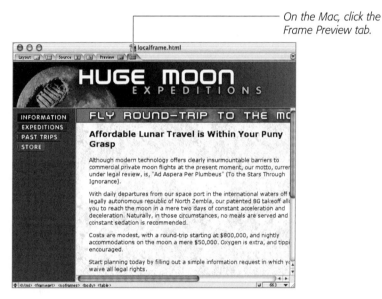

On the Mac, click the
Frame Preview tab.

The Mystery of the Macintosh GoLive Preview Set

The Frame and Frame Set Inspectors contain a bit of mystery; they're both full of buttons that appear to duplicate other features. But the choice to use VCR-style buttons stumps us.

In the Frame Inspector, clicking the Preview Frame button causes it to appear "pressed" while previewing is active. In the Frame Set Inspector, however, the same functionality requires two buttons: Preview Set, which resem-

bles a "play" button, and Stop Preview, which looks like a "stop" button. Neither button appears pressed when active.

Hopefully, consistency and simplicity will improve in a future version. (We first noted this oddity in the first edition of the book, covering GoLive 4, and remain perplexed as to why it has lived on through versions 5 and 6. If it kinda sorta works, don't fix it, we assume.)

Download Preview

GoLive can preview external URLs inside of frame sets via the Download item on the contextual menu for an appropriate frame. Selecting Download triggers GoLive's Download Page feature (see Chapter 2, *Layout*), which creates a copy of that Web page on your hard disk.

Keep in mind that the file becomes part of your site, as if you had created it—images and all. If you specify a page that has the same name as one of your existing pages (which includes pointing at a root URL—like http://www.realworldgolive.com/—which GoLive automatically renames index.html), the program asks if you want to replace it.

Frame set and frame previews in the Frame Editor (Macintosh only). As you're working in the Frame Editor, you can opt to display the contents of the entire frame set, or just individual frames, to get an idea of how the frames interact with one another. You can't edit the referenced HTML files directly, but previewing them helps to establish the overall look of the frame set.

Click a frame border to bring up the Frame Set Inspector, then click the Preview Set button. Each frame containing a local file displays the page's contents. Clicking the Stop Preview button reverts back to the default file icon view (see Figure 9-11). To view the contents of selected frames, select a frame and click the Preview Frame button on the Frame Inspector. Click the button again to stop previewing.

Figure 9-11
Previewing individual frames

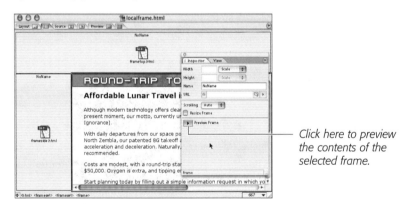

Click here to preview the contents of the selected frame.

Editing Frames

Real-world objects only go so far when used as computer-interface metaphors, and this is where the idea of the stained-glass window begins to break. Unlike solid windows made of glass and lead, frame sets feature the ability to move panes around easily, allow users to stretch their dimensions, load information in specific frames, and more.

Editing the contents of a frame. Rare is the occasion when all the HTML files you place into frames are in perfect shape. Invariably, something must change; when it does, simply double-click the frame to open its associated HTML file in a new window. GoLive adds a nice touch to this action: the new window appears the same size as your frame, in roughly the same location. You can open all your frame content files this way and work on them as if they were in a virtual frame set (see Figure 9-12).

Figure 9-12
Opening frames into individual windows

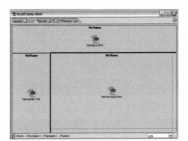
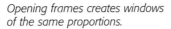

Opening frames creates windows of the same proportions.

Moving and Resizing Frames

Moving frames and frame sets is fairly intuitive; click within a frame to select it, then Shift-drag the selection to where you would like the frame to appear. However, you can only move individual frames within their parent frame sets. If you want a frame to appear in a separate nested frame set, use the single Frame icon to add a new frame where you'd like to move an existing one, make sure it's pointing to the same HTML source file, then delete the old frame (see Figure 9-13). To move an entire frame set, Shift-click and drag the frame set's border.

Resizing a frame is also easy, provided you're aware of how GoLive handles the settings that regulate frame size. When you add to an existing frame set by dragging the single Frame icon from the Frames palette, the Width or Height attributes in the Frame Inspector are set to Scale, which simply balances the size automatically with other frames in its row or column. In this case, although you can grab the divider and drag a ghosted version of it, the size won't actually change.

Figure 9-13
"Moving" a
frame into
another
frame set

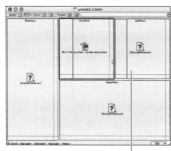

We want to move the MoonFull
frame into the left column frame
set, but MoonFull only moves
within its own frame set.

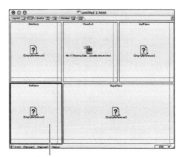

Use the single Frame icon from
the Objects palette to create a
new frame within the left column
frame set.

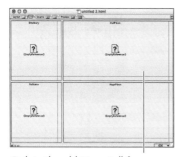

Delete the old MoonFull frame.

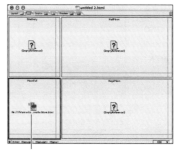

Rename the new frame to
MoonFull and set its source to
the original HTML file.

To make the size change permanent, you must first set the Width or Height options either to Pixels or Percent, depending on whether you want to set the sizes in absolute or relative terms. You can then either drag the frame border to set the size, or you can enter values directly into the fields. Switching back to Scale re-balances the frames.

If you build your frame set by dragging a prefab Frame Set icon from the Frames menu, you can just drag the borders to resize the frames, because at least one frame's Width or Height attribute is set to either Pixels or Percent.

Tip: Awkward Inspector Display When Resizing

To resize a frame, you need to click the frame's border. To select a frame set, you need to click the frame's border. Spot any similarities? Unlike resizing table cells, you can't resize a frame and view its exact pixel or percentage dimensions as you drag its border, because the Frame Set Inspector appears in place of the Frame Inspector as soon as you release the mouse button. So, if you're shooting for a specific width or height for your frame, it's better to enter that value in the Frame Inspector's Width or Height field.

Tip: Balancing the Scales

Web browsers like balance, because it means they don't have to work as hard to interpret the dimensions of a page. If you specify a frame's height or width in pixels or percentages, make sure at least one more frame in that row or column has its size set to Scale to avoid any potential browser problems.

Changing frame set orientation. GoLive 6 introduces a quickie method of rearranging your frames: the Orientation controls in the Frame Set Inspector (Figure 9-14). Select a frame set in the Frame Editor to see which orientation is currently active (either Horizontal or Vertical), and click the other radio button to change the frames' orientation. Before this simple little control, we had to delete frames and create new ones to achieve the same task.

Tip: Horizontal or Vertical?

When we look at two frames placed side by side, our first inclination is to declare them vertical, because the frames are tall and skinny. But according to GoLive's Orientation controls, we're wrong. The frame set is actually horizontal, because the frames appear side by side, like two rooms on the ground level of a building. When a frame set is vertical, the frames are stacked on top of each other.

Figure 9-14
"Moving" a frame into another frameset

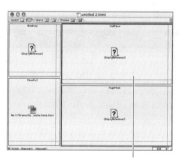
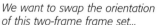

We want to swap the orientation of this two-frame frame set...

...although GoLive calls their orientation Vertical.

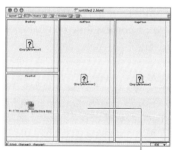

Clicking Horizontal in the Frame Set Inspector changes the orientation.

The third option, Matrix, deals primarily with your frames' appearance, rather than their structure. With Matrix selected, change the values in the Rows and Columns fields to create more space in the Layout Editor for more frames (see Figure 9-15). This automatically resizes the existing frames, but doesn't add any new frames in the newly-created space.

Figure 9-15
Previewing
individual
frames

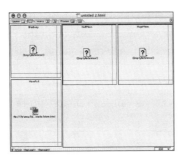

*Selecting Matrix and setting
Rows and Columns to 2
inserts extra space for more
frames at the bottom.*

You can also change the orientation method from the contextual menu: with the frame set selected, choose Set Horizontal/Vertical/Matrix Orientation (depending on which options are available); if just a frame is selected, bring up the contextual menu and choose a setting from the Frameset submenu.

Tip: Orientation Bug

For some reason, the Rows and Columns fields are activated when Horizontal or Vertical are selected. However, changing the values does nothing—it only applies when Matrix is selected. We suspect this is a simple oversight that will be corrected at some point. Remember, there is no spoon.

Controlling users' resizing options. Not all of the frame settings are intended to control the page from the designer's side. A unique feature of frames is the ability for users to resize their frames within Web browsers. Checking the Resize Frame box in the Frame Inspector gives users this option, and puts a small indented circle in the middle of the frame's border (see Figure 9-16). Since GoLive assumes that you want absolute control over your frame sizes, this option is turned off by default.

Tip: Making the Resize Frame Option Stick

You may have to turn on the Resize Frame option on both frames that share the resizable border in order to make it work. If one frame has Resize Frame turned on, but the other frame has it off, your users won't be able to move the border.

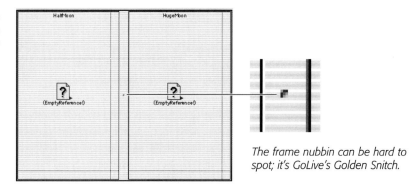

Figure 9-16
Resizable
frame indicator

The frame nubbin can be hard to spot; it's GoLive's Golden Snitch.

You can also control whether or not a frame's scrollbars are displayed in the browser. If the contents of the frame exceed the size of the window, browsers automatically show horizontal or vertical scrollbars. But you can force them to remain hidden by setting Scrolling to No, in which case the dotted-line scrollbar placeholders disappear. Similarly, choosing Yes draws scrollbars (even if they're inactive) every time, and the placeholders appear as solid lines. Since scrollbars in most browsers tend to take up a lot of space, especially in smaller frames, this feature can be useful for controlling a frame's appearance as well as its functionality. The Auto setting leaves the decision to draw the bars to the browser (see Figure 9-17).

The resizing and scrollbar options are also available from the contextual menu when a frame is selected.

Figure 9-17
Controlling
scroll bar
appearance
and seamless
frames

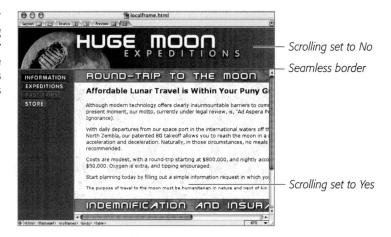

— Scrolling set to No

— Seamless border

— Scrolling set to Yes

Frame Borders

Frame borders can be part of how you navigate or interpret a page, and they can be modified in a few ways to control their effect and display. Click a border to bring up the Frame Set Inspector, where you can change the following options.

BorderSize. GoLive assigns borders with a default thickness of six pixels—big enough to grab and manipulate, but not so large they become obnoxious. Checking the BorderSize box lets you enter a pixel size to change the border's thickness. Often, designers set frame borders to zero so that the page doesn't blatantly look like it's been split into frames (see Figure 9-17, above). One downside is that zero-pixel borders can't be dragged to resize frames in most browsers, even if the Resize Frame box is checked.

BorderColor. If a border's size is set larger than zero, you can apply a color to it. Check the BorderColor box, then drag a swatch from the Color palette to its color field. Unlike table colors, where dropping a swatch onto a color field automatically checks the Color box, borders require that you first check BorderColor to select a color.

However, as interesting as this may sound, we were unable to get a colored frame to display in any modern browser except for Windows Internet Explorer 6. So, we can't recommend BorderColor as a design option. See the tip "Using Frames as Layout Elements" on the next page.

Also, with the widespread use of CSS-capable browsers, you can bypass primitive color settings and use CSS to define a frame set's background color. See Chapter 6, *Color*.

Border Skirmishes

If you play around with frame borders in GoLive, you'll discover that you can apply different attributes to separate borders within nested framesets. For example, a vertical border at left could be dark green, while a horizontal border at right could be bright yellow, and sized at 20 pixels.

What you see in your browser is a different matter; some programs we tested favored one setting over another. But which settings override others? Logically, it would make sense that the parent frameset would win out, but experience proves otherwise. In the example at the start of this sidebar, the bright yellow border wins out in Netscape Communicator 4.7, despite being the child frameset. The two border colors draw correctly under Internet Explorer 5.0, though.

As with too many aspects of HTML, the final results vary depending on which browser and platform you're using. Until the mythical day comes when all browsers treat HTML the same, you're better off testing your pages' effects with as many variations as you can get your hands on.

BorderFrame. The BorderFrame setting is a bit confusing on the surface, and requires a brief dip into the HTML being used in the page. Some settings, like table border sizes, are only set numerically; telling a browser to render a table with a border of zero effectively produces a borderless table. In the case of frame borders, two triggers come into play: the numeric size, and also an on/off toggle for displaying the border. In HTML, the Frameborder tag can have a value of "1" or "Yes" to indicate that a border is visible, or "0" or "No" to hide the border.

Therefore, if you *really* want your borders hidden, you need to set GoLive's BorderSize to 0 and specify that the BorderFrame is set to No. This also applies to border colors; if you specify a border color but BorderFrame is set to No, the color doesn't display (though in some browsers, a larger-sized BorderSize setting causes that much space to be filled with the browser's default background color).

Framespacing. Although it doesn't appear in the Frame Set Inspector, you can adjust the framespacing value from the Outline Editor. Select the frame set block and bring up the contextual menu; from the Add Attribute popout menu, select framespacing and enter a value in the field that appears. Framespacing increases the size of the frame borders in Internet Explorer (Netscape ignores the attribute). In fact, if you haven't applied any frame border settings, then enter a framespacing value, GoLive assumes that you really intend to change the BorderSize value when you return to the Frame Editor (though the source code remains unchanged). Similarly, applying a BorderSize setting automatically creates an equal framespacing value. Why use framespacing instead of the border commands? Honestly, we have no idea. But the capability is there if you want to experiment.

Tip: Using Frames as Layout Elements

A good way to avoid some of the unpredictability of how browsers display frame borders is to circumvent the border settings altogether. If you want a thick black border separating two vertical frames, for example, you can create a frame set containing three frames, with the borders hidden. The left and right frames hold the page's contents, as you would have done with a two-frame frame set. Then specify that the middle frame's width is 10, and use a source HTML file that contains nothing but a background color of black. You've cut down the number of variables at work, and you can also reuse that black-background page in other frame sets.

Naming and Targeting Frames

We've covered the structure of frames and frame sets, and how to manipulate their appearance. Moving still further away from our stained-glass metaphor, frames are designed to interact with one another so that all of them in combination work together as a whole on the page. To use a common example, if you're using a vertical frame to the left as a navigation bar, clicking a link should change the contents of a main content frame to the right. To accomplish this, you have to identify each frame with a unique name; otherwise, the link's destination page is likely to override your frame set and fill the entire window.

When you create a new frame set, each frame is titled "NoName" in the Frame Inspector's Name field. Whenever we build framed pages, one of the first things we do is name the frames to prevent confusion later in the process: simply type in a new name.

Creating frame links. Linking to a frame is essentially the same as linking to a file (see Chapter 1, *Going Live*), only in this case, you must specify a name to go along with the link's source. This is why naming frames is so important.

To start, open a frame's HTML file by double-clicking the frame. For purposes of explanation, let's assume that you want to create a link in the leftmost frame, titled "Left," that displays a new page as the contents of the bottom right frame, titled "Middle" (see Figure 9-18). Perform the following steps to create the link.

1. Select the text or image to be linked, and choose New Link from the Special menu, or click the New Link button on the Text or Image Inspector.

2. On the Link tab of the Text or Image Inspector, enter the link's destination in the URL Getter by typing the filename or using the Fetch URL (Point & Shoot) tool.

3. Specify the intended frame by entering its name in the Target field. If your frame set file is still open, the popup menu at right includes the names of all frames at the top of the list. In our example, use "Middle" as the target.

4. Be sure to save the content file.

Tip: Multiple Open Frame Set Files

When you have more than one frame set file open, the Target popup menu lists all the names available. If your frames share the same names across several files, close the frame set files that you're not using to make sure the link is pointing to the correct frame.

Figure 9-18
Targeting
frames

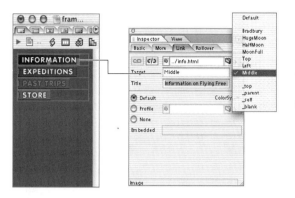

*The names of
the frames in
the active
document are
displayed in
the Target
popup menu.*

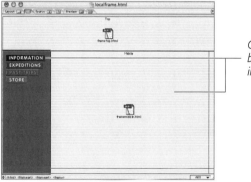

*Clicking the link in a Web
browser loads the destination
into the "Middle" frame.*

Now, when you click the link, your browser first looks for a frame with that name before loading the page. If one is found, the contents are loaded into that frame.

Tip: Renaming Frames

If you rename a frame, you run the risk of breaking the links to it. GoLive's ability to manage links automatically throughout a site is great, but unfortunately the feature doesn't extend to target names. The good news is that you can easily use the Element tab or Find & Replace tab of the Find feature to find the old frame name and replace it with the new name across all the files within your site (see Chapter 19, *Managing Files, Folders, and Links*).

Special built-in targets. The Target popup menu also features four targets that let you direct the contents of a link without using a specific frame name.

- **_top** directs your browser to load the targeted page into the existing window, overriding the frame set.

- **_parent** acts like _top, but is applied when you have nested frame sets, loading the contents into the parent frame set.
- **_self** replaces the contents of the frame containing the link with the targeted page.
- **_blank** loads the targeted page into a new browser window.

Are You Game for Frames?

Over the last few years, we've grown accustomed to looking at the Web on our computers, though it's more accurate to say that we look through our computers to glimpse the Web. With frames, you can multiply that view dramatically, using the same screen space to display and interact with more of the Web at the same time.

CHAPTER 10
Floating Boxes

In Chapter 8, *Layout Grids*, we covered one way of achieving precise positioning using complicated tables known as layout grids. Although grids do a good job of gaining control over where objects are placed on a page, they remain, at best, a sophisticated hack: imagine building a road not by laying asphalt in a continuous path, but by constructing a maze of guardrails that prevents your car from going anywhere other than the designated route. For the most part, layout grids work, but there's also a more advanced way of controlling your page: floating boxes.

You can put objects or text into a floating box, then position the box anywhere on a page. Floating boxes use Cascading Style Sheets (CSS) to specify pixel coordinates, so you're not limited to inserting them into a position forced by the word processor-style sequence of HTML. And the amount of code required to make a floating box appear is simpler and more standardized than grids, meaning less strain on the browser, which creates a greater chance of it looking like you expected.

The only real disadvantage is that you and your site's visitors must use version 4.0 or later of Netscape and Microsoft Internet Explorer to view floating boxes. People without 4.0 or later browsers (or the Opera browser's 5.0 or later release) see lumps of material scattered around the screen. Although most U.S. Web users are running these modern browsers, take heed of your audience—especially a worldwide one—before committing to floating boxes.

Creating Floating Boxes

Creating a new floating box is just as easy as adding nearly every object in GoLive: drag the Floating Box icon from the Basic tab of the Objects palette into the Layout Editor (see Figure 10-1); you can also use the Insert Object option on the contextual menu. GoLive inserts a small yellow placeholder icon, which indicates the spot in the HTML code where the contents of the floating box are inserted. However, the placeholder's location doesn't affect the positioning of the box on the page.

You can type or drag any kind of object into the floating box. If you drag in objects larger than the box, the box's size increases to fit them (see Figure 10-2).

Tip: Text Sizing in Floating Boxes

By default, a floating box begins with precise pixel measurements (100 pixels wide and tall, to be precise). When you type text into the box, it automatically resizes if the text runs longer than the box's measurements. However, plain HTML text is a slippery devil: depending on the browser and operating system, some text may display larger than the box. This is one reason why we've seen the light and make a point of specifying all text within floating boxes with CSS styles that use absolute pixel sizes. Another option, if you have a more flexible layout, is to set the box's width and height fields to Auto or Percent (see "Resizing," later in this chapter).

Figure 10-1
Dragging in a Floating Box icon

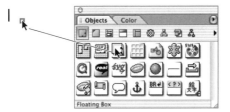

What's New in 6

Floating boxes have received a number of changes and improvements in GoLive 6, especially in the Floating Boxes palette. The visibility and locking controls have been simplified a great deal from previous versions, and a new Hierarchic menu item displays the relationships between nested floating boxes.

For those who want more control over their boxes, GoLive 6 provides access to the CSS controls that have lurked beneath the surface since floating boxes came into being. By selecting a box's name in the CSS Editor, you can set attributes via the CSS Style Inspector, such as the alignment and spacing of text within the box, plus a host of other settings

Figure 10-2
Resizing the
floating box

*Default
floating box*

*Floating box
automatically
resized*

Floating Boxes Palette

The Floating Boxes palette serves two purposes: it's the hiding place for some handy floating box preferences, and it provides a single location from which to help manage multiple boxes that may overlap or be spread throughout your page (see Figure 10-3).

Figure 10-3
Floating Boxes
palette

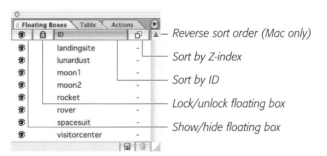

— *Reverse sort order (Mac only)*
— *Sort by Z-index*
— *Sort by ID*
— *Lock/unlock floating box*
— *Show/hide floating box*

Creating and removing floating boxes. The buttons at the lower-right corner let you create or destroy floating boxes from the palette. Click the New Floating Box button to make one appear on your page. To delete one or more boxes, select their names in the list and click the Remove Selected Floating Boxes button.

Floating box IDs. Each floating box on a page shows up in the Floating Boxes palette; its name, which is assigned to it in the Floating Box Inspector, appears in the ID column. You can change these names at any time through the Inspector (we discuss names a bit later in the chapter).

With multiple boxes listed, click the ID column heading to list the boxes in alphabetical order. Clicking it again re-sorts the list into reverse-alphabetical order. You can also change the sort by clicking the ID column title.

Visibility. Clicking the eye icon next to a floating box's name hides both the box and its contents. However, this doesn't make the box invisible on the Web page—the controls in the Floating Boxes palette only apply to editing in GoLive. If you have several floating boxes, especially if they overlap, it's easier to hide the ones you're not actively editing. If you're looking to hide the box's contents on your page, use the Visible checkbox in the Floating Box Inspector.

Tip: All for One

If you Command-click (Mac) or Control-click (Windows) any visibility icon, all floating boxes on the page appear or are hidden together. The same holds true for the padlock icon.

Locking. The second column in the palette controls whether you can edit the floating box. Clicking the padlock area enables its "locked" setting, and you won't be able to move, resize, or edit its contents. In fact, you need to click the box's yellow icon in order to even select it.

Lock and Unlock Visibility. By default the visibility and locking settings only stick while you're in the Layout Editor—if you switch to another editor then switch back, the boxes become visible and unlocked. However, you can get around this fickle setting by choosing Lock Visibility from the popout menu, which also applies to when you preview a DHTML animation (more on that topic in Chapter 26, *Creating Animation with DHTML*). Choose Unlock Visibility to turn this setting off.

Tip: Locksmith

Even with a floating box locked in the Floating Boxes palette, you can bypass the setting and have your way with it. Simply click the box's name in the palette, which makes it completely editable. When you deselect it, the lock remains in place until you unlock it or click the name again. This way you can tweak boxes without constantly locking and unlocking them.

Z-Index stacking order. The column to the right of the name (click the hyphen or number there to select it) indicates the box's Z-Index, or stacking order (see Figure 10-4). Floating boxes can be stacked, but without a Z-Index value, GoLive has no way of knowing which boxes sit on top of which. The number can be anything, and matches the Z-Index value in the Floating Box Inspector.

Figure 10-4
Z-index
stacking
order

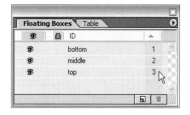

As with the ID column, clicking the Z-Index heading icon sorts the list in either ascending or descending order. Clicking the heading again reverses the sort order.

Floating box hierarchy. If you choose not to assign a Z-Index value, you can still control the boxes' stacking order from within the Floating Boxes palette. More importantly, you can also easily see which floating boxes have been nested within other floating boxes. From the palette's popout menu, choose the Hierarchic option (see Figure 10-5). This view also allows you to drag and drop the box names to specify their order (see Figure 10-6). To view them all at the same level, choose the Flat option (which is the default).

Figure 10-5
Choosing the
Hierarchic
option

Figure 10-6
Dragging and
dropping box
names to
change order

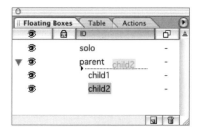

We still recommend using a Z-Index value as a more thorough alternative to creating stacking order, but adjusting the hierarchy can be a good quick-and-dirty method of experimenting with floating box layer positioning when you're designing a page. And being able to see which boxes exist within other boxes is invaluable.

Floating Box Grid Settings. With the Floating Boxes palette visible, select Floating Box Grid Settings from its popout menu at the upper right. Although you can move a floating box anywhere on the page, it can be helpful to use a grid for positioning. As with layout grids, you can set the grid size, the horizontal and vertical visibility, and whether objects snap to the grid. To make sure objects don't bleed into each other, check the Prevent Overlapping box. With these options enabled, a grid appears when you drag a floating box (see Figure 10-7). These settings apply only to the active document.

Figure 10-7
Floating Box
Grid Settings

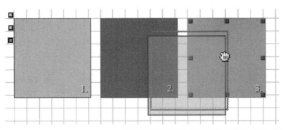

Convert to Layout Grid. In addition to using a grid for reference, you can opt to abandon floating boxes altogether and convert the page to a layout grid. Select Convert to Layout Grid from the Floating Boxes palette's popout menu. Fortunately, when you invoke this command, GoLive creates a new untitled document containing the grid, leaving the original and its floating boxes intact.

Tip: Collision Alert

If you have overlapping floating boxes, GoLive doesn't let you convert the page to a layout grid. Move the boxes away from each other manually, or by using the options on the Align palette.

Tip: Invisible Layout Grid Lines

If the Floating Box Grid Settings do not have the visibility options turned on, the layout grid you create will similarly feature hidden grid lines. To make the grid lines show up, enable them in the Floating Box Grid Settings, or simply toggle the controls in the Layout Grid Inspector once you've made the conversion.

Editing Floating Boxes

Like so many actions in GoLive, multiple methods of doing things are available. You can position and resize floating boxes using the mouse, the keyboard, or by entering values in the Floating Box Inspector or the Toolbar.

Naming

You can (and should) name each floating box to better identify it in the Floating Boxes palette. But it's also useful and necessary to name them when creating animations; see Chapter 25, *Creating Animation with DHTML*. When you create a new box, GoLive automatically increments the name (such as layer, layer2, layer3, etc.).

Tip: Duplicate Boxes

If you've created a floating box and need another one just like it, simply copy the box's yellow icon, move your cursor, then paste the new box; or select the icon and choose Duplicate from the Edit or contextual menu. Not only does it share the same dimensions and content as the first one, the name is automatically incremented based on the original name. This makes it easy to set up a series of similar floating boxes that are named sensibly, such as Navigation1, Navigation2, etc. Even if you begin with a box named Navigation42, GoLive correctly assumes that the next pasted one should be Navigation43.

Positioning

If you mouse over any of the four borders of a floating box, the cursor changes to a left-pointing gloved hand (see Figure 10-8). This indicates you can drag the box anywhere on the page.

Figure 10-8
The gloved
hand

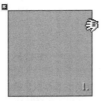

Tip: Boxes Overboard!

You can also drag a floating box partially off a page, provided that enough of the box remains sufficiently visible to grab with the mouse pointer. This technique is frequently used in animations, where an object appears from one edge of the screen; see Chapter 25.

The Floating Box Inspector, of course, allows you to set the left and top origin position of the box in pixels. But you can also change the box's dimensions in pixels, as a percentage of the browser window, or as an automatic resize to fill the necessary space (see Figure 10-9).

Figure 10-9
Changing
the box's
dimensions
using the
Floating Box
Inspector

Press the arrow keys to move boxes in one-pixel increments; holding down Option (Mac) or Alt (Windows) shifts the box according to the grid values found in the Floating Box Grid Settings dialog box. If the Snap option is enabled for horizontal or vertical spacing, holding down the modifier key achieves the opposite effect.

Tip: Multiple Box Keyboard Manipulation

The keyboard modifiers for positioning (and resizing, as discussed later) also apply when you have more than one floating box selected.

You can also use the positioning tools located on the Transform and Align palettes, as well as the Toolbar. We cover these operations in more detail in Chapter 8, *Layout Grids*.

Tip: "Centering" a Floating Box

Being able to put an object anywhere on the page by using a floating box is an impressive advantage—but also a serious liability if you're trying to dynamically center the object on a page that's designed to accommodate varying browser window widths. In many cases, you can't center the object on the page, because the floating box is positioned at specific pixel coordinates. However, it *is* possible, depending on your design.

Create the floating box and set the Left value to 0 in the Floating Box Inspector. Then, set the Width value to 100 Percent, which pushes the right edge of the box against the far side of the window. Add an object to the box, making sure that the objects inside are centered within using the Align Center button in the Toolbar. When you preview the page in a Web browser, the object remains centered even if you change the size of the window (see Figure 10-10).

Figure 10-10
Centering a
floating box
on a page.

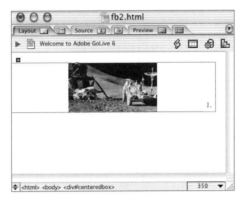

Behind the Box

Floating boxes use a somewhat elegant and simple approach for inserting a precisely positioned item on the screen. (This explanation requires some knowledge of CSS, which is in Chapter 27, *Defining Cascading Style Sheets*.)

First, all the material that appears in the floating box is inserted in the HTML using a Div (division) container. The Div tag is used just for CSS to help divvy up areas of a site into self-contained blocks. Each floating box is assigned a unique identifier in the Div tag.

Next, the positioning and other characteristics of the box are written to the page's style sheet as an individual style that has the corresponding unique identifier.

For instance, if we named a box "bingle," in the Head section of the page in the style decla-

ration you might see this in the HTML code:

```
#bingle { position: absolute;
top: 17px; left: 24px; width:
100px; height: 100px; visibility:
visible }
```

The box itself would be represented in the HTML as:

```
<div id="bingle">Whole lotta
shakin' goin' on</div>
```

Dragging or reshaping the floating box or changing specifications in the Floating Box Inspector causes the style #bingle to be rewritten. Editing the contents of "bingle" changes the material in the Div container labeled "bingle".

It's surprisingly straightforward, but again, not something you generally want to manage by hand.

Resizing

For precise control, change the width and height values in the Floating Box Inspector, and specify whether the dimensions should be expressed in pixels, by percentage, or automatically.

As with layout grids, floating boxes can be resized using the mouse. When you mouse over any of the control handles on the box, the cursor changes into an arrowhead (see Figure 10-11). Dragging resizes the box. Adding the Shift key constrains the resizing to the proportions of the existing box.

Figure 10-11
Resizing a
floating box
using the
mouse

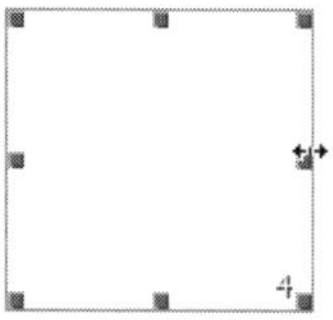

To resize using the keyboard, hold down the Shift key and press the arrow keys. As with positioning, the resizing increments are based on the settings in the Floating Box Grid Settings dialog box.

If you change the Width or Height fields to Auto or Percent, the appropriate control handles disappear, so you can't drag that dimension any more but must set it through the Floating Box Inspector.

Z-Index

Floating boxes may overlap one another, and you control their stacking order by entering a value into the Z-Index field (Z is the front-to-back dimension on a Web page).

The higher the number, the closer to the top the floating box, um, floats (see Figure 10-12). Numbers do not have to be sequential; you can assign numbers 7, 21, and 50 to three boxes, and that still places them in order from bottom to top (or most occluded to least).

Visibility

You can hide the contents of the floating box both in the Layout Editor and in a browser window by unchecking the Visible box. (This setting is different from the visibility control on the Floating Boxes palette, described earlier.) Turning off visibility enables you to later make items appear when called by an Action or during an animation.

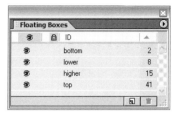

Figure 10-12
Using
the Z-Index
to control
stacking order

Color

A floating box's background color may be set by dragging a swatch into the Color field. Click the field once to enable its active color mode, where you can dynamically apply colors to the box's background by clicking color samples in the Color palette.

Tip: Color Is CSS

Unlike virtually every other color setting in GoLive outside the CSS Editor, the Floating Box Inspector's Color field actually sets the CSS property for background color in a floating box (see Figure 10-13).

Figure 10-13
Changing the
color in the
Floating Box
Inspector
changes the
CSS property.

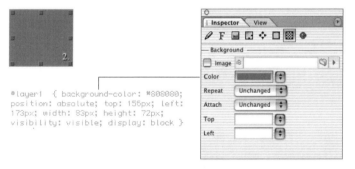

Background Image

Floating boxes are like mini-HTML pages, and can have their own tiled background images (see Figure 10-14). Set the background image for a floating box exactly as you would for an HTML page: browse or Point & Shoot from the URL Getter to specify an image.

Animation Settings

A chunk of the Floating Box Inspector includes features that relate to using floating boxes in Dynamic HTML (DHTML) animation. We address this advanced feature at length in Chapter 25. None of these options affects using floating boxes for absolute positioning on a page.

Figure 10-14
Setting a
background
image in a
floating box

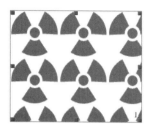

A Floating Box Doesn't Drift

It's ironic that in order to achieve precise positioning, we turn to a tool that offers the most flexibility for locating objects on a Web page. As advanced Web browsers continue to proliferate, the day may come when all of our pages are built out of floating boxes. In the meantime, though, we continue bobbing in this sea of code and grabbing onto floating boxes whenever we need a handle on more page control.

Editing Floating Boxes Using CSS

Without Cascading Style Sheets, we wouldn't have floating boxes. The precise-positioning features of CSS are what let you place a box anywhere on the page. When you create a floating box, you're creating a new ID style that describes the properties of the box—the Floating Box Inspector is really just a nice interface for controlling a limited subset of all possible CSS settings. In previous versions of GoLive, you needed to delve into the source code to apply additional settings beyond those specific in the Inspector, but GoLive 6 offers a better, sensible alternative.

In the Layout Editor, click the Open CSS Editor button to view a list of styles in your page; floating boxes appear as IDs (they begin with a pound sign), and include "Floatingbox rule" in the Info column. Selecting one displays the CSS Style Inspector, which contains posi-

tioning controls as well as the full complement of font, spacing, margin, border, and the rest of the options found in that Inspector. Want to set all text in your floating box to Verdana at 12 pixels, centered in the box? Use the Font and Text panels to apply the settings.

GoLive will also hijack but preserve any ID selectors you specify that have Absolute positioning set along with the Visibility property set to Visible. Once this ID is pointed somewhere on a page, like as part of a hand-coded Div section, GoLive internally thinks of it just like a floating box the next time you switch from Layout Editor to HTML Source Editor or close and open the page.

To be honest, we're crazy about editing extra floating box properties through the CSS Editor. It makes formatting within floating boxes more consistent and easier to define.

Templates

We've seen it happen. A designer builds a site, publishes it to the Web, and then hands the site files over to the client who will manage the day-to-day updates. The trouble is, there's no guarantee that your client knows as much about HTML as you do, so it's likely they will come calling in the future asking you to repair the damage they unintentionly inflicted while updating their content.

GoLive 6 added a new kind of template for pages which can limit what content on a page can be updated. You can easily assign regions that are editable, leaving the rest of the page off-limits.

Tip: Layout Editor Only

Not to throw cold water on a hot feature so soon, but keep in mind that Template regions only work their magic in the Layout Editor. You can easily go into the page's source code and edit whatever you please, or remove the region-identifying tags entirely.

Creating Template Regions

Ever the megalomaniacal control freaks, we like to dictate which areas of a page can be edited by others (or sometimes even by ourselves: clients aren't the only ones who sometimes inadvertenly mangle code). GoLive accomplishes this by letting us assign named Template regions.

In the Layout Editor, highlight a section of your page. It can be a range of text, a table, the contents of a floating box, or nearly anything else. Then, bring up the Template Regions palette and click the New Editable Region button. You can also use the Template submenu of either the Special menu or the contextual menu, though we prefer being able to view the list of regions in the palette (see Figure 11-1).

Your selection changes color to indicate that it's now a region, which is named according to the first few words of selected text. If no text is selected, the region is named, simply, "Region". Click the name in the palette and type a more descriptive name, if you want.

Figure 11-1
Template
region

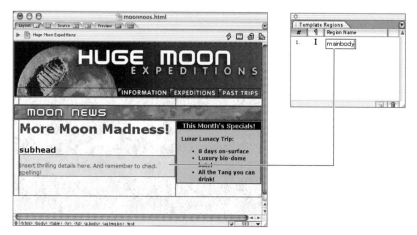

You can turn off GoLive's behavior of naming regions based on their selected text. In the Template Regions palette's popout menu, deselect the Selection Defines Region name option.

Tip: Template Names

The GoLive documentation says that spaces and underscores are not allowed in Template region names, though in our testing they seemed to work just fine. That said, it's our habit not to use spaces anyway when naming objects, so in this case it's acceptable (though not ideal) to not use underscores either. "Better safe than stupefied," is what we say on deadline.

Three types of regions are available, depending on what you've selected: inline, paragraph, and object.

Inline. Highlighting only a few words or characters and clicking New Editable Region creates an inline region, indicated by an "I" icon in the Template Regions palette (see Figure 11-2). The chief advantage of inline regions is that someone can edit the text within the region, but cannot create new paragraphs by hitting the Return or Enter keys. (However, you *can* insert line break characters to approximate paragraphs, if you want to cheat.)

Paragraph. If you highlight an area containing one or more paragraphs, you create a paragraph region, indicated by a paragraph symbol in the Template Regions palette (see Figure 11-2). Paragraph regions are much more flexible than inline regions: you can add objects such as tables, images, and layout grids, while still constraining the section of a page that's editable.

Object. Selecting an object such as a table or image and clicking New Editable Region creates an object region (see Figure 11-2). Object regions are identified in the Template Regions palette by a small square icon.

Figure 11-2
Region types

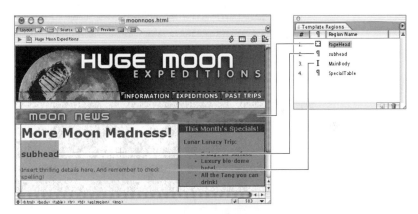

scaled, but cropped depending on the new dimensions; and Show All resizes the image, but retains its proportion, to ensure that the entire image appears within the dimensions (see Figure 11-3).

Figure 11-3
Scaling smart
images

Original

Exact Fit

No Border

Show All

Tip: Floating Box Regions

Assigning Template regions to floating boxes is somewhat inconsistent in the initial release of GoLive 6. You can select the contents of a floating box and create a region, but on the Mac, you cannot create a region out of the box by clicking the box itself. With the contents defined as a region, you cannot reposition the box on your page by dragging it to a new location; however, you can change the size and position values in the Floating Box Inspector. We attribute these inconsistencies to new-featuritis, and expect that future revisions of the program will clean up floating box template region behavior.

Selecting Template Regions

Two options in the Template Regions palette's popout menu control how region contents are selected. Enable the Auto Selection option to automatically select the entire contents of a region when you click on it. Or, with your cursor active within a region, hit the Tab key to move between different regions on your page; to deactivate this feature, disable Cyclic Tabbing from the popout menu. Of course, you can also click a region's name in the Template Regions palette to select it.

Locking and Unlocking the Template

When you're working in a Template, choose Lock Page from the Template submenu of the Special menu or the contextual menu to prevent any changes outside of the editable regions you've set up. Essentially, this lets you preview how a page created from your template will behave.

To unlock the Template, choose Unlock Page from the same Template submenu.

Saving the Template

Templates aren't saved differently than other pages—nothing specifically identifies a page as a Template. However, if you save the file into the Templates folder located in your site's data folder (found in the Site window in the Extras tab), GoLive treats the page as a Template (see Figure 11-4).

Figure 11-4
Templates folder in site

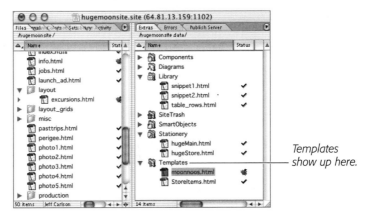

Templates show up here.

Creating Pages Based on Templates

Once your template page is set up, it can be used to create any number of new pages that share its design. There are a few methods of creating a new page based on a Template.

- From the File menu, select the New Special submenu and choose Page from Template. By default, the Open dialog box displays the contents of your site's Templates folder.

- From the contextual menu, select the New submenu, and then select the New from Template option; choose from the list of files in the site's Templates folder.

- Go to the Site Extras tab of the Objects palette. From the popup menu at the bottom of the palette, choose Templates to see the pages in the Templates folder. From here, you can drag a page icon to a new blank page (see Figure 11-5), to the Files tab of the Site window, or to the Navigation View if it is visible.

- In the Extras tab of the Site window, open the Templates folder and double-click a Template file. GoLive prompts you about whether to make a new page or edit the existing page; click the Create button. This also applies to double-clicking a Template icon in the Site Extras tab of the Objects palette.

Figure 11-5
Applying
Template to
blank page

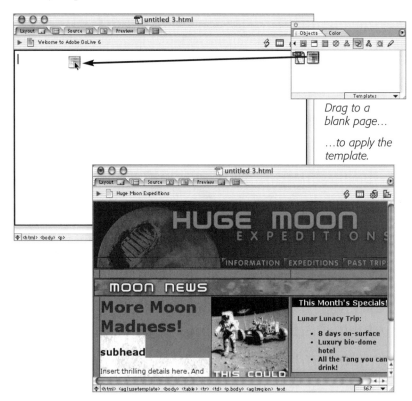

Drag to a
blank page...

...to apply the
template.

Tip: A Permanent Temp(late)

If all of your pages need to be based on one Template, you can configure GoLive to automatically create a new page using the Template's layout. Open GoLive's preferences and click the New Document checkbox in the General pane. Use the Select button to navigate to your Template file.

After opening, save the new untitled page, which contains everything on the Template; only the regions you specified are active.

Applying a Template to an Existing Page

If all you wanted to do was apply a Template to a blank page, you could use stationery files. However, Templates allow you to apply themselves to an existing page and merge the contents of the Template and the page.

For example, suppose someone on your team is responsible for writing a daily journal entry, and it's your job to apply that content to your site's home page. Instead of working in the layout itself, the other team member could write up the day's entry in a blank page by itself. When it's time to merge the two, simply drag your Template from the Site Extras tab of the Objects palette to the open journal file; you can also choose Apply Template from the Template submenu of the Special menu or the contextual menu. GoLive displays a dialog asking which Template region should be used to accommodate the journal text (see Figure 11-6). Select a region name and click OK; the journal page now contains the entire page, but with the journal text in its proper place.

You can also get slightly tricky by naming multiple regions in the journal file. If the region names match the ones in the Template, each region is updated with its corresponding text (see Figure 11-7, next page).

Figure 11-6
Adding text
to a Template

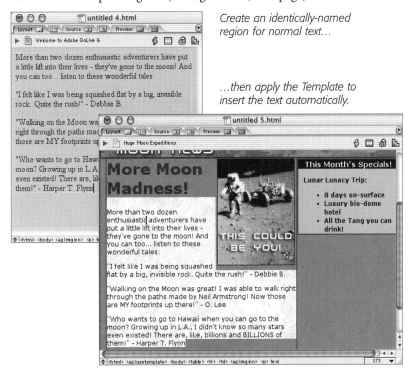

Create an identically-named region for normal text...

...then apply the Template to insert the text automatically.

If you have text or objects in the journal file which don't correspond to a region name in the Template, GoLive alerts you with a dialog. Choose one of the Template's regions, which is where the new material appears. Click OK.

Figure 11-7
Adding text
to multiple
Template
regions

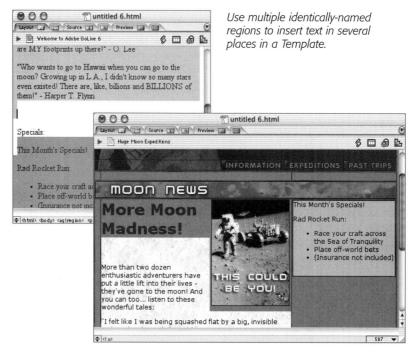

Use multiple identically-named regions to insert text in several places in a Template.

Tip: Mixing Region Types

It's not necessary to match region types when applying a Template: content in your page that's been specified as a paragraph region, for example, can replace the contents of an inline region in your Template.

Updating a Template

When you create a page based on a Template, a link is established between the two. Any changes you make to the Template, such as resizing a smart object image, are reflected on the pages it spawned. Of course, this being GoLive, there is more than one method of getting to your original Template.

- The simplest method is to double-click the file from the Extras tab of the Site window or the Site Extras tab of the Objects palette. GoLive asks if you want to create a new page based on the Template or modify the Template itself; click Modify.

- Open a file that was created using the Template. Then choose Open Attached Template from the Template submenu of the Special menu or the contextual menu.

Make any changes to the Template, then save or close the file. Its offspring are automatically updated.

Detaching a Page Template

If you decide you don't need the structure afforded by Template regions on a page, you can easily remove the editing restrictions. With your page open, choose Detach from Template from the Template submenu of the Special menu or the contextual menu. The region-specific source code is removed from the underlying HTML, leaving you with a standard Web page that contains everything from the Template.

Changing Highlight Coloring

Web pages come in all colors, making it difficult to distinguish Template regions when the background color is close to GoLive's default region highlight colors. The Highlight palette offers an easy solution.

Bring up the Highlight palette and switch to the Colors tab. Two settings in the center apply to Templates: Editable Regions and Locked Regions. Drag a new color from the Color palette to one of the color fields to change it, or click the field and then use the eyedropper that appears when your cursor is in the Color palette.

Another option is to show only the region's border. Click the Show Only Border On/Off button to the right of the Opacity slider to enable this type of highlighting (see Figure 11-8). If you don't mind the colors as they are, but want to change their intensity, drag the slider next to the color field to change its opacity.

Figure 11-8
Showing only
region borders

*Show Borders
Only On/Off*

A Region for Living

GoLive has long possessed the capability to build pages whose designs are modeled on pre-existing Stationery, but now you have the option of controlling how those pages are edited. Whether you're handing files off to a client or maintaining a smooth editing workflow among your team members, Template regions promise to make updating content much easier.

Rich Media

When you're building a multimedia Web site, you can wind up with all sorts of content: Acrobat PDFs, Flash files (SWFs), QuickTime movies, Real audio and video files, and lots of other bits and pieces. GoLive offers support for previewing, inserting, and editing a whole range of rich media.

Browser Plug-ins

At this point in the history of the Web, using browser plug-ins—modules added to a browser to handle specific file formats—is no big deal. Let's say you come across a page or link that utilizes a plug-in. If the file is one that your browser can handle natively, or via a plug-in that's already installed, it simply handles it. The file then plays within the browser window (for Flash files, for instance), or an appropriate application is launched that can handle the file (for PDFs, for instance).

GoLive supports any multimedia file that Netscape's browsers or Internet Explorer can handle, from SVG to Flash to Beatnik. GoLive works in much the same way as a browser. If you've inserted the plug-in file into the Plug-ins folder within the GoLive application folder (see Figure 12-1, next page), you can view your media files using GoLive's Layout Preview. If these plug-in files aren't placed there, you see only a generic plug-in icon.

Adding plug-ins to GoLive is just as easy as adding them to your browser. Either place them directly into the GoLive Plug-ins folder via the plug-in's installer, or duplicate the files and move them into the folder. Plug-ins placed here while GoLive is open don't become active until you quit and relaunch the program.

Figure 12-1
Plug-ins folder
location under
Windows and
Mac OS

Figure 12-1
Plug-ins folder
location under
Windows and
Mac OS

Adding Plug-in Objects to a Page

Flash, Real, QuickTime, and SVG plug-in media files are very different breeds of animals, and GoLive acknowledges that fact by adding specific plug-in items in the Objects palette, in addition to a generic plug-in item. That said, only one Inspector is needed to deal with these different media types.

Drag the Plug-in icon from the Objects palette's Basic tab to the Layout Editor to create a new generic plug-in. The placeholder icon that appears includes a question mark in the top right corner until you specify a file using the URL Getter in the Basic tab of the Plug-in Inspector or by choosing one of the Source Link options from the contextual menu (see Figure 12-2). Alternatively, you can drag a media file from the Site window or a directory location on your hard drive.

Tip: Organizing Plug-In Files, Part 1

If you drag a file onto a page and it only appears as a text link, you do not have the proper plug-in stored in the GoLive Plug-Ins folder. To rectify this, either add the plug-in to the folder (then quit and restart GoLive), or use the Plug-in icon from the Objects palette, and navigate to the plug-in.

Editing QuickTime Movies

GoLive also offers you the ability to create and edit QuickTime movies directly via the Timeline Window. In fact, we've been known to launch GoLive to perform quick movie edits. However, in the interests of keeping this book to a more manageable length, we cover that subject in a chapter called *QuickTime Editing*, available at realworldgolive.com/six/ as a free download.

Figure 12-2
Defining
source of
plug-in using
contextual
menu

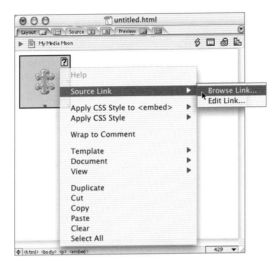

Plug-in icon

After the source file is defined, the question mark icon disappears and the file's name is placed in the upper-left corner of the placeholder. In addition, the generic puzzle icon becomes active instead of dimmed. Depending on what kind of file you reference, GoLive switches the plug-in icon to something more specific (yet still rather generic) for plug-in media that match items from a list of icons for recognized MIME types (see Figure 12-3).

Figure 12-3
Plug-in icons

Tip: A MIME You Look Forward to Seeing

MIME started its life as Multipurpose Internet Mail Extensions, a standard promulgated by a few prominent email gurus (including one of Glenn's idols, Nathaniel Borenstein). MIME was an attempt to bring order to mail attachments, allowing any mail user to encapsulate all kinds of content as parts of an email message and have any MIME-compliant mail reader understand enough about the attachment to, at worst, turn it into a separate file, and at best, decode, play, or display its content.

This standard was useful enough on its own, but the emergence of the Web with lots of operating systems and lots of rich media brought MIME to the forefront as a standard that enables all kinds of software—email clients, browsers, FTP software, etc.—to correctly mix, match, and exchange files without losing their essential nature.

Basic Tab

If you add a plug-in file that is recognized by GoLive, the inactive Player and Medium fields are pre-filled with the plug-in that should play the file, and the type of multimedia file you're linking to, respectively. GoLive gathers this information via the Plugins pane in Preferences, where you can assign a plug-in to play media based on the file extension (like .wav or .mov). If you link to a file without an extension, the field remains blank.

The MIME type should also be filled in, but you need to check the box to make it active and add it to the source code. If the MIME type doesn't appear automatically, check it to make it active, then either enter the MIME type in the field or select one from the popup menu (see Figure 12-4). See the sidebar, "Adding an MP3 File," later in this chapter, for an example of setting up a Plug-in object that GoLive doesn't automatically recognize. Checking MIME also changes the placeholder's generic plug-in icon from gray to more active.

Figure 12-4
Selecting a
MIME type

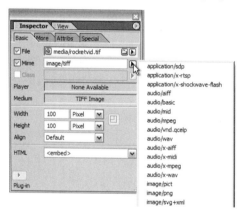

Tip: Recognizing Plug-in Files, Part 2

As mentioned before, the question mark icon in the top-right corner of the placeholder also disappears once linked to a known file (i.e., one found within your site). However, if you're linking to a URL outside the site, the question mark remains; check MIME and select the correct file type to make it go away.

GoLive enters a multimedia file's dimensions into the Width and Height fields if they're available. To change dimensions, enter values into either or both of these fields, or drag the placeholder icon by one of the blue handles. Select either Pixel for fixed dimensions, or Percent to resize the plug-in file relative to the size of the viewed page. Note that selecting Percent eliminates the placeholder icon's blue handles. To align the object on the page, select an option from the Align popup menu.

To preview the object in the Layout Editor, click the Play button at the bottom-left corner of the Plug-in Inspector, which is accessible on all the Inspector's tabs. Turn off previewing by clicking the depressed Play button, which brings back the placeholder icon. Preview is also turned off if you click away from the Layout Editor to one of the other editors, then return to the Layout Editor.

The HTML popup menu at the bottom should automatically be filled in with the required tag according to the plug-in file's MIME type. Embed is used as the default tag to bring in multimedia files to a page. If Object is selected (or if you have the choice between Embed and Object, such as for Flash files), the Class field becomes active, allowing you to specify the class ID or select an ID from the popup menu (see Figure 12-5).

Figure 12-5
Selecting a class ID

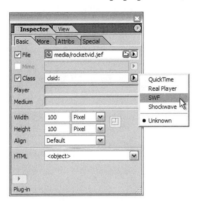

Tip: Objectifying Plug-ins

If you create a generic plug-in placeholder, change its HTML tag from Embed to Object, click on another tab in the Document window, then return to the Layout Editor, the plug-in placeholder becomes an object.

More Tab

Click the Plug-in Inspector's More tab to add a name to the object (see Figure 12-6, next page). You can assign a destination link for a page that includes instructions for installing the object's plug-in for users who don't already have it; check Page and enter the URL, or navigate to it. If you need to assign a link to a plug-in's code base (such as the location of the Flash player ActiveX control that the browser can download if not installed), check Code and enter or navigate to that URL. The Palette menu configures whether the plug-in appears in the Foreground or Background palette. If left as Default, the palette appears in the background. To add blank space surrounding the plug-in file, type values

Figure 12-6
Plug-in
Inspector's
More tab

in the HSpace and VSpace fields. If you want a multimedia object to play in the background (such as a sound file), check Is Hidden. Checking Is Hidden for a visual object defeats the purpose of including it on the page, as it is invisible—but it is possible.

Tip: Audio Control

The Is Hidden command seems like a great idea for giving your page a soundtrack—you know, establish the mood, make the page more interesting, etc. However, be courteous by using Is Hidden sparingly, and give the viewer the option to turn the sound off whenever possible.

Attribs Tab

The Attribs tab allows you to configure a plug-in's attributes manually if you're working with a multimedia plug-in not recognized by GoLive. Click the New Attribute button, type the attribute name in the Attribute field, then type its value in the Value field. For example, a common attribute is Autoplay, which starts the plug-in file once the page is loaded; enter either true or false as its value. To modify an attribute, select it from the list and edit either of the two fields. You can also re-order them using the arrow buttons at the lower left of the palette. To delete one or more attributes, select an item from the list and click the Remove Selected Attributes button (see Figure 12-7). You can also find a Special tab, which remains blank for unrecognized plug-ins. This tab changes depending on the type of plug-in.

Audio Tab

If you add an audio plug-in file (such as AIFF or WAV), you're still working within the Plug-in Inspector. However, the Special tab morphs into the Audio tab, from which you can configure the following attributes (see Figure 12-8):

Figure 12-7
Plug-in
Inspector's
Attribs tab

Figure 12-8
Plug-in
Inspector's
Audio tab

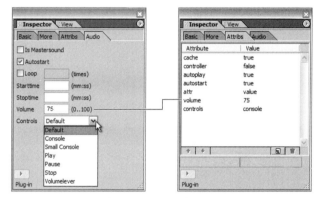

Attributes and values also appear in the Attribs tab.

- Is Mastersound groups sounds together using the More tab's Name attribute. In addition, checking this option allows you to spread the controls for a single sound around a page (such as placing the Play, Stop, and Pause buttons in different table cells). If you use this attribute, remember that all sounds in a group must use the Name attribute, and only one sound within the group can have Is Mastersound checked. (This only works with Netscape browsers.)

- Autostart plays the audio as soon as the page begins to load.

- Loop repeats the audio over and over, unless you specify a number of loops in the text field.

- Starttime and Stoptime values specify when to begin a sound clip at a certain point within the file and when to stop it at another point. Disregard GoLive's example to the right of each field. The values should be typed in a minute:second:1/100-seconds format (i.e., 01:30:05 to start or stop at one minute and thirty-5/100 seconds).

- Leave the Volume field blank to default to 100-percent volume; or, specify a desired percentage (0 to 100).

- The Controls popup menu allows you to specify a player interface. Console displays the default player interface with stop, play, and pause buttons and a volume lever, while Small Console displays a thinner version with only stop, play, and volume controls. Choosing one of Play, Pause, Stop, or Volume Level displays only that interface item. Note that this is a Netscape-only attribute.

Specialized Plug-in Inspector Tabs

The specialized plug-in items added to your Objects palette arsenal don't change much of the Basic, More, and Attribs tabs found in the Plug-in Inspector. However, each one (QuickTime, Flash, Real, and SVG) adds its own tab, overwriting the Special tab, as well as making some slight modifications to attributes in the first three tabs. The following sections detail these specific plug-in items.

Tip: QuickTime Plug-In

When you add a QuickTime movie to your page, it also uses the Plug-in Inspector to set playback attributes.

Flash files. Drag an SWF icon (no, it's not a code from the personals section of a weekly newspaper, but a Flash file) from the Objects palette to your page. After adding the file's location to the File field on the Basic tab, you should see a preview of the file with its default dimensions in the Layout Editor (see

Adding an MP3 File

One of the most common audio formats today is MP3, which compresses well while maintaining good audio quality. Unfortunately, GoLive doesn't automatically recognize the MP3 format. But you can still add MP3 files to your pages using GoLive's standard plug-in.

1. Drag the Plug-in icon from the Basic tab of the Objects palette to your page.

2. In the Basic tab of the Plug-in Inspector, use the URL Getter to specify an MP3 file.

3. Click the Mime button; from the popup menu to the right, select "audio/basic".

4. Switch to the Audio tab in the Inspector; Autostart is automatically checked.

5. Save your page and preview it in a Web browser.

MP3s aren't set up to play as they load, so you have to wait for the entire file to download before your music starts playing. Keep that in mind especially for larger audio files.

Figure 12-9). The Mime field is filled in with "application/x-shockwave-flash", while "clsid:D27CDB6E-AE6D-11cf-96B8-444553540000" is added to the Class. The HTML menu defaults to choose both Embed and Object; the latter is required for referencing the Macromedia Flash player ActiveX control that is needed by Internet Explorer and America Online browsers for Windows.

On the More tab, the Page field is prefilled with a link to download instructions, while the Code field includes a link to the Flash ActiveX control (Windows browsers only) that can be downloaded if not already on the viewer's system.

Figure 12-9
SWF preview
and specific
Plug-in tabs

*SWF files are
previewed in the
Layout Editor.*

Click the SWF tab to modify Autoplay (corresponding to Play on Attribs) to start the file playing automatically (also see Figure 12-9). Check Loop to have the file play over and over. The Quality field controls the appearance and playback speed of a file. Select Default to use the player's settings, or choose from the following:

- Best provides the top combination of appearance and playback speed. This option is entered by default.

- High emphasizes appearance over playback speed.

- Auto High emphasizes appearance, but improves speed when the frame rate drops below a specified frame rate.

- Auto Low emphasizes speed but improves appearance when the Flash player determines a viewer's system can handle it.

- Low emphasizes speed over appearance.

The Scale field controls how the Flash file appears if its original dimensions are different from those specified in the Basic tab's Width and Height fields.

- Default displays the file in the specified area and maintains the original aspect ratio; a border may appear on two sides of the file.

- No Border scales the file to the specified area and maintains the original aspect ratio, though some portions of the file may be cropped.

- With Exact Fit, the file displays exactly in the specified area, though no attempt is made to preserve the original aspect ratio and distortion may occur.

QuickTime movies. From the Basics tab of the Objects palette, double-click or drag the QuickTime icon to the Layout Editor. You can also drag a Quick-Time file from the site window or the Desktop, or bring up the contextual menu and use the Insert Object command.

Adding a QuickTime icon displays the Plug-in Inspector, and fills in much of the information there. In the Basic tab, the Mime field reads "video/quick-time", and Embed is selected from the HTML menu; the More tab remains unchanged. The Autoplay option on the QuickTime tab is enabled, but Show Controller remains turned off (see Figure 12-10). Here's the skinny on configuring the QuickTime tab's other attributes:

- Checking Show Controller reveals the QuickTime playback controls when the plug-in is viewed in a browser. The playback controls add 16 pixels to the height of your object.

- Checking Cache allows the file to be cached by the browser while playing.

- Autoplay (checked by default) allows the file to start playing immediately. Unchecking this option lets the viewer decide when to start playing a file. (Make sure if you uncheck Autoplay to also check Show Controller, or else the file just sits there.)

Figure 12-10
QuickTime-specific Plug-in Inspector tabs

QuickTime files do not display the movie controller by default.

- If you check Loop, the file repeats itself endlessly. In addition, if you check Palindrome, the file repeats back and forth (i.e., reversing itself when it hits the end; perfect for discovering backward messages in your favorite Beatles songs).

- If Play Every Frame is checked, the browser doesn't take any shortcuts by omitting frames from your file (a trick used to improve playback).

- Check Link to add a destination URL to the file (by adding the location into the Link field, or navigating to the page via Point & Shoot or browsing your hard drive), as well as set a Target (typing the information in the text field or choosing an item from the popup menu).

- Click the Open Movie button to preview the file in a GoLive window.

- Set a background color for the movie by checking BGColor and dragging a swatch from the Color palette into the preview field.

- Type a value into the Volume field at which you want the sound to be played back. A value of 100 places the volume slider at the top, while 50 places it in the middle and 0 (zero) places it at the bottom, thus playing no sound. Leaving the Volume field blank produces a default 100-percent QuickTime volume. If you're looking for some Neil Young feedback, you don't get it here; a value greater than 100 just places the volume control at 100 percent.

- Type a value in the Scale field to increase the size of the QuickTime pixels. A value of 1 is the default, while 2 doubles the size, and so on.

  After configuring the attributes for a file, click back to the Attribs tab and notice all attributes that were marked are mirrored in the attributes list.

Tip: Easy Movie Borders

You can easily create a colored border around your movie. Choose a color using the BGColor field, then go to the Inspector's Basic tab and increase the Height and Width values depending on how thick the border should be. For example, to create a two-pixel border around a 100 by 100 pixel movie, adjust the Height and Width values to 104, giving two pixels on each side (see Figure 12-11).

Figure 12-11
Adding a border to a QuickTime movie

Tip: Mac OS X Previewing

If you're running Mac OS X, GoLive doesn't automatically display QuickTime movies in the Layout Preview. To remedy this, open your hard disk, open the Library folder, and then open the Internet Plug-Ins folder. Copy the file "QuickTime Plugin.plugin" to the Plug-ins folder in your GoLive application folder, then relaunch GoLive.

Tip: QuickTime Editing

As we mentioned at the beginning of this chapter, you can find information about editing QuickTime movies within GoLive by downloading the QuickTime Editing chapter from realworldgolive.com.

Real files. Adding the Real item from the Objects palette adds "audio/x-pn-realaudio-plugin" to the Basic tab's Mime field and sets the HTML menu to Embed. On the Real tab, check Autostart to begin playing the file immediately. Checking No Labels stops display of such information as title, author, and copyright (see Figure 12-12).

Select a type of control button you want to include with the file from the Controls menu. Only one control is allowed per Real placeholder icon added to the page; to add more controls, you must add more Real plug-in items. For instance, to set up the basic playback interface for a streaming audio file, you'd add two Real items from the Objects palette. Add the first and link to the Real file in the Basic tab's File field. On the Real tab, choose Control Panel from the Controls menu and give this Real object a unique name in the Console field (or choose either _master or _unique from the popup menu). After adding the second Real item, choose Status Bar from the Controls menu and make sure to give this item the same name in the Console field.

Tip: Real Formatting

Real objects can be formatted on a page much like form objects—add spaces or paragraph breaks between items, or place individual objects into a table layout.

Tip: Real Names

Though you must use the same console name for all Real objects, you only need to add file reference information to just one of the objects.

Here's a rundown of the various Real items that can be selected via the Controls menu (we've intentionally left out self-explanatory items such as Pause Button and Rewind Control):

Figure 12-12
Real-specific
Plug-in
Inspector tabs

- **Image Window** provides a contextual menu that allows the viewer to control playback in the playback area using controls such as Play and Stop.

- **Control Panel** (or Default) displays the default RealPlayer control panel, which contains Play, Pause, Stop, Fast Forward, and Rewind buttons, Position and Volume sliders, and a Mute button that appears when the speaker is selected.

- **Play Button** displays a Play/Pause button.

- **Play Only Button** displays just a Play button.

- **Mute Control** displays a Mute button.

- **Mute Volume** displays a mute button and volume slider.

- **Position Slider** displays a slider indicating the location in the file of the current data being played.

- **Clip Information** displays an information field for information on the Real media clip.

- **Home Control** displays the Real logo.

- **Info Volume** displays presentation information as well as a volume slider and a mute button.

- **Info Panel** displays the presentation information panel.

- **Status Bar** displays informational messages, the network congestion LED, and the position field, which indicates the current place in the presentation timeline along with total clip length.

- **Status Field** displays the message text area of the status bar. If no status field or status bar is embedded, error messages display in the browser's status bar.

- **Position Field** displays the clip's current place in the presentation time line and the total clip length.

From the Console popup menu, choose _master to group the control with other controls on the page, or _unique to keep it separate. Choosing default assigns no Console attribute.

SVG files. Scalable Vector Graphic (SVG) files use an open-standard vector graphics language (based on XML) which allows you to include rich and sophisticated graphic elements, from filter effects to dynamic charting, using just plain text commands.

Tip: Mommy, Where Do SVGs Come From?

LiveMotion and Illustrator can both create SVG files; even GoLive 6 can create them when you export site diagrams (see Chapter 18, *Diagramming and Mapping*). SVG is a next-generation replacement for PostScript and complementary to SWF.

There's not a whole lot going on with SVG-specific options. The Basic tab displays "image/svg-xml" in the Mime field. In the SVG tab, check Use Compressed SVG if you link to a compressed SVGZ file (see Figure 12-13).

Figure 12-13
SVG-specific
Plug-in
Inspector tabs

How Rich Is Your Media?

The benefit of using plug-ins is being able to handle a wide variety of media (existing and not yet imagined) within GoLive, so you aren't forced to hand-code all of the various controls and attributes needed. This helps you focus on creating rich media, instead of merely coping with it on your page.

Code and
Servers

PART 2

CHAPTER 13

Forms

Most interaction on the Web involves users clicking links. Pressing buttons is fine when you're in an elevator, or after putting your money in a soda machine (unless the dreaded "selection unavailable" sign lights up). But most Web sites eventually need to gather more than clicks from their users; they need names, addresses, shirt sizes, movie preferences, and credit card numbers—for some, *especially* credit card numbers.

Users can enter text and make choices via HTML forms, which consist of an opening and closing tag (comprising an HTML container) and any number of structured elements that allow users to enter information or select items from a list. A form may also contain one or more buttons—graphical or plain—for submitting the form, and may include buttons to clear all values in the form or trigger programmed actions.

GoLive offers a straightforward method of graphically constructing forms. You drag and drop elements from the Forms tab of the Objects palette onto a page and customize their values via individual Inspectors. You do have to tweak almost every element you drag into place—by adding settings, resizing fields, or typing in precise sequences of data or directory paths—but GoLive's management of the process lets you create complex forms without much fuss.

If you open a page that contains an existing form, GoLive displays all the form's parts using GoLive symbols, and all elements are as editable as if you'd created the page using GoLive's form tools. (Some exceptions having to do with the Form object are discussed later in this chapter.)

GoLive's Preview window gives a reasonable indication of the appearance of form elements, but if you try to type or select items, the preview is less exact. It's much better to test forms in actual browsers, especially since different browsers offer different support and display of the various form elements.

In addition to constructing the forms themselves, you can write JavaScript code or use a built-in GoLive Action that validates whether a user has entered information into a given form field, and if so, whether what's entered conforms with what you expect. For instance, if you ask for an email address and get back something that contains spaces and no at-sign symbol (@), a JavaScript script could pop up a dialog box that asks the user to re-enter the address in that field.

Parts of a Form

GoLive supports all standard form elements and attributes, which are contained in the Objects palette's Forms tab and modified via various Inspectors. GoLive also lets you use form features from HTML 4.0 that are supported to varying degrees by browsers.

A form comprises two parts: an enclosing container (made visible as a surrounding box) and a set of fields. You make a container by inserting a Form object (see Figure 13-1). Many forms can co-exist on a single page, each in its own Form container. (Nesting forms in HTML is a no-no, but GoLive allows you to do so. A browser won't like it, resulting in a failed form submission.)

Figure 13-1
Form object

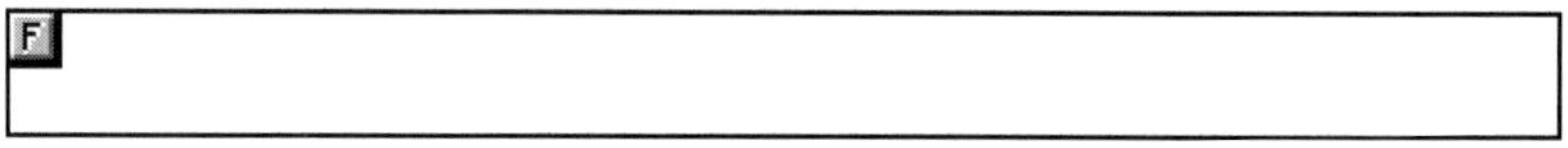

The Form object including its enclosing box

The fields may be any of a dozen or so types of input elements, including text fields and buttons, discussed in "Input Elements," later in this chapter.

What's New in 6

Adobe tweaked its support for forms but didn't make any fundamental changes. Two cosmetic changes are big improvements, however. First, you can now apply CSS classes to forms without any fuss. Select the form element and use the CSS palette to apply a class. In GoLive 5, you had to edit by hand to accomplish the same results.

Second, the Form object now offers an Inventory button, which brings up a dialog that displays the names of the objects contained in the Form object. Also, you can preview how a form submission URL will look when submitted by a browser.

Tip: Form Elements and JavaScript

GoLive offers support for adding JavaScript "handlers" to form elements; these provide actions when a user selects items in a list, checks a box, or submits a form. These handlers have to be entered through the JavaScript Inspector's Events tab, explained in Chapter 24, *Authoring JavaScript*.

Tip: Where to Find Form Pieces

All the pieces to create forms are found in the Forms tab of the Objects palette (see Figure 13-2). Any item referenced in this chapter as something you can move into place must be dragged from this palette; or, you can double-click the item to have it inserted wherever your cursor is in the text.

Figure 13-2
Forms tab of
Objects palette

Tip: Using Tables to Format Forms

The GoLive manual wisely suggests dropping your form elements into a table; otherwise you can't line up text and fields. You can see some examples of setting up form elements in a table in "Building Forms Using Tables" in Chapter 7, *Tables*.

Form Submissions and Servers

When a user clicks a form's Submit button, the Web browser sends the contents of the form to a specified server script or program as a long series of text containing the names of all the form elements and the values a user has entered or chosen. The server processes and acts on this information in some fashion; it might store the form's contents in a database, send email with its details, or deliver a custom page that depends on values selected in the form. The server, after processing the form, typically returns a Web page, though it could also provide a file to download, a movie or audio file to play, or something more complex.

GoLive allows you to create forms graphically, but it lacks support for integrating forms with Web servers. You can use Dynamic Content to connect a database to a form (see Chapter 23, *Building Dynamic Content*), but most people want to pass information from a form to a CGI (Common Gateway Interface) script that runs on a Web server. It's important to be clear at the outset that GoLive offers no features to help with this task.

You must work with a programmer or system administrator (or learn scripting yourself) to connect the data that comes out of a form submission with a script that performs an action.

Form Object

To set up a form, first drag a Form object to your page (see Figure 13-3). The Form object contains the HTML for opening and closing the form on the page. All your input tags, described below, get inserted into the Form object's container.

Figure 13-3
Dragging the
Form object
into page

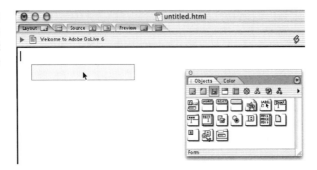

Figure 13-3
Dragging the
Form object
into page

Tip: New Endings

GoLive has gone through a few iterations of how to set up forms. In GoLive CyberStudio 3, dragging a Form icon on the page automatically inserted a </FORM> tag at the end. This got confusing, as the end wasn't explicitly shown.

GoLive 4 added a Form End icon that looked like a little slash-F. But you had to manually drag the icon to the correct place.

GoLive 5 introduced the Form object to contain all the elements of a form visually, a scheme that GoLive 6 uses as well. Older forms still open fine in 5 and 6, but your close form tag might float as a grayed-out element if your form doesn't conform to GoLive's current notions (see Figure 13-4).

Figure 13-4
Broken tables
and forms

*Form elements run off and tags are mismatched,
and the table itself is broken.*

*The close form tag is
here in the page.*

With the Inspector palette displayed, selecting the Form object brings up the Form Inspector (see Figure 13-5), which includes five items you can set, plus a button that leads to more information about the form.

Figure 13-5
The Form
Inspector

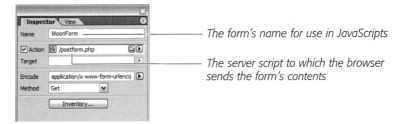

————————— The form's name for use in JavaScripts

————————— The server script to which the browser
sends the form's contents

Name. Naming a form isn't required; in fact, all your forms could have the same name. But if you want to use JavaScript to modify or interact with a form, it's a good idea to name each form differently and, probably, descriptively (see Chapter 24).

Action. When you click a submit button, your browser bundles up the data you've entered and sends it as part of a regular request to the Web server. But the browser needs to know what script to request to pass the information to, which is what the Action field provides.

Tip: Action and Actions

The Action field has nothing to do with GoLive Actions, which are prefabricated JavaScript tools. The Action field tells a browser where to send the contents of a form when submitted.

The Action field typically specifies the location of a processor: a script or program that's accessed on the same Web server on which the form is located—but not always.

If the processor exists on the same machine, you would generally enter a full path from the root of the server, such as /cgi-bin/form-process, and then use the Edit URL dialog (by choosing Edit under the URL popout menu in the Inspector palette) to choose Make Absolute. (See Chapter 19, *Managing Files, Folders, and Links,* for an explanation of absolute and relative links.) You can also browse to find a script to link to, or use the Point & Shoot tool, but typically you directly enter a path provided by your system administrator or Webmaster.

If the program is located on another machine, you need to enter a full Web address starting with http:// or https://.

Tip: Avoid mailto

It's possible to make a form's action be a mailto: link, but we warn against that. Unless the user's browser is correctly configured to send email, it won't work; the user gets an error. Even if it will work, most browsers pop up a security dialog box warning that the form is being sent via email. It's much more reliable to use a script, even one that just emails you the form contents, as that will work 99.99 percent of the time.

Target. With framesets, you can use the popup menu, located to the right of the Target field, to target the returned page (see Chapter 9, *Frames*). This menu includes four standard target destinations plus any frames you have already created; or, you can type an alternate destination into the Target field.

- **_top** loads the page within the current window, but independent of the current frameset.

- **_parent** loads the page within the frame containing the current frameset when you're using nested framesets.

- **_self** loads the return page within the same frame as the form.

- **_blank** works independently of frames, opening a new browser window to load the return page.

Encode. A Web browser has to turn any "illegal" characters in a form—certain text and non-text characters that can't be sent through standard Web protocols—into representations that can be sent. It encodes these characters in one of two ways, available from a popout menu next to the field.

Encoding and Decoding in Perl

If you've seen text like "%2E" in a URL, then you were looking at part of a browser's encoding efforts; the % sign means that the two following characters are the hexadecimal (base 16) number for a specific ASCII character code. In this case, %2E is the code for the equals sign (=). (Unicode 2-byte characters used for non-Roman alphabets have a somewhat similar method that's too involved for this aside.)

We don't want to scare anyone, but it's often tricky to track down how to encode or decode URLs correctly on the server side. Here's the perl code if you're scripting using that language for a CGI.

```perl
sub URLencode {
    my ($urle) = @_;
    $urle =~ s/([\W])/"%".uc(sprintf("%2.2x",ord($1)))/eg;
    return $urle;
}
sub URLdecode {
    my ($urle) = $_[0];
    $urle =~ s/%(..)/pack("c",hex($1))/ge;
    $urle =~ s/\+/ /g;
    return $urle;
}
```

The default encoding is the same as the "application/x-www-form-urlen-coded" option in the popup menu (see the sidebar, "Encoding and Decoding").

The other method of encoding, "multipart/form-data," is used to transmit files to a Web server correctly by identifying where they start and end. (We cover this a bit later in the chapter).

GoLive provides a field here to enter another value in case a new method is developed, but we haven't seen any yet.

Method. You can have a Web browser send data to a server by one of two methods: Get or Post. The Get method sends form data as part of a standard file request to a server. The browser appends all the data to the end of the file request for the script you specified in the Action field.

The problem with Get is twofold. First, you expose all your information in the URL, which can look ugly and might display passwords or other private information on screen or in a browser's cache or history file. Second, Get requests are limited to less than 256 characters on older browsers, so form data could be truncated.

The solution is to use Post, which is the better choice in almost every case. With a Post request, the browser still asks the server to process the data with a specific script, but it sends the form data as a separate stream of text, hidden from the user, and with no apparent limit. (We did have problems with Netscape 1.0, but none since.)

Inventory. The Inventory feature, new to version 6, provides a rundown and a preview of form submissions (see Figure 13-6). This feature is handy, as you often create a form in GoLive and need to pass information off manually (by paper or in email) to a system administrator who creates the back-end server processor.

Figure 13-6
Form Inventory

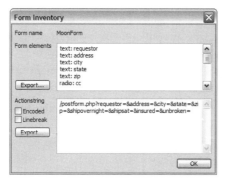

The Inventory dialog box is divided into a top and bottom part. The top lists the type of each form element coupled with its name. Unnamed generic items like Reset are omitted. This list orders elements as they occur in the HTML.

The bottom of the dialog box shows the query that the browser constructs from your form and sends to the Web server.

Tip: Query Construction

A Web query is constructed by taking the field names as they occur in the form, putting an equals sign after each name followed by the value, and using ampersands (&) to separate field/value pairs.

Checking the Encoded box converts special characters to the equivalent needed to transmit them as a Web request. (See the tip above, and the sidebar, "Encoding and Decoding.") Checking Line Break splits the query at each ampersand for legibility.

Clicking Export for either panel produces a text file that contains the identical information as in the corresponding panel. You can also select the text in the panel with the cursor and copy it to the clipboard. (If you're a Windows user and you don't name the file with ".txt" at the end, you cannot open it easily in a standard text editor.)

Input Elements

Once your form is all set up and ready to submit, you need to add elements that a user can type data into or select values from. If you've ever worked with FileMaker Pro or Microsoft Access, many of these terms, types, and concepts will be familiar to you.

Input elements may contain preset data, like the months of the year in a popup menu, or they may require a user to enter data from scratch, like a last name. HTML provides several kinds of input elements tailored to each of these needs. We've divided them into similar categories.

To access settings for each type, drag the element into an HTML page, make sure the Inspector palette is displayed, and select the item to bring up the Inspector; each element has its own Inspector options.

Text Fields

Text fields allow users to type any arbitrary bunch of text, like someone's name, email address, or credit card number. If you want the field to appear with a value already filled in or selected, enter that information in the Content field (Mac) or Value field (Windows) of the Inspector.

The number of characters shown onscreen is set via the Visible field. You can also drag the handle on the field's right side to resize it interactively; the number of characters changes in the Inspector as you drag the handle. Unfortunately, each browser interprets width slightly differently, so there's absolutely no guarantee that setting Visible to "10" allows for only or as many as 10 characters to be visible onscreen. Setting the field size with Visible doesn't constrain the user from exceeding that length. You can limit the number of characters a browser accepts in a field by entering a maximum number in the Max field.

HTML uses the password field to hide the contents of a field as a user types in text. GoLive supports this feature with the Is Password Field checkbox, which replaces the letters typed with characters (usually bullets or dots). GoLive offers both a Text Field icon and a Password icon in the Object palette's Forms tab, but you can change the state of either one later using this checkbox.

Tip: Password Isn't Encryption

If you use the Password field, be aware that it's not as secure as it may sound. All a password field does is prevent someone from reading a password as it's typed. The value in a password field is not encrypted or hidden when the browser transmits it to a server; it's sent in plain text, so it could be intercepted or logged in some fashion, though that's unlikely unless you're working with an open wireless network. Many sites combine a password field with an SSL secure server as the right mix of caution and protection.

Naming Elements

All input elements share one attribute: Name. When a form is submitted to a server, the name identifies which field a value came from. Because of this, you should name elements carefully. Sometimes scripts require highly specific names for different fields, and a Webmaster may need to tell you exactly what to name each item.

If you're using the Field Validator Action for form verification (discussed later in this chapter), your script will most likely address each element by the name you provide. Radio buttons are the one exception to this rule, as they share a group name that identifies members. But you still have to choose that group name. See "Checkboxes and Radio Buttons," later in this chapter.

Text Area

For longer text entry, like user comments on a feedback form, use the Text Area field. You can roughly control the dimensions of a Text Area field by specifying its width in characters in the Inspector's Columns field, and its height in lines of text in the Rows field, or by dragging its control handles. However, as with text fields, every browser interprets these dimensions differently.

You can set text to wrap automatically to the next line as a user types or pastes it in by setting Wrap to Virtual or Physical. Physical forces the browser to insert hard returns (like pressing Return) at each line break that you see on screen; Virtual just previews by wrapping without changing the actual text sent to the server.

Setting Wrap to Off turns off automatic line wrapping, so text just keeps scrolling off the left margin as a user types (see Figure 13-7 for the differences).

Figure 13-7
The Wrap attribute in different browsers and platforms

Netscape Navigator 6.2 (Windows) ignores Wrap settings.

Internet Explorer 6 (Windows) honors Wrap settings.

Internet Explorer 5.1 (Mac) honors Wrap settings.

GoLive's preview doesn't quite match how various browsers display Wrap values.

If you leave Wrap set to Default (Mac) or Standard (Windows), some versions of Netscape Navigator interpret this as Off, while Internet Explorer automatically wraps.

The Content field lets you prefill a value to be displayed whenever the user retrieves the page, which the user can replace.

Tip: W3C Rap on Wrap

"Users should be able to enter longer lines than this, so user agents should provide some means to scroll through the contents of the control when the contents extend beyond the visible area. User agents may wrap visible text lines to keep long lines visible without the need for scrolling." —W3C on Wrap.

Translated, this means, "The browser is responsible, but we're not going to provide you an attribute to allow a designer to define this behavior." See www.w3.org/TR/REC-html40/interact/forms.html#h-17.7 for more information.

Lists

Forms can present lists of items for a user to choose from in two formats: a popup menu or a scrolling list (called a "list box" by GoLive). The main difference between the two styles is that popup menus allow a single choice, while scrolling lists can be set to allow one or more selections. The HTML is almost identical for both formats.

You can drag either a Popup or List Box icon from the Forms tab into a form and use the Inspector palette to change one into the other (see Figure 13-8). Browsers typically display a popup menu when the Rows value is set to 1 and Multiple Selection is unchecked. If more than one row is set to display or multiple selections are allowed, browsers tend to display a scrolling list.

GoLive honors this behavior in its previews. With Multiple Selection checked, a user can select multiple items from the list by holding down the Command key (Mac) or the Control key (Windows) and clicking on items.

Figure 13-8
Popup menus
and scrolling
lists

Mac Internet Explorer

Popup menus and scrolling lists display differently in each browser, depending on how many rows are displayed and whether Multiple Selection is checked.

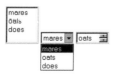

Windows Internet Explorer

The settings are, from left to right in both illustrations: Multiple Selection, show four rows; no Multiple selection, show one row; and Multiple selection, show one row. (One row is empty in each example.)

GoLive automatically inserts three placeholder items in the list of items when you create a Popup or List Box element: first, second, and third. You can create an indefinably large number of items for a list. The text in Label shows up on the Web page; the text for Value represents what's sent to the server if that option is chosen.

Click the New Item icon (it looks like a page) to create a new list item and edit it. To edit an existing item, select it in the list and type over the current value in the field at the bottom of the Inspector. You can also select an item and duplicate or delete it by clicking the appropriate button: the plus sign or trash can, respectively.

If you want to change the order in which items appear in the list, select one or more and use the up and down arrows to rearrange them. The order shown in the Inspector palette corresponds exactly with the order of items on the page.

You can change the number of rows displayed in a list by entering a new value into the Rows field in the Inspector, or you can drag on the handle at the bottom of a list box.

To preselect an item so that it's highlighted in a list or displayed in a popup menu, select it and click the checkbox to the left of the entry fields in the Inspector. Or, you can double click to the left of the item in the list itself.

If you preselect more than one item without having Multiple Selection checked, GoLive automatically checks the Multiple Selection box for you. If you uncheck that box with multiple items selected, GoLive removes the check from all items in the list except the first (see Figure 13-9).

Figure 13-9
Preselecting
multiple items
in a list

Select a single item and Multiple Selection can remain unchecked.

Add another preselected item, and GoLive checks Multiple Selection.

Tip: Wrong Label

What GoLive calls the Label in the Form List Box Inspector is not the same as the HTML 4.0 attribute for items in a list called Label. The Label in the Inspector is really just text that is inserted as part of the form; the HTML 4.0 attribute, by contrast, allows you to specify text that appears in a new hierarchical menu feature described in "HTML 4.0 Features," later in the chapter. This new feature must be handcoded; don't get confused by GoLive's label for Label.

Checkboxes and Radio Buttons

The alternative to lists and popup menus are checkboxes and radio buttons. In both cases, you're presenting a set of choices to a user to select from. With lists, you have to toe the HTML line, using the limited formatting available for popup menus and list boxes. With checkboxes and radio buttons, however, you can create any text and image layout that you want, and place the boxes or buttons in the right proximity for a user to select.

Checkboxes are binary choices: they can be checked or unchecked. Each checkbox on a page operates, by default, independently from all others. Radio buttons, by contrast, are groups of choices: each group can have only one item selected. Checkboxes are like multiple-selection lists; radio buttons act like popup menus.

Checkboxes and radio buttons each have a Value attribute, which is what the browser sends to a server when the form is submitted. You can precheck or preselect these elements by checking the Selected box in the Inspector.

Radio buttons are created in named groups with at least two members. A single radio button makes no sense, as one member of a group must always be selected, and a single-member group can't have its button unselected.

You can create a radio button group by dragging the Radio Button icon from the Forms tab onto a page and bringing up the Form Radio Button Inspector. Entering any text in the Group field creates a new group, which is automatically added to the popup menu next to the Group field. For the next button you create, you can select the group from the popup menu to the right of the field, or you can copy and paste an existing radio button that's part of a group to speed up creation.

Laying out checkboxes and radio buttons requires some extra work in spacing. You want to prevent the label for the button or box from being confused with one on the right or left. We often insert non-breaking spaces (Option-space or Alt-space, or " " in HTML) to better distance one button from the next (see Figure 13-10). It's also easier if you use a table and cells to control placement.

Figure 13-10
Non-breaking
spaces for
button
legibility

Credit Card   ○ Visa ○ MasterCard ○ Amex ○ Diner's Club   *With plain spaces*

Shipping Options   ○ UPS ○ FedEx ○ Airborne
                     ☐ Overnight ☐ Saturday Delivery ☐ Insured ☐ Unbroken

Credit Card   ○ Visa   ○ MasterCard   ○ Amex   ○ Diner's Club   *With non-breaking*

Shipping Options   ○ UPS   ○ FedEx   ○ Airborne   *spaces*
                     ☐ Overnight   ☐ Saturday Delivery   ☐ Insured   ☐ Unbroken

If you use the Label element, described under "HTML 4.0 Features," later in the chapter, you can associate a bit of text which, when clicked, also selects a radio button or checks a box.

Standard Buttons

Two buttons have traditionally been used in HTML forms to perform actions: a submit button sends a form to the server; a reset button causes the browser to empty or reset to default all the field values. Submit Button and Reset Button icons can be dragged directly from the Forms tab onto an HTML page. Selecting either button with the Inspector displayed brings up the Input Button Inspector.

You can convert a Submit Button into a Reset Button by clicking the appropriate radio button in the Input Button Inspector. The Normal option invokes an HTML 4.0 kind of button that has no built-in behavior, but which can be coded for behavior via JavaScript or GoLive Actions; we explain how to use it under "HTML 4.0 Features."

If you check the Label box, you can change the text that appears inside the button to anything you wish. We often change Submit to "Send the Form" and Reset to "Erase All Entries" to reduce visitors' confusion.

You can also use a custom image as a submit button by dragging the Form Input Image icon onto your page. This item can only be used to submit, not reset. GoLive presents you with a full array of image options in the Form Input Image Inspector, but not all browsers support special attributes for this kind of image.

Tip: Spittin' Image

GoLive offers two image icons in the Objects palette, depending on the context, but they're exactly the same. The only functional difference between the Image icon on the Basic tab and the Input Image icon on the Forms tab is that the latter automatically checks the Is Form box on the More tab in the Inspector. So if you already have an image on your page that you want to use as a submit button, simply check the Is Form box, which is quicker than deleting the existing image, dragging the Input Image icon from the Forms tab, and linking to the image again.

Hidden

Some server programs require a bit of extra identifying data to be sent along with a form, which the user shouldn't be able to see or modify. To include this information, use a Hidden Input tag. GoLive represents hidden items with a small H, which, when selected, activates the Form Hidden Inspector.

Set the Name and Value as instructed by your system administrator. Often, a hidden field is inserted as a placeholder in a template that a server program uses to insert identifying data.

Upload Files

You can let users upload files via a Web page using the File Browser element. When a user clicks the Browse button, the browser displays a file dialog in which the user can choose a file. The file chosen is inserted into the field portion of the element; you can use the Visible field or drag the control handle to display more or fewer characters of the file name.

When the user clicks a submit button, the browser transmits the file as part of the form data. You must set Encode to "multipart/form-data" in the Form Inspector for file upload to work. The server also must be configured to interpret the file data.

The script connected to this form needs to interpret MIME data, which identifies the file's type and its start and end, and write the file appropriately to disk or otherwise manipulate it. Ofoto.com, for instance, lets you upload a file that the company stores locally and allows you to crop and rotate, and add a frame to it.

Key Generator

GoLive includes the Key Generator icon to be thorough, but it appears that support for this feature is limited to Netscape 4.0 and earlier, and documentation is scarce—sort of an evolutionary dead-end. For more information, see home.netscape.com/eng/security/comm4-keygen.html.

HTML 4.0 Features

Forms have changed little since the early years of HTML, but the HTML 4.0 specification, a guideline to implementing standardized advanced HTML features, added refinements and new tags to improve form structure and usability. Not all browsers support all HTML 4.0 features, but as each newer release appears, we're seeing more and more implementation.

Formatting Form Fields

At first glance, form fields appear immutable and often somewhat ugly. But you can control their appearance to varying degrees by using Cascading Style Sheets (CSS). You can define CSS class selectors and then apply them to individual form elements by first selecting the element, and then using the CSS palette (see Figure 13-11).

This support is new to GoLive 6, and GoLive's preview doesn't display the formatted results. To see the formatting, load the page in a browser, making sure that any externally referenced style sheets are in the correct path.

For more on CSS and defining classes, see Chapter 4, *Text and Fonts*, and Chapter 27, *Defining Cascading Style Sheets*.

Figure 13-11
Setting CSS for
form elements

The tag name appears in this column.

The best place to check for support of specific features is at the wackily named Blooberry.com's Index DOT Html site, which has a section dedicated to form tags at www.blooberry.com/indexdot/html/tree/forms.htm.

You should also test all forms in target browser versions to make sure they work as expected. You can often include more advanced HTML 4.0-based tags which, even when they aren't supported by older browsers, don't disrupt the display of the form.

Most of the HTML 4.0 features that relate to existing elements are grouped in the Focus section of various Form Inspectors. Some features are new elements that provide new capabilities.

Tip: Learning HTML 4

Of the myriad books about HTML that burden bookstore shelves, we have consistently recommended one title as the best HTML reference you can buy. *HTML 4 for the World Wide Web: Visual QuickStart Guide, 4th Edition*, by Elizabeth Castro (Peachpit Press, ISBN 0201354934) offers easy-to-understand information about the current specification. (We have a link to buying this book online at realworldgolive.com/books.html.)

Focus and Field Modifiers

Focus refers to which field or element is currently selected or in the process of being edited. Any item that's being manipulated—like a checkbox being selected—gets highlighted in some manner and has the focus put on it (see Figure 13-12). GoLive lets you apply focus settings to most fields that allow input; Focus is located in the lower section of each form element Inspector. The kinds of focus are broken into discrete settings.

Figure 13-12
Focus on fields

Focus can be on any element, including checkboxes and radio buttons.

Tip: Mac Focus

Macs used to be the exception on focus: Windows and Unix browsers would highlight form elements and links when tabbed to or selected or clicked; Mac Internet Explorer and Netscape did not. That changed with the appearance of IE 5 and Netscape 6, which both show focus clearly.

Tabbing Chains

You can help users fill out a form by letting them press the Tab key to jump through fields in a specified and logical order. This is especially handy when using tables and forms together, as the sequence of tabbing from field to field might run from left to right across columns, while the items occur in more logical order (like name, address, city, state, zip) from top to bottom.

GoLive offers two ways to set the tab order. You can select an item, check the Tab box in its Inspector, and number the item in the order you want it to appear (see Figure 13-13). The tab numbers have to follow one another in increasing order, but don't have to be the next higher number. So whether you number tabs 10, 15, 20, 25 or 1, 2, 3, 4, both work the same way. This can be

Figure 13-13
Tab order

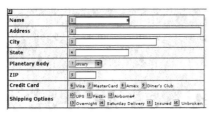

A form with Tabulator Indexing turned on

You can set tab order directly from any form element Inspector.

helpful if you plan to insert fields later and want to leave a gap in numbers so you don't have to renumber the entire form.

You can also use a point-and-click method to set tab order, either by selecting Start Tabulator Indexing from the Special menu, or by clicking the icon to the right of the Tab field in any form Inspector. If an item has already been assigned a number, that number appears in the Layout view adjacent to the item in a yellow box; otherwise, a question mark is displayed in the yellow box. As you click from item to item, the current number is assigned to that element, and the counter increases.

Clicking the icon in the Inspector again or selecting Stop Tabulator Indexing from the Special menu turns off the tab-order display and brings everything back to normal.

Tip: Click to Increment

Whenever you have tabulator indexing turned on, every click increments the tab order counter, whether you click on an item that already has a number or just click anywhere on a page. However, the gap between numbers doesn't affect tab order. So each time a user presses Tab, the browser determines the next highest numbered field, and moves the focus there.

Readonly

Checking Readonly in fields that support this attribute causes compatible browsers to display the field and any content you pre-filled, but does not allow modification. This might be useful for showing the user information in the same manner as the rest of a form and implying that it's being submitted as part of the form data. It's only handy as an attribute you can set via a JavaScript.

Disabled

Checking Disabled grays a field out and makes it uneditable. Since JavaScript can turn the disabled status of a field on or off, programmers might want to use the Disabled checkbox to keep certain fields inaccessible, and then activate them based on a user's actions; Readonly might also be appropriate.

For instance, if you provide a user login where a radio button allows users to choose between logging in and changing their password, you might want the new password field to be disabled unless the user clicks the correct radio button (see Figure 13-14), as explained here.

1. On your HTML page, name the Change Password checkbox "changepass" and click Disabled in its Inspector.

Figure 13-14
Setting up a
way to toggle
a disabled
field

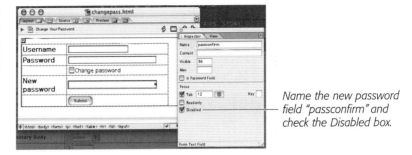

Name the new password
field "passconfirm" and
check the Disabled box.

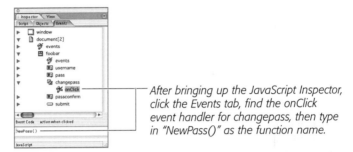

After bringing up the JavaScript Inspector,
click the Events tab, find the onClick
event handler for changepass, then type
in "NewPass()" as the function name.

2. Click the Open JavaScript Editor button, click (depending on platform) New Script Item or Create Script—the script and bean icon at the top of the Editor—and then click the Events tab in the Inspector.

3. Expand the view under document, your form name (FormName by default), and the checkbox that you've named changepass.

4. Select onClick and enter "NewPass()" in the Event Code field.

5. In the JavaScript Editor where you earlier created a new script, enter this as the script's contents:

```
function NewPass () {
    if (document.forms[0].changepass.value == "yes") {
        document.forms[0].passconfirm.disabled = false;
    } else {
        document.forms[0].passconfirm.disabled = true;
    }
}
```

Keystrokes

Users can move to a specific field or element by pressing a keystroke combination if you assign a letter in the Key field. On the Mac, a user types Command plus that key; under Windows, Alt plus that key. If you use this shortcut, you need to mention it alongside the element, as there's no other indication.

Keep in mind that most alphabetic Command and Alt key combinations are already assigned, so this feature doesn't provide much utility.

New Buttons

Standard HTML forms can have buttons that submit and/or reset a form, or an image that serves as a submit button. HTML 4.0 extends the standard button and adds a new, rich media button.

If you drag a Submit or Reset icon to your page and click Normal in the Input Button Inspector, you're actually turning the button into an HTML 4.0 button—the underlying HTML changes the button to a, well, "button" type of button. This kind of button has no action associated with it, like submit or reset; it can be used with JavaScript to trigger actions to better simulate an interactive user interface.

The rich media button is simply called Button in the Forms tab. This kind of button supports content inside its frame, which includes anything you can express in HTML, like images or even QuickTime movies. This button can be set via the Form Button Inspector to work as a submit or reset button, or like the Normal button described just above (see Figure 13-15).

Figure 13-15
Form Button
and its
Inspector

Smart Object used
as a Button

Better Labeling and Grouping

HTML 4.0 adds interface subtleties that make an HTML form look more like a program's dialog box—more familiar and easier to use at the same time.

List Hierarchies

In a popup menu, items are all displayed at the same depth—flat. HTML 4.0 adds tags and attributes to lists so you can code submenus without losing legible display in previous browsers. GoLive lacks support for these two features, resulting in the need for hand coding (see Figure 13-16).

Figure 13-16
Optgroup tag

```
<SELECT name="Shipping">
<OPTGROUP label="UPS">
<OPTION label="UPS Ground"
value="UPS Ground">UPS Ground
Shipping (3-10 days)
<OPTION label="UPS 2-day"
value="UPS 2-day">UPS Blue Label (2
days)
<OPTION label="UPS overnight"
value="UPS overnight">UPS Red Label
(overnight)
</OPTGROUP>
<OPTGROUP label="US Postal
Service">
<OPTION label="USPS First Class"
value="USPS First Class">USPS First
Class (3 to 7 days)
<OPTION label="USPS Priority Mail"
value="USPS Priority Mail">USPS

Priority Mail (2 to 3 days)
<OPTION label="USPS Express Mail"
value="USPS Express Mail">USPS
Express Mail (1 to 2 days)
</OPTGROUP>
<OPTGROUP label="FedEx">
<OPTION label="FedEx Two-Day"
value="FedEx Two-Day">FedEx Two-Day
(afternoon following next day)
<OPTION label="FedEx Standard"
value="FedEx Standard">FedEx
Standard (next business day after-
noon)
<OPTION label="FedEx Priority"
value="FedEx Priority">FedEx
Priority (next business day morn-
ing)
</OPTGROUP>
</SELECT>
```

The HTML above produces the menu at left in a fully HTML 4.0-compliant browser, such as Internet Explorer 5.1 for Mac OS X.

The Optgroup tag allows you to group a list of elements into submenus. Label becomes the submenu name. <OPTGROUP> can have a number of elements, and is then closed with its mate, </OPTGROUP>.

The Label attribute of the Option tag gets displayed as the submenu item, while the Name's value is sent as form data if that item is selected. In older browsers, the text following the Option tag gets displayed, and the Label attribute and Optgroup tags are ignored.

Label

A label is a piece of text that may be associated with a given field, such as a checkbox or radio button. Clicking the text has the same effect as clicking the field, bringing the focus to that field, or, in the case of a button, selecting or checking it.

GoLive uses a form of Point & Shoot to create the association between a label and its object. If you bring up the Form Label Inspector, you can point-and-shoot onto the element you want. Later, pressing the Show button draws a line to the associated object.

The value that GoLive automatically creates for the Reference field is best left alone, as it requires hand tweaking the associated field's HTML in Source view if you want to change the reference name.

Fieldset and Legend

You can group elements together into nifty boxed sets, just like GoLive does in its Inspector palettes, by using the Fieldset icon. Dragging this icon onto the page creates two different HTML tags: the Fieldset tag groups the set of items; the Legend tag provides the label for the set.

Unchecking Use Legend removes the text and deletes the tag. Checking it again restores the text you originally entered. You can also position the legend by selecting from the Alignment popup menu.

Form Validation

It's one thing to ask people to enter information you need from them; it's another to expect that they get it right. Some percentage of people, especially when you look at the cross-section of user experience level, will always type the wrong thing in the wrong place. Or even the most sophisticated user can make a typo. (This explains the frequent request to enter your email address twice in a row on many sign-up forms.)

To avoid asking questions when it's too late—after the form has already been submitted to the server—and to offload a server task to the browser, you can use JavaScript and/or a GoLive Action to validate a form. Form validation uses code to check what someone has typed in and see if it conforms to what you were expecting. If it doesn't, you can prompt the user to re-enter, or, with simple JavaScript, reformat what they entered.

Tip: Using Actions

If you're not familiar with GoLive Actions, the following information might be slightly obscure. We devote all of Chapter 26 to applying Actions later in the book. You may want to glance ahead and run through some of the examples first before trying to sort out the Field Validator Action.

Field Validator Action

The Field Validator Action examines a form and field that you define to see whether the value a user has entered or chosen conforms to guidelines. You first attach the Action to a trigger—or particular behavior—such as entering or leaving a field, or clicking the Submit button (see Figure 13-17).

Tip: Blurry Vision

We like to focus in on blur as a trigger for form validation: blur is the opposite of focus in JavaScript's terms, and JavaScript underlies all Actions. If your cursor is in

Figure 13-17
Form Button
and its
Inspector

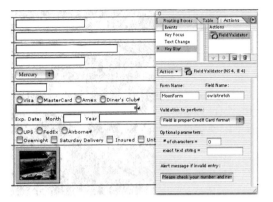

When the cursor leaves the field (Key Blur), the Field Validator Action confirms whether a valid credit card number was entered and alerts the user to re-enter if it wasn't.

a field, or if a button or other item has focus on it, leaving that field or clicking elsewhere blurs that focus. Actions (and JavaScripts) can be triggered by a blur.

1. Select a form element, such as a text field.

2. Bring up the Actions palette.

3. Select a trigger, such as Key Blur.

4. Click the New Action button which looks like a tiny page.

5. Select the Field Validator Action from the Action popup menu under the Getters submenu.

• Steps 1 and 3 vary from field to field, but steps 2, 4, and 5 are always the same.

The Field Validator Action has four separate parts (not neatly divided):

Form Name and Field Name. You need to name your form something unique as described earlier in this chapter, so that you can uniquely reference it here. Likewise, each field in a form should have a unique name.

Validation to Perform. This popup menu lists the kinds of validation you can perform. Most of the options are self-explanatory, such as Field Is Not Empty or Field Has This Many Characters. The proper email format option ensures that only legal characters and an at-sign (@) are in the field entry. The proper credit card format is debatable: we'd rather use JavaScript to avoid making users enter credit cards in the format that GoLive requires.

Optional Parameters. These two items correspond to specific validations selected from Validation to Perform. Enter the number of characters if you've

selected Field Has This Many Characters. Enter an exact text string if you selected that option.

Alert Message If Invalid Entry. GoLive will use a popup alert message to
warn users if their entries don't conform to the requirement. This Action does
not submit the form to the server if the condition isn't met; rather, users are
left on the page they were on and can correct the data and try again.

Tip: When to Validate

There are two schools of thought about when to validate a field entry: when the
user leaves that field or when the user submits the form. If you choose the former, you might drive someone crazy with an alert every time they tab; choose
the latter, and you might have to pop up several alerts warning of many different kinds of errors.

JavaScript Validation

If you don't know any JavaScript at all, you may still want to play with form
validation, as you can typically use recipe scripts to check results. With
JavaScript, you can check a wider variety of behavior and even offer more
flexibility in what a user enters than the Field Validator Action can handle.

Because we can't teach you all of JavaScript in this section or this book, we
provide a few examples below and in Chapter 25, *Authoring JavaScript*.

Validation Code

Validating form field entries requires you to know the name of form elements
and how to test them. We recommend naming all elements in a form as well
as the form itself, and we assume you've done that for the purposes of these
examples.

Tip: Counting on Numbers

You can address form elements and forms by the order in which they appear,
too, but that's tricky and time-consuming. Shifting field order or adding or removing fields or forms changes the numbering.

Let's look at a simple example to illustrate how you can perform multiple
tests to validate entries. Assume that if users check a box, they must also fill
in a field. If they leave that field blank, we want to tell them to fill it in (see
Figure 13-18).

Figure 13-18
Form Button
and its
Inspector

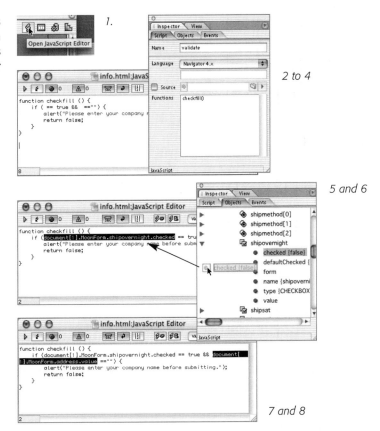

1.

2 to 4

5 and 6

7 and 8

1. Open the JavaScript Editor by clicking the script icon in the document layout window.

2. Click the New Script Item (Mac) or Create Script (Windows) button to create a new head script.

3. Enter this text:

```
function checkfill () {
    if ( == true && =="") {
        alert("Please enter your company name before
submitting.");
        return false;
    }
}
```

4. In the JavaScript Inspector's Script tab, name the script "validate".

5. In the JavaScript Inspector, select the Objects tab, and expand the document view, then the form view, then the checkbox view.

6. Drag the item labeled "checked" under the checkbox name into the second line of your script after "if (" and before "== true".

7. Expand the item for the text field in the JavaScript Inspector.

8. Drag the item labeled "value" into the script after what you typed.

You've now set up a validation script. But you still need to trigger that script by a user action.

Triggering Validation

You can set up a trigger for a JavaScript form validation script in two ways: by using normal triggers attached to objects on a page (the raw JavaScript method) or by using a GoLive Action to call a JavaScript function.

JavaScript trigger. Each object on a Web page has properties associated with it, including behavioral triggers (see Figure 13-19).

New in 6: FormName Name

GoLive 6 automatically names forms when you insert a Form object. To delete a form name, select it in the Layout view and remove the name via the Inspector.

1. Open the JavaScript Editor by clicking the script icon in the document layout window.

2. Click the Events tab of the JavaScript Inspector, then expand the document view, then the form name's view.

3. Expand the Submit button's view.

Figure 13-19
JavaScript
trigger for
function

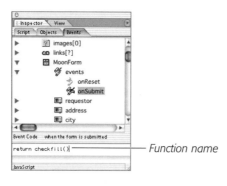

— *Function name*

A Script to Test Forms

This isn't a programming book, so we're not revealing the secrets of server scripts that process forms via CGI. These scripts vary by platform and server setup. You may not even have access to install programs on your site's Web server.

However, we want to give you a little help, as testing forms can be mystifying. If you are using a Web server on which you can run scripts and the perl scripting language is installed, you can enter and run the following script. (This script is also found at realworldgolive.com/simplecgi.txt.)

Enter everything exactly as seen here, remembering to use straight quotation marks, not curly, typographer's quotes. The first line requires the path to your system's copy of perl; under Unix or Mac OS X (via its Terminal program), you can enter "whereis perl" and replace "/usr/local/bin/perl" (the first line) with the results.

This script, when called via the Action attribute in a form that a Web browser submits, simply produces an alphabetical list of all the field names and values submitted by the form. This gives you a chance to run a test and make sure the values are being transmitted properly.

```perl
#!/usr/local/bin/perl
if ($ENV{'REQUEST_METHOD'} eq "GET") {
    $in = $ENV{'QUERY_STRING'};
} elsif ($ENV{'REQUEST_METHOD'} eq "POST") {
    read(STDIN, $in, $ENV{'CONTENT_LENGTH'});
}
@in = split(/&/,$in);
foreach (@in) {
    s/\+/ /g;
    local($key, $val) = split(/=/,2);
    $key =~ s/%(..)/pack("c",hex($1))/ge;
    $val =~ s/%(..)/pack("c",hex($1))/ge;
    $in{$key} .= " and " if (defined($in{$key}));
    $in{$key} .= $val;
}
print "Content-type: text/html\n\n";
print "<HEAD>\n<TITLE>Results of form</TITLE></HEAD>\n<BODY
BGCOLOR=\"#FFFFFF\">\n<TABLE BORDER=\"1\" CELLSPACING=\"2\"><TR> <TH
VALIGN=\"TOP\" ALIGN=\"LEFT\">Field name</TH>\n<TH VALIGN=\"TOP\"
ALIGN=\"LEFT\">Value</TH></TR>\n";

foreach (sort { $a cmp $b } keys %in) {
    print "<TR><TD VALIGN=\"TOP\" ALIGN=\"LEFT\">$_</TD>";
    print "<TD VALIGN=\"TOP\" ALIGN=\"LEFT\">$in{$_} </TD></TR>";
}
print "</TABLE></BODY>\n";
exit 1;
```

4. Select onClick.

5. Under Action at the bottom of the Inspector, enter

```
return checkfill()
```

Your trigger is all set up: when a user clicks the Submit button, the browser runs the validation script. If it returns false (the box is checked and the field is empty), then the form isn't submitted.

GoLive Action trigger. You can also use an Action to trigger your script, though it's less efficient (see Figure 13-20).

Figure 13-20
Action trigger
for function

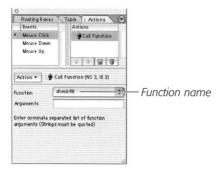

— *Function name*

1. Select the Submit button in the document layout.

2. In the Actions palette, select Mouse Click.

3. Click the New Action button.

4. Select Call Function from the Actions menu's Specials submenu.

5. Select "checkfill" from the popup menu that lists available scripts.

Form a Line

Since forms make up a significant portion of the Web's interactivity, the importance of getting them right is paramount. GoLive's approach to forms makes them easy to construct, maintain, and modify, and in the process you'll find that it helps you make them good-looking as well.

CHAPTER 14

Source Editing

Updating software is a matter of addition: new buttons, new menus, new look, new features, even new spins on old features. So imagine our surprise when we learned that one of GoLive's features does absolutely nothing—which is exactly what it should do. Adobe calls it 360Code, a slick way of saying that GoLive doesn't modify the underlying HTML code unless you ask it to.

Why is this important? HTML is the language of the Web, the set of directions that browsers interpret as Web pages. In some ways it's like PostScript, the page-description language used in desktop publishing to describe to a printer or imagesetter what a printed page looks like; the printer builds a picture of that page from the PostScript "recipe" and outputs it.

Unlike PostScript, however, HTML is accessible to Web designers and even average mortals. In fact, despite visual editors like GoLive, designers find themselves hand-tweaking HTML code to fine tune it, or include functionality offered by JavaScript, XML, ASP, PHP, JSP, ColdFusion, or other varieties of Web content. Using GoLive's source code editing tools, you can write and edit the code directly, add attributes to tags, and check the HTML's syntax for errors.

Accessing Source Code

GoLive offers five main approaches for interacting with a page's underlying HTML: the Split Source pane in the Layout Editor, the Source Code Editor, the Outline Editor, the Source Code palette, and the Visual Tag Editor. Other helpful methods of accessing code include the Markup Tree bar and GoLive's powerful search and replace functions. There's no "right" option; it's largely a matter of your own personal preferences, though each has its advantages.

Split Source pane. Some people can look at a page of HTML code and mentally see the page that it creates; others spend long, happy days in the Layout Editor without viewing a single bracketed tag. Most of us, however, open the door between the two rooms several times a day (and, yes, we occasionally slam the door), twiddle with the code, then preview the results. Now, you can view your layout and its code in the same window by activating the Split Source pane. Either select Show Split Source from the View menu, or click the Show/Hide Split Source button at the lower-left corner of the Document window (see Figure 14-1).

Figure 14-1
Show Split
Source

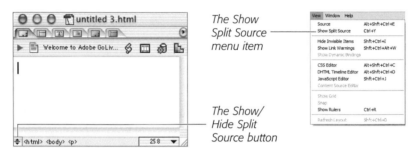

The Show Split Source menu item

The Show/ Hide Split Source button

Source Code palette. Similar to the Split Source pane, the Source Code palette presents a view of your code in a separate palette. If your screen real estate allows it, having the Source Code palette and the Layout Editor open at the same time lets you view more of both (see Figure 14-2). Select Source Code from the Window menu to display the palette.

Figure 14-2
Layout Editor
and Source
Code palette

The Source Code palette shows the contextual selection from the page.

Tip: Palette and Editor

If you switch to the Source Code Editor while the Source Code palette is displayed, the palette becomes blank, since your code is then fully displayed in the Document window.

Tip: Edit in Layout Preview (Mac)

Normally, the Layout Preview is only good for viewing your page as it would appear in a browser. However, you can make changes to the HTML in the Source Code palette or the Split Source pane and view the change in the Layout Preview.

Source Code Editor. If you want to immerse yourself in code without the pesky distraction of what your page actually looks like, switch to the Source Code Editor. Click the Source tab in the Document window, or choose Source from the View menu.

Tip: Source Editor Shortcut

We've been asking for this feature for years: press Command-Option-E (Mac) or Alt-Shift-Control-E (Windows) to switch to the Source Code Editor. Unfortunately, there isn't yet a keyboard shortcut to switch back to the Layout Editor, but we're ever hopeful.

Visual Tag Editor. To tweak a single tag manually, bring up the Visual Tag Editor from the Special menu. This dialog box lets you type attributes for whatever tag surrounds your cursor (see Figure 14-3).

What's New in 6

Apparently, some designers using GoLive 5 did not think it offered enough ways to get at a page's source code. In addition to the Source Code Editor and the Source Code palette, GoLive 6 boasts one of the program's best features: the Split Source pane, which lets you view the layout and source within the same Layout Editor window. If that's not enough, use the Visual Tag Editor to tweak the attributes of the tag belonging to whatever is selected in the layout.

Selecting Upper Block, a new entry in the Special menu, lets you highlight objects controlled by a tag higher up in the HTML page's hierarchy. For example, select a word and choose Select Upper Block to highlight the paragraph tags enclosing the word, or invoke it again to select the table cell that contains the paragraph.

We're also happy to see an improved Syntax Checker, which takes advantage of the Highlight palette to help you pinpoint errors in your code.

Figure 14-3
Visual Tag
Editor

Outline Editor. A novel approach to editing source code, the Outline Editor builds an outline of your page's structure (see Figure 14-4). Although we don't use the Outline Editor for creating pages from scratch, it has been extremely helpful at times when trying to troubleshoot why a page doesn't display correctly in browsers.

Figure 14-4
Outline Editor

Markup Tree. The purpose of the Markup Tree, which is located in the Status Bar at the bottom of the Layout Editor, is to give you a quick overview of the HTML hierarchy above the placement of your cursor in the Layout Editor (see Figure 14-5). On a standard page, you're likely to see only the HTML, Body, and P tags listed. The palette really comes into its own when you're in the midst of a complex nested table or similarly more advanced formatting. Clicking a tag automatically selects that area or object on the page in the Layout Editor.

Figure 14-5
Markup Tree

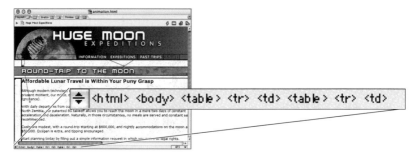

New in 6: Markup Tree on Status Bar

In GoLive 5, the Markup Tree was in its own palette, but it was quite difficult to use contextually. Putting it in the status bar makes much more sense.

Viewing Options

The Split Source pane, Source Code palette, and Source Code Editor perform the same tasks in different areas in GoLive, so it makes sense that they share the same options for viewing the code. The following settings, with a few exceptions, can be accessed from the Source Code palette's popout menu, the View palette (when one of the three areas is active), or from the contextual menu.

Tip: Code Settings Around GoLive

When you make a change to the viewing options in one of the code editors, the setting is applied to the others. For example, if you turn on line numbers in the Source Code palette, they will also appear in the Split Source pane the next time you click on it.

Toolbar. Available in the Split Source pane and Source Code Editor, this option displays a toolbar at the top of the pane/window containing buttons for colorizing text (see "Syntax Colorizing"), and toggling the Word Wrap and Line Numbers settings (see Figure 14-6). The toolbar also includes the Start Check Syntax button, which we deal with later in this chapter.

Figure 14-6
Highlight
buttons

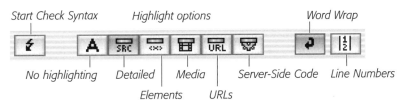

Start Check Syntax   Highlight options   Word Wrap

No highlighting   Detailed   Media   Server-Side Code   Line Numbers

Elements   URLs

Local Mode. By default, the Source Code palette shows as much HTML surrounding the position of your cursor as the window size allows. Depending on the amount of code, however, you may not immediately see where you're typing. Selecting Local Mode in the Split Source pane or Source Code palette displays only the code selected in the Layout Editor. GoLive is pretty strict about how this works. if nothing is selected, the palette is empty; selecting a word displays only that word. But when you select an object (such as an image or table), or even a range of formatted text, the applicable HTML tags appear (see Figure 14-7).

Figure 14-7
Local Mode,
Word Wrap,
and Line
Numbering

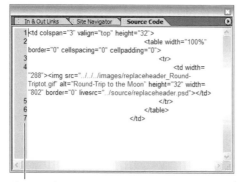

Line numbers

Tip: The Missing Link

If you select a linked bit of text in the Layout Editor, the Source palette set to Local Mode shows just the text, not the surrounding A tag and Href attribute. Include the characters just before and after the link in your selection to display the A tag.

Word Wrap. Unless GoLive stretches across multiple 21-inch monitors, there are some lines of HTML that won't fit the width of the Source Code palette. Selecting Word Wrap from the popout menu wraps the text to the current window size (see Figure 14-7, above). We leave this turned on since there's no reason to worry about line ending unless you're formatting pages with the Pre tags.

Display Line Numbers. Some people prefer to use line numbers to help track down problems in their code. With Display Line Numbers activated, a column of numbers appears along the left side of the source code. If you have Word Wrap turned on, the line numbers correspond only to lines ending in line breaks (see Figure 14-7, above).

Dim When Inactive. A nice, subtle preference is Dim When Inactive, which shows the HTML text at about half the intensity of normal text when the Split Source pane or Source Code palette isn't active. Not only does this make it easy to tell when you're editing the source code, it also minimizes the distraction of all that code when you're not working with it directly (see Figure 14-8).

Syntax Colorizing

To make the code display more legibly, GoLive offers options to highlight different parts of HTML syntax in different colors. These options appear on

Figure 14-8
Dim When
Inactive

Dimmed text

the Toolbar in the Source Code Editor and Split Source pane, as well as the View palette and the Code Coloring submenu of the contextual menu (see Figure 14-9).

Figure 14-9
Code Coloring
submenu in
the contextual
menu

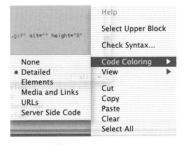

Tip: Colorizing and Highlighting

While syntax colorizing helps to make a page of source code easier to read, a more powerful tool is the Highlight palette. You can specify elements and objects to be shown in the Layout Editor, but those also carry to the Source Code Editor when it is displayed (see Figure 14-10). Consult Chapter 2, *Layout*, for details of the Highlight palette.

By default, the Detailed option is chosen, which makes GoLive color HTML by category: black for text, blue for HTML tags, green for special characters (like), and so on. There are four other options; only one form of highlighting may be active.

- Set your code to black text by choosing None (in the Toolbar, the command is called the Colorize Nothing button).

- Colorize only HTML tags by choosing Elements.

Figure 14-10
Highlight
palette

- Highlight just links and pieces of media (images, QuickTime files, etc.) by choosing Media and Links.

- Highlight links only by choosing URLs.

- Highlight code that activates instructions from the Web server by choosing Server Side Code.

Editing Source Code

Those familiar with HTML are likely to edit the code by typing tags and text directly into the Split Source pane, Source Code palette, or Source Code Editor. But you don't need an encyclopedic memory of the language to edit the source.

Tip: Quicker Keyboard Navigation (Mac)

You can move around using the arrow keys, of course, but they alone won't get you very far. Adding Option to a left or right arrow key moves the cursor from word to word. Command-left arrow or -right arrow takes you to the beginning or end of a line. Option-up arrow or -down arrow moves your cursor one full screen's distance (like the Page Up and Page Down keys); using Command instead jumps to the top and bottom of the document (like Home and End).

Tip; Quicker Keyboard Navigation (Windows)

GoLive for Windows offers fewer navigational keystrokes. Control plus the left or right arrow key moves the cursor from word to word.

Drag icons from the Objects palette. Nearly any icon from the Objects palette can be dragged onto one of the source code editing windows to insert its code. For example, dragging the Image icon produces the following HTML at the point where the icon is dropped:

```
<img src="(EmptyReference!)" width="32" height="32"
border="0">
```

This feature can be particularly handy when you're not sure of an element's tags and attributes, such as when you embed a QuickTime movie (see Figure 14-11). True, you can accomplish this in the Layout Editor as well, but if you're already editing the source, you may as well stay in the Source Code Editor.

Figure 14-11
Adding code
from the
Objects palette

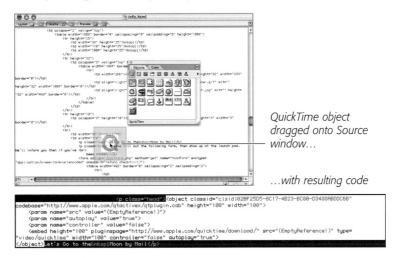

QuickTime object
dragged onto Source
window...

...with resulting code

Apply styles to highlighted text. You can also edit the appearance of text on your page using the text formatting controls covered in Chapter 4, *Text and Fonts*. Select some text, then choose formatting from the Toolbar or the Type menu. However, you can't toggle formatting on and off as you can in the Layout Editor. Clicking the Italic button in the Toolbar will add <I> and </I> around your selected text, but clicking it again doesn't remove it—in fact, it adds those tags again.

Drag and drop links. When you're creating links, GoLive offers another helpful tool: you can drag and drop a file from the desktop or a site window to create a link to that object. In this case, GoLive uses the file's name as placeholder-linked text; to make the link apply to an existing object or text, simply move the <A HREF> code in front of your desired link (see Figure 14-12). Don't forget to place the </A> closing tag after the link.

Select Upper Block command. This feature also works in the Layout Editor, but it's a code-specific action. With a range of code selected, choose Select Upper Block from the Special menu. The HTML element that contains your

Figure 14-12
Drag and drop
files to create
links

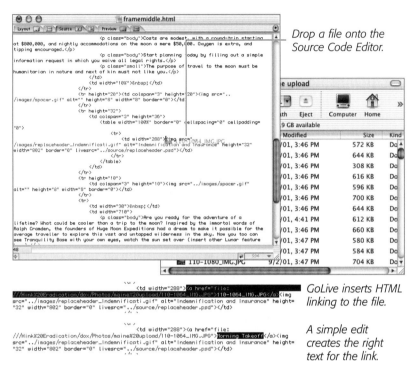

Drop a file onto the
Source Code Editor.

GoLive inserts HTML
linking to the file.

A simple edit
creates the right
text for the link.

selection becomes selected. For example, with a word highlighted on a basic page, choosing Select Upper Block selects the word's paragraph; choosing the option again selects the table cell, since the paragraph was located within an individual cell (see Figure 14-13).

Figure 14-13
Select Upper
Block

With a single word
highlighted, Select
Upper Block...

...selects the whole paragraph, but
when chosen again...

...selects the table cell in which
the paragraph is located.

The Noedit tag. Although GoLive is good about leaving a page's source code alone, there may be times when you want to be absolutely sure the program doesn't change a range of text, especially when using the Pre tag to format text with hard returns. At times like that, use the Noedit tag. Either type <NOEDIT> and </NOEDIT> around the text, or drag the Tag icon from the Basic tab of the Objects palette onto your page. The text enclosed within the Noedit tag doesn't appear in the Layout Editor, but you can feel secure that it's protected in its virtual source wrapper.

Formatting Source Code

Although Web browsers don't care about the appearance of HTML—you can, in fact, omit line breaks and other empty space between tags and get the same result—people who hand-edit code often prefer to control how it's displayed. Some people like to see elements like tables and forms indented for easier identification, while others prefer every line to appear flush left but with generous amounts of white space before and after.

The key to reformatting code lies in the scary-sounding Rewrite Source Code command located under the Edit menu. Whenever you invoke Rewrite Source Code, GoLive reformats your HTML code based on the settings found in the program's preferences and in Web Settings. GoLive displays an alert to point out that rewriting the code cannot be undone, so have a backup of the file handy in case you want to reverse the formatting you've applied. Don't worry, though: unless you've completely trashed your Web Settings information, your HTML appears clean and orderly on the other side.

Web Settings. GoLive's preferences let you specify how code shows up in the different source code views, including colors for syntax highlighting, typefaces, and whether tags appear bold or not To control how new code is written, as well as how it's optionally rewritten, take a trip to GoLive's Web Settings. Although we cover these options to some degree in Chapter 28, *Controlling Web Settings*, their usefulness applies most when editing source code.

The Global tab of the Web Settings window is devoted to source formatting (see Figure 14-14). Here, you can specify options such as the case for tags and attributes (UPPER, lower, or Capital), and the method of indenting text.

The Markup tab contains the definitions for the tags themselves, and this is where you can fine-tune the way your code displays on a tag-by-tag basis.

Basic tab. Clicking a tag name brings up the Web Settings Element Inspector. For the most part, you should probably avoid changing the settings here since they derive from the HTML specification. But do pay attention to a few items.

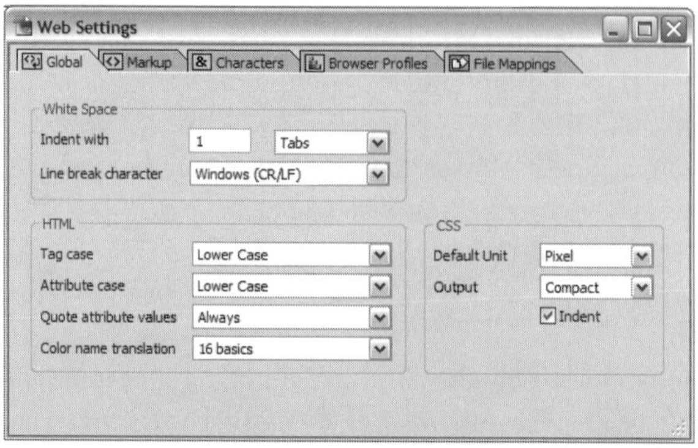

Figure 14-14 Global tab of Web Settings

Tip: Mind Your Ps

The <P> tag gets special treatment, since it lets the body section of the page accept text. If you open a blank, default GoLive page, a <P> and </P> tag set is already inserted. This allows you to begin typing or adding elements right away when you're in the Layout Editor.

In the Web Settings Element Inspector's Basic tab, <P> adds two options: Avoid every first <P>, and Avoid every last </P>. This protects the original tags from reformatting by the other specifications found in the Basic tab. Otherwise, you run the risk of deleting the tags that are holding the body together.

Tip: Removing the Default <P></P> Tags

As we just said, every blank page's body section includes a paired set of P tags by default. But some people don't need the ubiquitous tag pair, especially designers creating documents containing DHTML or other code variants.

Multiple Text Indent Controls

Indenting source code is one of those personal preferences that seems to polarize HTML coders. Is a page more readable when sections are indented to indicate their structure, or does the added horizontal space cause your eyes to zigzag down the screen? GoLive offers no fewer than three methods of controlling how source code is indented.

In Preferences, the Source section includes an Auto Indent checkbox where you can specify how many characters make up a Tab character.

In the Global tab of Web Settings, the Indent With value determines the base number of Tab characters or spaces used when applying indents for each tag set (see next item). To make your source run flush left against the window, set this value to 0 (zero).

The Output tab of the Web Settings Element Inspector lets you choose to indent the text between open and closed tag sets.

If you change these settings, they are applied to new documents; to make them stick to current pages, use the Rewrite Source Code command under the Edit menu.

To get around them, create a new blank file, delete the <P></P> pair, then save the file. In the General section of GoLive's preferences, check the New Document box and specify the file as your default. From now on, every new page will be created without the tags. (You can do this for any object on any page—if each page of a site needs your company logo in the upper-left corner, you can add the HTML that defines the logo and set that file as the default.)

Output tab. A more dramatic method of controlling the code formatting is found on the Output tab of the Web Settings Element Inspector. The Separation options dictate how much white space (line breaks) appears before and after each instance of a tag (see Figure 14-15).

Figure 14-15
Separation
options

- **None.** Text surrounding a tag runs right against the tag's brackets.

- **Small, Medium, Large, X Large.** The size differences refer to the number of line breaks separating the tag and its surrounding text. Small adds one line break, Medium adds two breaks, etc.

- **Before Start, Behind End, Behind Start, Before End.** These options determine whether the tag shares the same line with its preceding text and following text.

- **Indent Content.** With Indent Content checked, GoLive indents the content between open and close tags to increase its readability and visually cement the relationship to the tag.

- **Color.** Choose a custom color for that tag to appear when the source view option is set to Elements (see "Syntax Colorizing" earlier in this chapter).

Visual Tag Editor

Sometimes you want to view as much code as will fit in your window, but other times it's easier to edit just one tag or a small block of HTML. In the latter case, use the Visual Tag Editor to spot-edit your code (see Figure 14-16). With your cursor positioned in the Layout Editor, choose Visual Tag Editor from the Special menu, or type Command-Shift-E (Mac) or Alt-Shift-E (Windows).

Figure 14-16
Visual Tag
Editor

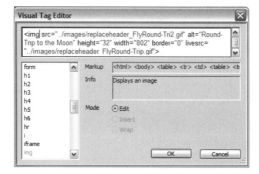

You can type a tag into the text field at the top of the screen (GoLive even provides the tag's brackets), or double-click a tag name from the list at left (see Figure 14-16). When you add a tag and type a space, the list changes to include attributes that GoLive recognizes for it; for example, selecting "font" from the list and adding a space brings up attributes such as size and color. Double-clicking an attribute inserts an equal sign (=) and quotation marks, where you can type the attribute's value.

The Visual Tag Editor also includes a markup tree similar to the one found at the bottom of the document window. It shows you the hierarchy of tags leading to where your cursor is located; click a tag name to select and edit it in the text field.

The Info area is a particularly nice touch: click a tag name or attribute in the text field to view a brief description of what it does. The Mode buttons indicate whether you're editing an existing tag or inserting a new tag. If you select a range of text or objects in the Layout Editor and then activate the Visual Tag Editor, the Wrap button tells you that the tag you add will surround your selection (for example, selecting text and adding the Strong tag in the Visual Tag Editor automatically supplies the closing </STRONG> code).

With the tag edited, click OK to add it to your page and dismiss the dialog box.

Outline Editor

Click the tab to the right of the Source Code Editor tab to open the Outline Editor. At first, you might wonder what alternate dimension you just stepped into. You're met with a collection of hierarchical "container tags" that can be collapsed by clicking the toggle triangle to the right of the beveled tag handle. For instance, clicking the toggle triangle of the Head container tag closes all the code associated with the Head tag (which appears indented below it), plus the closing Head tag. Meanwhile, the Body tag is still visible. To close the containers for the entire page, click the toggle triangle on the HTML container (see Figure 14-17).

Figure 14-17
Viewing code in the Outline Editor

A selection viewed in the Outline Editor…

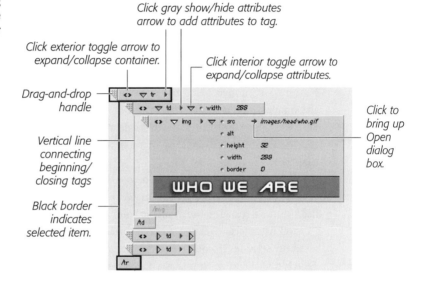

Click gray show/hide attributes arrow to add attributes to tag.

Click exterior toggle arrow to expand/collapse container.

Click interior toggle arrow to expand/collapse attributes.

Drag-and-drop handle

Click to bring up Open dialog box.

Vertical line connecting beginning/ closing tags

Black border indicates selected item.

…then viewed in HTML Source Editor…

```
<tr>
                                <td width="288"><img src="images/headwho.
gif" alt="" height="32" width="288" border="0"></td>
                                <td align="right" width="100%"><img src=
"images/headspacer.gif" alt="" height="32" width="100%" border="0"></td>
                                <td align="right" width="460"><img src=
"images/headright.jpg" alt="" height="32" width="460" border="0"></td>
                        </tr>
```

Tip: Expand or Contract All

Hold down the Option (Mac) or Shift (Windows) key when switching to the Outline Editor to show the entire outline either expanded or contracted (it applies the opposite setting of how it was previously displayed).

Your work in Outline mode is to configure code in containers. Each tag may have its own attributes; it may also contain other tags and text. All the values attached to any tag are accessed through popup menus on the containers.

Tip: Expand Attributes

You can hold down the Option or Shift key when clicking an element's toggle arrow to expand the entire hierarchy of that element. For example, clicking the Body tag expands everything within it, including tables and paragraphs.

It's a bit daunting, but the Outline Editor can be very helpful for moving large sections of code (by grabbing the handle of a container tag and dragging it to a desired spot). It's also helpful for beginning coders who gain the benefit of using a container's popup menus to see what attributes can be used with a particular tag. Some programmers also favor an object model where they know exactly what they're getting into so they're not just typing, but actually manipulating elements.

Say you want to add an alignment attribute to the Img tag shown in Figure 14-17, above. Click and hold the show/hide attributes triangle. This is the smaller, gray triangle to the right of the HTML tag—not to be confused with the larger, outlined toggle triangle at the front of the container. Holding this triangle brings up a popup menu of available attributes. Select Align from that menu (see Figure 14-18).

The Align attribute is then added to the container's list of attributes, from which you can click the gray triangle to its right and call up another popup list, this time showing the available values for the attribute.

You could also click the space to the right of the gray triangle and type the attribute's value. If you've entered the value name incorrectly, the Outline Editor doesn't warn you that you've made a syntax error. The only way to check errors is to return to the Source Code Editor and run the Syntax Checker (see "Checking Syntax" later in this chapter).

Figure 14-18
Modifying
code in the
Outline Editor

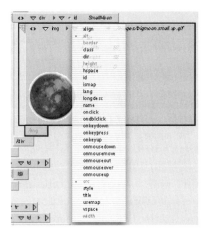
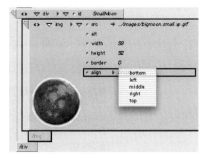

Adding an attribute to the Img tag (left), and then adding the attribute's value (right)

Adding and Editing Elements

When you switch to the Outline Editor, the Toolbar contextually changes to become the Source toolbar, from which you can insert elements, attributes, text, comments, and custom elements (for XML, ASP, PHP, etc.). You can also access these Source toolbar items from the contextual menu.

Most HTML tags are binary, meaning they operate in a matched opening and closing pair. In the opening tag, attributes appear (if any are needed) that modify the tag, such as width and background color for a Table tag. Inside the pair, the information in question appears, such as the text for a link or elements in a table cell. The pair of tags forms a container—sound familiar?

Some elements (such as Img) are called unary because they stand on their own without requiring a closing tag. (There are also a few tags, such as P, that can operate either way, due to early confusion over the direction of HTML.)

Clicking the Toggle Binary button adds a closing tag to an HTML element that doesn't necessarily require a closing tag. For example, click a P tag to select it (a black boundary surrounds the entire element), then click the Toggle Binary button from the Toolbar to add a closing tag directly below the selected tag.

Checking Syntax

Even the most code-hardened programmer isn't immune from introducing errors in source code. Typos, elements that weren't closed, improperly nested tags…these things do happen. GoLive's Syntax Checker can help spot those errors for you to fix. It can also look over your code to see if your page complies with several different browser specifications. Although not a substitute for testing on multiple platforms and browsers, the Syntax Checker can help identify elements that could give you trouble.

To check for errors in the HTML, choose Check Syntax from the Edit menu, or display the Highlight palette and click the Syntax button. (You can also press Command-Option-K on the Mac or press Alt-Shift-Control-B under Windows.) The Syntax Check dialog box appears (see Figure 14-19).

Tip: Check Anywhere

The Syntax Checker works in any of GoLive's editors, not just the Source Code Editor.

The Syntax Checker looks for two things when examining a page: the general "well-formedness" of the code, such as making sure tags are closed and nested properly, and the compatibility of the code with various browsers. The

Figure 14-19
Syntax Check

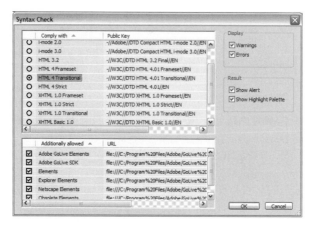

options in the compatibility list correspond to common Document Type Definitions (DTDs). The default, !DOCTYPE assigned, matches whichever Doctype you've chosen for the page. To check against another DTD, click its radio button. The last three items in the list check against well-formedness of code as displayed in Internet Explorer and Netscape browser versions.

Tip: Changing Doctype

As we mentioned way back in Chapter 2, *Layout*, to change a page's Doctype, select an option from the Doctype submenu of the Document window's popout menu.

The list at the bottom of the Syntax Check dialog box provides for additional compatibility factors. These take into account GoLive-specific code such as Livesrc (the image attribute that specifies the source file for a smart object), and prevents the Syntax Checker from flagging perfectly legal tags that you'd normally strip out before uploading to your Web server or that a browser would ignore.

Tip: Uncheck the Extras

If you're looking to eradicate any code that doesn't belong to these specifications—especially something like HTML 4.0 Strict—uncheck the options in the list at the bottom before you run the Syntax Checker.

When you check a page's syntax, GoLive examines the browser or Doctype compatibility information stored for each markup tag in Web Settings. It uses this information to determine whether any given bit of HTML or other markup language should be marked as an error or with a warning for a particular range of browsers. So, if you have a custom tag that's not in Web Settings (or if a tag is misspelled in your code), you will receive a warning that GoLive doesn't recognize the tag.

GoLive also warns you when the contents of attributes don't work with the browser set you selected. For example, if you've applied a lean rollover to an image and check against Netscape 2-4, the Syntax Checker points out that the attribute "onmousedown" isn't supported by Netscape 3.x or Explorer 3.x.

What's the difference between an error and a warning? In general, errors flag problems with tags, while warnings point out concerns with attributes. So the <TABLE> tag misspelled as <TBLE> generates an error, but if the tag's background color attribute is set to "whte" instead of "white," GoLive calls it a warning (see Figure 14-20).

Figure 14-20
Warnings and
Errors in the
Highlight
palette

Bad color name

Bad tag

Tip: Displaying Warnings and Errors

The Highlight palette doesn't distinguish between warnings and errors, and GoLive itself always says that it found some number of "error(s)." The only way to tell the difference between the two is to uncheck Warnings or Errors in Syntax Check before checking the page.

The Result options define how errors are displayed. Clicking Show Alert pops up an alert summarizing how many errors or warnings were found. Show Highlight Palette displays the palette if it isn't already visible. If you turn this option off, the errors on your page are just highlighted without any description.

Tip: Annoying Alerts

For our part, we tend to turn off the Show Alert option. We don't particularly need to know how many errors were found, and we especially don't want to have to dismiss an alert window to find out. Since the Highlight palette tells us the same information, we stick with its superior notification.

Tip: Syntax Error, or HTML Spec?

In some cases, what may appear to be a syntax problem is actually valid HTML, causing GoLive to not flag what appears to be a problem. For example, the HTML 3.2 and 4.0 specifications for a table requires that it begin with <TABLE> and end with </TABLE>. However, the rows and cells within the table, expressed as <TR> and <TD>, don't require closing tags—although most coders consider it good form to include them. To make these (and other) tags required, go to Web Settings, locate the tag, and select Required from the End Tag popup menu in the Web Settings Element Inspector.

Macros

If you spend a lot of time working in one of the three text-editing views—Source Code Editor, JavaScript Editor, or the Source tab of the CSS Editor—you can set up shortcuts or "macros" to insert longer bits of commonly typed text. This tool is handy if you have a logo image or boilerplate text that appears frequently.

Macros have a short name, which you type, followed by a key combination to transform what you typed into the text it stands for. For instance, in the Source Code Editor, you can type the letter A plus Command-Shift-M (Mac) or Control-Shift-M (Windows) to insert

```
<A HREF="http://where"></A>
```

with the word "where" highlighted (see Figure 14-21). You can also type "A" and then select Use Macro from the Special menu.

Figure 14-21
Using text
macros

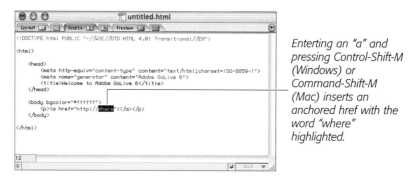

Entering an "a" and pressing Control-Shift-M (Windows) or Command-Shift-M (Mac) inserts an anchored href with the word "where" highlighted.

Creating macros. You can define your own macros by editing the appropriate file in the TextMacros folder in the Settings folder found in the GoLive application's folder. GoLive has four folders here, which contain macro definition files:

- **All.** The Default.macro file holds macros that work in all three editors.
- **CSS.** The CSSSource.macro file includes macros for the CSS Editor.
- **JavaScript.** The JavaScriptSource.macro file defines macros for the JavaScript Editor.
- **Markup.** The MarkupSource.macro file applies to the Source Code Editor.

Macros consist of the macro name and the macro's content surrounded by a unique character or delimiter that defines the start and end of the macro. You can insert marks in the macro that cause text to be highlighted or the cursor to be positioned in a location after GoLive inserts the macro.

If you want to write a macro that inserts a specific font set in a Font tag whenever you type "f1" but requires you to enter a size, you enter it into either the MarkupSource.macro file or the Default.macro file:

```
f1 '<font face="Geneva,Helvetica,Arial,Swiss, SunSans-
Regular" size="%size%">'
```

The single quotation marks indicate the beginning and end of the macro. The percentage signs mark the area to highlight after insertion. You can also just position the cursor in the right place without providing helpful text by inserting a vertical bar:

```
f1 '<font face="Geneva,Helvetica,Arial,Swiss,SunSans-
Regular" size="|">'
```

The GoLive online help offers extensive insight into the nomenclature, syntax, and special conditions affecting macros.

Find and Replace

In case you hadn't noticed, most Web pages tend to require a lot of code to operate, which means it can be harder to find the sections you're looking for when editing the HTML. GoLive offers several methods of searching for text and elements—so many, in fact, that we've had to scatter them throughout the book where they're most applicable, even though they all come up in the general Find dialog box.

In this chapter, we talk about the Find dialog's Find & Replace and Element tabs. We cover regular-expression pattern matching, an option for finding complicated strings of characters in several places in GoLive, including the Find feature, in Chapter 22, *Advanced Features.*

Invoke the Find feature by selecting it from the Edit menu, or by pressing Command-F (Mac) or Control-F (Windows).

As a somewhat faster method of searching, select a range of text in your code and choose Find Selection from the Edit menu. The next occurrence is highlighted, without you ever needing to bring up the Find dialog box at all.

Find & Replace Tab

For longer pages or pages on which you need to change the same element multiple times, consider using the Find & Replace tab (see Figure 14-22). It offers some simple and powerful controls for locating items on a page.

Figure 14-22
Find & Replace tab

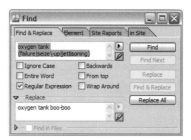

Find field. Enter the text you want to find here. The Find field keeps track of your most recent searches, so you can "replay" them by selecting from the popup menu next to the field. To edit a longer string of text, click the Edit Field button (indicated by the image of a pencil) to bring up an Edit dialog.

Ignore Case. Checking this box ignores the capitalization both in what you've entered and what's on the page. So searching for "EaRtH" matches earth, EARTH, Earth, and eArTh.

Entire Word. This option limits the find to whole words, which are defined as characters between white space (returns, spaces, and tabs).

Regular Expression. GoLive offers the powerful option of using regular-expression pattern matching to specify wildcard patterns to find (and replace) items in text. We devote a section to its power and complexity in Chapter 22, *Advanced Features.*

Backwards, From Top, Wrap Around. If you check Backwards, GoLive searches from the current point in the text to the start of the document. Checking From Top searches from the start of the document to the bottom.

To search the entire document in either direction, regardless of where your cursor is located, check Wrap Around.

Find button. Click Find to find the first instance of the text in the Find field. When a match is made, the document window moves to the foreground by default. You can change this behavior in the Find section of GoLive's Preferences using the When Match Is Found popup menu.

Find Next button. This button finds the next instance of your search text. A more practical incarnation of this command is to use Command-G (Mac) or Control-G (Windows) with the Document window frontmost to find the next occurrence without switching back to the Find dialog box.

Replace field. Finding isn't enough: the Find & Replace tab can handle the useful task of replacing items wherever they occur on a page or in selected instances. Click the expansion triangle next to the word Replace at the bottom of the Find dialog box to open the Replace field if it's not already expanded. As with the Find field, recently used Replace entries appear in the popup menu to the right of the field.

Replace button. Click this button to replace the current instance, and leave the cursor at that point on the page.

Find & Replace. This button performs the replace operation, and then performs Find Next.

Replace All. It's dangerous, tempting, and generally useful: clicking Replace All changes all instances in the document that it finds. Just in case, make sure you have a backup copy of the file before replacing all. (This is especially critical when using Find & Replace on multiple pages, discussed later.)

Element Tab

It's one thing to perform a search for a word like "mocha" and replace it with "espresso" throughout a page or site. But what if you want to change all table borders sized 4 points down to 2 points? You could jump into the Source Code Editor, search for the following code, and change its value from 4 to 2.

```
border="4"
```

But that would also change the size of image borders, leaving you to construct more elaborate searches or make the adjustments by hand.

A better method is to use the controls found in the Find dialog's Element tab (see Figure 14-23). Unlike the straightforward Find command, the Element feature's controls understand HTML and tag structure.

Figure 14-23
Setting up
search
elements

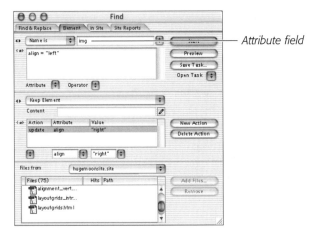
Attribute field

Defining search elements. Choose either Name Is or Name Matches from the Element Name popup menu. Type the name of the tag in the field. Alternately, you can choose a tag name from the popup menu to the right of the field.

Tip: Regular Expressions

You can also enter regular expressions in the name field; this is covered in Chapter 22, *Advanced Features*. For instance, entering ".*" allows you to search for an attribute that might occur in any tag, as ".*" matches any tag's name.

If you're searching for a particular attribute of that element, select its name from the Attribute popup menu, or type its value into the Attribute field (see Figure 14-23, above). This menu changes depending on which tag name is selected. The Operator popup menu defines the relationship you're applying to the search. You can set up more than one attribute at a time using the operators "and," "or," "not," or "()" between each attribute definition.

If you want to find a Font tab that contains both a Color and Size attribute, enter Font in the Name field and the following in the Attribute field:

```
color <> "" and size <> ""
```

You can also find all instances of the tag without any attributes or their values by leaving the Attribute field blank.

Defining actions. With the search defined, it's time to take action. In the Action section of the dialog (the middle), select one of the following actions from the popup menu.

- **Keep Element:** does nothing to the tag name itself, but makes it possible to change the attributes. This is the most typical setting; most tasks involve changing attribute values.

- **Rename Element:** retains the tag's attributes, but changes the name of the tag itself. Enter a replacement name in the New Name field.

- **Delete Element:** removes the entire element, including start and end tags.

- **Replace Element by Its Content:** removes the start and end tags, but keeps the information appearing between them. This is a great way to remove A tags around anchors or links while leaving the text intact.

- **Delete Content Only:** keeps the start and end tags, but deletes the information they enclose.

- **Replace Content:** leaves tags intact and changes only the element's content.

Click the New Action button to define how the element changes. The Action popup menu gives you the option to set, update, or delete an attribute's value. The Attribute popup menu is similar to its namesake in the Search section above. If you want to add a Color attribute to all Font tags, for instance, whether or not the Font tag had a Color attribute already, you would leave the Attribute field blank and use the Set choice for the action.

Finally, type the text to be changed in the Value field; the popup menu to its right lists predefined options when applicable. To add more actions, click the New Action button.

Tip: Changing Color Values (Mac Only)

If you're specifying a new color, such as for a font or background, drag and drop a color swatch from the Color palette onto the Value field to insert its hexadecimal value. However, be sure to clear the field first, or else the value is added to the existing contents.

Performing the search. When your search criteria is all set up, the last step is to choose the files on which the search will run. Click the Add Files button to select the files from your hard disk. On the Mac, you can also click and hold the Page icon in an open document window, and then drag that into the files list area.

If you have a site file open, choose the site's name from the site popup menu. You can also drag files from the Site window into the file list.

Unfortunately, even with only one file open, you must still add it to the list—GoLive doesn't automatically assume that you want to use that file, like the Find & Replace tab does.

To remove a file, select it and click the Remove button.

When your elements and attributes are all set up, you can optionally click the Preview button, which performs the search but doesn't apply the changes; the file list shows the number of changes in each file. If you're ready to make the changes, click the Start button. Be sure you have a backup of your files, as the search action offers no undo once you've applied it. (If the file you're editing is open when the change occurs, you can select Revert to Saved from the File menu, but we would caution you not to count on that option as your first line of defense.)

Using and saving tasks. The Element search and replace feature is especially useful if you find yourself regularly modifying or cleaning up Web pages created by others. To store the definitions for later, click the Save Task button. When prompted to name the task, save it to the Find by Element Tasks folder located in GoLive's Module's folder.

To retrieve a saved task (including a handful that Adobe included with GoLive), select one from the Open Task popup menu. If you don't see the one you're looking for, select Browse from the menu and locate the task file on your hard disk.

Tip: Saved Task Locations

Tasks can be saved anywhere, but they'll only appear in the Open Task menu if they're located in the FindByElementTasks folder.

Tip: Clear Element Fields

If you've performed a complex Element search and want to start fresh, you need to manually delete the data in the fields. Or do you? We've created a task called ClearFind that resets the Element dialog box. Download the file at realworldgolive.com/six/element.html.

Getting Back to the Source

You can scream, "Pay no attention to the geek behind the curtain!" all you want, but designing for the Web means you must face HTML source code at some point. GoLive's source-editing features become more robust with every new generation of the program—whether by manipulating the text or keeping its paws off—which means you can move between the two worlds with ease.

Dynamic Content and Databases

GoLive gives Web designers several tools to make pages visually dynamic: GoLive Actions, DHTML animation, and browser plug-ins. But, up until early 2000, using GoLive to add dynamic content that would pull information from a database via a server required you to hand-code server-side scripts.

Adobe wanted to make GoLive the center of all Web design and management activities, and so they built a powerful technology into the program that allows you to interact directly with a database, using the same drag-and-drop ease with which you can add Actions to a page.

Dynamic Content is Adobe's solution. This GoLive module allows you to build and maintain complex sites much more efficiently by linking to a database via several scripting languages. The database may store some, most, or all of your site's content. This can give users access to hundreds or thousands (or millions) of records via a few template pages you create and maintain.

When you need to change or add more data, you simply edit the database, which you can do directly using the database's own software, or via another set of database administration Web pages. The information can then be made available instantly to site visitors—no more tedious HTML page editing!

And since the layout and visual appearance of the content is controlled by a few template pages, when you want to change how the content is displayed, you edit the templates—not individual static pages.

Tip: Static Pages

Adobe included a way to turn dynamic pages from a server into static pages, which can be handy in some circumstances. The Page Generator feature is discussed in its own sidebar, "Generating Static Pages," near the end of this chapter.

Because the configuration for Dynamic Content is so extensive, we've split the more administrative and technical tasks into another location, Chapter 23, *Building Dynamic Content.* That chapter covers installing and configuring scripting languages and databases, and setting up data sources that can be linked into individual pages.

This chapter works with the individual page elements you can use to place information on a page, display results, and capture information from special Dynamic Content form tags and text bindings.

Be forewarned: there's a pile of configuration and learning before we can present practical examples of how to pull it all together. Get a mug of coffee or cocoa, and prepare to plow through this in a few readings, not all at once.

Tip: Follow Along Online

To make it easier to understand the concepts here, many of the examples can be found in their raw form on our Web site (realworldgolive.com) so you can see the code and elements. Our practical examples, near the end of the chapter, are available along with their source databases (in a form that can be imported into a SQL database) so you can install and try them out on your own.

Basics

Databases can be daunting if you haven't encountered them before. You may think you've worked with a database before, such as when you edited records or created layouts or reports in FileMaker Pro or Microsoft Access. In fact, those programs combine the database itself (the bits of individual data structured into fields, records, and tables) with the graphical interface or front-end that lets you edit the data and the structure. In most cases throughout this chapter, when we talk about a database, we're talking about using the raw data, not interacting with a front-end application. Let's conduct a quick, high-level review to put us on the same page.

Structure

Databases are structured into tables and fields, and data is stored in a sequence of records.

Tables. Relational databases, the kind that Dynamic Content works with, use a separate table for each distinct kind of data (see Figure 15-1). If you have a customer database, for example, you would have one table that contains all of your customers, another for invoices, another for service records, and so

Figure 15-1
Database
structures

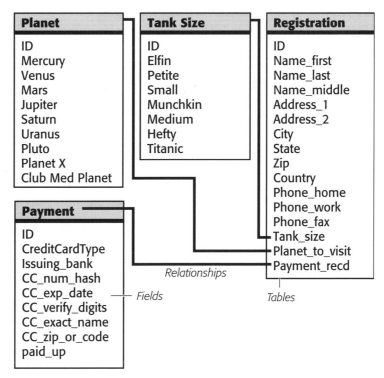

forth. Different items in different tables may link to each other so that you can answer questions such as, Which customers live in Minnesota and ordered more than $100 worth of merchandise this year?

Tip: Databases: the SQL

The language that lets you ask these questions is SQL (pronounced "sequel," but never spelled that way) or Structured Query Language, which will be covered in greater depth later in this chapter.

Tip: Flat Files

If you're used to databases like FileMaker Pro, which are called flat databases, you may recognize tables: each file in a flat database program is just like a table (see Figure 15-2).

Fields. A table is divided into fields, which uniquely categorize the data (see Figure 15-1, above). A field might be limited to a certain kind of data, like text, a date, or a number. Typically, every table has a field called ID that's uniquely numbered to cross-link entries across tables.

Figure 15-2
Familiar
structures

Records. A record is an instance of a set of fields in a table inside a database, comprising a unique set of data recorded discretely from all others. When you talk about having 1,000 customers in your database, each customer comprises a single record.

Tip: XML Data

GoLive can extract data from structured files encoded using XML. With an XML file, the fields and records are intertwined. This issue is covered in Chapter 23.

Operations

The Dynamic Content (DC) feature lets you perform essentially three kinds of operations on information stored in one or more databases:

- **Retrieve records.** You can display the information from a database, like entries in a catalog or listings. You can show all matching records on a single page, a range of records, or a limited number of records per page. Next and previous links allow you to use a single template to walk through multiple pages.

- **Search for or match records.** The contents of a database can be searched for matching characteristics through queries and filters.

- **Modify entries.** Records can be updated, new records inserted in a database, or existing entries deleted.

That's the long and short of what DC does, but it forms the majority of the kinds of tasks you need a database for on a Web site.

Interface

Before we get too far into the workings of DC, let's quickly review the parts you work with in GoLive.

- **Content Source Editor.** This palette contains the linkages between databases defined in Site Settings (described in Chapter 23) and groups of fields by table or query that you define for use in a page. Click the Open Content Source Editor button in the Layout Editor, or choose Content Source Editor from the View menu, to display the palette (see Figure 15-3). (Although the palette's title bar reads Content Sources, GoLive calls it the Content Source Editor everywhere else in the program, so we're sticking with that name.)

Figure 15-3
Content
Source Editor

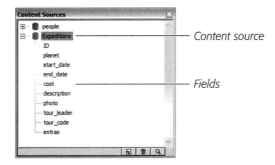

- **Dynamic Bindings palette.** Individual items on a page are linked, or "bound," to fields or special DC objects through the Dynamic Bindings palette. Select Dynamic Bindings from the Window menu to display it (see Figure 15-4). This palette also displays error messages for objects in a page even when those objects can't otherwise be configured.

Figure 15-4
Dynamic
Bindings
palette

When you first display it, the Dynamic Bindings palette is fairly small. However, as you'll see, it can eventually contain several different controls—but the palette doesn't automatically resize. We recommend that you resize this palette vertically to make sure you're not missing any controls we talk about later.

- **Dynamic Content Toolbar.** This abbreviated Toolbar, available by selecting Dynamic Content Toolbar from the Window menu, allows you to toggle online and offline status (in which you communicate with scripts or not); toggle dynamic highlighting of DC objects; and click to bring up the Dynamic Content pane of Site Settings (see Figure 15-5).

Figure 15-5
Dyanmic
Content
Toolbar

Site Settings Dynamic Content pane

Highlighting

Online/offline

We recommend turning dynamic highlighting on before trying to perform any dynamic tasks. It's one of the most helpful kinds of highlighting in GoLive, showing you visually when an object is linked or unlinked, or an error is present.

- **Content Source Inspector.** You use this Inspector, which appears when you select an item in the Content Source Editor, to set up which fields are displayed and filtered, or to link to other resources, depending on the type of data source (see Figure 15-6).

Suggestions

Here are a few practical ideas about what you might use Dynamic Content for, in case you aren't already burning with desire to add it (or even if you need to add fuel to your fire).

Form feedback. If you want to accept input from users through a feedback form, you could wire a script that would deliver information to you via email. With DC, you can let users enter their information and have it added to your database directly. Meanwhile, you can use a private page to query the database, and use the database interface itself or a custom script to extract details for a customer mailing.

Catalog. If you're selling or displaying any collection of items, DC lets you define a simple template for display, including multiple rows and automatic division of

Figure 15-6
Content
Source
Inspector

your content into pages with a limited number of items on each page. This grouping avoids you having to reconstruct pages as the database grows and shrinks. You can also tie in a DC-enabled search, allowing users to self-service their queries.

Content management. Because DC is so flexible, you could manage a news site or other content-based site entirely through tables in a database, allowing multiple individuals to enter and edit entries that visitors to the site call up, and allowing visitors to search the database for matching stories.

Workflow

To place content from databases on a page, you need to follow a sequence of steps in your workflow to create an appropriate page, add in content sources, define containers and field objects, and end up with a finished page you can upload to the site (see Figure 15-7).

Content sources define which records will actually be retrieved from the databases. Containers or tables hold the records. Individual form elements and text placeholders display fields or accept new values for fields.

Remember that we're assuming your servers and databases have already been configured, as explained in Chapter 23, *Building Dynamic Content.*

Creating Pages

Adobe wisely suggests that you start your workflow by creating a normal HTML page with dummy content, formatted to show results. You can create form entry fields, tables, CSS styles, and all of the normal components of a page, and test them for design purposes.

Figure 15-7
Connecting
database
elements to
parts of a
GoLive page

1. Drag a Content Source into
the Head section of a page.

2. Connect a database table. The Content
Source Editor display the table's fields.

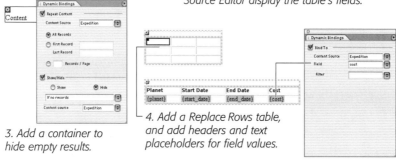

3. Add a container to
hide empty results.

4. Add a Replace Rows table,
and add headers and text
placeholders for field values.

Planet	Start Date	End Date	Cost
Venus	2022-04-01	2022-08-01	1500343
Neptune	2012-04-01	2014-03-31	100000003
Planet X	3001-04-01	4001-04-01	34

5. Preview the results in a browser.

The form elements, especially, can be useful (see Chapter 13, *Forms*). If you're accepting input from a user, you can completely mock the process up before ever linking database content in.

When you have your pages designed and ready to go, it's time to shift into dynamic overdrive.

Converting Pages

In order to put dynamic content on a page, you need to convert pages from normal HTML into PHP, JSP, or ASP pages. GoLive doesn't let you create new script pages from scratch; you have to take an existing page or create a new HTML page and then convert it.

With a page open, the Dynamic Bindings palette offers to convert the page to any of the scripting languages you've linked to for the site (see Figure 15-8). Select a language from the popup menu, then click the Convert Page button. Only languages you have set up on your site show up in this popup menu.

After conversion, you can switch back to a normal HTML page by selecting Make Static from the palette's popout menu (see Figure 15-9). GoLive strips out all the special DC-specific code from the page in this process.

Figure 15-8
Available
languages in
the Dynamic
Bindings
palette

Figure 15-9
Making a
page static

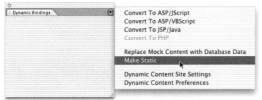

Yes, this palette is entirely empty when nothing on the page is selected; you select Make Static from its popout menu.

You can also convert the page into other scripting languages, but not all options are available in each type of conversion: filters specific to one language (such as formatting a date) are removed when converted into another.

If you choose Replace Mock Content with Database Data, GoLive performs a full retrieval of your page as if it were displayed via a browser, and replaces the contents with the extracted information.

Tip: Real Preview

The Preview mode in the document window retrieves database information for a true preview of the page with the current settings; that's the better approach to take to see what your page would look like filled in.

Tip: Don't Mock Me

Replacing mock content with actual entries is useful, but it rewrites the code on the page. It is vitally important to save before choosing this option, and not save afterward unless you're attempting to make a static page. Choose Revert to Saved from the File menu to reload your dynamic page.

You can automatically convert a site into static pages via templates and variables using the Page Generator feature, discussed in the sidebar, "Generating Static Pages," at the end of this chapter.

Linking Content Sources

The first task at hand is to link-in chunks of the database. Click the Content Source Editor button in the Layout Editor to bring up the Content Source Editor (see Figure 15-3, earlier in the chapter).

In the Content Source Editor, you create links between GoLive and parts of the database or other resources connected to the site in Site Settings.

Tip: Set Up in Advance

The steps that follow start at the point at which your databases are ready, your scripting language is set up, GoLive's scripting support is installed, and you've defined databases in the Site Settings. Yes, we reminded you about this already, but this is tricky stuff—if you're not properly set up, the steps in this chapter won't work.

Tip: Duplicating Content Sources

After configuring a Content Source, you can drag it to the Library tab of the Site window or the Objects palette to store it as an object that can be used on other pages. There is no sitewide management tool for Content Sources in this release.

SQL for Starters

SQL, or Structured Query Language, is a straightforward method of asking questions of a database. The language allows you to retrieve information through intersection: you can ask, for instance, for the first and last names of all customers who live in Seattle, and the response from the database is structured by fields and rows.

This handy language, developed decades ago, has become practically universal, meaning that you can ask the same question of many different kinds of databases that contain the same data and get the same results.

A query written in SQL might look like

```
select * from 'people_fields'
where city = 'seattle'
```

The asterisk indicates the database should retrieve all fields; "from" tells the database which table to look at (in this case, a single one); and "where" defines the parameter (in this case, records in which the city field is Seattle).

More usefully, if you only want to retrieve certain fields from a large table, you can write a query like

```
Select field1, field2, field3, field4
from 'hurking_table'
```

This reduces the amount of information GoLive reads about the table, which can make it more easily manipulated.

Learning a few SQL queries could make a huge difference in your ability to customize dynamic content and build complete systems. At the risk of sounding like the end of an afterschool special: if you'd like to learn more about SQL, try the technical tutorial at the MySQL.com site: www.mysql.com/documentation/mysql/bychapter/manual_Reference.html#Reference, or Sams Publishing's book *Teach Yourself SQL in 10 Minutes* (visit realworldgolive.com/six/books.html for a link, or find the book via its ISBN, 0672321289).

Create Content Source

Click the Create New Content Source button to get started. The Content Source Inspector allows you to choose the database and other values associated with this source. GoLive inserts a Content Source object into the Head section of the page that corresponds with the link you create.

Each Content Source represents a pool of records that you can format on a page or range of pages. You can have many Content Sources on a single page, each of them representing a different pool of data.

You can name the item anything you want; this name is used as a mnemonic as you link items on the page.

The icon for a Content Source appears like a little yellow cog in the Content Source Editor until it's linked in, after which it looks like a cylinder—the universal symbol for a database.

Select Type

The Type popup menu is where you link the data source defined in Site Settings to the content source itself. There are seven possible choices from this menu that vary depending on which language or languages you have set up in Site Settings.

Tip: Choose Wisely

If you select an option which doesn't correspond to your data source, you're out of luck: the results are unpredictable and certainly meaningless. You need to go back and reselect the correct options.

ADO Database (ASP), JDBC (JSP), and MySQL (PHP). These database types correspond to the conduits Adobe supports that connect these languages to database servers.

From the Database popup menu, select the name of the appropriate database set up in Site Settings. If it does not appear in the list, select Refresh Database List. If it still doesn't appear, return to Site Settings (or have your administrator return there) and confirm that the data source is linked correctly.

From the Table popup menu, select the table in the database that contains the records you want to work with on the page. You can also select Custom SQL, which allows you to compose a query in this widely supported standard language (see the sidebar, "SQL for Starters").

With a table selected or query entered, the Filter Records area of the Content Source Inspector displays the appropriate fields.

Each field can be filtered in a sophisticated fashion by selecting it and then entering a legal pattern, or choosing one of several options from a popup menu. We talk more about filtering when we discuss specific tasks, such as creating links from page to page later in this chapter.

The four options from the popup menu below the filter area in the Inspector correspond to four different methods of matching information stored as part of the state of the page by the scripting language:

- **Match request parameter 'field'.** If you pass a value in a form field, this filter allows you to display results based on that value. For instance, if you were looking through a list of furniture stores, and wanted to see only those in Poughkeepsie, you could pass that city name in a URL that this filter would capture. (We discuss this in much greater depth below.)

- **Match cookie 'field'.** You can store values in cookies via Actions or scripts, and then use this filter to match up the stored value with database results. (See Chapter 26, *Applying Actions*, on how to embed information in cookies using Actions.)

- **Match session variable 'field'.** At this writing, Adobe is unable to explain how this works. Scripting languages like the ones supported by GoLive can often automatically create a unique session identifier when a user starts working with pages coded in that language. However, Adobe didn't provide enough information or tools to work with this feature, despite its inclusion. Look for third-party extensions to take advantage of this feature.

- **Match application variable 'field'.** Adobe also offers little insight into this option, which allows you to filter based on settings that relate to the scripting language and the environment in which it's running on a server.

You can sort the results by one of the fields, in either descending order (alphabetically or numerically, last to first) or ascending order (the default).

Clicking Test Content Source brings up the first record in the set of data that matches the parameters. It's also a great way to test your query to make sure that it works.

Tip: Quote "Bug" Unquote

If you enter a value in the field at the bottom of the Filter Records area that contains double quotation marks ("), GoLive lets you test it just fine, but the scripted page generates an error. This is a bug: GoLive must escape (put a backslash before) any double quotes and does not. You can avoid this problem by simply using single quotes (').

Tip: Pre-Query

You can build a database table that is the result of a query in the database, and contains the same structure as if you had asked the database a question. Because some queries are quite complicated and may take unnecessary resources, you may want your database administrator to create this kind of table for you.

For instance, you can use the sum() feature to add up values; this operation can take the same amount of time and processor power to perform on every page load. Instead, the results can be calculated, stored in a static table, retrieved directly as needed.

Navigation Block View (all). Block is used as a higher-level navigation tool to move among large sets of records. If you have, for instance, 10,000 records in a set, using Dynamic Content's forward and back buttons only allow you to navigate through small sections at a time.

The Block option lets you create chunks, essentially, so you can reference records as sets divided into the units that you specified as the number of records per page.

Navigation Block is rather hard to describe on its own because it requires so much configuration to demonstrate. We provide a fully populated example in "Practical Dynamic Content," near the end of this chapter.

XML (all). XML data sources are static, and you can only retrieve data in the order they appear in the XML itself. The options for this type allow you to select the data source that correctly binds the XML elements, and then a file that contains the XML data.

Custom Merchant Shopping Card and Custom Merchant Order Form (all). These options correspond to a commercial system that Adobe supports through partner businesses. Consult Adobe's documentation and Web site for more information on using this separate for-fee service.

Binding Results

We know the first chunk of this chapter was a lot to get through to reach this point, but you've arrived! Now you can start linking data to areas of a page, an action that GoLive calls "binding."

GoLive binds several kinds of objects to display or accept data.

- **Containers.** Each set of results on a page has to appear inside a container or a table, either of which is itself bound to a Content Source. You can have multiple containers on a page each bound to a separate set of records, allowing you to combine interesting types of data in one place. Containers can also selectively show or hide HTML contained within them based on settings you define to show errors or more information depending on the set of records retrieved.

- **Tables.** HTML tables are used to display repeating sets of records. You format a single row in a table, and GoLive uses that as a template to repeat rows of content; or, to repeat cells in columns horizontally.

- **Text.** GoLive can insert text anywhere that represents the contents of a field, with or without a filter applied. It can also display error messages, record numbers, or other values derived from the Content Source.

- **Links.** You can use links in sophisticated ways to create next and previous record links, links to other templates, and links that embed variables so that you can control what values are displayed even on the same page.

- **Image references.** Bound images use a field in a database to point to the location of an image in a URL path; GoLive doesn't support images embedded in databases themselves. (GoLive can use Altercast, a server system that Adobe sells, to create dynamic images through the Variables feature; more on this later.)

- **Form elements.** A dynamic content page isn't restricted to just displaying data. By including Form elements, you can provide a mechanism to add, edit, or delete records from the database via the Web.

Containers

Think of a container as a bucket that contains all matching records for a given Content Source (see Figure 15-10). You can place multiple containers on the same page, and they can reference the same or different Content Sources.

Containers are required for controlling the number of records displayed, referencing record numbers, and conditionally displaying or hiding records. If you don't use a container, all the records in the table or query are connected to the bound items. You can put any variety of content in a container; in that sense, it's almost like a floating box.

Tip: When to Omit

You don't need a container for a record detail page in which a single result is shown.

Figure 15-10
Container

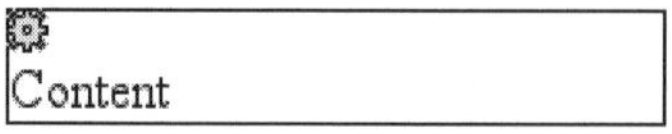

Content

Containers come in three varieties in the Dynamic Content tab of the Objects palette: Container, Hide Content, and Repeat Content. These three icons actually produce the same result with different settings already applied in the Dynamic Bindings palette.

Drag a container into a page that's set up for ASP, JSP, or PHP. GoLive places an outlined box with the DC cog wheel icon in its upper left corner and the word "Content" contained within it as text. The text isn't bound to anything; it's just a placeholder.

The container object works just like a form object: the bounding box around it expands and contracts to contain HTML. Objects in the box, like fields and text bound to database fields, use the container to point to which records they refer to.

To link a container to a Content Source, select the container by clicking its icon and view the Dynamic Bindings palette (see Figure 15-11). You can choose Repeat Content, Show/Hide, neither, or both via the palette. Choosing neither is a possible, but inappropriate option, since the container would contain no records whatsoever.

Figure 15-11
Binding
content
sources to
containers

Repeat Content

Repeat Content is the basic method of including information about multiple records. Typically, you nest a table (see "Tables," below) that displays the multiple rows or cells full of information; tables can also stand on their own without a container.

You can choose to include all records in a container, which is essentially the same as omitting a container altogether; a range of records, numbered by the order they are filtered and sorted in the Content Source; or a certain number of records per page, which is often the best option.

When you show a limited number of objects per page, this page serves as the template that users see when they navigate back and forth among groups of records. The special link options for display first and last records, and next and previous pages of records rely on containers on dynamic template pages.

Show/Hide

A container can selectively appear or disappear on a template based on factors chosen from the popup menu. You set the condition, and choose whether to Show or Hide the container based on that condition (see Figure 15-12).

Even though you can show records just with tables, these show/hide options let you nest a table inside a container that can be selectively displayed, preventing an empty table with headers from appearing.

Figure 15-12
Show/Hide
popup menu
options

If first record, If last record, If no records. While self-explanatory in nature, this popup menu can be used to hide and show next and previous page buttons or links if you are, in fact, on the first page (no previous pages), last page (no subsequent pages), or blank page (no results whatsoever).

In fact, you could use containers that hold just HTML and no record placeholders to display a special message when no match or results are found, while simultaneously suppressing your results formatting and buttons.

If many records. This condition is true if the number of records in the set defined by this container is greater than (but not equal to) the number you enter.

If field has error. Individual fields can return errors, and this condition is an excellent way to display special information in case of an error.

If field is empty. No data in a specific field creates a match.

If field matches. You can enter a value that a field needs to match, such as "on" or "yes," for this field to be true. This condition could display extra information for records that have extended details in another table, for instance.

Always. To test a container, you can set the container to Always to make sure it works as expected.

Custom. You can compose an expression (the kind of value that would get placed after an "if" statement) in the appropriate language for the page. For instance, if you wanted to only display certain information based on whether a user had a cookie indicating he was authorized, you might write a statement in PHP that otherwise hides a container:

```
!empty($HTTP_COOKIE_VARS['auth_user']) &&
$HTTP_COOKIE_VARS['auth_user'] == "yes"
```

You could also use a custom condition in combination with a parameter variable passed in a URL to create a single template page that would activate different regions for detail page containers and pages containing lists of records.

Tables

When you're retrieving multiple, identical records from a database, such as a list of some kind, an HTML table is the ideal way to present the same information row after row. Inch by inch, row by row, we're going to watch our tables grow.

GoLive offers two different ways to connect to a table: Replace Rows and Repeat Cells. You can drag one of two icons corresponding to these items into a container or onto a page. Or, drag a table onto a page and use the Dynamic Bindings palette to check Replace Rows or Repeat Cells.

Tip: Tables Need Containers

If you place a table on a page outside of a container, you cannot use the navigation links to connect to other records.

Tip: Exclusive Choices

The GoLive developers made Replace Rows and Repeat Cells checkboxes in the palette, but you can't select both at once, only either or none.

Tip: Radio Buttons

Radio buttons that are dynamically constructed from data in a table must be placed in a table using either Replace Rows or Repeat Cells in order to show the full complement of options.

Replace Rows

You can insert as many rows as you want before the row that contains bound elements, but you must put all bound elements in a single row (see Figure 15-13). You can overcome this limitation by nesting another table inside a single row in the bound table to better control output structure.

Figure 15-13
Binding
elements in a
table

— Header row
— Placeholder text

Dragging a bound element into a row or using the Dynamic Bindings palette to bind an element in a row turns that row into the repeated one if it's the topmost row with bound content.

Sound a little confusing? It gets worse: content in subsequent rows, even if it remains present and highlighted, isn't displayed, but its appearance is unchanged. Click on one of those subsequent rows' bound elements, and the Dynamic Bindings palette reveals the truth.

You can choose a Content Source and then set the record display for that table, just like a container. The values here override a container display; a table and a container should probably be set to the same values, however.

Finally, rows below a replacement row are ignored.

Repeat Cells

Repeat Cells inserts a single field into sequential cells (see Figure 15-14). You can set the number of cells inserted per row, and the number of rows on a single page.

Figure 15-14
Repeating cells

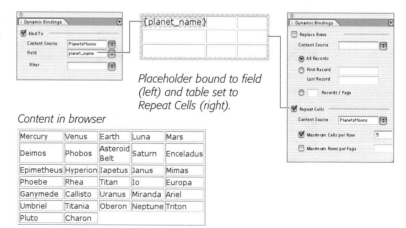

Placeholder bound to field
(left) and table set to
Repeat Cells (right).

Content in browser

Text

GoLive can insert a placeholder for the actual contents of a field from a Content Source. Inserting your cursor anywhere on a page that GoLive can insert placeholders—like the first row of a bound table—causes a Bind To checkbox to appear in the Dynamic Bindings palette.

Check the box to insert a generic placeholder (see Figure 15-15). Select a Content Source and field, and that field's name is displayed.

Figure 15-15
Generic
placeholder
text

Text bound to field

Text placeholders can also display special items, such as a record number (the currently displayed record), a record count (the number of records in the set), or the first and last records on the page (to show a range). You could format these results to note, "Displaying records 35 to 49 of 3,700," for instance.

Yet another option is to fill a field with an error message corresponding to a given field in a table. In all honesty, we haven't yet figured out how to use this; check our Web site for this chapter and see if it eventually made sense. (Even Adobe doesn't seem to know: it appears only cursorily in the documentation.)

Links

GoLive uses links to provide automatic navigation through records. The template you create to display information can be reloaded via a link with parameters that display the next set of records, an empty record for data entry, or the details of a record. Many other combinations are possible through the use of Actions, cookies, and parameters passed through a URL.

You can select objects and create a link or drag one of several icons from the Objects palette: Show Previous Record, Show Next Record, or Show Details of Current Record (see Figure 15-16). The Dynamic Bindings palette has three areas that correspond to the text that's linked (Bind Link Text To), the URL connected to with the link (Bind Link Destination To), and what happens when you arrive (Link Action).

Bind Link Text To

The contents of the link can be derived from a database field selected in this area.

Figure 15-16
Link objects

Show Previous Record, Show Next Record, and Show Details of Current Record

You can also select options after creating a link from the Link Action menu.

Bind Link Destination To

The link destination can also be extracted from a database record. If you check URL is Relative to the Site Root, you need to provide a field value that is truly relative in that fashion.

> **Tip: Recommend Root Relative**
>
> We recommend this approach. It may involve slightly more text in the database, but it ensures that all URLs always work as long as the site structure remains the same. On the contrary, if you want portable pages that can always point relative to the location of your dynamic templates, then you can leave that box unchecked.

Link Action

Don't confuse the word "action" in this context with GoLive Actions. It just means, "what the link does to the resulting page's display."

> **Tip: Actions and Bound Links**
>
> You can add any GoLive Action to a bound link, which allows you to add cookies, set variables, open popup windows, and all the other goodies that Actions can offer. See Chapter 26, *Applying Actions*.

Show Details of Current Record. Use this option to bring up a detail page. Combine it with an Open Window Action to have a nice popup window with the detail. This link typically points to another page, although you could hide and show containers to have it work with a single template.

Show Details of Empty Record. This special Link Action is required when you are using bound form elements to allow a user to enter a new record. You must use this option to link to a blank form on which a user can enter information from scratch. Otherwise, the entry of a new record will fail.

Show Next Record, Show Previous Record, Show First Record, Show Last Record. These four options are largely self-explanatory (but we're compulsive sometimes, so we discuss them anyway). Typically, these options point to the same page on which they appear; the bound areas are replaced with the appropriate records.

You can use containers to show and hide first, next, previous, and last options depending on whether records are available.

To move forward and backward by larger units you must use a Navigation Block View content source. See "Showing Records and Details," later in the chapter, on how to configure that option.

Images

GoLive can't (yet) extract images from a database, but it can use a URL that points to an image somewhere in a static Web site. GoLive inserts that reference to display it in Layout Preview.

Drag a Bound Image icon into the appropriate position, or select an existing image and check Bind To in the Dynamic Bindings palette (see Figure 15-17).

Figure 15-17
Image
bindings

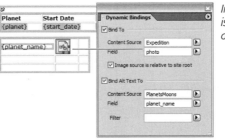

Image source URL is bound to field, as is Alt text.

Check Image Source is Relative to Site Root if the database field contains a full URL starting at the root of the site (like "/foo/bar/fee.gif"). You can store and name images anything you want because the path is completely specified.

Because Alt Text is important for making Web sites accessible to people with various impairments, as well as making it usable by text browsers and low-bandwidth users, GoLive includes the Bind Alt Text To option. Check this box to include a field from the database that describes the image in question. Typically, this is just another field in the same Content Source.

Tip: Dynamic Variables Graphics

A thought may be wandering through your mind: if images and graphics created in Photoshop, Illustrator, and LiveMotion can be changed dynamically with smart objects and variables (see Chapter 5, *Images*), couldn't I make images on the fly with a database?

Not so fast, pardner! Yes, you can, but you need another server component, called Altercast, which Adobe offers, to create on-the-fly images using variables. Altercast isn't a complete server system, like the Workgroup Server; rather, it's a component that a developer has to build into a larger system. For more information about this option, consult Adobe's Altercast information at www.adobe.com/products/altercast/.

If you add a link to an image, the Dynamic Bindings palette expands to include Bind Link Destination To and Link Action, just as with links. (See "Links," earlier in this chapter.)

Form Elements

One of the main activities you probably want to perform with Dynamic Content is offering a Web interface to update, delete, or add records. Fortunately, GoLive is up to the task using familiar form elements.

You can create a form without any bound content and later bind each element (see Figure 15-18). You can also create bound elements and use the Library tab of the Site window or Objects tab to reuse them later without having to specify their values each time (see Figure 15-19).

The Dynamic Bindings palette, as with text placeholders, lets you specify the Content Source, a field (or record item or error), and whether errors are displayed for troubleshooting (see Figure 15-18 again).

Figure 15-18
Binding form
elements

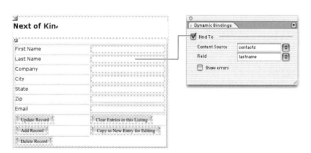

Figure 15-19
Storing
elements in
the Library tab

All form elements are available as their bound counterparts except Keyset Generator, which is a deprecated item, and Fieldset, which could be useful but just isn't available.

To get started with a form, make sure you've inserted a Form object that contains all the form elements (see Figure 15-18, above). GoLive automatically creates the appropriate link to a script page; you should not edit the Action field in the Form Inspector (see Figure 15-20).

Figure 15-20
Form object
pointing to
script page

Fields to Forms

Several form elements can be connected directly to form fields to be pre-filled or to accept input. The contents of these fields depend on the action that loaded the page, which is discussed under "Bound Actions," later in this chapter.

Bound Text Field, Bound Password, Bound Text Area. These items are filled or pass along text. Quite simple. If a user enters text containing hard returns in the Bound Text Area, you may need to use a Filter to map returns when results are displayed. (See the sidebar, "Filtering Information.")

Bound Checkbox, Bound Radio Button, Bound List Box, Bound Popup. These items can be hard-coded into a page, and map only exactly to items that are fed out by the database. If there's a mismatch between the values, items aren't checked or displayed.

If you define a checkbox, it's checked if the field value matches the text in the Value field in the Form Check Box Inspector.

Radio buttons, list boxes, and popup menus can be statically defined in their respective Inspectors, or they can be built on the fly from information stored in a database table. See "Dynamic Menus and Radio Buttons," just below.

Bound Hidden. Use the Bound Hidden icon to pass information that doesn't need to be displayed, such as a parameter, along to a server.

Bound Label. A Label that points to another field can be filled with dynamic content. The pointer always points to the same place, however.

Dynamic Menus and Radio Buttons
Radio buttons, popup menus, and list boxes can be constructed from information in a table. You might even go so far as to create a database that's nothing but tables of list values that you bind to these kinds of objects.

Filtering Information

The Filter popup menu is available for several kinds of items in the Dynamic Bindings palette, including placeholders and text. Filtering takes the results of a field and postprocesses it before displaying it on the page.

Encode String as HTML. Instead of inserting the contents of a field so that a browser would interpret the results as HTML, the scripting languages encode special characters, like the less-than sign, to display in their true form.

Encode URL String. The contents of the field are rewritten to work as part of a URL. (See Chapter 13, *Forms*, for more on URL encoding, including some sample perl code.)

Map Application-Relative Path. This filter rewrites the text in a field to be preceded with a dot and a slash (./), which indicates that the file is stored in the same path as the HTML file you're viewing in a browser. We're not sure why

this is called application-relative, because it's unclear which application is being referred to.

Convert Line Endings. Hard returns in the database entry are preserved and formatted as the HTML line break style of your choice. Checking Use   in White Space turns extra spaces (beyond one in a row) into non-breaking spaces. Use
 Tag puts the line break tag after the end of each line. Use <P> Tag replaces two hard returns with a paragraph tag. Encode as HTML works just like Encode String as HTML above.

Truncate Text (Extra Filters submenu). Truncate Text allows you to specify the maximum number of characters in the field, and to add a suffix (like an elipsis) at the end of the cut-off text.

Regular Expression Match and Regular Expression Replace (Extra Filters submenu). Both of these filters use the regular expression pattern

For instance, if you need to use a list of U.S. states in a number of different forms, you can reference the same table for each of them to construct the popup menu.

The only necessary values in a table mapped to one of these list elements is an ID number (always needed for uniqueness) and a field that contains the values that should be inserted into the form when constructing the element. You can also add columns that correspond to the labels displayed corresponding to each value in a list box or popup menu (see Figure 15-22).

Tip: Selective Filtering

You can filter a table that contains values for a radio button group, list, or menu through the Content Source Inspector. See the sidebar, "Constructing by Filter."

matching built into the various scripting languages. It's very similar, but not identical to, the patterns we describe in Chapter 22, *Advanced Features*. Enter a pattern in Search For within the quotation marks. Checking Ignore Case, uh, ignores case (capitalization is irrelevant).

With Match, enter a true and false set of text for "If found, emit" and "If not found, emit". GoLive substitutes that text for the entire database field. If you want to replace just part of a field, use Replace. The Replace With pattern can include some of the text matched. For instance, using PHP, if the Search For pattern is "(GoLive)" and the Replace With pattern is "Adobe \\1" all instances of "GoLive" become "Adobe GoLive".

See www.php.net/manual/en/function.ereg. php for PHP pattern replacement details. ASP and JSP lack similar definitive descriptions.

Currency, number, percentage, date, time, and currency filters (PHP/JSP submenu). JSP- and PHP-based pages can filter fields for dates, time,

date and time combos, and currency. Available options appear under a JSP or PHP submenu.

Currency symbols are inserted in the Web server's national flavor. Currency, number, and percentage can have their floating points set (Digital after Decimal), the decimal point (which is a comma in some countries), and the separator for thousands (a period in some countries).

Date, time, and date and time have options for formatting from the popup menu depending on language (see Figure 15-21). The fields that contain these items should be structured as date and time or combined fields in the source database to ensure the filter gets the right input.

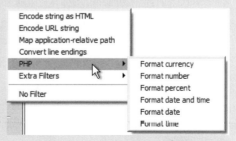

Figure 15-21
Formatting menus for PHP

Figure 15-22
Building dynamic menus

Checking Construct Dynamically causes GoLive to build a menu from a table's values, including setting the value.

Constructing by Filter

You can use the filter options in a content source coupled with cookies or parameters to selectively display values for dynamically constructed form elements.

Say you want to build a set of questions, each of which depend on the previous answer; each page you navigate through could be filtered based on the answer on the previous page.

For instance, if you want to provide custom options based on the computing platform of a visitor, you could ask for their platform on the first page and store that in a cookie. On subsequent pages, the filter in Content Source could be set to filter to the specific platform.

You would set up a table with a few fields, like at right, to create a custom menu for Mac and PC users asking them their platform.

On the first page in this sequence, you might ask which platform a user works with. That value could be written to a cookie or passed as a parameter. On the page on which this form element appears, in the Content Source Inspector for the items in this field, you would set up a filter for this table based on the Name field. Choose a Match option depending on whether you chose to use a cookie or a parameter. When this page loads, only the appropriate options show (see Figure 15-23).

The only downside of this approach, versus, say, a JavaScript-driven menuing system, is that you must load a new page for each subsequent question or direction. However, the benefit is that a single change in the database allows you to add an option, rather than re-coding one or more pages.

ID	Value	Name	Platform
1	win95	Windows 95	pc
2	win98	Windows 98	pc
3	winme	Windows ME	pc
4	winxph	Windows XP Home	pc
5	winxpp	Windows XP Pro	pc
6	win2k	Windows 2000	pc
7	macold	OS 8.5 or earlier	mac
8	mac86	OS 8.6	mac
9	mac90	OS 9.0	mac
10	mac91	OS 9.1	mac
11	macosx100	OS X 10.0	mac
12	macosx101	OS X 10.1	mac

Figure 15-23
Filtering dynamic menus

Bound Radio Button. Radio buttons work like small record sets, which, in fact, they are. To create multiple radio buttons from a table, add a Replace Rows or Repeat Cells element.

Put a Bound Radio Button in a single cell and use the Dynamic Bindings palette to set the Bind To option to the appropriate field containing the value. Set Construct Dynamically to the table that contains the possible values for the radio buttons.

Place the cursor in the same cell as the Bound Radio Button if you want to use Repeat Cells, or the same or any other cell in the row to work with Replace Rows (see Figure 15-24). Now select the same table from the same Content Source in the Dynamic Bindings palette, and choose the field that has the label text for these particular radio buttons.

Figure 15-24
Repeating dynamic radio buttons

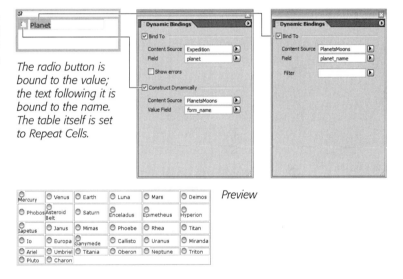

The radio button is bound to the value; the text following it is bound to the name. The table itself is set to Repeat Cells.

Preview

Cool, huh? It just presents only the necessary options. There's no way to automatically select a radio button, though, which is a minor problem that can be solved with JavaScript or a server-side scripting language.

Bound List Box and Bound Popup. Creating dynamically constructed list boxes and popup menus is much, much simpler. Just insert one of these objects, check Construct Dynamically, and choose the appropriate fields from the table for values (what's sent to the server) and labels (what's displayed in the popup menu).

Bound Actions

We get to the heart of the matter here: a user telling a browser to tell a script how to handle the data in the current form.

Three objects can have form submission behavior bound to them: Submit Action, Button Action, and Image Action. The objects correspond exactly to the Submit, Button, and Image icons in the Form tab of the Objects Inspector.

With one of these objects on a page, the Dynamic Bindings palette changes to show a checked Action box with a menu of possible behaviors beneath it (see Figure 15-25).

We're interested particularly in the submenu that corresponds to your scripting language, ADO Database, JDBC Database, or MySQL Database (see Figure 15-25 for MySQL). Another submenu corresponds to ecommerce options available through Adobe business partners.

Five options can be selected from this submenu:

- **Update Record.** Update the record that's currently displayed with the changes entered in the form. The record that's displayed can be from any of the bound link Link Actions, such as Show Next Record.

- **Add Record.** Clicking a submit button set to Add Record creates a new record with the current page's values. You need to start with a blank form, which was created through a bound link to the template page that is set to Show Details of Empty Record.

- **Delete Record.** Deletes the currently displayed record.

- **Clear Form Data.** Loads an empty form page.

Tip: Reset Form

The Reset icon from the Form tab of the Objects palette can be used on a record page to empty the values displayed without deleting or changing any entries in the database.

Figure 15-25
Action
submenu by
database

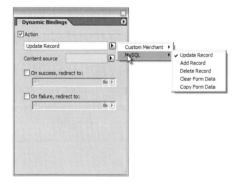

- **Copy Form Data.** Extracts data from the current record, loads a new empty page, and fills it with that content. (This isn't the same as duplicating the record, as the copied content is only inserted—with or without your modifications—when you submit it.)

GoLive can redirect a browser to another page after the action completes: you can set one for success, when the action is carried out as expected; or set another for failure; or set both of these options. Whichever option is not set causes the same template to be reloaded after the page is submitted.

Practical Dynamic Content

This chapter has felt somewhat theoretical, we're sure, unless you're familiar with making and linking database content. In this section, we present a few practical examples, which can be found in their original form on the Web, to walk you through common tasks.

You can find these examples on our Web site at realworldgolive.com/six/dc/ including the various stages corresponding to steps.

All of these examples assume that you have created a site and configured it for access to the databases in question via Site Settings.

Showing Records and Details

If you have a number of records—whether a few or a few million—one of your goals is to display this information in a comprehensive form that your site visitors have access to. Typically, you want to show summary information for a range of records on a page, allow navigation back and forth by ranges, and show the details of individual records.

If you want users to be able to search on fields, see our search example, later in this section.

In our example, visitors to the Huge Moon Expeditions site can browse through upcoming trips and see more details about each one.

1. Create an ordinary page in a DC-enabled site.

2. Design how you would like a table display of your content to look. You can design as many rows as you like, but only one row can have database content in it. The others are just headers. Use embedded tables to provide more advanced formatting, as you can put text placeholders in nested tables in the same row.

3. Design a display for record navigation in a table using a single cell that will be repeated in the final layout. The design can include a page number for the current page containing a subset of records, or it can contain a range, as in "records 51 to 100." The numbers are replaced through text binding in the final layout.

4. Convert the page to the scripting language used in your site.

5. Create a Content Source and link it to your database table; for example, "expeditions".

6. Create a Content Source and select Block Navigation from the Type popup menu. Link this to the table Content Source you just created in step 5. Let's call this block "ex_block".

7. Create a container. Bind it to "expeditions". Check the Repeat Content option and set the record set to "5" Records/Page.

8. Drag your two tables into the container.

9. Select the table that contains "expeditions" content. Bind it to the "expeditions" Content Source.

10. Go through each cell in the database replacement row and set the text to be replaced by the appropriate fields.

11. Select the table that contains the Block Navigation design and bind it to "ex_block".

12. Select just the text to be replaced by a page number and turn it into a link. From the Dynamic Bindings palette, check Bind Link Text To and choose "ex_block". Select "[Record Number]" from the field popup menu. For Bind Link Destination To, choose "ex_block" and "Link_URL".

   If you want to use a range of records to link to, duplicate step 12 for both the starting and ending number, choosing "[First Record on Page]" and "[Last Record on Page]". Create a link of the whole piece of text before setting it to "Link_URL".

13. Create a new page that displays the details of the record. Design it to hold as much of the data as you want to display in this detailed format. Because only a single record appears on this page, you can format it with or without a table in any fashion you like.

14. Convert the page to a scripting language.

15. Copy the Content Source for "expedition" from the range of records page by using copy and paste.

16. Create a container and drag all the display content inside.

17. Set the container to Show/Hide and choose Always from the popup menu.

    If you want to have an option to show information in case part of the record is empty, in step 17, set the container to Hide if Field is Empty. Choose a field that should always contain data. Then create another container with content, such as an error message, that shows when the field is empty. You can also create a custom test in the scripting language for more flexibility.

18. Bind each area of the detailed display to the appropriate field in the "expedition" database.

19. Return to the range of records page and link in some bit of text in the row that contains the record summary. You could, for instance, add an image or even text reading "Detail" which you would add a link to.

20. In the Text or Image Inspector, link the URL to the detail page.

21. In the Link Action part of the Dynamic Bindings palette, set the action to Show Details of Current Record.

Accepting Form Input

A question we're constantly asked is: how do you record form input from a Web site? The good news is that it's quite simple with Dynamic Content.

In our example, we ask visitors who come to the Huge Moon Expeditions site to fill out a contact form to request more information about our faux tours.

1. In your database, create a separate table for the form entry information, and one table each for the values that you want for radio buttons and menus or lists. The database needs to have write access configured for the particular user/password combination you use in your production site; otherwise, visitors can't supply their data.

2. Design a form that contains all the fields you want users to enter.

3. Convert the page to the appropriate scripting language for your system via the Dynamic Bindings palette.

4. Create a Content Source. Link the Content Source to your database's table for form entry.

5. Create a container.

6. Drag the form inside the container.

7. Delete the word "Content" from the container.

8. Check the Show/Hide box and set the popup menu to Always.

Tip: GoLive Manual Omission

If you religiously follow the steps in the GoLive 6 manual (online and in print) to create a form that displays and updates content, you may note that they omitted the equivalent of steps 5 to 8 without which the whole thing doesn't work.

9. Go through each of your fields and link them to the corresponding fields in the form input database table.

    If you have any dynamically constructed lists, bind them to the appropriate table that contains their values.

    If you have radio buttons that need to be created from a table, insert a table, bind it to the radio button's database table, move the radio button and mock text into the upper-left cell, and set your parameters for repetition and formatting.

10. You need your page to load as an empty form that's ready to submit its content to the database, but because we're not linking from a database page to reach this point, we need to force GoLive's code to create an empty form addition page. Adobe offers several suggestions, the easiest of which is to add a "broken" filter to your Content Source. In the Content Source Inspector, select the ID field or any text field, and in the filter area at the lower right, enter =\"emptyrecord\"; this assumes there's no value "empty-record" in that field.

11. Set your Submit button in the Dynamic Bindings palette to be an Add Record action.

    You can also use the Field Validator Action (or an Action Group) attached to the Submit button to check that fields are appropriately filled in before editing.

12. Set your On Success and On Failure links to provide useful information: On Success can redirect to a thank you page; On Failure can inform the person that something is wrong, ask them to notify the system administrator, and to send email. (Even better, your On Failure page can use JavaScript or an ASP/JSP/PHP script to page your system administrator.)

You can duplicate the form you've created, add some more buttons for different actions, and couple it with a search and display interface to have private control for reviewing and editing form information.

If you want to pass the form results on to another program, you need to write a SQL script or use a database connection program to extract the data. For instance, in a Unix environment, you can use a crontab entry (a scheduled event) to run a SQL command on a database and then email the results as an attachment to a specific address or upload them to a specific location.

Searching Records

Creating searches can be as simple as using the Filter area of the Content Source Inspector and a plain form.

1. Create a scripting page with a form in it that contains the fields on which you want to search. Matches are precise, so if you include multiple fields, all fields must match, not just one or more.

2. Connect the Form object's Action field to the same page.

3. Set the Form Method to Get.

4. On the same page, create a record display as described in "Showing Records and Details," earlier in this chapter.

5. Select the Content Source that's bound to the container on the page.

6. **PHP:** Select each field in which you want to match. We suggest using a separate form for each field for the least coding and most flexibility. In the Filter area at the bottom of the Content Source Inspector, enter:

    ```
    rlike '{$_GET["field"]}'
    ```

    Replace "field" with the name of the field in question. The keyword "rlike" means to match any part of the result.

Tip: And/Or?

If you're willing to edit the source code, you can use multiple fields as filters and change the "and" in a SQL statement embedded in the Content Source source code to an "or." In this snippet, for instance, the value entered in the "keyword" form field can match parts of either the "firstname" or "lastname" fields in the "people" database.

```
<?php // GoLive Content Source

$contacts = WrapMySQLDatabaseResults("temp", "select *
from people where firstname rlike '" . $_GET["keyword"] .
"' or lastname rlike '" . $_GET["keyword"] . "'",
"block=25","contacts");

?>
```

To make this work on the same page in PHP, you need to add a statement that fills in the "keyword" slot when the page is first loaded to avoid an error. Just above where you see that Content Source statement in the HTML, add this PHP code:

```
<?php if (empty($_GET["keyword"])) $_GET["keyword"] =
"null" ?>
```

ASP, JSP: Select each field in the Content Source Inspector's Field area, and choose from the popup menu at the bottom Match Request Parameter 'field'. GoLive automatically changes "field" to the selected field.

You should set two containers on the results page as discussed earlier in this section: one would show only if there were any results; the other would explain if there were no results.

Troubleshooting

A lot can go wrong with dynamic content, but luckily GoLive's interaction means that you see the problems—and solve them—before a user ever does.

Generating Static Pages

Although it may seem counterintuive to talk about static pages in a chapter on datbases, the two are related. In many cases, when details in a database are updated infrequently or only in specific areas, creating a system in which visitors actually interact with a database server may waste your resources.

Instead, you can perform a single task in which a list of queries—for example, a list of all product numbers in a catalog—is performed at once, creating static pages with the results.

GoLive's Page Generator feature does just that. You provide an HTML file with an HTML table with at least three columns: the first is named "Template" and the last "Output file". The middle one or more columns are variable names for a query.

If your site used a URL path such as

```
http://hugemoonexpeditions.com/
catalog.asp?id=54
```

where the "id" variable controlled which products were displayed, you'd create an HTML table like this:

```
Template  ID   Output file
http://hugemoonexpeditions.com/
catalog.asp   54    item54.htm
http://hugemoonexpeditions.com/
catalog.asp   52    item52.htm
http://hugemoonexpeditions.com/
catalog.asp   51    item51.htm
```

Because you can direct a Content Source to filter data based on a URL, you can use Page Generator in combination with Dynamic Content to create these static pages.

Here's how to set up a DC template to create your source, assuming the above values (the URL and the ID field) would be correct.

1. Choose a Content Source from a database: select it in the Head section and choose Copy from the Edit menu. (This will not work with XML data sources.)
2. Create a new page.
3. Convert the page to the scripting language that you used on the page from which you copied the Content Source (Dynamic Bindings popout menu).

HTTP Error

When you open a page and receive an HTTP Error dialog box, it usually indicates that the server is misconfigured in one of several ways. The Response Details section at the bottom may help you figure out which problem is the culprit.

- **Server not running.** This may seem obvious, but after restarting a crashed machine, you may need to also restart the server software.

- **Configuration change.** Someone has changed the server configuration without your knowledge.

The dialog box offers three choices for proceeding. Continue Online retries the URL noted in the URL field. If the server problem has been resolved,

---

4. Paste the Content Source into the Head section.

5. Create a container.

6. Bind the Content Source to that container with the option All Records.

7. Create a ReplaceRows object in that container.

8. In the top row, enter from left to right in those cells, Template, ID, and Output file.

9. Delete the third row.

10. In the second row, from left to right, enter the URL http://hugemoonexpeditions.com/catalog.asp (or whatever's appropriate, obviously); bind mock content to the ID field of your Content Source; and enter "item" plus the same mock content plus ".htm".

11. Save the page, upload it, and view it in a browser.

12. Save the page from the browser to a path you can reach from GoLive.

To set up the template page to work with Page Generator, you need to add a filter to the ID field. You may want to duplicate a real template on your site to create this Page Generator-oriented page. The URL of this template is what you entered above for URL, of course.

1. Select the Content Source.

2. In the Content Source Inspector, choose the ID field.

3. In the field at the bottom, select Match Request Parameter. GoLive fills this in as "Match request parameter 'ID'".

Now it's time to generate the pages.

1. Select Page Generator from the File menu.

2. For URL List File, choose the page you created from the template above and saved locally (or a hand-created table).

3. For Save Path, choose a directory in which you want the output files saved.

4. Skip Folder can be set to remove levels of directories in a path to avoid nesting directories too deeply. If your template URL contains, for instance, "/asp/catalog/code/woof/bark/" in it, you can set Skip Folder to 5 and remove those five nested levels.

5. Click Generate; GoLive retrieves each page and creates a static HTML file.

Those static pages can now be fed off any Web server quickly requiring no database resources whatsoever.

this now works. Go Offline turns off the interactive part of Dynamic Content, without solving the problem.

The Troubleshoot button brings up the troubleshooting page for diagnosing further ills. Of course, if a server problem prevents the server from running requests, this option does no good. (See Chapter 23, *Building Dynamic Content*, for more on that topic.)

Bugs in the Content Source Inspector

If you see green error bugs in the Content Source Inspector, click the Test button to have GoLive display the errors it found in one or more fields.

For instance, we named some fields with reserved words, or words that the scripting language or database server reserves for its own special purposes, and GoLive warned us.

Dynamic Bindings Errors

The Dynamic Bindings palette displays contextual errors even for items that it otherwise has no settings. For instance, if you have highlighting turned on for Dynamic Content, and the Form object is outlined in red, selecting it shows why the DC module is "angry" (it's red, so that's anger, right?).

If you have a single form with different Content Sources referenced by the bound form elements, the Dynamic Bindings palette mentions this fact.

Go Dynamic

Using Dynamic Content requires a lot of coordination, but once the parts are configured, you have an enormously powerful and flexible tool at your disposal that you can use to create sophisticated sites presenting millions of results and accepting dynamic feedback.

Languages and Scripting

Web development these days isn't just about writing fancy (yet clean and nimble) HTML code. Viewers expect rich, interactive pages and personalization features. Now that the Internet can be viewed using an ever wider assortment of devices, it's important for Web publishers to be multi-lingual in order to write code that can be understood and rendered correctly by desktop PCs, PDAs, and cell phones.

You can add interactivity using Java applets (which are cross-platform) and ActiveX controls (a Microsoft technology that, oddly enough, can be read primarily on Windows browsers). GoLive also offers significant support for embedding content and structuring output with several other kinds of advanced Web features: XML, a content-encoding standard; server-side scripting languages, including ASP (Active Server Pages, Microsoft's solution), JSP (JavaServer Pages, Sun's solution), and PHP (PHP: Hypertext Preprocessor, the open-source community's solution), and i-mode, a markup language similar to HTML that's optimized for viewing on handheld devices.

Java Applets and Objects

Before getting into the nitty gritty of GoLive's tools for configuring Java and W3CObjects (as the GoLive manual refers to them), let's identify what these distinct technologies represent:

- The Java programming language was developed by Sun Microsystems to be platform independent. Small Java "applets" (which provide a range of functions from groovy animation to database mining) can run on any compatible browser across most platforms. When hooking a Java applet into a GoLive page, look for a file with a .class extension (which compiles Java's bytecode).

- Objects, or W3CObject controls, refer to executable, object-oriented "controls" such as Microsoft's ActiveX. Unlike Java, these items must be developed and compiled for a specific platform; so far, that's mostly Windows. An outgrowth of Microsoft's Object Linking and Embedding (OLE) technologies, ActiveX controls can be inserted into Web pages to offer new features. The Windows Update function in Windows that scans your local hard drive and downloads appropriate Windows patches is an example. The main difference from Java is that ActiveX controls can also interact with a wide range of programming languages and applications (including, of course, those created by Microsoft).

GoLive, for the most part, treats these two media objects much like it does plug-ins and images. Simply drag either the Java Applet or Object icon from the Basic tab of the Objects palette into the Layout Editor, and the appropriate Inspector is called up. The Basic tabs of the two Inspectors are similar, but with a few important differences, at least on the Mac side (outlined below); the Windows version of the Object Inspector adds buttons to the bottom of the Basic tab that let you create and configure a control (see Figure 16-1).

- In the Base field, type or navigate to the location of the applet or object. In GoLive for Windows, click the Select button to bring up the Insert Object dialog box, from which you can add or create an object or ActiveX control (detailed in the "Object Inspector Specifics" section, later in this chapter).

- Type values in the Width and Height fields; you can also choose between a fixed pixel or percentage measurement using the popup menus.

Figure 16-1
Object
Inspector

- In the HSpace and VSpace fields, you can add blank space (in pixels) surrounding the object; in the Object Inspector, you can also add a border.

- The Align popup menu offers you the usual attributes for placing your object.

- Type a unique identifier in the Name field.

You can further modify these objects and applets by adding attributes via the Properties tab of the Object Inspector and the Params tab of the Java Applet Inspector. Click the New button, then enter the attribute in the Property (Object) or Name (Java) field and its value in the Value field. Be sure to click New when you add an attribute to avoid typing over the attribute you just set (see Figure 16-2).

Figure 16-2
Adding an
attribute

Java Applet Inspector Specifics

In the Alt Text field of the Alt tab, you can add a plain text message that displays when a user disables the browser's Java functionality and then loads the page.

To format a rich HTML message containing formatting or images, check Show Alternative HTML. A text box appears within the Java Applet placeholder. Like Alt Text, it displays when Java is turned off or is not supported by the user's browser; however, you can use HTML code to format the message's appearance.

Click within the box and type or paste your code, or drag tag icons from the Objects palette. If you supply a notation in the Alt Text field and a rich HTML message, they both appear in a browser that's not showing Java.

Tip: Java Display Bug

If you switch to another editor within the GoLive document window, then return to the Layout Editor, the Java Applet placeholder returns to its normal icon. Check the Show Alternative HTML option again to display the work you've already done, then add more if needed (see Figure 16-3).

Figure 16-3
Now you
see it...

Java Applet in Layout Editor

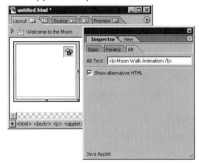

Switching to another editor and back...   *...changes the checkmark and image.*

Tip: Userdef Java Files (Mac only)

If you created a Java applet using a definition file, click the Userdef tab to display its operators. The Userdef tab does not appear in GoLive for Windows.

Object Inspector Specifics

On the Mac, you can only specify the location of an object using the Base field on the Object Inspector's Basic tab. However, the Windows version of GoLive offers a more direct route—due largely to the fact that ActiveX is first and foremost a Windows standard—via the Select button at the bottom of the Basic tab. In fact, you must use this route to add ActiveX controls and objects.

Clicking the Select button or double-clicking the Object placeholder icon brings up the Insert Object dialog box, which gives you three options: Create New, Create from File, and Create Control (see Figure 16-4). If you want to

Figure 16-4
Insert Object
dialog box

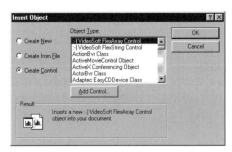

add an ActiveX control, choose Create Control, scroll through the list of controls available on your system, and select a control type. Choosing Create New allows you to begin from scratch, while choosing Create from File loads an object into your page.

After adding a control or object, you can configure it by adding attributes on the Properties tab. Some ActiveX controls also allow you to open a Properties dialog box associated directly with the control; the Properties button on the Basic tab becomes active if this is the case (see Figure 16-5).

Figure 16-5
Built-in
controls

Click an active
Properties button...

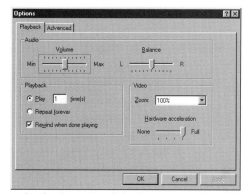

...for the Properties dialog box.

Server-Side Scripting Support

Server-side scripting languages are a way to embed instructions in a Web page that are carried out before the user ever sees the page. The scripts can contain substitution commands, so that placeholders on a page display the time and date, a user's name, or extract information from a database.

GoLive has essentially three kinds of support: ignore, preview, and database integration.

- **Ignore.** GoLive simply ignores most server-side scripts, due to what it calls its "360Code" feature which leaves markup code alone that doesn't have anything to do with HTML.

- **Preview.** GoLive can preview SSIs (server-side includes) with a module that comes with version 6. SSIs are server directives that are specific to each kind of server software, like Apache.

- **Database integration.** GoLive 6 ships with Dynamic Content, a module that allows you to reference and preview content extracted from a database or XML data file directly in pages using GoLive as the window. We cover Dynamic Content in the previous chapter, *Dynamic Content and Databases*, and in Chapter 23, *Building Dynamic Content*.

Languages

Primarily, programmers work with five server-side scripting languges: ASP, ColdFusion, JSP, Lasso, and PHP. Programmers may also work with SSIs for particular brands of server software.

ASP. Microsoft invented this language, and it can be used with practically any Web server software shipped with Windows 98 and later, although configuration varies. GoLive and Dreamweaver UltraDev support ASP for Dyanmic Content. ASP code looks like this on a page:

```
<%=Request.form("yourname")%>
```

ColdFusion. Allaire originally developed ColdFusion as a rich language to work with databases back in a time when it was extremely hard to write conduits between databases and Web pages. The language has grown and diversified over the years, and after Macromedia and Allaire merged, ColdFusion became a supported language in Dreamweaver UltraDev. Cold Fusion code looks like this:

```
<cfset DSN="NextX">
```

JSP. JavaServer Pages are a way to extend the use of the Java programming language to company-wide operations. Some firms now use Java for all server-side and internal programming tasks; JSP allows them to access Java-based programs with reusable, identical code from other parts of their operations. JSP is a supported language in Dynamic Content and Dreamweaver UltraDev. JSP code looks like this:

```
<% String userID = request.getParameter("USERID"); %>
```

Lasso. The Lasso programming language is part of an end-to-end system that includes plug-ins for GoLive and server software. It's developed by Blue World Communications. We discuss it thoroughly in Chapter 23, *Building Dynamic Content*, as an alternative to GoLive's built-in database support. Lasso code looks like this:

```
[Shown_NextGroup]
```

PHP. PHP is an open-source replacement for ASP that arose from the Internet community of open-source programmers. It's a very simple language to learn, but has powerful database features and rich programming options. GoLive supports PHP in its Preconfigured Servers and Dynamic Content; Dreamweaver

UltraDev can use PHP for database integration through a free third-party extension. PHP code looks like this:

```
<?php if(file_exists('topten.txt')) readfile('topten.txt'); ?>
```

SSI. Server-side includes are a way to use a server without any additional scripting language to insert special text or other information. SSIs aren't as rich as the other programming languages, but they're simple ways to include text or run scripts that generate text output that a server puts into a page.

Technically, SSI can include all of the programming languages above, but in general practice it refers to just this limited set of features available in a server with no add-ons.

Tip: Using SSI Previews

If you want to use SSI with GoLive and see a live preview, you need to install the SDK (Software Developer's Kit) that's one of the options if you choose Custom Install when installing GoLive 6. With the SDK installed, go to the GoLive application folder, dive into the SDK folder, and find the Translate SSI folder nested in the Examples folder. Drag the whole Translate SSI folder into the Extend Scripts folder, for which you find an alias in the main application folder.

Quit GoLive and run it again. Switch to the GoLive program, open Preferences from the Edit menu, select Modules, and scroll down to Extend Scripts. Check Translate SSI. Quit GoLive and run it again to activate the Module.

Apache documentation on SSI can be found at httpd.apache.org/docs/mod/mod_include.html. Apache SSI code looks just like it's a comment:

```
<!--#include virtual="/cgi-bin/example.cgi?argument=value"-->
```

XML

XML (or eXtensible Markup Language) is the greatest thing since spatially divided grain-based baked food products—or so its proponents maintain. Based loosely on SGML (Standard Generalized Markup Language), XML is a human-readable, machine-understandable, general syntax for describing hierarchical data that lets users define and tag discrete categories of information using simple text labels.

Huh?

In other words, XML is customizable (i.e., "extensible") code that looks like regular text and which you can read, but there's no implication built into the format that describes how the data should look (as in HTML). Instead, XML just describes what the data consists of.

For instance, <H3> in HTML always means a heading level 3, and virtually all browsers interpret it as such—it has a fixed meaning that defines both the content and its display (bold and a font size of about 14 points). Whereas, in XML, you might define a headline in some fashion, like <BOOKTITLE>, but that definition wouldn't inherently describe its output, just that the enclosed information was, in this case, a book's title. (It could also be the name of a type of flower, because the tag's name is entirely arbitrary; but it's not likely.)

XML documents always reference a separate file, called a DTD (Document Type Definition) that list the vocabulary allowed in the XML file and the parts and pieces of tags. It's sort of like a simplified dictionary for a language: there might be only a hundred words, but those hundred words fully describe any kind of item that might be represented in the XML file.

Instead of relying on (and conforming to) the fixed code of HTML from which each browser or other interpreting software has to decipher what <P> and <A HREF> mean, you create your own XML language in a DTD that describes the data that's being presented (rather than telling the browser how to present it). Thus, if a DTD had definitions for booktitle, price, and pagecount, a XML data file might start:

```
<booktitle>Real World Scanning and Halftones</booktitle>
<price currency="us">29.95</price>
<pagecount>464</pagecount>
```

Any kind of information can be structured using tags, and any kind of display program (a browser or word processor) or interpreter (like a database or a price-comparison engine or whatever) would be able to process or display information in a document using definitions identical to those in the program that created the document. In fact, HTML has been reformulated into XML as XHTML (extensible HTML) for just this purpose: to create a version that can be passed around as easily as XML using existing XML software, browsers, and database interpreters.

The portability of XML allows many different programs (from standard Web browsers to mobile phone microbrowsers) to access the same data without using proprietary formats, making it easier to exchange rich information across systems and to reuse the same information in many different places without rewriting it for each purpose.

Tip: More XML Information

We really can't teach you XML in a few pages, but we can point you in the right directions for learning more about it. The World Wide Web Consortium (W3C) offers extensive documentation, examples, and other information at its Web site at www.w3.org/. A great starting point for learning about XML is the page at www.w3.org/XML/1999/XML-in-10-points.

XML in Editable Pages

If you open a file with an .xml extension (such as one of the files in your site's settings folder), GoLive opens the page in the Outline Editor (see Figure 16-6). Click the expansion triangle at the far right of an element to view its attributes. To add new elements and attributes, click the New Element button from the Toolbar (see Figure 16-7).

Alternatively, switch to the Layout Editor, which offers a similar—though less detailed—view of the page (see Figure 16-8). Selecting an item brings up

Figure 16-6
Opening XML

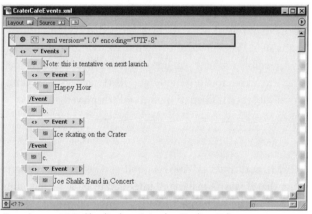

Opening an XML file displays it in the Outline Editor.

Figure 16-7
New Elements

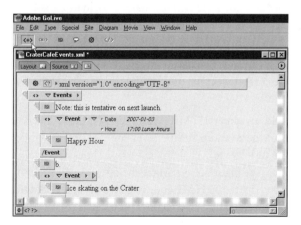

the XML Item Inspector, where you can assign a name to the element, edit attributes and values, and add or delete attribute/value pairings from the list.

Figure 16-8
XML file in
Layout Editor

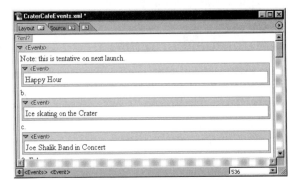

XML as Data Sources

GoLive can use XML data files—files that contain one or more records with consistent tags—instead of a database as a source for Dynamic Content. This is incredibly useful if you have access to the output of a database without having live access to the actual data. XML data sources can't be queried against for a subset of information, but only displayed.

XHTML

HTML continues to enjoy a good run, as markup languages go, despite the fact that it wasn't originally intended to be a display language. To add more structure, the W3C recommends using Extensible HTML (XHTML). A page that uses XHTML for structure and CSS or XSL (Extensible Style Language, a kind of XML for style definitions) for formatting is better suited for being used across multiple devices and platforms, such as PDAs or mobile phones.

There are two methods of building XHTML pages.

- From the New Special submenu of the File menu, choose XHTML Page. The correct Doctype information is included at the top of the file's source code.

- Build a regular HTML page, then use the Convert to XHTML option from the Markup submenu of the Document window's popout menu. The Convert to XHTML dialog box appears, containing conversion settings (see Figure 16-9). Mark the options you wish to use, depending on how strict the XHTML code needs to be, and click OK.

Figure 16-9
Convert to
XHTML

It's esoteric, but you could author all of your documents in XHTML for maximum compatibility and then use an XSL transform document to turn it into standard HTML when it's requested from a server. If this makes no sense to you—and it shouldn't—try www.xml101.com for more on XML, XSL, and XHTML.

Wireless Web Languages

Usually when you think of the Web, you picture someone viewing it with a laptop or desktop computer. But as various devices become smaller and more powerful, the Web is migrating to a host of other platforms, such as cellular phones. GoLive offers support for HTML-like markup languages that are optimized for these devices.

The Windows version of GoLive includes a handful of emulators for viewing wireless-ready code. The Access Compact Viewer, which is available in the Wireless Emulators folder on the GoLive installation CD, can be set up to launch from GoLive's Show in Browser button.

i-mode (CHTML)

i-mode, also known as Compact HTML (CHTML) is the format used primarily by mobile phones connecting to Japan's NTT DoCoMo service. i-mode is very similar to HTML, so you can develop sites and pages as you normally would in a regular HTML page. To distinguish the page as intended for i-mode devices, however, perform the following two actions after creating a new document in GoLive.

1. Change the page's document type by selecting one of the i-mode options in the Doctype submenu of the Document window's popout menu (see Figure 16-10). This adds the appropriate information at the beginning of the file to identify it to browsers.

2. Some HTML tags aren't recognized by i-mode devices, so GoLive includes an option to display only appropriate icons in the Objects palette. From the palette's popout menu, go to the Configure submenu and choose an i-mode version.

Figure 16-10
Changing
to i-mode

Select an i-mode option in the Doctype submenu.

Choose an i-mode version in the Objects palette.

Since i-mode is currently used primarily in Japan, GoLive also includes support for creating i-mode pages that include emoji, small icons used in place of words. First, however, you need to activate that support: in GoLive's preferences, choose the Modules option and enable the Encodings module and i-mode Emoji under Extend Scripts; quit and restart GoLive.

To add an emoji, drag the i-mode Emoji icon from the Basic tab of the Objects palette to your page. In the i-mode Emoji Inspector, click a symbol from the grid (see Figure 16-11). By default, all symbols are shown, but you can reduce the clutter by selecting an item from the Category popup menu.

XHTML-Basic

Another method of producing wireless content is XHTML-Basic, which is the W3C's recommendation for markup being read by devices that don't fully support HTML.

To create a new XHTML-Basic page, select XHTML-Basic Page from the New Special submenu of the File menu. Unlike i-mode, the correct Doctype information is already included in the page. However, you need to set up the Object palette to display only appropriate tags; go to the Object palette's popout menu and select XHTML-Basic 1.0 from the Configure submenu.

Figure 16-11
i-mode Emoji
Inspector

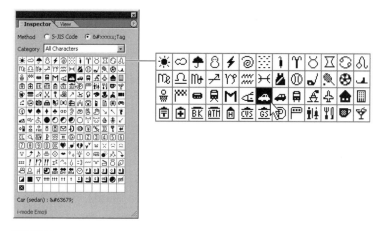

WML

WML, or Wireless Markup Langauge, is yet another language for creating wireless-ready pages, though it differs significantly from i-mode and XHTML-Basic. A WML page is known as a deck, which then contains different cards. When a WML page is accessed by a user's device, the deck and all cards are downloaded.

To work with WML pages, you first need to enable the WML module in GoLive's preferences (it's listed under Extend Scripts). This provides a new WML Elements tab in the Objects palette, which contains the commands used by WML (see Figure 16-12).

Figure 16-12
WML Elements
tab

Create a new WML page by choosing WML Deck from the New Special submenu of the File menu; the Document window contains only the Layout Editor, Source Code Editor, and Outline Editor. Since WML is a structural language based on XML, you must use the icons in the WML Elements tab to build the hierarchy of cards and elements within the deck (see Figure 16-13, next page).

Tip: More WML Info

See the WAP Forum Web site (www.wapforum.org) for more information on Wireless Markup Language.

Figure 16-13
Building a
WML page

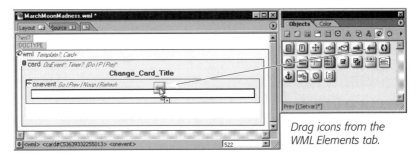

Drag icons from the
WML Elements tab.

SMIL

SMIL (Synchronized Multimedia Integration Language, pronounced "smile") is a markup language used for creating multimedia presentations. With SMIL, you can build a page that has several multimedia elements—such as streaming audio and video—and make them play at specific times and on different layers.

Adobe calls its SMIL Module a preview intended to give you an insight into working with SMIL as it becomes more accepted, but not to produce final documents with it.

To create SMIL pages, you first need to set up GoLive to handle them.

1. Quit GoLive if it's running.

2. Locate the SMIL Authoring folder in GoLive's application folder on your hard disk.

3. Move the SMIL Module file to the Modules folder, and then start up GoLive.

Tip: SMIL at Startup

When you copy the SMIL Module to the Modules folder, GoLive automatically activates it when you relaunch the program; you don't have to go into GoLive's preferences to turn it on.

With GoLive set up, choose SMIL Document from the New Special submenu of the File menu to create a new page. In the Objects palette, display the SMIL tab to reveal SMIL-specific icons. Dragging the icons to the Layout Editor adds them to the page, just as if you're working with an HTML page.

Tip: More SMILs

Included in the SMIL Authoring folder is a SMIL Authoring.pdf document that explains how to create SMIL pages in depth. Rather than repeat the information here (and add yet more pages to this already sizeable tome), we recommend consulting the PDF for SMIL specifics.

¿Habla Usted Java...i-Mode...XML? ¡Sí!

The Web pushes onwards from its HTML base into other realms (it is the *Worldwide* Web, after all). Combining scripting languages, applets, scriplets, XML, and telephones seems daunting until you try, because GoLive does most of the work for you. Telepathic holographic interfaces aren't yet supported, but we fear it's just a matter of time.

Sites and Groups

PART 3

Managing Sites

The basic units of the Web are pages and sites. A page is a discrete file that contains HTML; it stands alone as a unique object. Sites are collections of pages, images, media, and other files (CSS style sheets, JavaScript libraries, etc.) that collectively form a navigational whole in which all (or most) elements can be reached in some manner by starting at the home page or root of the site.

Sites can exist as a few pages on one server in someone's basement in Twin Falls, Idaho, or comprise hundreds of thousands of pages on servers around the world. But what differentiates a site from a random list of files is that pages link to each other in an organized fashion.

GoLive uses this notion of linked pages in its approach to site management. In GoLive, you create a site file that stores all the information about the objects and links found in a site's HTML, media, and code files; you point to a site folder that contains the actual site documents; and GoLive creates a data folder where all special templates and reusable items for a particular site reside, along with a settings folder containing items as disparate as server connection values and site settings.

You can always see precisely which files are in your site and the relationships between them and other linked files and objects. Behind the scenes in the site file, GoLive maintains a database of this information, which allows it to manage aspects of a site that are embedded in individual HTML and media files. Change the name of a file and GoLive can update references to it everywhere, including within PDFs, SVG files, Flash (SWF) files, and Quick-Time movies. Update a recurring element, like a navigation bar, and GoLive can update it on all pages on which it appears.

This aspect of site management is highly satisfying, saving enormous amounts of labor and reducing mistakes. Creating new objects is a snap, as is updating thousands of links on thousands of pages and prototyping multiple designs while working out a new Web site.

This chapter covers how GoLive deals with a site: where all the parts live, which commands are available, the specifics of working with the site management tools, and how the program divides different aspects of site management into sections.

This part of the book covers the individual aspects of site management:

- Prototyping and mapping a site using the Diagrams tab (Chapter 18).

- Working with files, folders, and links, including templates and troubleshooting using the Files, External, Extras, and Errors tabs (Chapter 19).

- Synchronizing your local copy of a site with a remote Web server using the FTP and WebDAV tabs (Chapter 20).

- Working in groups by installing the included Workgroup Server (WGS), which allows collaborative site design and maintenance, as well as storing and making available older versions of each file on the WGS (Chapter 21).

Site Building Example

The process of creating a site in GoLive is a straightforward affair, so let's walk through building and uploading a site. In this example, let's assume you have some content already assembled that you want to turn into a GoLive site (see Figure 17-1, page 436).

1. Import the site. Choose New Site from the File menu, select the Single User radio button, then choose Import from Folder in the next screen. Select your folder, the home page, and the location to store GoLive's files.

2. Edit files. Open files, change their contents, add links, and save them. Add a CSS external style sheet to all the HTML pages in the site.

3. Move files. Reorganize the site so that all of the images are in a single folder.

4. Add files from elsewhere in the site. Copy media and files into the site.

5. Manage Components. Store repeated HTML elements in Components.

6. Use Stationery and Templates. Add new pages based on a consistent design to the site.

7. Fix errors. Find missing files and links, and hook them up.

8. Clean Up Site. Use the Clean Up Site feature to make sure everything needed for the site to work is in place, linked, and ready to go.

9. Examine the site map. Find problems and clean up the hierarchy.

10. Connect to an FTP server. Choose a server and upload changed files, or the whole site if it's the first time.

Site Setup

Before you start working on a site, GoLive wants you to identify the files that comprise it (if any) and a location to put all of its associated files and folders. You can start in one of several ways depending on whether you already have a site you want to bring into management under GoLive, or you're starting from scratch.

Site Wizard

GoLive uses a step-by-step set of dialog boxes to help you choose from the many options in creating, importing, or linking to a site (see Figure 17-2).

GoLive splits sites into two categories in the wizard's first screen: what it calls single user sites, which are really just sites that reside locally on your own hard drive or perhaps a networked drive; and workgroup sites, which take advantage of GoLive's bundled Workgroup Server (WGS), allowing collaboration and automatic revision storage as files are edited.

In this section, we cover setting up local, single-user sites; using the WGS deserves a chapter to itself, coincidentally located in Chapter 21, *Working in*

What's New in 6

Miracle of miracles, many Site window behaviors are now undoable either through the Undo menu or the History palette. We still recommend frequent backups, but at least you can walk back a step or more without the penalty of resorting to one of those backups.

The site settings folder is a new addition, externalizing a number of site preferences as structured XML files, including settings for connecting to servers. You probably don't want to touch these by hand.

You can now import existing sites via FTP or plain HTTP; GoLive 5 could handle FTP only.

The HTTP feature is frighteningly powerful: you can suck down a site from anywhere and turn it into a GoLive site. (Kids, don't steal sites.)

The Workgroup Server (WGS) included with GoLive 6 changes how you build, connect to, or import a site. The WGS lets you store your files and archive older revisions of each file through a simple approach that allows many people to work with a single set of files at once. Or, you can even set it up on your own machine, and use WGS to appropriately archive your previous revisions. Because of all the cases now possible, you have more choices when setting up a site.

Figure 17-1
Site folders
(see previous
pages for full
explanation)

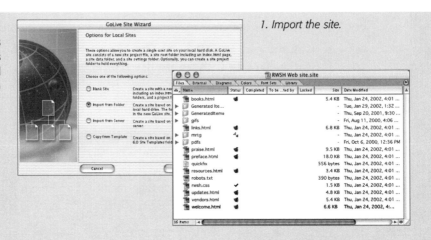

1. Import the site.

2. Edit files.

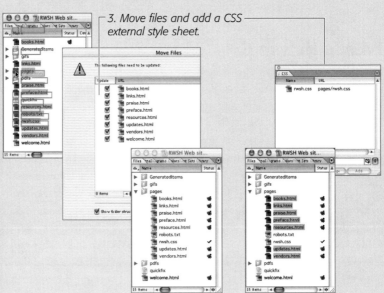

3. Move files and add a CSS external style sheet.

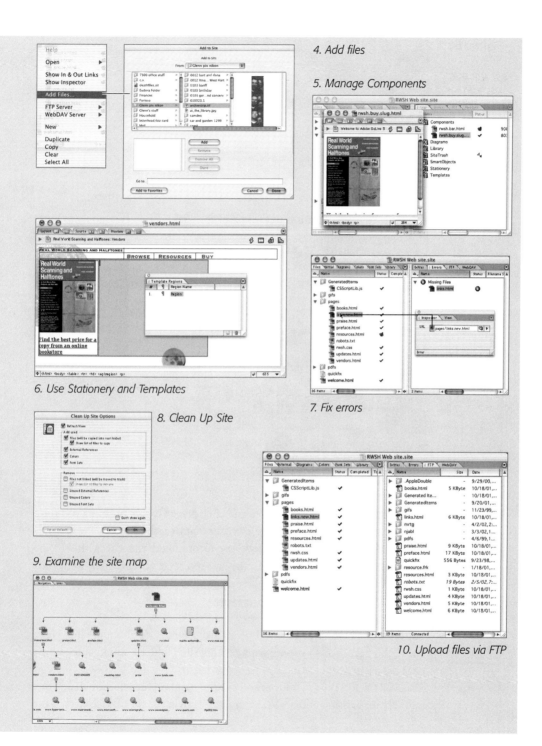

4. Add files

5. Manage Components

6. Use Stationery and Templates

7. Fix errors

8. Clean Up Site

9. Examine the site map

10. Upload files via FTP

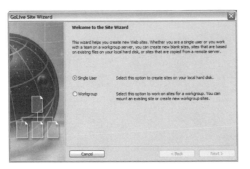

Figure 17-2
Site Wizard
opening
screen for
creating a
New Site

Groups. Most of the features in the rest of the chapter, however, apply to both local and workgroup sites.

Choose Single User and click Next.

Starting a Site

You have four options for starting with a locally stored site (see Figure 17-3).

Figure 17-3
Options for
Local Sites

Blank Site. If you select Blank Site and click Next, GoLive prompts you for a site name and then just writes skeleton content to each of the locations mentioned in "Finishing a Site," below. We recommend you check the Create Project Folder box when naming the site to create an enclosing folder for those four items; the enclosing folder is named whatever you call the site plus a space and "folder".

Import from Folder. Select the Import from Folder option and click Next, and GoLive asks you to specify your existing site's folder location and a home page file inside that location.

Click the top Browse button, and use the standard file selection dialog box to find your existing folder. GoLive creates its own site files and folders at the same level as your existing site folder, so you may want to create a new folder that contains just the existing site before importing into GoLive; this prevents new items from mingling with older files and folders.

Tip: Double Importing

If you try to select a folder that contains an existing, open site, GoLive waggles its finger at you via an alert dialog and doesn't let you proceed.

The home page should be the first page users retrieve when they type in your URL without a page selected, such as http://realworldgolive.com. GoLive considers the home page as the root of all navigation and links. Choose this page by clicking Browse at the bottom right.

If the home page in the folder you're importing is named the same as GoLive's default home page (index.html), GoLive automatically chooses it and displays it beneath Please Select the Home Page of the Existing Site. (This only works for index.html, even if you've chosen a different default home page value in Preferences or Site Settings.)

If you don't have something you consider a default home page or want to defer that decision, check the Create Generic Home Page box. We discuss making the decision about what your home page is in Chapter 19, *Managing Files, Folders, and Links.*

Import from Server. After choosing Import from Server and clicking Next, GoLive offers a choice: FTP or HTTP. This is a fascinating choice (and new to GoLive 6).

If you choose FTP, you're presented with GoLive's typical FTP connection dialog, described in Chapter 20, *Synchronizing Sites.* When you click the Browse button, GoLive connects to the FTP server using the settings you provided. You can browse the remote directories and files to find the home page.

With the HTTP option, you can download part or all of a Web site located anywhere on the Internet. Specify the URL of the starting point. The import options control how much of the site is retrieved. Get Levels refers to the hierarchical depth to which GoLive follows link-to-link, starting at the home page. Get Entire Site ignores the numbers of levels and grabs as much as it can.

Only Get Pages Under Same Path assures that GoLive doesn't retrieve files from elsewhere on the same server if they're not in the same or lower directory than the one you entered for the URL. Finally, Stay on Same Server keeps GoLive from heading off to linked images or files found elsewhere.

Tip: Ownership

This is a powerful feature and one that should be used with care; you should only download content that you own or have permission to use. It warrants saying even after all these years: the Internet doesn't remove copyright protection, and there have been many lawsuits in which people have been sued for taking one person's content and repurposing it for themselves.

It's one thing to look at someone else's source code to see how they accomplished their design; it's another thing entirely to pull down their hard work, make a few modifications, and call it your own. We're not lawyers and this isn't legal advice, so consult an attorney if you have questions.

Tip: Importing Sites Appendix

Making imported sites sing can be a more or less difficult task depending on the size and age of the site. This process includes rooting out dead files, bad links, old image maps, and many other examples of rot.

Copy from Template. Selecting Copy from Template allows you to choose a prefabricated site template while viewing a preview of its structure and layout. GoLive creates a copy of this template, including all its files, Stationery, Components, and whatnot, for your own use. GoLive includes several site templates for you to get started, located in the Site Templates folder within GoLive's application folder; or, of course, you can create your own templates (see the sidebar "Creating a Site Template" on the next page).

Finishing a Site

In the first three options, the end of the process (which usually comes after hitting Next) involves saving to a specific location; Copy from Template requires that you name the site on the screen where you select the site template. When you choose a site name, it's used as the base for creating all the site folders and the site file. The default name is "New Site" which creates a "New Site.site" file, a "New Site" folder, a "New Site.settings" folder, and a "New Site.data" folder (see Figure 17-6, after the next page).

The Advanced button brings up the Advanced URL Handling dialog box. The option Check URLs Case-Sensitive ensures that upper- and lower-case aren't used interchangeably to refer to the same file; Unix doesn't like that much, and other platforms have different opinions.

UTF 8 lets you create non-Western European sites, especially important when using non-Roman characters. The %HH Escaping option ensures that URLs can be properly passed and parsed by a Web server. GoLive's approach isn't the best, as it should only be encoding a few characters, not all, as it says.

Click Default Values to return to the options available in a clean installation.

Creating a Site Template

Creating a site template is extremely simple. You may want to create one for in-house projects, especially on an intranet, where you want everyone to start with the same set of files, structure, graphics, Stationery, and Templates.

First build a site with pages, links, objects, Stationery, Diagrams, Templates, and Components in as generic a fashion as you want. Then copy that site's enclosing folder—the one that contains the site file, and all of the site folders—into the Site Templates folder in the GoLive application folder (see Figure 17-4). The site is now available as a template.

To customize the preview display, make two screen captures of 72 pixels square of the site's structure and navigation (or of anything you

want, really). Save these somewhere handy; they can be located anywhere, but inside the Site Templates folder probably makes sense. Open the site template's site file, and then hold down the Shift key and click the Site Settings button on the Site Toolbar. This enables an additional setting that allows you to enter a description and link to the screen captures (see Figure 17-5).

The new GoLive 6 Templates feature works in perfect harmony with site templates. GoLive Templates are pages with locked and unlocked areas which you, as a designer, define. Users can, by default, only make changes in areas that are set up for editing, allowing parts of a page to not be manipulated by accident or by design. See Chapter 11, *Templates*, for more on this feature.

Figure 17-4
Site Templates folder

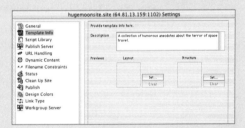

Figure 17-5
Accessing site template settings

Site File and Folders

As we mentioned earlier in the chapter, GoLive creates four items on your local hard drive for your site (whether local or on a WGS): the site file, the site folder, the site data folder, and the site settings folder (also see Figure 17-6).

Figure 17-6
Site folders

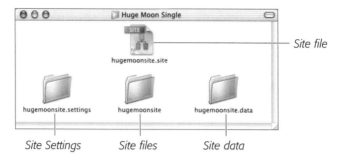

Site file

hugemoonsite.site

hugemoonsite.settings   hugemoonsite   hugemoonsite.data

Site Settings   Site files   Site data

Tip: Changing Site Names

The names of the site file, site folder, site settings, and site data folder are coordinated to start with the same text. Although you can change these outside of GoLive, we don't recommend it. If you change the name of the site folder, GoLive asks you to locate it the next time you open the site file; if you change the name of the site data folder, a new, blank one is created. If you really need to change the root name of your site, be sure to make the change on all four elements. GoLive asks you to specify the site folder once the next time you open the site file, but from then on the change sticks.

Site file. The site file contains the database of items found in the site: a list of HTML files, images, and other documents, and their internal references; the list of external links, colors, and font sets; the structure of any site maps or designs you're working on in the Diagrams tab; and all your local preferences.

The site file can be saved after changes are made to any of the attributes that are part of it. Its save-to-disk behavior is a little too transparent for us cautious types, though. If you quit without saving changes to the site, GoLive saves changes to the site file anyway, but doesn't warn you about saving changes. However, you can manually Save the file at any point after changes are made.

Tip: Cross-Platform Site File

You can open the same site file on either Macintosh or Windows, but if the files aren't in precisely the same place with the same names, you may have to use Refresh View or Reparse to force an update. We discuss these options later in this chapter.

Tip: Long Save

Yes, it can take inordinately long to save the site file. GoLive likes to perform a variety of clean up and confirmations before it writes out to disk, and site files can be several megabytes in size. Try not to force quit, Control-Alt-Delete quit, or otherwise bail in the middle or you may have to reconstruct your site file.

Tip: Save Often

Your site file isn't automatically saved until you exit the program, and you could easily spend hours working in GoLive without a save—which we don't recommend. Since the site file contains all the above-mentioned items, you lose any information not contained in the Web site itself that you may have manipulated.

For instance, if you create folders to organize your links in the External tab and unceremoniously crash, those folders will not appear when you reboot; the links will still be intact if they're present in the site's individual HTML files, but not if you created them from scratch in order to add them to pages.

Tip: Site File Backup

The site file is automatically backed up when you close it or quit GoLive. It's also backed up when you open the file, which can add tens of seconds to either process. It's only a small time loss, so we recommend leaving this option on unless you have a really great backup procedure in place. You can disable backups by unchecking Automatic Backup of Site File in the Site pane of the Preferences dialog.

You can wind up with many backup copies, we've discovered; on drives with less space available, go to the site folder's enclosing folder and clean out the old backups from time to time.

Tip: Where to Store the Site File

The site file should be stored one folder level above the site folder (see Figure 17-7). We once received email from a poor soul who had stored his site file in his site folder, and every time he uploaded his site to his FTP server, the several-megabyte site file went with it.

Figure 17-7
Positioning
the site file

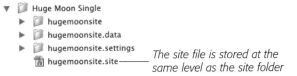

The site file is stored at the
same level as the site folder

The site file, when opened in GoLive, is represented by the Site window. The site itself, comprising real documents and folders, is stored entirely in the site folder.

Site folder. This folder contains all the files that comprise your Web site. It is essentially a local, identical representation of your remote Web site, with all files and folders intact.

If you reference files that live outside the site folder by browsing via the URL Getter, GoLive offers a few tools to copy or move them into the site folder before you upload your site or synchronize it. See the discussion of the Clean Up Site feature in Chapter 19, *Managing Files, Folders, and Links.* Ultimately, anything you reference locally has to be copied into the site folder so that it can be uploaded to your Web server.

You can, conversely, keep files in the site folder that you don't upload to the Web site. We discuss how to prevent files from being uploaded in Chapter 19, and Chapter 20, *Synchronizing Sites.* (You can run into trouble here with references to files, like aliases, symbolic links, and shortcuts; we also discuss solutions for maintaining references in Chapter 20.)

Site settings folder. The site settings folder holds XML documents that contain data used for site-specific settings, like the organization of the External tab, FTP servers, and other preferences. By externalizing these and storing them with the individual site, it makes the entire site much more transportable.

Site data folder. The site data folder holds the GoLive miscellany (Stationery, Components, in-progress design prototypes, even trash), operating as a temporary holding bin before you empty it.

You can view the contents of the site data folder by opening the split-pane view of the Site window: click the two-way arrow at the lower-right corner of the window (see Figure 17-8). The Extras tab shows the several folders contained in the site data folder, even if those folders are empty: Components, Diagrams, Library, SiteTrash, SmartObjects, Stationery, and Templates.

Figure 17-8
Splitting the panes

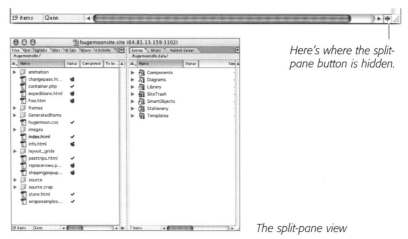

Here's where the split-pane button is hidden.

The split-pane view

Site Window

Regardless of whether your site is local or on the WGS, GoLive displays a site with the same organization. The five tabs in a Site window each handle specific aspects of site management (see Figure 17-9). (The sixth tab, Library, let you store text and HTML "snippets" you might want to use later.)

Figure 17-9
Site window
tabs

The five tabs starting at the left of the Site window—Files, External, Diagrams, Colors, and Font Sets—divide into three categories.

- **References and files.** The Files and External tabs help you manage HTML files, and folders containing items, media and other files, email addresses users can click on, and any external URLs.

- **Diagramming and mapping.** The Diagrams tab offers a graphical and outline view of the navigational structure and linking relationships among all the elements in a site. It also offers powerful tools for prototyping and extending sites with the ability to test and stage changes.

- **HTML attributes.** The Colors and Font Sets tabs provide a central location to view the Font tag's Face attribute and the general Color attribute applied to text, tables, and other items anywhere in a site. Because these are HTML properties that can't be modified centrally, only viewed, we put coverage of them into the appropriate chapters: Chapter 4, *Text and Fonts*, and Chapter 6, *Color*.

By centralizing all this management into one window, it's a simple task to view all the elements by category in a site. For instance, you can change a reference to another Internet location with a single Point & Shoot action, or move all images from one nested folder to another and have GoLive rewrite all the pointers in one fell swoop.

References and Files

The Files tab in GoLive shows all the files that make up the site and that are stored on your local hard drive or on a remote Workgroup Server, depending on your configuration. The Files tab also manages all references made inside HTML files that point to other objects on your site, such as other HTML pages, GIF and JPEG images, SVG files, Flash SWF files, and PDFs.

If you click the split-pane button in the Site window, you can examine or select errors, Stationery, Diagrams, Templates, SmartObjects, items thrown in the GoLive trash, Templates, and Components; you can also access an FTP file list displaying the contents of remote FTP servers, and interact with a WebDAV workgroup file server (see Figure 17-10). The FTP and WebDAV tabs let you manage uploads and downloads to your Web site.

Figure 17-10
WebDAV and
FTP tabs

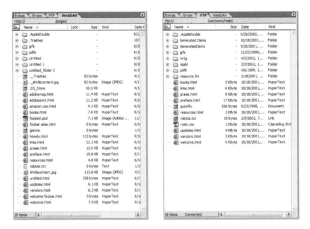

The External tab shows all URLs that reference external Web pages or other objects like FTP servers and PDFs. Any item inside an HTML hyperlink that starts with a resource identifier link, such as http://, ftp://, or mailto:, gets extracted and turned into an object you can manage in the External tab.

GoLive can handle links embedded in several kinds of media files: Quick-Time, SVG, Acrobat PDF, and Flash SWF files. This media file management means you can update URLs and internal references to files on the site without having to go back to the source program and data to recreate a new media file.

Diagramming and Mapping

The Diagrams tab serves two separate functions: site prototyping and site mapping. The prototype feature lets you drag in blank pages, objects representing server and network resources, stationery, and templates, and create links between them, essentially populating a Web site before you have all the content to put into place. It also allows you to directly modify those pages in a prototype "stage" so you can test them locally before incorporating them into your Web site. You can add them to your live site and then remove them, too, if you need to make more revisions.

The other feature of the Diagrams tab shows a graphic relationship between pages and objects in a site through either a navigational view (top-down from the home page showing the main links) or through a links view which shows all inbound and outbound links from every page and object.

Both views offer significant opportunities for visualizing what's going on without resorting to paper and pencil.

For more detail, see Chapter 18, *Diagramming and Mapping.*

HTML Attributes

The Colors and Font Sets tabs land in the same bucket because both let you view a summary of a single HTML attribute. The Color attribute used to be found attached to many different HTML tags, including those for table cells, page backgrounds, and individual text ranges.

The Font Sets tab shows a summary of the contents of the Font tag's Face attribute. Font sets are lists of font names that were formerly the dominant way to control a Web browser's display of text.

The Colors and Font Sets tabs both offer tools to create and name specific uses of colors or font sets, and extract a list of all those items used in a site. Changing the values of a color or font set applies the change throughout your site, though sometimes with unexpected results.

A better method of accomplishing site-wide, page-wide, and world-wide font and color management is to use Cascading Style Sheets (CSS), which is supported in all modern browsers. We provide a full accounting of using fonts and colors throughout a site in Chapter 4, *Text and Fonts*, and Chapter 6, *Colors*. See Chapter 27, *Defining Cascading Style Sheets*, as well.

Library

The Library tab is an odd bird. When you drag text or HTML objects into this tab, GoLive turns them into incomplete HTML files, which it automatically names "snippet" plus a number and ".html". You edit these snippets via the Layout Editor. The functionality is identical to the Library tab of the Objects palette.

For instance, you could create a table with complex formatting and drag it into the Library tab. When you want to use this table again, you simply drag it from the Library tab into a document window, and GoLive faithfully duplicates it for you (see Figure 17-11). Because the Library tab and the HTML cuttings stored in it belong to a site, you can use this distinctly from global clippings you store in the Object palette's Library tab. Also, you can send these Library items along with a site, or use them as part of a WGS site.

Figure 17-11
Adding items
from the
Library

If you drag a table into the Library tab, GoLive creates a file from it. You can then modify the table to meet your needs.

Drag the Library item from the Library tab onto a page...

...and GoLive inserts the objects in the file, just as if you pasted the underlying HTML.

Site Preferences

GoLive offers a number of application-wide site preferences that affect your current site and new sites created later. Many preferences are found in the Preferences dialog box reached via the Edit menu. In Preferences, click the Site icon, or the triangle (Mac) or plus sign (Windows) next to it (see Figure 17-12). You should also examine site-specific Site Settings, reached by clicking the Site Settings button or from the Site menu.

Figure 17-12
Site
preferences

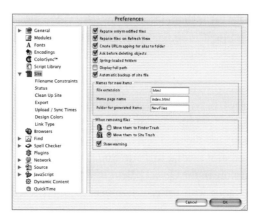

New in 6: Site Settings Mirror Prefs

GoLive 6 now offers more control over site-related settings that were formerly only set on a global program basis. This includes useful settings like Script Library, which was tricky to modify site by site.

Site-Based Settings

Many of these settings can be applied globally in Preferences. But you should think of those as defaults rather than constants. Preferences changes apply only to sites created or opened after the settings are changed.

We recommend setting local settings in Site Settings for many items to ensure consistency over time. In many cases, you must check a box to indicate that you wish to make site-specific changes. Once the box is checked, you can modify the values in that panel.

- **General (Site Settings only).** Home page setting.

- **Script Library.** Where and what to name the external script library used for Actions and DHTML. (See Chapter 24, *Authoring JavaScript*, Chapter 26, *Applying Actions*.)

- **FTP & WebDAV Server (Single User).** Choose the FTP and/or WebDAV server appropriate for your site via a popup menu that contains values set in the Edit menu's Servers item. (See Chapter 20, *Synchronizing Sites*.)

- **Publish Server (Workgroup).** Select the server to which your workgroup site should be published. This setting is made on the WGS itself; selecting Edit from the popup menu list of servers (if any) takes you to the administration page of the Web site. (See Chapter 21, *Working in Groups*.)

- **URL Handling (under General in Preferences).** This setting controls how GoLive changes, excludes, or encodes URLs. (See Chapter 1, *Going Live*.)

- **URL Mappings (Single User, Site Settings only).** Other sites can be linked via aliases and folder references to a site you're working on to preview and provide cleaner links. (See Chapter 19, *Managing Files, Folders, and Links*.)

- **Dynamic Content (Site Settings only).** To use dynamic content from databases, you need to upload and configure a variety of files. The Dynamic Content setting walks you through that process and lets you modify settings after they're initially made.

- **Filename Constraints, Status, and Clean Up Site.** These options control or reveal information about individual files and other objects on a site and are fully detailed in Chapter 19.

- **Export (Single User)/Publish (Workgroup).** Takes the contents of a site and reorganizes it for output (including stripping special information inserted by GoLive) and restructures the hierarchy into a variety of origami. For local, single-user sites, Export copies these files to a local folder that you specify. For workgroup sites, Publish controls how the server restructures the files in a site before the server uploads them to your live Web site. (See Chapters 19 and 21.)

- **Design Colors and Link Type.** These settings primarily set the appearance of items in the Diagrams tab; consult Chapter 18, *Diagramming and Mapping*, for details.

- **Upload/Sync Times (Single User).** Most of the options in this pane are familiar from the Export or Publish pane: you control which files are uploaded or have their modification time synchronized with their locally stored counterparts. You can also set HTML stripping options. (See Chapter 20.)

- **Workgroup Server (Workgroup, Site Settings only).** With WGS-based sites, you can control how frequently the local information you're working with is updated from the remote server, and how you're communicating with the mother ship that is WGS. (See Chapter 21.)

Site Pane

The Site pane contains behaviors that have nothing to do with HTML or code, but rather how GoLive's Site user interface and local parsing work. These settings can only be set globally, not site-by-site.

Reparse Only Modified Files, and Reparse Files on Refresh View. These two options control how often GoLive checks the source HTML to see if changes were made that it hadn't tracked internally. (See Chapter 19, *Managing Files, Folders, and Links.*)

Create URL Mapping for Alias/Shortcut to Folder. URL mappings are a highly powerful, yet confusing feature for splitting content over multiple Web sites, for which we provide some step-by-step clarification in Chapter 19. The main URL Mappings setting is found in Site Settings.

Ask Before Deleting Objects. If this isn't checked, you can delete items with impunity without any warnings. Danger, Will Robinson! Starting with GoLive 6, you can undo many operations several steps back—including restoring deleted files under some circumstances. But you can't reverse all of history, and it may not always work. An ounce of caution, etc., etc.

Spring-Loaded Folders. If this option is checked, folders automatically open when you drag files over them or use the Point & Shoot tool and hover over them.

Display Full Path. This option is checked by default, placing the full path above the Path icon at the top left of each pane in the Site window. Unchecking it keeps the Path icon in place, but hides the path. In the FTP and WebDAV tabs (Single User) and Publish tab (Workgroup), GoLive shows the protocol (ftp or http) and fully qualified URLs.

Automatic Backup of Site File. As mentioned earlier in this chapter, checking this option (which is on by default) creates a backup of the site file every time you open or close it. This adds time to both operations, but it ensures that you always have a recent copy.

Names for New Items. These three fields control how new, blank pages are created when dragged from the Objects palette's Site tab, added from the Site menu, or otherwise plopped into a site. File Extension controls the part of the file that defines its content after a period; this is almost always .html, even on Windows boxes, but DOS demands just .htm.

The Home Page Name defines what a new, default site uses as its home page file name. The Folder for Generated Items field lets you chose a name where new, unlinked pages appear in the Files tab's folder hierarchy.

When Removing Files. These radio buttons allow you to select a Trash folder for your deleted files: either the internal one in the site data folder handled by GoLive (Move Them to Site Trash); or your system's own waste elimination device (the Desktop Trash on Macintosh, the Recycling Bin on Windows). For the latter option, select Move Them to Finder Trash on the Macintosh or Move Them to System Trash under Windows. Unchecking Show Warning removes files without displaying a warning when you delete them. These options are covered in depth in Chapter 19, *Managing Files, Folders, and Links*.

Site Features and Objects

The same site feature or object can be found in several different places in GoLive, sometimes under a different name in each place. Some commands are available only from the Site menu, while others might be activated from the Site menu, the Site toolbar, and the contextual menu. Objects can be inserted by dragging from, or double-clicking in, the Site tab of the Objects palette, and sometimes by selecting an option from the contextual menu.

The Site menu, the contextual menu, and the Site toolbar display choices in gray that aren't available for the tab you have selected; the menu items may change their contents as well. The Site tab of the Objects palette lets you drag objects that aren't applicable, but when you release them, they snap back to the Objects palette; if they're appropriate, the whole tab highlights on its edges, just like dragging files into a folder on the Desktop.

Most of the subjects below are covered in greater depth in Chapter 19, where we address links, file management, and other topics.

Tip: Diagram Menu

The Diagram menu and the Diagram tab of the Objects palette contain all features and objects needed for the Diagrams tab of the Site window.

New in 6: Heaps of Diagram Icons

The previous version of GoLive introduced what it then called Designs, and in this release, Diagrams. GoLive 6 includes a number of specialized icons in the Diagram tab of the Objects palette for customizing site maps and prototyping sites.

Here are all the site-specific commands found on the Site menu, Site toolbar, contextual menu, and Site tab of the Objects palette, and where we address them fully throughout the rest of this part of the book.

New Generic Page, URL, Address, Color, Font Set, Library item, and folders for each. The Site menu's New submenu creates all the objects you need in each tab except Diagrams. The submenu only shows appropriate objects for the tab you're viewing (see Table 17-1). You can also insert them from the contextual menu.

If you want to group any items in any of the tabs except Diagrams, add a folder in the tab by any of these methods:

Tab	New object
Files	Generic Page
External	URL or Address
Color	Color
Font Sets	Font Set
Library	Empty document

Table 17-1
Tabs and their objects

- Select Folder from the Site menu's New submenu.
- Click the New Folder button in the Site toolbar.
- Select New Folder from the contextual menu.
- Drag the Folder or one of the four Group icons (URL Group, Address Group, Color Group, and Font Set Group) from the Site tab of the Objects palette into the appropriate Site window tab.

Tip: Plus Approval

If you're dragging the right type of folder for the correct tab, the folder icon adds a plus sign next to it. Otherwise, releasing the folder in the wrong tab does nothing.

In the Files tab, creating a folder is exactly like adding a level of hierarchy to the navigation or creating a folder on the Desktop.

Creating a folder from a menu or the toolbar creates the contextually appropriate folder for grouping items in the External, Color, Font Sets, and Library tabs. If you want to work more graphically, just drag the right item from the Objects palette.

Refresh View, Reparse All, Create Thumbnails (Files and Extras tab). With the Files or Extras tab selected, the Refresh View option can be selected from any menu or clicked in the Site toolbar. Refresh View checks the site folder or site data folder for new or removed items that were changed without GoLive's involvement. Hold down the Control or Option key to change the Site menu's Refresh View to Reparse All, which rereads the HTML that underlies the site. This step is useful when hand-editing in another program or using the Find feature to make changes in the source code.

Holding Command-Option (Mac) or Control-Alt while selecting Refresh View changes it into Create Thumbnails. Thumbnails are created automatically whenever you modify and save an HTML page in GoLive, but this option allows you to create all the thumbnails for every page in a site all at once. (You can also make them one page at a time.)

Removed Unused…, Get…Used (External, Colors, and Font Sets tabs). If you delete URLs, addresses, colors, or font sets from pages in your site, they persist in the appropriate tab; or, if you create new objects and don't apply them to pages, they also remain. Selecting Remove Unused… deletes any item that isn't used somewhere in the site.

Clean Up Site. Clean Up Site offers the same kind of functionality as Remove Unused…, but it allows you to remove all kinds of unused objects simultaneously, including files that aren't linked into the navigation hierarchy.

Change References. Selecting this option from the menu or clicking the Change References button in the Site toolbar brings up a Change References dialog box that allows you to change all instances of an internal or external link.

Finder/Explorer. Mac users see a Finder item, while Windows users see Explorer in the Site menu. The options in this submenu and in the Site toolbar correspond to showing, explaining, and opening items from the desktop within GoLive. We cover this mostly in Chapter 19, as well as the two platform-specific appendixes on Mac and Windows.

FTP Server and WebDAV Server. The FTP and WebDAV features get full coverage in Chapter 20, *Synchronizing Sites*.

Settings. The Settings item brings up Site Settings, which contains any preferences customized for your site (covered earlier in this chapter).

Set Your Sights

With the big picture in mind, let's set our sights on setting up sites, and walk through the details of each aspect of creating, maintaining, and updating sites using GoLive.

Diagramming and Mapping

You can build a site two ways: as accretions of links and pages that you add and name chaotically as the need arises, and not according to any system or schedule; or, as a carefully thought-out set of sections and pages which are consistently structured, named, and linked, and which correspond to an overall navigational theme that users can handle.

Can you tell our bias?

Actually, like most Web designers, we work in a state that is often a combination of anal-retentive and free-love hippie-child. Depending on the site's size and our available time, we can either cobble together pages and graphics to produce something; or, spend months with programmers, editors, and information architects trying to figure out how to build a site that can expand sensibly for months or years.

We all yearn for a tool that would answer both needs: a kind of electronic paper and pencil that would let us draw in a site with quick strokes, making multiple illustrations, each serving its own purpose, and erasing and redrawing lines and boxes as the design progresses.

The electronic design sketches would eliminate the tedium of drawing each individual box or line, and as we move pages around, the lines would redraw themselves. Sounds like an unreachable ideal, but GoLive's diagramming features aren't too far from utopia.

With GoLive's Diagram options, you can map the outlines of a site, including creating links and hierarchical relationships between pages, scripts, databases, and other media types with a minimum of effort. Type a few keystrokes and move the mouse, and your diagrammed site is completely reorganized on screen.

GoLive's goal is to let you use templates and blank pages to sketch in the structure of a site, and identify the relationships between parts. You can edit Web pages directly in a staging area, as well as create links, and nothing is committed to the existing live site until you're ready. This lets you test and work on the structure and content without disturbing the rest of the site.

GoLive lets you develop any number of sets of these diagrams at the same time without interfering with one another. When you're ready, you can stage these diagrams into the live site, while still being able to revoke a diagram after it's become live.

These diagrams can be used as roughs for clients or for yourself to preview how new features and sections of a site might look and work. In a collaborative environment, different people could open the same site file (over a file server, for example) and create and annotate different designs.

Tip: Normal Linking

You can, of course, still add pages and links to the live site without using these design features; we discuss how to do that in the next chapter, *Managing Files, Folders, and Links*.

The Diagram menu includes one site mapping view, Navigation. Another view, Links, can be reached via a tab after selecting Navigation. The Navigation view lets you add pages and pending links to the live site. The Links view of a Web site displays the full inbound and outbound links for every page. To bring up either view, click the Navigation View button on the Toolbar.

What's New in 6

The Diagrams feature was called Designs in GoLive 5; Diagrams is a bit more descriptive of the actual function. This feature is now much better designed to create site maps for output. New icons represent different kinds of files, such as ASP scripts or databases. New text and graphics tools let you define levels in a hierarchy and place text on the page.

The Master tab, introduced in the diagram window, allows you to put objects on a diagram that aren't checked in when a diagram is staged. This provides a better way to label elements or even include decorative items, like a legend.

The diagram window automatically breaks its display into pages for better output, and you can export a design to a vector file (PDF or SVG formats) for editing.

New in 6: Diagrams

The Diagrams tab was called the Site tab in GoLive 4, and the Designs tab in GoLive 5, both of which were confusing. You had the Site tab, the Site window, the Site menu, and so forth in 4; and then the Design tab in a design window in the Design tab in GoLive 5. GoLive 6 cleans up the nomenclature by renaming the tab to Diagrams, and adding a Diagram menu.

Tip: Family Resemblance

GoLive follows the standard Web design practice of naming pages "parents" that are above other pages in a hierarchy; the pages below parents are their "children." "Siblings" are pages down a level in the hierarchy from a parent that are all linked from the same parent, and may be linked to each other (see Figure 18-1).

For instance, a parent could be the home page, with the children being the section divisions that are all siblings to each other. GoLive allows left and right siblings that indicate previous or next items in a sequence, such as a tutorial that has an organized flow of pages.

Figure 18-1
Family
resemblance

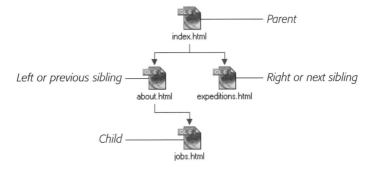

Tip: Extracting Sites

Unfortunately, there is no facility to build a new design based on existing sites or sections.

Creating Site Diagrams

The diagram features in GoLive are built around the idea that you start with a site map on paper or in your head, and you add sections (pages with special properties) and pages to flesh out that map, including the relationship between pages as siblings, parents, and children. You can also add pending links between pages that get stored for later application to items on the page. And you can leave notes like stickies all over a design, either attached to a page or just floating out there in space.

The basic order of prototyping a site is outlined below. The first three steps can happen concurrently (see Figure 18-2). You can also use step 1a to create a master page on which you then base subsequent diagrams.

1a. Add sections and pages that correspond to all the pages necessary in the new site or area you're creating.

1b. Create pending links between pages that correspond to connections you need to make in the actual content of a page.

1c. Nail down the overall structure and prettify the appearance using tools to clean up alignment, distribution, and display, and add visual groups to lump content together. Customize with the View palette.

2. Fill pages with content and add the pending links to the items on pages.

3. Send in digital form to clients and/or others for comments. (If you're working alone, just look at it yourself.) Make remarks using the Annotations feature (see Figure 18-3), and export as a PDF or SVG file to exchange with collaborators or reviewers.

4. Test and confirm that all content is good, and that all comments in annotations are answered.

5a. Submit the diagram from the staging area into the current local version of the site in the Files tab. Confirm that everything works as you expect.

5b. If there are any problems, revoke the diagram (which moves the files out of the live site back into the staging area), and make notes and/or corrections. Repeat steps 5a and 5b as necessary (see Figure 18-4).

6. Upload the new files to your live site via FTP or WebDAV, or to a Workgroup Server (WGS).

Tip: Revisionist History

Most of the actions you can perform in the Diagrams tab are fully undoable (i.e., you can revert after committing to the action), from dragging objects around the tab, adding and removing pages, and changing links. Consult the History palette to go backward and forward.

Managing Diagrams

Like many features in GoLive, the Diagrams tab appears to have no functionality when you first open it. It's a *tabula rasa* (blank slate), which can be

Figure 18-2
Prototyping
a site

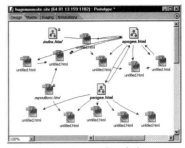

Step 1a: Add sections and pages.   *Step 1b: Create pending links.*

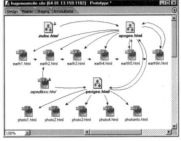

Step 1c: Nail down structure.

Figure 18-3
Annotating a
design

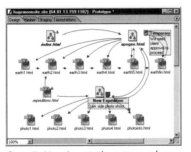

Step 3: Use Annotations to mark up a design for review and feedback.

Figure 18-4
Submitting a
design

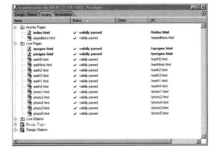

Step 5: Submit design.   *Step 6: Upload new files.*

daunting. But it's easy to start adding to the tab and to get up and running with prototyping.

Tip: True Names

Adobe names only certain parts of items found in the Diagrams tab, so we had to invent a little terminology for clarity. We call the open window of an individual diagram the diagram window (lowercase to indicate it's generic). At times we wound up referring to the Design tab in a diagram window in the Diagrams tab. It can get long-winded, so we try to only talk about the Design tab or the Design tab in a diagram window.

Adding a diagram. With a Site window open, select New Design Diagram from the Diagram menu or contextual menu (see Figure 18-5). A new diagram is empty, and represented by a icon in the Diagrams tab's diagram list. The Diagrams tab can hold multiple diagrams, which are initially sorted alphabetically by name, although you can sort by modification date as well.

Figure 18-5
Adding a diagram

Add a new Design Diagram by choosing New Design Diagram from the Diagram menu (left) or the contextual menu (below).

Opening a diagram. Double-click the diagram icon to open a diagram window in which you create your diagrams and relationships between parts, as well as stage and annotate diagrams. There are four tabs corresponding to these tasks in every diagram window: Design, Master, Staging, and Annotations.

Deleting a diagram. Select one or more diagrams and choose Clear or Delete from the Edit menu or contextual menu, or simply press Command-Delete (Mac) or Delete (Windows). GoLive prompts you about whether you want to delete the diagrams; this action can be undone.

New in 6: Undo Delete

GoLive 6 lets you undo deletion of diagrams.

Changing a diagram's name. The diagram's name is highlighted after creation so you can directly edit it. You can also select the name later and modify it, or use the Site Diagram Inspector.

Building Site Diagrams

The Design tab of a diagram window provides you with a drawing pad in which you can sketch out the structure and content of your new site, new section, or new pages. The Design tab contains a placeholder grid when first opened.

Dragging icons from the Diagram tab of the Objects palette creates diagrams. You can drag in pages, text blocks, grouping elements, and icons that represent a whole range of special files for scripting or connecting to Web pages. You can create a superset of pages, called a section, which assigns properties to any subpages created in that section.

You can also drag in Stationery and Templates, as well as pages you've already created that are listed in the Files tab of the Site window. Links can be created automatically when you insert new pages, or by using Point & Shoot to connect pages.

Once placed, you can drag pages all over the diagram and GoLive preserves the relationships between them, redrawing any link lines as needed. When you've achieved optimal results, you can clean up the Design tab through alignment and distribution features. It's a visual tool, so don't be afraid to act visually.

New in 6: Master Elements

In addition to creating diagrams, you can lock any object you place on a page as a master element. These elements are locked in place, and cannot be linked to or from in the Design tab. The advantage here is being able to assign something like an annotation that repeats when the diagram spans multiple pages.

Viewing Diagrams

The Design tab works like a big canvas, similar to the canvas or pasteboard found in desktop publishing programs. You generally see only a fraction of the canvas at any given time (depending on the size of your window and the complexity of your diagram). GoLive provides several tools you can use to pan and zoom around.

Drag. Holding down the spacebar turns the cursor into a grabber hand just like in other Adobe applications (see Figure 18-6). You can then click and slide the view around.

Figure 18-6
Dragging the
design area

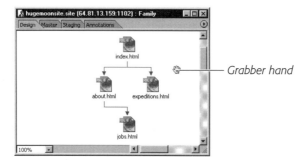

Grabber hand

Zoom menu. The Zoom menu, located at the lower-left corner of the Design tab, allows you to select a magnification amount; the default is 100 percent, where thumbnail previews are displayed at 72 dpi.

The Zoom menu offers preset enlargement and reduction factors: 10, 20, 50, 80, 100, 125, 150, 200, 300, 400, and 500 (see Figure 18-7). You can also select Fit Site in Window or Fit in Window, and GoLive reduces the site map to very tiny proportions to accommodate the window size. The Zoom menu displays the currently selected percentage.

Figure 18-7
Zoom menu
presets

Tip: Distorted Views

The page thumbnails GoLive creates are sized for 72 dpi at 100 percent view in the Design tab, and end up pixilated at larger sizes.

Magnifying glass. Holding down Option (Mac) or Shift (Windows) turns the cursor into a zoom-in magnifying glass to enlarge the site map. Clicking once zooms to 200 percent and changes the icon to a zoom-out magnifying glass which, if clicked, zooms back to 100 percent.

You can also zoom to higher magnifications (up to 500 percent) by clicking and dragging to create a marquee, which fills the window with the selected area.

Site Navigator palette. For true ease in panning around the site map, invoke the Site Navigator palette from the Window menu (see Figure 18-8). The Site Navigator gives you a thumbnail of the entire diagram canvas, with a marquee that you drag to control the section that appears in the main window.

Figure 18-8
Site Navigator
palette

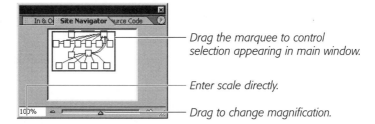

— Drag the marquee to control selection appearing in main window.

— Enter scale directly.

— Drag to change magnification.

When you drag the marquee, the diagram window scrolls as you drag; or just click points on the site thumbnail, and the Design tab or Master tab instantly changes its focus to display that section.

Zoom options are available at the bottom of the palette. Clicking the larger and smaller "mountain" buttons increases or decreases the diagram window's zoom factor by standard increments. Or, you can use the slider to dynamically change the zoom value. Just to round things out, you can enter a value into the Zoom field at lower left. The palette is resizable within small bounds (see Figure 18-9). If you need a bigger preview, try the Panorama pane.

Figure 18-9
Resizing the
Site Navigator
palette

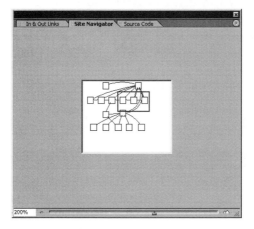

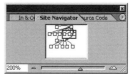

You can only resize the palette within certain bounds.

Panorama pane. The Panorama pane works remarkably like the Site Navigator palette, but it's an integrated part of a diagram window and shows a larger area (see Figure 18-10). It's also a proxy for selection, just like the Table palette is for tables: you can select items in the Panorama exactly like you would in the main diagram window. You can even use the Point & Shoot tool or resize items.

Figure 18-10
Panorama
pane

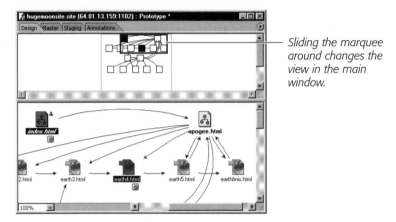

Sliding the marquee around changes the view in the main window.

Display the Panorama pane by checking its box in the Design tab of the Design View palette. (See "Design View Palette," later in this chapter.)

Pages and Icons

The simplest way to start a diagram is to add pages and icons—whether empty or derived from Stationery, Templates, or "sample" files—to the blank diagram canvas.

Pages are homely objects: they simply represent a blank Web page. Icons are more complicated, as they represent all manner of other kinds of script files and resources. But underlying these icons is nothing unusual; it's all about graphics to make a better site map and to mnemonically remind you of what should be linked to what.

Tip: Adding Custom Icons

GoLive lets you add your own icons. Search the online help for "adding custom objects."

Adding by dragging. Drag any icon from the Diagram tab of the Objects palette, or drag Stationery or a Template from the Site Extras tab (see Figure

18-11). GoLive inserts an object, named "untitled" and an appropriate extension (such as "untitled.html"), to represent these new items.

Figure 18-11
Adding pages
by dragging

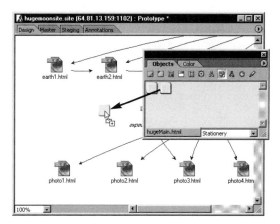

If you drag near an existing item, a new relationship is added via links, depending on the point on the compass you drag to, and indicated by a solid bar near the existing icon. Dragging to the top creates a parent relationship; to the left, a previous sibling; to the right, a next sibling; and below, a child (see Figure 18-12).

Figure 18-12
Dragging
relationships

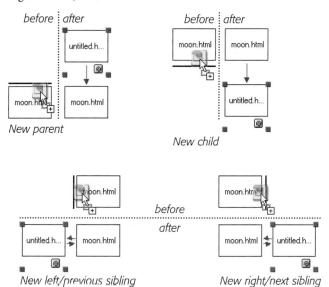

If the item you drag near is derived from Stationery, the new page is also copied from the same Stationery; likewise for Templates. If the page is a section, the section rules for naming and folders apply.

Adding by menu. You can also add items by choosing from the Insert Object submenu of the contextual menu (see Figure 18-13). Specific page relationships can be created by selecting an existing page and then choosing from the Diagram menu or contextual menu's New submenu.

Figure 18-13
Listing pages
from the
contextual
menu

Tip: Adobe, Name Your Kids Right

Although both contain the same options, the New submenus of the Diagram menu and the contextual menu use different names and orders for creating new relationships. The Diagram menu's New submenu lists Next Page, Child Page, Previous Page, and Parent Page. By contrast, the New submenu of the contextual menu lists Child, Next, Previous, and Parent.

Tip: Remembering Relatives

The GoLive engineers threw in a neat feature for helping you create site sketches. Create a page and then add a parent or child to that page. Drag that parent or child left or right, up or down. Now, create the next relationship from it—GoLive remembers the direction and distance you dragged, and adds the latest item in that same direction (see Figure 18-14). Pretty nifty!

Just like with dragging in a new page, if the page you selected is derived from Stationery or a Template, the new page uses the same Stationery or Template; if it's a section, the new page uses the section's rules, as described below.

Figure 18-14
Predicting
positions

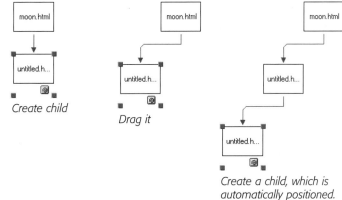

Create child

Drag it

Create a child, which is
automatically positioned.

Adding by Toolbar. With a page or item selected, click any of the four icons corresponding to parent, child, or next or previous sibling from the Toolbar to insert a page.

Duplicating. Select an item and choose Duplicate from the Edit menu or contextual menu. Or, you can engage in some complicated finger work: select a file and keep the mouse button held down (this part is critical) and while dragging press the Control key (Windows) or Option key (Mac). Notice that the cursor changes to add a plus sign next to it; it's now a duplicating tool. ("What's that? What do you know about my duplicating ray?"–Roy Lichtenstein.)

Adding master items. The Master tab in a diagram window contains items that you want to have appear in a printed or exported diagram, but that you don't want to check into an actual site. This is useful for adding text (like the page title) that needs to appear on multiple pages when printed, for example. Select any page or icon that you've added to a page and choose Master Item from the contextual menu (see Figure 18-15, next page). Or, drag an item directly to the Master tab, which pops to the front and adds your item as a master item. Four crop marks surround master items to indicate their kind.

You can revert an item back to a normal page icon by selecting Master Item again to uncheck it. Master icons can't be linked.

Page and Object Inspectors

With items on the page, you can now start manipulating them. Pages and other objects have almost identical Inspectors with some slight differences in their leftmost tabs (labeled Page and Object, respectively).

Figure 18-15
Adding a
master item

Select a page or item that you want to use as a master item and choose Master Item from the contextual menu.

Tip: Different Page Inspector

Pages have their own special Page Inspector, which is entirely different from the Page Inspector associated with the Files tab in a site window (see Chapter 19, *Managing Files, Folders, and Links*).

Page or Object tab. The basic attributes for a page or object's source and nature appear on this tab (see Figure 18-16).

Figure 18-16
Page and
Object tabs

Page tab   *Object tab*

- **Name.** The Name field has nothing to do with any underlying HTML; it's used only in the Design tab when you view the name of files by their "design name." (See "Design View Palette," later in this section, for details on customizing the display using the Design View palette.)

- **Type (objects).** This popup menu shows the kind of object displayed, which you can change at any time by selecting another item. Your custom items show up in this menu as well.

- **Target Dir.** By default, new items are created in your default directory for new pages and objects; this is set in the Site pane of Preferences in the field marked Folder for Generated Items. If you enter a name in Target Dir, however, GoLive puts this item into the directory you specify. You can use any of the URL Getter features (browser, direct entry, Point & Shoot, or the Link popout menu) to select or create a directory.

Tip: Staging Items

Under "Staging," later in the chapter, we discuss how you move a diagram into the live site. If you've specified new directories, GoLive creates them, but it doesn't delete them if you revoke the diagram.

- **File Name.** The file name is the actual name of the file. Changing it here modifies the item's file name on disk or in a workgroup site.

Tip: Hold Back

The Diagram tab doesn't honor Filename Constraints; it allows you to name a file anything. Read about Filename Constraints in Chapter 19, *Managing Files, Folders, and Links.*

- **Page Title (pages).** The page title is the text placed between Title tags in the Head section of an HTML page. (This is one of about nine ways to change the title of a page in GoLive.)
- **Create From.** Pages and objects can have a derivation which is set via this part of the Inspector. Once you add an object to a site, but before you edit it, you can change the place from which it derives its content; after editing the page, these checkboxes are grayed out. Stationery and Template are popup menus, while Sample is a source that you duplicate through reference.

Tip: Mandatory Create From

At first glance, it looks as if it's mandatory to select an option to Create From for pages, while it's optional for objects. In fact, if you create blank pages on their own, none of the three options is checked in the Page Inspector.

Layout. The Layout tab controls the display of the selected item or items in relation to other items. Changing settings on a parent page changes the behavior of the children.

- **Draw Links As.** The three modes for links are Lines, Connectors, and Outline. Lines shows all pending links between items. Connectors point to a single item without an arrowhead just to demonstrate some relationship. Outline explicitly shows the parent, child, and sibling relationship between items.

- **Icons for hierarchies.** The four icons below Draw Links As rearrange children into single or double rows. With Lines selected above, only the left two single-row options are available.

- **Stagger.** Checking Stagger offsets the display of children.

- **Auto Position.** This option forces items to be correctly positioned when added or modified.

- **Honor Page Breaks.** Because diagrams can automatically break themselves into pages for output or export, this option makes sure that children don't straddle page breaks.

- **Align Children and Center Children.** These two checkboxes are exclusive of each other: you can either center children on their connecting lines, or have them all lined up in the same plane as the icon you chose above.

- **Honor Grid.** All icons sit locked to gridlines.

- **Spacing.** You can offset icons by a given horizontal or vertical distance in pixels (you can only apply a value to one or the other, however).

- **Line Drawing.** The arrowheads for the connecting lines can be set to none, square, or angled (see Figure 18-17).

Figure 18-17
Arrowheads

None   Square   Angled

Graphics. The Graphics tab sets the font, color, fill, and line width for selected items. Pages and objects use only the Text Color and Font Size fields.

- **Line Color, Fill Color, Header Fill Color, Text Color.** These options can be set via the Color palette, which is brought to front when you click the swatches.

- **Line Width.** Line widths can be set to selected sizes or typed in.

- **Font Size.** Any text in the selected item can be changed in size.

- **Default Settings.** Clicking this button resets the settings to their default.

- **Apply to All.** Any children of the page or item in question receive the settings when you click Apply to All.

Sections

Pages are fine, but you have to add them one at a time and name them individually. What if you create a template for an entire set of pages—a new section of the site—and want to add five or even 50 pages for that section? The Section feature helps with that task.

Sections look and act like pages, but they have additional properties assigned to them in the Section tab of the Section Inspector that allow you to automate adding new pages as children. Adding pages then becomes a cookie-cutter operation in which the section is the template for the naming, location, and contents.

Adding sections. You add a section to a diagram through two methods: drag the Section icon from the Diagram tab of the Objects palette into the diagram window (see Figure 18-18), or select Section from the Insert Object submenu of the contextual menu. You can also convert pages into sections; see below.

Figure 18-18
Adding a
section

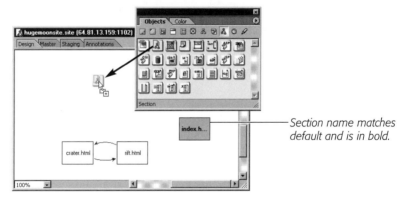

Section name matches
default and is in bold.

The section symbol on a page has a special icon that looks like a site hierarchy; the name is also in bold type. Sections are named by default with the home page name specified in the Site pane of Preferences. This is a small problem, as you have to either pay close attention to the file or select it and check out which Inspector palette appears.

Section Inspector's Section tab. All the properties of a section are defined through the Section tab of the Section Inspector (see Figure 18-19).

Figure 18-19
Section tab

- **New Filename.** The name you enter here becomes the stub prefix for any pages created through this section. If you enter "scooby", pages are created named "scooby.html", "scooby1.html", "scooby2.html", and so forth. If you add items to a section, the numbering is preserved, but the appropriate extension, like ".php", is added.

Tip: Same Names

Adding items to a section in this way acts a little strange when you're creating child pages, because the file name's numbering scheme only works within relationships. So, adding a sibling page to "scooby.html" results in "scooby1.html", but adding a child to "scooby1.html" gives you another "scooby.html" page (see Figure 18-20).

Figure 18-20
Odd names for
child pages

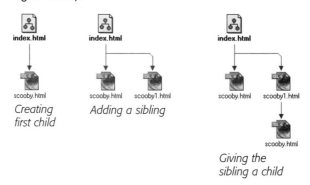

- **Folder.** You can use Point & Shoot, direct entry, browse, or the Link popout menu to choose a folder in which these pages should be stored in the site.

- **Stationery and Template.** Any Stationery or Templates in the site are available through these popup menus. Choosing an item here creates new pages using that Stationery or Template.

- **Generate Links.** The section page is the parent, in this case, so selecting items from the Parent popup menu controls which visual links are drawn between the section and the pages you're creating. The None option is self-explanatory; for the rest, see Figure 18-21. The Sibling popup menu affects all the pages created in the section: The To Next Sibling option links just from one page to each subsequently created page; To Adjacent Siblings links bi-directionally (see Figure 18-22).

Figure 18-21
Link types

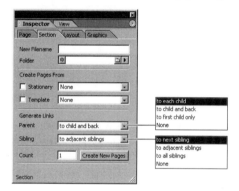

Figure 18-22
Sibling
relationships

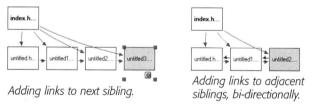

Adding links to next sibling.

Adding links to adjacent siblings, bi-directionally.

- **Create New Pages.** The section menu gives you a shortcut to creating new pages, as discussed just below. Enter the number of pages to create and click Create New Pages.

Adding pages to sections. You add single relative pages to a section by selecting the section and choosing one of the options from the Diagram menu or contextual menu's New submenu, or by dragging any icons from the Diagram tab of the Objects palette, or any Stationery or Template onto the section. With a section selected, the rules of that section apply to any new page created when it's selected or dragged onto.

These methods create just a single new page or object. To create multiple pages, choose New Pages from the Diagram menu or contextual menu with any item selected. The New Pages menu treats every object as if it were a section, and the dialog box that it brings up exactly mirrors the Section tab of the Section Inspector (see Figure 18-23).

Figure 18-23
The New
Pages dialog
box

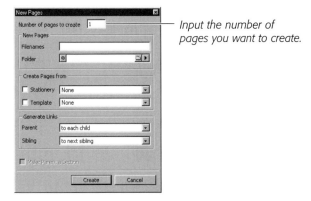

Input the number of pages you want to create.

Converting items to sections. If you want to convert the selected item to a section, check the Make Parent a Section box in the New Pages dialog box mentioned just above, or select a page and choose Convert to Section from the contextual menu.

Links

Pages by themselves are certainly nice, but they only have worth once they've been linked to other pages and other items. In the diagram window's Design tab, you're creating pending links, or links that you later apply to text and images on the page you're linking from. These pending links appear in two places: in the visual preview you edit in the Design tab of a diagram window, and in the Pending Links palette, discussed below in "Adding Pending Links."

GoLive offers three kinds of links in the Design tab: hyperlink, navigation, and tour. Navigation links include parent, previous, next, and child, which GoLive breaks out as separately defined items. You can also define your own link styles to color-code certain links differently than others; or, you can redefine the colors so that parent and child links are more distinct.

Only the hyperlink and navigation link options work as pending links; the tour link and any links you define on your own are for visual impact only.

Link Inspector. Selecting one or more links brings up the Link Inspector, which has blessedly few settings. Link Type defines the kind of link out of six defaults or any user-defined link types. You can change a link from one type to another through the popup menu.

Tip: Defining New Links

You can define new link types or change the color or name of an existing type through the Link Type pane in Preferences (global) or Site Settings (per site). You can't delete or rename the six defaults, although you can change the color assigned to them.

Deflection describes the angle of arc assigned to a link. You can use the prefabricated values in the popup menu or simply drag the handle in the middle of a link to arc it out or in with a much higher degree of control.

The Arrowhead menu lets you select no capper, or a square or angled one.

The Graphics tab is explained above, in "Pages and Icons." For lines, only the line width option can be changed.

Adding navigation links. Navigation links are added when you drag a page onto another page, by selecting New Pages from a menu, or by using the Create New Pages button in the Section Inspector. These links appear green by default.

Adding hyperlinks. Use Point & Shoot to add links to other items in the diagram. These appear blue by default.

You can't Point & Shoot anywhere except in the diagram window, because you can only link to other files in the same diagram sandbox. Once you drag anchors in, which are proxies for real pages on your active site, you can link to and from them (see Figure 18-24). See "Anchors," next page.

Figure 18-24
Anchors

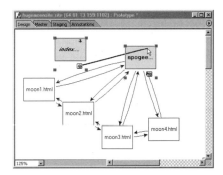

Adding tour and custom links. The only way to add custom links is to convert a link you've made through the methods described for hyperlinks and navigational links. Select the link or links, bring up the Link Inspector, and choose your new link type from the popup menu, such as Tour.

Adding any type of link by selection. Another way to create links is to select two or more pages and choose Add Design Line from the contextual menu; it's not available from any other menu. You can choose any type of link from the submenu to add. The order of selecting pages determines the direction of the arrows of the links you add (see Figure 18-25).

Figure 18-25
Page selection
order

Anchors

If you're creating an annex or new section for an existing site, you need to link the new pages to at least one point on an existing page—otherwise, how does a user navigate to your new section? You create these links through anchors.

Unlike an HTML anchor, which is a link destination within a page, a diagram anchor is an alias or shortcut to a file in the existing site. Drag a file from the Files tab or the Navigation or Links views into the diagram window's Design tab, and GoLive creates an anchor (see Figure 18-26). You can then use Point & Shoot to link the anchor to an existing page. This adds a pending link on the anchor page. You can have as many anchors as you like. Anchors are easy to identify: they have a section icon, bold italic type for their name or label, and an anchor icon directly adjacent.

Once the anchor is created, you can treat it just like any other page in a diagram. You can Point & Shoot links to it from other pages, or use any of the options to create new navigational relationships. You can even use the New Pages menu item to convert the anchor into a section.

Figure 18-26
Creating
an anchor

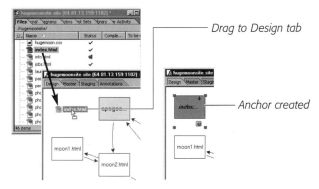

Drag to Design tab

Anchor created

Adding Pending Links

After you construct a set of linked pages, you need to fill them with at least *some* content. The links you've added visually are recorded by GoLive as pending links, accessed through the Pending Links palette. Open any page in the Design tab and select Pending Links from the Window menu.

The Pending Links palette shows every link to other HTML pages, objects, and media files already present on the page, but, more importantly, it also displays pending links to other objects on the site (see Figure 18-27).

Figure 18-27
Pending tab

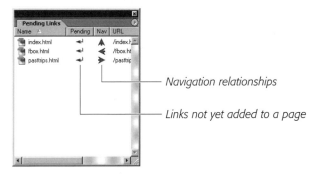

Navigation relationships

Links not yet added to a page

Tip: Navigation Additions

Because you can add links to the existing site via the Navigation view, the Pending Links palette is applicable for those relationships you create as well. See "Mapping Sites," later in this chapter.

Tip: The Old In & Out

While you're editing a page in the Design tab, the In & Out Links palette is a useful tool to help figure out what links are already on a page. It's discussed in great detail in Chapter 19, *Managing Files, Folders, and Links*.

The Pending Links palette has four columns:

- **Name.** The link's name.

- **Pending.** A blue arrow means that the link is still pending and hasn't been added on the page itself to text or an object.

- **Nav.** This column only applies to pending links added via the Navigation view; see "Mapping Sites," later in this chapter.

- **URL.** Displays the full local path to internal links or media files.

You add objects from the palette into an open page in one of the following three methods. After applying any of them, the pending icon disappears from that object in the palette (see Figure 18-28).

Figure 18-28
Adding
pending links
and objects

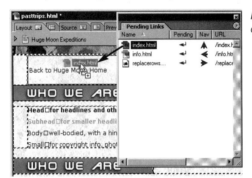

*Pending link gets
dragged onto a page.*

*Pending link no longer
appears pending.*

Dragging. Drag the link from the Pending Links palette into the page. GoLive creates a hyperlink using the link's file name.

Selection. First, select text to be linked on the page. With the Page Inspector visible, drag a pending link from the palette onto the selected text.

Other tabs. You can drag pages from the Files tab, Navigation view, or Links view onto an HTML page (whether you have something selected on that page or not). This isn't the most efficient method, nor does it directly use the Pending Links palette, but it does remove the pending status from the palette's corresponding item after you've dragged the object into the page.

Collection

The collection options center around selecting one or more files and identifying them as a set you can reselect later. You can make, edit, and retrieve collections in the diagram window as well as the Navigation view and Links view.

Tip: Spotlight Display

Collections are useful in conjunction with the Spotlight display option in the Design tab of the diagram window or the Navigation view. Spotlight can highlight a variety of relationships, including collections (see Figure 18-29). Which set is spotlighted is set via the View palette.

Figure 18-29
Spotlight
display

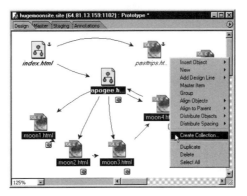

Creating a collection. Choose one or more pages and select Create Collection from the Diagram or contextual menu. Provide a unique name for the selection; you can even select a unique color when these items are spotlighted.

Unchecking Add Selection lets you simply create a new entry without adding the selected objects. Spotlight Collection highlights this set in the Design tab.

Editing collections. You can't edit the actual files chosen by a given selection through the Edit Collections menu item in the Diagram. Instead, you can change the collection's default name and assign a different color to the selection.

Toggling collections. The Toggle Collection submenu, available only in the contextual menu, allows you to change the contents of a selection. Select one or more items, and then view the Toggle Collection submenu. Selecting any item in the list that is unchecked adds the current selection to that set; likewise, choosing a checked set (which means the selection is already part of the set) removes it from that set (see Figure 18-30).

Figure 18-30
Toggling
selections

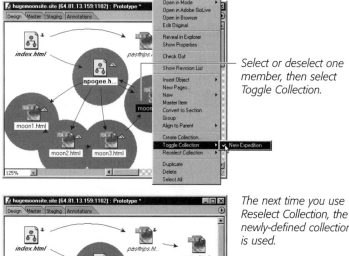

Select or deselect one
member, then select
Toggle Collection.

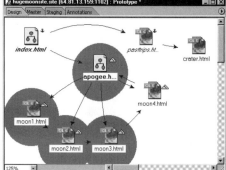

The next time you use
Reselect Collection, the
newly-defined collection
is used.

Reselecting collections. Choose a collection from the Reselect Collection submenu in the Diagram or contextual menu. The pages in the chosen selection are then highlighted.

Grouping

The grouping features allow you to create a colored container into which you place items; or, you can select items and have a visual container drawn around them. Groups don't affect any underlying HTML or other code. They're all about appearance and organization.

Creating a group. There are three ways to create groups (see Figure 18-31):

- Drag a Group icon from the Diagram tab of the Objects palette; or, double-click that icon. You can drag files into the newly created group.

- Select one or more items and select Group from the Edit or contextual menu.

- Select one or more items and click the Group icon under the Grouping area in the Transform palette.

Figure 18-31
Creating
groups

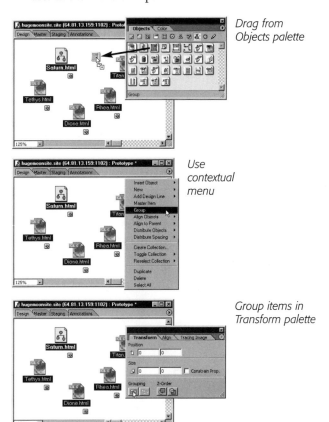

Drag from
Objects palette

Use
contextual
menu

Group items in
Transform palette

Modifying a group. You can drag items in and out of a group at will. The group's borders highlight if the items are inside the group. If you set a group to automatically resize , when you slide items around, the group's borders enlarge or shrink.

You can also drag groups around a diagram, in and out of other groups, or near other groups to bump them out of the way if Auto Resize is enabled.

Group Inspector. The Group Inspector has two tabs: the Group tab and the Graphics tab. In the Group tab, you can name a group and set the name's alignment in the title bar. Unchecking Display Title Bar removes the group's title bar as well as the name it contains. Auto Resize controls whether the group changes shape as you drag items in and out of it.

The Graphics tab controls the fill color for the body of the group (Fill Color), and the title bar (Header Fill Color). You can also set text color and font size.

Ungrouping. Select a group by its edge or title bar and choose Ungroup from the Edit or contextual menu. You can also click the Ungroup button in the Transform palette under the Grouping area.

Deleting a group. Select any edge of the group or the group's title bar and press Delete or select Clear or Delete from the Edit menu or the contextual menu. This removes the group and all of its enclosed items.

Formatting

For printing and exporting diagrams, GoLive offers some text features and bracketing tools that provide better commentary outside of the icons and links that you're otherwise limited to (see Figure 18-32).

Figure 18-32
Formatting

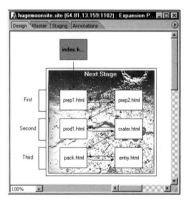

Box. The Box object lets you place formatted text on a page, which you control via the Box Inspector. You can force text to stay on a single line, to resize dynamically with the text that's entered, and to align left, center, or right. You can also provide a margin, and set text to bold or italic.

Boxes support background images, useful for designing site maps. The text box can be sized to fit the image through the Size to Image checkbox.

Boxes typically are turned into master items to keep them out of the staging area, even incidentally.

Level. Level is a resizeable symbol that can encompass hierarchical depths for better labeling. You can resize these brackets by dragging.

The Level Inspector allows the entry of text, which can be set to run in a single line by checking Single Line (see Figure 18-33).

Figure 18-33
Level Inspector

The three vertical placement icons at left control whether text is placed at top, in the middle, or at the bottom. Text can be aligned across the horizontal dimension as well, and set to bold and/or italic.

Margin Width controls the offset of text, but it only affects the bracket itself if you check Center Bracket.

Levels, too, are often set as master items.

Alignment and Distribution

Like any good page-layout program, GoLive offers tools to better shuffle icons around on screen to clean them up. The alignment and distribution tools, available from menus and palettes, are exactly the same as those available for objects in layout grids. Would we be so crass as to waste your time and several pages by repeating that information here? No way! (See Figure 18-34, next page; also see "Working with Grid Objects" in Chapter 8, *Layout Grids*.)

Also, you should know that GoLive likes to let the pages rock and roll in the Design tab of the diagram window. Every time you move any file or add one, GoLive seems compelled to rearrange all the links and icons near whatever you changed.

Figure 18-34
Alignment and
distribution

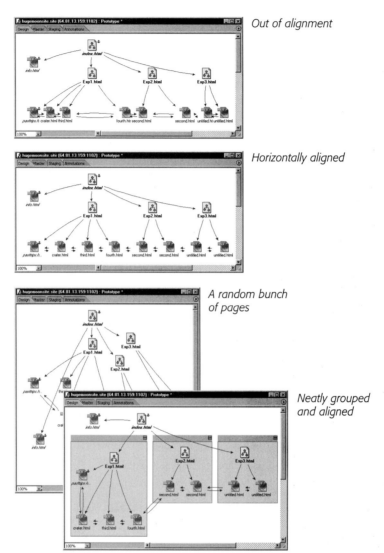

Out of alignment

Horizontally aligned

A random bunch
of pages

Neatly grouped
and aligned

The way to avoid this behavior is to turn off Collision Avoidance (unchecking both Horiz. and Vert.) in the Grid tab of the Design View palette, and to uncheck Auto Resize in every group you create; you can't set that as a default behavior. There is no simple way to lock a file or link's position in the diagram window.

Design View Palette

So far, we've discussed only how to manipulate objects, but GoLive also offers a large list of display options to customize how you view pages and their relationships in the main diagram window. Display the View palette to see three tabs: Design, Display, and Grid.

Tip: Panorama

The Design View palette also affects the Panorama pane, described below.

Design Colors

The Design View palette doesn't set the colors for everything in the diagram window. GoLive's Design Colors settings let you set the background color for all the panes and windows in the Diagrams tab, as well as the colors for links and items (see Figure 18-35).

You can set global defaults for Design Colors through Preferences or Site Settings. Open the Site pane in Preferences, or open Site Settings, and select Design Colors.

The colors in the Background Colors column set the background for the panes or windows noted. The Item Color swatch sets the default color for pages added to a diagram. The Link Colors swatches affect the Navigation view and Links view colors: the Navigation field colors all links in Navigation view; Links covers all links in Links view; and Pending covers pending links when displayed via the View palette in the Navigation view.

Default Design Link Colors control the links in a diagram window's Design tab.

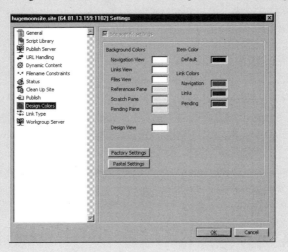

Figure 18-35
Setting
Design Colors

Design Tab

The Design tab controls the overall display of the Design tab of a diagram window.

Spotlight. With a set selected in the Collection popup menu, GoLive puts large circles around the items in that set (see Figure 18-36). This makes it easy to switch around to look at different parts of your diagram as you're building a site to stage out.

Figure 18-36
Spotlight

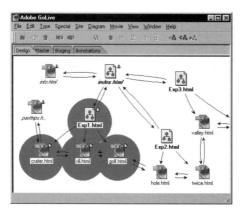

Orientation. The Tall and Wide settings for orientation affect how the panes arrange themselves, but have no impact on whether links get made from left to right or top to bottom (see Figure 18-37). In the Navigation view and Links view, Orientation affects the display of pages.

Show Panes. GoLive uses four panes in conjunction with the Design tab of a diagram window. In the Design tab of the View palette, two are available: Panorama and Reference (Scratch appears, but is grayed out).

- Panorama is also discussed earlier in the chapter in the section, "Viewing Diagrams." It's a proxy for selection, meaning that you can select items in it just as if you were selecting them in the main window. You can drag items around, delete them, group them, and edit links.

- Reference shows any media items included on a page, such as images and QuickTime movies.

Display Tab

The Display tab formats the individual items in the diagram window's panes.

Figure 18-37
Orientation

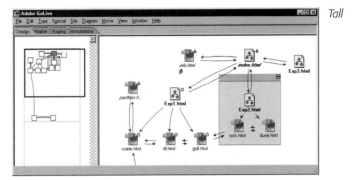

Tall

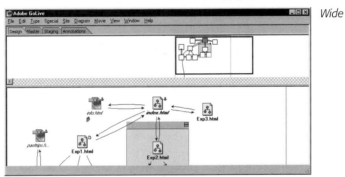

Wide

View Master Items. Objects in the Master tab, which aren't part of a site when staged, can be toggled on or off.

View Page Breaks. GoLive breaks the diagram's Design tab into printable pages. You can see these or not, although it's useful to avoid mysteries as objects leap across the breaks.

View Staging Icons. A small icon next to each item in the diagram indicates its status, if one is appropriate. We recommend turning this off when printing or exporting to keep the map cleaner. (For an explanation of icons, see Chapter 19, *Managing Files, Folders, and Links.*)

Show Items As. The Show Items As heading offers five options (see Figure 18-38, next page):

- **Icons:** the icons for objects as seen in the Desktop. The name appears below the page.

- **Thumbnails:** a small rectangle containing page thumbnails, if available, with the item's name below the box. (See the sidebar, "Thumbnails.")

Figure 18-38
Show Items As

Icons   *Thumbnails*   *Frames*   *Ovals*   *Icon Frames*

- **Frames:** a box with the page's name inside of it.

- **Ovals:** big ol' ovals with the page's name nestled in the middle.

- **Icon Frames:** a rectangle divided vertically, with a tiny icon at left and the Item Label at right.

Item Label. The Item Label can be set to Page Title (the name in the Title tags), the File Name (the actual name of the file), or the Design Name (the name set in the Name field of the Page or Object tab of either the Page, Object, or Section Inspector). If you set Item Label to Page Title and the page has no title, GoLive wisely displays "No Title." Ditto for Design Name, which displays "No Name."

The two checkboxes below the label choices control how text is displayed around the item icon or frame (see Figure 18-39). Icons and Thumbnails can set Overhang Text so that a label extends beyond the width of the item. Frames and Icon Frames can display Multi-Line Text within their boundaries.

Frame Size. The Frame Size controls the height and width of the page icons in the diagram window. We don't find much reason to change these unless we want to see more of a thumbnail's preview.

Thumbnails

Thumbnails are tiny previews of HTML pages that GoLive can generate from the pages' contents. We discuss this feature thoroughly in Chapter 19, *Managing Files, Folders, and Links.* However, thumbnails get used in the Diagrams tab, too, if you set the Show Items As option to Thumbnails in the Design View palette or References View palette. You can create thumbnails for pages in the Design tab by selecting Update Thumbnails from the Diagram menu. This can take quite a while to carry out, as GoLive has to open each page, then render and store each thumbnail.

A simpler way to create a thumbnail for a particular page is to open it, make a small change, and save it. GoLive then automatically creates a thumbnail.

Figure 18-39
Item Label
choices

Huge Moon Expeditions

Overhang Text

Multi-Line Text

Item Color. You can choose a custom color for each page in a diagram window. This option is disabled if you are viewing items as icons.

Grid Tab

The Grid tab handles the interaction of objects (see Figure 18-40).

Figure 18-40
Grid Tab

Grid. The Horizontal and Vertical grid settings work here just as in layout grids: they control the minimum increments to which items get snapped. You can turn off both grid settings to move items around willy-nilly.

Collision Avoidance. This feature allows you to drag pages wherever you want in the diagram window without two items overlapping. However, if you want to group related pages together in a small space, make sure the Collision Avoidance box is unchecked.

> **Tip: Avoiding Avoidance**
>
> If you're trying to create a neat, permanent display of your diagram, you really should disable Collision Avoidance. Otherwise, every new link or page can cause other pages to jump about.

Canvas Is Single Page. The diagram window can be printed and exported, but you can opt out of the default display that breaks the canvas into pages. Check this box and you can disable page breaks.

The Page Rows and Columns fields and their corresponding Auto boxes let you limit the number of pages created. Auto extends the canvas as needed; uncheck one or both boxes and change the Page Rows and Columns values to set explicit ranges.

References View Palette

The Reference pane has its own View palette to handle the objects it shows. This is due, in part, to a broader array of files that might show up in this pane. The main diagram window and Panorama show only Web pages. The Reference pane can show any media file or external reference that is already linked to a Web page, that is pending, or is to be linked.

To use the References View palette and the Reference pane follow these steps:

1. Select View from the Window menu, or click the View palette's tab in the docked Inspector palette (it's there by default).

2. Open a diagram and click the Design tab. The View palette is now the Design View palette. (Design is a holdover from the last release of GoLive in which the diagram features were called design features.)

3. Check the Reference box in the Design View's Design tab.

4. Click anywhere in the Reference pane, which is now displayed. The Design View changes to the References View palette.

References Tab

The References tab works like a stripped-down version of the Display tab of the Design View palette, described earlier. Orientation modifies how the various panes are displayed in the diagram window.

Display Tab

The Display tab picks up some features from the corresponding tab in the Design View palette.

Graphical or Outline. Graphical view is the default for this pane. Selecting Outline shows the items in the Reference pane as a list with all their properties, just like items shown in the Files tab (see Figure 18-41). See Chapter 19, *Managing Files, Folders, and Links*, for more information about these properties.

Figure 18-41
Outline view

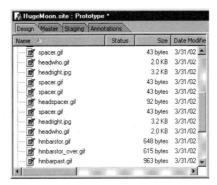

Shows Items As. Four of the five Design tab display options can be used in the Reference pane.

Item Label. Because the items included in the Reference pane aren't prospective pages, the Design Name option is excluded here. You can show either the File Name or Page Title.

Cell Size, Item Color, and Frame Size. You can use the same options here as in the Design View palette.

Filter Tab

The Filter tab is common to the Reference pane as well as the Navigation view and Links view. This tab allows you to select which files and link types appear.

Each of the checkboxes is a toggle, controlling whether the file type listed is displayed in the current pane or view (see Figure 18-42, next page). The Toggle Media and Toggle Links buttons don't work exactly as expected. They don't actually toggle the settings (turning inactive ones on and active ones off), but rather turn them all on or all off.

The media types are pretty straightforward: GIF, JPEG, and PNG are image types. Link types include the two references found in the External tab—URLs and email addresses—and missing files. The two grayed out items, Links to Self and Cyclic Links, are explained under "Links View," later in this chapter.

Staging

If you made it this far, the rest is a lot easier. Most of the work you do on a diagram site is in the Design tab of a diagram window. But when you've tweaked

Figure 18-42
Filter tab

the diagram as much as it needs and you're ready to link it into your existing site, switch to the Staging tab for some straightforward action, Jackson!

Tip: Anchors? Away!

Remember that you can't stage your site until you have created at least one pending link between an anchor and a page in your diagram. See "Anchors," earlier in the chapter.

Staging a site causes GoLive to copy all or selected files in your diagram to either the default folder for new files (as defined in the Site pane of Preferences) or to folders you specified for each file or section when creating them. GoLive keeps track of which files it copies so that it can move them back to the staging area upon request.

The Staging tab has five folders: Anchor Pages, Live Pages, Live Objects, Design Pages, and Design Objects. Anchor Pages contain any anchors you've dragged into the Design tab; these pages appear as aliases or shortcuts, just like they do in the Design tab. Live Pages and Live Objects show the pages and objects that you've staged, even though they are actually now located in the site folder itself. The Design Pages and Design Objects folders show the hierarchy of pages and objects before they are staged into the live site. You can sort files and folders in this tab by any of the column headers.

Check Staging

This option—found in the Toolbar, the Staging submenu of the Diagram menu, and the popout menu of a diagram window—confirms that the contents of the files in your site are up to snuff. The Status column shows typical file problems; for an explanation of these codes, see "Status Icons" in Chapter 19, *Managing Files, Folders, and Links.*

Any problems with staging are reported in the Check column:

- **File in use.** Close the file; GoLive needs all files to be closed in order to stage an item.

- **Target folder.** GoLive can't create the folder you specified for that item in the Target Dir field of the Page or Object tab of the Page, Object, or Section Inspector. Check that you're not asking it to create something impossible.

- **Section name.** The section name you've chosen is already in use in the location you want to locate a section. Rename the section or opt for a different directory through the Section Inspector's Page tab.

- **Stage in scratch.** If the file isn't linked to a navigation hierarchy starting with an anchor page, this error shows up. What it means is that when you stage that item, it doesn't have a connection to the site.

- **File rename.** GoLive needs to rename the file when the diagram is staged.

Submitting a Diagram

You can copy files from your diagram to the live site in one of three ways:

- **Submit All, Submit Items.** Choose one of these options to copy all or just selected files to the default New Files folder or any folders you specified in the live site.

- **Submit Items to Scratch.** The Scratch pane of the Navigation view replaces the old missing files display, showing all files in a site that aren't linked to the main navigation tree. With files selected, this option copies the selected files in the Design Pages folder to the live site whether or not those files selected are linked to an anchor. You can then create pending links to the file or files via the Scratch pane of the Navigation view or any other linking method.

Recalling a Diagram

As with submitting, you have a few options for recalling a diagram. When you recall a diagram or files in a diagram, GoLive moves these files back to the staging area, removing them from the live site.

Choose Recall All to copy all files back to the staging area, or Recall Items to retrieve just the selected items.

Annotations

Like any good piece of electronic paper, you can put electronic sticky notes on it (and they don't even leave adhesive on the screen!). Annotations let you apply notes that can be displayed in a variety of configurations attached to pages or areas of the drawing board.

Tip: In Latin, Post Id

We can't call them what you think they should be called or a certain Minnesota-based firm's lawyers would be after us. Besides, if we revealed the name here in this book, we'd have to also go on the Web and post it.

Add an annotation by dragging an Annotation icon from the Diagram tab of the Objects palette. If you drop it anywhere in the diagram window, it stays put. If you drag it near a page, you see an annunciation-style focus (cue angel choir) appear around the page indicating that the note will be stuck to that page when you release the mouse button (see Figure 18-43).

Annotations can be grouped, selected, aligned, and distributed along with page icons (see Figure 18-44).

Figure 18-43
Annunciation of the annotation

Figure 18-44
Moving annotations with pages

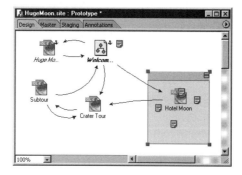

Annotation Inspector

The Annotation Inspector lets you set the parameters associated with an annotation, such as the text and positioning.

Subject. The subject is the header for the annotation and is displayed separately from the text. It should be relatively short, as it's the item by which the annotation is listed in the Annotations tab.

Alignment. The subject can be aligned left, center, or right by clicking one of these three icons.

Text. The text is the body of the annotation and can be any length.

Display Subject and Display Text. Checking neither, either, or both of these boxes controls whether the respective item displays in the Design tab (see Figure 18-45). These two options are available as Expand Subject and Expand Text in the Annotation submenu of the contextual menu.

Figure 18-45
Annotations
with subject
and text

Subject and text
displayed

Subject hidden and
text displayed

Subject displayed
and text hidden

Subject and
text hidden

Position. You can set the position of the text attached to the annotation to be to the left or right of, below, or centered over the icon (see Figure 18-46, next page).

Graphics tab. The Graphics tab lets you set each annotation to a different colored text or fill, so you can create annotations custom to each collaborator on a site, for instance, when you're building a workgroup site.

Figure 18-46
Annotations
with subject
and text

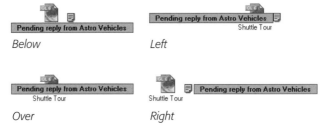

Below

Left

Over

Right

Tip: Resizing Annotations

When you select an annotation that has the subject or text (or both) displayed, a small blue square appears at the lower right corner. Drag the box to change the width of the annotated text.

Annotations Tab

The Annotations tab is the control center for annotations, making it easy to review them all in one place. You can see that there aren't a whole lot of options, but we can suggest a few things.

When you or other designers in your workgroup add annotations, start the subject with your initials or a number (with leading zeroes). This helps organize annotations when it's time to review them. Otherwise, annotations are alphabetized entirely by text or subject (depending on which column you choose; subject is the default).

We imagine that in future release of GoLive, you could set a status to an annotation and/or display only active annotations that haven't been dealt with.

Mapping Sites

Although GoLive offers a powerful prototyping tool, it can't show or modify pages in your existing site. To visualize and add pending links and new pages to your current site, you need to use one of GoLive's two mapping views: Navigation and Links. Both views are available from the Diagram menu, or from the popout menu in any diagram window.

Tip: One Item to Rule Them Both

The two mapping views are reached via a single item, Navigation. To show the Links view, you must bring up the Navigation view and then click the Links tab.

The two views represent two distinct approaches. Navigation shows the top-down organization of a site, where the home page is the root, and pages are shown linked by their relationship to one another. Navigation also allows you to add new pages and pending links in a similar manner to a diagram window. The Links view works much like the In & Out Links palette, showing all the inbound and outbound links from every page. This makes it easy to see the relationship of any page or file in a site to every other file.

Views Interface

The Navigation and Links views share many features in common for viewing and handling files.

Opening. Double-clicking a file in either view opens it. If it's an HTML file, it opens in GoLive. For other files, the preferences you set take precedence for controlling which applications open which files (see Chapter 19, *Managing Files, Folders, and Links*).

Revealing files. Simply selecting a file and choosing Reveal in Site from the contextual menu reveals it in the Files tab of the Site window (see Figure 18-47). This saves a vast amount of time by allowing you to use either view as a navigation map for your site. No more clicking through endless folders and scrolling. You can select one or more files at the same time. You can also choose to reveal files in the Finder (Mac) or Explorer (Windows), in addition to showing the file's properties in either operating system.

Figure 18-47
Revealing files via contextual menu

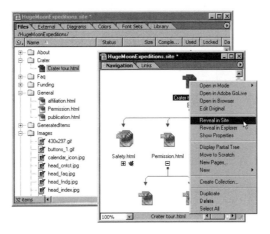

Tip: Roomy Mess

After we've messed around in the Navigation or Links view, we find our Files tab to be really out of sorts—practically every folder is opened. On a big site, it's a mess! But there's a simple solution. 1. Click anywhere in the Files tab. 2. Select All from the Edit or contextual menu. 3. Press Command-Option-left arrow (Mac) or Control-Alt-left arrow (Windows). This collapses all the folders back down again, closing each one as GoLive carries out the task. When you reopen any folder, the ones beneath it are also closed.

Tip: Colored Icons

If you assign any Status labels to pages or files, the Navigation and Links views display those items using the color associated with that label. It's a handy way to see what's going on all at once, especially when scanning via the Panorama pane.

Graphical view. The Graphical option in the References View palette's Display tab displays pages as icons, thumbnails, frames, or ovals. You can control spacing and the size of the preview, just like in the Reference pane discussed earlier in this chapter.

You can open and close files above and below a given page by clicking a plus sign or minus sign. If the plus sign is showing, that means files exist as children below that page in the Navigation view, or that the page has additional links inbound or outbound in the Links view (see Figure 18-48).

Figure 18-48
Revealing files
via contextual
menu

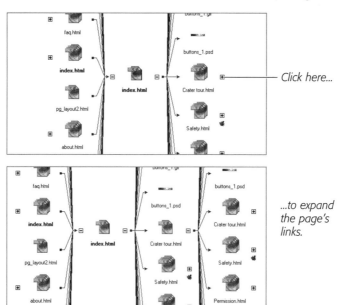

Click here...

*...to expand
the page's
links.*

Selecting any page and clicking the Unfold All button in the Design Toolbar completely expands all links below the current one in the Navigation view, or just a single level in the Links view.

Tip: Expanding Graphical View

Although the Graphical view doesn't offer a method to collapse or expand all from a given point, there is a simple way out. Switch to Outline, collapse or expand as needed (all or some), and then switch back to Graphical.

Outline view. The Display tab's other option is Outline, which turns the view of relationships (link or navigation) into a file list with status and other information, just like in the Files tab. Opening a file by clicking its triangle (Mac) or plus-sign (Windows) shows the children (Navigation view) or outbound links (Links view). You can also use a variety of keyboard shortcuts to expand and collapse single and multiple levels (see Table 18-1).

Table 18-1
Keyboard shortcuts for expanding and collapsing in Outline view (any pane)

Windows	Mac	Action	Result
Alt	Option	click closed icon	expand all from that point
Alt	Option	click open icon	collapse all from that point
Right arrow	Command	select one or more files	expand selections one level
Left arrow	Command	select one or more files	collapse selections one level
Control-Alt-right arrow	Command-Option-right arrow	select one or more files	expand all selections
Control-Alt-left arrow	Command-Option-left arrow	select one or more files	collapse all selections

Collections. You can use the Create Collection and Reselect Collection features just as you can in the diagram window's Design tab.

Page and other Inspectors. Selecting an item brings up the appropriate Inspector with the same range of offerings as if you were in the Files tab and had selected one or more files.

File commands. You can apply any file-based command located under the Site menu's Finder (Mac) or Explorer (Windows) submenus, the Edit menu, the Toolbar, and the contextual menu. You can also use the Change References command, or the Point & Shoot icon in the In & Out Links palette, to redirect files and links, including pointing at files in the site map itself (see Figure 18-49).

Figure 18-49
File-based
commands

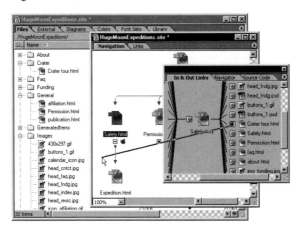

Deleting files. If you press the Delete key or choose Clear from the Edit or contextual menu, the selected file or files are thrown into whichever trash you specified (see "Trash" in Chapter 19, *Managing Files, Folders, and Links*).

GoLive warns you about deleting files, but if you have multiple items selected, all of them are thrown into the trash, and you have to sort the trash to restore their locations. The History palette and Undo don't help out here.

If you choose to use GoLive's Site Trash in the Extras tab, which is the program's default, you can drag any item you trash back to where it belongs in the Files tab.

Navigation View

The Navigation view organizes the contents of a site hierarchically starting with the home page. Each link from the home page is listed as a child; each page in the site is listed just once, as the child of the first page that links it (see Figure 18-50).

This is not always how a site is organized. For instance, if you use a common navigation bar on every page, those items are referenced just from the first page on which they appear. The Links view (described in more detail

Figure 18-50
Navigation
View

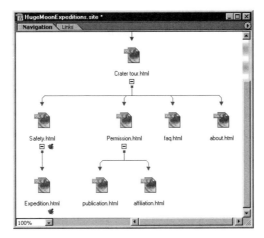

later) helps sort through that particular set of issues, however, by showing every link.

Fortunately, virtually every aspect of the interface for Navigation view is identical to the Design tab of a diagram window. You can zoom, use the Site Navigator palette, add panes through the References View palette, use the grabber hand to move pages around, etc. However, there are a few key differences:

• Navigation view shows only pages that exist in the live site; the Design tab shows diagram pages that are in the staging area.

• You can't rearrange pages in Navigation view; they are locked to the grid. You can change spacing, however.

• The Scratch pane (grayed out for the Design tab) can be enabled in Navigation view, showing files in the site folder that aren't linked into the navigational hierarchy. These can then be dragged into the Navigation view to be added as pending links to existing pages.

Customizing View

The References View palette for the Navigation view matches the Design tab's Design View palette closely, so we won't repeat the identical items (see Figure 18-51, next page). Consult "Design View Palette" and "References View Palette," earlier in this chapter.

Display Partial Tree. This feature, available only in the contextual menu, truncates the Navigation view from the current selection on down. This allows you to see just a piece of the site at once. The option is a toggle, so selecting it again—which unchecks it—restores the full site map.

Figure 18-51
Navigation
View's Site
View
Controller

Tip: Partial Escape

You can also narrow your focus by selecting one or more pages and hitting the Esc (Escape) key to display only those files.

Tip: Print Partial

It's much easier to print out part of a site with Display Partial Tree selected. That way, you can show just what you think is most important.

Tip: Table of Contents

The Navigation view offers a table of contents builder that's based on the files you're showing in that view when you select Create Table of Contents from the Diagram menu. The TOC GoLive generates is a linked-up HTML page; hopefully, a future release will add placeholders, so you can update a template with new pages without having to regenerate and rebuild a file.

Navigation tab. The Navigation tab offers a great and unique feature that you'll find yourself using all the time: Spotlight. By selecting one of the six options for Spotlight you can view relationships between multiple pages in an extremely clear highlighted fashion (see Figure 18-52). GoLive puts a spotlight or highlight around the items in question; in the case of Pending, it actually adds more link arrows. The six types of Spotlight work as follows:

- **None.** Enough said.

- **Family.** Choosing Family and selecting a single page highlights the parent, siblings, and children of that page, if any or all of those exist.

- **Incoming.** Selecting any file highlights all files or items that point to that file; this works for media, objects, and HTML pages.

Figure 18-52
Spotlighting
Options

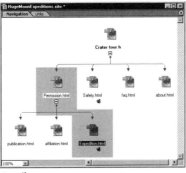

Family

Incoming

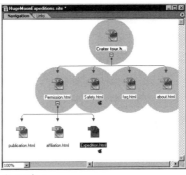

Outgoing

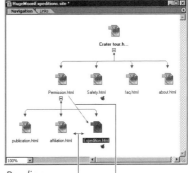

Pending —

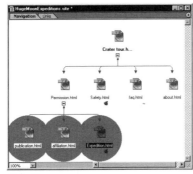

Selection

- **Outgoing.** Ditto as Incoming, but selecting any file highlights anything the file links to.

- **Pending.** Pending puts a spin on Spotlight by introducing a link between all files that have pending links to one another. This is a great aid for figuring out what's left to link in. Unfortunately, you can't drag files from the Navigation view onto pages to create links.

- **Collection.** Remember our friend Create Collection? Well, not only can you select multiple files and create new collections of selections in the two maps of your site, but you can also Spotlight any collection you've already made. The Collection option doesn't reselect the files; it just highlights them.

You can also show all three panes listed in the Navigation tab: Panorama and Reference, which work just like they do in the Design tab, as well as Scratch.

- **Panorama.** Panorama is even more useful in Navigation view, as the number of files shown at once can be staggering. We like to select items in Panorama or hover over them to see their names. It's a great way to select multiple items with a marquee, too (see Figure 18-53).

Figure 18-53
Panorama
Selection

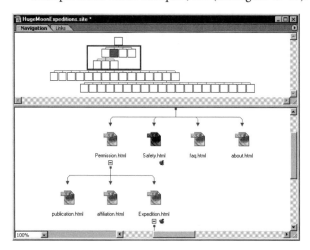

- **Scratch.** Scratch shows all pages in the site that aren't linked into your main navigation hierarchy (see Figure 18-54). You can drag pages out of any of these into the main navigation window to add new pending links (see "Adding Links and Pages," later in this chapter).

- **Reference.** Reference works just the same as in the Design tab, showing any items referenced on the selected page or pages.

The Orientation radio buttons let you swap the direction of the view's hierarchy.

Display tab. This tab is discussed under "References View Palette," earlier in this chapter. The only unique aspect is that with Outline selected, you can't display the Panorama pane through the Navigation tab of the References View palette.

Figure 18-54
Scratch pane

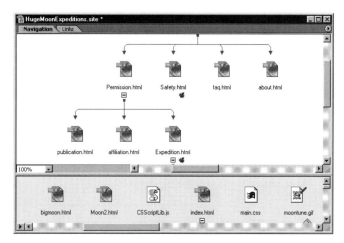

Filter tab. This is identical to the Reference and Pending tabs' Filter tab described under "References View Palette," earlier in this chapter. The HTML Pages checkbox is disabled because you really have to show HTML pages to show the Navigation view!

Adding Links and Pages

The Navigation Hierarchy mode lets you add entirely new pages to a site just as you would in the Design tab of a diagram window. (You have to set Navigation view to Graphical in the Display tab of the References View palette.)

You can drag in a Page icon or any object icons from the Diagram tab of the Objects palette or a Stationery or Template file from the Site Extras tab of the Objects palette. Or, even drag one from the Reference pane. You can also drag in files from elsewhere in the Navigation view. Or, you can select a file and click one of the New buttons (Next, Previous, Child, and Parent Pages) in the Design Toolbar. That enough options for you?

Unlike the Design tab, you must drag the item you're adding on top of an existing file. Blank items, Templates, and Stationery are added to your default new files folder, while other items already exist in the site; so, a pending link is simply added, but the file itself is otherwise unaffected.

With Orientation in the Navigation tab set to Tall, dragging left adds a pending parent link, top and bottom add pending next and previous links, and dragging right adds a pending child link. With Orientation set to Wide, the traditional top: parent, left: previous, right: next, and bottom: child relationships apply.

Tip: Media Connections

If you drag a file on top of a media file, you can only drag it to the parent, next, or previous compass points. Media can't have children—a sad, but true fact. The same behavior happens if you drag in a media file on top of other files, HTML or otherwise, in the Navigation view.

Granted, you can have links that come out of a PDF, SWF, or QuickTime file, but you cannot create these as pending links in the Navigation view because GoLive can't access pending links for anything but HTML files.

The pending links you add via this method still have to be put on a page just as with any other pending link.

Links View

The Links view is a hall of mirrors: links linking to links linking to links (you're back on the chain gang). The Links view lets you see the full panoply of media and HTML references to and from any item or page in a site. Many of the features work like those in Navigation, so we've highlighted just the unique parts here in the main display window and the References View palette's Links and Filter tabs.

Links display. The main display shows files with link lines between them. It also shows the status icons next to each file.

You can select any file and choose Move to Center from the contextual menu to make the world rotate around it: GoLive shows just the inbound and outbound links for that file (see Figure 18-55). It's the equivalent of Show Partial Tree in the Navigation view.

Tip: Link Escape

Similar to the Navigation view, selecting a file and pressing the Esc (Escape) key is the equivalent of selecting Move to Center from the contextual menu.

Selecting a file can appear odd: because each file can show up many times in the Links view, selecting a single file actually selects all instances of that file in the current display. Any changes you make to the file obviously affect all views of it because it's really the same file (see Figure 18-56).

Links tab. The Links tab of the Links View palette lets you turn Incoming Links and Outgoing Links on or off. Turning both off is senseless, as you

Figure 18-55
Using Move
to Center

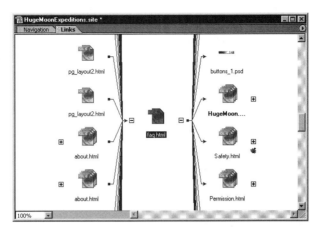

Figure 18-56
Selecting a file

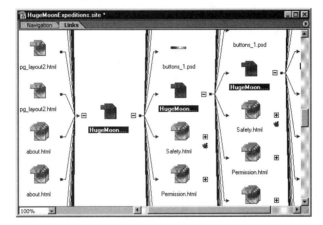

*The same file
can appear
many times,
so all instances
are selected.*

would be left with a single page in the middle; however, these are checkboxes, because you need to be able to have both or either turned on.

The Explore choices are split between Multiple and Single Link Paths. If you have Multiple Link Paths selected, each time you click a plus sign to open a node, it simply opens it without affecting any other items displayed. With Single Link Path selected, all other open nodes at that level are closed when the new node is opened (see Figure 18-57, next page).

Filter tab. Two options in the Filter tab are only available for the Links View palette: Links to Self and Cyclic Links. If you enable Links to Self, GoLive shows incoming and outgoing links that point to the file from which those links emerge (see Figure 18-58, next page). Turning this off can simplify the display, although it reduces the amount of information you're seeing, too.

Figure 18-57
Choosing
Link Paths

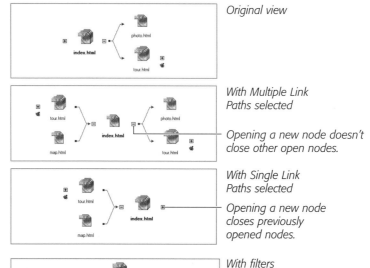

Original view

*With Multiple Link
Paths selected*

*Opening a new node doesn't
close other open nodes.*

*With Single Link
Paths selected*

*Opening a new node
closes previously
opened nodes.*

Figure 18-58
Filtering links

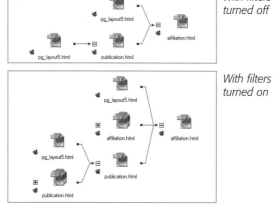

*With filters
turned off*

*With filters
turned on*

If you turn on Cyclic Links, GoLive displays self-referencing links. For example, suppose you have a navigation bar with three links that appears on every page. If you've selected one of those three linked pages, the Cyclic Links option displays that page as if it were a separate page, because the link to itself is present.

Printing and Exporting

Much of the changes for the Diagrams feature between versions 5 and 6 of GoLive improved printing and formatting. Throughout this chapter, we've described different items specifically designed to assist in this process of printing; GoLive 6 also added an export option which turns diagrams into PDFs or SVG files.

Output Options

Let's recap the long list of features designed to help you create better output, whether to a printer or a vector file.

Page breaks. A diagram is divided into pages by default. You can turn this off in the Design View palette, or leave it on and have GoLive automatically split the diagram into as many pages as it needs to, or as you specify.

Page breaks are based on your current Page Setup selection for page format. Selecting a new page size causes GoLive to prompt you whether you want to reposition the items in your diagram.

Headings (Mac Only)

GoLive for Macintosh has settings in the Page Setup dialog box that allow you to customize the text that appears on the top and bottom of each page (see Figure 18-59). (GoLive for Windows lacks these options, although Windows previews output in a sort of funky manner.) GoLive offers choices for the left, middle, and right of the header and footer:

- **Date:** the current date
- **Title:** the site file's name
- **Username:** Whatever name is entered in File Sharing (Macintosh)
- **Page Number**

You can also set whether a line appears below the header and above the footer.

Figure 18-59
Print options

Macintosh print options

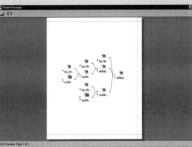

Windows print preview

Master tab. The Master tab of a diagram window lets you place items on it that aren't part of the staging and check-in process, but are simply displayed.

Box and level. The Box icon lets you place text arbitrarily on the page, while the Level icon can be resized to place brackets around levels of a site.

Graphics tab. Every object in the Design tab of the diagram window has a Graphics tab in its Inspector, which allows you to control aspects of that item's line thickness, font size, and/or fill color, depending on what's appropriate.

Design Colors. Whichever colors you choose in the Design Colors settings for backgrounds and items appear in the output or export as well.

Better sizing. Icons, lines, and boxes all look better at multiple sizes than they used to so it's easier to print smaller or larger versions of a map.

Tip: Selected Sections

When you want to print just selected portions of the site map, collapse the hierarchies that don't need to appear on the printout.

Tip: In & Out Printing

You can also print a links display using the popout menu of the In & Out Links palette. This can useful for printing just the relationships to one file.

Print

When you're ready to print, you can simply bring the diagram window to the front and choose Print from the File menu.

Windows (most versions) and Mac OS X have print preview features built into their printer drivers, which makes up for GoLive's lack of a preview.

Export

If you'd like to manipulate a diagram further in Illustrator, or merely create an interchange format that allows you to digitally pass the diagram on (Annotations intact), select Design Diagram from the File menu's Export submenu.

This Export option lets you turn your diagram into a site map as live as you want it. You can choose either SVG or PDF as the file format; both work natively in most browsers, although they do require free plug-ins for the few folks who have neither.

In the Export Options dialog box, checking Preserve Background Color does just that.

The links in your diagram can be directly mapped to a live site by checking Make Diagram Objects Into Links, and populating the URL Getter with a legitimate path. This could be a local path if you're handing this site out to others on your network who have access to same the files, or if you're testing it locally.

Annotations can be kept intact by either choosing Static, which uses your current opened-and-closed decisions on the live diagram; or Live, in which Annotations are closed, and clicking the Annotation in the exported file displays its contents.

The Big Picture

By combining prototyping in your diagram stage and mapping your completed site, you can achieve a real big picture—graphical, even—of how your site is built and continues to be expanded. Using these features, you not only get to work out ideas, but put them into action with a minimum of fuss.

Managing Files, Folders, and Links

The heart of site management is tracking connections. Managing this process is what GoLive does best, by offering many different kinds of graphical views of the files that comprise your site, internal and external links connected to and from those files, and tools that let you move and link at will. GoLive accomplishes these tasks by hiding things from you. It keeps a lot of information behind the scenes where you don't even have to know about it.

When you create any site, you're really creating a set of relationships between resources. Some of these resources may be files stored on the Web server itself, like HTML pages and GIF images; others may be documents stored elsewhere on the Web or on an intranet, like a PDF file containing a form that a user can print out, or a simple Web page with more information on a subject.

GoLive provides management tools for local files that reflect the contents of your Web site as well as a view into all of the "external" resources your site links to elsewhere on the Web.

This chapter covers working directly with files and folders (or directories), managing and updating links, creating and working with Stationery and reusable Components, troubleshooting errors, and cleaning up sites by stripping out the dead brush.

Files Inside GoLive

An ordinary document on the Macintosh or Windows Desktop doesn't have much intelligence. On its own, a file might have an icon and a file extension or file type that identifies its creator or kind to the operating system. But unless a file is opened by an application which can act on the data in that file, the Desktop can't peer inside and tell you what's what. However, when that same file is viewed through the Files tab in GoLive, it exhibits lots of smarts, revealing links and other object relationships.

The Files tab of the Site window mimics the display of files and folders in the Mac OS Finder or in the My Computer window under Windows. Files can be moved up and down folder levels, renamed, and deleted.

GoLive maintains a hidden database in the site file, stored on your local hard drive, that contains every link and image reference in all HTML files. If

What's New in 6

Although the basics are the same for working with files, folders, and links—and have been since version 3.0—Adobe continues to add small and large improvements that make it easier to do precisely what you want without workarounds.

GoLive continues to muddle the differences between relative and absolute links. This is explained in great detail later in this chapter, but users familiar with GoLive 5 should take note. In that version of the program, GoLive included an Absolute Link button in any Inspector palette field from which you selected a URL. When selected, it forced a given link to include the entire path from the root of the site to the given file or folder.

In GoLive 6, that simple (and misnamed) button has been replaced with a more complicated behavior: you have to select the Relative menu item from the Link popout menu to the right of the URL field. Or, you can Option (Mac only) click the Browse button to bring up the Edit URL dialog box and click the Make Absolute button. Both methods are tedious.

The Edit URL dialog box has changed substantially from GoLive 5. Instead of being a simple field in which you could see the full URL at one go, in GoLive 6, Edit URL offers more elaborate URL and path control. You can switch

between GoLive's Absolute and Relative links, as noted above, but you can also edit URLs with attributes, variables that get sent to a server.

The Styles tab of the File Inspector has been removed; its functions appear in the new CSS palette. With the Files tab displayed and files selected, the CSS palette allows global addition or removal of external style sheets. (With text selected on an individual page, the CSS palette shows available class selectors, instead.)

The Extras tab of the Site window has squeezed in several new folders, including the Library folder (which corresponds to the Library tab, formerly the Custom tab, on the left-hand side of the Site window), and the Templates folder.

Templates are new to GoLive 6.0: they allow designers to specify areas of a page as locked and uneditable, while other parts can be edited by a user. From a site perspective, Templates can be used almost identically to Stationery, and controls for adding Templates to a site or applying them to a page are found in the same places as Stationery controls.

The Detach Selected Components and Detach All Components menu items in the Special menu allow you to convert Components into plain HTML.

you have the right GoLive Modules loaded, other kinds of links are managed as well, including URLs embedded in QuickTime movies or Flash SWF files (see Chapter 22, *Advanced Features*, for more on modules).

Because every link and image is managed by this internal database, whenever you act on a file, GoLive prompts you to update all applicable references to that file. If you agree—which you almost always should—GoLive rewrites every link within HTML or supported media files, like PDFs and QuickTime movies, to reflect your changes. GoLive also updates its internal list.

For instance, let's say while building a site you put all images at a single folder level, the main level of your site. This is pretty typical for a small site that gets big over time. You may suddenly find yourself with hundreds of files at the main level and want to reorganize them to make the site's files display for easier browsing.

Due to the way GoLive tracks references, you can just drag and drop to your heart's content in the Site window. In this case, you could:

1. Create a folder named "images" in the Files tab.

2. Drag all your image files into it (see Figure 19-1).

3. GoLive prompts you to change all of the HTML and media files that contain links pointing to those images.

4. Clicking OK allows GoLive to rewrite the links and move the files.

   Everything on the site remains correctly linked.

Figure 19-1
Reorganizing files in the Files tab via drag and drop

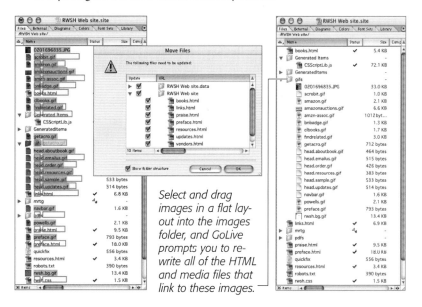

Select and drag images in a flat layout into the images folder, and GoLive prompts you to rewrite all of the HTML and media files that link to these images.

Working with Files in a Site

Opening the Site window displays the Files tab, which shows the list of files already in the site; if you start from a blank site, the Files tab displays just an empty home page (see Figure 19-2).

The Files tab is the theater in which you stage your show: all the images, documents, and directories, as well as other media you might employ, all strut about in this space. GoLive is your assistant director, allowing you to move the players about at will, tracking their locations, and helping you stay in charge.

Root Location

Every site has a root: the place from which you measure outward and downward. On a Web server, your site's root location is the directory in which your Web files are located, and to which the Web server starts looking for files when it receives a request for your domain name or site.

Similarly, the root location of your site on your local hard drive contains the collection of Web files and nested folders in a given directory. All files are referenced from that directory, either at the same level or deeper, in nested folders. Folders might be nested many layers deep, but they're always identified starting from that main, root folder which marks the headwaters of the site (see Figure 19-3).

Mac and Windows both show the enclosing folder when you hold down the Path button.

The Mac root from the local site to the hard drive can be shown by Command-clicking the Site file's name in the titlebar.

New in 6: Relative Menu

In GoLive 5, you made a link relative to the root of a site (starting with a slash, but no http at the beginning) by pressing the Absolute Link button. That simple button is gone in 6, replaced by the Relative menu item and Edit URL dialog box's Make Absolute button.

When you create a new link within a page and have the Relative item unchecked in the Link popout menu, the URL is displayed with the full path from the root to the current location, through any intervening directories—even if the link is in the same directory as the file itself (see Figure 19-4). For example, suppose you're working in a file called "hobbes.html" located in the "comics" folder, which itself is in the root of the site. Linking to a file called "calvin.html" in the same folder would normally display just the file name in the URL field of the Inspector. However, with Relative unchecked, the URL would show: "/comics/calvin.html".

Figure 19-4
Relative
checked and
unchecked

Relative checked

Relative unchecked (relative to root)

Tip: Root's Root

In traditional computer parlance, "root" refers to the base level of your hard drive, like "C:" in Windows or "Macintosh HD" (or whatever you may have renamed your hard disk) on the Mac. GoLive is smart enough to treat your site file's directory as the root for its Web site. See the sidebar, "Absolute Versus Relative," for a more detailed explanation.

Tip: Make All Relative

You can bypass changing the relative state of individual links by setting the program preference Make New Links Absolute. It's off by default, and can be checked in the URL Handling setting of the General pane in Preferences. This is one of GoLive's "from now on" global preferences: it doesn't change any existing links, only links created from that point forward in any site or on any page.

Tip: Testing Absolute Links

If you link to an image or media file with Relative unchecked, you cannot preview it locally in a browser. Unlike GoLive, browsers assume the root of an Absolute link is the top of the hard drive; GoLive automatically "deflects" that in order to preview. To test GoLive-style Absolute links in a browser, you must upload the files to a server.

In the upper left of the Files tab, GoLive displays a Path icon, above which is the name of the current root folder (see Figure 19-5). Double clicking any folders in the Files tab zooms them to fill the screen as the main view. You can then hold down the mouse button on the Path icon for about two seconds and GoLive displays a hierarchical list of folders back to the root (see Figure 19-6). This is also true for all of the tabs in the Site window, such as the Extras tab or External tab.

Once you're down a level or more below the root in any folder in any tab, you can navigate back up by clicking the Path icon to move up one level, or by holding down the Path button and selecting any higher-level folder from the popup list.

Figure 19-5
Files tab's full
path display

GoLive uses a different Path icon under Windows (left) and Mac (right).

— Path icon —

Figure 19-6
Path from root

Hold down the mouse button to get the path popup.

Tip: Showing the Path

The default for GoLive is to show a file's full path. Uncheck Display Full Path in the Site pane of the Preferences dialog box or uncheck Show Path in the View palette, and the path display disappears. The Path icon remains, however. Each of the other Site window tabs shows a corresponding directory or folder path from the root as well, such as the fully qualified URL for FTP or WebDAV (see Figure 19-7).

Figure 19-7
Display Full
Path options

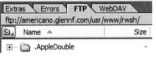 

Display Full Path checked   Display Full Path unchecked

Home Page

The home page of a site is almost always in the root, and it forms the basis of the navigational hierarchy of the site. The home page is the point from which you navigate "down" to the rest of the site. GoLive creates a default home page if you create a blank site, but you can choose any page to be the home page, even in a fully built-out site.

1. Select any HTML file in the Files tab.

2. Bring up the File Inspector, if it's not already visible.

3. From the Page tab, check the Home Page box.

    You can also use the contextual menu's Set as Home Page item.

File Information

Each file and folder is shown in the Files tab with several characteristics in columns (see Figure 19-8).

Figure 19-8
Files tab

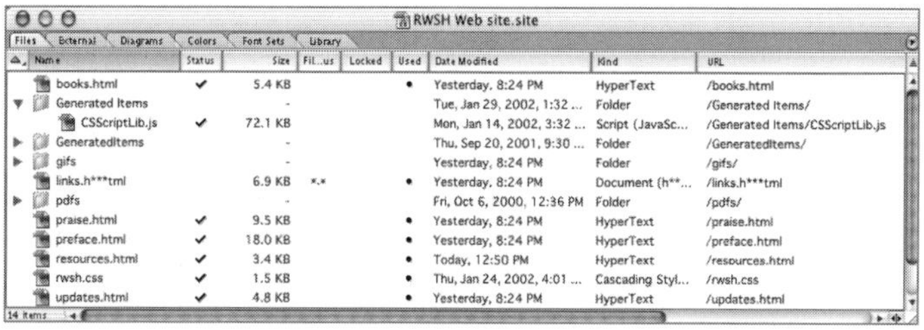

- **Name:** select the file or folder name to make it editable

- **Status:** indicates the current state, such as if the file contains broken links or all links work, the file is empty, and so on

- **Completed:** when used with the Workgroup Server, you or another user has marked the file as ready to put on the live site

- **To Be Edited by:** when used with the Workgroup Server, you or another user has requested the file should next be edited by the specified user

- **Size in bytes**

- **Date Modified**

- **Locked:** whether the file is editable or not

- **Used:** whether a file is referenced in the site from the navigational root

- **Kind:** document, folder, HTML file, etc.

- **URL:** the path from the root of the site

- **Filename Status:** whether the file or folder's name meets the file name constraints set for this site or globally (see "Filename Constraints," later in this chapter)

    The View palette allows you to toggle the visibility of any and all of these columns. Clicking the column's name sorts the items alphabetically, by size, or

Table 19-1 Absolute and relative references	Type of link	User is at...
	Relative	http://www.etaoin.com/shrdlu/welcome.html
	Relative folder	http://www.etaoin.com/shrdlu/welcome.html
	GoLive Absolute	http://www.etaoin.com/pdevil/welcome.html
	Relative with ".."	http://www.etaoin.com/pdevil/welcome.html
	Real absolute	http://www.etaoin.com/pdevil/dvorak.html

Absolute Versus Relative

All references in GoLive, whether they're hypertext links or media links, fall into one of two categories (see Table 19-1, above):

- **Absolute:** the entire URL is specified, including what's called a "scheme": http, ftp, file, etc., such as http://www.bootyc.com/foo/bar/path.html or ftp://ftp.windbagx.com/mish/e/gas/nonsense.pdf
- **Relative:** just the part containing a file name or a path to a file name is included, like "bar/path.html" where "bar" is a folder

A relative reference uses context: where you are within a site tells a browser where to search for the link. If you're at http://www.bootyc.com/foo/welcome.html, the relative URL in the example above treats "bar" as a folder without having to know about the enclosing "foo" folder, and path.html as a file in that folder.

GoLive mixes up the issue by calling a certain subclass of relative URL "Absolute," counter to the HTML specification that defined these terms. Every URL field has a Link popout menu with a Relative menu item on it. When that's checked, you get the standard relative path from the current location. When it's unchecked, GoLive generates a reference that includes a path all the way back to the root location of the site. This doesn't turn the file reference into a true, absolute URL shown above (sometimes known as a fully qualified URL); rather, Absolute provides a relative-to-the-root path. (You can also use the Edit URL dialog box and click the Make Absolute or Make Relative buttons to switch between the two kinds of relative paths.)

So in the above example, if we made path.html into a GoLive Absolute link, the URL would turn into:

```
/foo/bar/path.html
```

This kind of reference always works, no matter where in the directory the linking file is located. Using GoLive's Absolute link makes your files somewhat more portable without adding too much of a management burden, as GoLive can cope with its own form of Absolute as well as any kind of relative link to a file on the site. You can also easily rewrite Absolute links into relative ones by using Change Reference, described later in this chapter.

You can force GoLive to make all new links Absolute ones by checking Make New Links Absolute in the URL Handling settings of the General pane in the Preferences dialog box.

Link in HREF is...	User winds up at...
letterpress.html	http://www.etaoin.com/shrdlu/letterpress.html
oldstyle/numerals.html	http://www.etaoin.com/shrdlu/oldstyle/numerals.html
/shrdlu/welcome.html	http://www.etaoin.com/shrdlu/welcome.html
../shrdlu/welcome.html	http://www.etaoin.com/shrdlu/welcome.html
http://www.qwerty.com/index.html	http://www.qwerty.com/index.html

by date depending on the contents of the column. Items in expanded folders are first sorted by the folder's property (name, status, and so on), and then by the items in the folder.

Click the column name again, or, on the Mac, click the pyramid button at the right of the headers, to reverse the sort order. Hover over the division between columns and drag to resize their widths. Hold down the Command key (Mac) or Control key (Windows) to rearrange the order of the columns from left to right. On the Mac, a grabber hand appears with the Command key down, but not under Windows.

Tip: Tabbing Through Files

Pressing Tab and Shift-Tab moves you forward alphabetically through files and folders regardless of how you've sorted the file display, unlike the down and up arrow keys which always move sequentially. If you have a folder expanded, tabbing still hits files alphabetically, so don't be surprised if you tab from "about.html" in the root level to "arden.gif" in the "images" folder.

Tip: Switching Sides (Mac)

Pressing Option-Tab toggles between the left and right panes of the Site window if the right pane is open.

Tip: Item Count

We're not sure how useful this is, but the lower-left corner of the Files tab displays the item count, or the number of items currently displayed in the Files tab.

Tip: Magic Fingers

Typing the first few letters of a file name selects the file in the list. The letters you type show up briefly in the item count box in the lower-left corner of the Site window.

Viewing Folder Contents

Double-clicking a folder in the Files tab expands it to fill the tab and updates the file path shown above the Path icon (see Figure 19-9). You can click the expansion triangle (Mac) or plus sign (Windows) to show nested items inside folders in the same view (see Figure 19-10).

Figure 19-9
Opening a
folder

Windows display of closed and opened folder

Mac display of closed and opened folder

Figure 19-10
Expanding
folders

Clicking the plus sign (a triangle on the Mac) expands the folder's contents.

Tip: Files Tab Display

Although the Files tab looks almost identical in Mac and Windows versions, they both pick up "local" conventions. Mac users are accustomed to seeing right-pointing triangles which indicate that the user can click and expand the display to see nested contents underneath, as in a folder. Windows users are accustomed to a plus sign in a box for the same effect. The two icons work identically (see Figure 19-11).

Figure 19-11
Triangle and
plus sign

Macintosh expand triangle

Windows plus sign in a box

Revealing and Opening Files and Folders

With a file or folder selected, you can manipulate a file in various ways, from revealing its enclosing folder on the Desktop, to duplicating it, to opening it in the application that created it.

Tip: Many Places to Select

Most of these options can be accessed through both the Edit menu and Site menu's Finder (Mac) or Explorer (Windows) submenu, and under slightly different names in the contextual menu (right-click under Windows or Control-click on the Mac) when files are selected (see Figure 19-12). They are also paralleled in the Site toolbar; here, they appear on the left-hand side with different names and in a different order than in the Site menu and contextual menu.

The Finder (Mac) or Explorer (Windows) submenu in the Site menu offers three options when you select one or more items in the Files tab: Reveal Object, Show Object Information, and Launch File.

Figure 19-12
Some of the
many ways of
opening

Mac contextual and Site menus

Windows contextual and Site menus

Tip: Multiple Objects

Although Show Object Information is pluralized to Objects if you have more than one item selected, you cannot get info on multiple items at once. Instead, GoLive selects or shows info for one after another. (Further, in Mac OS X, you can only view information about one file at a time.) Under Windows, you can select Reveal Object and have GoLive open multiple items at once, but not on the Mac.

The Edit menu makes available Clear (Mac)/Delete (Windows), Duplicate, and Select All for files and folders. Clear and Duplicate work on multiple selections; Select All doesn't require any selection to work.

Reveal Object(s). Selecting this command opens the item's enclosing folder in the Desktop with the item selected in it (see Figure 19-13). The contextual menu puts the option under the Open submenu, where it's called Reveal in Finder (Mac) or Reveal in Explorer (Windows); it's only available when a single item is selected. The same is true for the option when found in the Site toolbar.

Figure 19-13
Revealing
objects on
Desktop or in
Finder

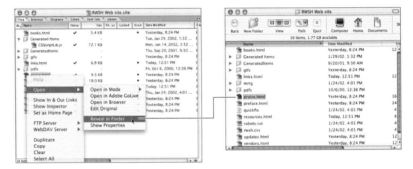

Select a file and choose Reveal in Finder from the contextual menu to open the appropriate folder with the item selected.

Tip: Reveal by Command (Mac)

You can quickly reveals a folder's enclosing location or a file in a folder by Command-clicking the item in a Files tab.

Show Object(s) Information. This option brings up the Information or Info window on the Macintosh or the Properties window under Windows, showing the file system characteristics and values, such as modification date, permissions, and file size. GoLive has Inspectors that do much the same; see "Inspectors," later in this chapter. This option is called Show Properties in the contextual menu's Open submenu, which is available only for single selections. The Site toolbar calls it Show Information in Finder (Mac) or Explorer (Windows).

Launch File. The most complex option is Launch File, as it relies on quite a bit of underlying detail to work correctly.

Selecting Launch File or double-clicking a file opens the file in the application specified in the File Mappings tab in Web Settings (accessed from the Edit menu). In brief, you can set GoLive to open certain kinds of files and choose applications (or use defaults) to open others. If no program is set, different options control what happens when you double-click the file.

Using the contextual menu shows two to five options under an Open submenu, and only when a single item is selected (see Figure 19-14). These options are Open in Mode (one of the Document window modes for HTML files only), Open in Adobe GoLive (if it's a file type GoLive has built-in support for), Open in "Program Name" (if another program is listed in File Mappings), Open in Browser (GoLive opens the file in the default browser), and Edit Original (which opens the item using the program that the operating system thinks created it). For file types GoLive doesn't support and for which it has no program associated, the Open in Adobe GoLive and Open in "Program Name" options are both omitted.

Figure 19-14
Contextual
menu for
opening

Open in Mode	▶	———— *Appears for HTML files*
Open in Adobe GoLive		———— *Appears if GoLive has built-in support*
Open in Browser		———— *Always appears*
Edit Original	°	———— *Launches file from Desktop*
Reveal in Finder	°	
Show Properties	°	

Tip: File Icons (Mac)

The Site window's Files tab displays the files as the Macintosh Finder sees them, which means you may see different icons for the same type of file, like a GIF or HTML document. The most common example on our systems is a mixture of HTML files that show icons for GoLive and the text editor BBEdit. (The icons are just a reflection of what program that file has been associated with in the file's internal Creator flag; see Appendix A, *Macintosh Issues & Extras*, for an explanation of this subject.)

If you were to double-click a file in the Finder, the program associated with the icon opens the file. But within GoLive's Site window, the File Mappings setting overrides the file's Finder flag every time. This way, you don't have to worry about accidentally launching a different program for the same type of file.

Tip: Alternate HTML Editors

File Mappings and contextual selection are especially useful for setting an alternate HTML editor. If you set up a program for the .htm and .html extensions in File Mappings settings, GoLive opens the files with those extensions in the

Status Icons

The Files, External, and Diagrams tabs share a set of icons which indicate the status of a file's links or an actual link (see Figure 19-15). Files can have multiple states, but only one icon is displayed for a given item.

Folders can also have status icons, which look like smaller versions of file status icons with an expand arrow. They show whether the folder contains files with links that are broken, has empty files, is in the process of having its external links verified, or has files that should be in the folder but are missing (also see Figure 19-16).

Checkmark. All the item's links are up to date and GoLive confirmed that the item is where GoLive points to it on the local hard drive.

Green bug. A page's links to some items are missing. In the Layout Editor, clicking the green bug or Link Warnings icon in the Toolbar highlights all the broken links on the page with a colored outline (see Chapter 2, *Layout*). In the Site window, clicking the green bug in the Toolbar displays the Errors tab in the right pane. In the External tab, the URL has been tested and failed. You can also click the green bug icon in the Highlight palette.

Yield sign. The page is empty; typically, it was created from a template or through the Diagrams tab. It could also have been created by dragging a Generic Page icon from the Site tab of the Objects palette into the Files tab.

Stop sign. When this icon appears in the Files or Designs tab, the file is missing; the icon also shows up in the Missing Files folder in the Errors tab. (See "Errors," later in this chapter.)

Question mark. This icon gets attached to a file when GoLive can't find the actual item on the local hard drive. It shows up in the Errors tab and in the In & Out Links palette.

Crossed-out folder. This icon, which symbolizes orphaned files—ones that aren't stored in the site folder but are referenced by the site from somewhere else on the local hard drive—helps you troubleshoot before uploading a site to a server.

Filename Warnings. The Filename Warnings icon appears only in the Errors tab of the Site window to indicate which files in your site don't conform to the file name settings you set up globally or for this particular site. (See "Filename Constraints," later in this chapter.)

Two-way arrows. In the External tab only, a two-way arrow icon means that the link is in the process of being verified by GoLive.

program you set as your new default HTML editor. This program also shows up in the Open submenu, where you can choose to Open in Adobe GoLive instead.

Clear (Mac)/Delete (Windows). Selecting Clear or Delete prompts GoLive to ask if you want to delete the selected file or files. The files are moved to the trash location specified in the Site pane's setting in the Preferences dialog box.

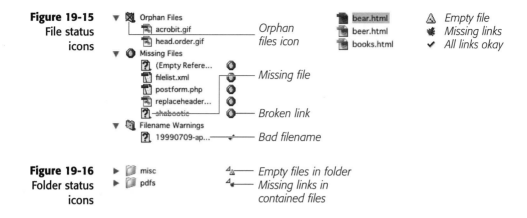

Figure 19-15
File status
icons

Orphan files icon

Missing file

Broken link

Bad filename

Empty file
Missing links
All links okay

Figure 19-16
Folder status
icons

Empty files in folder
Missing links in contained files

Duplicate. The selected item or items are duplicated.

Select All. All items in the Files tab are selected. Pressing Command-A (Mac) or Control-A (Windows) accomplishes the same thing.

Inspectors

The Files tab features two Inspectors that help you examine and modify the properties of files and folders: the File Inspector and the Folder Inspector. For HTML files, there are three tabs in the File Inspector: File, Page, and Content; for media files, just the File and Content tabs appear. If you have Filename Constraints enabled, the Name tab also shows up for any kind of file. (This is different for certain special kinds of media; see Chapter 12, *Rich Media*.)

Tip: Multiple Selections

Selecting multiple files or multiple folders disables most of the options in the File and Folder Inspectors except for Status, Publish, and the Mac-only options.

Basics. The File tab of the File Inspector is almost identical to the Folder Inspector's only display: the Folder tab (see Figure 19-17). The Name field allows you to change the file's or folder's name.

Tip: Renaming

You can also change the name of an item by clicking on the name portion in the file list and waiting for it to highlight, then editing or typing over it. GoLive prompts you whether it should rewrite any links pointing to that item after you press Return or Enter.

Figure 19-17
Basic items in
File tab of File
Inspector

When you highlight a file in the Site window to change its name, only the main part of the name is highlighted, not the extension, like .html. Although it takes a little getting used to, especially for those of us who find ourselves retyping ".html" all the time, this feature makes it faster and easier to change file names without entering the wrong extension.

The URL field, which can't be edited, shows the location of the file or folder relative to the site's root. This is the same information as in the URL column of the Files tab.

Aliases and Shortcuts

Most platforms let you create pointers to files that serve as proxies for them: the Macintosh uses aliases and Windows uses shortcuts (see Figure 19-18). However, GoLive treats both kinds of pointers as plain files, showing the File Inspector's File and Content tabs when an alias or shortcut is selected.

GoLive lets you map folder aliases to other sites if you've split your content among multiple Web servers; and it supports, to some ex-tent, links that are used on Web servers to point to content elsewhere on your Web site.

But support remains a bit tricky to sort out, and we'd recommend not using aliases at all, and only folder aliases for URL Mapping, described later in this chapter. We also provide a much fuller explanation of how links and pointers work in uploading and downloading sites in "Aliases, Shortcuts, and Symbolic Links" in Chapter 20, *Synchronizing Sites*.

Figure 19-18
Shortcuts and
aliases

Windows shortcuts have a small arrow in a box over the regular icon.

Mac aliases have an arrow as well, but it's very subtle in OS X.

You can set a color (Mac) and name (both platforms) via the Status menu. The color and name allow you to sort items by Status and identify, for instance, the stage of a project's files (such as, "completed" or "first draft"). The colors also show up in the site mapping display; see Chapter 18, *Diagramming and Mapping.*

Tip: Status Symbols

Status is a built-in feature of Mac OS 9 and earlier that allows you to set a color and name label to any file or folder on the Desktop. Adobe tried to have the best of both worlds by duplicating these status names and colors in GoLive for Windows; it also supports them in GoLive under Mac OS X, which doesn't have status labels on the Desktop either. You can't edit the basic Status settings in GoLive, although you can create new ones.

See Appendix A, *Macintosh Issues & Extras,* for more details.

The Publish popup menu controls whether a file or folder is uploaded to a Web server when you use the built-in FTP features of GoLive. (See Chapter 20, *Synchronizing Sites,* for an in-depth discussion of this option and how it interacts with other GoLive preferences.)

The Created and Modified fields, which can't be edited, show the date and time of the file's creation and last changes.

The Size field appears only in the File Inspector, not the Folder Inspector, and simply shows the size of the file in bytes.

The Stationery Pad checkbox and the Type and Creator fields appear in the File Inspector only on the Macintosh; for a discussion of them, see Appendix A, *Macintosh Issues & Extras.* They don't affect how you work with files or folders.

Page tab. The Title field shows the page's title, which you can edit here without opening the file.

Tip: Count the Ways

We joked with the GoLive engineers that there were seven ways to change the title of a page. They disagreed: more like eight or nine! Among the many methods, you can open the file, click the Page icon, and rename it via the Page Inspector; or just click the title text next to the Page icon and edit it directly. There's also the Title tag in the Head section, which you can edit via the Title Inspector, and many, many, perhaps too many, more.

The file's encoding, or the language and character set in which the document was authored, appears for reference in the Page tab. It can only be changed by opening the file and selecting another option from the File menu's Document Encoding submenu, or by selecting the Encoding item in the Head section and using the Inspector palette. See Chapter 2, *Layout*, for more on encoding.

The Home Page checkbox lets you change the root page for your site, or the page from which all the hierarchical links are mapped for uploading referenced files or creating a site map. However, you can't simply uncheck the box with the home page selected. Instead, select the page you want to become your new home page, and check the box there; that file name turns bold in the Files tab, and the other page's Home Page box becomes unchecked. (You can also reset your home page via the Site Settings, discussed in Chapter 17, *Managing Sites*. Or, you can select a page in the Files tab, and choose Set as Home Page from the contextual menu.)

Content tab. A preview of the content of the file appears here if GoLive knows how to preview it (see Figure 19-19). For HTML files, GoLive must already have opened, modified, and saved the file for a thumbnail to show up; or, you can click the Update Thumbnail button (the arrows chasing each other) for an instant preview.

For other media, the appropriate module must be loaded to offer a preview. For instance, without the QuickTime Module loaded, QuickTime movies and sound files don't offer preview controls in this tab (see "Modules" in Chapter 1, *Going Live*.) PDFs have a stylin' preview: a mini-browser that lets you page through thumbnails of the file.

Figure 19-19
Content
previews

HTML preview

JPEG preview

QuickTime preview

Tip: Know Thy Password

If your PDF is password protected, you cannot preview it or otherwise edit it in GoLive without entering the password or clicking Cancel. Pressing Control (Windows) or Command (Mac) while clicking Cancel bypasses all the rest of the password prompts for the site.

If you display an image type GoLive knows about, the Content tab can offer some additional information, such as the pixel dimensions of the image. Images are shrunk to fit the Content tab, but you can click the unnamed four-arrows zoom button to expand the image to its full size or reduce it to fit in the window. Click and drag the image to pan it around the pane when you're viewing at its full size.

CSS Palette

Cascading Style Sheets (CSS) let you control type and paragraph formatting through a single set of specifications that can be stored in an individual file or linked to an external CSS document that many pages can share. The CSS palette lets you select one or more files in the Files tab and link them collectively to an external style sheet (see Figure 19-20).

New in 6: CSS Palette

The CSS Palette replaces the Styles tab found in GoLive 5. The CSS palette is contextual. With files selected in the Files tab, you can add external style sheets to pages. With text selected in the Layout Editor, you can apply class selectors to ranges of text or other objects.

1. Select one or more files in the Files tab.

2. Select an external style sheet GoLive knows about from the popup menu at the bottom of the palette; or, Point & Shoot or browse to find a style sheet; or, type in a URL of the style sheet

3. Click the Add button.

For more on CSS in general, or external style sheets in particular, consult Chapter 4, *Text and Fonts*, and Chapter 27, *Defining Cascading Style Sheets*.

Figure 19-20
Linking external style sheets via the CSS palette

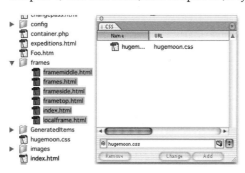

Tip: Rearranging Precedence

Style sheets are applied to a page in the order they occur using strict precedence rules. This allows you to override settings with other settings for the same item (such as a local page having a different text color for a heading 1 selector). Unfortunately, the CSS palette doesn't let you re-order external style sheets. If you enter these external items in the wrong precedence order, you must either delete them all and add them again correctly, or open each page and use the Style Sheet Editor's precedence-changing Move Up and Move Down arrows.

Adding Files to the Site

GoLive lets you add content to the Files tab in several ways, making it convenient to use whatever method you prefer. The methods include:

- Choosing Add Files from the contextual menu while right-clicking (Windows) or Control-clicking (Mac) with no selection or a folder selected in the Files tab.

- Dragging and dropping items from the Desktop into the Files tab.

- Creating new, blank files to fill with content.

- Using Stationery or Templates to create new pages.

- Copying files from the Desktop into the Web site folder, bypassing GoLive.

Using either the Add Files command or dragging items into the Files tab copies the files in question rather than moving them.

Tip: Hooking Content

When files are added via the first two methods, GoLive scans them for links and adds those relationships to the site file. If you add files to the Web site folder on the Desktop, you have to go through a few more steps, described below, to hook in the content of the files.

Add Files. The only method to add files to your site from within GoLive is the Add Files feature. You can choose Add Files from the contextual menu with nothing or a specific folder selected in the Files tab when you click. The dialog box allows you to navigate to files and add them to the list by selecting them and clicking Add (see Figure 19-21).

Clicking Add Folder adds the folder's contents to the list, including nested subfolders; clicking Add All adds the entire current contents of the file browser's display, including all nested subfolders. You can individually remove items by selecting them and clicking Remove, or delete your entire selection of files by clicking Remove All.

Figure 19-21
Adding files

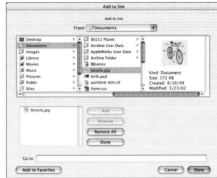

Windows   *Mac*

Clicking Done copies all the items, wherever they are, to the site folder; the files appear immediately in the Files tab and are located at the root level of the site folder, unless you're viewing the contents of a subfolder, in which case they're copied into that folder. Clicking Cancel is the equivalent of clicking Remove All and Done: the end result is no action taken.

Dragging into Files tab. Sometimes, it's just easier to find what you need on the Desktop, select it, and drag it into the Files tab. GoLive is perfectly content to let you act this way; in fact, it's just as good as using the Add Files option.

Before dragging items into the Files tab, it's a good idea to arrange the window so that you can see the area you're dragging into when you're on the Desktop. If you want to nest the items inside a folder—that is, not put them at the root level of the site—open that folder (Mac) or select it from the Explorer (Windows) so it's the only thing in the Files tab (see Figure 19-22).

Items you drag are immediately copied to the site folder and appear in the Files tab. If any of the files are HTML or media files that include embedded links, GoLive brings up the Copy Files dialog box and notifies you that the links need to be updated (see Figure 19-23). Generally, you click OK. Clicking Cancel halts the copy, so if you want to copy the files without updating links, uncheck the boxes for those files (or the box at the top for all files), and then click OK.

Dragging into the Desktop folder. Although we think it a bit uncouth, you can bypass GoLive altogether and copy or move files directly into the site folder on the Desktop. The problem with the direct route is that when you return to GoLive, the program doesn't know the files have been added. Don't worry! There's a solution: select Refresh View from either the Site menu or the contextual menu to force GoLive to rescan the directory.

Figure 19-22
Dragging files
into an open
folder

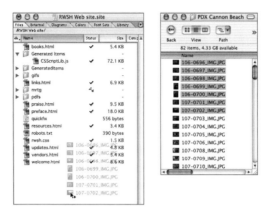

Figure 19-23
Updating links
in added files

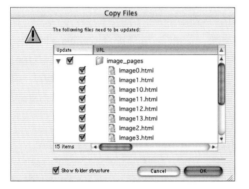

Adding empty files. When you're prototyping a site to build out content, it can be useful to add empty files that will eventually include real content. Using the Diagrams tab, you can add templates or completely blank pages with link placeholders (pending links) to other items in the site. (See Chapter 18, *Diagramming and Mapping*, for the details on prototyping.)

You can also drag a Page icon directly from the Object palette's Site tab; Go-Live creates an untitled page with a yield icon in the status column indicating that it has no links or content. If you double-click the Generic Page icon, the program creates an untitled file either in the root level, or nested in a selected folder. GoLive neatly selects the name of the file for immediate editing, as well.

Adding Stationery or Templates. GoLive lets you create fully editable or locked templates which are stored in folders in the Extras tab of the Site window. You can drag Stationery (editable) or Templates (locked areas) from their respective folders into the Files tab, or double-click the item to create a new copy that you can save in the site. See "Stationery and Templates," later in this chapter.

Moving Files

Because GoLive tracks every link in every file, moving and reorganizing items in a site is a cinch. Select any file, folder, or set of items, and drag it to a new location; GoLive prompts you with a dialog asking which files should have their links rewritten to reflect these new locations. This list includes files you're moving as well as any files that link to the selected files. GoLive rewrites links embedded in a variety of media when moved, too, including PDFs, QuickTime movies, and Flash SWF files, depending on which modules are loaded. (See Chapter 12, *Rich Media*.)

Unless you have a specific reason not to, you should click OK when GoLive asks you to update links; otherwise, the links break, and GoLive reports missing and orphaned files (see "Errors," later in this chapter).

Creating Links

It's also a snap to add links through the URL Getter, which is GoLive's bar in the Inspector containing all the methods of linking files. You can use Point & Shoot visual linking; direct entry, where you type in a path; and Browse, through which you find a file on a local or remote hard drive (see Figure 19-24).

Figure 19-24
URL Getter

Add Link | Point & Shoot   Direct entry   Browse/Edit
Remove Link

Link popout menu

GoLive also offers a method of creating placeholder links in the Designs tab when you're prototyping sites, briefly discussed here.

Point & Shoot

Point & Shoot navigation lets you simply drag a line from any link field or URL Getter or from certain selected items directly to the object you want to link. It's as simple as that. Although you can use Point & Shoot on individual open pages to make anchors—specific locations on a page to jump to—it's most powerfully employed in creating hypertext links and links to media files.

Tip: External Links

Everything described in this section that works for local links in your site functions just as well for external URLs found in the External tab. See "External Links," later in this chapter.

Point & Shoot button. The most common use of Point & Shoot is via the URL Getter in the Image Inspector's Link tab and Text Inspector's Basic tab, although the field and tool are found in the Map Area Inspector for individual mapped areas, and numerous other places in the program (see Figure 19-25).

Figure 19-25
Some of the many appearances of Point & Shoot navigation

Point & Shoot navigation is available, for example, in the Map Area Inspector, the Link tab of the Text Inspector, and for each of the links in the In & Out Links palette.

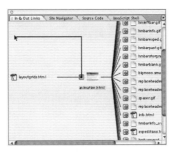

Click and hold on the Point & Shoot button (identified as Fetch URL by its Tooltip), then drag your mouse pointer onto the Site window—after a few seconds' delay, that window comes to the front. If you drag on top of the Files, Diagrams, or External tab, GoLive switches to that tab; then you can drag to items in those locations. If you drag on top of a folder, after a slight pause, GoLive opens the folder to reveal its contents. Dragging over the Path icon lets you move up folder levels as well. You can even drag your cursor onto the Select Window icon in the Toolbar, and GoLive swaps the Site window in front.

Tip: Disabling Spring-Loaded Folders

You can disable the ability to drag onto folders and tabs to open them by unchecking Spring-Loaded Folders in the Site pane of the Preferences dialog box. We prefer keeping this feature active, as it allows us to move items around easily without perfectly positioning everything first.

When you hover over a linkable object, like an HTML file, the item highlights (see Figure 19-26). If you release the Point & Shoot tool's link line on top of that item, the link is added into the URL Getter's direct entry field.

Figure 19-26
Adding a link
via Point &
Shoot

Adding the link (left);

the new link (top)

If you release the mouse button on top of the wrong kind of item—for instance, a font set in the Font Sets tab—or if you release it without having anything selected, the line retracts.

Point & Shoot shortcut. With any text selected on an HTML page, holding down the Command key (Mac) or Alt key (Windows) turns the cursor into a Point & Shoot tool (see Figure 19-27). You can drag from that text onto any kind of object or tab as described above to complete the link.

If you drag to a location on the same HTML page or on another open HTML page, GoLive creates an anchor link pointing to that exact location on the page. A user who clicks the link is taken directly to that spot.

Previously Selected Links

The Link popout menu on the Inspector palette shows a list of the most recently selected items in any site. These items include HTML pages, media files, and external URLs (see Figure 19-28). A longer list is categorized below that into submenus such as HTML Files and Misc URLs.

Figure 19-27
Point & Shoot
shortcut

Holding down Command (Mac) or Alt (Windows) changes the cursor to a Point & Shoot tool.

Dragging Links

Although it's not quite as elegant, you can drag a file or folder from the Files tab directly into an HTML page. Wherever you release the mouse, the item's name is inserted in the direct-entry field, and it's automatically linked back to the source. You can then rename the link.

Figure 19-28
Link popout
menu

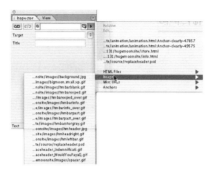

Tip: Dragging Images

If you drag an image of a type recognized by GoLive onto a page, GoLive automatically inserts the appropriate Smart Object and brings up the Save for Web dialog. See Chapter 5, *Images*, for details on importing image files.

Browsing

Clicking the Browse button (the icon that looks like a folder) brings up a dialog box from which you can select a file. The file doesn't have to be in the site folder to select it. However, if you choose an item that's not in the site folder, it shows up in the Orphan Files folder in the Errors tab, and you must eventually copy it over (using Clean Up Site, for instance) to keep the site working when you upload it.

Direct Entry

You'd hardly believe it in a graphical program like GoLive, but you really can just type in links in the URL Getter's direct entry field instead of using Point & Shoot or drag and drop. Of course, that's about as déclassé as paying with green paper at the supermarket these days (you should see the looks we get). It's almost always better to use Point & Shoot because it constructs the links perfectly. But, you can certainly type a file name in the same folder, an Absolute-style path, or a URL for a file location elsewhere.

Editing

Selecting Edit from the Link popout menu brings up the Edit URL dialog box displaying the full text in a larger, modal dialog box (see Figure 19-29). On the Mac, you can also click the Browse button on the URL Getter while holding down the Option key.

The Edit URL dialog displays the URL at the top and offers Make Absolute and Make Relative buttons. These two buttons, active for URLs that point to files in the local Web site, flip between a relative-to-the-root path that

Figure 19-29
Edit URL
dialog box

includes all the folders (if any) from your root to this particular link, or a relative path that's relative to the location in which the file you're linking from is stored. For more information on this, see the sidebar, "Absolute Versus Relative," earlier in this chapter.

Tip: Up a Level

GoLive follows the Web convention for relative links, so if you want to refer to a file located in a folder level up from where the linking file is located, insert two dots and a slash (../); this means "go up a folder level." For instance, if you want to link to "wonderbro.html" two levels above in the "jerry" folder, use a link like

```
../../jerry/wonderbro.html
```

We received email on our GoLive discussion list from a user whose Web hosting company told him that the ".." was some weirdo Mac thing. It's not. It's a) Unix in origin and b) completely standard on virtually every Web server.

Edit URL also allows you to add or edit parameters on the end of a URL. Parameters are used to pass information to a Web server or server script that modifies the information displayed in the resulting page. Many kinds of servers and scripts require parameters, and GoLive's approach makes it easier to enter them or change them one at a time. GoLive previews the actual URL at the bottom of the dialog box with all the special punctuation that packs it together.

Pending Links

In the Diagrams tab, you can add pending links, or placeholders where links should be added to final pages, as you prototype a site's structure. By creating these in-process links, you can later go back and turn the pending links into actual ones by inserting items on the page and adding the links to them.

For instance, when you're prototyping a site, you might know that page A needs links to pages B, C, and D, but the elements that will link to B, C, and D aren't yet created. After you create those elements, you can go to the Pending tab of the Page Inspector and connect the items with the pages they point to. Chapter 18, *Diagramming and Mapping*, covers this subject in great detail.

Modifying and Examining Links

The features for looking at existing links and modifying them are equally as strong as the tools for creating links. For examining links, GoLive offers the powerful In & Out Links palette; for modifying existing links, you can use either the In & Out Links palette or the Change References feature.

In & Out Links Palette

The In & Out Links palette is your best friend in managing a site. It can show all the inbound connections to a given file. For HTML and media files with embedded URLs, it also shows all the items the file links to (see Figure 19-30).

Invoke the In & Out Links palette from the Windows menu. Select any file in the Files tab or any design in the Designs tab to create a display in the In & Out Links palette of all the inbound and outbound links relating to that file.

Select Palette Options from the popout menu to specify whether the palette should show inbound or outbound links at all, and, if so, which kinds of outbound links to display. Filter the external links and other types by unchecking them to unclutter the display of outbound links.

You can also use Palette Options to choose to show an icon for a file instead of its thumbnail (if any). Unchecking URL at Bottom disables the display of URLs as you move your mouse off items in the palette.

Selecting the file at the center brings up the File Inspector. Selecting one of the linked-to or linked-from objects makes that object the star, putting it in the central position of the In & Out Links palette.

Any item that is linked to, including the selected item if it has any inbound links, has a Point & Shoot icon next to it. By using Point & Shoot, you can redirect the link that points at that object to any other object. This allows you, for instance, to update an old external link on a page by viewing it in the In & Out Links palette, and just dragging the Point & Shoot link line onto the External tab and on top of the correct new external link. (You can also click the Change References button or select that from the Site menu; this action automatically enters the reference for the current item in the center of the In & Out Links palette as the value for Change All References To.)

Figure 19-30
In & Out Links
palette

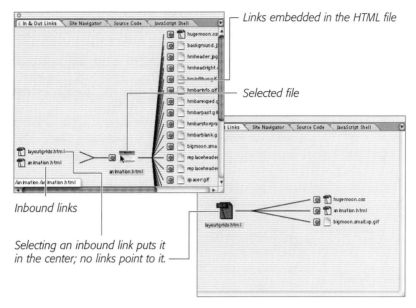

Links embedded in the HTML file

Selected file

Inbound links

Selecting an inbound link puts it
in the center; no links point to it.

This feature is especially useful for troubleshooting errors.

1. Select the file with an error from the Errors tab in the Site window. The In
   & Out Links palette displays all the files that point to the missing or broken item.

2. Use the Point & Shoot icon to reconnect the error icon to the correct item.

3. GoLive rebuilds the links. Voilà!

Tip: Printing Links

The popout menu of the In & Out Links palette has a Print option that prints
precisely what's displayed in the window. This can be useful as a mini-site map,
although you can customize it more completely in the Links view via the
Diagram menu. Selecting Print brings up the Print dialog box.

Change References

The Change References feature allows you to change a reference throughout a
site to another reference. It even works within the In & Out Links palette.
Bring up the Change References dialog box by selecting it from the Site menu
or clicking its button in the Site toolbar.

With an item selected in the Files, Site, or External tab, or with an item
showing at the center of the In & Out Links palette, choose Change
References to display the dialog box with the Change All References To field

prefilled with the selected item (see Figure 19-31). That field can't be modified if an item was selected when you chose Change References. GoLive generates an error if you have an item selected which has no inbound links, as there's nothing to transform references to.

Figure 19-31
Change
References
dialog box

Existing link

Replacement link

With nothing selected and nothing in the In & Out Links palette, bringing up the dialog box allows you to type, browse, or Point & Shoot a value for the Change All References To field. In either case, you can navigate the replacement value for the Into References To field.

Tip: Not "To" Clear

Let's be clear: Although both fields of the Change References dialog box use the preposition "to," the top field (Change All References To) means "from the current setting" and the bottom field (Into References To) means "to this new setting."

Change References, like some site features, can be reverted via the History palette and Undo features. But it can be a big change, so be sure to make a backup first, just in case.

Cleaning References

One of the best ways to use Change References is to clean up older HTML pages that might have a variety of references to the same file. Our friends at Adobe suggest using Change References typing in all the old references one at a time in the top field, while leaving the bottom field set to your new value. For instance, if we want a whole variety of files to point to /foobar/sniggle.html, we might search for these three URLs:

```
http://www.snark.com/foobar/
sniggle.html

/home/users/wumpus/foobar/
sniggle.html

~wumpus/foobar/sniggle.html
```

Then we could replace those, one at a time, with the new location. This works site-wide and cleans up the management task of having lots of different URLs that point to the same file.

If you want to ensure that everything's normal after using Change References, use Reparse All as described in "Tuning Up," later in the chapter.

Filename Constraints

Filename Constraints allows you to make sure that any file or folder name you choose can be uploaded correctly to the specific server hardware configuration you're working with, whether Mac, Unix, DOS, Windows, or something more unusual.

The "constraints" refer to which characters (letters, numbers, or symbols) a given platform and operating system can handle correctly, and the length and format of the name. For instance, Unix file names can be up to 256 characters long and contain any character except a forward slash (/). But DOS names must not include all sorts of characters, and must be eight characters at most, followed by a period, then followed by a maximum of three characters.

Tip: DOS Folders

Most of these constraints are true for both files and folders, except in DOS where folders can be a maximum of eight characters total.

Tip: Giving DOS a Boot?

Few people use DOS in any of its forms, but DOS file name limitations can crop up in older programs or in the oddest places, even though Windows itself has long abandoned filename constraints.

GoLive comes with several prefabricated sets of constraints for the major platforms and some good combinations of the major platforms. The explanations that Adobe provides for each set is top notch, noting all the peculiarities of the required naming scheme.

Filename Constraints manifests itself in several places in the program, so let's cover each in turn.

Tip: Fixing Bad Names

Because Filename Constraints is an integral part of GoLive, you can fix a "bad" file name by simply editing the name in the Files tab. You can't create bad file names for Windows or Mac OS on those platforms, as GoLive won't allow you to rename files to names that can't work on those two platforms; and, you can't even create files or download them with "illegal" names.

Tip: The Overlong Name (Mac OS X)

Mac OS X allows you to name files in the Finder with more characters than some Mac programs like GoLive can handle. OS X bypasses this limitation by offering the program a second, shorter name that ends with a # followed by a number. This can cause problems on uploading files. Be sure to keep your names legal, and use GoLive to double-check this for files named or renamed in the Finder.

Preferences. Filename Constraints preferences are found in both the Preferences dialog box's Site pane under Filename Constraints, as well as in each site's Site Settings (see Figure 19-32).

Figure 19-32
Filename
Constraints

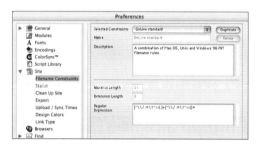

Tip: Site Versus Global Settings

As with other site settings, you can edit sitewide settings via Preferences to make global changes that affect all open sites or sites opened subsequently; or you can make changes just to the currently opened site by editing the Site Settings for that site.

From the Selected Constraints popup menu, you can select the most appropriate setting for the Web server you're uploading or transferring your files to. If you don't know, ask your Webmaster, ISP, or system administrator.

The best choice is GoLive Standard, which only allows file names that work on Unix, Mac OS (9 and earlier), Mac OS X, and Windows 98/NT and later machines. Since the vast majority of Web servers are running on one of these operating systems, you should never have problems.

If you want to create your own sets, you have to click the Duplicate button; there is no new set button. The Maximal Length and Extension Length fields control the number of characters in each part of the name; the Regular Expression field uses a regular expression as discussed in Chapter 22, *Advanced Features*, to identify legal patterns in file names.

Filename Warnings. One of the easiest ways to find any items in your site that don't meet the constraints is to look at the Errors tab in the Site window. If any non-conforming files or folders exist, the Errors tab shows a Filename Warnings folder containing all the bad files. Selecting a file allows you to edit the faulty file name in the File Inspector.

File Inspector's Name tab. When you select a non-conforming file or folder in the Errors tab or the Files tab, the File Inspector's Name tab explains that the file name or folder violates the site or global constraints.

Filename Status column. By default, the Filename Status column is not displayed in the Files tab. In the View palette, select it from the Show Columns popup menu to display it. It shows the standard red *.* icon for any file or folder not up to snuff.

New in 6: OS X Constraint

OS X can't accept file names with a slash in them, because the underlying Unix operating system uses a slash to mark the separation of directories in a path, just like in Web URLs. The constraint added in GoLive 6 allows long-file names, which OS X does allow, but disallows colons (a Mac OS 9 holdover) and slashes.

Windows users shouldn't feel left out: GoLive 6 still shows Windows 98/NT because ME, XP, and 2000 didn't change file name requirements.

Tuning Up

After you've done quite a bit of work in the Files tab, it could seem, well, a bit out of sorts. Generally, GoLive tracks all the elements in a site, but if you've clicked Cancel here and unchecked a box there, and edited your HTML in a text editor way over there, some of your links and files might need a bit of tidying.

GoLive offers a few tools for helping in that department. Here are three tips for cleaning up missing files or deleted files, updating problems, and missing thumbnails. (We offer more tips under "Errors," later in this chapter.)

Refreshing Site

If you've added content by dragging it into the Web site folder or manipulated files without using GoLive, you need to refresh the site. Refreshing forces GoLive to re-examine all of the items in the folders that comprise the site.

Select Refresh View from the Site menu or click the Refresh View button in the Site toolbar. Refresh View is context-sensitive: if you've selected a folder's contents so that it fills the file list, only that view is updated. Refresh View also works to update items in the Extras tab if the highlight is on that tab (by clicking anywhere in that tab), or if a nested folder is displayed or selected.

Reparse All

If you've been a little naughty and worked on raw HTML in an editor other than GoLive's Source Code Editor, GoLive isn't up to speed on the contents of that file. You have two choices:

- **Tedious:** You can open any files you've edited elsewhere, make a small change (like typing and erasing a space character), and then save it.

- **Efficient:** Hold down the Option key (Mac) or Control key (Windows) and select Reparse Selection or Reparse All from the Site menu.

Reparse walks through selected or all of the site's HTML pages and recreates the invisible GoLive database of links and other information.

Tip: Modified Files

If you check Reparse Only Modified Files in the Site pane of the Preferences dialog box, GoLive checks the modification date of the file against its record of the last time it dealt with the file. If the modification date is more recent, only then does it reparse the file. We're not sure why you'd want to turn this off.

Tip: Reparse that Refreshes

If you check Reparse Files on Refresh View in the Preferences dialog box's Site pane, then Refresh View and Reparse All have the same functionality.

Creating Thumbnails

GoLive automatically makes thumbnails—tiny previews—of HTML pages after you've modified them at least once in the program and saved those changes. These thumbnails are used in the Content tab of the File Inspector as well as in one of many possible views in the Site tab.

However, if you've brought in HTML from other sources, GoLive hasn't had the opportunity to create a preview for the file. Press Command-Option (Mac) or Control-Alt (Windows) and then select Create Thumbnails from the Site menu; this option only appears when these keys are depressed.

For larger sites, creating thumbnails can take some time, as GoLive has to open every page, internally render a preview, save the preview, and move on. GoLive puts up a progress bar to show you how far it's gotten on larger sites. You can cancel the operation midstream. Keep in mind that your site file can balloon in size if you've created lots of thumbnails.

Tip: Individual Thumbnails

You can make individual page thumbnails by selecting the page in the Files tab, choosing the Content tab of the File Inspector, and clicking the Create Thumbnail button, which looks like two arrows chasing each other's tails.

External Links

So far, we've been talking largely about links to and from local resources stored on your hard drive and typically represented in your Site window. But many sites contain extensive links to other Web resources; others may simply have a few scattered URLs throughout the site. Managing these resources is eased with a couple of GoLive features, using the same controls for adding and modifying external links as those you use for internal links.

Two of the biggest problems in keeping a site fresh and functional are tracking when those links go bad, and changing links throughout the site when the original reference changes. GoLive automates both features in the External tab.

Let's walk through managing link objects, editing the values stored in them, and then discuss link validation.

Tip: Making an Email Link

Another type of "external" link is the email link, which works a bit differently than other links in GoLive. Select the text you want to make into a link, and then click the New Link button in the Text Inspector. Enter mailto: followed by the email address, such as (without the quotes) "mailto:billg@macrohard.com". If you have Auto Add "mailto" to Addresses checked in the General Preferences pane's URL Handling settings, you don't even have to include "mailto:"—just the email address will do.

Link Objects

When you import a site, GoLive automatically generates a list of external references (see Figure 19-33). It also adds external references as you enter new items in files in your site. The External tab shows both "external" URLs—links to other sites referenced from your site—as well as any email addresses that you can click on as links (ones you specified using "mailto:").

The External tab also has a column indicating whether a given address or URL has been referenced or "used" somewhere in the site. The Status field indicates whether or not the link has been confirmed as good using GoLive's link validator tool, discussed later in this section.

Figure 19-33
External tab

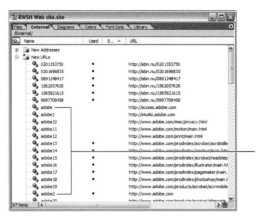

When there's more than one link to the same domain or host name, GoLive adds a number to the object's name.

Grouping. If you have a large number of external references, you might want to group them by category for easier viewing. With the External tab active, click the New Folder button in the Toolbar, name the folder, and then drag and drop your external URLs and email links into them.

You can also drag in a URL Group or Address Group folder from the Site tab of the Objects palette. If you select a group, the Group Inspector appears, allowing you to change the icon for the group; the functionality is identical whether you choose URLs, Addresses, New URLs, or New Addresses. Really, none of these names matter; it just makes it easier to visually inspect which links are in which categories.

Updating. If you've added or removed external URLs or email addresses from your site after importing or creating it, you can select either Get References Used from the Site menu to update the External tab, or Remove Unused References to delete entries you are no longer using anywhere in the site.

Tip: Clean Up

The Clean Up Site feature allows you to group features like removing unused references, getting used references, and other cleaning operations for font sets, colors, and files into one dialog box. See "Clean Up Site," later in this chapter.

GoLive adds new addresses and URLs to the first group it finds tagged as New for that category; if no such groups exist, GoLive creates them as needed.

If you use Remove Unused References and you've created placeholder items in the External tab that haven't been added to pages in the site, those items are removed from the tab and can't be restored.

Creating. It's easy enough to create links from scratch. Drag an Address (for email) or URL icon into the External tab, or double-click either icon to insert one. Use the Reference Inspector to edit the value or the shortcut name that appears in the External tab. Addresses must start with "mailto:", which GoLive prefills when you add an empty Address icon.

Renaming. You can name the link objects anything you want via the Reference Inspector. References are named, by default, with part of the host-name after "www.", or for names like "store.apple.com", with the start of the name. For multiple URLs with similar names, the program adds a number following the name (see Figure 19-33, above).

Managing Links

Each URL or email address in the External tab consists of two parts: the name that GoLive or you assign to it (which appears in the Name column of the tab), and the actual URL or address (which appears in the URL column).

GoLive tracks the URL or address so that each one is unique in the site, regardless of the name assigned to it. The URL or address is centrally managed so that changing it in the External tab changes it wherever it appears throughout the site.

You can modify the values for URLs that aren't referenced in the site (ones you've created from scratch to insert later), as well as ones that have links to them using a few methods.

Tip: Viewing References as Links

The In & Out Links palette works just as well on URLs as it does on files. Select an item from the External tab and bring up the In & Out Links palette to see all the files that reference that URL (see Figure 19-34). Using Point & Shoot, you can redirect links to an external reference just as you can to an internal page or object.

Figure 19-34
Showing
external links
in the In & Out
Links palette

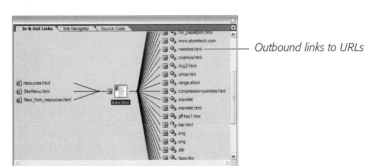

— Outbound links to URLs

Reference Inspector. The Reference Inspector appears when you select either a URL or an email address in the External tab. It allows you to change the name of the object, or the URL or address the object represents. The Edit button allows you to bring up a dialog box for easily editing longer Web locations.

If you edit the URL field and that URL is used anywhere in the site, GoLive brings up the Change Reference dialog box letting you know and approve which files need to be rewritten to reflect the new URL. If you only change the URL on certain pages, instead of accepting all of the ones that GoLive proposes, it leaves the original link in place (with the files you chose not to modify still pointing to it), and then creates a new External object with your new value; the files you chose to change now point to it.

Let's say you have several links that point to a certain external Web page. Then you decide some links should point to a different link. You can edit that first link in the Reference Inspector and then choose only the pages you want to change to the new URL from the Change Reference dialog box. GoLive creates a new URL entry and changes five pages to point to it (see Figure 19-35).

Tip: Use Edit URL

URLs are often too long to fit in the URL field of the Reference Inspector (see Figure 19-36). Clicking the Edit button brings up the standard Edit URL dialog box that allows you to see the entire URL and edit it, as well as modify parameters.

Change References. You can select an item in the External tab and click Change References in the toolbar to choose which reference to point to. This is identical to using the Reference Inspector, but offers a clearer way to see what you're doing (see the "Change References" explanation, earlier in this chapter).

Point & Shoot. You can use Point & Shoot in the In & Out Links palette or Change References dialog box to link to a new URL or address.

Checking Links

GoLive can automatically check whether external links still exist, or whether they've become "cobwebs"—links that no longer bring up pages or sites that no longer exist.

In the External tab, select Check External Links from the Site or contextual menu (see Figure 19-37). Each URL displays a double-arrowed icon in the Status column to indicate that the address is due to be checked. GoLive tests each link, displaying green bug icons to indicate bad links, and checkmarks to note good links.

Figure 19-35
Splitting one
URL into two

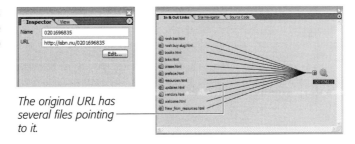

The original URL has
several files pointing
to it.

Edit the URL but only
check some of the files
to have the reference
rewritten in just those
cases.

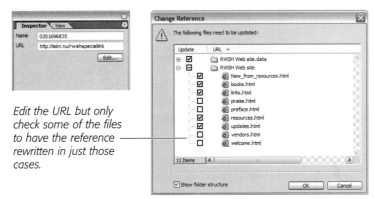

GoLive creates the new object leaving the original one in place.

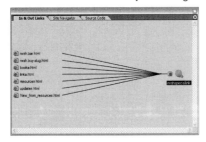

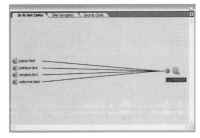

Figure 19-36
Edit URL
dialog box

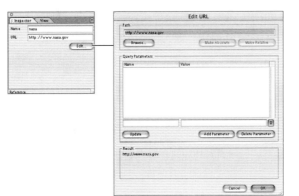

Use this dialog box
to edit or enter
longer URLs.

Figure 19-37
Check Links

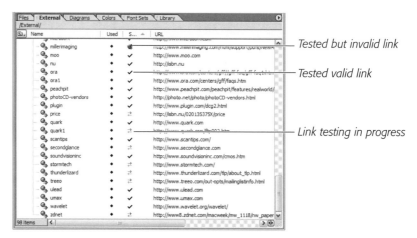

Tested but invalid link

Tested valid link

Link testing in progress

Importing Bookmarks from Browsers

Instead of tediously copying Web addresses from a browser into GoLive when you're adding external links to a page, you can create bookmarks in your browser, import them directly into GoLive's External tab, and drag them or link to them via that interface. GoLive can import both Netscape and Microsoft formatted favorites lists or bookmarks files (see Figure 19-38).

We've found that each browser and platform stores bookmarks in a different place. Rather than try to find this file, use your browser to export favorites to a separate file, the location of which you can specify.

- In Netscape, you typically use the Bookmarks menu to bring up Manage Bookmarks, and then select Export Bookmarks from the resulting File menu.
- In Mac Internet Explorer, choose Organize Favorites from the Favorites menu, and select Export Favorites from the File menu.
- In Internet Explorer for Windows, select Import and Export from the File menu and via the Wizard, choose Export Favorites.

Once you've exported the file from your browser, select from the File menu's Import submenu the item Favorites as Site Externals. Choose the bookmarks file you export. GoLive churns a while for longer lists. When it's done, you see all of your bookmarks organized in the same folder structure as they were in the browser.

Figure 19-38
Imported bookmarks

External tab preserves same folder structure as in browser's bookmarks

Once you initiate a check, there isn't much else to be done. The only way to cancel the process is to close the site file. Unfortunately, you can't check only a few URLs; it's check all or nothing.

If you have a number of links, the checking can take a while, so you may not see problems immediately; Adobe recommends increasing the memory allotted to GoLive for Mac OS 9.2 or earlier to help avoid problems with larger sites. (Windows and Mac OS X automatically allocate necessary memory.)

If you have a slow connection to the Net, cheer up: GoLive doesn't take much longer to test links than on a fast connection, because it only has to send a tiny amount of information to validate the link.

Tip: Link Validators

Link checking utilities we've found useful are VSE Link Tester for the Mac (www.vse-online.com/link-tester/index.html) and the free (but somewhat out of date) Xenu's Link Sleuth for Windows (home.snafu.de/tilman/xenulink.html).

Right Pane of the Site Window

The Site window has both a left pane (shown as the full window when you open a site file) and a right pane, which you choose to display manually. Click the split-pane icon at the lower-right corner of the screen (see Figure 19-39). The right pane of the Site window contains the FTP and WebDAV tabs, which we discuss in Chapter 20, *Synchronizing Sites*; the right pane also contains the Errors and Extras tabs, which are covered later in this chapter.

Figure 19-39
Right pane of
Site window

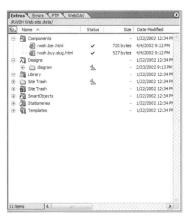

Extras tab displayed

The Files and Extras tabs never leave the Site window, but the five other tabs in the left pane (External, Diagrams, Colors, Font Sets, and Library) and the three others in the right pane (Errors, FTP, and WebDAV) can be torn off as self-standing windows (see Figure 19-40).

Figure 19-40
Tearing off
windows

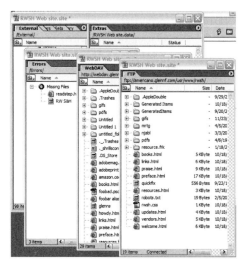

If you drag any of the torn-off tabs back into the Site window—overlap the torn-off tab on top until you see a snap-in outline—they are put back into place in the same order as their default. If you close a torn-off tab, you can bring it back up by selecting its name from the popout menu in the upper-right corner of either pane (see Figure 19-41). You can also restore the default display by selecting Default Configuration from that popout menu.

The Errors tab is a centralized place to troubleshoot a site's file problems, and the Extras tab contains templates, designs, and trash.

Figure 19-41
Window
popout menu

Errors

GoLive uses the Errors tab to show problems where files are located—or not located—on the site. Open the split-pane view by pressing the split-pane icon at the lower-right corner, then click the Errors tab. GoLive lists three kinds of errors there (see Figure 19-42):

- Missing files, where GoLive can't find the file referred to by a link that's supposed to be in the local site folder.

- Orphaned files, where the file referred to is located outside of the site folder on the local hard drive.

- Illegally named files, according to the Filename Constraints preferences (discussed earlier in this chapter under "Filename Constraints").

The Errors tab uses the same columns and interface as the Files tab. You can rearrange, resize, and turn columns on and off in the display by dragging and using the View palette.

Figure 19-42
Errors tab

Tip: Move to the Left

We recommend moving the URL column to the immediate right of the Name column as it's the piece of information you can use best to troubleshoot problems.

Missing Files

Selecting a file with a question mark or icon next to its name in the Missing Files folder brings up the Error Inspector. You can browse, edit the path, Point & Shoot, or type in a new name to fix the error (see Figure 19-43). You can also bring up the In & Out Links palette, and use Point & Shoot to specify a replacement file or relink to the correct file on your site.

There's even a third option: select Change References from the Site menu and use that interface, described earlier in the chapter, to update the link.

Figure 19-43
Fixing Errors

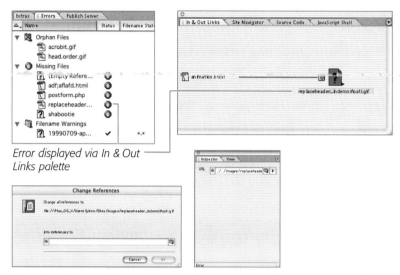

Error displayed via In & Out Links palette

Use either Change References or the Error Inspector to link to the correct file.

If you need more information about which link has gone bad, you can use the In & Out Links palette to find files that reference the link. Open one of those files, click the Link Warnings icon on the Toolbar or in the Highlight palette, then troll through the page to find what was linking to the missing file (see Figure 19-44). (This is often easier than trying to figure out what a file named "oc8989aa.hml" is supposed to contain.)

Omitting Certain Files

If you purposely aren't keeping local copies of certain files, you may want to exclude them from showing up in Missing Files through GoLive's URL Handling feature. Don't confuse URL Handling with File Mappings (which programs open which files) or URL Mapping. URL Handling lets you exclude certain patterns or URLs from GoLive's missing-file checker.

Go to the Preferences dialog box, and under the General pane, find the URL Handling set-

tings. Add an item like a file name or a specific extension (.pdf if you want to exclude all PDFs, for instance), and click OK. If you have a site file open, you are then prompted to decide whether to apply those changes to all open sites. Usually, the answer is yes.

We often map "/cgi-bin/", because the scripts referenced inside GoLive typically are not stored in the local folder, but are on the Web server in that special directory.

Figure 19-44
Troubleshooting
bad page links

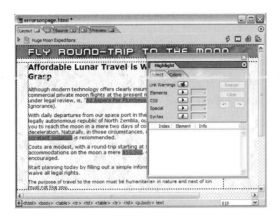

Orphaned Files

Orphaned files are located outside the site folder, and may contain content that you've collected from other sources, such as networked volumes on file servers. However, before you upload the site, you need to make sure that GoLive has incorporated the orphaned file so that it gets properly referenced on the Web—otherwise, users will get an error message when they click the link to the orphaned item.

You can choose one of four approaches to correct orphaned files.

> **Tip: Workgroup Orphans**
>
> We're not talking in this tip about children put into hard labor, but rather orphaned files for sites managed by Adobe's Workgroup Server, discussed later in this part of the book. Because workgroup sites keep all live files on the Workgroup Server, you should ensure that files you add from your local hard drive aren't orphaned, but are copied into the site.

- **Copy them locally.** If you simply drag the orphaned file icon from the Errors tab into any location in the files list side of the Files tab, GoLive makes a local copy of the file and links it in.

- **Clean Up Site.** The Clean Up Site feature has an option that allows you to copy any external files (into the default "NewFiles" folder in the site) to correct this problem wherever it appears. It's equivalent to selecting all of the orphaned files and dragging them over, but much simpler. See "Clean Up Site," later in this chapter.

- **Export Site.** You can hold off dealing with this problem until you're ready to transfer the site and use the Export Site feature, which makes a copy of your site. As one of the options, you can specify Export Referenced Files That Are Not Part of the Site; see "Export Site," later in this chapter.

- **Leave them alone.** This only works if you're willing to have broken links on your Web site, though we expect you're probably not.

Extras

Have you found yourself acting somewhat robotic in your Web design and production work, repeating the same activity over and over again with no end in sight (or site)? GoLive offers two site features to relieve tedium caused by a human being having to act like a computer: Stationery and Components, both found in the Extras tab. It also has two associated features, Templates and Library, which can be used in conjunction with repeated elements.

Tip: Extra Extras

The Extras tab also contains other folders that represent different objects or program areas which GoLive stores and manages, including the Designs folder (Chapter 18, *Diagramming and Mapping*), and SmartObjects folder (Chapter 5, *Images*).

Tip: Site Trash

The Site Trash folder also lives in the Extras tab. So, for the purpose of consistency and perhaps due to a lack of organizational imagination, we discuss it in this section, as well.

Stationery allows you to label and store specific HTML files as templates that you can use as new, blank pages in the Files tab and the Designs tab. Components are HTML snippets that you insert in Web pages which are managed from a central location. Changes to a Component update all pages on which that Component is placed.

Templates are documents that contain predefined areas or text blocks that prevent a user from editing those parts of the page or specifically allow them to enter text. Templates can be used in an organization where a designer creates a page, makes it into a template, and allows others in the organization to update only what they need to. (See Chapter 11, *Templates*, for more on defining and using templates.)

Tip: Stationery or Template

Stationery and Templates might appear identical at first glance, but there's an important difference. Any part of a page created from Stationery may be moved, removed, deleted, or manipulated. Only specific areas on a Template can be modified.

New in 6: Templates

Templates are a new feature in GoLive 6 for creating manageable cookie-cutter pages.

The Library contains short snippets of HTML that you may have dragged off a page or entered manually. GoLive doesn't manage Library elements the way it does Components; rather, it copies and pastes items from the Library into pages you're working on as a one-time deal. After that, they're on their own.

Tip: Library Doubling

Oh, yes, there are two Library locations in the Objects palette. The Library tab of the Site window stores site-specific HTML blurbs. The Library tab of the Objects palette stores program-wide HTML blurbs. You can drag items from one into the other, and from the Library tab of the Objects palette into the Library view of the Site Extras tab. Help us, please! We're drowning!

Components, Stationery, Library, and Templates all show up in the Extras tab as folders and in the Objects palette's Site Extras tab as individual objects (see Figure 19-45). You can select which of the four types you're viewing through a popup menu at the lower right of that tab. Hovering over any item in that tab displays the item's name in the lower-left corner of the Objects palette. All items except Library snippets are shown with preview icons of their contents, if a thumbnail exists.

Figure 19-45
Extras folders
corresponding
to repeatable
items

You can save a file in progress directly into the Stationery, Components, or Templates folder by selecting any of these folders from the Site Folder popup menu in the Save As dialog box (see Figure 19-46).

Figure 19-46
Save As special
popup menu

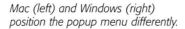

*Mac (left) and Windows (right)
position the popup menu differently.*

Stationery and Templates

Making Stationery is straightforward; Templates are a bit trickier. To make Stationery, create a file in GoLive that contains all the elements you want on every page, including Components (described below). To make a Template, consult Chapter 11, *Templates*, for the blow-by-blow details.

You can turn a page into something GoLive recognizes as Stationery or a Template by any of these methods:

- Save the file in the Stationery or Templates folder (see above).

- Save the file in the root of the site, and then drag it to the Stationery or Templates folder in the Extras tab. GoLive moves the file, rewrites references, and, on the Mac, changes its icon. (If you Option- or Alt-drag a file, GoLive copies it and turns the copy into a Stationery file.)

- Check the Stationery (Mac OS 9) or Stationery Pad (Mac OS X)box in the File Inspector (Mac). This doesn't move the file, but it does give it Stationery properties, which may not be the best idea; we don't recommend it.

Tip: Desktop Stationery (Mac Only)

The Stationery attribute is set at the file level, so you can examine and change this setting on the Desktop. On the Mac, select the file and from the File menu choose Get Info (OS 8 and 9) or Show Info (OS X).

Applying Stationery and Templates

When you double-click a Stationery or Templates file in the Extras tab, GoLive asks if you want to modify the file itself or create a new document (see Figure 19-47). If you click Create, the program opens a new, untitled document window with the name "untitled". GoLive adds a number to the document name if you've opened previous new documents during the same session.

Figure 19-47
Prompt when
trying to open
Stationery

After editing this untitled document, selecting Save or Save As brings up a prompt for a file location and name. After you save the file, it acts just like any other HTML file. If it's a Template, the attributes for editable regions of the page are retained regardless of where it's saved or how often it's edited.

You can also drag Stationery and Templates from the Site Extras tab of the Objects palette into the Files tab; GoLive creates a copy of the file called "New from" (Mac) or "from" (Windows) plus the file's name.

Tip: Don't Drag

If you drag Stationery or a Template from Extras to the Files tab, GoLive moves the file itself, which is not what you want if you mean to create a new document.

Applying Stationery and Templates in the Diagram Tab

You can drag Stationery or Templates into diagrams either from the Site Extras folder or the Site Extras tab of the Objects palette. We cover using files in this manner in Chapter 18, *Diagramming and Mapping*.

Components

Components let you reuse the same piece of HTML over and over again while centrally managing the piece through a single editable file. When you edit the Component, every occurrence of that Component throughout a site is automatically updated with the new HTML.

Components can be as small as a single piece of text or a tag, or as large as an entire page including all the appropriate page tags, like the Head tag (see Figure 19-48). Typically, you'd use Components for any kind of element that repeats exactly on every page it appears. You can't use Components to insert, for example, a menu bar with section-based rollovers, unless you devise separate Components for each section. But if you use one menu bar for the entire site that doesn't identify sections, you can certainly include it.

Tip: Copyright Component

The best example we can think of for a Component? A copyright statement. Most of the sites we design have a copyright and contact notice at the bottom

Figure 19-48
Component
preview and
underlying
code

*The preview
of a Compo-
nent; note
the corner
triangle*

```
<!DOCTYPE html PUBLIC "-//W3C//DTD HTML 4.01 Transitional//EN">
<html>
    <head>
        <meta http-equiv="content-type" content="text/html;charset=ISO-8859-1">
        <meta name="generator" content="Adobe GoLive 6">
        <title>Welcome to Adobe GoLive 6</title>
        <link href="../../hugemoonsite/hugemoon.css" rel="stylesheet" media="screen">
    </head>
    <body bgcolor="#ffffff" leftmargin="0" marginheight="0" marginwidth="0" topmargin="0">
        <p><img src="../../hugemoonsite/images/hmheader.jpg" alt="" height="104" width="740"
border="0"></p>
    </body>
</html>
```

*The Component's
raw HTML includes
Doctype, Html, Head,
and Body tags, which
are stripped off when
the Component is
inserted on the page.*

of every page, no matter how many thousands of pages there are. Using a Component for this enables us to modify the date or contact person once and watch 1,000 pages get rewritten automatically on a particularly large site.

Tip: JavaScript References

Because Components are embedded multiple times, you have to reference all the JavaScript that a Component uses through an external link to a JavaScript file rather than embedding every page or embedding in the Component itself. In order to do this, every page on which you use a Component needs to have a reference to a shared JavaScript file; see Chapter 24, *Authoring JavaScript*, on how to create this reference.

Creating Components

Since Components are pure HTML, they can be created in two simple ways.

• In the Layout Editor, create what you want visually, use the Page Inspector's HTML tab to turn the page into a Component, and save it in the Components folder.

• In the Source Code Editor in GoLive or in a plain-text editor (such as NotePad, SimpleText, or BBEdit), enter the HTML code directly, and save or drag the file into the Components folder.

You can and should include all of the folderol that a normal HTML page needs, like the Head, Body, Title, and Html tags, because GoLive knows to automatically strip that information before inserting the Component in a page. GoLive needs the surrounding tags to seamlessly preview Components when you open them.

Using the Page Inspector. You can take a page you're viewing in the Layout Editor and turn it into a Component with the Page Inspector's HTML tab.

1. With the HTML page open and set to the Layout Editor, click the Page icon.

2. Bring up the Page Inspector, and click the HTML tab (see Figure 19-49).

3. Click the Settings to Use Page as a Component button. If the settings are already correct, the button is grayed out.

4. Note that Import GoLive Script Library is selected. This is necessary if you use any GoLive Actions on your page; it prevents GoLive from writing the JavaScript libraries into the HTML page you're turning into a Component. This code would otherwise wind up on the individual pages where the Component appears.

5. Save the page in the Components folder ending the name with .htm or .html, even though you're not loading it directly into a site. With an .htm or .html extension, when you open the file, GoLive lets you edit it visually.

Figure 19-49
HTML tab

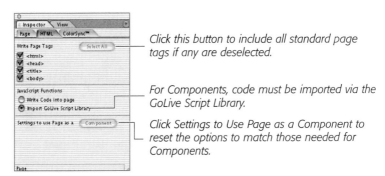

Click this button to include all standard page tags if any are deselected.

For Components, code must be imported via the GoLive Script Library.

Click Settings to Use Page as a Component to reset the options to match those needed for Components.

Writing raw HTML for a Component. If you're familiar with HTML, you can type code directly into the Source Code Editor or a regular text editor and save it in the Components folder. Or, you can create what you need visually in the Layout Editor, switch to the Source Code Editor, and delete excess HTML.

Adding a Component to a Page

GoLive offers two ways to add Components to the Layout Editor.

- **Site Extras tab of Objects palette.** With Components selected from the popup menu in the lower right of the Site Extras tab of the Objects palette, drag a Component onto the page.

- **Smart placeholder.** Drag the Component icon from the Smart tab of the Objects palette. Use Point & Shoot to connect the placeholder to an item in the Components folder of the Extras tab.

On big projects, it's not uncommon for one person to build separate pages that reference an object (like a navigation bar) being built by another team member. Using the Component placeholder lets you point to a blank file that later becomes an actual object without having to go back and reassign the link later. As soon as the Component is ready, GoLive can update the entire site to reflect the new element.

Tip: Can't Drag This

If you drag and drop a Component from the Components folder in the Extras tab into the Layout Editor, a linked filename is inserted, for some reason. In GoLive 5, this was another way to insert a Component.

Component Code in the Page

Components are inserted distinctively into a page both visually in the Layout Editor and Layout Preview, and textually into the HTML.

Visually, a Component appears as a dotted outline around its contents, with a green triangle in the upper-left corner (see Figure 19-48, earlier).

In the underlying HTML, GoLive inserts the contents of the Component surrounded by Csobj open and close tags (see Figure 19-50). The Csobj tag is used only by GoLive, and can be omitted when you export or upload pages. It contains a set of attributes that describe the path to the Component, its dimensions, and some other housekeeping information that GoLive requires.

Always Use Absolute References

The one real limitation we've run into in creating Components is that because they live outside of your site folder, which contains all of the site's pages and media, references to images and other files might show a full path from the root of your hard drive instead of a relative path.

Components, when inserted into a Web page, may continue to show the local reference to an object instead of a relative reference that works when the page is uploaded to a Web site.

We've gotten around this problem by always using GoLive-style Absolute links for all references in a Component. This ensures that wherever the Component is inserted, the paths to the referenced items work because they're all referenced from the root level of the site.

For each link in the Component, bring up the appropriate Inspector palette, and in the Link tab, uncheck Relative from the Link popout menu. The less tedious way to do this is to bring up Preferences or Site Settings and check Make New Links Absolute in the General pane's URL Handling settings (at least while you're creating a Component).

Being Absolute forces GoLive to write nice, clean HTML that references all files in a way that never breaks due to a problem with a path, and all browsers support.

Figure 19-50
HTML for a
Component on
a page

```
    <csobj occur="10" w="603" h="104" t="Component" csref="file:
///Mac_OS_X/Users/glenn/Sites/hugemoonsite on 64.81.13.159/hugemoonsite.data/Components/topbar.
html">
        <p><img src="file:///Mac_OS_X/Users/glenn/Sites/hugemoonsite on 64.81.13.
159/hugemoonsite/images/hmheader.jpg" alt="" height="104" width="740" border="0"></p>
    </csobj>
```

Tip: Memories

The Csobj tag commemorates those days, long ago, when GoLive was called GoLive CyberStudio (hence, the item is a "CyberStudio Object"). After Adobe acquired GoLive, Inc., and CyberStudio 3.1, it dropped the product name in favor of the more exciting company moniker.

Because of these extra GoLive-only tags, the resulting HTML can make site validators gag. However, GoLive allows you to strip out these tags when uploading to an FTP or WebDAV server, or when exporting the site into a fresh folder.

1. For FTP, click Upload to Server; for WebDAV, click Synchronize All or Upload Modified Items; for Export, select Export Site from the File menu's Export submenu (see Figure 19-51).

2. Click the Strip Options button.

3. Check the Adobe GoLive Elements box.

You can also strip comments, spaces, and linefeeds in most cases without harming the HTML's appearance, although we've found weird bugs with table cells and line returns.

Figure 19-51
Stripping
HTML

Tip: Strip Preferences

You can set your preferred HTML stripping options for Export and Upload globally in Preferences under the Site pane, or locally for a given site in Site Settings through Upload Settings.

Tip: Full Astern!

The only reason not to compact your HTML on uploading to an FTP or WebDAV server is if you foresee ever needing to download it back from the server. Very few sites we know modify files on the server themselves; most of the time, files are edited on the local machine that has GoLive or another editing program on it, and uploaded when they're ready to go live (as it were).

Because you've stripped out the special code that allows GoLive to remember that part of the HTML is a Component, you'd have to do some refurbishing to restore files locally from a remote server.

Updating Components

It's quite simple to update any Component (see Figure 19-52). Display the Extras tab and open the Components folder. Double-click any of the Components you've created. Make any changes you want.

When you press Command-S (Mac) or Control-S (Windows) or select Save from the File menu, GoLive reviews its internal database to see which files need to be changed and brings up the Updating Component dialog box which shows all the files that need to be changed. The default is to show the files organized by folders, including any folders in the Extras tab; if you uncheck Show Folder Structure you can see an alphabetical list of items to update.

Figure 19-52
Updating
Components
throughout
a site

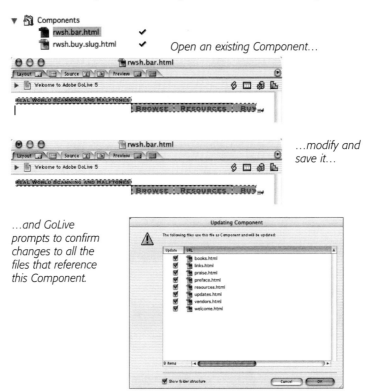

Open an existing Component…

…modify and save it…

…and GoLive prompts to confirm changes to all the files that reference this Component.

Tip: Sort by Update

You can sort by either the URL or Update field in the Updating Component dialog box by clicking the field's name at the top of the box. Sorting by Update allows you to see which items you have or haven't checked.

Select the files to update. You can choose all or none, or select individual files or folders. Click OK, and GoLive shows a progress bar as it updates the files referencing this Component. Click Cancel and GoLive doesn't save the file or make any changes.

Tip: Sync after Update

After updating a Component, you should synchronize your site via FTP or Web-DAV, or using the Workgroup Server, since every page referencing that Component now needs to be transferred to the server. Upload to Server, WebDAV Upload Modified Items, and various Check In options all grab the correct files, as GoLive has modified each of them locally.

Detaching Components

If you've wound up with a Component on a page that you want to edit directly on that specific page, you don't have to copy and paste, edit HTML, or otherwise look under the hood. Instead select the Component and choose Detach Selected Component from the Special menu.

GoLive rewrites the underlying code so the HTML chunk no longer references the original Component. It is now editable.

New in 6: Detach

This option is new in version 6. It's a nice alternative to the messy editing that would otherwise be required.

You can also choose Detach All Components from the Special menu, and turn the entire page into an editable construction.

This step cannot be undone, so save the page first; you can Revert to Saved (File menu) if you truly need to return to the past.

Site Trash

When you delete a file from the Files tab or Diagrams tab of the Site window, or from most of the Extras tabs' subfolders, GoLive offers a number of configurable options for disposing of that file.

You can have the program toss the file in the Desktop trash (the Mac Trash icon or the Windows Recycle Bin); or, you can keep the trash a little closer by using GoLive's built-in SiteTrash folder in the Extras tab of the split-pane (see Figure 19-53).

Figure 19-53
Site Trash

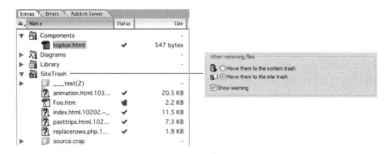

The option of where the deleted files go is set through the Preferences dialog box in the Site pane, in the area marked When Removing Files. If you select Move Them to the Finder Trash (Mac) or System Trash (Windows), GoLive immediately moves files into that location; if you select the other (default) option, Move Them to the Site Trash, the items are stored in the site data folder's SiteTrash folder.

If you uncheck the Show Warning box, files you delete are moved without comment to the appropriate trash. If you are set to toss deletions into the Site Trash, right-click (Windows) or Control-click (Mac) the SiteTrash folder in the Extras tab, and select Empty Trash from the menu. This doesn't actually empty the trash, but rather moves it to the Desktop trash.

The safety mechanisms built into deletion are noteworthy, as they give you two to four options to say no or recover items before they're gone for good. (Of course, you made a backup, right?)

Sitewide Finding

GoLive's Find feature has three tabs that let you examine usage of given text or HTML throughout a site, and/or make sitewide changes with a click of one button. A fourth tab works to find files in a site. We cover the basics of the Find feature in Chapter 14, *Source Editing*, and more advanced uses in Chapter 22, *Advanced Features*.

The Find & Replace tab in the Find dialog box lets you search for any arbitrary text, whether HTML or text in a document, and replace it in a single file or an entire site, and anywhere in-between.

The Element tab is specific to HTML, and allows you to find and replace, update, or delete any attribute in any HTML tag. This can be useful in targeting individual kinds of tags or attributes.

The Site Reports tab uncovers errors and other specified items to help debug site problems or determine the usage of certain objects throughout a site.

Find is located in the Edit menu, or by pressing Command-F (Mac) or Control-F (Windows).

Find & Replace

Click the Find & Replace tab, then click the expand control next to the Find in Files checkbox (see Figure 19-54). The Find & Replace tab now displays controls that allow you to find and replace text in more than one file.

Figure 19-54
Finding in site
in the Find &
Replace tab

Click Find in Files to find
and replace in files.

Tip: Some Reversion

Sitewide Find & Replace is not reversible—you cannot revert to previous copies of the files after performing replaces. This is why we suggest that you always make a backup of your site before making significant sitewide changes. Consult Chapter 17, *Managing Sites*, for solutions on making backups before proceeding.

The options below control how files are processed.

Find in Files. Once you add files to the file list, checking this box lets you toggle between finding across many files or finding within the file that's currently open and in the frontmost window.

Script of String. If your pages use special encoding for other languages or alphabets and Treat Files In is set to Layout Mode, select the correct script (i.e., language or encoding) before performing searches.

Treat Files In. If Treat Files In is set to Source Mode, GoLive examines the underlying HTML of each page. If it's set to Layout Mode, the program looks only at the textual content of the pages, ignoring all HTML formatting.

Setting GoLive to Source Mode can be dangerous unless you're searching for highly specific bits of HTML code.

Selecting then Replacing

Your first task is to choose the files you want to search. Either add files one at a time by clicking the Add Files button, or add every HTML file in a selected site window by choosing that site from the Files From popup menu. You can also drag files from the Files tab into the Find & Replace file list, or drag them from the Desktop into the file list.

Remove files from the list by selecting one or more files and clicking the Remove button. As you add and remove files, a counter in the Files heading displays the current number of chosen files (see Figure 19-55).

Figure 19-55
Number of
files in list

Number of selected files

Finding in Files. Clicking Find All starts the process of scanning through each file; click Stop to halt the operation midway through. If there's one or more matches on the Find term, the number of matches or hits is displayed next to the file name. A counter in the Hits heading shows how many matches were made. An arrow points to each file as it is processed (see Figure 19-56).

Figure 19-56
Processing the
file and
number of
matches

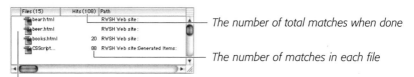

The number of total matches when done

The number of matches in each file

An arrow appears here while searching is underway showing which file is in use.

You can also use Find to get the first instance, and Find Next to step through each successive instance of a match. If you choose this method, each file with one or more matches is opened in turn.

Replacing in Files. Click Replace All, sit back, and watch the results. When GoLive is finished, it will provide a summary of the number of instances changed (see Figure 19-57).

Figure 19-57
Number of
replacements

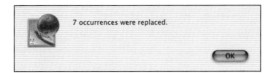
7 occurrences were replaced.
OK

You can step through changes visually file by file if you click the Replace button (which replaces but doesn't find the next instance) or click the Find & Replace button (which replaces and then finds the next instance), just as you would in an individual file.

Element

The Element tab is a ridiculously powerful tool that can strip your socks off while you're still wearing your shoes (this is only a small exaggeration). What Element brings to the table, as thoroughly discussed in Chapter 14, *Source Editing*, is the ability to target the contents of HTML tags and make intricate changes. You can find just Font tags where the text color is blue and change them to red, or find every instance of a width attribute in any tag that's set to 100 pixels and change it to 120 pixels.

Element offers a sitewide find-and-replace option that's very similar, but not identical, to Find & Replace (see Figure 19-58). You can add an entire site by choosing the site name from the Files From popup menu. Or, if you leave that menu set to Custom, you can add files by clicking Add Files. The number of files in the selection area is shown after the column header labeled Files.

Clicking the Start button causes GoLive to work on each file, and show an arrow pointing at the file currently being modified. The number of matches per file is shown in the Hits column next to that file. The overall number of

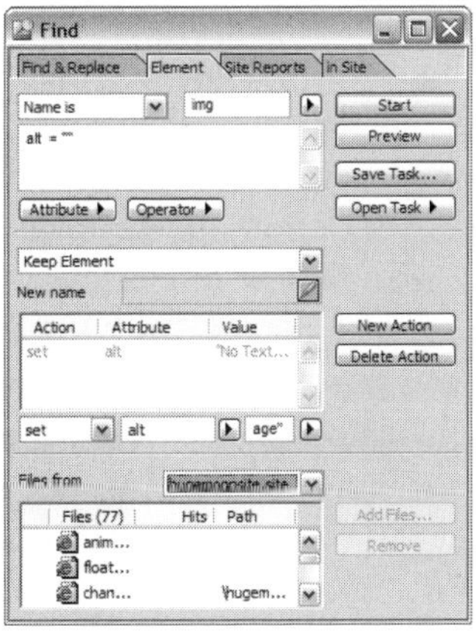

Figure 19-58
Element tab

matches is shown after the word Hits in that column. Preview shows what change would take place by quantity in each file, and also checks the syntax of your query.

Site Reports

The Site Reports tab automates a lot of debugging typically necessary to make a site bulletproof. It also helps find missing pieces that you know are somewhere, or it can simply produce a report about the frequency of certain elements or features you've used (see Figure 19-59).

The Site Reports tab searches the entire site without showing specific file-by-file results or allowing you to choose individual files. It has six tabs, corresponding to different aspects of site management.

You can save and load queries, which helps you create complex choices that you don't have to re-enter from scratch each time.

Before choosing criteria, you can select whether you want any or all of the criteria to be matched, which corresponds to an "or" or an "and" request of the criteria you enter.

File Info. Three checkboxes let you choose files by parameters related to file size, download time (based on specific download speeds), and modification or creation dates.

Errors. You can identify several kinds of errors. First, find pages that have something wrong with their title, such as untitled or one that includes the familiar Default Title error which affects potentially hundreds of thousands of pages on the Web. (Search for exactly—with the quotation marks—"Welcome to Adobe GoLive" at www.google.com to see what we mean.)

Second, you can find common image errors. You may want to omit these three attributes from an image, but they speed display and make pages useful for folks who can't or don't want to view images.

Finally, you can tag pages with errors or warnings as determined by GoLive's built-in HTML database in Web Settings.

Site Objects. Site Objects allows you to select items that appear in multiple tabs in the Site window: Components, email addresses, fonts and font sets, and colors. Fontset and Site Color correspond to the names of items in the Colors and Font Sets tabs; Font, Name, Value, and Color correspond to individual items that you select or define.

Figure 19-59
Site Reports

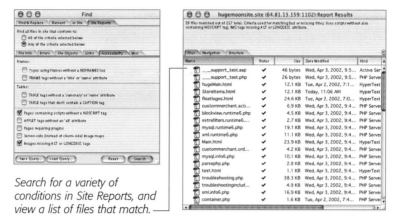

*Search for a variety of
conditions in Site Reports, and
view a list of files that match.*

You can also view files by navigation or link hierarchy.

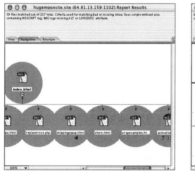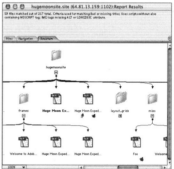

*Files that match conditions are
spotlighted in the navigation view.*

Tip: Retrieve Email

Before searching on email addresses in the Site Objects tab, remember to switch to the External tab and select Get References Used from the Site menu. This ensures that any email addresses you may have added when editing pages are available in the Containing Addresses popup menu.

Links. You can search for pages with any external links, but oddly not individual links. You can also search for specific extension and protocol types. This is useful if you want to know every page that references a Word document (.doc) or a secure site (https:).

Accessibility. The options listed in this tab correspond to common choices and omissions in Web site design that render pages unusable to a large section of the population who may be using alternate pointing equipment, be unable to type, or use a reader that speaks the contents of pages.

New in 6: Accessibility Checking

Bravo Adobe for adding this tab in GoLive 6 that should make it a breeze to improve how a person who cannot directly navigate pages through vision and typing can access a Web site. The U.S. government among many governments now promulgate rules by which electronic media must be rendered accessible for both governmental sites and sites developed under contract for agencies. For more information on this important topic, visit the World Wide Web Consortium's area for accessibility: www.w3.org/WAI/Policy/

Misc. This last option is fascinating. It's a nice option to be able to see everything that has a navigational relationship away from a file, in part just to make sure that your navigational scheme works.

Site Report Results

Click the Search button to perform a search. The results appear in a window with three tabs corresponding to three views of the results: Files, Navigation, and Structure (see Figure 19-59, earlier). The View palette offers identical options for these three tabs as for the Files tab, and the Diagram menu's Navigation and Links view (except cyclical links), respectively. (The Site Report's Files tab lacks Filename Status, Used, and Locked.)

The Navigation tab is locked in Spotlight mode—explained in Chapter 18, *Diagramming and Mapping*—highlighting the files in the navigational hierarchy of your site that match the criteria in your search. The Structure tab is similar to the Links view found in the Diagram menu, but it shows just the files that meet your criteria; nothing else.

Tip: Separate Windows

You can carry out as many searches as you want, and the results of each appears in a separate window.

Selecting files in any of these tabs works just like selecting them in the Site window tabs or Diagram views they mirror. You can also use contextual menus.

Selected items in any tab may be turned into a collection via the contextual menu's Create Collection item or the popout menu's Create Collection from Results item, just as in a design in the Diagrams tab. See Chapter 18, *Diagramming and Mapping*, for details on this feature.

The popout menu and contextual menu also allow you to export results as an HTML file or a tab-delimited file which can be imported into Excel or a database. Choose the appropriate option from the popout menu, or, in the contextual menu, select the option from the Export Results As File menu item.

Find Files in Site

For truly large sites, you might prefer an option to navigating up and down folders in order to find a specific file or two. The In Site tab of the Find dialog box allows you to do just that (see Figure 19-60).

The menus to the right of Find Item Whose let you define the search by Name or URL, and then by whether a file contains, is (read: is exactly), begins with, or ends with the text you enter below it. The popup menu to the right of that text field shows the last few searches you've performed.

Figure 19-60
Find files
in site

Export Site

Although GoLive works hard to keep a site clean, small, and efficient, you can wind up with extra files littering your site folder, jumbled HTML, and lots of embedded code that only GoLive could love. Fortunately, Adobe included a way to separate the wheat from the chaff through their Export Site feature. Export Site takes all of the files in the site and creates a duplicate with filtered HTML and a file structure you specify.

Configuring Export

Select Export Site from the File menu's Export submenu. A dialog box appears with several options in multiple categories that allow you to choose how your HTML files are cleaned up, and how the site is structured (see Figure 19-61).

Hierarchy. Since GoLive maintains its own internal database of files and links within a site, there are a couple options for the exported site's structure. The default is to stick with your current structure (As In Site), but you can also collapse your site in two ways. GoLive automatically rewrites all internal references in the process of exporting.

Figure 19-61
Export Site

Clicking Strip Options brings up further choices.

If you choose Separate Pages and Media, GoLive puts all HTML files into a folder called Pages; everything else on the site goes into a folder called Media. If you check Export Linked Files That Are Not Part of the Site, GoLive also creates a folder called Other into which it copies files from outside of your site folder referenced in the site. The home page is placed at the same level as the two folders (see Figure 19-62).

Figure 19-62
Separate pages
and media
option

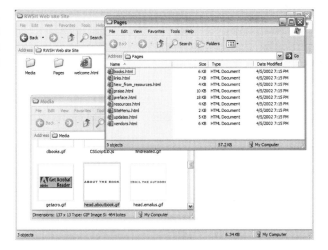

Tip: Choose Your Own Names

GoLive understands that we all have personal preferences. For example, we tend to store graphics in a folder called "images" in our sites, but we know others who use "gifs" or "graphics" instead. You can set the names of the folders that the Separate Pages and Media option creates through the Preferences item in the Edit menu. Click to expand the Site category, and select Export.

You can also select Flat, in which case all of the files in the site, including the home page, are placed in the same folder (see Figure 19-63).

Figure 19-63
Flat option

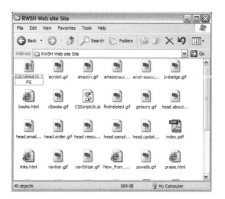

Publish state and links. In Chapter 20, *Synchronizing Sites*, we include an extensive discussion of how you can set and use the Publish state on files to control whether or not they are uploaded to an FTP or WebDAV server when you choose Upload to Server. These same parameters apply here.

If the Publish state of files and folders is set to anything but Always and you check both Folders and Files under Honor "Publish" State Of, the Publish state limits which files are uploaded.

The Export Linked Files Only checkbox is grayed out if you check the Honor "Publish" State Of boxes, as the Publish state takes precedence.

You can uncheck both Publish state options and then check Export Linked Files Only to export only those files that are part of the site's hierarchy, which can be viewed in the Diagrams tab's Navigation View. If you uncheck this box, all the site's files are exported.

Strip Options. Clicking the Strip Options button brings up the Strip Options dialog box, which offers some HTML cleaning tools; this dialog is identical to that used for FTP Upload. By checking different items, you can strip out any GoLive-specific tags during export, like those used for inserting Components; comments you've added to annotate your page; and extra spaces, tabs, returns, and linefeeds, collectively known as "white space."

Tip: Unnecessary White Space

HTML doesn't necessarily require extra spaces or linefeeds between items, which are put in just for readability (like when you're using the Source Code Editor to read raw HTML). You can reduce the size of a page by about five percent or more by removing these excess characters. Browsers shouldn't rely on this spacing to display pages correctly, but we have found exceptions where an extra or missing line return changes table formatting in Netscape.

Tip: Necessary White Space

The one exception to the "white space" rule is when you're using the Pre tag to format text. The Pre tag, listed as Preformatted in GoLive's Header submenu under the Type menu, lets you use the Return or Enter key to signify the end of the line instead of the HTML tags BR and P. GoLive is clever enough to avoid removing these necessary returns.

Tip: Global White Space

The Global tab of the Web Settings dialog box (found under the Edit menu or by pressing Command-Shift-K on the Mac or Control-Shift-K under Windows) lets you set how GoLive formats HTML for all pages created or modified after you change settings. Thus you can reduce the amount of white space used in your pages and then reformat your site; see Chapter 28, *Controlling Web Settings*.

Strip GoLive Data from Media Files removes any special codes that GoLive embeds into rich media for managing links in those files. The Flatten Script Library option shrinks GoLive's external JavaScript library to include just the code necessary for pages in your site; otherwise, it can include all JavaScript needed for any GoLive Action or DHTML behavior.

New in 6: New Strip Options

Both stripping GoLive data from media and the automatic option for flattening the script library are new in GoLive 6.0; they're both sensible additions for trying to export a clean, simple site.

Don't Show Again, Show Options Dialog, Site Settings, and Preferences. As with other dialog boxes in GoLive, checking Don't Show Again allows you to set and use your global preferences for exporting a site without accessing the dialog boxes again. You can also set your preferences in GoLive's Preferences with the Export settings under the Site category; or, by checking Site Specific Settings, you can have export preferences that work just on the current site. The options in both Preferences and Site Settings are identical to those that come up by default when selecting Export Site. However, there's an additional checkbox labeled Show Options Dialog which allows you to display the export options again after checking Don't Show Again.

During and After Export

Click the Export button to start the export process. GoLive first prompts you for a location to save the file in which the exported site is nested. GoLive doesn't copy anything in the site data or settings folders, nor does it copy the site file. Choose a location and a folder name and click OK.

If you've checked Flatten Script Library, GoLive first displays a dialog showing its progress in scanning all the files in the site for script references. It then brings up a progress bar that initially reads "Preparing". The bar offers more information if the operation takes more than a few seconds. The program rewrites and strips the files according to the options you choose in the Export Site Options dialog box.

When GoLive finishes exporting, it pops up a dialog box describing any unusual behavior, such as files that were exported but aren't referenced in the site (see Figure 19-64). Clicking OK dismisses the box; clicking Details creates an HTML file showing any problems plus the options you chose to create the exported site (see Figure 19-65).

Figure 19-64
Export report

Figure 19-65
Export details

Clean Up Site

Clean Up Site acts like a gardener: it roots out weeds (unused links, colors, email addresses, and font sets), while planting seeds (adding files and objects referenced in the site but not in the site folder). You can control Clean Up Site to a high degree, plucking out just the items that are necessary to keep your site tidy. Select Clean Up Site from the Site menu.

New in 6: No Warning!

We discovered during beta testing that the GoLive team turned off the default display of the Clean Up Site Options. When you select Clean Up Site, the basic clean-up operations are carried out without notice. To change this back, bring up Preferences (Site pane) or Site Settings and modify the Clean Up Site settings so that the Show Options Dialog is checked at the bottom.

The Clean Up Site Options dialog box allows you to (see Figure 19-66):

- Refresh the root folder, updating the GoLive site file to reflect any changes you might have made on the Desktop to the files and folders that comprise the local copy of the site. (This is exactly like selecting Refresh View from the Site menu, Site toolbar, or contextual menu.)

- Add files that are referenced in the site but not located in the site folder, and remove files not referenced in the site but which are located in the site folder.

- Add all elements used in the site that aren't already present, and remove unused ones.

Figure 19-66
Clean Up Site
Options

Clean Up Site lets you activate or deactivate the add and remove functions for each kind of behavior described above, on a tab-by-tab basis. That is, you can remove all unused font sets, but leave unused colors, external references, and unreferenced files.

Clean Up Site's options for adding and removing files are similar to Export Site, except that with Clean Up Site they apply to your current working version of the site stored locally—Export applies only to an exported copy.

Add Used files. By checking Files under Add Used, any files not found in the site folder that are referenced in the site are automatically copied into the site folder, and all references to them are rewritten. Checking Show List of Files to Copy previews and offers a choice of which files to copy over. (This option corresponds to the Export Site's checkbox labeled Export Linked Files That Are Not Part of the Site.)

Remove Files Not Linked. You can automatically remove files that aren't used in the hierarchy of files and links descending from your home page by checking Files Not Linked under Remove. As with adding used files, checking Show List of Files to Remove lets you preview which files are going to be moved to the trash, and selectively change that list.

Add Used and Remove Unused objects. For both the Add Used and Remove Unused areas, GoLive offers items corresponding to three Site window tabs: External, Colors, and Font Sets. These checkboxes correspond exactly to Get …Used and Remove Unused… items under the Site menu in those tabs.

Don't Show Again, Show Options Dialog, Site Settings, and Preferences. As with other dialog boxes in GoLive, checking Don't Show Again allows you to set and use your global preferences for exporting a site without accessing the dialog boxes again. The Show Options Dialog checkbox makes changes in your global Preferences when selected. You have to return to Preferences or use Site Settings to display the dialog in the future.

URL Mappings

Sometimes you may have split the content for your site among different servers; for instance, commerce pages may be located on a secure server while the rest of the site uses a normal Web server. (Don't say it's "insecure," as that phrase gives the shakes to those who are nervous about credit cards being stolen.) You might also manage content centrally, but locate it on several intranet Web servers with different names.

Whatever the reason, you don't want to create a separate GoLive site for each project, as the sites share many of the same files, graphics, and pages, and may even link extensively to each other.

The GoLive developers added URL Mappings to let you easily manage multiple sites without having to rewrite URLs or have many site files. URL Mappings causes GoLive to address files properly under any given folders in your site.

Take a simple case: you have your secure commerce Web pages in a folder called https and your regular content in a folder called http. These folders both live in the root level of your Web site.

First, you need to set up URL Mappings by bringing up Site Settings and clicking the URL Mappings pane. Click the New button to create a new mapping. Enter the fully qualified URL in the top field; in this case, that's "http:// secure.rwsh.com". In the bottom field, use the Browse button to navigate to the folder called https in your site's root. This URL will now be tacked on to the front of any link in that folder; the https part of the path is eliminated.

Now click New again and add the http folder. Type in "http://www.rwsh. com" in the top field and navigate to the http folder in the bottom. Click OK.

You're now ready to link between the two sites in the folder. Create a link that references the secure site. You can see in the Text Inspector that the link is correctly made with just the URL plus the page name, as the welcome.html file resides at the top level of the https folder.

How to upload these sites? Rob Keniger, an Australian GoLive power user who gave us the clarity of mind back in the year 2000 (so long ago) to understand URL Mapping, noted that on his Web server, he has a "web" folder that contains two folders named (as in this case) http and https. Each of those folders forms the root of the two Web sites; that is, the servers point inside them as the root. This allows him to use GoLive to update both sites simultaneously.

In many cases, however, your content may reside on two different sites, in which case you may need to use the FTP Browser or create multiple FTP server settings and switch between them as you upload files. (It may also behoove you to use Upload Modified Files, which doesn't check the remote files' modification date and time.)

Tip: Automatic Mappings

If you check Create URL Mapping for Alias/Shortcut to Folder in the Site pane of the Preferences dialog box, GoLive can automatically build mappings for folder aliases or for your shortcuts between parts of the site. The program prompts you to update all open sites; click OK to add the mappings to the site's settings. This technique can sometimes be easier for existing sites that you're splitting up, or site elements that you're duplicating between multiple sites.

Single File Ahead

Link management is GoLive's single most powerful feature; with control of it, you can maintain sites of hundreds, or even several thousands of pages without breaking a sweat—though you might make the argument for a faster machine despite GoLive's agility. Even the best program needs a little help from the processor.

Synchronizing Sites

Trapeze artists may perform their best work without a net, but Webmasters typically work both with the Net and with a net to prevent errors in their work from becoming immediately apparent to their Web site's next visitor.

When you're modifying a site, you're first making changes on a local copy stored on your computer's hard drive or a local area network (LAN). Any changes you make must then be synchronized with the Web server that handles actual requests from visitors. This Web server could be down the hall or across the planet, or even the same machine you're running GoLive on.

The standard method of transferring documents to remote file servers is via File Transfer Protocol, or FTP. A more recent development, WebDAV, is giving FTP a run for its money by offering better information about files and including built-in collaborative tools. GoLive offers two ways to connect to FTP and WebDAV servers: one for synchronizing your site's files with the Web server; the other for accessing arbitrary FTP and WebDAV servers to upload or download files, saving you the need to run a separate program.

Tip: Local Remote

If your Web server is located on a LAN, you might be able to copy your files to it through a Windows shared volume, Samba, an AppleShare file server, NetWare, NFS, or other programs with trademarked names. GoLive doesn't offer you any help (unlike Dreamweaver); it can't synchronize to a folder on a network drive. You might instead use the Workgroup Server in this scenario, which we discuss in Chapter 21, *Working in Groups*. We discuss other solutions later in this chapter.

WebDAV itself is used in two ways within GoLive: as a tool for collaboration, in which one or more users check files in and out of an actual live Web server with WebDAV support built-in; or, as part of the separately controlled Workgroup Server (WGS) that ships with GoLive 6.

Tip: Why Use WebDAV and Not WGS?

If you use the Workgroup Server, you have entirely separate controls from accessing a WebDAV site. We discuss WGS controls in Chapter 21. The advantage of using WebDAV's built-in GoLive features lets you work with an existing Web server installation; lets many kinds of tools work with that same installation (not just GoLive or Adobe products); and it requires less system administration than running a regular Web server plus WGS.

How It Works

FTP and WebDAV servers are pieces of software that run on server machines and allow files and directories of files to move back and forth between a client machine (the computer you're working and running GoLive on) and the server machine where the Web server typically also resides.

The software acts as an intermediary between the server's file system (and the related permissions to write files to that system), and users who need to upload and download files. The server might provide access both to hard drives directly connected to it and other storage available over a network or the Internet.

Both FTP and WebDAV require client software on your computer which communicates with the server software. The client interprets messages from the server and handles sending and receiving files.

FTP is an old and well-supported standard for exchanging files using rules at the server level to mediate which files a user has access to, including deleting, overwriting, and retrieving. WebDAV has those abilities as well, but adds

What's New in GoLive 6

Our most-asked-for feature materialized in GoLive 6: you can now tell GoLive that a file stored on your hard drive is up to date without having to re-upload the file to the server. The Sync Modification Times option lets you bypass a very tedious routine that could crop up when recreating a site file, moving files around, or having a variety of problems with your FTP site.

The Workgroup Server (WGS) employs WebDAV as a method of transferring files back and forth, even though it doesn't use the WebDAV tools that first appeared in GoLive 5. It uses slightly different controls for more powerful results. We discuss this fully in Chapter 21, *Working in Groups*.

file locking and other file details so that multiple people can edit a group of files at the same time without worrying about whether they have the latest "live" version of the file.

FTP

An FTP server lets you log in, tracks your actions, and handles the transfer of files and other details. The FTP server also protects the server machine on which it runs from unauthorized access, so users can't go messing with files that don't belong to them.

The FTP client talks to the server in a special language that's part of the FTP protocol and allows the two to understand each other. Fortunately, this language is hidden from view most of the time. The only time you see it is in error messages. But you don't otherwise need to know anything about this lower-level communication to understand what's going on.

FTP clients can be pretty stripped-down, requiring some obscure typed commands, as with the Unix "ftp" command or the similar program found in Windows 98/NT and later as ftp.exe (in Windows\System or similar locations). But FTP clients can also be highly graphical, hiding all the low-level FTP client/server commands entirely from view.

Tip: Graphical FTP

Some FTP clients for Mac and Windows—like Interarchy for Mac (www.stairways.com) and Ipswitch's WS_FTP Pro for Windows (www.ipswitch.com/Products/WS_FTP/index.html)—let you access remote files through an interface that resembles the Macintosh or Windows Desktop.

Hopefully, you won't need to use anything but GoLive's FTP clients, but we've found it useful on many occasions to have an easy-to-use FTP program lying around for emergencies and special cases.

Most of what an FTP client accomplishes is sending and receiving files; ditto for the FTP server. The built-in GoLive FTP clients handle that part fine, but they also offer limited control of lower-level settings for file access control.

WebDAV

WebDAV uses the same underlying method as the Web itself for exchanging files: HTTP (Hypertext Transfer Protocol). This is neither better nor worse than FTP, but it's one fewer thing to worry about for sysadmins, because they can use the same tools to administer access to a Web site and a WebDAV server.

Using Web transfers also tends to not raise red flags on firewalls, as the Web protocol is almost universally allowed to pass without comment or concern. This can be an advantage for networks that carefully lock down access.

A WebDAV server keeps a separate storehouse of information about the files it manages called metadata (data about data). This storehouse includes whether a file is locked or not. WebDAV servers can also store information about when and by whom a file was modified.

Because WebDAV uses the Web itself to transfer files back and forth, user accounts and security are provided in the same way as for a Web site. A Webmaster typically has a tool or a program that lets him or her create user accounts and passwords.

In future releases of the WebDAV specification, the protocol's promoters plan to add versioning and merging, which would allow a server to keep all revisions of a file (typically as diffs, or the differences between each draft), or allow multiple people to work on a file at the same time and merge the differences. Some WebDAV servers can already store multiple versions of a file, such as the Workgroup Server.

Tip: Installing WebDAV

To read more about WebDAV and find out how to install a non-Adobe server of your own, visit www.webdav.org.

Network Status

The Network Status display provides more information about what's happening behind the scenes when you connect to FTP and WebDAV servers. It's only when the network fails, a server won't let you connect, or some other untoward event occurs that you should need to consult the Network Status window.

To bring up Network Status, select it from the File menu. You can configure what shows up in the display from the Preferences dialog box's Network Status settings under the Network pane (see Figure 20-1).

If you really want to see everything that's happening, check Warnings and Status Messages. The former shows you messages a server sends your client when it doesn't like something but is willing to proceed anyway. Status messages indicate successful activities, like securing a lock or uploading a file.

The top pane shows the individual messages and warnings; the bottom pane displays the information received from the server. This information can help you or a system administrator troubleshoot thorny, frustrating problems which are all too common in file transfers.

Figure 20-1
Network
Status and
preferences

Configure Network Status's verbosity and depth in the Preferences dialog box (right).

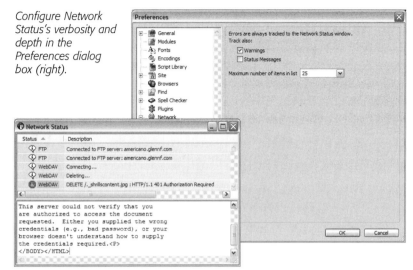

The icons conform to general standards, showing a stop sign for errors, a yield sign for warnings, and a talking head for status alerts.

Tip: Status Slowdown

Adobe engineers report that enabling Warnings and Status Messages can substantially slow down file transfer time. Keep these options disabled unless you really need to know what's happening to debug a problem.

Built-In Clients

GoLive offers two different methods of working with FTP and WebDAV. These methods may seem redundant, but both offer distinct advantages. The site-based FTP and WebDAV clients, accessed through the split-pane view on the right-hand side of the Site window, retain settings for a site. You can use these clients to synchronize the site's content on your local hard drive with the files and directories on a remote Web site.

The Site window's FTP and WebDAV settings are displayed by selecting the Settings item from the Site menu (see Figure 20-2), or by clicking the Site Settings button on the Site toolbar, and choosing FTP & WebDAV Server. If you click the FTP Server Connect/Disconnect or WebDAV Connect/Disconnect button on the Site toolbar without entering settings, you are presented with the Settings dialog box set to the FTP & WebDAV Server pane.

On the other hand, the stand-alone clients—called the FTP Browser and WebDAV Browser—let you easily connect to any server to which you have

Figure 20-2
FTP Site
Settings

been granted access, regardless of whether it's associated with a GoLive site file. Since we often find ourselves uploading and downloading files, the browsers can often save us the trouble of launching a separate application.

To access the stand-alone FTP client, type Command-Shift-F (Mac) or Control-Shift-F (Windows), or select FTP Browser from the File menu (see Figure 20-3). The WebDAV Browser is accessed by typing Command-Shift-W (Mac) or Control-Shift-W (Windows), or by selecting WebDAV Browser from the File menu (see Figure 20-4).

Setting Up a Connection

GoLive centralizes the entry of all server information for both FTP and WebDAV via the Edit menu's Servers dialog box. Bring up this dialog box and click the New Item button to create a new entry. Select an item and start editing in the fields below it to make live changes to that server. To remove them, select one or more server entries and click Remove Selected Items.

Figure 20-3
Stand-alone
FTP client

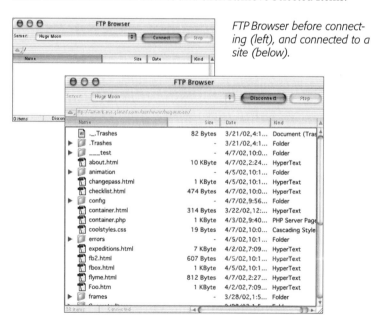

FTP Browser before connecting (left), and connected to a site (below).

Figure 20-4
Stand-alone
WebDAV client

When you want to use one of these servers in any area of GoLive that requires the use of a server, you can just select it from the popup menu.

New in 6: Central Servers

The Servers feature takes GoLive 5's mess of places where you could enter server information (at least five different areas) and puts them into one central, easy-to-update location.

To connect to any FTP or WebDAV site, you typically need three pieces of information: the FTP server name in Internet form, a username, and a password. You may also need to specify a path to a directory, especially in the case of WebDAV.

Tip: Paths for Servers

FTP servers can redirect an FTP client to the appropriate path for your account automatically, but WebDAV servers typically don't, so it's more important to get that path correct.

Nickname

The Nickname field is where you set the name that appears in various popup menus around GoLive when you're selecting which FTP or WebDAV server you want to work with. Make it descriptive: short, sweet, and smart.

Server

The server is the machine that's running FTP or WebDAV software. You need to enter its full name, like "ftp-www.earthlink.net". If you get a DNS error or a "server not found" error, double-check the address.

Directory

The Directory is the path from the root, or top level, of the server to the folder where your Web site files live. This pathway often bears little or no resemblance to the URL for your Web site. Servers can be configured to hide most directories from users, only letting them have access to a fraction of the remote files and folders for added security.

Tip: Automatic Paths (FTP)

Most of the time, you can just enter your account name and password, leaving Directory blank, and the FTP server automatically brings up the directory for the account. The FTP Browser and the Site window's FTP tab both show the path including the directory, even if it's not explicitly entered. (see Figure 20-5).

Figure 20-5
Path to FTP
files

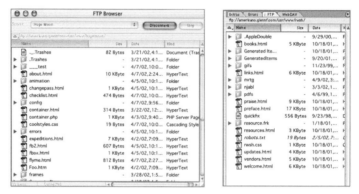

The FTP Browser (left) and FTP tab's view of files is similar, but not identical.

Tip: Display Full Path

The Display Full Path checkbox in the Site pane of the Preferences dialog box controls whether you see the full path at the top of the Site window's left and right panes. We recommend checking it: it's another helpful indicator of what's going on while you work.

If you need to enter a directory name, you have to ask the system administrator or Webmaster for the path; it's rarely intuitive, and there's no standard location for where files are found.

Tip: Entering a URL

You can paste in a URL, like ftp://water.forchocolate.com/www/nino/pinto/ into the Server field, and GoLive converts it to the correct Server and Directory information that it needs (see Figure 20-6).

Figure 20-6
Pasting URL
for conversion

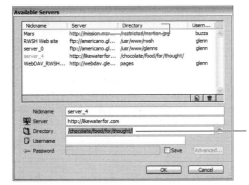

When you paste in a URL like
http://likewaterfor.com/
chocolate/food/for/thought/,
GoLive converts it to the
necessary format.

Tip: Forward, Slash!

Keep in mind that GoLive requires you to enter all paths in the default Unix/
Web format. Each directory is separated by a forward slash (/), even if the remote server is running some flavor of Windows or runs on a Mac. So a Windows
NT file path like C:\inetpub\wwwroot\site1\html\ would get entered as /inet-
pub/wwwroot/site1/html/ as an FTP path.

Username and Password

A system administrator or ISP should have given you a username or account
name and password when you were set up with file server access. These details
are typically the same ones you use for email. If you don't have these or get an
error when using them, it's time to check back with whomever operates your
site's systems.

The username and password allows a server to determine if you have permission to create new files, overwrite old ones, create directories, and perform
other file-related tasks (see the sidebar, "May I, Please?," later in this chapter).

If you don't check Save, you are prompted during each session for the
password the first time you try to connect to the server. After you enter it
once, you can connect, disconnect, and reconnect without re-entering it.
Closing the Site window or quitting GoLive resets this information, and you
have to enter the password again on your next use.

Tip: Anonymous Access

Not all servers require a username or password; some repositories of files offer
anonymous FTP access, where you log in as "anonymous" using your e-mail address as a password. However, it's extremely unlikely that you would ever be interacting with Web site content on a WebDAV or FTP server without an account
controlling access to the files.

Tip: Keychain (Mac)

Mac OS 9 and X incorporate a feature called Keychain that allows you to store passwords securely on your Macintosh by locking them with a passphrase and "strong" encryption. (We can refer you to book-length works on encryption if you're interested.) GoLive takes advantage of this feature, allowing you to store FTP and WebDAV passwords in the Keychain.

Bring up the Preferences dialog box, and in the Network pane check Use System Keychain for Passwords. If you want an extra level of alerts, check the Ask Before Adding Passwords box. See Appendix A, *Macintosh Issues & Extras*.

Tip: Saving Passwords

We don't recommend you check Save Password on a machine that's not physically secure—other than a Macintosh running Mac OS 9 or X using Keychains (see above). That is, if your machine is used in an environment where others have ready access to it, you're better off entering the password each time. Leaving the password on the machine allows anyone to connect to your live Web site and make changes, including—depending on how the server is configured—deleting all your files. (For many people, this isn't an issue unless you work in a college dorm, have really serious enemies in your company, or have a three-year-old who likes computers.)

Proxy

Your network administrator may tell you that you have to use a "proxy server" to access FTP and Web (and WebDAV) servers outside of your local network. If so, you need to set this in the Network pane of the Preferences dialog box. Check the Use FTP Proxy box and/or Use HTTP Proxy (for Web and WebDAV) and enter the values for Host and Port provided by the administrator (see Figure 20-7).

Figure 20-7
FTP proxy settings

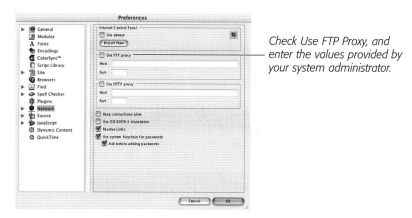

Check Use FTP Proxy, and enter the values provided by your system administrator.

Tip: Internet Config (Mac only)

If you're using Mac OS 9's Internet control panel or OS X's Network system preference for your settings and need to configure an FTP or HTTP proxy, see Appendix A, *Macintosh Issues & Extras*.

Advanced Settings (FTP)

Additional options for FTP connections appear when you click the Advanced button in the Available Servers dialog box. These options can help you connect to an FTP server that dislikes the default settings used by all FTP clients.

Use Passive Mode. The Use Passive Mode option reduces the variety of different conversations required to make FTP work between a client and server. Instead of using several different channels (think about someone juggling a bunch of phone receivers to have multiple dialogs), passive mode restricts all coverage to one channel which firewalls typically allow to pass without comment. If you can't make a clean connection with an FTP server, try this option; there's no penalty.

Keep Connections Alive. FTP has the unfortunate tendency to disconnect after arbitrary amounts of time, often set by the remote system adminstrator, or by default for a particular kind of FTP server. This option, when checked, tries to keep a continuous link to the remote server.

Tip: Unexpected Disconnect

GoLive doesn't provide a warning when the FTP server has booted you off. Most FTP servers disconnect after 10 or 20 minutes of idle time; others may disconnect after hours. If you try to act on files in the FTP window after a disconnect, GoLive displays the error message, "Unexpected Disconnect".

Use ISO 8859-1 Translation (Mac only). This option ensures that characters in the special Macintosh encoding set are mapped appropriately for the FTP server to handle them.

Resolve Links. With this option checked, GoLive follows down the path of symbolic links (also known as aliases or shortcuts) to figure out where the actual file on the FTP server resides. (See the sidebar, "Aliases, Symbolic Links, and Shortcuts," later in this chapter.)

Tip: No Port in a Storm

GoLive 5 and earlier allowed you to set the TCP/IP port on a per-server basis. This port is used as a conduit to connect to an FTP server. This is an incredibly obscure setting, and only a system administrator should tell you to use anything but the built-in default.

There's an easy fix if you do need a custom port number: add a colon and the number at the end of the server URL when you set up a server. For instance, "ftp://howdydo.com:1402" sets GoLive to connect via port 1402.

Connecting to the Server

Once you've set up all your parameters, connecting and disconnecting to a server is merely a matter of clicking a button or selecting a menu item.

Selecting

You can select the server you set up in GoLive's settings by selecting its name from the popup menu in whichever client or setting you're working with, whether it's one of the browsers or in Site Settings. For sites, you can also choose the nickname of a server from the FTP Server or WebDAV Server submenus in the Site menu.

New in 6: Multiple Servers

GoLive 6 allows you to choose among multiple servers quickly and easily when working with a site. It seems unlikely that you'd really need to upload the same content to multiple places, but we know folks who need this for testing: they synchronize first to their test site, and then, when everything works, they upload to their live site.

Connecting

To connect, you have many options:

• Click the Connect button in the FTP Browser or WebDAV Browser.

• Click the FTP Server Connect/Disconnect button in the Site toolbar.

• Click the WebDAV Server Connect/Disconnect button in the Site toolbar.

• Select Connect from the Site menu's FTP Server or WebDAV Server submenu.

• Select Connect from the contextual menu's FTP Server or WebDAV Server submenu.

If you get an error on connecting that isn't something obvious like "incorrect password," check out "Troubleshooting," later in this chapter.

Disconnecting

To disconnect, you have an equally large and parallel set of choices:

- Click the Disconnect button in the FTP Browser or WebDAV Browser.
- Click the FTP Server Connect/Disconnect button in the Site toolbar.
- Click the WebDAV Server Connect/Disconnect button in the Site toolbar.
- Select Disconnect from the Site menu's FTP Server or WebDAV Server submenu.
- Select Disconnect from the contextual menu's FTP Server or WebDAV Server submenu.

Abort

You can abort during the connection process by clicking Stop in the progress dialog box, which is labeled Uploading or something similar depending on the action you're carrying out. You can also press Command-period on a Macintosh or the Esc key under Windows to stop the process. (Abort, Command-period, and Escape are also used to stop other FTP behavior in progress.)

Local FTP

Because GoLive can't synchronize over a LAN like Macromedia Dreamweaver can, you might think you're out of luck. Not so! It's a trivial matter to set up your own local FTP or WebDAV server on virtually any computer. Because you're working over a LAN, you won't suffer from bandwidth problems, either. (You can also use the Workgroup Server that comes with GoLive, which has its own set of pros and cons, discussed in Chapter 21, *Working in Groups.*)

The trick is that the same machine your Web site lives on, or the file server from which the Web site references its files (such as a network volume on an NT, NetWare, or AppleShare, NFS, or Samba file server), needs to run the FTP or WebDAV server. Then you set up GoLive to communicate with that server.

For Mac OS 9, check out NetPresenz, a $70 FTP and Web server (www.stairways.com/netpresenz/). For Windows NT, 2000, or XP Professional, you can use a built-in FTP server that ships with the software. For Unix, almost every installation comes with wuftpd, a free FTP server. Mac OS X comes with built-in FTP support as its default method of file sharing.

For WebDAV servers, check out webdav.org/projects/, which should list the most current servers available, and see the sidebar, "WebDAV for Apache," below. You can compile or purchase Web servers with WebDAV support for all platforms; some options are entirely free.

Of course, there's some system administration cost associated with this. Someone has to figure out how to appropriately configure the FTP or WebDAV server. But it can provide you with LAN-based synchronization that would otherwise be unavailable in GoLive.

File Handling

Now that you've connected to a server through FTP or WebDAV, you can manhandle the directory's contents as much as you want—within the constraints set by the system administrator or Webmaster, of course.

FTP servers can separate out several different kinds of file changes. For instance, an FTP server treats deleting, overwriting, creating, and renaming a file as different activities, and can limit different users to varying activities. WebDAV is more lumpy, with users having the ability to write (delete, overwrite, create, or rename) or not, and/or lock or unlock files and directories so that others know whether those files are checked out or not.

The FTP or WebDAV server's configuration for your account establishes how you can act. You may be able to upload files to certain directories of the Web site, for example, but not others. The server might let you delete files in one folder, but not in another.

All of these parameters get defined by the system administrator or Webmaster, so you have to consult with them to apply parameter changes. If you're running your own FTP or WebDAV server, however, you control the

WebDAV for Apache

We've really tried to avoid this being a technical manual, but we'd like to provide some information on how to add WebDAV service to a free Apache server. When the previous edition of this book was published, an extension to Apache had just been released in its 1.0 form. This extension has been updated over the last 18 months, and continues to be improved; it provides all the necessary features so that GoLive can interact with on a WebDAV server.

(Folks, don't try this at home unless you've compiled software before or have a Linux box and want to experiment with this type of thing. However, any system administrator who has ever compiled Apache should have little or no trouble installing this simple add-on.)

Tell your system administrator to visit www.webdav.org/mod_dav/, which is the official

home page for the release. Installing mod_dav requires recompiling Apache 1.3, which is actually a relatively simple thing to do. Have the sysadmin follow the directions in the Install file that comes with the package. It requires him or her to separately configure mod_dav and compile it into an existing Apache build directory.

After compiling mod_dav and then recompiling Apache to include it properly, the Apache configuration file (often called httpd.conf) needs to be updated, which requires a bit of reading and experimentation. Fortunately, the mod_dav instructions give most of the answers.

If you're running Apache 2.0, which was released just as we finished this edition, WebDAV support comes with the server source code and can be enabled with a simple switch at the time of configuring for compilation.

means of access, and need only fiddle with settings to make sure you have enough permission to carry out your tasks (see the sidebar, "May I, Please?" later in this chapter).

With the FTP or WebDAV client windows open, you can now examine and manipulate files, folders, and links (see the sidebar, "Aliases, Symbolic Links, and Shortcuts," later in this chapter).

Status (FTP Only)

A status field at the bottom of the FTP tab and FTP Browser shows how GoLive is currently interacting with the FTP server (see Figure 20-8). The messages include, "Connecting…", "Connected", "Downloading Files", and other standard behavior. At any point while the status field shows an action in progress, you can click the Stop button to cancel the operation.

Figure 20-8
FTP status

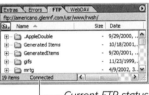

— *Current FTP status*

Locking (WebDAV Only)

WebDAV allows you to lock files and folders on the WebDAV server so that other users can see who is currently working on a file or directory. It also prevents them from editing the file or folder.

Select any files or folders in any combination and choose Lock or Shared Lock from the contextual menu; this is the only way to lock or unlock an item (see Figure 20-9). You unlock items the same way: select them and select Unlock from the contextual menu.

Force a lock's removal by selecting Reset Lock Status from the contextual menu. This is ill advised unless you're sure the lock is assigned incorrectly.

GoLive displays an icon for both kinds of lock in the Lock column of the WebDAV Browser or tab (see Figure 20-10). Lock is exclusive; Shared Lock allows others to work on a file while knowing that you've got it checked out as well. If you own an exclusive lock, you see a pencil, indicating you can write the file. An exclusive lock owned by someone else appears as a padlock icon. A shared lock shows up as two overlapping faces, like a group icon; it also has a pencil with it if you have permission to edit that file.

The lock ownership is shown with detail in the Lock tab of the File Properties Inspector, discussed below.

Figure 20-9
Locking and
unlocking files
via WebDAV

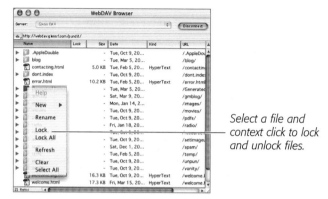

*Select a file and
context click to lock
and unlock files.*

Figure 20-10
Locked files

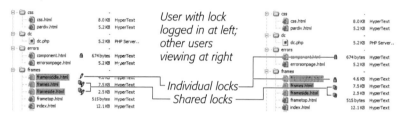

*User with lock
logged in at left;
other users
viewing at right*

Individual locks
Shared locks

Selection

The FTP and WebDAV clients show you the number of items in the current window just as the count appears in the Files tab (see Chapter 19, *Managing Files, Folders, and Links*). This appears at the bottom left of all clients (see Figure 20-11).

Figure 20-11
Selection
count

— *Count of selected items*

Refreshing

An FTP or WebDAV session can get out sync if changes may be taking place on a server, or if you take our suggestion and use FTP and WebDAV on the same Web server for different purposes. You can refresh the file list in any client window by clicking in the window and selecting Refresh View from the Site menu or contextual menu.

Live Editing

When you double-click any file in the FTP or WebDAV file list, GoLive downloads it to a temporary files location, nesting it inside folders that exactly match the directories in the path to that file via the remote server. GoLive also retrieves any graphics necessary to make the page display correctly and rewrites the links on the page to point to the local temporary storage of those files. (In fact, it's just like the Download Page feature under the File menu; see Chapter 2, *Layout*.)

Tip: Locked While Editing

In the case of WebDAV, the downloaded page is automatically exclusively locked while it is open so that someone else can't edit it. When you save, the file is unlocked.

Tip: Temporary Images

The temporary images directory is set in Preferences in the General pane under Images settings. It's the Import Folder. See Chapter 5, *Images*, for more on this setting.

After making any changes to this file, selecting Save will re-upload it to the same location you downloaded from. The danger with editing files in this manner is that image links are incorrectly rewritten to point to the temporary location; you can keep an eye out for this by using the In & Out Links palette to see the media file links from the page (see Chapter 19).

Live editing works with all the clients, and it's a neat trick despite the pitfalls. It combines the advantages of local editing with immediate updating. If you edit a file this way that's part of a site, you can use the Incremental Download item in the FTP Server submenu of the Site menu, or the corresponding button in the Site toolbar, to get the latest version to replace the local hard drive's copy of the file. Or, just drag the file over to the Files tab (see below for more on both options). Or, select the files and choose Download Selection from the FTP Server submenu.

Tip: GoLive Code

Remember that if you have special GoLive code embedded in an HTML file to support Actions or Components or other features, and you've stripped this on upload, you will lose all of this code if you then edit live off the server and download the resulting file into your local copy of the site.

Adding or Uploading

You can add files and folders from the Desktop or the Files tab by dragging them into the client window. The WebDAV clients warn you about overwriting files, while FTP doesn't seem to care—it assumes you know what you're doing.

The more sensible way to add files is to use the synchronization features, described later in respective FTP and WebDAV sections. Synchronization ensures that GoLive gives you a realistic and extensive confirmation of all the changes you're about to make. If you don't have permission to create or overwrite files, you get an appropriate error when you attempt it, such as "553 /usr/www/spamalot/guineve.html: Permission denied" (see Figure 20-12).

Figure 20-12
FTP error

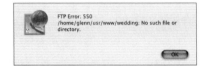

Unfortunately, you can't drag aliases or shortcuts into the FTP or WebDAV browsers or tabs and have them appropriately point to another file (see the sidebar, "Aliases, Symbolic Links, and Shortcuts," later in this chapter). A system administrator with direct access to the Web server file system has to create pointers, whether in Unix or any other operating system.

Downloading

Any file or folder can be downloaded via FTP to your local hard drive by dragging it onto the Desktop or into any open Site window, regardless of which GoLive FTP client you're using. If you drag a folder, all the contents are recursively copied; that is, all of the nested items, no matter how deep, are also copied.

If you drag an item into the Files tab of the Site window, and an item with the same name already exists, GoLive asks you whether you want to replace it.

When you drag a pointer or link from any WebDAV or FTP client onto the Desktop or into the Files tab, GoLive copies the file that the link on the Web server points to, rather than making a local alias or shortcut to the item. If the link points to a folder, it copies its entire contents.

Creating Folders (FTP only)

In the FTP clients, you click the New Folder icon in the Toolbar to create a new folder. The default name is "untitled_folder"; each subsequent folder gets a number added to it, like "untitled_folder2" and so on.

If you have a folder selected in any client when you add a new folder, GoLive nests the new folder inside the old one and names it by default just as above. GoLive automatically selects the folder you've just created, so you need to click elsewhere in the browser or tab if you want to create additional empty folders to avoid nesting them.

Moving

You can drag any file in any client window and move it to any folder depth. GoLive doesn't offer the same spring-loaded folder action in these windows as it does in all the tabs and windows elsewhere in GoLive, so you will have to click on the folder-expansion icon to display a folder or a file nested down more than a single level (see Figure 20-13).

Figure 20-13
Dragging files
across folder
levels

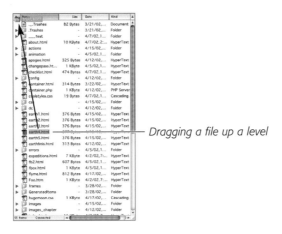

Dragging a file up a level

If you are nested down a level from where you want to relocate a file, drag that file onto the Path icon first to get to the right level, and then drop the file in the main window of that directory. If you've expanded the folder view and can see the directory level you want to relocate the file to, you just drag the file into the main window (see Figure 20-14).

Figure 20-14
Moving a file
into a
subdirectory

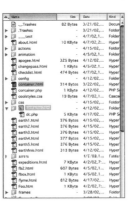

Tip: FTP Can't Move

Technically, FTP servers don't support moving a file. GoLive is actually copying the file to the new location and then deleting it from the old location. Because of FTP restrictions, you may not always be able to move files.

Renaming

You can rename a file in any client by clicking on the file's name. The file's title highlights, and you can type in a new name.

Tip: No Rename

If you don't have renaming permissions on the server, GoLive displays an error.

Tip: Don't Rename on Server

Renaming or moving items on the server is dangerous, because GoLive won't rewrite references to those items as it does when you rename or move files or folders in the file system part of the Files tab. You should only rename or move items on the server when you're trying to fix a problem or move a file or folder to a different name so that you can copy a different version of it to the Web site.

Deleting

Deleting files on a server requires specific permission. If you don't have permission, GoLive displays an error. If you do have permission, GoLive asks you, "Do you really want to delete the selected item(s)?"

Tip: No Undo Delete

You cannot revert after deleting a file from the server like you can when you delete a file out of the Files tab, so make sure you're doing the right thing before you click OK. One strategy we've found useful is dragging outdated files into a folder called, predictably enough, "oldfiles". We occasionally go through that folder and toss old items, but having them available for a while ensures that we don't lose any work in case we need to go back a few revisions to restore data.

FTP Inspectors

For viewing detailed properties of items accessed via FTP, GoLive provides three FTP Inspectors, one each for pointers, files, and folders. (If you don't know what a pointer is, see the sidebar, "Aliases, Symbolic Links, and Shortcuts.") These Inspectors are named FTP Link, FTP File, and FTP Folder, respectively (see Figure 20-15).

Figure 20-15
FTP Inspectors

FTP Link Inspector   *FTP File Inspector*   *FTP Folder Inspector*

The Inspectors collect details about the items and present them through a consistent interface regardless of whether you're accessing a Macintosh, Windows, Unix, or even a tiny matchbox-sized FTP server on the other end.

All three Inspectors show the modification date of the item, if available, and the URL to reach the item via FTP. The time might not match exactly what you think; remote FTP servers keep their own track of time and time zone. You can't copy and paste the URL; it's just there for reference.

They also show the permissions "map": who may read, write, and execute the file, folder, or link (see the sidebar, "May I, Please?", later in this chapter). Changing the set of permissions requires you to click the Set Rights button. For folders, you can also change all permissions for every file and folder inside of it, no matter how many levels deep those files and folders are nested, by checking the Recursive box.

Depending on how the FTP server is set up, you may not be able to change permissions at all. If you can't but need to, there's no way to change this in GoLive. You have to ask the system administrator responsible for the server to add "chmod" and perhaps "umask" support. (If they don't know what this means, you may just be out of luck.)

Tip: Execution Orders

You may wonder why all Web site folders accessed through a Unix FTP server have Execute checked for all three kinds of users. It's an obscure but important attribute; folders that contain items which everyone everywhere can access (whether as read-only or as modifiable items) must be set as executable. It's just one of those things that doesn't make specific sense on the surface, but is required for low-level FTP operations. So don't just uncheck Execute and click Set Rights because it looks wrong, as that will bar all access to the folder.

The FTP Link Inspector also shows the object pointed to in the Target field in the form of a URL. The FTP File Inspector reveals the file size of the selected document.

You can change an item's name on the FTP server by changing it in the appropriate FTP Inspector or by clicking the file name and typing a new one. However, making a change in this manner won't rewrite links from other files that point to it.

WebDAV Inspectors

GoLive offers as much information as it can about files and folders stored on a WebDAV server through the single Resource Properties Inspector (see Figure 20-16).

Aliases, Symbolic Links, and Shortcuts

Your mother may have told you that pointing isn't polite, but it is efficient at indicating exactly what you're talking about. Every major operating system lets you create multiple pointers to the same document, program, or folder so that you don't have to make multiple copies of the thing itself, but, rather, can reference it from many places at once.

Apple added aliases back in Macintosh System 7 so that users could, for instance, put links to their most common programs and documents in a single place, or get to a specific deeply-nested folder without opening window after window. Microsoft added the same functionality starting in Windows 95 through shortcuts. Unix has pretty much always had symbolic links.

What's the difference between aliases, shortcuts, and symbolic links? Not much. They all point to an actual resource and can be moved around and still retain their link to that resource. But they only occupy a few bytes and they don't duplicate the contents of the resource.

The biggest difficulty we find with pointers is that GoLive, since its 3.x incarnation, always downloads everything found underneath a pointer through its FTP clients. That is, you can't set it to only download the pointer itself, which would logically turn it into an alias or shortcut depending on whether you're running GoLive on a Mac or under Windows. (WebDAV doesn't display pointers, so it's a non-issue.)

When you attempt to upload an alias or shortcut, GoLive turns it into a plain text file on the FTP or WebDAV server, which doesn't serve much of a purpose either; or, it may balk at uploading it at all, saying, "not a plain file."

The FTP and WebDAV protocols don't allow you to create pointers, either; you have to get a system administrator to make them on the Web site file system.

We provide some strategies for dealing with both shortcomings in the respective "Synchronizing" sections for FTP and WebDAV later in this chapter.

Figure 20-16
Resource
Properties
Inspector

File tab   *Special tab*   *Lock tab*

Tip: Many Servers

Since WebDAV is a protocol, not a product, there are many implementations of it. Many of the features shown in this Inspector may not be populated with some servers and may have excruciating detail with others.

File tab. Normal file properties are displayed here, including name, full URL reference, creation and modification datestamps, and size. You can modify the name of the remote file by editing it in the Name field; we don't recommend this, however, as it doesn't update the local file name.

Special tab. The Special tab offers information that may be stored about a given file, such as the language, resource type, and so on. With the Apache WebDAV server, only Etag (a special, unique property assigned to a file transaction) and content type (the MIME type of the file) appear. (For more on MIME types, see "File Mappings" in Chapter 28, *Controlling Web Settings.*)

Lock. This tab shows the current outstanding lock or locks. The properties assigned to a lock include an owner, permissions (such as write), a scope (whether it's shared or exclusive to a single individual), a duration the lock is allowed (which can be "infinite"), and a lock token (used for internal record keeping). If an item has multiple shared locks, they all show up here.

Tip: XML in Action

The information shown in the Lock tab is generally stored as part of an XML document. It's a good example of how rich information can be stored in XML instead of requiring complex proprietary databases or other structures. WebDAV servers and clients can both read and write XML, so you don't need to use a particular WebDAV server.

FTP Synchronizing

GoLive includes a simple, powerful set of controls for keeping your local copy of the content and the remote Web site content synchronized over FTP. These features let you synchronize in either direction, and offer some control over what gets uploaded from the local version of the Web site.

Tip: Site Window Sync

Note that synchronization only works with the FTP tab, not the FTP Browser, because you need a local set of files to compare.

Tip: Your First Time

The first time you perform Upload Modified Items with a given site file, GoLive automatically uploads everything, even if the remote files have identical modification dates. GoLive has to make a record in the site file of the fact that it did synchronize once. There's an override for this, however; see "Sync Modification Times All/Selection," below.

If you upload via FTP, only the files on your local hard drive that meet certain criteria compared to those on the FTP server are uploaded. There are four options, coupled with an extra to reset some of GoLive's internal records.

These options are reachable through the Site menu's FTP Server submenu, the Site toolbar (all except Sync Modification Times Selection/All), and the contextual menu's FTP Server submenu (see Figure 20-17).

Figure 20-17 FTP upload options

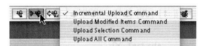

- **Upload Modified Items.** GoLive compares the modification date and time of each local file with its counterpart (if any) on the FTP server. If the local file is newer, it uploads it. This operation can take quite a while with larger sites, as GoLive must check the timestamp on every file on the FTP server. You can bypass this check by using Incremental Upload, or reset the time by using Sync Modifications Times.

Tip: Merging Updates

If you've edited both the file on the FTP server and in your local copy of the site, GoLive won't harmonize the differences and merge the file. You have to do that yourself, using Microsoft Word's Merge Documents feature or other software.

That's why it's wise to always keep track of the latest "live" version of the file, or which copy has been most recently modified.

- **Incremental Upload.** GoLive only uploads files that have been modified in the local site folder since its record of last uploading, but it doesn't check the modification time on the same files stored on the server. This is a way to add missing files quickly.

- **Upload Selection.** Choose some items in the Files tab and invoke this option to force an upload of the selected items.

- **Upload All.** This option combines Export and Upload. GoLive does a full export of the site to a local folder and then uploads the entire site. This could be useful if your remote site had become very out of sync and you wanted to simply start from scratch. You could delete the remote site entirely and then select Upload All. However, choosing Incremental Upload would accomplish the same result.

- **Sync Modification Times All/Selection.** Choosing either of these options forces GoLive to update its internal tracking timestamp for all or selected files in the local copy. This allows you to bypass re-uploading files that you know are already in sync.

New in 6: Sync Saves

We've seen many cases in which GoLive loses track of when a file was modified on the remote server, typically after a crash in which the GoLive site file wasn't saved after an upload. FTP also lacks a good way to tell client software what the server thinks the current time is; GoLive uses some clever tricks to determine this offset, but sometimes misunderstands the difference. Sync Modification Times solves this whole category of problems, eliminating lots of wasted re-uploading time, and it's something we've been begging Adobe to add since GoLive 4.

In contrast, the single option for downloading, Incremental Download, only retrieves files from the FTP server that GoLive thinks are newer. (The timing issue may be problematic, though; FTP servers and your local machine can occasionally be out of sync, although GoLive tries to compensate.) You can also choose files and select Download Selection.

Tip: Beware Downloading

Watch out for downloading files if you've used any of the HTML code-stripping options—see the Strip Options section later in this chapter for more details.

Getting Set to Synchronize

When you're ready to upload, select which upload option to use in the Toolbar, and then click the upload buton. If you're just trying to resync file timestamps, select Sync Modification Times from the FTP Server submenu. In both cases, you're presented with an Upload Options or Sync Times Options dialog box with identical choices.

Publish State and Linked Files

The two checkboxes for Honor Publish State and Upload/Sync Linked Files Only represent just two separate methods of deciding what to upload or on which files to sync time, even though you can check or uncheck combinations of them (see Figure 20-18). These options are more about deciding what *not* to select than which items are actually acted on.

Figure 20-18
Upload
options

The Honor Publish State checkboxes mediate whether files and folders that have Publish set to Never or If Referenced (files) or If Not Empty (folders) get uploaded or synced.

If you check Honor Publish State for Files or Folders, GoLive relies on the Publish flag set for each item, which is set to Always by default.

Figure 20-19
Setting the
Publish state

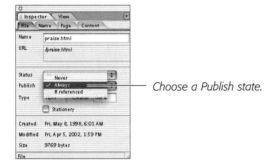

Choose a Publish state.

Figure 20-20
Setting
multiple
Publish states

This Inspector appears when you have multiple files or multiple folders selected, allowing you to set the Publish state for all at once.

- If the Publish flag is set to Always, GoLive always uploads or syncs the item if it meets the criterion (modified, incremental, selected, or all).

- If the flag is set to Never, the item (and its contents, if it's a folder) isn't uploaded or synced regardless of the selected criterion.

- If it's a file and set to If Referenced, GoLive uploads or syncs it only if the item appears in the navigation hierarchy; that is, if the item is referenced from any link descending from the home page you've defined. You can view the navigation hierarchy via the Diagram menu's Navigation view item.

- If it's a folder, and Publish is set to If Not Empty, and the folder has any contents, GoLive creates the folder on the FTP server if one doesn't already exist. However, this option only matters if all the items inside the folder aren't set to upload or sync on their own. GoLive creates any necessary folders for enclosed items that get uploaded or synced.

- If you check either Files or Folders under Honor Publish State, the Upload/Sync Linked Files Only setting is grayed out. (By the way, Windows shows Pages and Groups, which means the same thing, but is an accidental leftover from GoLive 4 and 5, still not fixed.)

With Honor Publish State's settings off and Upload/Sync Linked Files Only checked, GoLive only transfers or resets the time stamps for files that meet the upload or sync criterion and that are in the link hierarchy as described just above. If a new file is in a folder that doesn't exist on the FTP server, this option automatically creates that folder.

Show List of Files to Upload/Sync

When either uploading or syncing files, having this option checked displays all files that are affected. You can then deselect individual files by unchecking them. You can view files by folder or as a flat list omitting folders—which are created as necessary on the FTP server—by unchecking Show Folder Structure (see Figure 20-21). We prefer to view by folder as it's a cleaner organization and we can turn off an entire folder using this method.

Figure 20-21
Flat and
structured
upload

Structured by folder showing just necessary items to upload.

Flat list omitting folders.

Tip: Uncheck All

If you want to uncheck all files, it's better to uncheck Show Folder Structure, uncheck the box at the top of the list—which unchecks all files—and then check Show Folder Structure again (see Figure 20-22). It sounds complex, but you get used to it, and it's more efficient than unchecking each folder one at a time.

We always leave Show List of Files to Upload/Sync checked so we can make sure the right files have been swept up in the net.

Strip Options (Uploads Only)

You can filter your HTML at the time you upload it to strip out extra spaces, GoLive-specific tags and attributes, and embedded comments, as well as clean up GoLive's JavaScript library (see Figure 20-23). This stripping action is useful in three respects:

Figure 20-22
Unselecting all
uploads

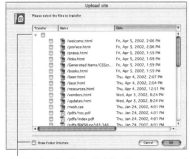

1. Show files to upload with Show Folder Structure checked.

2. Uncheck Show Folder Structure and then uncheck the top Upload box.

3. Check Show Folder Structure again, and now you can choose individual folders to upload.

Figure 20-23
Strip HTML
Code dialog
box

1. It doesn't expose to the world (the world that views source on HTML pages) information you may have inserted in a page for your own reference.

2. It removes GoLive tags, making your HTML that much cleaner (and able to pass validation checks some companies require for their HTML pages).

3. It makes pages slightly smaller, and can dramatically reduce the JavaScript library, reducing download time by microseconds to seconds for users.

    Strip Options has five checkboxes. The first three apply only to HTML pages.

•   **Adobe GoLive Elements.** This removes any GoLive specific code, such as embedded references to Components or other GoLive tracking information.

This option helps keep HTML validators from choking on your HTML. (See the "Export Site" section of Chapter 19, *Managing Files, Folders, and Links*, for more details on this as well.)

- **Comments.** Embedded comments may boost page size; this checkbox removes those. (Some comments are critical, however, for content-management system templates.)

- **Spaces.** Spaces are optional within HTML with some exceptions. Removing them can reduce a page size by a few percentage points or more.

May I, Please?

Every computer that lets users access its files remotely has a built-in set of policies that control which users can access and modify files. These policies are called file permissions, and correspond to settings attached to each file and directory. (Mac OS 9 is the sole exception in which file permissions are set just by folder, not file.)

For users who haven't had to deal with remote files over a network, file permissions can be intimidating. The Mac and Windows systems generally let you read, write, delete, and overwrite all of the files on the local drive; you can lock files in different ways on both with a little effort. But when you share your files or access shared files, there has to be some intermediation so that any user passing by can't destroy your Web site.

File permissions define who owns a particular file or directory, what group (if any) may have special access to it, and how the rest of the world can interact with it. The owner, the group, and the world can each have separate permissions set for access. The owner and groups are typically set up by user accounts on a system; the owner is a login name for a particular user, while a group contains any number of users and/or other groups, depending on the operating system.

Each platform has somewhat different ideas about permissions (see Table 20-1). GoLive maps this behavior by showing group read and write permissions checked for any file you select and view with the FTP File Inspector. If you try to change the settings and click Set Rights, you get an error: "FTP Error: 404, Parameter Not Accepted."

Table 20-1 Permission categories by platform	GoLive calls it	Owner	Group	Other	Permissions
	Mac OS 7 to 9.x	User	Group	Everyone	Folder only
	Mac OS X	User	Group	Everyone	Files/folders
	Windows 98/ME	*	*	*	Folder only
	Windows XP/NT/2000	User	Group	Everybody	Files/folders
	Unix/Linux	User	Group	World	Files/folders

*Windows 98/ME supports password-based file sharing and permissions, but FTP servers running under Windows 98/ME may map different permissions settings onto files and folders.

- **Strip GoLive Data from Media Files.** GoLive can embed some of its own code into media files, including GIF, JPEG, PNG, SWF, and SVG files. Check this to extract that information before upload.

- **Flatten Script Library.** The Script Library is a text file that GoLive uses to centralize all of the JavaScript code needed for its DHTML animation, Actions, and other snippets throughout the program. This file can get large over time if you add and remove Actions in your site's pages. Flattening the Script Library examines all HTML in a site and determines which specific code is needed; it can reduce a 50K file down to 1K. (We talk about flattening extensively in Chapter 26, *Applying Actions.*)

Tip: Download after Stripping

The downside of stripping out HTML chunks when uploading is that your remote page no longer matches your local page. If you have to download that page back to your local hard drive, the page may be missing critical Components you use throughout a site; these appear as just regular HTML when the GoLive tags are stripped.

Don't Show Again

Checking this box allows you to bypass the Upload/Sync Options dialog box the next time you upload; GoLive follows the settings you've checked or unchecked. If you check this box, you must go to the Preferences or Site Settings dialog box to force GoLive to once again show you the dialog box each time (see Figure 20-24).

Uploading Process

As noted earlier, there are four ways to upload files via FTP. Choose the most appropriate method from the FTP Server submenu of the Site menu or from the popup menu that emerges from the FTP Upload button to the right of the FTP Server Connect/Disconnect button.

Figure 20-24
Don't Show
Again

If you check Don't Show Again in the Upload Options dialog box, you have to check the Show Options Dialog in Preferences to restore it.

GoLive then presents you with the Upload Options dialog box, followed by the file list, as described above.

First Time

The first time you transfer a site to a remote server, GoLive transfers all the files and creates all the directories, essentially initializing the site.

Tip: Bypass First Upload

Even if all the files are identical on the local hard drive and remote FTP server, GoLive wants to synchronize them in order to set up the modification time-stamp for each file. You can bypass this by selecting Sync Modification Times All from the FTP Server submenu.

Choosing Files

It's a good idea to choose to upload all files that GoLive suggests, as the program usually figures out which ones are the right ones. If you upload some and not others, you face the problem that some of your links won't work on the live site.

You can select the files that you want to upload and use the Upload Selected Files option to bypass GoLive's inclination to upload all files.

Out of Sync Uploads

If you delete or reorganize your content in the Files tab, GoLive can't track these changes and fix them remotely. This means that if you remove a file in the Files tab, it won't be automatically removed from the FTP server when you synchronize.

Similarly, if you move content around, such as transporting all your images from the root level of the Web site to their own folder, GoLive doesn't reshuffle them per your new local arrangement on the FTP server. Instead, it treats the new folder as a new object, and wants to upload it and all the contents.

To fix this problem, you have to delete, rename, or move the corresponding files on the server. Or, you can delete all the items affected, and use the Upload All feature to reinstall a clean copy. This latter solution is easier, but it can take a while if the site is large and you don't have sufficient bandwidth.

If you need to create new pointers, delete old ones, or move existing ones via GoLive—well, you can't. The FTP protocol, as we noted earlier, doesn't have a provision for coping with pointers. You have to ask your system administrator to make these changes on the server itself. (If the system administrator is someone other than yourself, ask politely.)

Tip: Staging Site

To avoid problems that sometimes happen when taking content live, we suggest (if possible) setting up a mirror or "staging" site for help with synchronizing. You can use this location to test the upload and make sure everything worked right. You can then use a stand-alone FTP program to copy the files to the real Web site.

It's possible to set up a staging site to test new content by having a directory pointed to by a separate Web server. Or, you can even nest your test inside a folder on your main Web site. It may sound like a bit of extra work now, but trust us: experience has taught us the value of mirroring sites in progress.

Uploading to Multiple Servers

Updating a site that's split between multiple servers can be tricky, and may involve the use of the URL Mapping feature. We discuss this feature and its implications in Chapter 19.

Exporting

If you want to restructure your site to use a flat organization, such as putting all the media files in one folder and all the pages in another, but keep your local copy intact, you can export your site and then upload those files to the server using the FTP Browser. See the "Export Site" section of Chapter 19.

Downloading

On occasion, you may need to edit a file on the Web server itself, rather than editing files locally and uploading them. Or, a server might generate files for you automatically that you need to retrieve.

By clicking Incremental Download in the Site toolbar or selecting that item from the Site menu's FTP Server submenu, you can download all files from the server that were modified more recently than the local copies.

Tip: Sync Down

If GoLive's idea of "more recently" isn't quite right, use the Sync Modification Times feature to fix it. Even though synchronization seems like a feature related to uploading files, it's just as valuable when downloading because GoLive uses the same timestamp for incremental downloads.

GoLive also downloads any folders and files which aren't found in the local copy of the site.

You can also select one or more items and choose Download Selection from the FTP Server submenu.

Tip: Overwriting Home Page

In order to overwrite the page you chose as your home page (see Chapter 19), you must use the Download from Server feature. The workaround is to choose any other file in your site, bring up the File Inspector's Page tab, and check Home Page. You can now download the real home page, and then reverse the process to make it the home page again (see Figure 20-25).

Figure 20-25
Downloading home page subterfuge

1. Select another page to substitute as your home page for this subterfuge.

2. Drag the home page from the FTP tab into the Files tab.

3. Reset your home page back to the real McCoy.

Avoiding Pointers

The Incremental Download feature downloads everything that's not present in the local copy, including pointers. We haven't figured out a workaround that prevents this behavior, and it can generate an awfully long list of files to review.

The solution, if you have a lot of links or many files nested underneath them, is either to drag specific files you need from the FTP tab to the Files tab, or to uncheck inappropriate items from the files list that appears when you use Incremental Download.

Out of Sync Downloads

As noted earlier, GoLive doesn't synchronize file deletions or move between local and remote copies. So if you have some orphan files on the Web site, the Incremental Download command tries to download these files, as there are no local copies. Either delete these from the Web site, move them, or uncheck them from the files list displayed after you select the command.

WebDAV Synchronizing

Compared to FTP synchronization, WebDAV is a walk in the park. You have fewer options, but it's a lot more visual about what's happening.

Synchronizing, Uploading, Downloading

After you connect to the WebDAV server through one of the methods discussed earlier, you have three options for synchronizing: Synchronize All, Upload Modified Items, and Download Modified Items. The three buttons in the Site toolbar correspond to these three items; the WebDAV submenu of the Site menu and contextual menu also makes available the same options for items selected in the Files or WebDAV tab.

Tip: FTP/WebDAV Combo to Solve Problems

With WebDAV, you can't modify permissions through an Inspector, but you can still get errors when you don't have the right file permissions when you attempt to delete, download, upload, or overwrite files. Sometimes, we set up both an FTP server and a WebDAV server pointing to the same directory: we use the FTP Inspectors to change permissions and WebDAV to handle synchronization.

Choosing any of these options brings up the same dialog box for uploading and downloading (see Figure 20-26). The only difference is that choosing Synchronize All looks for modified files both locally and remotely, while upload and download look on just the local or remote directories, respectively.

Upload and download actions. This dialog shows a list associating all local and remote files with a clickable icon in the middle between them that indicates the action to take place. There are four possibilities for each file: upload, download, skip, or delete.

A fifth icon, a yield sign, appears for files that are located in both locations and have different modification times; yield is the same as skip, as GoLive doesn't act on those files without guidance.

Figure 20-26
WebDAV
Synchronize
dialog box

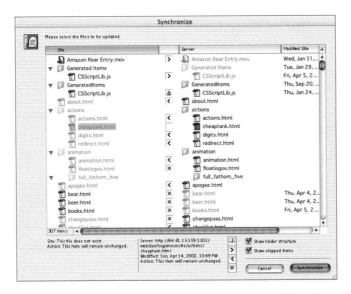

You can click the icon to cycle through any available options, or select one or more files and click the icon in the legend below the files list to set that option for the entire selection. If the yield sign is displayed, clicking the icon still rotates through available choices.

If you select a folder and click any of the icons at the bottom, any actions you select are applied to all nested files, even though an icon doesn't show up for folders.

Show Folder Structure. If you check this box, the Synchronize dialog box shows you the files organized by folders, including nested folders. Unchecking it shows you the alphabetical listing of all files.

Show Skipped Items. Items that don't need to have an action performed on them, or ones that you manually chose and clicked the Skip button, can be omitted from the file list by checking this box. Unchecking it redisplays them in case you need to make changes to their upload and download behavior as well.

Information. When you select a file, GoLive displays a fair amount of information in two areas at the lower left of the Synchronize window. On the left is information about the local file ("site"); on the right, about the remote file ("server"). The text describes precisely what GoLive will do.

Errors. Errors are displayed in the Network Status dialog box with a lot of detail—hopefully enough to troubleshoot or report to a sysadmin.

Selecting

You can choose files in either the Files or WebDAV tab and drag them over to the opposite tab. GoLive brings up a transfer progress bar and asks if you're sure you want to copy the files. Often, this involves GoLive first deleting the existing files and replacing them with the ones you want to copy.

Exporting

WebDAV synchronization doesn't allow you to strip HTML code like you can with FTP. To achieve that, export your site using the Export Site feature and then upload it via the WebDAV Browser. See Chapter 19.

Out of Sync

WebDAV suffers from the same problem as FTP: when you delete files locally, they are not deleted on the WebDAV server; when you move files locally, they aren't moved remotely. The Synchronize dialog box offers the ability to delete files, but this still doesn't synchronize them.

If you wind up out of sync, you may need to delete files remotely and then upload them again from the local directory using Synchronize.

Troubleshooting

Some common problems with FTP and WebDAV that GoLive can't control might plague you. Here are the symptoms, and what you can tell a system administrator to do to fix it.

GoLive passes through errors that the server reports. Many of these are semi-opaque, and provide little information for troubleshooting the problem. However, Network Status can provide quite a lot of information, as you can review it for the actual messages sent back by the server in a transcript of the session.

For a list of all FTP error codes, see the following page at our Web site for reference: www.realworldgolive.com/ftpcodes.html. This list is abstracted from the FTP protocol description. A system administrator may want the specific code, so the more information you can provide, the better.

WebDAV's errors are more descriptive, tending to mirror or be identical to those created by a Web server. Anything that doesn't make sense, report to the system administrator.

Connection

Connecting to a server should be straightforward, but there are enough variables to complicate the process.

Wrong username or password (FTP). If you enter the wrong username or password for FTP, GoLive should tell you specifically that either the username or password is incorrect. If you think you're using the right information, confirm it with the system administrator. We've found that a typical cause for a wrong username or password is incorrect capitalization. Often, it's critical to type a username or password exactly, with the same caps and lower case, as what's provided to you. It's also easy to hit the Caps Lock key by accident, as you can't see what you're typing when you enter the password.

Wrong username or password (WebDAV). For WebDAV, GoLive fails to provide any warning unless the server balks. We've found that with the way Apache is set up, for instance, you receive no warning, but you cannot edit any files without then generating errors in the Network Status window.

Wrong host name. If you enter the host name incorrectly you should get a DNS error, which means that the domain name you entered with that particular machine or host name doesn't have an Internet address. Double check the information provided and contact the system administrator if it persists.

No response from server. The first time you try to connect to a server, if you don't get a response in a reasonable period of time, it might be that the server is down or not reachable from your Internet location. If this persists, contact the system administrator with the dates and times you tried to connect. It's possible that an Internet firewall is blocking connection to that particular server or all kinds of FTP and Web connections.

User not authorized (FTP). Systems often have to be configured to allow users to access them via FTP. Your account may be properly set up, but when you try to connect you get "530: Login failed: user not authorized." The system administrator will need to double check his or her settings for your account to confirm you have access.

The server did not send a root resource... (WebDAV). If you connect to a server that isn't running a WebDAV component, you may get this error. Check that you're connecting to the right place.

GoLive can't support server. From your perspective as a user, the server's operating system and type of software are invisible. However, there are dozens (maybe hundreds) of different FTP server software packages, and GoLive only supports the most popular for Unix, Linux, Windows 98/NT/2000/XP, and Mac OS 9 and X.

The GoLive manual doesn't provide a list of supported servers, but you may get no error—and no connection—when it encounters one that uses a different format from the established standards.

WebDAV is a newer standard with more uniformity and fewer options, so GoLive should support any WebDAV compliant server. However, we're sure quirks will appear.

File List

After GoLive connects to the server, it should quickly display a list of items in the directory you've connected to. If you don't get this list, the problem could be one of the following situations.

Permission problem. The account's directory isn't set up to allow you "read" access, meaning that you can't see the files in them. The system administrator must make system changes to make this work for you.

Proxy server or network interference. Networks with firewalls, proxies, or other intermediaries might require you to check Use Passive Mode in order to make an FTP connection work, or you may have to configure a Web or FTP proxy in the Network pane of Preferences. In these cases, you might be able to connect to the server, but it won't download or upload files, and it might not be able to send a file list.

Method Not Allowed (WebDAV). WebDAV servers have to be configured to allow WebDAV access to directories. If the one you attempt to access isn't configured correctly in general or for your username and password in particular, WebDAV offers an error like "PROPFIND / : HTTP/1.1 405 Method Not Allowed". Check with your sysadmin.

Unknown mystery (FTP). Sometimes on the Macintosh, we find that we just can't use FTP any longer. Connections get made, but no file lists are ever transferred. Rebooting the Mac through a normal restart from the Finder usually fixes the problem. We haven't found an explanation for this behavior, even after years of looking for one.

Can't Access Directory or Upload

You may find that there are areas of a site you can't reach via FTP or WebDAV, or certain directories won't allow you to upload files. Both of these problems are permission related, and require the system administrator to change permissions to allow you or your group read, write, and/or execute permission to the appropriate directories.

Upload directive (FTP). Additionally, if you can't upload, many FTP servers require a separate "upload" directive that allows a user to login and upload to specific directories. If the directory isn't specified in that directive, the user can't add, overwrite, delete, or rename files.

Configuration for upload (WebDAV). A WebDAV server has to be configured to allow users to perform each kind of file activity, including adding new files to the directory. This directive might be missing.

Web site is inaccessible (FTP). You may find that Web surfers can't reach files on your Web site. GoLive allows you to change file permissions as long as the FTP server is configured to let you change them. If users can't reach your site, make sure the files you've added are set, under the FTP File or FTP Link Inspector, to Read for Other. For folders, both Read and Execute must be checked for Other.

If you click Set Rights and get an error, then you will need the system administrator to make the permissions changes for you.

For Mac OS 9 Web servers, you only need to set folder permissions via the FTP Folder Inspector to Read and Execute as files lack permission controls.

If you're using WebDAV, you can't change file permissions. This is why we recommend having both FTP and WebDAV access for your sites.

Locked and (Up)loaded

With a mastery of staging and synchronizing in hand, keeping your site up to date involves a minimum of effort and maximum of aplomb.

It's important to remember that even experienced Internet hands find themselves flummoxed facing file transfers on occasion, as the number of potential problems in correctly setting up FTP or WebDAV access on a server can be manifold. However, a good network or system administrator can make your part of the job easy: figuring out what goes where and when it needs to get put there.

CHAPTER 21

Working in Groups

No Web site is an island, entire of itself; every site is a piece of the Internet, a part of the main. Therefore, do not call for whom last updated the Web site; it may have been thee.

The GoLive Workgroup Server (WGS) tries to answer that perplexing bit of philosophy: who did what when, and why? (And often: how?) You can now answer those questions by setting up software on a server machine (which could even be the machine on which you routinely work) that coordinates multiple users working with an entire GoLive site.

The WGS stores the files, updates them to a Web server (which could also be on the same machine), and mediates access—including checking files in and out—among various GoLive and non-GoLive users. It also tracks files, storing multiple revisions of each file for later retrieval in case you need to backtrack.

The WGS maintains a database of links between objects, just like in a site file for a single-user site. This lets you take advantage of the WGS for performing certain kinds of maintenance operations, such as Clean Up Site and exporting a site with code-stripping options, without waiting around for your own machine to complete these sometimes lengthy tasks. You're pushing your workload off to another machine while you continue on more important duties.

The WGS performs all these tasks ably and simply. In fact, you'll be surprised how you ever managed to run a Web site without it.

In this chapter, we cover setting up the server, walking through each of its configuration parts; managing a site via GoLive's connection with the WGS;

and then collaborating with other users, whether they're using GoLive, Photoshop, a WebDAV client (including the one built into Mac OS X), or (gasp) Dreamweaver.

Tip: WGS Serves You

The WGS isn't a substitute for a Web server; it's a piece of intermediate software, handling the interaction between users and the Web server itself. It's a combination of a repository and an active part of your site design and maintenance process.

Setting Up WGS

Installing WGS should be a snap: run the installer, enter your serial number, and wait a bit while files are copied and services are started up. You need to make a few choices in this process that are worth reviewing, however. After the program is installed, the Workgroup Server Monitor starts, stops, and monitors its status.

Tip: Static IP

You almost definitely need a static and routable IP reachable by the rest of the Internet assigned to the machine that's running WGS. If the WGS is behind a firewall that locks down ports, or if you use a dynamically assigned address, it will be almost impossible to reach.

If your server is located on a local network in which only local users need to reach it, then you can manage with a NAT (Network Address Translation) assigned address. These addresses are often offered up in conjunction with a DHCP server and begin with 10.0 or 192.168.

The WGS installs under modern server-style systems only: Windows 2000 or XP, or Mac OS X 10.1 or later. The reason for this is simply support. Those platforms (2000 and XP have the same underlying OS code) are robust enough and have enough of the right supporting pieces already included to allow smooth operation with the right amount of speed.

Tip: Server Setup

Even if you don't already have a server on which you can run WGS as an extra component, think about buying some slightly older (cheap) hardware to set up a dedicated machine that could double as a file server. Windows XP and OS X both cost about $200 for install-from-scratch versions; couple the OS with $400 to $800 worth of hardware (an old Pentium III or an early model G4 tower), and you've got a perfectly good system.

Installing

The installer for WGS offers very few choices until you reach the point where it asks you for port numbers; this looks slightly different under Mac and Windows (see Figure 21-1). Port numbers are like doors in an office building; the building is at a certain address (an IP number) and each door has its own number that someone can knock on to engage in services. The WGS is entirely administered via a Web interface at the default port or a port you specified.

Tip: Changing Ports

Adobe assigned a default of port 1102 for Web-based administration (setting up sites and accounts) and WebDAV client access, and 1103 for restarting the server, which only the Workgroup Server Monitor uses. (See Chapter 20,

Figure 21-1
Installing the
Workgroup
Server

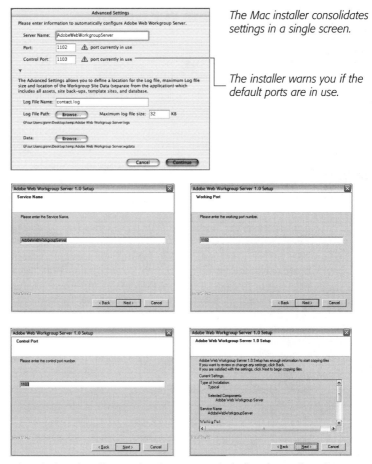

The Mac installer consolidates settings in a single screen.

The installer warns you if the default ports are in use.

The Windows installer requires four screens including the confirmation.

Synchronizing Sites.) There's no good reason to change these unless you have a particular firewall situation that blocks certain ports. Consult your system administrator, or add 1102 and 1103 to your list of allowed ports for access.

Waiting

The installer first copies and installs a rather large number of files, and then WGS on its first run configures and modifies these files. Even when you think the process has halted—have patience. It can take as long as 10 minutes for the initial install, during which the machine looks idle much of the time.

After your installation, GoLive opens two windows: a browser window for login, and the Workgroup Server Monitor.

Workgroup Server Monitor

The Workgroup Server Monitor offers up your window into whether the WGS is operating as expected (see Figure 21-2). It allows you to start and stop the server. It may seem odd to have this separate control panel, but think about it: since it's a Web-based tool, you wouldn't be able to debug or start the WGS without a separate tool.

The monitor offers just a few options: a status message at the top, and then buttons labeled Start, Stop, Refresh, Minimize, and Exit. Refresh needs explanation: the monitor doesn't continuously poll the status of the server; it only checks at the time the monitor is launched. Clicking Refresh rechecks to see what's up. Exiting the monitor doesn't quit or stop the server.

Tip: Administration

Use the File menu's Open Workgroup Administration menu item to launch a browser window pointed to the WGS's appropriate port. This is especially useful if you've chosen a port that's not the default and—perhaps—forgotten its number!

Figure 21-2
Adobe Web
Workgroup
Server

Tip: Smell the Java

The WGS is entirely JavaServer Page (JSP)-based, which made it easier for the GoLive team to deploy it uniformly on different platforms and systems.

First Login

The browser window that opens after the installation is complete lets you login to the WGS. The next section discusses configuration, but you should first login using one of the default accounts.

The WGS ships with three enabled default accounts: system, admin, and go-live. The passwords are, predictably, "admin" for admin and "golive" for golive. Admin is an administrator account that allows you to configure the server. The golive account is a plain user account set up just to show you a normal account.

The System account is used for internal maintenance and setup tasks, and on your first login, you're asked to change the password as part of the setup procedure. You should never login as System.

Go ahead and login to the admin account, change the password, and start configuring the site.

Tip: Turn "admin" Off

We recommend quickly adding a new user account with the administrator option set and disabling the admin and golive accounts as a pure security measure. Most server systems stopped shipping with easily guessed or identical login/user passwords long ago after hackers started exploiting this weakness. See "Users," later in this chapter, for editing user accounts.

Connecting Remotely

If you want to set up your server from a location other than the machine on which WGS is installed, you can control it just as well over the Web: the WGS doesn't care whether you're accessing its administrative controls from Ultima Thule or Umatilla (but not Uma Thurman).

In your Web browser, enter the fully qualified host name of the server (like goliveserver.necoffee.com) and the port number (1102 by default) like so:

```
http://goliveserver.necoffee.com:1102/
```

You can also find this precise information on the page that's launched locally when the server starts up (see Figure 21-3).

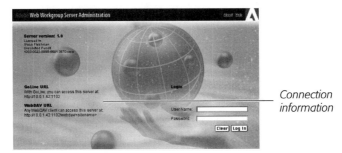

Figure 21-3
Main Web
administration
screen

Connection information

Configuring WGS

Before you can use WGS as a server, you need to set up the various details that let the server publish workgroup sites —copy the site's files and folders—via FTP or to folders also located on the same machine.

The WGS offers two options for configuration: a Setup Wizard, which walks you through basic options to configure the server and multiple sites and publish settings; or via the individual settings. We're giving the Setup Wizard a pass as it's self-explanatory and well-documented in the user manual.

Tip: After Wizard

Even after you've walked through the Setup Wizard, you still need to change or add options via the individual settings.

The WGS organizes its configuration into a logical division.

- First, you configure users. Each user has access to a certain set of sites (or none at all), and may also be allowed to have overall administration access to the server.

- Next, you define sites: new sites, old sites, imported sites. Users are assigned to sites here, allowing them to make changes. You can also change options for how these sites are published to the servers or paths you've set up just as you could in the Export Site feature used for single-user sites.

- Finally, you set publishing options for where the site is uploaded to via FTP, or published to locally in a file path to a folder. GoLive calls these locations or servers Publish Servers.

You can also configure some basic preferences, perform maintenance, and view the activity log. It's easy to modify any of these settings after an initial setup, with simple links and setup pages for adding and removing users, sites, and publish servers.

Users

Anyone who wants to access workgroup sites, whether through GoLive or a WebDAV client, must have a user account. GoLive allows you enter a variety of information about users in its configuration setup.

Click the Users icon at left to view a list of existing users (see Figure 21-4). Clicking the edit icon at left allows you to modify current users; the trash can at right prompts whether you want to remove the user or not.

Click the New User link near the Users icon at left to create a new user. The only required fields are a full name, login name, and password. Unchecking Enabled disables the account, which can be useful if you have occasional users. The Administrator checkbox allows you to turn a regular user into one who can modify these and other WGS settings.

Figure 21-4
User
administration

— Delete User

— Edit User

— New User

Tip: Administration

If your account has the Administrator box checked, your interaction via GoLive or a WebDAV client is identical; the extra privileges allow you to login over the Web to the WGS server administration system.

After creating a user or when editing an existing user, you can change the sites they're associated with by clicking the edit icon to the left of that user's name. A list of all sites appears under Assigned Sites, and you can check or uncheck which sites this user is allowed to work with. Click the Save button to commit changes made to a user's details or that user's assigned sites. Cancel reverts to the previously saved settings.

Sites

The Sites section coordinates all the details associated with sites that the WGS manages. There are three aspects to each WGS-managed site:

- The original source of the site's file (omitted for a blank site). This is specified only once when creating the site.

- The users who may then edit the site's files. Users are assigned only when a site is modified, not when it's initially created. Users can be added or removed at any time without affecting any other aspect of the site.

- The path or FTP server to which the site's files are published when modified. You can publish a site to many locations; a publish server or path is required when first setting up a site, after which you can add or modify publish servers. Publish happens on request via GoLive or the administration server; it can't be scheduled to happen automatically.

Creating a New Site

The WGS offers four options that are almost identical to the new site options for a single-user site described in Chapter 17, *Managing Sites* (see Figure 21-5). Because the WGS manages where files are stored locally, there's much less to be concerned about.

Figure 21-5
Creating a
new site

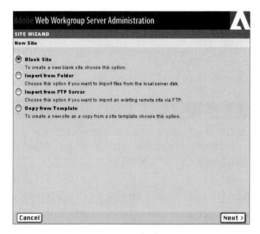

Tip: Wait, Wait!

It can take an inordinate amount of time for the WGS to import a site, especially a large one, even from local files. We've sat and watched for dozens of minutes before the site was successfully turned into a workgroup site. So don't get impatient. You only have to import once.

- **Blank Site.** Creates a new, empty site.

- **Import from Folder.** Imports data from a folder on the local server. The path needs to be typed in; you can't navigate to find it. Under Windows,

the path will start with a drive name, like "C:\documents\sites\
richardstarkey\"; in OS X, you'd specify with forward slashes, such as
"/documents/sites/petebest/" (see Figure 21-6). You can copy sites stored
elsewhere to the WGS machine to take advantage of this option.

Figure 21-6
Import from
Folder

- **Import from FTP Server.** Take a site stored remotely on FTP and copy it
  locally. Enter your FTP information just as you would when settings up an
  FTP server in GoLive proper (see Figure 21-7).

Figure 21-7
Import from
FTP Server

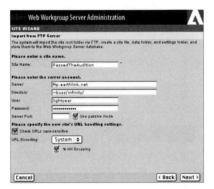

Tip: Importing Other Sites

Although the WGS can't import a site stored locally on another machine or import it via HTTP, there's a simple solution. First, import the site into your own
copy of GoLive. Second, use the Convert to Workgroup Site from the Site menu's
Workgroup submenu. We discuss this option further in "Working with WGS."

- **Copy from Template.** Use a site template shipped with GoLive, or one you
  (or your firm) has developed to create a blank site with all the trimmings.

Tip: Your Own Templates

You can copy your own site templates by placing them in the wgdata's
"sitetemplates" folder from the root of the WGS installation (see Figure 21-8).

Figure 21-8
Finding the
sitetemplates
folder

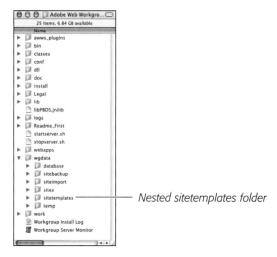

Nested sitetemplates folder

The WGS site templates require two additional files: the .info file that's a one-line text description of the site, and the .smd file which is formatted as XML and contains an outline of everything in the site. Adobe hasn't provided details yet about creating these files; check their tech support guidance online, or visit our Web site's section for this chapter for updates.

After choosing your options for creating a site, GoLive asks you to choose where you will publish the site's contents. The Publish Server is either a path on the local machine to a root folder or a remote FTP server.

Tip: Publish to Many

You can set up multiple Publish Servers per site, but in the initial setup you must specify at least one. You can add more later, or modify existing Publish Servers.

If you're choosing a local folder (which GoLive confusingly lists as the File option), you need to enter a path to that folder in the format that the operating system requires, as noted above under Import from Folder (also see Figure 21-6, above).

Items created in the Publish Servers area are available to the corresponding workgroup's users when they choose to publish updated files or entire sites.

Tip: OS X Paths (Mac only)

In OS X, paths to folders must be specified in the Unix style. If you're running the WGS on a server in which "bill" is the user from which Web sites are being fed, for instance, your path would be

```
/Users/bill/Sites/sitename
```

Tip: Make a Folder

Create the folder that you're pointing to when you enter a path in the Location field before creating that Publish Server. Otherwise, GoLive displays an error that the location doesn't exist.

Modifying Sites

Once a site has been created through the above methods of converting a single-user site, the Sites panel shows a list of all sites with editing and deletion options (see Figure 21-9). The tiny icons correspond, left to right, to Edit Site, Clean Up Site, Duplicate Site, Create Site Backup, and, at far right, Delete Site. You can also click the site name to edit its settings.

Figure 21-9
Site
administration

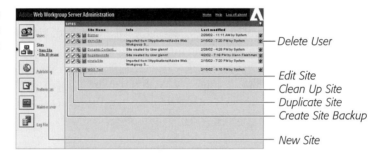

— Delete User

— Edit Site
— Clean Up Site
— Duplicate Site
— Create Site Backup

— New Site

Edit Site. When you edit the site, you can change a variety of parameters, but also set which users have permission to work with a given site (see Figure 21-10). This is the flip side of the ability to assign a user to multiple sites. (Kudos to the developers for offering both directions for assigning sites and users.)

Figure 21-10
Editing a
site's users

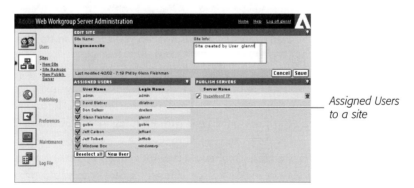

Assigned Users
to a site

When you choose to edit a site, an additional option appears below the Sites icon: New Publish Server. This is a bit of a hack for the WGS, as it should probably appear at right under the Publish Servers list (see Figure 21-11).

Figure 21-11
Adding a new
Publish Server

Click that New Publish Server link to add more locations or FTP servers to publish to. Under the Publish Servers heading, click the Edit Publish Server or Delete Publish Server icons to the left and right of Publish Server names for those corresponding activities.

Clean Up Site. Because the WGS maintains a database of the relationships that tie sites, links, and site elements together, you can use the Clean Up Site feature just as you would on a local site.

Tip: Clean Up Locally

If you select Clean Up Site from the Site menu in GoLive with an open workgroup site, the results are the same as choosing this feature via the server administration tool if your user account has Administrator privileges.

Tip: Can't Clean Other Sites

The WGS server administration tool lets you select Clean Up Site for sites that you aren't connected to. But when you click Clean Up, the server presents an error explaining you aren't assigned to that site.

Rescan Root Folder checks to see whether any links were added or changed from the WGS's internal map of these links. This feature helps when you edit and copy files to the WGS without using the Check In and Check Out features.

The Add Used checkboxes allow you to scan files on a site and extract or copy anything referenced but not actually appearing as part of the site. (The first item makes no sense, however: how can you copy orphaned files that aren't on the WGS?)

Remove Unreferenced deletes files, links, colors, and font sets that were used at one point and no longer have a connection to the navigational hierarchy (for files) or any files on the site (the other items).

For more on Clean Up Site, read that section of Chapter 19, *Managing Files, Folders, and Links.*

Duplicate Site. You can take an existing site and make an exact copy. We'd suggest it would be better to create either a site template if you need to ever copy the site more than once, or to use Create Site Backup for a snapshot of the current site.

We can see it would be useful to duplicate a site that you're splitting in two so that some of the content remains on one site and some on another, however.

Create Site Backup. This lovely feature lets you take a snapshot of all the files in an existing site and store that as a discrete unit you can revert to later, if need be. Click Create Site Backup, add some annotation about the particular purpose of the backup (if any), and click Save. GoLive copies the files to a unique location.

Tip: Scheduling Backups

Unfortunately, the WGS doesn't offer scheduling features, and because of the way in which site backups are triggered, we can't see a way you could script or otherwise trigger a site backup to happen on an automatic basis.

Site Backups

If you later need to revert to one of the site backup snapshots you made via Create Site Backup, click the Site Backups link next to the Sites icon at left, and click the Restore Site Backup icon to the left of the appropriate backup.

To regain disk storage space, delete site backups by clicking the trash icon to the right of each backup. You can only delete one backup at a time.

Where Files Are Stored

As a point of interest, the WGS stores its files in easy-to-find locations. The application is installed under Windows at C:\Program Files\Adobe\Adobe Web Workgroup Server\ and under Mac OS X in Applications/Adobe Web Workgroup Server/. In the application folder, a folder named "wgdata" stores the actual site information. (We've found a folder called "wgdata1" as our live WGS folder after reinstalling the server on one of our systems; it was obviously attempting to not overwrite the original data.)

In the "wgdata" folder, WGS organizes live sites in the "sites" folder, and creates a backup in the "sitebackup" folder. Sites are structured the same way they are locally, with revisions numbered sequentially in the file name.

Publishing

Site publishing involves taking the current state of a site and using FTP or local file copying to move any files changed since the last publish operation to those locations.

Because you set up Publish Servers locally on a site-by-site basis rather than globally, when you click the Publish icon, you first choose your site, then the particular Publish Server (see Figure 21-12).

Figure 21-12
Choosing a
Publish
Server for a
particular site

Site Specific Settings

If you've read Chapter 19, *Managing Files, Folders, and Links*, this next screen, Site Specific Settings, looks entirely familiar. It's almost identical to the options found for FTP Upload and Synchronize Modification Time, Export Site, and Strip Options all combined in one.

For more depth on each of these options, consult Chapter 19, which has several pages devoted to each of the areas mentioned.

Publish Conditions. Publish Conditions affect which files are uploaded. Each file and folder can be set to a particular Publish state, which restricts or allows that file or folder to be transferred based on circumstances. For instance, you can set files to never upload, and folders to upload only if not empty.

Publish Referenced Files Only makes sure that only files that are part of the site's navigational hierarchy are uploaded. Publish Referenced Files That Are Not Part of the Site likewise uploads files outside of the site's structure that are needed; it's unclear how this works when those files are not actually stored on the WGS itself.

Hierarchy. This innocuous set of fields and checkboxes hides a powerful feature. In GoLive, you can export a site to a separate folder while choosing these options. However, it's a time-consuming process at the end of which you're left with a folder which still must be separately uploaded via FTP.

With the Hierarchy section in the WGS, you can take your more complicated site and restructure it each time the site is uploaded. There are some good reasons for setting up one site identically to your GoLive hierarchy and another to be, say, entirely flat (no folders); this process removes the hassle.

Choosing As In Site mirrors the site architecture; Separate Pages and Media puts HTML and markup language files in one folder, and media in another; and Flat puts all folders at a single folder level.

You can name the folders that markup pages and media files are stored in via Folder Name for Pages and Folder Name for Media. The Folder Name for Files Not in Site field sets the location for files referenced outside the site that are included.

Strip HTML Code and GoLive Data. The Strip options remove extras found in the HTML that can affect code validation (checking that the HTML conforms to specific intranet standards, for instance), or that make files human-readable but are unnecessary for browsers to interpret.

Checking Adobe GoLive Elements extracts embedded GoLive tags for Components and other placeholders. Spaces and Comments remove sometimes-useful information: spaces have an effect in certain parts of HTML; comments may be used for embedded server-side codes.

Strip GoLive Data from Media Files removes any special information GoLive has embedded to track data in those files.

Publish Mode. This option, when checked, forces a full reload of a site. There aren't too many good reasons to do it, unless you notice that the WGS has somehow gotten out of sync with the remote server or the local file that's used as a Publish Server. If files have been deleted in either location, it may be worth checking this option once and immediately publishing.

Publish Reports

The Publish Reports link allows you to review a history of upload or copy operations, and check over errors (click the Errors link), the duration of the upload, and who initiated it (see Figure 21-13). Any assigned user to a site can publish the site, so these reports establish a paper trail of who published what when.

You can filter reports by site to avoid looking at long lists. You can also delete reports one by one by clicking the trash icon next to each report. (Again, you must delete individually; you can't delete multiple reports.)

Figure 21-13
Publish reports

Preferences

Preferences for the WGS are fairly stripped down. You can reset the ports on which the WGS serves its data. The three levels of log detail (Warning, Error, and Info) are progressively more verbose for following WGS events. And the FTP Proxy is a preset method of using a company pass-through FTP server where it's appropriate; you'll know if you need it.

Maintenance

Adobe had good foresight in including these options in the very first release of the WGS. Many developers don't think until later that anything could go wrong with their precious little software. As we all know, bugs happen, and in a system as complex as WGS—which is interacting with remote servers, paths, Java, WebDAV, etc.—we're glad they didn't have an ego.

Synchronize Site

Choosing this option, selecting a site, and clicking OK causes the WGS to double-check its database (essentially, its own GoLive site file for that site) against the files stored locally that represent the site. This is the equivalent of Refresh View in GoLive itself.

The WGS offers a report of what's wrong (if anything). Clicking Synchronize allows it to fix its database; clicking Cancel lets you walk away.

Clean Up Revisions

Because the WGS can keep up to an infinite number of versions of each file on a site, you may want to occasionally clean house and throw away older versions or a number of versions beyond a certain limit.

Choose the site and the data or number parameter, and click Delete.

Reset User Locks

Ken checks out a bunch of files. Ken shuts his computer down and locks his office and leaves for the day. That dratted Ken! Fortunately, the WGS is smarter than Ken. Select the user you want to reset locks for and click the Reset button, and that person's live files are now dead.

When Ken returns and is soundly berated, he can use the Compare to Server from the Site menu's Revisions submenu for each file to see what, if anything, he needs to go back and change.

Log File

The log file is where WGS operations and errors are listed chronologically, depending on which options you chose under Preferences for the level of detail.

If you have problems with the WGS and consult Adobe Technical Support, they'll almost certainly want to know what the log file has to say about it.

Working with WGS

To start working from GoLive with a Workgroup Server, you first need to create a local site that has a relationship with the WGS. After creating the site, you can then check files in and out, and watch what other users are doing, as well as revert to older versions of a file or tell someone else what their next task is.

As an added bonus, several other software programs, including practically everything out of Adobe, work with WGS as if it's a plain old WebDAV server. This means that you can build a multi-program collaborative workflow without changing how anyone else in the group has to accomplish what they're supposed to.

Creating a Workgroup Site

GoLive offers four options for creating or starting to interact with a workgroup site. These options are distinct but similar to the single-user site options.

Select New Site from the File menu, then choose Workgroup as your site type. Click the Next button to continue (see Figure 21-14).

- **Blank Site.** Choosing this option creates a new blank site on the WGS.

- **Mount.** Copy the site files for an existing workgroup site to your machine in preparation for editing.

Figure 21-14
Creating a new
workgroup site

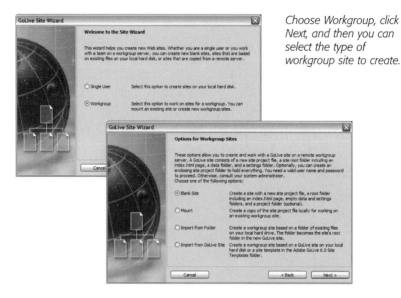

*Choose Workgroup, click
Next, and then you can
select the type of
workgroup site to create.*

Tip: Mount via File Menu

The File Menu offers a shortcut for this mounting process; select Mount Workgroup Site from its menu, and you're halfway there.

- **Import from Folder.** Take a local folder and convert it into a WGS site.

- **Import from GoLive Site.** Take an existing GoLive site or template and make it a WGS site.

Tip: Convert by Menu

You can also open a GoLive site and choose Convert to Workgroup Site from the Site menu's Workgroup submenu.

Tip: You Can Tell by Looking (Windows only)

Workgroup sites have a unique icon in their upper-left corner under Windows that combines a normal site icon with a network connection at the bottom.

If you want to take a site that's in a folder on your local hard drive and import it as a WGS site, you can either use the Import from Folder option above, or you can copy that folder directly to the WGS server (via whatever other methods you've installed for sharing files on that machine) and use the WGS administration tool to create a WGS. In both cases, the WGS has to copy the files; it's a toss-up as to which is easier. (We like to offload tasks to the WGS wherever possible, though.)

Tip: Import via HTTP

The WGS can't import a site by downloading it via HTTP, as you can with a single-user site (see Chapter 17, *Managing Sites*). You can get around this limitation by first creating a single-user site imported from HTTP, and then converting it to a workgroup site.

Regardless of which option you chose, you are subsequently asked to enter your WGS server name or IP address, its port (remember: default is 1102), and your login information (see Figure 21-15). Each workgroup site you work with can be on the same or different workgroup server.

Figure 21-15
Logging into
the Workgroup
Server

Tip: Caps Lock

If your password isn't saved, and the site doesn't mount when you retype it, check that Caps Lock isn't on. We know, this sounds like a no-brainer, but we've done this a million times, and still scream at the machine, "Why won't you accept it!?!" Then we realize we're typing SHMOO instead of shmoo.

In each case, you are also asked where on the local hard drive you want to save the copies of the WGS files as they're in process (see Figure 21-16), and then any advanced options for URL encoding or parsing (see Figure 21-17).

Figure 21-16
Saving the
workgroup site
to a local
location

Figure 21-17
Advanced URL
Handling

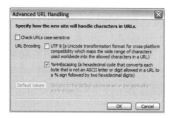

After you've chosen and stepped through the workgroup creation process, your copy of GoLive and the WGS transfer the appropriate files back and forth. Be patient, as always: the WGS may spend a while building or copying files.

To open a workgroup site after you've closed it, just navigate to the appropriate location on your local hard drive and open the site file.

Workflow

Your local copy of the workgroup site is just that: a local copy. The WGS is the repository for all files. When you check files in and out, the WGS keeps track and stores older versions of files as they're replaced. You can keep part of the site or a whole copy locally, and even control when and to where the WGS publishes that workgroup site's files.

But let's be clear: the WGS is the brain of this body; GoLive users are fingers and toes. The WGS has to be appropriately and carefully administered; going behind its back in copying and updating files defeats its purpose and can easily put various collaborators out of sync. (There are tools to fix this, of course.)

Let's start with the basics of working with files and publishing updates, and move into troubleshooting when things go awry.

Site Settings and Administration

A few overhead details can help as you plow into the next section.

Show Deleted Server Files (Revisions submenu). While you can delete files from the WGS, this option displays deleted files in the Revisions list as dimmed objects. This lets you see if something was deleted that shouldn't have been.

Change User (Workgroup submenu). This allows you to login as a different user, or allows another user on the same machine to log in under his or her own name.

Change Password (Workgroup submenu). You can change your password through this method instead of using the Web-based administration tools.

Open Workgroup Administration (Workgroup submenu). Choosing this item opens a Web browser that points to the appropriate server and port so you can log in and administer the server if your account has those privileges.

Workgroup Server (Site Settings). You can change which user is logged in via this area, or change the site refresh interval (and whether it's refreshed at all). The refresh isn't of files in the Files tab, but rather of GoLive-specific items, like external links. To see an updated Files tab view, click Refresh View with the Files tab selected.

File Interaction

When you have a workgroup site open, notice a few changes in the display. The FTP and WebDAV tabs on the right-hand side of the Site window are replaced with a single Publish Server tab. The left-hand side has a new tab, User Activity. The Files tab's Locked, Completed, and To Be Edited By column heads actually have values in them; the latter two columns appear when you enable a Workflow Module. Your Site window has become a control panel for interacting with the WGS.

Tip: Trash in Site Folder

It's vitally important that the WGS is set to move deleted files to the site trash instead of the computer's trash; in GoLive's Preferences, set the Site pane's When Removing Files option to Move Them to the Site Trash, instead of the Finder or System Trash. The WGS uses this preference to determine whether it actually deletes files when they're removed from the site, or continues to store them for later retrieval. (You can, of course, empty the trash in GoLive and flush those documents out to sea.)

Tip: Page Context

One of the most useful occurrences of the contextual menu happens when you're editing a page and want to access the workgroup features, like Compare to Server. Rather than sort through the Site menu, right-click (Windows) or Control-click (Mac) on the Page icon to see only the appropriate options. It's even more stripped down than the Files tab's contextual menu.

Checking out and working locally. Checking out files allows you to own the live copy of the file by locking it on the server. You can then edit the file locally, save it, and check it back in to make it the current live file.

When you check pages out, copies of media files (images, movies, etc.) associated with that page are also downloaded if they aren't already part of the local copy of the site.

There are many ways to check out files.

- **Open and start editing.** You can select any local file, open it, and start typing or adding objects. GoLive asks if you want to check out the file—the answer is almost always yes. (If you select no, your changes aren't saved to the server.)

- **Select one or more files and folders and choose Check Out.** The Check Out option in the Site menu, the contextual menu, and Workgroup Toolbar lets you check out and lock all the files in your selection, whether nested in folders or not. (Folders are not checked out.)

- **Choose Check Out All from the Site menu.** This is a big step to take, especially in a large site; it may take a very long time to accomplish.

Make any changes you like to a file, including throwing it away. As long as you've checked it out, you're the master of that file.

In fact, you can walk away with those checked out files by selecting Work Offline from the Site menu's Workgroup submenu. When you return to a live connection, select it again to uncheck it and start communicating with the WGS again.

Tip: Resetting Locks

As we note earlier in the chapter, you can reset the locks for a specific user (that laggard, Ken) via the workgroup administration server if you have Administrator privileges.

Workflow palette. The Workflow palette lets you pass information about a file's status to other users. First, you have to enable it, however; it's turned off by default in the shipping version of GoLive. Bring up Preferences from the Edit menu, click the Modules pane, scroll down to the Extend Scripts folder, and check Workflow. Click OK, quit GoLive, and run GoLive.

Bring up the Workflow palette from the Window menu (see Figure 21-18). You can enter the person who should next edit the file and the percentage

Figure 21-18
Workflow palette and its Files tab fields

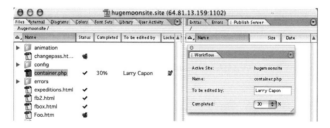

of the work in that document that you think is done. These two values show up in two new columns added to the Files tab by the Workflow Module: To Be Edited By and Completed.

Add files. If you drag files into the Files tab from the Desktop or use the Add Files feature (contextual menu or in the File menu's Import submenu as Files to Site), GoLive responds with a dialog asking if you want to check the files in. But you have no real choice: the boxes for the files are checked and disabled.

GoLive displays an uploading message that doesn't show the completion percentage as files are transferred.

Compare to Server. If you aren't quite sure what changes you've made, you can use the Compare to Server feature under the Site menu's Revisions submenu for text and markup files. It's also available in the contextual menu and the Workgroup Toolbar.

The Compare to Server feature displays a quite interesting dialog box that shows all the changes in the underlying HTML, XML, or other text, comparing the latest copy of a Web page on the server to the one you're working on (see Figure 21-19). You must save the file before you can compare it to the server's copy.

Figure 21-19
Compare to
Server

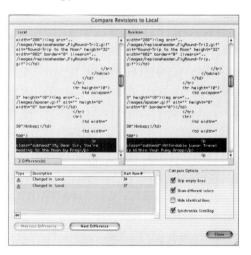

Tip: Identical Files

If you've made no changes, GoLive chirpily brings up a dialog box that informs you that the files are identical.

The feature shows you side-by-side views of your local copy (left) and the copy on the server (right), which it confusingly calls "Revision" (instead of "last version" or "last revision").

In the lower left, you can select the listed items to see where the changes occurred, or use the Previous Difference and Next Difference buttons to walk backwards and forwards.

The Compare Options checkboxes at lower right control the display and interface. Uncheck Skip Empty Lines to display all of the HTML code. Uncheck Show Different Colors to make it harder to mentally parse the code. Check Hide Identical Lines (unchecked by default) to remove HTML that's not relevant. Finally, Synchronize Scrolling makes it easier to perform side-by-side comparisons.

Click Close, your only option, to exit.

Tip: Pencil and Paper

You can't edit the HTML in either left or right pane, so take notes. It's one of the few places in GoLive where you aren't offered a live-edit option.

Checking In. When you've made all the edits you want and saved the files (closing is optional—GoLive prompts), you can check them back in to the server. You have a couple methods of moving files back into the clutches of the WGS.

- **Select one or more files and folders and choose Check In.** The Check In option works with multiple items or just a single one, and appears in the Site menu, the contextual menu, and Workgroup Toolbar.

- **Choose Check In All from the Site menu.** All checked-out files are copied over. This may take quite a while, depending on how many files you have checked out.

GoLive shows a list of all files (even if there's just one) that you're checking in. The list can be shown flat or by folder hierarchy, and individual items can be checked or unchecked, just like uploading via FTP.

When you check files in, the WGS moves the current version of the file into its revisions pile, and makes your version the live, unlocked version that the next person checks out.

It's a good idea to take GoLive up on its suggestion and make some comments about the version you're checking in, as you can review those comments later in the Revision List if you need to revert to an earlier version (see Figure 21-20).

Figure 21-20
Reviewing
revisions

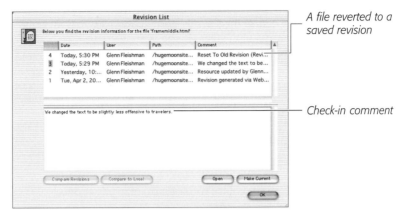

A file reverted to a
saved revision

Check-in comment

Undo Check Out and Revisions. Change your mind on some changes? Before checking in, you can choose Undo Check Out from any of the menu locations or toolbar; this reverts your local copy to the last revised copy and removes your ownership on it. You can give up on all checked out files via Undo Check Out All in the Site menu.

Revisions offers a more flexible option. You can choose Revision List from any Revisions submenu or the Workgroup Toolbar to view a list of all the versions of that file the WGS has stashed away. The comments that you entered (if any) when you checked a file in can be viewed to help determine which revision you need.

In the Revision List, if you're working with a markup or text file, you can choose a revision and click Compare to Local. Up pops the Compare Revisions to Local dialog box, which should be familiar from the "Compare to Server" section, earlier. You can also choose any two revisions in the list and compare them to each other.

Tip: Superb Feature

If for no other reason than Revisions, the price of GoLive is worth it. Heck, there's no good way for the average user to easily manage multiple versions of a file. And here Adobe goes and throws the tool in for free! It's an incredible boon to those of us managing sites and trying to stay sane.

Tip: Site Backup

Remember way back in discussing site administration earlier in this chapter we mentioned that there's a simple way to create full site backups at the WGS? We suggest creating these as frequently as daily as just another piece of peace of mind.

Of course the flip side of site backups is that they only include the current live version of the files. All the revisions remain with your live site, still accessible; the backup is really a snapshot.

Download and Remove Local File. Whenever you check out a file, GoLive automatically downloads the latest version to your local folder. If it's an HTML file, all associated media files are also downloaded.

As the site is changed by multiple people, even though your Files tab is updated to reflect what's on the WGS itself, you may not have a local copy of all the files. You can use the Download feature to make sure you have part or all of the site copied to your local machine at once.

Tip: Working Offsite

If you're working away from the network containing your WGS, or you're going to be using a network with minimal bandwidth, Download ensures you possess local copies of the site's files before you suck data through a straw. You might need to edit small HTML files on the road, but there could be megabytes of images linked to those files, and it's best to have them on hand before you depart.

You can't choose whether to store files locally or not as a preference, but you can select multiple files and choose Remove Local Files from any of the various menus. Likewise, if you've gotten rid of local copies and you want to refresh without checking these files out, select one or more and choose Download.

You can perform this operation en masse through Remove All Local Files and Download All in the Site menu.

Tip: Saving Private Bandwidth

GoLive should offer an option to reduce bandwidth use within a workgroup site. While these remove and download options help, it would be better if you could choose to track and download the updates for certain files automatically, or none at all.

Checking up on other users. It may sound Big Brother-ish, but the User Activity tab of the Site window shows you a list of all the assigned users for a site, and lets you see which files they have checked out. This saves yelling out, "Hey, who the heck has the Johnson file?" (especially if your collaborators are in another office, city, or continent).

Site-editing features. Remember that all site-editing features available for regular sites are also available for workgroup sites. You may need to download all files locally before using options like Flatten Script Library or Clean Up Site. Updating a link, for instance, can prompt GoLive to ask you to check out a number of files, which it needs to rewrite with the new link location.

Publishing

With a workgroup site open, the FTP and WebDAV tabs disappear from the right side of the Site window and are replaced by a single Publish Server tab (see Figure 21-21).

Figure 21-21
Publish Server
in the Site
window

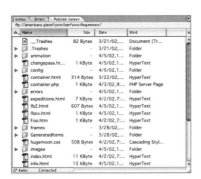

The Publish Server's list of files (left) and the Site Setting to choose it (above).

The Publish tab, the Publish Server Connect/Disconnect button in the Toolbar, and the Publish submenu all work similarly to how you interact with an FTP server, with one important difference: when you publish a workgroup site, you're actually telling the WGS itself to copy files from its master cache.

This is a huge benefit when your WGS server is located on either a fast or slow link. If it's on a fast link, such as at a co-location facility or corporate headquarters, but you're on a slow link or dialing in, you can effectively use the WGS's higher speed to move files that much faster.

If the WGS is on a slow link, then you can force it to spool the files out over FTP without tying up your local copy of GoLive. You can merrily proceed to other tasks, while the WGS handles the operations for you.

Publish Servers (Site Settings). To set up publishing, open Site Settings and select the Publish Server pane. The popup menu in this pane shows available Publish Servers that were set up on the WGS. You can also select and switch between servers from the Publish Server submenu in the Site menu.

Tip: FTP Only

Although you can select Publish Servers that are local folders from this menu, the name says it all: FTP Publish Servers. You must have administration permission and use the Publish feature via the Web administration tool to publish these sites.

If you select Edit Servers, GoLive opens a window in your Web browser that points to the WGS's administration tool where, if you have administrator privileges, you can add Publish Servers after logging in.

Publish (Site Settings). The Publish pane of Site Settings offers the same controls found when editing the settings for a Publish Server via the workgroup administration tool (see "Publishing," earlier in this chapter). There are just two important differences to point out.

First, the Publish Mode option on the workgroup administration server isn't available in Site Settings. To push all files out, you must select Upload All from the Site menu's Publish submenu.

Second, the Publish Linked Files That Are Not Part of the Site option actually works locally in GoLive, copying the files necessary from other locations on your hard drive and uploading them. (Clean Up Site works as well.) This checkbox, while available on the WGS, has no effect there.

You might note (as our third of two points) that Flatten Script Library is unchecked and grayed out. You can't perform this function when publishing a site; rather, you must select it separately and possibly download all files soon.

Publish (menus and toolbar). After selecting a Publish Server, you can click the Publish Server Connect/Disconnect button on the Toolbar, or select the Connect option from the Site menu's Publish submenu. Although the Publish Server tab in the Site window looks much like an FTP server, and the Inspectors are labeled like an FTP server, you can't download files from the Publish Server.

You have three upload options: Upload Modified Items, Upload Selection, and Upload All. Just as with FTP, modified items are documents that have changed since the last recorded upload. The Workgroup Publish Options dialog offers the defaults you selected in the Publish pane of Site Settings.

When you click Publish, GoLive transmits instructions to the WGS to copy files via FTP to that particular Publish Server, and you've gone live.

Tip: Everybody Can Publish

The WGS only offers two user types: administrator and regular. Regular users assigned to a site can publish a site to any defined FTP Publish Server.

Other Applications

GoLive is the head librarian in this WGS system, with full control of the card catalog. But under-librarians scurry around in the woodwork, adding new books and checking out ones it wants.

Other programs with WebDAV support have full access to the WGS for checking files in and out, adding files, and viewing files. This includes dozens of programs, as well as built-in operating system support in Mac OS X and Windows XP!

You need to use a special URL to access the WebDAV features, which the Workgroup Server Administration tool displays on its home page for reference. It's always the URL for the WGS plus "/webdav/" plus the exact site name. If you've created a site called "Dexter" and your server is at 192.168.0.1, and you're using all the defaults for the WGS, the root URL would be:

`http://192.168.0.1:1102/webdav/Dexter/`

You can tack on paths and filenames after that, depending on where your files are stored. Include any spaces in the site name.

Tip: Spaced Out

Spaces may confuse some WebDAV clients, so we recommend not naming a site with spaces in it.

Even though you can't access version information from these other programs and interfaces, WGS continues to store each older version of the files you work with as they are checked in. GoLive provides access to these older versions.

Tip: ARMed and Ready

To work best with other Adobe products, enable the ARM Module in the Preferences Modules pane; it's off by default. Bring up Preferences, check the box next to ARM, click OK, quit GoLive, and run GoLive again. GoLive now warns you whenever it opens a workgroup site that the ARM Module might interfere with already-checked-out files. You should check in all of those files in other programs before proceeding. GoLive also lets you disable ARM support for a session, too, by clicking No at the warning prompt.

Photoshop 6

Photoshop 6 offers minimal support for WebDAV, but it works just fine with WGS. All these options are found in the Workflow submenu of the File menu.

If you have an existing file you want to add to a site, select Add to Workflow. The file is uploaded and checked out. Enter the IP number of the WGS; Photoshop can't handle domain names. Include the full path with the filename.

Open from Workflow downloads a file and allows you to work on the file through a local copy. It's essentially like checking a file out. Undo Check Out reverts to the copy saved on the server and unlocks your file.

Check In uploads the modified version of the file.

Illustrator 10, InDesign 2, LiveMotion 2, and Photoshop 7

Illustrator 10, InDesign 2, LiveMotion 2, and Photoshop 7 have complete WebDAV support built right in. The Preferences for these programs allow you to turn workgroup features on or off via the Workgroup pane. You can also set defaults, such as automatically checking files out as needed, or asking first. You can turn down the level of prompts so that as you work with native files and images placed in those files, you're never asked anything at all.

To start working with a workgroup, select Workgroup Servers from the File menu's Workgroup submenu; this submenu is where all the workgroup features reside (see Figure 21-22). (Illustrator 10 calls it Manage Workgroups, but it's otherwise identical.) In Workgroup Servers, create a New Server and enter the WebDAV URL for the WGS. If you click the Advanced button, you can set a custom location to store downloaded workgroup media files locally.

Figure 21-22
Workgroup submenu in Adobe programs

Tip: Shared Settings

These workgroup settings are shared among all four programs; once they're set up in one program, a workgroup server appears in all of the applications.

Each time you connect to a workgroup server, the program prompts for a user name and password; there's no facility to store this information permanently. Also, we've found that these programs prompt at least twice when we initially connect to Save As or Place a document from the WGS.

Create a new document in any of the four programs, and you can save that document onto the WGS via the Workgroup submenu's Save As item.

The program informs you where the local file is stored. When you open the local copy of the file, the program tries to check it out of the server so you can edit it live locally.

If you have existing documents on the WGS, you can select Open from the Workgroup submenu. Choose a server (or set one up) via the Server menu at right. The display is refreshed to show all documents the program can open. If you change the Files of Type menu, you can examine more of the files on the server, although a given program can't open anything but its own supported file formats; InDesign, for instance, can only open InDesign files.

If the lock has been reset on your file, the program brings up a Collision Error dialog box that queries how to proceed: discard changes and download a new copy; update the server with your copy; or save the local file under a different name.

Tip: Photoshop Document Popup

Photoshop sports a tiny server-like document icon at the bottom of all its windows. From this popup, you can select all of the Workgroup options found in the File's Workgroup submenu.

When you check a file back in or cancel your ownership of the file (via Check In or Cancel Check Out), the program closes your local copy. Select Revert to continue your hold on the file but reopen the previous version of the file.

With an open document in Illustrator, InDesign, or LiveMotion, the Place menu becomes active, allowing you to put media items from the WGS into a native document. InDesign and Illustrator have just a simple Place menu item, while LiveMotion offers several: Place, Place Sequence, and Place as Texture.

Verify State displays the status of the file you're working on, such as whether you have the latest copy checked out (see Figure 21-23).

Figure 21-23
Verify State in
Photoshop

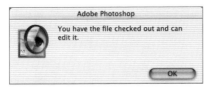

Just as in GoLive, you can select Work Offline to retain ownership and work on the file without a live connection to the server. The Logoff All Servers item closes any documents opened via WebDAV.

Dreamweaver 4

In Dreamweaver 4, you can assign a site to a WebDAV server as its synchronization method. When setting up or editing a site, choose WebDAV in the Remote Files pane (see Figure 21-24). Click Settings and enter your WGS URL as above and your username and password. Make sure in the main pane that Check Out Files When Opening is checked.

Figure 21-24
Remote Files
pane in
Dreamweaver

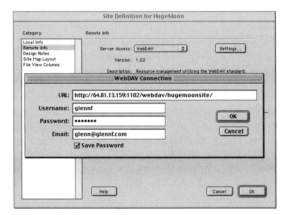

Open the site and click the Connects to Remote Host button (two cables plugging into each other). You see a list of files at left comprising the WGS site, including checkmarks next to any checked out files (see Figure 21-25).

Figure 21-25
WebDAV file
listing in
Dreamweaver

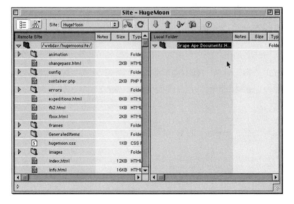

Dreamweaver's normal WebDAV features all apply: click Refresh to update the remote display; select files (locally or remotely) and click the Check Out File(s) button; likewise, select files and click Check In to return them to the WGS repository. Checkout files have a black (instead of red) checkmark next to them in the local file pane.

You can even use Dreamweaver's Synchronize feature to coordinate files in both directions, which is especially useful if you make extensive local revisions, rather than checking in each file individually.

Mac OS X

In the Finder, select Connect to Server from the Go menu (Command-K). In the Address field, enter the full URL including "http://". The operating system will ask you for your name and password (see Figure 21-26). Once mounted, the WGS acts precisely like a regular mounted hard drive.

We've definitely noticed some flakiness in OS X 10.1.3, the latest version at this writing, in which we could not get a legitimate WGS server to mount; yet at other times, we've had no problems.

Figure 21-26
Mounting the
Workgroup
Server in
Mac OS X

Windows XP

Open any folder and select Map Network Drive. Click the Sign Up for Online Storage or Connect to a Network Server link. Use the wizard to go to the Where Do You Want to Create This Network Place screen and then select Choose Another Network Location (see Figure 21-27). You know, just where you'd expect it.

Enter the full URL in the next screen and Windows XP prompts you for the username and password. You can open the folder when you finish, and it adds the WGS server location as a Web Folder.

WebDAV Clients

If you don't have access to any of the above, you can download a WebDAV client that works like an FTP transfer program. The best place to look for these clients is at the home of WebDAV, www.webdav.org.

Figure 21-27
Mounting the
Workgroup
Server in
Windows XP

*Some of the many steps to mount a WebDAV
server in Windows: In My Network Places,
double-click Add Network Place, enter the
address, type in a password, give it a name
and it shows up in the list of volumes.*

Workgroup It, Baby! Yeah!

The WGS server incorporates features not available elsewhere for love or
money in a simple, easy-to-install package. We predict it will transform the
way that people collaborate, even when they're all by themselves.

Advanced

PART 4

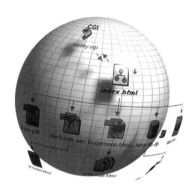

CHAPTER 22
Advanced Features

GoLive appears to have no end of features, and the more you learn about the program, the more it seems you need—or want—to learn about how to use it more effectively.

In this part of the book, we cover the most difficult-to-learn parts of GoLive, most of which involve a greater knowledge of general Web protocols and standards. GoLive insulates you from the real nitty-gritty, providing a friendly interface that lets you manipulate sophisticated controls behind the scenes. But we'll try to introduce you to the GoLive approach and to show you what's behind the curtain, so you can twist the dials and knobs yourself.

The chapters that follow provide an introduction and an inside look at:

- **Dynamic Content:** setting up databases to work with Dynamic Content, including the prefabricated set of database links and connectors that ship with GoLive 6.

- **JavaScript:** scripting tips using GoLive's tools for editing and inserting JavaScript.

- **Animation:** animating objects on a page with Dynamic HTML (DHTML).

- **Actions:** how best to use GoLive's built-in Actions for handling complex coding behavior.

- **Cascading Style Sheets:** creating a single, consistent source for text formatting across a page or an entire site.

- **Web Settings:** understanding GoLive's sophisticated approach to internally representing structured elements used in the program for coding and previewing.

GoLive's Secret Weapon

This chapter covers a significant advanced feature that doesn't fit neatly into other categories, but certainly goes beyond the kinds of tasks that a user doing page layout and site management might encounter on a regular basis.

We're talking, of course, about regular-expression pattern matching: Go-Live's version of a powerful tool for matching patterns in a number of places in the program, including sitewide find and replace.

To the uninitiated, this capability can look like a cat walked across the key-board and miraculously fixed elements within a page or site; but, in reality, it's one of the most powerful methods for making complex and extensive changes without hand editing.

Regular-Expression Pattern Matching

Regular-expression pattern matching is often found only in the most advanced text editors and word processors, such as BBEdit and Microsoft Word. It's also called "regexp" for short, and known as "grep" (global regular expression pattern matching) in the Unix command-line world.

Regular expressions are wildcard patterns that can match a variety of text that meets their parameters, instead of just an exact set of characters or run of text. For instance, you could find all tags in an HTML file by specifying a pattern that begins with a less-than sign (<), is followed by any text except a greater-than sign (>), and then ends with a greater-than sign.

You can search for or use regular expressions in several places in GoLive: in the Find field of the Find & Replace tab in the Find feature; in the Element tab's Attribute field in the Find feature; in Filename Constraints for legal file-names used in a site; in the Regular Expressions preferences for setting up pre-fabricated Find patterns; and in the Spell Checker's Pattern Dictionary for ignoring patterns that you don't want to spellcheck, like URLs.

Patterns

Patterns are combinations of characters which, when composed correctly, can match ranges of text. These patterns also include wildcards, which match text that you don't exactly specify. There are five types of wildcards in GoLive:

- Number of characters to be selected by a match

- A range or set of characters to match

- Optional selection that doesn't have to be found to create a positive match

- Start or end of line

- Definite selection

Tip: Reserved Characters

Certain punctuation characters have special meanings in a regular expression to identify groups of characters or other wildcard behavior. These are called reserved characters, as they're reserved for these special purposes. In order to use one of them literally, like a parenthesis in a phrase you want to match, you have to proceed the character with a backslash, or \. So, for instance, if you want to search for "http://www.phlegmatic.com/", you'd enter in the Find field:

```
http\:\/\/www\.phlegmatic\.com\/
```

Tip: Tag Brackets

Although < and > and : don't appear to be reserved characters, we've occasionally found problems searching on them. So just to be on the safe side, we often put a backslash in front of punctuation. GoLive treats backslash plus any character as that character, so adding a backslash doesn't introduce new problems.

Number of Characters

Three symbols control the amount of text selected: the asterisk, the plus sign, and the question mark (*, +, and ?). Let's introduce these first, and then show examples below, under "Pattern," where they make more sense.

Asterisk. An asterisk matches zero or more instances of the preceding character or characters in a pattern.

Plus sign. A plus sign matches one or more instances of the preceding character or characters in a pattern.

Question mark. A question mark makes the preceding character optional. If you precede the question mark with text enclosed in parentheses, the entire text in parentheses is optional.

Ranges

GoLive offers a wide set of character selectors for creating ranges of characters to match. These include selecting any single character, any character in a specified range or set, any character not in a specified range or set, and special selectors that choose all digits, all white space, only returns, and the like.

Period. Entering a period selects any single character. For instance, finding for

```
peters.n
```

matches "peterson" and "petersen" but also "petersbn". To find a run of zero or more instances of any character, you use the very simple expedient of adding an asterisk, as in

```
peters.*
```

which in this example would find "peterson" as well as "petersburg", but it also selects everything to the end of the line. (You need to use negation, below, to limit the number of characters matched.)

Square brackets. You can insert any characters or a range of characters inside square brackets—[and]—to select a range of text that matches only the characters in the square brackets. If you don't put a +, *, or ? after it, it finds just one character that's inside the brackets. Finding for

```
peters[eo]n
```

matches only "peterson" or "petersen".

Negative square brackets. If you put a caret (^) at the start of text inside square brackets, GoLive finds only characters that aren't found in the square brackets. This can be useful for trying to find everything up until a terminator. For instance, if you find for

```
<[^>]+>
```

GoLive matches just the interior of a tag. The "[^>]+" means, "match everything except a greater-than sign," so the pattern matches everything in the interior until it reaches the closing greater-than sign.

If you want to find only whole words that are or start with "peters", you could search for everything up until a space; this also matches up to the end of a line for words that end with a hard return:

```
peters[^ ]*
```

Special matches. GoLive also offers a number of special selectors that correspond to any digit, any white space (tab or space characters), any line break, any tab, and many of their negations (see Table 22-1).

Optional Selection

GoLive offers two ways to indicate whether a pattern or range of characters is optional when identifying a match.

Table 22-1
Special matches

Character	Description
\d	Matches any digit
\D	Matches anything but a digit (the same as [^\d])
\w	Matches any alphabetic character, uppercase or lowercase (i.e., A-Z or a-z)
\W	Matches anything but alphabetic characters (the same as [^\w])
\s	Matches white space, which in GoLive is just tabs or spaces
\S	Matches anything but white space (the same as [^\s])
\r	Used with Find & Replace in the HTML Source Editor, matches line breaks, regardless of platform
\t	Used with Find & Replace in the HTML Source Editor, matches tabs used for indentation
\x00 - \xff	For characters that you can't enter from the keyboard, you can enter their base 16 or hexadecimal value to match them. This is rarely needed in GoLive.

Vertical bar. The vertical bar, or |, lets you specify a set of possible matches. For instance, if you wanted to match either the Src or Href attributes in order to change the items they link to, you could find for

```
(HREF|SRC)\=\"
```

You only need to enclose choices in parentheses if there is text before or after the matches that isn't part of what you want to look for. If you wanted to search for Real World Adobe GoLive or Real World Adobe InDesign, you would use parentheses like this

```
Real World Adobe (InDesign|GoLive)
```

Parentheses. If you enclose text in parentheses and follow it by a question mark, the entire bit in parentheses becomes optional. If you want to find any instance of Ezra Stiles College where folks might have forgotten the Ezra, you would search for

```
(Ezra )?Stiles College
```

Start or End of Line

Two special characters help you identify the start or end of a line or filename: the caret (^) for the start of a line or paragraph and the dollar sign ($) for the end of a line or paragraph. This is especially useful with Find & Replace, but it can also be useful when finding the start or end of a complete filename in Filename Constraints.

The use in Find & Replace varies by whether you're in the HTML Source Editor (line based) or Layout Editor (paragraph based) when searching on an individual page, or whether you have the Treat Files In popup menu set to Source Mode or Layout Mode when working on a sitewide operation.

Definite Selection

In the Find & Replace tab, surrounding something by parentheses in the Find field with Regular Expression checked lets you insert that text in the Replace field by typing a backslash (\) followed by a number indicating that particular parenthetical set's position in the Find field. These are called back references.

For instance, you might want to find every instance of text that matches a URL and enclose it in Teletype tags. You wouldn't want to run a separate search for each URL; instead, you can use regular expressions to specify the URL generically and then drop in the matched URL as part of your replacement text.

Although GoLive uses parentheses for three purposes—two of them described under "Optional Selection," earlier in this chapter—any use of them always creates a back reference. So if you're using parentheses to indicate a choice among options, you still have to consider it when counting. For example, changing the start of an absolute reference would look like this in the Find field:

```
(A|IMG) (SRC|HREF)\=\"\~foobar\/
```

In the Replace field, you'd put

```
\1 \2="/~hagar/
```

Find & Replace

You activate regular expressions in the Find & Replace tab by checking the Regular Expression box (see Figure 22-1). You can then enter search patterns into the Find field and replacement values in the Replace field, including back references to any selected patterns.

Tip: Ignore Case Applies

Ignore Case still applies to regular expressions, so check or uncheck this as applicable; for HTML tags, you should almost always leave it checked. GoLive creates consistently formatted tags per the settings in the Global tab of Web Settings, so if you're working with a page that hasn't been created by GoLive or had the Rewrite Source Code command applied, Ignore Case is even more important. (See Chapter 14, *Source Editing*, for more on making GoLive rewrite source code.)

Figure 22-1
Activating
Regular
Expressions

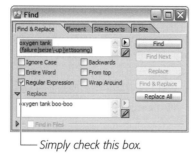

└─ *Simply check this box.*

Figure 22-2
Find pane's
Regular
Expressions
settings

Items in the Regular Expressions settings show up in the popup menus to the right of the Find and Replace fields with the names assigned to them.

Prefab Find Regular Expressions

GoLive's developers provide a set of prefabricated regular expressions in the Preferences dialog box's Find pane under Regular Expressions settings (see Figure 22-2). You can select these items from the popup menus to the right of the Find and Replace fields in the Find dialog box.

The names that appear in the menus are assigned in the Regular Expressions settings Name column. You can add common expressions here, as well.

Element

The Element tab of the Find feature lets you use regular expressions in just one place: the Attribute field. (You can't pattern match the name or contents of attributes, nor can you replace using patterns matched.) See Chapter 14, *Source Editing*, for more on the Element tab.

Spellchecking

There are some items you don't want GoLive to flag as spelling errors. For instance, GoLive comes with a built-in set of regular expressions that allows its internal spellchecker to ignore anything that looks like a URL. Otherwise, if you included a human-readable URL in the text of your pages, GoLive would flag it as an error. You can also enter more complex technical requirements, or even specific words.

The list is found in the Preferences dialog box under the Spell Checker pane in Regular Expressions. The items here are negative settings, meaning that any pattern you enter is ignored.

Filename Constraints

Filename Constraints is explained fully in Chapter 19, *Managing Files, Folders, and Links*. It lets GoLive easily flag any files that have characters in their names that a given operating system (like MS-DOS or Unix) would find so distasteful, it would prevent you from uploading or transferring the files. You can define your own sets to meet company specifications for file naming, for instance, and use regular expressions to ensure compliance.

The settings for Filename Constraints are found on a global basis in the Site pane of the Preferences dialog box. You can also create site-by-site settings by selecting the Filename Constraints pane in Site Settings for any given site, and checking the Site Specific Settings box.

Ever Advancing

When someone tells us a particular program fulfills a user's every need, we get skeptical. In the case of GoLive, however, our skepticism has been put aside for the time being. Granted, GoLive probably doesn't do everything a designer could want, but it comes pretty darn close.

Building Dynamic Content

The most powerful new set of features in GoLive 6 is grouped together as Dynamic Content. Dynamic Content allows you to create template pages in GoLive that display information derived from database interactions. Better still, you can create forms in which information can be modified or added to a database, or records removed.

GoLive accomplishes this immense task by linking databases and structured data sources through server-side scripting languages that support processing queries via a Web server. In Chapter 15, *Dynamic Content and Databases*, we covered how to add dynamic content to your page in GoLive; in this chapter, we cover how to set up and work with the database servers.

The previous release of GoLive handled just a limited kind of Microsoft ASP (Active Server Pages) interaction and required a lot of hand-tweaking by users to set up and configure GoLive's relationship to a database.

GoLive 6, however, expands the support to two new languages: PHP (PHP: Hypertext Preprocessor, we kid you not) and JSP (JavaServer Pages), as well as building in an entire live test suite for each language that allows you to fully debug any configuration before committing to it and rolling it out to designers working on individual pages.

Adobe has gone one step further and included preconfigured servers (which it calls GoLive Preconfigured Servers in a nice literal approach) which combine the MySQL relational database with an Apache Web server configured to work with PHP and a JSP server (Tomcat). You could get these software components separately for free, but not configured in this synchronized fashion ready to install with a couple of clicks.

The preconfigured servers are installed identically under many versions of Windows and Macintosh OS X 10.1 or later. This prefab package lets you test out working with databases and processing languages through examples that Adobe has provided. With some simple modifications, you can turn them into actual production systems.

Dynamic Concepts

The three scripting languages that GoLive supports rely on a combination of two factors: the scripts and configurations are included in individual pages uploaded to a Web server that a visitor never sees; and, the Web server, database server, and GoLive itself can be located on the same machine, or split among any number of machines.

In the case of PHP and JSP, a properly equipped Web server has support built in (or compiled in if you're handy; see later in this chapter) to work with one or both of those languages. With ASP, Microsoft supports it in its Internet Information Server (IIS), which can be turned on or off.

The database server can be located practically anywhere, although in practice, most smaller systems host both the database and Web server on the same machine, or at least on physically proximate machines. The database server can be any of a number of flavors, as long as they are supported directly (like MySQL) or through a standard interface, such as ODBC (Open Database Connectivity) or JDBC (Java Database Connectivity), both of which GoLive can work with through the scripting languages.

Each of these scripting languages works by combining the script itself (or a reference to an external file containing a script) with values embedded into an HTML page. So when you view the page as source in GoLive, you can see a variety of code and placeholders; but when processed by the server and fed to

What's New in 6

Dynamic Content was called Dynamic Link in GoLive 5, and it offered minimal features. It worked only with ASP, and didn't self configure and test. GoLive 6 swapped the name for an upgrade (content is more descriptive than link), and added integration with the JSP and PHP scripting languages.

With the addition of JSP and PHP, more database types were opened up to direct access. JSP can access many databases directly via the JDBC translator, while PHP can talk to MySQL. The new Dynamic Content module handles XML neatly, letting you transform records in a structured file into entries on a page.

Figure 23-1
Building and
configuring
Dynamic
Content

1. Install servers and languages.

2. Configure servers for access.

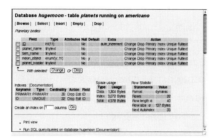

3. Build or link databases.

4. Set up GoLive to work with
Dynamic Content.

5. Add languages
to GoLive, ap-
propriate to the
servers
referenced.

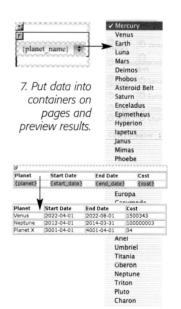

7. Put data into
containers on
pages and
preview results.

6. Add data sources that
reference individual databases
or structured records.

a Web browser, you'd see that the underlying HTML looks completely normal and has all the appropriate spots filled in with content. None of the code appears to the browser at all.

The server knows a requested page has server-side code in it because the file name ends with an extension of ".asp", ".jsp", or ".php" instead of ".html". A directive in appropriately configured servers recognizes the extension and hands off pages to the right interpreters.

Who Uses Which Language?

Each language allows human-readable scripting that can be quickly modified or visually inspected. When a server receives a request for a file containing one of these languages, it interprets the page, replacing symbols and code on the page with HTML or other markup languages.

Beyond these similarities, however, there's a slightly different audience for each of the supported scripting languages.

ASP. ASP is typically used in organizations that have standardized on Windows NT or 2000 for their internal servers. ASP can be used throughout an organization, and programmers who have been trained in it can write scripts that work for both internal purposes and external Web sites.

Being Dynamic

Not all sites need to be database-driven. Good candidate tasks for using a database include product catalogs, press release archives, employee bios, and current job listings; that is, any set of information that has multiple items with similar characteristics.

Though the Dynamic Content interface is simple and easy to use, a few caveats remain:

- It does not create the database for you; you must own the appropriate database software and know how to use it before you can do anything with Dynamic Content. (We discuss that in this chapter.)
- The Dynamic Content system supports

ASP, JSP, and PHP. But not every system administrator allows programs written in these languages to run, nor will it necessarily be easy to meld GoLive's code with an existing operation.

- When you use the visual Dynamic Content tools, you are limited to a narrow subset of server capabilities: basically getting data out of and into a database, and displaying it on a Web page. All three languages support an enormously larger set of options than GoLive accesses, but these options require learning the languages and writing your own scripts.

Tip: VBScript and JScript

GoLive supports ASP via two kinds of scripting languages: VBScript (Visual Basic scripting) and JScript (Microsoft's version of JavaScript). The JScript option is new. The VBScript support remains because Dynamic Link in GoLive 5 only worked with VBScript, and Adobe apparently didn't want to abandon earlier users.

ASP is also used by individuals and organizations that have a Windows XP, NT, 2000, or similar server with the IIS system installed. Because this is preinstalled, it's an easy way to set up a Web site as part of the whole system.

Some companies also sell software that allows ASP to run under Unix systems, such as Sun Microsystems's ChiliSoft ASP package (www.chilisoft.com).

Average human beings can learn how to code basic ASPs through a variety of books and courses. It's possible to immediately put into practice some simple ASP commands, and to build more complicated systems.

ASP code tends to live on individual pages in a site, although better-written sites reference common sets of functions in external files to reduce the management problem of updating code on many pages. You can manage ASP from within GoLive transparently; GoLive leaves ASP code alone when it's encountered.

GoLive Versus Dreamweaver

Comparisons are constantly made between GoLive and Macromedia Dreamweaver and Dreamweaver UltraDev, a package that adds a set of database scripting tools.

GoLive 6 moved the program closer to Ultra-Dev, which supports ASP and JSP, as well as the ColdFusion scripting language, which is a well-evolved and widely supported product made by Macromedia (it merged with the language's creator, Allaire).

When you review the two tools side by side, GoLive has most of the same features, but Ultra-Dev is slightly more evolved because it can talk directly to a database rather than speaking through an interpreter. GoLive has to use scripts to talk to databases, which adds to latency and slows down development.

Some of UltraDev's tools are also superior for streamlining the building of database pages. In UltraDev, a single palette displays all the available bindings that can be added, while GoLive requires you to select or insert items and then use a more complicated set of popup menus.

UltraDev goes one step further in its bundled package in which it allows direct program development of scripting code with Jrun, Macromedia's JSP server software, and ColdFusion. This allows a programmer to write code, test it live, and integrate it in the same interface with Dreamweaver.

At some point, Adobe will have to integrate that next step, and offer ASP, JSP, and/or PHP programming tools that will work from start to finish entirely within the system.

JSP. JavaServer Pages are found in organizations that have bought into Sun Microsystems's Java programming language for operating their servers. An enterprise (or corporate network and systems) version of Java has been extremely popular because of its ease of learning, compact code, speed, and widespread support.

JSP is supported through several commercial packages, as well as Tomcat, an open-source, free package that implements all of the necessary pieces.

JDBC works with JSP to talk to databases through a standard interface for making queries and updating data. Some databases have a specific JDBC interface; others can work with a JDBC-to-ODBC converter that talks through these two parts to have a conversation.

JSP requires real programming knowledge, as Java is a higher-level language and requires fairly extensive study and practice to master.

Most of the code for JSP is in the back-end: the JSP processor, like Tomcat, uses sets of files that it has access to in order to execute the commands found in JSP files loaded by users.

PHP. PHP was designed, like ASP, to allow server-side processing of embedded commands in Web pages, so you could plop in the current date and time, perform calculations, or interact with a database.

And, like ASP, PHP is easily learned: the syntax is not horribly complicated, and you can quickly pick up a few commands that spice up Web pages or allow you to solve problems that would require oceans of JavaScript. (JavaScript best solves user-side interaction: clicks or mouse actions that do things; PHP solves server-side interaction: information to display, process, or retrieve.)

GoLive also passes through embedded PHP scripting without comment (no joke intended), so you can embed PHP instructions directly into GoLive-managed Web pages.

Setting Up Dynamic Servers

To work with Dynamic Content in Golive, you need at a minimum a database, a Web server, and support for one of GoLive's supported scripting languages.

Tip: Structured Data

The term *database* is a pretty strict one, but GoLive uses the term loosely. Because some of these scripting languages have enormous support for documents structured using XML, you can, in fact, treat data formatted in XML files as de facto databases.

There are lots and lots of ways to put together the packages you need to work with GoLive. We discuss just a few popular configurations that should be enough for most users working on their own.

Because GoLive can work with such a large variety of systems, any more sophisticated information technology person with an existing database system should be able to also set up linkages for more complicated arrangements that will also work. For instance, the Oracle database system has all the necessary hooks through the ODBC standard to work with ASP, JSP, or PHP.

Tip: Firewalls

Installing servers typically requires changes in a personal or corporate firewall because servers communicate via ports. When configuring a system, pay close attention to which Internet addresses and which users have access to systems to avoid compromising your databases or Web servers.

Tip: License to Database

Many of the open-source or freely distributable packages listed below (including all the software shipped as part of the preconfigured servers) require acceptance of a software license. Because these products distribute their actual source code, they also limit in various ways the methods by which new products that incorporate the source code may be resold or distributed.

This does not affect your use of scripts, however. The licensing issues only affect modification, sales, and distribution of the underlying system, not the scripts you write that rely on this. If this is confusing, join the club.

Installing Preconfigured Servers

Adobe's made this task pretty simple for us all by including a standard set of preconfigured servers that can be installed through a few clicks. This set of servers works under most versions of Windows (98, XP, NT, 2000, etc.) as well as with Mac OS X 10.1 or later.

Locate the Preconfigured Servers folder on the disc that's bound into the back of the Adobe Web Workgroup Server manual. The folder contains two items: Dynamic Content and Extras. The Dynamic Content folder contains a single installer that, when run, allows you to install Apache, Tomcat, and PHP. Apache is an open-source Web server which, in this installation, is customized to work directly with the open-source PHP language. Tomcat handles JSP requests as a freestanding server.

The Extras folder contains MySQL, a free database server that can also be installed through a single process. If you want to use MySQL with PHP, the standard configuration already supports it.

Tip: Password Protect MySQL

Make sure to set up a password for MySQL as described in the installation procedure and documentation.

To use MySQL with JSP, copy the MySQL JDBC driver to your JSP server as described in the MySQL JDBC folder in the Extras folder.

Working with the Servers

The preconfigured servers require a few choices about the ports on which they will work. A Web server, for instance, is typically installed at port 80, the default for Web servers on the Internet. However, if you are already using a built-in Web server in the operating system or one you've installed on your own, you either need to disable the other server or install the new one at a special port.

The default ports for Tomcat and MySQL should be used, as they are generally reserved for their purposes. If you are already running copies of these software packages, you need to choose other ports.

GoLive includes several scripts to halt, start up, and restart these servers. When you install JSP support for a site, for instance, you have to then restart the Tomcat server to have it reload its support files.

You can walk through a number of examples developed by Adobe that are installed along with the Preconfigured Servers to get a feel for both how to structure dynamic sites and how to code pages in GoLive. When you finish

Critical PHP Bug Fix

The version of PHP that came with the 6.0 release of GoLive shipped just after a critical bug was discovered in PHP that allows hacker access in certain circumstances. Adobe may have updated their package before you read this part of the book (check their Web site), but you can also fix the problem by turning off a setting that allows files to be uploaded.

In the preconfigured servers folder, navigate down to the php_server folder, and then the apache folder. At that level, the installation placed a file called php.ini. Edit this file with a text editor. Scroll down to the part of the file that reads:

```
; Whether to allow HTTP file
    uploads.
file_uploads = On
```

Simply put a semicolon at the start of the file_uploads line so it now reads:

```
; file_uploads = On
```

Save the file. You should now restart Apache using the stop and start or restart scripts. Unless you're intending to receive files from users, this option doesn't need to be on in any case.

If you do need to receive files via the Web, then consult "Installing Custom Servers," later in this chapter, in which case you can get the latest, fixed version.

installing the servers, a browser should launch automatically pointing to the home page for these examples. If not, follow the instructions in the folder to visit the example Web sites.

Customizing the Preconfigured Servers

The Adobe package can be easily customized to support your own sites running on the same servers with Apache/PHP or JSP. It requires a little hand-editing of text files, though.

Create a folder on the server to contain your site files. This folder will be where you place the live files for the site and the location or path you define under Servers. If you're also running GoLive on the same machine, you can define this as a local path when you set up database sources in Site Settings (see later in this chapter). For this example, let's assume your path is "/short-site" on the Mac (a "shortsite" folder at the root level of the boot drive) and "c:\shortsite" under Windows.

Adding a path to create an Apache subsite. If you want to set up your Web site to offer files at its hostname plus this path, here's how. If your hostname is http://www.weebles.yz, the site example shows up at:

```
http://www.weebles.yz/shortsite
```

Tip: Root URL

If you need to set up new servers that work at the root of a site (no path following the hostname), you need to learn a little more about system administration than we can cover here. You have to configure DNS and make more substantial changes to this configuration file.

1. Use a shortcut to edit the Apache configuration. This is named differently on each platform, but should look like Edit Apache Config or a similar name. Double-click this.

2. In the Apache configuration file, which is just a long text file with directives, scroll down to near the end where you find a comment that reads

   ```
   # Alias for Apache docs
   ```

   Put the cursor just above that and enter this text with your own values. (You can find this on our Web site to copy and paste into place.)

   ```
   Alias /shortsite "/shortsite"
   <Directory "/shortsite">
     Options Indexes FollowSymLinks MultiViews ExecCGI
     AllowOverride All
     Order allow,deny
   ```

```
 Allow from all
</Directory>
```

On a Windows machine, change the first two lines to read

```
Alias /shortsite "C:\shortsite"
<Directory "C:\shortsite">
```

3. Save the document.

4. Restart the Apache server using the stop and start Apache scripts, or the restart Apache script.

Adding a path to create a Tomcat/JSP subsite. If you want to feed out JSP pages, you can reconfigure the server as installed to handle those as well.

1. Use a shortcut to edit the Tomcat configuration. This is named differently on each platform, but should look like Edit Tomcat Config or a similar name. Double-click this.

2. In the Tomcat configuration file, scroll down to near the end where you find a comment that reads

```
<!--Virtual host example
```

Put the cursor just above that and enter this text exactly as it appears. (You can find this on our Web site to copy and paste into place.)

```
<Context path="/shortsite"
 docBase="/shortsite"
 debug="1"
 reloadable="true" >
</Context>
```

On a Windows machine, change the second line to read

```
 docBase="C:\shortsite"
```

3. Save the document.

4. Restart the Tomcat server using the stop and start Apache scripts, or the restart all servers script.

Installing Custom Servers

It's likely that the preconfigured servers will be more instructive than productive for existing operations which may have some parts of their process already in place. In those cases, you might want to try to install your own servers or configure existing systems to work with GoLive.

In the interests of brevity and sanity, here are several combinations of free, simple, and relatively easy-to-put-together packages for Windows, Linux/ Unix, and Mac OS X.

Tip: OS 9 Servers? (Mac only)

There are ways to serve content from Mac OS 9, but OS X's Unix underpinnings put it squarely into the server category. Switch to OS X 10.1 or later in order to actually build production-quality servers you can provide access to for in-house and external users.

Roll your own Apache, PHP, and MySQL

Glenn's been a system administrator (not entirely by choice) since 1994 when he started a Web development company. Although the preconfigured servers are quite nice, he decided to poke around to find the right combination of options to create his own special blend on our office's Red Hat Linux box.

This combination should work under pretty much any standard Linux distribution and many commercial Unix systems as well.

Tip: Use the Stock Install

Because the GoLive Preconfigured Servers already put together Apache, PHP, Tomcat, and MySQL for Windows and Mac OS X, you may want to rely on them for those two platforms.

When Glenn configures a server, he starts by creating a directory called /usr/construction in which he can place and compile all the source code. He then downloads the following packages that allow a secure server compilation and installation of Apache and links PHP into that setup as well:

- **Apache 1.3** (current version: 2.0.35), httpd.apache.org. Version 2.0 of Apache was released just as we finished this edition, and these instructions will change for that version; see our Web site for the revised details as the latest version includes several of the modules below in its distribution.

- **OpenSSL 0.9** (current version: 0.9.6c), www.openssl.org. The group behind OpenSSL ships new versions every few months. This package offers free support for secure servers (SSL). You can omit this package and the following one if you don't care about secure support.

- **Mod_ssl** (current version 2.8.7), www.modssl.org. This code is a module for Apache that links in SSL support using the OpenSSL software. Find the version that corresponds to your release of Apache. Omit for plain HTTP.

- **PHP 4**, www.php.net. Download the source code.

- **Sablotron**, www.gingerall.com/charlie/ga/xml/d_sab.xml. Sablotron is needed to support XML and XSLT content source parsing. You can omit this component without affecting the rest of the process.

- **MySQL**, www.mysql.com. You can download complete binary installations that require a simple installation, as well as source code.

- **Tomcat for JSP**, jakarta.apache.org/tomcat/index.html. Although we don't offer advice on configuring JSP, you can download this package from scratch to try your hand at it if you're already a Java wizard.

Follow these instructions to create your custom server installation:

1. Gunzip and untar these files in your construction directory.

2. Change to the Apache directory and run ./configure; this sets Apache up to handle the PHP installation.

3. Jump up a level and change to the OpenSSL directory. Run its configuration process; see its Readme and Install documentation. Skip this step to omit SSL support.

4. Change to the Sablotron directory, and configure with this command:

   ```
   ./configure --disable-javascript
   ```

   Then compile and install it.

5. Change to the PHP directory, and enter the following (make changes to the newest version numbers if newer versions are available). Remove the "openssl" line and the "\" on the previous line if you're not including SSL support. Omit the lines "--enable-xslt" and "--with-xslt-sablot" to exclude XML data source processing.

   ```
   ./configure \
     --with-mysql \
     --with-apache=../apache_1.3.23 \
     --with-config-file-path=/etc \
     --enable-magic-quotes \
     --enable-debugger \
     --enable-track-vars \
     --with-db3=/usr/local/BerkeleyDB.3.1 \
     --with-openssl=../openssl-0.9.6c/ \
     --enable-xslt \
     --with-xslt-sablot
   ```

6. Change to the /usr/construction directory and install the file below as apache-configure (making changes for version numbers as needed).

Remove the "openssl" line and the "\" on the previous line if you're not in-cluding SSL support.

```
#!/bin/sh
cd mod_ssl-2.8.7-1.3.23
./configure \
    --prefix=/usr/apache13 \
    --verbose \
    --enable-module=expires \
    --enable-module=usertrack \
    --enable-module=rewrite \
    --enable-module=status \
    --enable-module=proxy \
    --enable-module=so \
    --activate-module=src/modules/php4/libphp4.a \
    --with-apache=../apache_1.3.23 \
    --with-ssl=../openssl-0.9.6c
cd ..
cd apache_1.3.23
make
make install
```

7. Run the program:

```
sh ./apache-configure
```

The script compiles and installs the software.

8. Set up the configuration files. Apache includes documentation and sample files in the path /usr/apache13/conf (if you installed using the above settings). Make sure and use the directives required to pass PHP code on to the PHP processor.

    PHP has its documentation online and you can edit the /etc/php.ini file to meet the requirements of GoLive, which will tell you the settings you need to change as appropriate.

Built-in ASP Service

Windows XP Professional, NT, 2000, and later versions of all of these operating systems come with Microsoft's Internet Information Server (IIS) which supports the ASP language.

Tip: Personal Web Server

The Personal Web Server (PWS) available in some configurations can also work with ASP in Windows versions not designed as servers.

If you didn't purposely install IIS when you set up your system, open Control Panels, and use Add/Remove Software to select the Windows Components option. You can then select IIS from the scrolling list, dig up that OS installation disc you've been using as a coaster, and install it.

The administrative tools for IIS are extremely primitive and frustrating. From Control Panel, choose Administrative Tools. Use Internet Information Services to set up virtual directories and scripting access (see Figure 23-2).

Our advice for this area is to read Microsoft's documentation and, perhaps, buy a book. Running IIS looks simple, but it's not for the faint of heart, as numerous system administrators have related to us.

Figure 23-2
Internet
Information
Services
administrative
tool

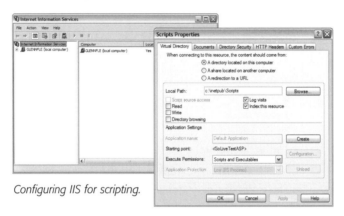

Configuring IIS for scripting.

Tenon iTools

Tenon offers iTools for OS X, a package that includes Apache configured for secure commerce with a number of other server tools. What's more important, however, is that they also bundle software from Halcyon Software called iASP that adds full ASP support along with integration with JDBC database drivers and other hooks to Java and JSP. The full iTools package is $400. See www.tenon.com/products/itools-osx/.

Mac OS X Server

Apple sells a preconfigured package with loads of Unix servers that includes graphical server administration tools. This includes Apache, PHP, JSP, MySQL, and many other packages.

The server software sells for about $500 for a version that handles 10 simultaneous users, or $1,000 for unlimited users. Visit www.apple.com/macosx/server/specs.html for full details.

Working with Databases

Because GoLive works with these three scripting languages, which themselves can talk to practically any database directly or through translators (ODBC and JDBC), you have a high degree of choice if you're starting from scratch, or lots of flexibility if you're working with existing sources.

GoLive can talk through ASP, JSP, and PHP to four kinds of structured data sources:

- **ADO Database Query.** ActiveX Data Object (ADO) is how GoLive labels databases that can be reached via ODBC or the Windows OLE DB driver including Microsoft Access and SQL Server, Oracle, FileMaker Pro, and many, many others. This option is available with ASP-enabled sites.

- **JDBC Database.** The JDBC interface allows a JSP server to talk to databases directly or via an ODBC translator.

- **MySQL Database Query.** This is the standard interface for PHP sites to talk to the MySQL database.

- **XML Data Source.** All three languages (with the appropriate extensions) can parse XML as if it were a database and retrieve data out of it as if it were comprised of fields and records.

Tip: Commerce for Hire

Don't get too excited about the CustomMerchant options listed as a database option. This option only works with an Adobe business partner that provides GoLive turnkey integration of a shopping cart and payment system. It's available for a fee, and, while cool, is not a generalized solution for shopping or buying, which it might appear to be at first glance. Read their documentation for more on using this system.

Connecting

If you have existing databases, you need to jot down several details:

- The IP address of the server and the port to which you can connect. The port is often set to a default for that type of server, like 3306 for MySQL.

- The name of the database.

- An account name and password.

If you don't have all of this information, you almost certainly cannot use a database as a source.

Building

Although building databases is beyond our book's scope, there are plenty of resources (books, Web sites, and classes) that teach you how relational databases are constructed and how to work with them. However, we have to share one tip.

Our colleague in Australia, Rob Keniger (bigbangextensions.com), suggested a truly marvelous tool for us to work with the combination of PHP and MySQL: phpMyAdmin (phpmyadmin.sourceforge.com). A simple set of free PHP scripts, this tool offers Web-based interaction with a MySQL server, making it as easy to work with as FileMaker Pro.

Tip: Unique ID

Each table in a database should have a field that acts as its unique identifier. GoLive works with tables that lack this field, but it does complain about it. The unique ID is needed to cross-reference records between tables.

Setting Up GoLive

Once you have all the server components installed and clearing their throats, you still must spend some time learning GoLive's methods of communicating with the various parts of these database operations.

Checklist

Before you get started, you need to ensure the following conditions are met:

1. The Dynamic Content Module is turned on in GoLive. It's on by default in new installations.

Tip: Restoring the Module

If you've turned Dynamic Content off to streamline GoLive's operations, open Preferences, select the Modules pane, and check the box next to Dynamic Content. You have to quit GoLive and launch it again to activate Dynamic Content.

2. You have ASP, PHP, and/or JSP installed on the servers you're working with. In the case of JSP, the JSP processor is up and running.

3. Your database, MySQL, Microsoft SQL, or otherwise, is configured to accept queries from the Web server's IP address. Or you have a valid XML source in a place you can reach it via a URL.

4. The Web server is reachable from your current location; no firewall or other filter prevents you from reaching it.

5. You have FTP or WebDAV access to a remote Web server, or you're running the scripting language off a local server that you can copy files to directly through a file path.

If all of these statements are true, you're ready to get started.

Dynamic Content Wizard

The Dynamic Content Wizard can walk you through the necessary steps to install DC support on your Web server. While you answer questions and proceed, GoLive installs scripts, retrieves tests, and gives you tips or non-GoLive instructions to finish a configuration.

You can use the wizard by bringing up Site Settings and clicking the Dynamic Content pane. If you already have a configuration finished or in process, the link for the wizard is in the upper right; otherwise, the whole window is devoted to explaining the wizard (see Figure 23-3).

Click the cog wheel to start the wizard.

Figure 23-3
Starting the
Dynamic Site
Wizard

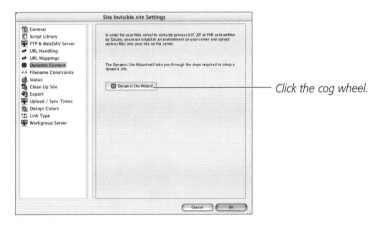

Click the cog wheel.

Choosing a Language
The first screen offers you some help and instructions, and allows you to choose which processing languages you will be using: ASP, JSP, or PHP (see Figure 23-4). You can choose any combination of these languages.

Tip: Fixing Broken Dynamic Link Sites

As we finished preparing this edition of the book, several readers wrote us desperately trying to fix GoLive 5 Dynamic Link sites that they had imported into GoLive 6 and refreshed using Dynamic Content. The problem was in the scripting

Figure 23-4
Adding the
scripting
language

If a language is already installed, unchecking it causes the wizard to remove scripting support.

language choice: GoLive appeared to automatically switch their sites to JScript, which broke them. We recommended they manually change the option to ASP/VBScript in the Site Settings Dynamic Content pane, and they were then able to bring their sites back to working condition.

Connecting to the Server

The wizard requires you to choose how GoLive communicates with the dynamically enabled server: via FTP, WebDAV, or a local path for locally served sites (see Figure 23-5). If you don't have your FTP or WebDAV server set up yet, you can select Edit Server from either menu to bring up the Servers feature in which you can define new servers without leaving the wizard. For workgroup sites, you can select an already defined Publish Server.

Figure 23-5
Server file
transfer
selection in
workgroups
and single-user
servers

Workgroup sites show available Publish Servers, but you can't configure more from this menu.

Your Site's Web Address

GoLive needs to retrieve files both during testing and in routine development of dynamic content pages. Enter the URL that these pages can be retrieved from (see Figure 23-6). If pages are nested in a subdirectory, make sure to correctly specify the entire path to the site.

Figure 23-6
Entering the
Web address
of the dynamic
server

Preparing the Server

In the next screen, GoLive tries to upload and retrieve the appropriate files for the scripting language you chose. You may receive a variety of errors at this stage if these files fail to upload or fail to return the appropriate values.

Generally, GoLive displays the actual Web page it returned, which contains a detailed description of the error to help with troubleshooting.

Tip: FTP Timeout

If you wait a while between starting the wizard and/or use the Back button after this stage to return to an earlier part of the process and then walk away, the FTP server may time out. When you click Next again, you receive an FTP Disconnect message. Clicking Back and Next again should refresh the server connection and reupload the necessary files.

Security Setup

If GoLive successfully uploads and tests the files, the Security Setup screen appears (see Figure 23-7). This screen allows you to control access to the authoring features in GoLive to ensure that random people can't reconfigure your site.

The most restrictive choice is Allow Only This Address, which is prefilled. We're more likely to enter values in Allow Only This Subnet. If you're not a system administrator, you may need to ask someone for these specific values for your whole network; they're not intuitive.

Figure 23-7
Setting security
access to
underlying files

An Alternative: Lasso Professional

An alternative to Adobe's entire system is Lasso Professional, a set of software applications and server from Blue World Communications (www.blueworld.com). Lasso Professional bundles a MySQL server with Blue World's own rich programming language. Coupled with their Lasso Studio package, you can program the underlying system directly within GoLive.

The difference between Blue World's approach and Adobe's is that Adobe offers the minimum necessary pieces for ASP, JSP, and PHP written in those languages to support its database operations. Blue World, on the other hand, has provided practically its entire suite of commands in its own language through GoLive palettes.

So not only can you show database records, but you can also calculate math functions, manipulate queries through variables, or write complicated scripts entirely within our favorite Web management application. Because the process is drag, drop, and fill-in via an Inspector, average users can handle some fairly complicated transactions. (Someone could extend GoLive for its three supported languages, as well; there's no technical constraint.)

The idea behind Lasso is that you can build an entire system with a single engine behind it

that works in a supported, comprehensible, extensible way. You can, of course, build out systems using PHP, JSP, ASP, and other environments, but it's hard to find this kind of integration coupled with a developer community and good documentation. Also, Lasso has a variety of security options inherent in its design, whereas with the other scripting languages, security often has to be painfully overlaid.

The Lasso components you'd need comprise three parts: the server software, Lasso Professional Standard Edition, which runs under Windows 2000, XP, and Mac OS X ($1,200 to $2,000); the developer's software, used for implementation of Lasso-based systems ($350 to $1,050); and Lasso Studio for GoLive, the set of plug-ins and palettes ($300 to $350). You need a separate copy of the Lasso Studio for each copy of GoLive.

Blue World offers direct technical support for their entire configuration from end to end; the pricing above is based in part on how much support you purchase along with the product. If you choose any of the other methods described in this chapter, you'd have to purchase and find separate technical support for each component, and no one would advise you on integration.

We agree with Adobe: Allow Anyone is a dangerous choice, and you should use only in a case in which access to the server is controlled through other means already.

After installing these settings for the first time, this screen in the wizard changes to point you to the location of the security access files (see Table 23-1).

Table 23-1
Access files

Language	Location
ASP	\<site root>/config/include/friends.asp
JSP	\<site root>/WEB-INF/friends.xml
PHP	\<site root>/config/include/friends.php

You can edit these files locally in GoLive, but must re-upload them to the server to change access permissions. The files contain explanations on which values to enter.

Tip: Java Friends

Restart the JSP server after editing its friends.xml file.

Tip: Losing Friends

The single most common problem we've had with Dynamic Content is having the friends file overwritten, thus losing our custom access permissions. We'd suggest making a backup of your friends file after you edit it so you can easily restore it if your version is overwritten with the default.

Installing Files

After clicking Next on the Security Setup screen, GoLive installs the necessary collection of files on your server via the connection method you specified. This can take a while with a slow connection, but should be just a minute or so on a local network.

New in 6: Automatic Install

Users of Dynamic Link in GoLive 5 may recall the tedious process of getting this far with ASP files. GoLive 6 automatically configures and installs necessary files in the right location, tests them, and produces debugging and trouble-shooting results.

After using the wizard once, returning to the wizard process later, or using the Back button from a later screen, brings up a Troubleshooting section which allows you to test an installation (click Test) and receive feedback; or, you can click to reinstall the files from scratch, which isn't a bad idea when you're trying to eliminate variables from a wonky configuration.

Test and Troubleshooting

When you first set up a language linkage or when you click Test in the wizard or in the Dynamic Content pane with a language selected, GoLive uses a trouble-shooting script on the server to provide feedback about configuration options.

Typical problems include settings that need to be changed in the php.ini file, permissions for directories, and modules that need to be compiled into a server. You often need to restart a server (stop and start or restart, depending on the software) after changing settings.

The troubleshooting page is launched in a browser, and after you make changes to fix errors, you can hit reload in the browser to run the test again.

Modifying Choices

When the Wizard has finished its job, you're deposited in a newly populated Dynamic Content pane (see Figure 23-8). In this pane, you can change, re-move, and add to many of the choices you made using the wizard.

Enter a new Site Root URL at the top. When you click OK to close the Site Settings window, GoLive prompts you to update the scripting configuration files.

Change the type of Server Connection in the next area down. You can add, remove, or test scripting language connections in Server Processing Languages.

You can also click the wizard icon in the upper right of the pane to walk through adding to or modifying the options you already set.

Figure 23-8
Dynamic
Content Site
Settings

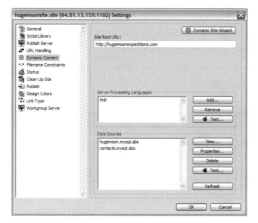

Data Sources

The Data Sources area of the Dynamic Content pane in Site Settings appears after you successfully add a scripting language (see Figure 23-1, earlier). This area lets you define the actual database or file sources that you link into an individual site, making records available for display and manipulation in GoLive.

Clicking New brings up selections appropriate for the scripting languages you've chosen (see Table 23-2). If you have more than one language installed, all of the appropriate options are available.

Table 23-2
Access files

Language	Access	ADO	JDBC	MySQL	XML	Commerce
ASP	●	●			●	●
JSP			●		●	●
PHP				●	●	●

Each type of database has a different configuration screen for the options you need to enter. All of them share the property of storing a local file that contains configuration information

---

Tip: No Write

The folder that stores configuration information should not be globally writable. That is, you don't want someone to be able to follow a path to the folder and overwrite your files (which will be named the same in all GoLive installations).

The files must be readable as they contain passwords for accessing your data sources; however, GoLive uses built-in scripts in those files to prevent access.

The Properties button allows you to edit settings after they're created. The Delete button's meaning is obvious, while Refresh rescans the configuration file to make sure no new sources have been added that it's missed, such as Access databases (see below).

The Test button works just as it does in a new data source window: it queries the data source and returns a sample record.

Creating Data Sources

We won't waste your time by repeating information that's available in meticulous detail elsewhere. The GoLive manual spends page after page covering, quite well, the details of connecting to each of these data sources. Instead, we want to provide a breezy overview of three types, and an in-depth look at XML data sources, which Adobe's manual and online help offer a fuzzier picture of.

In all types of databases, you're asked to provide a data source name, which GoLive appends the appropriate suffix onto. The data source name is the name of the file that contains the settings needed for the scripting languages to access the database, so it must be named something that's a legal file name on the server, typically with no spaces or special punctuation.

You also typically need a name and password to access the data source.

Tip: Failure to Connect

If you can't connect to a database, make sure it's configured to allow access from your location. Many databases restrict access based on an IP address.

Access Database. GoLive can talk directly to a Microsoft Access database as long as it's not password protected. Copy the database into the <site-root>/config/datasources/ folder on your server. Click Refresh in the Dynamic Content pane to force the database to show up in the Data Sources area. There are no configuration options for this type of source.

ADODatabase. This option lets you talk to data sources via translators that sit between the databases and the ASP code.

JDBC Database. The JDBC Database options use a driver in your JSP server to interact with the database. You need to know the name of this module (GoLive has some suggestions) and the path that the JSP server uses to talk to the database. You can set the number of threads to control the amount of simultaneous processing.

MySQL Database. A MySQL database with PHP requires just an IP address or host name with a port post-pended (like 192.168.0.1:3306); a database name; and a user name and password. It's one of the easiest items to configure.

XML Data Source. XML data sources aren't databases, but rather structured collections of data in a static XML file. You cannot query an XML file, but all three languages that GoLive supports have (or can add) parsers that can interpret XML data to extract information for display. See the sidebar, "Using XML Data Sources."

Custom Merchant Provider. As we note above, the Custom Merchant option allows you to create shopping carts and ecommerce transactions systems through an Adobe partner company.

Matching Data Sources to Content Sources

After creating data sources and clicking OK in the Site Settings dialog box, you can start creating pages in which you map data sources (databases and structured data) to content sources on an individual page (tables and regions in a specified data source).

We cover working with dynamic content on a page in Chapter 15, *Dynamic Content and Databases*, which is aimed at a more intermediate user who has not had to follow through on the work discussed in this chapter, but is ready to put Dynamic Content features to work.

Structural Reinforcement

With GoLive and some free or inexpensive servers, you can design and build world-class Web sites with vast amounts of data available to visitors without incurring likewise vast amounts of development and programming cost.

Authoring JavaScript

When you mention the word "programming" to most designers, their eyes glaze over. Programming is something for guys and gals in dark rooms who come into the office at noon or later, and emerge from their hideaways to search for caffeine and day-old pizza in the early morning hours. But mention graphical rollovers, form verification, and other nifty tricks that you can carry out in the browser, and the same designers get excited.

JavaScript, a simple scripting language, is a form of programming: defining structured sequences of events that use variable names to control behavior in the browser, thereby adding a lot of low-level, simple interactivity. Luckily, GoLive takes a lot of the sting out of JavaScript by providing tools to help make programming simpler, and predefined routines that involve setting values without messing with the underlying code.

In this chapter, we talk about the programming part of JavaScript, and how GoLive's tools help you write code and debug it. In the next two chapters we cover animation and GoLive Actions, both of which involve prepackaged JavaScript code. Consider this the primer that will help you better understand the whole subject. (If you haven't used JavaScript before, see the sidebar, "Learning JavaScript," before reading the whole chapter.)

Browser Support

Netscape invented JavaScript (originally calling it "LiveScript" before jumping on the Java bandwagon); it has nothing to do with Sun Microsystems' Java programming language, aside from marketing hype. Netscape's browsers all support JavaScript to varying degrees.

Microsoft also found JavaScript to be quite useful, adding support for what they call "JScript" since version 3.0 of Internet Explorer. Netscape and Microsoft jointly submitted the JavaScript specification to ECMA, a European technical standards body, to review and maintain as an open standard. You may sometimes run across the strange-sounding name "ECMA Script" which refers to the ratified standard version of JavaScript.

Tip: JavaScripting and Java Server Pages

Microsoft employs JavaScript on the server side—in scripts that run remotely on a Web server to carry out tasks—as one of the scripting languages supported by Active Server Pages (ASP) for server-side scripting. Netscape uses it as well with their server software.

But neither ASP nor the JavaScript support in ASP are the same as Java-Server Pages (JSP). JSP uses a Java engine on a server. It's distinct from ASP and has nothing to do with JavaScript either.

Unfortunately, the JavaScript road has a few potholes. Although it ostensibly works across browsers (Netscape and Internet Explorer) and across platforms (Mac, Windows, and Unix), different browser versions on different platforms support different versions of JavaScript.

And while both Netscape and Microsoft include JavaScript in their browsers, each added its own extensions to the standardized version. This mandates testing all your JavaScript scripts in as many different browsers as possible to ensure that they actually work. Many times, we've written simple scripts and watched them break on one browser, even as they work on seven others. It is possible for a skilled scripter to write JavaScript code to work around this problem, so that browsers capable of handling the script simply run it while browsers that can't are unaffected.

Over time, we've seen a convergence in standards, so that the newest browsers tend to support more or less the same features in the same way. But

What's New in 6

We're glad to say: not much. JavaScript support has always been good in GoLive, and Adobe has merely smoothed the edges to improve it.

The most significant change? The icon to launch the JavaScript Editor is now a script icon instead of the coffee bean that formerly (and confusingly) represented it.

What's Old in 6? The same missing feature that represents all links on a page by "links[?]" instead of unique names or numbers that you could use to attach triggers to.

you want to support at least a few versions of each browser, which means dealing with older incompatibilities you may no longer have to account for in Netscape 6 and IE 6.

Using JavaScript in GoLive

If you've decided to take the plunge and learn JavaScript, or if you're already an experienced scripter, you're all set. GoLive provides excellent support for adding scripts to your pages as well as editing them in three ways.

- Using GoLive's built-in JavaScript and DHTML Actions
- Writing scripts by hand using GoLive's JavaScript Editor
- Typing scripts directly into the HTML source code

Learning JavaScript

This chapter isn't intended to teach you JavaScript, but rather to teach you how to use JavaScript most efficiently in GoLive, while taking advantage of GoLive's graphical interface and JavaScript-management features.

If you already know JavaScript, terms like "handler," "procedure," and "variable" shouldn't frighten you. If those terms make you clutch your head and moan, we can recommend some resources for learning JavaScript before getting started.

If you've never touched a programming language before, there are classes and books designed to introduce programming basics using JavaScript's constructs. It's also not a hard language to learn if you've ever written in BASIC, Visual Basic, Fortran, Pascal, or C; you'll pick it up in hours.

JavaScript's popularity has helped create a huge number of excellent books to help you teach yourself the language. For new users, we recommend *JavaScript for the World Wide Web: Visual QuickStart Guide* (ISBN 0201735172), available from—you guessed it!—Peachpit Press. The authors (and our friends) Tom Negrino and Dori Smith assume no previous programming experience on the reader's part. They also include many example scripts that you can use as recipes to put directly into your pages.

Many Web sites also offer excellent tips and tutorials, as well as ready to use cut-and-paste scripts.

- Netscape DevEdge: devedge.netscape.com
- Web Review: www.webreview.com
- Webreference.com: www.webreference.com

You can find links to these sites and links to buy the book online (or you can buy from your local bookstore, of course) at realworldgolive.com/six/javascript.html.

Why Not Actions?

You may be asking yourself, "Why should I slave away writing scripts by hand if GoLive can do it for me with Actions?" While GoLive's built-in Actions can save time by giving you drag-and-drop functionality, there are major advantages to rolling your own scripts.

* JavaScript that is written by hand is almost always smaller and more efficient than that created by GoLive's Actions.

Client-Side versus Server-Side Scripting

You often hear the terms "client-side" and "server-side" bandied about when talk of scripting languages, Java, and Web server CGI (Common Gateway Interface) scripting comes up.

Client-side scripts are programs run on your computer. That is, the script is downloaded—usually as part of the HTML page, in the case of JavaScript—and then your machine executes the instructions in the program just as if you double-clicked on software on your desktop. Most JavaScript programs are simple sequences triggered by a mouse movement: for instance, the browser swaps out a different image while your mouse is hovering over a link.

The advantage of client-side programming is speed and flexibility; your machine doesn't need to contact another computer over the Internet or a company's intranet to carry out a task. And the tasks that JavaScript performs are often local tasks that don't need the involvement of a server. Do you really want to load a new page to display a larger version of an image or find out that you entered your Zip code in the wrong format? Not necessarily.

In server-side scripting or programming, the software runs on a server that you connect to over the Web. For instance, when you enter data in a form on a browser and then click submit, your browser sends all that data to a server. The server runs a program that examines the data and sends a response back to your browser. In a case like this, you're sending data that the server processes and stores or performs some action with, like adding your name to a mailing list.

Where this gets confusing is that JavaScript, Java, and other programming languages can be both client-side and server-side, but not simultaneously. Some servers use JavaScript programs (usually found client-side) to process form submissions. JavaScript is used in some other contexts, too, like validating form entries in Adobe Acrobat, and in writing special modules in GoLive. Java is used on the server as part of JavaServer Pages (JSP).

Where the action happens is key. In client-side programs, like JavaScript in HTML, your computer executes the program and produces results locally; with server-side programs, you have to send data to a server, have it run a program, and then get fed the response. Often, the bandwidth required to repeatedly pass basic data between a client and server can overshadow the utility of the software existing on the server's machine.

- The built-in Actions don't give you many options for dealing with multiple browsers and platforms.

- While there are many useful Actions, there are many more things you can do with JavaScript if you learn how to write it yourself.

- Actions can respond to many user events, but JavaScript itself responds to many more events, which you may want to call on to trigger scripts.

- The code that Actions create is very complex and essentially impossible to edit by hand. And, if someone does edit the script by hand, GoLive will no longer recognize it as an Action.

- If a page with GoLive Actions is opened in another visual editor, such as Microsoft FrontPage, the JavaScript may be changed and may no longer work properly.

We cover Actions more thoroughly in Chapter 26, *Applying Actions*, where we show you the best way to use these prefab bits.

Adding JavaScript

If you're a JavaScript Jedi Knight, you can simply click the Source Code Editor tab of the document window and start typing raw code. However, GoLive's built-in scripting environment offers nice features for both the novice and advanced scripter.

What about Other Scripting Languages?

What about other client-side scripting languages like Microsoft's VBScript? While GoLive doesn't offer direct support for adding VBScripts to your pages, it won't overwrite them or change them should you choose to type them in directly.

The same is true for ASP, JSP, and PHP code, as well as SSI (server-side includes). These languages can be embedded directly into HTML pages, but the code is executed by the server when the page is requested by a browser. The server treats the code as a set of instructions for manipulating the HTML page. The results of the program typically replace placeholders on the page (like a list of names as part of a database query replacing the contents of table cells).

The code, although embedded in the HTML page on the server, isn't sent to the browser; just the resulting HTML.

See Chapter 16, *Languages and Scripting*, and Chapter 23, *Building Dynamic Content*, for more about ASP, JSP, PHP, and SSI support.

Inserting a Script

You can add scripts written in JavaScript to either the head or body part of an HTML page. Generally, you insert scripts in the head part of the page to ensure they load first and are available when event handlers within the body trigger them.

When you add a script in GoLive, the program manages all the housekeeping tasks for you, like inserting a Script tag and comment tags into the HTML to surround the script.

GoLive offers the JavaScript Editor that lets you enter and modify body and head scripts (see Figure 24-1). The JavaScript Editor has a corresponding JavaScript Inspector, discussed at length in this chapter, which lets you choose JavaScript events, objects, and versions.

Figure 24-1
Script Editor

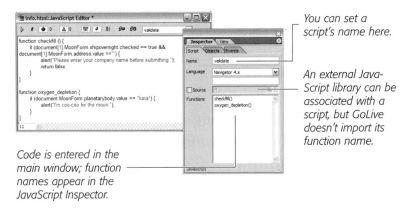

You can set a script's name here.

An external Java-Script library can be associated with a script, but GoLive doesn't import its function name.

Code is entered in the main window; function names appear in the JavaScript Inspector.

Tip: You Only Need One Script

You can get by with creating a single head script that contains all your JavaScript code. GoLive supports multiple scripts so that you can use different versions of JavaScript in each script, or even different scripting languages, such as Microsoft's close JavaScript relative, JScript.

Adding a head script. Click the JavaScript icon at the top of the Layout Editor to open the JavaScript Editor. Click the New Script Item (Mac) or Create Script (Windows) button to add a new head script. GoLive names it "Head Script 001" by default, but you can modify its name in the JavaScript Inspector.

You can also click the Toggle Head Section triangle in the head part of the Layout Editor, select the newly created script, and use the Head Script Inspector to name it (see Figure 24-2).

Figure 24-2
Head Script
Inspector used
with the Head
Section

Adding a body script. If, for some reason, you need to insert a JavaScript in the page's body, drag the JavaScript icon from the Basic tab of the Objects palette and drop it anywhere in the body of your page, but preferably before any event handler that needs to use it. The Inspector becomes the Body Script Inspector, and it allows you to name the script and specify a target browser and JavaScript version.

The Body Script Inspector lets you reference an external script, or, by clicking the Edit button, switch to the JavaScript Editor with that body script already selected. You can also bring up the JavaScript Editor at any time and select the script from the popup menu at the upper-right of the editor.

Choosing a Browser and Language Version

When you create a GoLive head or body script, one of the popup menus in the corresponding Inspector is for Language, which lists several browser versions. When you choose one, GoLive automatically places that browser's version or "flavor" of JavaScript in the text box below the menu and adds the same text to the "Language" attribute of the Script tag. This was intended to prevent a browser that doesn't support the specified level of JavaScript from executing the script.

GoLive helps you code by displaying only those items that are supported by the browser version you specified and any later version in the JavaScript Inspector's Events and Objects tabs. So, if you choose to target Netscape Navigator 2.0, for example, you don't see the Image object in the object list because that feature was not supported until Navigator 3.0.

The JavaScript version control isn't problem-free, though. There are substantial differences among various browsers' definitions of "JavaScript1.1," or "JScript," especially from platform to platform. Also, GoLive's method of blocking browsers still allows errors. If the Script tag says "JavaScript1.2" and the page is viewed in a 3.0 browser, the browser generates a "Function not defined" error when an event handler calls a function, because the browser ignores the head script containing the function, but not the event handler that calls the function.

We prefer adding JavaScript code that checks the browser version and exits without acting if the browser is too old to do what we want it to. We recommend forcing GoLive to write a generic JavaScript language setting by deleting the number following JavaScript in the text field below the Language menu (see Figure 24-1, earlier in the chapter). This allows all browsers that support any version of JavaScript to use event handlers without error, and your script can decide how to cope with them.

JavaScript Events and the Events Tab

Events are actions initiated by the user, or by JavaScript itself, that occur in the browser window. These include a mouse click, the browser loading a page, or even the cursor passing over an object (a "mouseover"). All JavaScript functions are triggered by events.

For an event to trigger a script, you add an "event handler" that GoLive inserts into an HTML tag. The Events tab of the JavaScript Inspector displays a hierarchical list of all the HTML objects on the page that can have event handlers attached to them. Clicking the arrows (Mac) or plus signs (Windows) next to these objects displays all the events they support. Clicking the event

Syntax Check

The Check Syntax button in the JavaScript Editor does not actually institute a check for bugs in your code. Syntax checking confirms that punctuation and commands all make sense in the context of the programming language. Missing parentheses or quote characters result in a syntax error. (Likewise the JavaScript Shell isn't for testing JavaScript, but rather for third-party developers who create Actions.)

While a syntax check catches many common mistakes, it won't determine whether a script actually runs in a browser. (There is a deep computer science theory called "the halting problem" that describes why it's hard to write a program that can check another program for whether it will actually run or not; checking for proper syntax is as close as you can get most of the time.)

Remember to test in every browser and platform the visitors of your site might be expected to use. For most sites, this means every version of Netscape and Internet Explorer since 3.0, and the latest releases of the Opera browser.

lets you see a definition of that event; you can enter the name of a JavaScript function in the text box below that gets inserted into the event handler (see Figure 24-3).

Figure 24-3
Events tab

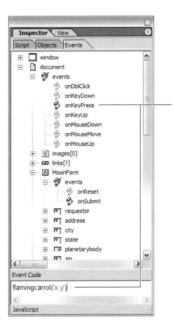

Clicking this event allows you to enter a function under Event Code—in this case, flamingcarrot(x,y)—which is called when a key is pressed.

External JavaScripts

If you're going to use the same script on more than one page, you can put it in a single file instead of repeating it on each Web page.

Create a text file with ".js" (the JavaScript extension that Web servers and browsers recognize) at the end of the file name and place your scripts in it. You can create a head script to use GoLive's JavaScript syntax and editing tools, then copy and paste its contents into the .js file.

To reference that JavaScript file, create a new, blank head script in the JavaScript Editor. Set your language and other options in the Java-Script Inspector. Check the Source box and use the Browse dialog or use Point & Shoot to link to your .js file. GoLive does not show the functions available in this external file; you have to remember to enter them into event handlers.

If you change your mind and want to bring the script back into the page, copy and paste it from the external file into a blank head script.

Older browsers didn't all support external script files, but you shouldn't worry about it these days, unless someone is running software so old they can barely visit any Web sites.

Tip: Broken Links

All regular links on a page are (unfortunately) represented identically in the Events tab, even though you should be able to differentiate them and attach handlers to any property. Links are listed as "links[?]"; we've complained about this to Adobe for years, and we hope they fix it some day. It's the single biggest flaw remaining untouched in GoLive (see Figure 24-4).

Figure 24-4
The confusing
links[?]

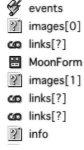

events
images[0]
links[?]
MoonForm
images[1]
links[?]
links[?]
info

The event handler associates a given JavaScript function—a self-contained piece of JavaScript—with an action occurring in connection with an object. For instance, you can specify a graphical rollover by attaching a "mouseover" event handler to a hyperlinked image. When a user moves the cursor over the image, this event handler gets triggered, and calls a script that swaps out the first image with another image.

You can also drag and drop an event from the Inspector into your code in the JavaScript Editor. GoLive automatically creates a new, empty function, and adds an event handler to the object which calls the newly created function.

JavaScript Objects and the Objects Tab

JavaScript views the browser window, the page loaded within it, and everything on the page as a collection of objects that it can retrieve information about and manipulate. This group of objects is referred to as the Document Object Model (DOM), and is structured in a hierarchical tree so that individual objects can be targeted by scripts. Think of the object reference as the item's address within the browser's neighborhood.

The Objects tab of the JavaScript Inspector displays a complete catalog of objects supported by the currently targeted browser—displayed in the same hierarchical order as the DOM—including any properties and methods that can be accessed by scripts (see Figure 24-5).

Figure 24-5
Document
Object Model
(DOM)

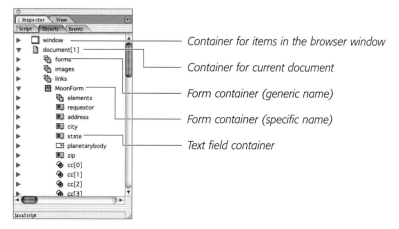

Container for items in the browser window

Container for current document

Form container (generic name)

Form container (specific name)

Text field container

By expanding the list, you can display any specific object on the page and drag and drop it into the JavaScript Editor to add the object reference to your script. You can choose to reference the object by name (if you've given the object a name within the HTML) or by index number, which GoLive displays. The index number changes as you insert or remove objects that appear earlier than the item in the page.

One reason we suggest appropriately naming form elements, like text-entry boxes, (see Chapter 13, *Forms*), is to use those names in JavaScript. The mnemonic device of having a name associated with a form element makes it easier to conceptualize how you're working with the element, rather than remember that it is element 12 in the form (see Figure 24-6). Also, adding or removing form elements changes the index number; the name stays the same.

You may note that below the window and document lists, there's an item called Other Objects. These objects are special JavaScript functions and references you may want to use in your scripts. Consult a JavaScript resource for the specifics on how to apply them. GoLive doesn't explain them or offer additional support: it just lets you drag and drop them from this reference list into a function instead of you having to type them from scratch.

The Future of JavaScript

Since JavaScript has proven to be so useful and easy to learn, you can be assured that any effort you put into learning to script will not be wasted. In fact, most Web developers now consider knowing JavaScript to be as essential a skill as knowing HTML itself.

Figure 24-6
Form elements
by number
and name

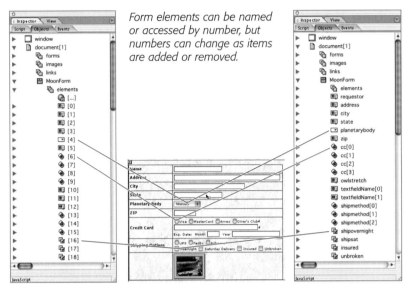

Form elements can be named or accessed by number, but numbers can change as items are added or removed.

As we take a look at Dynamic HTML—which browser vendors tout as one of the main ways to create client-side Web animation and interaction—in the following chapters, you'll see that DHTML is really nothing more than JavaScript combined with the positioning capabilities of Cascading Style Sheets.

With its wide support and continuing development, JavaScript isn't going away any time soon.

CHAPTER 25

Creating Animation with DHTML

It's a rare day when Netscape and Microsoft agree on something—anything—so when both companies decided several years ago that Dynamic HTML (or DHTML) would be the wave of the future for Web site design, and they incorporated DHTML features into the 4.0 (and subsequent) versions of their browsers, most designers took a long, hard look.

Initially, DHTML suffered from a lack of follow-through in its implementation, despite its great potential. Now a few years later, DHTML has permeated the Web strata so thoroughly that future generations will call 2001 and beyond The DHTML Age. The last two major releases of Internet Explorer, the 6.0 release of Netscape, and the Opera 5 browser offer almost complete and consistent support for DHTML features, making it possible to truly author a single page that works all the time for the vast majority of visitors.

DHTML allows the simple addition of certain multimedia categories to Web pages without plug-ins such as Shockwave or Flash, Java, or ActiveX. Much like a fax machine was originally the odd union of a slow modem, a cheap scanner, and a bad printer, DHTML combines some JavaScript features with HTML and the object-positioning features of Cascading Style Sheets (CSS) to create a whole that is a bit greater than its parts.

The DHTML Promise

By bringing positioning and scripting together to provide time-based animation controls within the browser, designers gain substantially more control over the layout and interactivity of their pages. DHTML lets a designer specify the absolute position of text and images; it provides dynamic control over font size, style, leading, and kerning; and it allows the animation of elements on the page by moving them along a path or hiding and showing them. You can even change the size and position of the browser window itself as part of a sequence.

DHTML requires a version 4.0 or later browser to work, but it's the 5.0 or later IE, 6.0 or later Navigator, and the last couple of versions of Opera (especially 5) that shine. These browsers have all toed the line pretty closely on a variety of W3C and related standards, and thus can handle the demands of DHTML.

Netscape 4's Last Breath

Netscape 4 is a dying browser as we write this. Although millions of people continue to use it, the irony is that Microsoft took the lead on implementing Internet standards long before Netscape. Netscape finally caught up (after its acquisition by AOL and long delays) with its 6.0 browser. Unfortunately, 6.0 and even 6.1 were buggy enough to turn people off. Netscape 6.2, however, the latest version as we write this, meets the spec quite well and works reliably.

But you still find a lot of holdout users who don't have the system strength to run Netscape 6.2, and have strong feelings about Microsoft that preclude them from running IE. It's too bad, as these users are the squeaky wheels that will never get any grease. Uniformly, when we receive email from a user that is having a problem with one of the sites we manage, it's a Netscape 4.x user.

For instance, one of Glenn's sites uses "::" in the path to separate information. This is legal according to all W3C documents. But Netscape 4.x doesn't like it and truncates the URL. He receives at least one email per week from a user complaining about the site not working.

Netscape's idiosyncratic choices in 4.x extended even to how DHTML was embedded in HTML. They relied on the proprietary Layer tag extension to HTML, an extension that Microsoft chose not to implement, and the World Wide Web Consortium (W3C) chose not to ratify as a standard. The W3C opted for the absolute positioning already built into the first Cascading Style Sheets (CSS) version, CSS1 (see Chapter 27, *Defining Cascading Style Sheets*). This meant that designers had to write convoluted code to get DHTML to work in IE 4 and Netscape 4.

GoLive's solution for getting around the cross-browser issue was to ignore the Netscape Layer tag completely and employ CSS Div tags to define independently layered page elements, which are represented in GoLive as floating boxes (see Chapter 10, *Floating Boxes*).

This turned out to be the right course of action: this is now how DHTML is made by default, and it works for about 97 percent of all users. The last three percent? They're going to be dragged kicking and screaming into the 21st century.

In Chapter 24, *Authoring JavaScript*, we say that writing your own JavaScripts often results in smaller, more efficient pages. However, in the case of DHTML animation, having a WYSIWYG tool that can write the code for you is truly a godsend (and once you take a look at the code required, we're sure you'll agree).

Although folks tend to lump animation and Actions together under the heading of DHTML, we think two distinct kinds of DHTML coexist inside GoLive: animation, in which you're moving objects around a page using floating boxes; and Actions, which are prefabricated, complex JavaScripts that handle a variety of tasks, like writing a cookie to a browser, or displaying a different image each day of the week.

This chapter covers DHTML animation; Chapter 26 addresses Actions.

Floating Boxes and Time Tracks

GoLive employs two interface elements to let you create and control animation: floating boxes contain the elements you want to animate, and timelines—called time tracks when referring to an individual object's timeline—control their speed and timing.

When you place any content into a floating box, whether images, text, form elements, even plug-ins or Java applets, GoLive dynamically controls the content's visibility and its absolute position within the window. You can also animate the box's content by moving it from point to point or along a path.

You can trigger animation automatically when a page loads, set a timer to delay it, run it once, have it loop, or give control to the viewer through mouse clicks and mouseovers. (For a refresher on floating boxes, see Chapter 10, *Floating Boxes*.)

Bring up the DHTML Timeline Editor by clicking its icon at the top right of the Layout Editor. When you open the DHTML Timeline Editor, all the floating boxes on the page are automatically listed by number in the order you added them to the page (see Figure 25-1). Each floating box has its own time track which allows you to animate each box independently. An arrow next to a time track indicates which floating box is currently selected.

Tip: Action Track

Above standard time tracks, there's a gray bar, which is the Action Track. This track allows you to choose Actions that are triggered at a given point in time during an animation. The Action Track is explained at the end of this chapter.

Figure 25-1
Timeline Editor

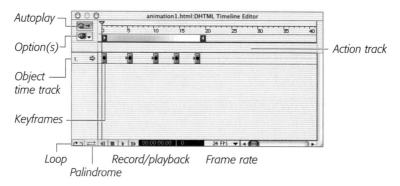

The keyframe is the "key" to controlling animation. If you've worked with animation or video-editing applications like iMovie, Adobe LiveMotion or Premiere, or Macromedia Flash or Director, you're already familiar with keyframes. If you haven't, keyframes may be a little intimidating at first.

A keyframe is a marker on the time track that tells GoLive at what location on the page you want your floating box to be at a given time. As you add keyframes and move the box to different locations, GoLive automatically determines the path of the box between keyframes (this is called "tweening" or "interpolation"). The greater the distance between keyframes, the more time it takes the box to move between the two positions. Keyframes can also be used to control more static properties of floating boxes such as visibility and layering order.

Setting Keyframes

Keyframes are set by moving the floating box to a new location and Command-clicking (Mac) or Control-clicking (Windows) the time track at the point in time you want the box to reach that position; or, you can Option-drag or Alt-drag an existing keyframe to the new time (see Figure 25-2).

To change the settings of a keyframe, select it and move the floating box; or go to the Floating Box Inspector to choose new position, visibility, path shape, and/or relative layer depth settings. Dragging keyframes closer together or farther apart lets you change the timing between two keyframes in the animation (see Figure 25-3).

At the top of the DHTML Timeline Editor is a time scale with numbers and tickmarks. Each tickmark indicates a frame of animation. By setting the distance between keyframes you can control the number of frames GoLive generates between the different locations of a floating box, thus controlling the flow of the animation. Setting the number of frames per second in the

Figure 25-2
Alt/Option-
dragging to
create a new
keyframe

Alt/Option-
dragging an
existing keyframe
creates a new one.

Figure 25-3
Changing
timing
between
keyframes

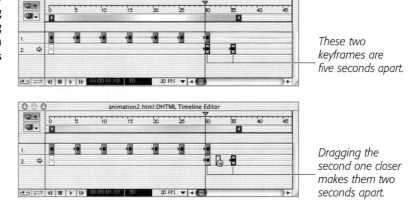

These two
keyframes are
five seconds apart.

Dragging the
second one closer
makes them two
seconds apart.

Frames per Second popup menu at the bottom of the DHTML Timeline
Editor determines the overall choppiness of the animation; more frames
means a smoother performance (see Figure 25-4).

Figure 25-4
Frame rate
menu

Tip: Frames and File Size

Unlike animated GIFs, adding frames to a DHTML animation does not increase
the file size of the page by more than literally a few bytes. However, moving images—especially large or multiple images—is very processor intensive. Even if
you set the frame rate to 30 frames per second, a viewer using an older computer may only see a choppy animation at 5-10 frames per second. Always try
to test animations on a computer that is close to the lowest common denominator of your audience.

A few controls in the Floating Box Inspector are used just for animation.

Depth. The Z-Index field lets you set the layer of a floating box relative to all other floating boxes on the page: the lower the number you enter, the deeper the layer. A floating box with a depth of 1 appears beneath a floating box with a depth of 2 (see Figure 25-5). Each keyframe associated with a floating box can have its own depth setting. This means that you can animate the depth of layers over time, making objects appear first in front of, then behind, other objects.

Figure 25-5
Changing the depth of objects

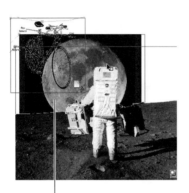 

This image has a lower setting in the Depth field than the others.

Changing this image's Depth value to be higher than all of the other objects places it (and its floating box) on top.

Tip: Depth Numbering

The Z-Index numbers don't have to be sequential. Boxes with depths of 42, 118, and 14321 appear in the same order as if they were numbered 1, 2, and 3.

Visible. The Visible checkbox determines (what else) the visibility of the floating box at any given time during the animation. As with the Z-Index setting, each keyframe can have its own visibility setting.

Tip: Start Invisibly

It is good practice to make all your page's animated floating boxes invisible while the page loads, and then start the animation when the page has finished loading using the Play Scene Action set to be triggered OnLoad (see "Triggering Actions" in Chapter 26, *Applying Actions*). This helps the animation run as smoothly as possible.

Animation. The Animation popup menu allows you to select whether the path originating from the keyframe point is sharp and angular (Linear, the default), smooth (Curve), or jittery and shaky (Random). You can also turn animation off by setting this value to None. Of course, each keyframe can have its own Animation setting, so your animation path can go from a straight line into a smooth curve into a jitterbug routine (see Figure 25-6).

Figure 25-6
Different types
of animation
paths

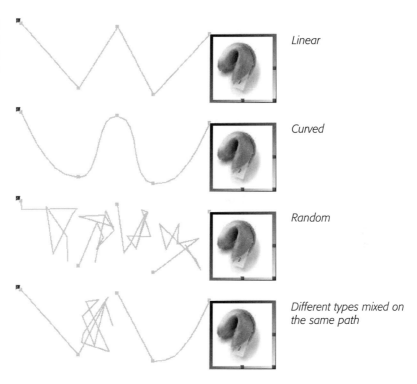

Linear

Curved

Random

Different types mixed on the same path

KeyColor. The Key Color field lets you change the color of the selected keyframe in the DHTML Timeline Editor by dragging a color swatch from the Color palette onto the field. This feature can help you track which keyframes feature specific events, such as a change in layering order or the arrival or departure of a floating box on a page.

Record. The Record button lets you create an animation path and all of its keyframes by dragging the floating box along the path you want it to travel. Position the floating box where you want the animation to begin, click the Record button, and drag the box around the page exactly as you want it to animate (see Figure 25-7). When you're done, release the mouse button to stop recording. The animation path appears in the layout and keyframes show up

Figure 25-7
Path using
Record

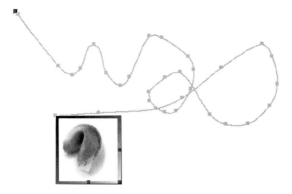

in the DHTML Timeline Editor. After recording, you can adjust a recorded animation just like any other by moving or deleting keyframes or selecting keyframes and moving the floating box.

Creating Animations

Building Web elements based on timelines can cause confusion for most traditional Web designers, especially if their primary notion of Web time is the long wait while inadequately-optimized Web pages load. So, let's run through a few examples.

For our first exercise, let's create an animation of the moon flying in from the left and stopping in the upper-right corner of the page. (If you want to follow along with this example, download the elements and the GoLive page from realworldgolive.com/six/animation.html.)

1. Add a floating box to your layout by dragging the Floating Box icon from the Basic tab of the Objects palette (see Figure 25-8). It doesn't matter where you initially drop the floating box on your page. The position of the top-left corner of the box is always calculated in relation to the upper-left corner of the window.

2. Drag the moon into the floating box. The floating box automatically grows, if necessary, to the dimensions of the image (see Figure 25-9).

Figure 25-8
Inserting a
floating box

Drag a floating box
onto the page.

Figure 25-9
Inserting an
image

Drag the image in.

Tip: Layering Floating Boxes

Since floating boxes are always in front of regular page elements such as text, images, and backgrounds, you may want to make the background of your images in animated floating boxes transparent for a better effect.

3. Name the floating box to make it easier to track (see Figure 25-10). GoLive automatically names the floating box "layer1" in the Name field of the Floating Box Inspector. Enter a new name reflecting its contents; in this case, "SmallMoon". (The name must be one word; if not, GoLive pops up an error message and resets the name.)

Figure 25-10
Naming a
floating box

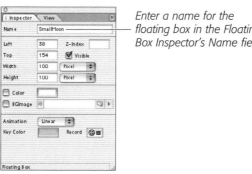

Enter a name for the
floating box in the Floating
Box Inspector's Name field.

Tip: Selecting the Floating Box

Sometimes it's tricky to know if you've selected a floating box or the image within it. For best results, use the Floating Boxes palette, which lists all floating boxes on your page. However, if you'd rather not open yet another palette, position the cursor in the Layout Editor so it is hovering over an edge of the box, then click when the cursor changes into a hand (see Figure 25-11).

You know you've selected the box if the Inspector palette changes into the Floating Box Inspector. You can also click the small floating box placeholder icon. If you click in the middle of the box, you select its contents, and could accidentally drag the image out of the box.

Figure 25-11
Selecting a
floating box

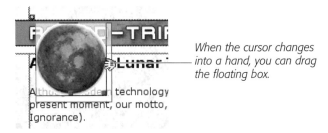

*When the cursor changes
into a hand, you can drag
the floating box.*

4. Bring up the DHTML Timeline Editor by clicking its icon; the floating box is automatically included as the first track, with the first keyframe inserted (see Figure 25-12).

Figure 25-12
Initial Timeline
Editor view

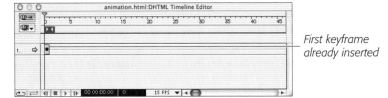

*First keyframe
already inserted*

5. Select the first keyframe in the SmallMoon track and position the floating box where you want it to appear in the window at the end of the animation. This approach may seem backwards, but makes it easier to move the logo in a straight line and make it end up where we want it.

6. To add another keyframe, Command-click (Mac) or Control-click (Windows) anywhere in the SmallMoon track, or Option-drag or Alt-drag the first keyframe to the point at which you want the animation to end (see Figure 25-13). This creates a keyframe with the logo in exactly the same position as the first keyframe, which is its final position.

Figure 25-13
Ending the
animation

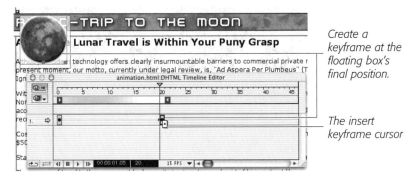

*Create a
keyframe at the
floating box's
final position.*

*The insert
keyframe cursor*

7. Move the moon to its starting point. Make sure the first keyframe is se-lected—it has a bold outline when selected—and drag the floating box with the moon far enough to the right so it is beyond the monitor size of most of your audience; 1,000 to 1,200 pixels should be plenty (see Figure 25-14). You can track the pixel location in the Left field of the Floating Box Inspector, or you can directly enter a value there.

Figure 25-14
Starting the animation off screen

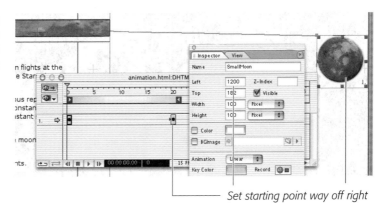

Set starting point way off right

If you move the box by dragging, make sure it's still the same distance from the top of the window as the ending keyframe by clicking each keyframe and checking that each number in the Top field of the Floating Box Inspector is identical.

Tip: Keyframe Connectors in the Editor

A light gray line in the Layout Editor connects keyframes. This is the animation path; the squares indicate keyframes. When we add more keyframes later on, you'll see that each square on the path corresponds with the box's position at that point in time.

These squares are indicators only and cannot be dragged to edit the keyframe data. You can only change keyframe attributes by dragging keyframes within the time track to change timing, clicking them in the time track and dragging the floating box to a new position, or modifying the values in the Floating Box Inspector.

8. Switch to the Layout Preview tab to preview the animation. To make the movement faster or slower, go back to the Layout Editor and drag the final keyframe to the left or right; you can also change the Frames per Second setting to change tempo (see Figure 25-15). Experiment until you like the results.

Figure 25-15
Stepping
through the
animation in
Layout Editor

The Time display at the bottom of the DHTML Timeline Editor tells you how long your animation runs in seconds. Remember, however, that the actual speed and smoothness of the animation depend greatly upon the speed of the viewer's computer.

Tip: Starting Animations after Page Load

By default, GoLive sets up an animation to play when your page loads. However, if you deselect the Autoplay button in the upper-left corner of the DHTML Timeline Editor (a film reel with an arrow pointing right), you can use an Action to trigger the start of the animation. If the button is depressed, click it to deselect the option. We cover this later in "Triggering an Action within an Animation."

Throwing Some Curves

To make our animation a little more interesting, let's add some keyframes.

1. Command-click (Mac) or Control-click (Windows) at several points on the time track.

2. Select each of the new keyframes and move the floating box into the new position to create a zigzag effect as the logo moves across the screen (see Figure 25-16).

Figure 25-16
Zigzag path

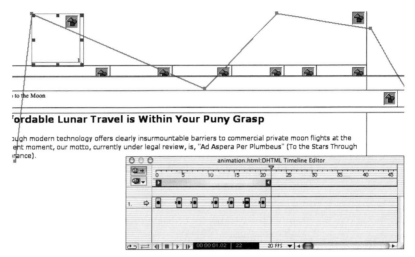

3. When you preview the animation, the logo follows the new zigzag path. (By first setting up a simple linear animation, it only took a few clicks and mouse movements to dramatically alter the logo's path.)

Changing Multiple Keyframes

By default, GoLive sets each new keyframe with linear motion between it and the next keyframe. To make the animation path curve between two points, instead of following a straight line, select the keyframe and choose Curve from the Animation popup menu in the Floating Box Inspector. You can make the entire path curved, or you can mix curved and linear keyframes. This can have some unexpected results, so you may want to experiment a bit to see what works.

Shift-click each keyframe on the floating box's path or drag a marquee around all of the keyframes, then select Curve from the Animation popup menu in the Floating Box Inspector. The animation path should now be curvy instead of straight (see Figure 25-17).

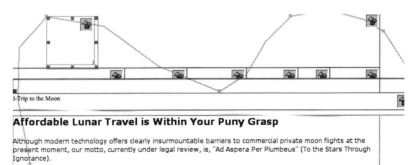
Figure 25-17
Curvy path

Tip: Avoid Random Motion

The Random option causes the floating box to move in a jittery fashion roughly along the animation path that changes randomly every time the animation plays. We don't recommend this feature (unless that's precisely the effect you're looking for) since you really don't have much control over the effect, and we've experienced intermittent browser incompatibilities.

Animating Multiple Elements

Our moon animation is smooth and silky, but what if we want to animate several images independent of each other? To illustrate this idea, let's show our logo assembling itself on the top of the page it appears. The overlaid graphics have transparent backgrounds, so the background rectangles won't cover the images below when we move them.

1. First we place three images on the page and align them in their final positions: the background of the logo, the footprint on the moon, and the logo's type (see Figure 25-18). We copy their keyframes as in the previous example to exactly position their end point.

2. The logo type flies in from the right and when it lands in place, the footprint "stamps" onto the moon (see Figure 25-19).

3. Finally, after the image assembles itself, all three floating boxes are hidden to reveal the underlying table and graphics (see Figure 25-20).

Avoiding Timeline Editor Interface Quirks

There are a few potentially confusing features of the DHTML Timeline Editor.

- The direction the Time Cursor moves— left to right—does not indicate the direction the animated element is moving. For example, in our first animation, the logo moves from right to left while the Time Cursor always moves left to right along the time-elapsed axis.

- The order of the time tracks in the DHTML Timeline Editor does not correspond to the stacking order of the floating boxes, only the order in which they were created. Use the Floating Boxes palette with its popout menu set to Hierarchic to show the order of stacking corresponding to the Z-Index field in the Floating Box Inspector.

- Selecting a keyframe moves the Time Cursor in the DHTML Timeline Editor to that keyframe's location, and it selects the floating box that corresponds to it. But the reverse isn't true; selecting a floating box does not select any keyframe. If you already have a keyframe selected and then click a floating box, the keyframe remains selected and changes in the Floating Box Inspector corresponding to that keyframe, not the floating box you've clicked.

Figure 25-18
The pieces to
assemble

The footprint
floating box

The background in
one big floating box

The logo floating box

Figure 25-19
Opening and
mid-range
appearance

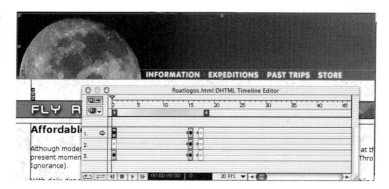

Figure 25-20
Replaced with
the static
background
image

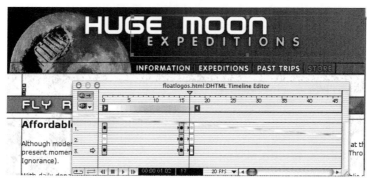

Tip: Layering Elements

Since keyframes can have independent Z-Index settings, you can change the depth of a floating box at any time during an animation. This can lead to some interesting effects, such as a moon orbiting a planet using only two graphics and a couple of floating boxes. The Floating Boxes palette can help you sort out which layer a floating box is currently on (see Figure 25-21).

Figure 25-21
Floating Boxes palette

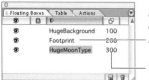

Each layer's name is listed, along with an eyeball to show whether it's visible and a lock to show whether it's editable.

The Z-Index value shows the order and depth of layers.

Animation Scenes

You can not only set multiple floating boxes to run at different times, but you can also build entirely different sets of floating boxes which GoLive calls "scenes." You might use this to have one element animate when the page loads and another when the user clicks a button. Or, after running an animation, use same elements again in an entirely different way on the same page.

Think of scenes as somewhat independent time tracks within the same page that can have a set of shared or separate elements, timing, triggers, and Actions. With scenes you can set up and trigger many different animations whenever and however you choose. Let's see how this works by adding a scene to our logo assembly animation.

Setting Up a Second Scene

1. The animation we've already created is called "Scene 1" by default. You can rename scenes by selecting Rename Scene from the Options popup menu (which appears as a film reel icon) at the top of the DHTML Timeline Editor (see Figure 25-22).

2. Add a new scene by selecting New Scene from the Options menu and name it "ClickAnimation". You see a new time track with both floating

Figure 25-22
Options menu showing scenes

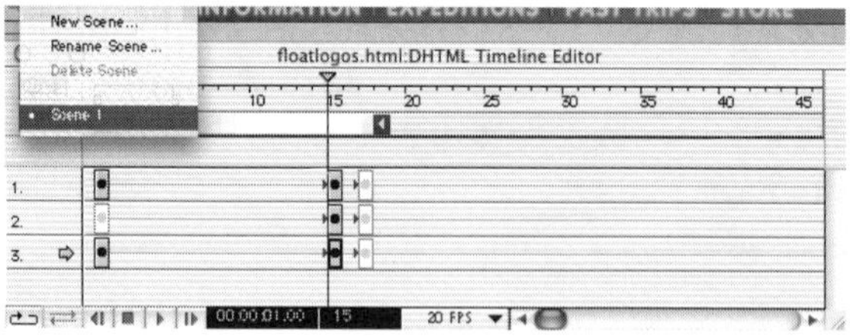

boxes listed as tracks, but with only the initial keyframe for the floating box. Our old animation is still there; use the Options menu to switch back to see it (see Figure 25-23).

Figure 25-23
New scene

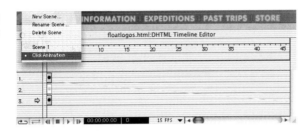

3. Let's create an animation using Record to move a small moon around and about the page. Select the default first keyframe of the logo background track and click the Record button in the Floating Box Inspector.

4. Drag the floating box around.

5. Release the floating box to stop recording. GoLive creates a new animation path and several keyframes (see Figure 25-24).

    You may want to delete excess keyframes, as Record creates more than are strictly needed—the more keyframes, the more browser computation.

Figure 25-24
Recording a
moving box

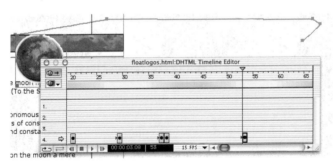

Using an Action to Trigger the Second Scene

Now we have two scenes that both play when the page loads. This obviously creates a conflict, so we need to make the second scene play when the viewer clicks the top of the page. To do this, we add an Action that uses the onClick attribute, and attach it to the main navigation image. (We add the Action to the navigation image because it shows up only after the first animation finishes.)

1. Make sure you turn off Autoplay for the Click Animation scene at the top of the time track.

2. Select the navigation graphic add a dummy link to it: just a #, for an empty anchor. (You can't attach an Action to a floating box, and you must have a link in order to attach an Action.)

3. Open the Actions palette and add a Mouse Click trigger.

4. Choose Play Scene from the Multimedia submenu of the Action menu.

5. From the Action configuration options that appear in the Actions palette, choose Click Animation from the Scenes popup (see Figure 25-25). (Actions are covered in depth in the next chapter.)

6. When you preview the page in a browser you should see the first scene animate in the window as before and stop. When you click the navigation header, the moon should cross heaven's bower.

Figure 25-25
Selecting an
Action for a
Mouse Click
trigger

Triggering an Action within an Animation

We've just used an Action to trigger an animation, but you can also use an animation to trigger an Action by using the Action Track, the gray bar near the top of the DHTML Timeline Editor. Assign an Action to a point in time by Command-clicking (Mac) or Control-clicking (Windows) the Action Track at the point in time that you want the Action to be triggered (see Figure 25-26).

To demonstrate, instead of using a Mouse Click to trigger the Click Animation scene, let's make the first scene trigger the next when the first is done playing (see Figure 25-27).

1. Remove the link from the navigation image, which automatically eliminates the Action attached to it.

2. With the DHTML Timeline Editor set to display Scene 1, Command-click (Mac) or Control-click (Windows) the Action Track just above the last keyframe of the first scene. The Action Inspector appears.

Figure 25-26
Adding an
Action to the
Action Track

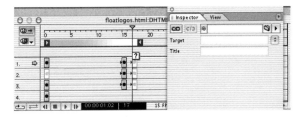

Figure 25-27
Setting the
Action and
choosing a
scene

3. Choose Play Scene from the Action popup menu under the Multimedia
    submenu and choose Click Animation from the Scene popup. When the
    page loads, the first animation sequence runs and then it triggers the sec-
    ond scene automatically.

    You can use the Actions track to trigger any of the other Actions as well,
    such as displaying an alert window at a certain point or playing a sound each
    time the animation loops.

The Hard Truth

As we said in last chapter, if you are a savvy scripter, you can write code by
hand that is much more compact and efficient. But even if you are savvy
enough to hand code, the DHTML animation scripting is complicated
enough that the time and effort GoLive saves you is worth the extra overhead.

Although GoLive makes it easy to create DHTML animations, try not to
go nuts adding lots of animation all over your pages unless you know that
your audience employs a fast network connection. If done in moderation—a
little bit here, a little bit there—DHTML animations can add style and impact
to your pages.

CHAPTER 26
Applying Actions

Back in the JavaScript chapter, we provided some persuasive reasons why you should hand code your scripts whenever possible. Now we're contradicting ourselves by advising you to consider GoLive's built-in Actions: prefabricated powerful JavaScript and DHTML behaviors that require no programming whatsoever.

What's the incongruity here? It's simple. Scripts created "by hand" offer more flexibility and control, and are almost always smaller, more efficient, and carry out their tasks faster than Actions. In addition, Actions are almost impossible to modify or update without using GoLive; if multiple people are maintaining a site, multiple copies of the software are needed. You can't get by, for instance, with one person using BBEdit, another using Dreamweaver, and the rest using GoLive.

But if you don't have the time, money, or inclination to build scripts from scratch; you're in a hurry and want to assemble prototype pages; or if you're in charge of updating your site and you have complete control over which applications to use—then Actions (and related smart objects) make it quick and easy to add functionality and special effects with drag-and-drop ease.

Actions are prefabricated sets of JavaScript and Cascading Style Sheets settings (otherwise known as DHTML—or Dynamic HTML—when they involve animation) that allow you to just plug in values and let GoLive write and modify the code. Your interface with an Action is through the Actions palette, which activates whenever you select an item that can have an Action attached to it. This palette provides you with all the necessary fields and menus to enter numbers, text, or other values specific to each Action.

Tip: Action Inspectors

For Head Actions, Body Actions, and Actions found on the Timeline Editor's Action Track, the old standby Inspector palette (in the form of the Action Inspector) handles configuring Actions.

GoLive comes with about 80 Actions that encompass a whole range of activities, like writing a cookie to a user's browser, handling conditions (like "if such-and-such happens, then do this other thing"), and forcing a page to load as the only thing in a window if it finds itself as part of a frameset.

Tip: Even More Actions

Adobe has also made additional Actions available free for downloading, and set up an area on their Web site as an Actions exchange for independent developers. See realworldgolive.com for links to that material.

In this chapter, we also talk about smart objects, which are even simpler-to-use Actions you insert to include the date or time at which the page was last updated, or redirect users if they're not using a browser you require. Smart objects also provide GoLive containers for placing Actions in the Head or body section of an HTML page.

Tip: Browser Compatibility

Most GoLive Actions only work properly in Netscape and Microsoft's 4.0 (or later) browser releases or compatible equivalents like Opera. We noted in the previous chapter that this currently encompasses the almost total universe of visitors. But GoLive provides nice legacy support by showing each Action's list of compatible browsers next to the Action's name.

GoLive automatically writes the code so the JavaScript is hidden from the few browsers that can't run it. However, this means that users with older browsers see nothing, rather than alternate content which could be displayed if the script were written by an experienced scripter. The Browser Detection Action lets you divert users with incompatible browsers to an alternate page.

Tip: Filtering for Compatibility

The Actions palette has an interesting item: Filter Actions. Select this and choose the browser version for Netscape and Internet Explorer to only see Actions that work with those versions or later releases.

Tip: Hand Editing

If any of the JavaScript code that GoLive Actions creates is modified by hand or by editing the file in another visual editor, GoLive no longer recognizes it as an Action and you can't edit it using the Actions palette.

Smart Objects

We need to introduce smart objects before we talk about GoLive's Actions, as some smart objects are required to use Actions properly. Smart objects are special GoLive elements. They insert or control internal objects (like date- and timestamps); act as a container for Actions not connected to a link in the Head section or body; and offer special options that regular Actions couldn't include, such as automatically redirecting a browser to another page based on the browser's platform and version.

Tip: Strange Objectfellows

GoLive groups these items together for no particular reason, except they don't really belong anywhere else, and you might use them in tandem quite often.

To add these objects to a page, click the Smart tab of the Objects palette and drag a smart object icon into the Layout Editor's body or Head section where you want it to appear. The Inspector changes to the name of the smart object and allows you to set its parameters.

Tip: Smart Object Compatibility

Unlike the Actions palette, the Smart Object Inspector doesn't indicate which browsers the smart object works with; it's critical to test them with many browsers.

Internal Objects

GoLive uses two smart objects to act as containers for content that the program updates. Neither of them uses JavaScript, nor are they really Actions.

Modified Date. Modified Date inserts the date and/or time that the document was last edited into a specific location on a page. It's not JavaScript or an

What's New in 6

Adobe added several new Actions in GoLive 6 and cleaned up the existing ones. The best new Actions involve layers and CSS-defined ID selections, which are uniquely named areas on a page. You can swap text, a modification time of the page, or the current time into either a layer or an ID selection via Actions.

The script library is now easier to work with on two counts: Flatten Script Library, which reduces the library's size to the absolute necessities, can be automated and is found in more places; and you can now set the location and name of the folder and script library file on a per-site basis.

Action, but a placeholder that GoLive uses to identify where to insert static text into the HTML each time the page is opened and saved. (To update the timestamp, just open the page; GoLive makes the change for you.)

You can select one of several formats for the date or time, and choose a language/country style from a popup menu (see Figure 26-1).

Figure 26-1
Modified Date
Smart Object

Tip: Mama Loshen

You have to have the appropriate languages or encodings installed to select some of the countries or languages.

This smart object cannot be accessed or used by other smart objects or Actions; it's really just text that GoLive inserts each time you update the page. Unlike a JavaScript (or an Action described later) that can display the current date and time, Modified Date is plain old HTML in a wrapper.

Component. The Component smart object is a placeholder for inserting a Component, a centrally-managed template for a fragment of a page. We cover Components and this placeholder thoroughly in Chapter 19, *Managing Files, Folders, and Links*.

Smart Photoshop, Illustrator, LiveMotion, and Generic Smart Objects. The smart objects for Photoshop, Illustrator, and LiveMotion let you embed links to native files for these three programs. (You must have the software packages installed for these icons to appear.) The Generic smart object handles other file types that GoLive can manage but aren't identified by program. Modifying the element causes your computer to open the element in the application that created it or in GoLive's Save for Web internal feature, make the changes to that element, save it, and reload it in GoLive. For a full explanation, see Chapter 5, *Images*.

Page Actions

The page-based Action smart objects are dissected later in this chapter in "Triggering Actions." The Body Action and Head Action allow you to insert an Action directly into the Head section or body of a page to trigger Actions based on activity (mouse movement, key presses, etc.) in the browser window.

Standard Actions

Browser Switch, Rollover, and URL Popup are essentially identical to any Action in the Actions palette. But limitations in the nature of Actions themselves required these special smart objects to work more closely with the innards of GoLive.

Browser Switch. You can use Browser Switch to detect which browser is loading the page (see Figure 26-2). The smart object can automatically redirect a user to an alternate page based on the combination of browser, platform, and version. If you check the Auto box in the Browser Switch Inspector, GoLive writes the JavaScript code to redirect any browser that can't handle the Actions, animations, or style sheets attached to the current page.

Figure 26-2
Browser
Switch Smart
Object

Browser Switch is the only option to display different content for users with older browsers, if you are not writing JavaScript yourself by hand. Also, 2.0 and older browsers on all platforms ignore the Browser Switch because they don't support the JavaScript necessary to make it work. (If more than five people in each state are still *effectively* using a 2.0 browser at this point, we'll eat a PDF.)

Rollover. Rollover is a simple way to create a button that changes its content based on a user action (see Figure 26-3). You can specify a default image (labeled Normal), an image that displays when the user has the cursor over the image (Over), and an image that displays when the user clicks the image (Down). JavaScript code swaps out the image displayed in the browser for another graphic when the specified mouse event occurs.

Figure 26-3
Rollover Smart
Object

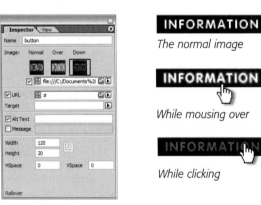

Set up images in the Inspector.

To use Rollover, create two or three images that have identical dimensions. (The browser scales the images to fit if they are not the same dimensions, but this may break the smart object in some browsers.) Click the buttons labeled Main, Over, and Down in the Rollover Inspector to define the appropriate image for each action.

You can specify a URL for the button to link to when clicked, or Actions for it to trigger. The Rollover Inspector also provides a place to enter a message that appears at the bottom of the browser window in the status field: check the Message box in the Inspector, and enter your text.

You can create these same effects with Actions as well, but since using this one smart object can take the place of up to five or six Actions per button, it can be much easier to use and set up.

URL Popup. The URL Popup smart object provides an easy way to include a popular Web site feature in which selecting an item from a popup menu instantly loads a new page upon release of the mouse button (see Figure 26-4). You can use the URLPopup Inspector (yes, the Inspector's name lacks a space) to enter a list of pages or sites, including locations in your own site.

Figure 26-4
URL Popup
Smart Object

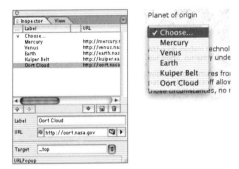

Click the New Item button to add values. The Label field contains the text that shows up on the popup menu. Select items and use the up and down arrows to re-order how they appear in the menu. Selecting an item and clicking Remove Selected Items or Duplicate Selected Items does the predictable.

The Target box at the bottom of the Inspector enables you to select whether the linked page is loaded in its own new window, or if it interacts within an existing frameset.

If a user has JavaScript disabled or is using an old browser, selecting an item from the popup menu has no effect; GoLive doesn't include a "Go" button or other submit button coupled with a CGI script that would provide an alternative for older browsers to use this method.

Triggering Actions

Since Actions are made up of JavaScript code, they must be triggered by specific events, such as a mouse click or a page loading. Let's walk through the different categories of event handlers and discuss how to apply them. To apply some of the Actions discussed later, you use items found in the Objects palette's Smart tab.

Event handlers are attached in one of three general ways: to a page, to text and image links, and to the Timeline Editor's Action Track. Page-based event handlers trigger Actions from browser-window activity, like loading a page. Text and image link event handlers respond to user activities, such as moving the cursor over an image. Action Track triggers are integrated with the

DHTML Timeline Editor, discussed in Chapter 25, *Creating Animation with DHTML*. A few JavaScript events available in browsers aren't supported by GoLive Actions.

Page Event Handlers

You can trigger Actions in four ways to respond to browser-window activity.

- **OnLoad:** when the entire contents of the page have finished loading in the browser window. This is handy for triggering a behavior only when the computer is at rest and has all its resources available.

- **OnUnload:** when the browser begins to access another page. Many adult Web sites use this technique to bring up another window, sometimes in endless succession, to keep users from ever escaping their sites. (Kind of like a Roach Motel with ads for pay-per-view channels.)

- **OnParse:** when the script is read by the browser, but before the rest of the page has loaded. This event handler lets you immediately trigger a behavior, which is useful on longer page loads. (This is a GoLive invention, by the way: it's not part of JavaScript, but a technique GoLive uses to simulate this trigger.)

- **OnCall:** when a specific function is called by name. This method allows you to trigger Actions stored in the Head section from anywhere in the page without having to write custom function calls.

You can use these events to trigger any arbitrary Action by inserting a Head Action or Body Action from the Smart tab of the Objects palette.

Drag the Head Action icon to the Head section of the Layout Editor. In the Head Action Inspector you can choose one of the four events described above, and then select a particular Action and configure it (see Figure 26-5).

For example, if you want to use one of these triggers to insert text into the body of a page, drag a Body Action into the appropriate location in the page's body. In the Body Action Inspector, select Document Write from the Action menu's Message submenu (see Figure 26-6); we describe how to configure Document Write in "Message Actions," later in this chapter.

Text and Image Link Event Handlers

Text and Image events are things users do that can be detected and "handled" by any range of text, image, or area of an imagemap that has a hyperlink attached to it.

Figure 26-5
Configuring a
Head Action

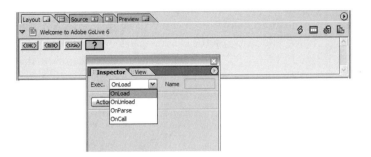

Figure 26-6
Writing text
into a page

- **Mouse Click:** the mouse button is pressed and released over the object the Action is attached to.

- **Mouse Enter:** the cursor moves over the object the Action is attached to (known as "mouseover" in JavaScript).

- **Mouse Exit:** the cursor leaves the object the Action is attached to (known as "mouseout" in JavaScript).

- **Double Click:** the mouse button is quickly pressed and released twice over the object the Action is attached to.

- **Mouse Down:** the mouse button is pressed and held over the object the Action is attached to, as if the user were dragging; this is the first half of the Mouse Click.

- **Mouse Up:** the mouse button, already pressed and held, is released over the object the Action is attached to; this is the second half of the Mouse Click.

- **Key Down:** any key on the keyboard is pressed.

- **Key Press:** any key on the keyboard is pressed or held down.

- **Key Up:** any key on the keyboard is released.

To attach an Action to a linked image, text, or imagemap area, select the object and bring up the Actions palette (see Figure 26-7). A scrolling list of valid events appears under Events. Select the event that is to trigger the Action, click the New Action button (which looks like a page with the corner turned up), and choose the Action you want the event to trigger from the Action popup menu. Finally, set its options.

Figure 26-7
Attaching an
Action

Select an object and
add a link.

Choose an event,
such as Mouse Click.

Click the New
Action button.

Choose an Action
from the popup
menu, such as
Field Validator.

Configure
the Action's
options.

You can add multiple events to a link object, and each event can trigger more than one Action. The order that Actions are executed is set by the order you add them to the event handler; you can rearrange their order by selecting Actions and clicking the up and down arrows near the New Action button. A bullet appears next to each event handler to which an Action is assigned.

Each area on an imagemap can have its own set of event handlers associated with it (see Figure 26-8).

Tip: Pound Away

You can get around the limitation of needing a specific link to assign an Action by linking the text, image, or imagemap region to just the pound-sign (#) character, which is known as the hash sign outside the U.S. (or the octothorpe by clever wits). This tells the browser to link to the current page; when the user

Figure 26-8
An imagemap
with an Action
attached to
an area

clicks the link, the Action is triggered, but a new page isn't loaded. Leaving the link set to "(EmptyReference!)" doesn't work: it shows a link warning and generates an error when someone tries to click it if there isn't a Mouse Click handler attached.

Form Element Event Handlers

Some form elements, such as text boxes, buttons, check boxes, radio buttons, popup menus—even the Form object itself, or the container surrounding form elements—can detect certain events. Some of these events are unique to form elements, and others overlap text and image handlers. The Actions palette shows these events contextually for whatever form element is selected; the form elements for each type of handler are listed in parentheses following the handler name.

Tip: JavaScript Alternatives

You can access these handlers via the JavaScript Inspector Events tab, too. You don't have to be a rocket scientist (or JavaScript programmer) to use these triggers now; you can use JavaScript recipes and then drag in the appropriate trigger from that tab.

- **Form Submit (Form object).** This handler triggers when the user clicks the submit button in a form, but before the information is sent to the server. This allows you to insert a verification check that prevents a form with bad values from being submitted.

- **Form Reset (Form object).** Ditto for the reset button.

Tip: Intercept Reset

We would argue that all forms should intercept a Reset click in order to confirm it with a simple yes/no alert. It's darned easy to erase several minutes of filled-in form content with a fatal, undoable reset. You could write the JavaScrpt to handle this once, and then reuse it indefinitely.

- **Mouse Click (Submit, Reset, Radio Button, Check Box).** Clicking any of these four form elements both affects the element (the submit and reset buttons look "depressed," the radio button is selected, or the box is checked) and triggers an Action.

Tip: Checking for Checks

We use the Mouse Click handler in some forms we work on to ensure that an exclusive choice was made. Radio buttons require that one of the group of buttons is checked. But sometimes, the choice isn't one or the other, but a number of elements out of a group. We use checkboxes to allow multiple choices and JavaScript to check whether options were chosen in the right combination. We can pop up an alert to notify someone if they chose the wrong combination; otherwise, we can allow the submission of the form.

- **Text Change (Text Field, Password, Text Area, Popup, List Box).** Select an item from a popup menu, or change the text in a text field or area.
- **Key Focus, Key Blur (Text Field, Password, Text Area).** Key Focus triggers when the cursor is placed in any of these three field types; Key Blur triggers when the cursor leaves the field. Under Windows (any browser), or Internet Explorer 5 or Netscape 6 or later for Mac, focus and blur occur as you tab from field to field. See Chapter 13, *Forms*, for a fuller explanation of these two terms.
- **Mouse Up, Mouse Down (Submit, Reset).** See these items in "Text and Image Link Event Handlers," earlier in the chapter.
- **Key Down, Key Up (Text Area).** See these items in "Text and Image Link Event Handlers," above.

Action Track Event Handlers

Actions within an animation are triggered by a timing event controlled by the Action's position in time on the Action Track in the Timeline Editor. See Chapter 25, *Creating Animation with DHTML*, for details on triggering Actions within animations.

Unsupported Actions

If you know JavaScript well, you may have noticed that several JavaScript events are not listed above, including onFocus, onBlur, onError, and onSelect. The built-in GoLive Actions lack support for these events, or only support them for certain items. For example, you can trigger an Action with onFocus attached to a text box in a form, but not with a window or frame. If you want to use them to trigger activities, you have to write the code yourself, inserting the triggers in the Source Code Editor.

Configuring Actions

All Actions and their options are configured through the Actions palette, or the Action Inspector if you are using a Head Action, Body Action, or the Action Track of the DHTML Timeline Editor. Each Action has its own set of text fields, popup menus, and buttons which set its parameters.

Before we get started explaining Actions, let's walk through the settings that apply to multiple Actions, and how to set up for using Actions.

> **Tip: Finding Actions**
>
> Some Actions are found only in the Smart tab of the Objects palette. These smart objects are a motley collection of Actions, GoLive features, and place-holders, which we explain in "Smart Objects," earlier in this chapter.

Field Entry Indicator

GoLive displays an icon next to many of the fields in an Actions palette; click the icon to change the kind of data you enter into the field (see Figure 26-9).

When the red "C" is displayed (the default), you generally type into the field to set the Action target or value. With some Actions, you can also use Point & Shoot to set the value, or even select a value from a popup menu.

With the blue ball displayed, GoLive provides a popup list of variables defined on the page that contain compatible values, such as a variable set to a URL for a field that requires a URL. This variable might be read from a cookie, for instance, passed from a previous time the user was on the page.

When the question mark in a green box appears, select an Action from a menu listing all the currently specified Actions. You must first select and configure other Actions before this option is available. Use this option when you have other actions set to execute "OnCall".

In some cases, especially with images, choices are available in a plain popup menu that doesn't offer these three indicators.

Figure 26-9
Field entry
indicators

Red C for direct entry

*Blue ball for
variable selection*

*Question mark in green box
for onCall Action selection*

Setting Up for Actions

Preparing your objects before applying Actions saves some frustration. Any item that you want to manipulate through an Action should already be inserted on the page and have a name, and one chosen by you instead of a default.

- **Images.** Enter a name in the Name field next to the Is Form checkbox in the Image Inspector's More tab. This Name field's location is a bit misleading. Although you can name a button that's used to submit a form, this identification information is also required for other tasks to pick out a specific image. Images are used by Actions as a container to swap other images in and out of, typically. You often want to fill an image with a placeholder or simply a transparent white GIF (see sidebar, "Set Image URL Tutorial," for details).

- **Forms.** Each kind of form item, from the form container itself to each individual field element, can take a name. Change the default into something simple and meaningful.

- **Layers.** Use the Floating Box Inspector to name layers. Actions can hide, show, and move layers, among many possibilities.

- **IDs.** Several Actions new to GoLive 6 allow an Action to target areas defined with a CSS ID selector. The ID selector lets you give a particular name to a part of a page or range of text. That name, a unique selector on the page, is used by the Action to swap out text or perform other activities. See Chapter 27, *Defining Cascading Style Sheets*, on how to create an ID selector.

Tip: Late Browsing

The three new GoLive 6 Actions that support inserting or modifying text by ID or layer name all require fairly recent browsers: Internet Explorer 5 or later and Netscape 6 or later, according to Adobe.

- **Scenes.** DHTML scenes, or sequences of activities grouping one or more layers, can be named in the Options popup menu in the DHTML Timeline Editor (upper-left, second button down). Scenes can be triggers; started or stopped; or used in combination with other behaviors.

  A bit of preparation saves fooling around later.

Alerts

One more note of interest: if you enter text into any Action that plans to display that information as part of a pop-up alert message, you must precede all apostrophes (') with a backslash. An apostrophe is used as a special character in JavaScript; text is contained between pairs of them. A backslash (\') tells JavaScript to not interpret it literally, but just to display it.

Actions by Category

While GoLive makes it easy to apply and configure individual Actions—and the online manual explains every last Action in excellent detail—the tricky part is learning how Actions can interact to combine them to build more complex functionality.

First, we take a look at all the available Actions, discussing what they do and the best ways to use them. Then, we show examples of GoLive gene splicing: using multiple Actions together and setting them up to add some serious capabilities to your pages.

Actions are categorized in GoLive by what they accomplish or the kinds of objects they work with. Getters retrieve something, such as a floating box position or a form value; Link Actions work with links or the contents of pages.

For each Action, we identify the most common or best way to activate it (OnLoad, OnUnload, OnParse, OnCall, Body, link triggers, form triggers, or even "any"), and then how to configure its parts.

Tip: Trigger Wisely

Most Actions can be triggered by anything, but many triggers just don't make sense. Do you want the page, when loaded, to bring up an annoying alert window? Probably not.

Tip: Download Examples

We've provided one example of each Action integrated in a site file at our Web site. Visit realworldgolive.com/six/actions.html. From there, you can view pages or download an archive.

Getters Actions

Getters gather information from the user via HTML forms and store that information in a page-based variable or a browser-stored cookie. Getters also let you detect the position of a floating box within the browser window.

Field Validator. *Trigger: any Form command, especially Form Submit.* The Field Validator Action allows you to confirm whether *(continued on page 742)*

Set Image URL Tutorial

Set Image URL lets you use any trigger on any link—whether an image or a text hyperlink—to display an image (see Figure 26-10). Typically, we'd use Mouse Enter and Mouse Exit to simulate a remote rollover: rolling over a link replaces an image elsewhere on the page into an existing image container. It might be better named Substitute Image instead of Set Image URL.

The images you substitute should be the same size as the original image. (Internet Explorer can automatically show the image at its own dimensions, but Netscape before 6.0 lacks this ability.)

To start with, create a set of links and an image (or images) that you are going to swap out with other pictures. In this example, we created a simple set of text links that swap out travel photos into the space at right. We use a floating box to hold the image to keep it positioned precisely.

The image we start with is a simple white-only GIF to create a blank space. In the Image Inspector's Basic tab, set Height and Width to the pixel dimensions that all the images share. This allows the substituted images to retain their correct dimensions when loaded. (This is a good trick for any image substituting Action, by the way.)

Name the image in the More tab. Next, choose any link on the page, and bring up the Actions palette. In this case, we're using Mouse Enter to trigger the Action, so that as a user sweeps his or her mouse over the link, the image comes up. (For a more sophisticated approach, you could load a thumbnail for Mouse Enter and the full resolution image only on Mouse Click.) For Mouse Out, we plop back the original white image, so that when someone is off the link, the image is no longer displayed.

Select Mouse Enter and click the New Action button. From the Action menu, select Set Image URL from the Image submenu. You can then select the image you originally named above to serve as the one that gets swapped out, and select the image to be swapped into its place. Select Mouse Exit, and follow the same instructions to put the white-only GIF back in its place.

Repeat this for each link. It's important to remember to select the image from the popup menu each time; it's easy to forget, and GoLive doesn't care if it's not selected. However, the JavaScript generates an error on loading into a browser if you fail to select the image name.

If you'd like to go one level more technical, you could use the Preload Image Action to bring in all the images you're going to swap while the page is loading. This wouldn't delay the page load, as Preload loads images in the background, but it would speed up the swap process, since the browser would have cached all the images.

From the Smart tab of the Objects palette, drag the Head Action icon into the Head section of the page. Select the Preload Image Action from the Action menu's Image submenu. Point & Shoot, enter the name of, or Browse to the first image you're swapping in. Repeat for each additional image. (You can copy and paste the Head Action so you don't have to drag it from the palette and reselect the Preload Image Action over and over again.)

There you have it: very simple, very straightforward, and a good building block for a more dynamic page. You can review these pages as part of our Actions site at realworldgolive.com/six/actions.html.

Figure 26-10
Fixing image size

Set the Width and Height values to the shared pixel dimensions.

Name the image map "sub".

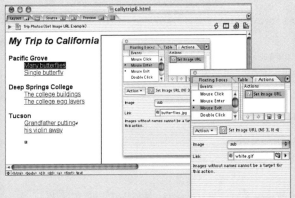

Set the Mouse Enter and Mouse Exit triggers for each link. Mouse Enter is set to the image that should load; Mouse Exit is set to the white placeholder image.

Set Preload Image Actions for each of the images on the page.

Mousing over a link displays the appropriate image at right.

(continued from page 739)   a user entered values that you expected for a given field, like all numbers in a credit-card field, or only numbers in a blank asking their age. We cover setting this Action at length, including some practical JavaScript combinations and alternatives, in Chapter 13, *Forms*.

Get Floating Box Position. *Trigger: any.* When triggered by an event, this Action returns the current top-left corner coordinates in pixels of the specified floating box. It can be used with Condition or Idle Actions to trigger an Action when an animated floating box moves to a certain position.

Get Form Value. *Trigger: any.* Get Form Value retrieves the value or contents of a specific form element (numbers entered in a text box, the chosen item from a popup menu, etc.) within a specific form. This is then combined with Condition or Idle Actions to produce results.

Image Actions

The Image Actions let you control the display of images on the page; they also let you change images via user events or other Actions.

Daily Image URL. *Trigger: Head OnLoad or Body.* This Action changes an image based on the day of the week. Select a named image as the location that GoLive swaps into.

Preload Image. *Trigger: Head OnLoad.* This Action loads an image into the browser's cache so it can be displayed quickly when called for by another Action, such as a rollover.

Random Image. *Trigger: Mouse Enter, Mouse Exit, Head OnParse, Body.* Random Image randomly switches among three different images when triggered. Used with a Mouse Enter and Mouse Exit, the image can change on each rollover; with an OnParse, just when the page is loaded. When it is used to randomly change an existing image on the page, all three images must have the same dimensions or the browser distorts the new image to fit the original graphic's area. The base image must not only be named but also have a link (even just "#") for randomize to work.

Set Image URL. *Trigger: any link trigger.* As one of our most requested explanations, we've devoted a sidebar to this Action; see "Set Image URL Tutorial," page 740.

Figure 26-11
Popping up a
customized
window

Open Window Prompt. *Trigger: link triggers, Head OnLoad.* This is a nifty tool for debugging and testing sites by prompting the visitor for a window height and width. Most users don't need this capability, so it's really intended for us designers.

PDF Redirect, SVG Redirect, SWF Redirect. *Trigger: Head OnParse.* These three Actions form a troika of plug-in detection. If the visitor's browser lacks the appropriate plug-in (PDF, SVG for Scalable Vector Graphics, or Flash for SWF format files), you can redirect them to a page that doesn't require the plug-in. Or one that berates them for not having all the plug-ins installed on their machine! The PDF Redirect also tells users where to download the Acrobat Reader. For SVG and SWF, you can also display an alert message with information.

Random Links. We're dubious about the value of this one. You can choose up to six links that open randomly each time the Action is triggered. Adobe makes some odd suggestions in its manual about how to use it. Although we're sure it could be used for fun walks through a Web site, we can also see how you might be tempted to redirect folks all over the place in a merry (but unsettling) chase.

Redirect Prompt. *Trigger: link triggers, Head OnLoad.* This nifty Action lets you construct a decision tree that could be used to build a quite sophisticated self-service help site for users of a product or service (see Figure 26-12).

Each question can have a set of legal answers which a user must enter exactly as you have entered them. If a user responds with a specific answer, you can redirect them to the appropriate page. ("Are you a Mac or Windows user?" "Do you have Internet Explorer or Netscape Navigator installed or both?")

To help users along the path, you can enter text that provides an explicit list of which answers are valid. You can also provide a response when they enter a

Figure 26-12
Redirect
Prompt

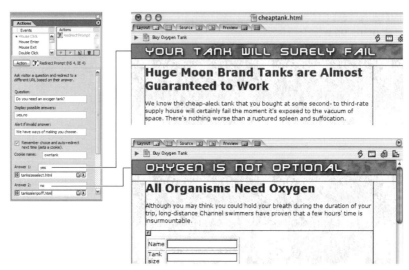

choice that doesn't match any of the up to five you've provided. Finally, you can set a cookie by name to recall their previous option. This could help someone slide down that decision tree quite quickly after their first visit.

SVG Redirect. See PDF Redirect.

SWF Redirect. See PDF Redirect.

Slide New Window. *Trigger: link triggers, Head OnLoad.* Almost identical to the standard Open Window Action, Slide New Window centers a new window in the screen through a sliding behavior. You have to try it to understand it.

Target2Frames. *Trigger: link triggers.* Target2Frames allows one link to change pages simultaneously in two different frames. For example, if you have a frame containing a navigation bar that shows options and a frame that contains some actual content, like an item in the navigation bar, you might want to design it so that the navigation bar presents different options when the user clicks to navigate to a different section of the site. With this Action, the user clicks a link and the Action changes both the navigation bar frame and the content frame.

TargetRemote. *Trigger: link triggers.* Used with the Open Window Action, this Action allows a user to click a link in one named window and have changes appear in another named window. For instance, you could have a small control panel in a pop-up window that controls what's displayed in the main window.

Text Swap (ID). *Trigger: any.* The Text Swap Action allows you to change out one bit of text with another, with two options: you can revert to the original text or remove it.

You specify the location of the text by using either a floating box name (a layer from the popup menu), or by typing in the name of an ID selector you've set up.

The new text you enter replaces the text in the layer or between the tags that define the selection for the ID. You can set the text to return to what it was following an interval in seconds, or disappear at the end of that period.

The controls are even more granular, allowing you to manually enter open and close tags that you'd like to be around the replacement text. This can help if you have some embedded code in the ID selection.

TimeRedirect. *Trigger: link triggers, Body OnLoad.* This action redirects the user to a different HTML page based on the time of day on the user's computer.

Message Actions

These Actions let you communicate directly with users through HTML within the page, the text in the status bar, and dialog boxes.

Document Write. *Trigger: Body.* You can use this Action to display customized HTML when the page loads. It has to be triggered via a Body Action, because HTML cannot be written to the page once it has finished loading. The HTML displayed may come from a variable, another Action (via a call), or text you type into the Actions palette yourself (see Figure 26-13).

Figure 26-13
Document
Write

Inserting text from a variable

Last Modified (ID), Last Modified (form). *Trigger: link triggers, Head On-Load.* The ID version of this Action inserts the modification date into an ID selector area or layer (see "Text Swap (ID)," above for ID/layer details); the form version pops the date into a named form field. You can choose a format for the date, include or exclude the day of the week, and have some preceding (Lead in) text.

Open Alert Window. *Trigger: link triggers, form triggers.* This Action opens a dialog box displaying a message, which the user can dismiss by clicking the OK button. Since every browser displays this dialog box differently, the only control you have over how it looks is the text contents (see Figure 26-14).

The useful tie-in with Open Alert Window is that you can draw the text from variable or field, allowing the outcome of an operation to be displayed to the user. (Look, ma, I'm programming!)

Figure 26-14
Open Alert
window

IE for Windows alert

IE for Macintosh alert

Password. *Trigger: Body.* Password allows you to protect pages on your site by using an encrypted password hidden in the JavaScript. Adobe gets around a few difficulties in this concept by requiring that you name a page with the same name as the unencrypted password plus a ".html".

Adobe ships a password generator in the form of a Web page called makepassword.html, located in GoLive 6.0/Modules/JScripts/Actions/Message. The output from this form is the encrypted information you place in the Encrypted Password field. Choose an alert message to confirm that the password a user entered was correct.

Set Status. *Trigger: Mouse Enter.* The Set Status Action lets you create a message at the bottom of the browser window in the status bar (see Figure 26-15). It's usually used in conjunction with the Mouse Enter event attached to a button to give the visitor a better idea of where the link takes them. The message can be derived from a variable or field, allowing cool combinations with other Actions, such as displaying a status based on results in a form.

Figure 26-15
Status display

Multimedia Actions

The Multimedia Actions deal with controlling floating boxes and animation (see Chapter 25, *Creating Animation with DHTML*).

Drag Floating Box. *Trigger: link triggers.* This Action lets a user drag a specified floating box. Unfortunately, the box's outline and contents are not visible while it is being dragged.

Flip Move. *Trigger: link triggers.* When triggered, Flip Move moves a floating box from one absolute position to another; when triggered again, the box moves to another position. If you specify the second place as the original location, it's as if you're flipping the box back and forth. You specify both positions and whether GoLive animates the transition. Click either or both Get buttons to retrieve the floating box's current position. Ticks, if set to a value greater than zero, defines how long the move should take in sixtieths of a second (1⁄60).

Float Layer. *Trigger: link triggers, Head OnLoad.* Coolo-beanos: lock a floating box in place using a relative offset from the edge of the browser window when the rest of the page scrolls. Adobe warns that for certain older browsers (Internet Explorer 4.5 and earlier), you need to move the box to its location first, via the Move To Action (see below).

Mouse Follow. *Trigger: link triggers, Head OnParse.* Mouse Follow sets a floating box to track the movements of a user's mouse. Creepy? Cool? Annoying? All of the above, depending on its use.

Move By, Move To. *Trigger: link triggers.* Move By moves a floating box a specified distance from its last position; Move To migrates a floating box from its current position to a set of absolute coordinates. Click the Get button to get the current position. Move To can be animated, like Float Layer. Both Move By and Move To can use the results of Actions or other values to specify their motions and the layer acted on.

Play Scene, Stop Scene. *Trigger: link triggers.* This pair of Actions triggers a DHTML animation timeline to start or stop. For instance, you might want an animation to play when a user clicks a button that reads "play animation." Or the opposite with Stop Scene. (There's an example of using Play Scene in Chapter 25, *Creating Animation with DHTML*.)

Play Sound, Stop Sound. *Trigger: link triggers.* This pair of Actions directs a specified plug-in to start or stop playing a sound. The plug-in must have the ability to respond to JavaScript and be named; check the plug-in's documentation to find out if it is compatible or not.

ShowHide. *Trigger: link triggers.* ShowHide toggles a floating box's visibility, changing its state from visible to invisible, or vice-versa; or, it forces a floating box to be shown or hidden, regardless of its current visibility.

SlideShow, SlideShowAuto, SlideShowAutoStop. *Trigger: link triggers, Head OnLoad.* This set of Actions works with a set of images numbered 01, 02, 03, and so on, all located in the same folder as a base image. The SlideShow and SlideShowAuto Actions take a base image as a starting point. The total number of images must be specified, and they must all be either GIF or JPEG; no mixing of types within a slide show. All the graphics must have the same dimensions or the browser distorts them to fit the area of the first image.

SlideShow lets a user click to walk through slides. Loop, Palindrome, and Play Backwards are complementary and exclusive choices. Loop continues the slide show from start to finish after the last image is shown. Play Backwards reverses the order. Checking Palindrome plays a slide show first from start to finish and then finish to start; Loop has to be checked for that to work.

SlideShowAuto starts running when triggered. You can specify a delay between slides in seconds, and use the SlideShowAutoStop Action attached to a button or link to pause or continue the show. You can also choose to loop the show around to the front again or not; the other two options aren't available.

Stop Complete. *Trigger: link triggers.* This Action stops all DHTML animation currently running on the page. It's polite to give the viewer the option to stop animation on a page, to keep it from transitioning from entertaining to annoying. Or, you can stop an animation automatically after a certain time has passed using the Condition Action.

Wipe Transition. *Trigger: link triggers, Head OnParse.* Wipe Transition lets you use a "wipe" style of transition when hiding or showing a floating box carried out in the number of steps you specify. You can hide or show the floating box by wiping in (show) or out (hide). The options are plentiful: left to right, right to left, top to bottom, bottom to top, or center out.

Others Actions

The Others Actions mostly act on the browser window itself.

Clock Date (ID). *Trigger: Head OnLoad.* You can place the local time and/or date into any layer or ID defined area. (See "Text Swap (ID)," above for configuring IDs or the custom open and close tags.)

The time displayed is taken from the machine that's displaying the page, not the server. Check either or both Show Local Time and Show Date; neither shows nothing. Use 24hr Format displays military style time. The Date Format and Include Day of Week options are self-explanatory.

Lead In Text precedes the date and is identical regardless of the time.

Digital Clock. *Trigger: Head OnLoad.* Create ten unique images to correspond to the digits 0 to 9. Put any four of these images on a page and name them uniquely in the More tab of the Image Inspector (see Figure 26-16). The images themselves should be either an umixed set of GIFs or JPEGs named 0.gif or 0.jpg through 9.gif or 9.jpg. Choose the folder in which these 10 images reside at the bottom of the Actions palette.

The base images for each of the four digits in the time predetermine the image dimensions for each digit. Images can all be different sizes if you like, however; set their dimensions to Image from Pixel in the Image Inspector's Basic tab, if so.

Select four images by the name you gave them in the More tab so that GoLive knows which images to swap out with the current time.

Figure 26-16
Digital Clock

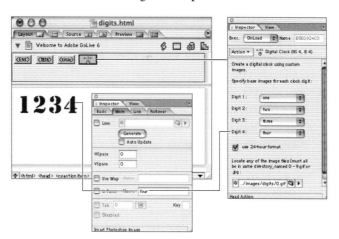

Netscape CSS Fix. *Trigger: Head OnLoad.* A Netscape 4 bug causes pages to lose most of their Cascading Style Sheet (CSS) formatting information when the window is resized. This occurs because Netscape 4.x reparses the page's HTML when the window's dimensions are changed, without taking into account CSS. To be safe you should add Netscape CSS Fix to every page that includes style sheets if you believe you'll have many 4.x visitors.

Print Document. *Trigger: link triggers.* Print the current frame or browser window in which the Action lies if the user is running Netscape 4 or later or Internet Explorer 5 or later.

Resize Window. *Trigger: link triggers.* This Action changes the size of the current window.

Scroll Down, Scroll Left, Scroll Right, and Scroll Up. *Trigger: link triggers.* This set of Actions scrolls the window down, left, right, or up by an amount in pixels at a speed you specify.

ScrollStatus. *Trigger: Head OnLoad, link triggers.* This implements one of the most-requested features of all time, or so we think. A few years ago, some brilliant mind figured out how to scroll stuff through the status field using JavaScript; this Action makes it simple, and offers choices for speed and direction. Use with care; it might annoy your visitors. Speed values vary from 1 to 1000, with one being fastest.

SearchEngine. *Trigger: link triggers, Head OnLad.* It's hard to express our limitless joy at this feature. This allows you to create a custom search form that links to results on any of several major search engines with an option to have the results pop up into their own window. The Action can take the output from a form to feed in as arguments. Or, you can enter your own search string, too, replacing spaces with plus signs (+). (We'd recommend checking on this Action frequently, as search engines change their formats all the time, and we'd guess this needs to be updated by the developers when that happens.)

Set BackColor. *Trigger: any.* Set BackColor changes the current window's background color. You can't change the background image using this Action, but you can use a floating box as a background and change it using the Set Image URL Action (see sidebar, "Set Image URL Tutorial," earlier in the chapter).

WorldClock. *Trigger: Head OnLoad.* This neat Action inserts the current time and date in clock format using the visitor's computer's own time. So if their clock is off, this display is off. You can use GMT offset to show the time anywhere in the world. The time can be inserted into a form element by specifying that form's and field's names, or in the status bar.

Specials Actions

There are always things that don't fit into a neat category. The Specials Actions relate to grouping and referencing other Actions.

Action Group. *Trigger: n/a.* The Action Group is a container that lets you group a set of Actions to be triggered together. After adding Actions, you can re-order them with the up and down arrow buttons.

Call Action. *Trigger: link triggers or inside Action sequences.* Call Action lets you start another Action by name which can be supplied as a named Head OnCall Action or via variables.

Call Function. *Trigger: any.* Use Call Function to trigger a function within a custom-coded JavaScript that you've inserted into a page. This feature allows you to write custom functions using the JavaScript editor for behavior not available in an Action, while integrating this custom feature with Actions to speed up the development process. You can pass values to the JavaScript while calling it, too.

Condition. *Trigger: any.* This Action tests the results of four actions: Intersection (to see if two floating boxes are intersecting, such as when an animation is playing); KeyCompare (if a specified key is being pressed); Timeout (if a certain amount of time has passed); or Test Variable (if a variable matches a value, such as true or false) (see Figure 26-17). You can trigger one Action if the condition is true and a different Action—or no Action at all—if the condition is false. Also, this is a great place to use Action Groups to create multiple results which themselves could contain nested Conditions.

Idle. *Trigger: Head OnLoad.* When placed in the Head section of the Layout Editor, the Idle Action monitors for the same conditions specified above in "Condition." You can specify an Action to trigger when the condition has occurred, as well as an Action to trigger over and over again if the condition is

Figure 26-17
Condition
example

Declare a variable in the Head section with onLoad set.

Configure an item on the page, such as this checkbox, that changes the variable's value.

Set up a condition to check whether the box was checked or not.

The results of truth

The results of falsehood

false. You can also set the Idle Action to continue even after the condition has been met, or stop after the first time it tests true. However, you cannot stop the Idle Action once it is set in motion; you have to wait until the condition is met and then only if you previously set it to stop. Once stopped, it can be restarted using Call Action.

The Condition Action and the Idle Action differ in their triggers: Condition is triggered directly from a specific test; Idle runs continuously, scanning for any outcome by those four Actions.

Intersection, KeyCompare, Timeout. *Trigger: Idle Action only (embedded).* These dependent Actions work within Idle to monitor active conditions on the current Web page. Intersection is true when two floating boxes cross paths. KeyCompare becomes true if a given key is pressed. Timeout lets a specified amount of time pass, and then declares itself true.

KeyCompare is tricky in two ways: first, you need to enter the ASCII code for the character, like 65 for A; and second, you can't specify a false response because the Action is always false until the key is pressed. False would be triggered immediately.

Variables

A variable is a container that lets you store text or numbers for use in other Actions. For example, you can ask a visitor what his or her favorite color is and store it as a variable using the Get Form Value Action. Then you can use that variable to change the background color of the page using the Set Back Color Action. In order to use a variable, you must first create and name it using the Declare Variable Action.

One shortcoming of variables is that the browser can't remember them from page to page; they only work within Actions called on the same page that the variable was created or modified. One way around this limitation is to store the variable's value in a cookie, a small bit of text that a Web server or JavaScript can ask a browser to store on the user's hard drive. Cookies can be named and can contain up to 4,096 characters of alphanumeric data (letters, numbers, and punctuation).

You can also assign an expiration date to a cookie, so that you can retrieve the stored value or update it for a fixed period of time. That might be an hour from when you set it, a week later, or even 10 years later (though the odds that someone will be using the same browser in 10 years is too small to measure, even with the most advanced computers). If you do not give the cookie an expiration date, it lasts only as long as the browser is open and running. When a user quits the browser or reboots their machine, the cookie expires and joins the choir invisible.

Cookies are stored for a specific site, and a browser reveals a cookie only when it returns to a page at the site for which the cookie was originally stored. Most cookies are set to be available on every page in the site. You update cookies by writing new values to them, which replace any value stored.

Declare Variable. *Trigger: any.* This Action creates a new variable; it can be stored in an existing cookie using Write Cookie. There are 12 possible types of variables, which we note below in Init Variable.

You can set a cookie name, too, for this variable to be stored in. Follow this Action with a Write Cookie Action to ensure it's stored by the browser.

DeleteCookie. *Trigger: link triggers, Head OnLoad.* To get rid of a cookie, use Delete Cookie with the name set to one you defined at some point in Visitor-Cookie or Write Cookie. It sets the cookie's expiration date to the current time.

Init Variable. *Trigger: Head OnParse.* Set the initial value of a variable with Init Variable. The types above in Declare Variable all apply. This Action provides the way to enter the specific data appropriate for each kind of variable. You can use direct entry to set a constant value whenever this Action appears; use Set Variable to move a value into a declared variable.

The 12 variable types are:

- **Boolean:** on or off, represented by a checkbox (checked is on or true; unchecked is off or false).
- **Integer:** a whole number with no fraction.
- **Float:** a number with a decimal fraction (a floating point number for the geeks).
- **String:** any text.
- **Layer:** a floating box; a popup menu shows all layers.
- **Layer Position:** a floating box's coordinates. Oddly, a Get box appears, but since you can't select a layer there, there's no way to use it to retrieve any current settings.
- **Image:** any name image; a popup menu lists all named images on the page.
- **URL:** a path or URL.
- **Color:** any color; use the Color palette to select.
- **Scene:** any DHTML Timeline scene; select from a popup menu.
- **OnCall Action:** any Head Action set to OnCall; select from a popup menu.
- **Function:** a JavaScript function defined in the JavaScript Editor, just as you could use in the Call Function Action; select from a popup menu.

Read Cookie. *Trigger: link triggers, Head OnLoad.* Get information for one or more variables stored in a cookie specified by name with Read Cookie.

Set Variable. *Trigger: link triggers, Head OnLoad.* Store a value in a variable with this Action. You may want to use triggers on a page that change the value stored in a variable to something other than what you specified in Init Variable.

Test Variable. *Trigger: Idle Action only.* With Test Variable, you can determine whether one of your variables meets, exceeds, or doesn't match a given value, and then behave accordingly. Your tests must match the kind of variable you're working with. You can't find out if a layer value contains a number, for instance.

TimesVisited. *Trigger: Head OnLoad.* This Action requires users to accept a cookie which tracks how many times they've been to that page. It updates the count each time the page is loaded. If you enter text in the 1st Time Visitor Message field, that text appears in an alert when the user shows up with no cookie. On subsequent visits, the Show This Message + Total Visits field can display text coupled with the count of their current visit in an alert dialog box. You can also show a message after a certain number of visits via the Optional Message field. You should name the cookie uniquely.

VisitorCookie. *Trigger: Head OnLoad.* VisitorCookie marks that a user has been to your site. After the first visit, the Action reads the cookie that notes that the user has been there before, and redirects the browser to another page that you choose. This lets you display a welcoming splash screen to first-time visitors, and then take them directly to the real main page when they come back.

WriteCookie. *Trigger: Head OnLoad.* WriteCookie creates a cookie on the user's computer with a name and expiration time (in hours) that you specify. The Domain must be set to the current site's domain (like peachpit.com) or a subdomain (like beta.peachpit.com). Set to any other value, it fails.

WriteCookie also lets you specify which pages on the site the browser reveals the cookie to; most of the time, you should set this to "/" to let the cookie be revealed on any page on the site. If Secure is checked, the browser should only send a cookie when a browser is communicating over SSL, but it's never been clear to us if that's ever worked as a setting in browsers.

Combining Actions

Actions don't do much by themselves; creating a variable or retrieving the position of a floating box may be interesting, but it certainly isn't useful unless you apply that information. The trick to unlocking the power of Actions is to create a group that works together to accomplish a task. Here are three examples to start you thinking about how to use Actions for real-world solutions. (Download the source materials for these examples from realworldgolive.com/six/actions.html.)

Rotating Banner Ads

Actions used: *Idle/Timeout, Random Image*

This first example randomly changes an image on the page—in this case a banner ad—at set time intervals.

At the top of your example page, place a banner ad that you want to be randomly replaced. For the Actions to work, the image has to have a name; select the image and enter "bannerAd" in the Name field next to the Is Form checkbox in the Image Inspector's More tab (see Figure 26-18).

Figure 26-18
Naming the
image

This Action needs to start running as soon as the page loads, so insert a Head Action, and bring up the Action Inspector.

Choose OnLoad from the Exec menu to trigger the Action as soon as the entire page has downloaded. Select Idle from the Action menu under the Specials submenu. We want the banner to change every 30 seconds, so make sure Exit Idle If Condition Returns True is not checked, and, in the Condition tab, choose Timeout from the Specials submenu of the Action menu. There is only one option to set for Timeout, the length of time to wait in seconds; enter 30 in the Timeout field (see Figure 26-19).

Figure 26-19
Setting Idle
conditions

After 30 seconds, the Idle Action triggers the Action specified in the True tab. Select the True tab and then choose Random Image from the Image submenu of the Action menu. Since you named the banner ad earlier, you can select it in the Base Image menu to target it. All that's left to do now is to specify graphics for the three random image slots (see Figure 26-20).

Figure 26-20
Filling out the
random slots

Save the page and preview it in a browser. If all went as planned, the banner should now change to one of three randomly chosen ads every 30 seconds. Because the images are chosen at random, you might see the same one twice in a row; be patient if it doesn't change after 30 seconds (or change the interval to a shorter period to preview the changes).

Open a Remote Control Subwindow

Actions used: *Open Window, Target Remote*

This example opens a small subwindow with a menu bar that functions like a remote control, so that when you click a button in the subwindow the browser loads a new page in the main window.

First, create a new page with menu buttons to be linked to other pages on your site. Don't link the buttons just yet (see Figure 26-21).

Figure 26-21
A page with
menu buttons

Add a link or button to your main page layout—for this example, add a text link—that you want visitors to click to open the remote-control window. You could also place this Action in the Head section with an OnLoad trigger to automatically open the second window when the page loads.

Select the link and open the Actions palette. Choose Mouse Click from the Events list and click the New Action button. Choose Open Window from the Action menu's Link submenu. Name the new window "remote" in the Target field and make it 100 by 200 pixels. Uncheck all the display options so that only the status bar is displayed (see Figure 26-22).

Figure 26-22
Setting up the
new window

Use Point & Shoot navigation or browse to the menu buttons page created earlier to use it as the link page that is displayed in the new window.

To make the buttons in the remote control window functional, open the menu buttons page you created earlier. Select the first button and make it a link. Open the Actions palette, add a Mouse Click, and select Target Remote from the Action menu's Link submenu.

The Target Remote action automatically targets the original window that opened our new subwindow, so just link to the page we want to display. In this example, we link to "rotatingBanner.html" (see Figure 26-23). As you can

Figure 26-23
Linking to the
page in the
main window

see from the options in the Inspector palette, if the original page contained frames we could also target a frame within that frameset.

Repeat this last operation with the rest of the menu buttons on the remote control page, then test your new creation in several browsers to see how it works (see Figure 26-24).

Figure 26-24
Testing remote
control

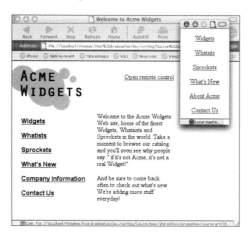

Storing Information in a Cookie

Actions used: *Declare Variable, Init Variable, WriteCookie, Set Variable, Read-Cookie, Set BackColor, Condition, Document Write*

To demonstrate how to get information into a cookie and read it out again later on other pages, create a page named askcolor.html that prompts users to choose between two colors. On the next page, we use Actions to set the background to the color they chose, as well as insert the color name in the page itself.

Let's start with the page where the visitor makes his or her choice. Drag a Head Action icon from the Smart tab into the page's Head section. In the Head Action Inspector, choose Declare Variable from the Variables submenu of the Action menu (see Figure 26-25). Give the variable the name "color", set the Type to String (to indicate we are storing text in the variable), and, in the Cookie field, type "colorPref". This last parameter doesn't actually create the

Figure 26-25
Setting up
Declare
Variable

cookie, but it does indicate which cookie ends up storing this variable's contents. Finally, choose OnParse from the Exec menu so the variable is created as soon as the browser reads this Action.

Next, we want to put a default value into the variable, so drag another Head Action into the Head section, and choose Init Variable from the Variables submenu (see Figure 26-26). Set Exec to OnParse, choose "color" (the name of the variable we just created) from the Variable menu, and type "nothing" into the value field. Now, when the browser reads these Actions, we have a variable named "color" which contains the word "nothing".

Figure 26-26
Setting up Init
Variable

Let's store this default value in a cookie in case the visitor decides not to choose a color. Drag yet another Head Action into the Head section, and set Exec to OnParse (see Figure 26-27). Choose WriteCookie from the Variables submenu and give it the name "colorPref". Because we also filled in the Cookie field on our "color" variable with the same name, the WriteCookie Action automatically links up with that variable and stores its contents in a cookie named "colorPref".

Figure 26-27
Setting up
Write Cookie

With these three Actions set up in the Head section, we can now build a form from which the user chooses a color (see Figure 26-28). Add a Form object from the Forms tab of the Objects palette to the body of the page. In the Form object, enter some text, such as "Which color do you prefer?" Add a paragraph break and drag in a Submit Button icon from the Forms tab. In the Input Button Inspector, choose Normal as the button type. Check the Label box and enter "blue" for the button label.

Figure 26-28
Making a color
choosing form

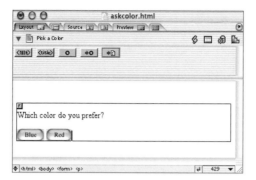

We need to add three Actions to the Mouse Click event for this button, so bring up the Actions palette, and, with the submit button selected, add the first Mouse Click event by clicking the New Action button (see Figure 26-29). Choose Set Variable from the Variables submenu, and choose "color" from the Variable menu, which should be the only choice. In this case we give the variable the value "blue" since that is the button the user is clicking.

Figure 26-29
Three mouse
click Actions to
handle the
color choice

Add another Mouse Click event to the button named blue, and choose Write Cookie. Just like before, type in "colorPref" for the name. This causes the word "blue" to overwrite the "nothing" we stored in the colorPref cookie earlier. For our last Mouse Click event, choose Goto Link from the Link submenu and enter the URL of our next page (in this case "showcolor.html") in the Link field.

Let's take a shortcut in adding a second button to the form. Select the Blue button and copy it (see Figure 26-30). Type a space after the existing button, and select Paste from the Edit menu. Select the second button and change its label in the Input Button Inspector to "red". Now we just have to make one change to this new button's Actions to store a different value in our colorPref cookie. Select the Red button with the Actions palette visible. In the Set

Figure 26-30
Configuring
the second
button

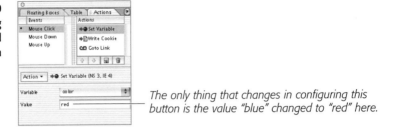

The only thing that changes in configuring this button is the value "blue" changed to "red" here.

Variable options, change the Value field from "blue" to "red". Now we can move on to the next page where we read the cookie and use the information we stored in it.

Create a new page and save it as "showcolor.html". Just as we did before, add two Head Action objects to the page to declare a variable named color and a cookie named "colorPref"; set it to "nothing", or just copy and paste the first two Head Actions from the askcolor.html page.

Next, add another Head Action and choose Read Cookie from the Variables submenu (see Figure 26-31). We assign it the name "colorPref" so that the browser can retrieve the cookie we stored earlier and place its contents (in this case either "blue" or "red") in the variable "color". Make sure all three of these Actions are set to Execute OnParse.

Figure 26-31
Adding Read
Cookie

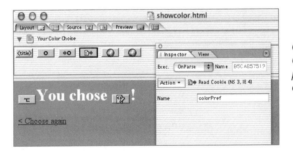

Configure the Read Cookie Action on the page that shows the color choice results.

Lastly, we add two more Actions to the Head section (see Figure 26-32). For both, choose Set BackColor from the Others submenu and set Exec to OnCall, since we trigger them later using another Action. Name the first one "BkgBlue", and set the color to whatever blue you like; name the second Action "BkgRed", and set its color to your favorite red.

We can now test to see what the user actually chose on the previous page. Drag a Body Action object onto the page, and choose Condition from the Specials submenu in the Body Action Inspector (see Figure 26-33). In the Condition tab, choose Test Variable from Variables and set Variable to "color"

Figure 26-32
Setting
BackColor

The two options for color results which are called from a conditional Action

Figure 26-33
Conditional
color setting

(it should be the only choice). We know that the value we got from the cookie and stored in the color variable is either "blue" or "red", so to test to see if the user chose blue, enter "blue" into the Value field, and set Operation to Equal.

If the variable "color" is "blue", the condition tests true. In that case, we want to call the Set BackColor Action to change the background color of the page to blue. Click the True tab and choose Call Action from the Specials submenu. Click the button next to Action until it is a green square with a question mark in it (see sidebar, "Field Entry Indicator," earlier in this chapter). Choose BkgBlue from the popup to target the Head Action that changes the background to blue.

We're assuming that if the color is not blue, it's red, so in the False tab (because true is blue), we can trigger a different Action. Choose Call Action, but this time set Action to "BkgRed".

Let's do one more thing with our cookie contents before testing these pages. In the body of showcolor.html, enter the words "You chose", add a space, and drag in another Body Action object (see Figure 26-34). In the Body Action Inspector choose Document Write from the Message submenu and click the little button next to HTML until it is a blue ball. By choosing "color"

Figure 26-34
Showing what
the user chose

from the popup menu, the browser inserts the word stored in the variable "color" into that spot on the page.

Let's test. Load askcolor.html into a browser, and click on either the Blue or Red button. If everything is configured correctly you should go to the showcolor page and it has the background color of your choice; it should also tell you at the top of the page "You chose blue" or "You chose red" (see Figure 26-35).

Figure 26-37
The results of choosing

Choose a color.   The color you chose.

Shifting Scripts to an External Library File

For a change of pace, let's finish up with a discussion of where GoLive sticks all the JavaScript necessary to handle Actions, smart objects, and DHTML animations. By default, GoLive stores all this JavaScript in the Head section of each page on which any of the objects or animations appear. Though convenient, this is wasteful, because if you use the same behavior on multiple pages, a visitor to your site has to load that code several times.

GoLive offers the option to externalize all this JavaScript in a separate file that a visitor's browser loads just once when he or she reaches any page referencing it. After that, it holds it in its local cache, speeding up the time to handle any Actions or other routines.

This external library enlarges as you work on the site. GoLive starts throwing everything and the kitchen sink into it. Fortunately, an option that appeared late in GoLive 5's testing cycle has been vastly improved in GoLive 6: Flatten Script Library. This feature lets you slim down the size of the library.

Moving Code

You can externalize the code of a particular page in your site, or a Component that contains elements requiring GoLive's JavaScript library. (This doesn't work for a single page; only for pages or elements contained in a site.) Open the page or Component, click the Page icon at the top of the Layout Editor, and then choose the HTML tab in the Page Inspector.

You can select one of two options under JavaScript Functions. The default, Write Code into Page, leaves all the JavaScript in the page's Head section. Choosing Import GoLive Script Library removes all code necessary for the page or Component's Actions, DHTML animations, and smart objects, leaving behind only some page-specific parameters. (You can set this choice for subsequently created pages in the Preferences or Site Settings under Script Library.)

Tip: Rebuilding

The Rebuild button in the Script Library pane of Preferences doesn't rebuild pages. It rebuilds the master list of Actions that shows up in the Inspector palette's Actions tab after you add a new Action to the appropriate folder.

GoLive adds a link from the page to a file called, by default, CSScriptLib.js, which it places into a folder in the root level of your site called Generated Items. You can change the name and the folder's name (it must stay in the root level) via the Script Library pane in Preferences or Site Settings.

New in 6: Generated Items

The folder containing the JavaScript library gained a space. In GoLive 5, it was called "GeneratedItems". The space shouldn't cause you any problems, but when you upgrade a site from 5 to 6, you'll find your old folder with your old GoLive Script Library in it. You can use Preferences to reset the location, too.

The changes are applied as soon as you choose any of these options, and made permanent when you save the page.

Tip: Library Privileges

GoLive automatically restricts access to the external code to browsers that support JavaScript 1.2 or higher, so even if the Actions you've used are compatible with some 3.0 browsers, the scripts are hidden from them. Only a very small percentage of users (probably below one percent) use 3.0 or earlier browsers.

Flatten Script Library

GoLive builds the script library from a larger collection of JavaScript it knows is needed for given Actions and animations. The script library can get larger than necessary, 50K in size or greater, and you're forcing your users to download this file each time they visit the site and use any page that references the library.

Fortunately, Flatten Script Library can squeeze that external JavaScript down to the smallest amount by analyzing every file in the site and confirming precisely what's needed. What's more, you can automate the process.

There are several ways you can use Flatten Script Library.

- Select it from the Site or contextual menu with the mouse or selection on the Files tab.

- Check it in Strip Options when uploading via FTP. It can be set each time, or as a global or sitewide preference via the Upload/Sync Times.

- Set it when you export a site. It's also settable each time or as a preference.

When GoLive flattens the library, it shows you a progress window as it processes each file. When it's done, it indicates the processing is complete by showing a lightning bolt next to a descriptive item.

Tip: Handwritten Libraries

GoLive's Script Library doesn't contain any JavaScript you added by hand or via the JavaScript Editor into a page. We recommend creating your own, separate JavaScript library file for your own reusable routines. Name it with ".js" at the end; consult Chapter 24, *Authoring JavaScript*, for more details.

Building Action-Packed Web Sites

Actions offer enormous help by bundling so many complex features into a few relatively simple-to-use tools. Although Actions don't solve every problem or provide an interface to every possible need, they're comprehensive enough to let non-programmers build sophisticated sites, and to let programmers quickly prototype new features without expending the effort to hand code advanced functionality.

Defining Cascading Style Sheets

Cascading Style Sheets (hereafter just CSS) let you control every aspect of the appearance of type and the position of objects on a page. When we wrote the first edition of this book back in 1999, most browsers were still just beginning to cope with CSS. Now, we've had three years of compatibility and stability. Most browsers since Internet Explorer 4.5 or 5.0 (depending on platform) and Netscape 6.0 handle almost all CSS specifications with aplomb; each subsequent release only gets better.

This support makes it easy to talk about and design with CSS. Earlier in the book, in the Building Pages section, we told you how to design CSS selectors for controlling text (Chapter 4, *Text and Fonts*), color (Chapter 6, *Color*), and interacting with floating boxes (Chapter 10, *Floating Boxes*). In Chapter 25 and 26, we addressed the role of CSS in relation to DHTML (positioning in animation) and Actions (using CSS in combination with Actions).

In this chapter, we're launching full-on into the CSS stratosphere: all of the specifications that you can set in GoLive, linking and editing styles, how the program previews them, and how you can go beyond GoLive's built-in features to add more advanced CSS features that the browsers uniformly support and support well.

Tip: CSS1 and CSS2

CSS is a specification created by the World Wide Web Consortium (www.w3c. org). The first formal spec was called CSS1, and the second spec, CSS2, has been widely supported for at least two years. CSS3 started making the rounds a few years ago, but the current status indicates little progress towards browser implementation. GoLive generally provides all CSS1 features, but in cases where the feature described is part of CSS2, GoLive is less likely to fully implement it, and you may have to enter the code by hand.

What CSS Looks Like

Although GoLive insulates you from underlying code that defines CSS-based styles, it's not a bad idea to first peek under the hood. This becomes especially important knowledge later when and if you decide to tweak the code by hand.

CSS has a very simple structure for defining the name of a style sheet and its properties within HTML:

```
selector { property: value }
```

The selector is the name of the style, which also defines what text gets selected by it. The selector can be the name of a tag, a unique identifier used once in a document, or a generic name that can be applied to any range of text or portion of a page.

The property is an attribute, such as font size or width of a rule. The value is the number or text that tells the property how to behave. It's defined in units appropriate to the property. (Selectors, properties, and values are described in more detail in "Creating Style Sheets," later in this chapter.)

You can have many properties in the same definition, each separated by semicolons:

```
EM.figures { color: olive; font-style: italic; font-
variant: small-caps }
```

Because browsers before about 4.0 don't support CSS, GoLive and other programs must hide style sheet code from these older browsers, just as with JavaScript and other scripting languages. GoLive inserts the style information into the head portion of an HTML page. A typical example looks like this:

What's New in 6

CSS support in GoLive 6 is more coherent than in any previous version. The CSS Editor offers better and cleaner access to editing and creating styles; the buttons to add items are now at the bottom of the editor instead of floating on a Toolbar. The CSS Style Inspector has essentially the same controls as last time, but the preview of CSS has improved somewhat, so more of what you specify can be viewed in the Layout Editor, rather than a browser.

CSS's big change is the CSS palette, which lets you apply class selectors to text or other markup objects, and assign external style sheets to one or more files in the Files tab of the Site window. The CSS palette's columns change based on the current selection making it clear whether a specific tag (like a form element) is chosen or whether it's a range of text and/or tags.

One small point: the import statement to link external style sheets still needs to be manually coded, but the CSS Editor now allows appropriate changes in the order of appearance.

```
<html>
 <head>
   <title>An Average Page</title>
   <style type="text/css" media="screen"><!--
      #headings { color: olive;
         font-style : italic;
         font-variant: small-caps }
      h1 { font-family:
         "Times New Roman", Georgia,
         Times; text-indent: 1pt }
--></style>
 </head>
 <body>
   <h1>How do you solve a problem
   like <span id="headings">
   Maria</span>?</h1>
 </body>
</html>
```

Displaying in Browsers

Browsers combine designer-defined style sheets referenced or embedded in a Web page with the browsers' own definition of elements (see Figure 27-1). Because you can use CSS to redefine the appearance of actual HTML tags as well as to tag ranges of text and regions on a page, the browser performs a complex series of analyses related just to style sheets before it ever displays a page.

Although we spend time later in this chapter talking about the specific rules that browsers apply according to the CSS specifications, let's walk through the logic that a browser applies to showing something as simple as an H1 HTML tag occurring at the top of a page.

- The browser first refers to built-in style sheets that contain the default values.

- Any external style sheets referenced on the page are loaded and examined in order for any references that would affect H1.

- The browser follows the same process for style sheets embedded in a page.

- Likewise, it checks for any style sheets attached to a specific instance of a tag where it appears on the page.

- CSS allows style sheets to override others out of order if they have an extra bit of emphasis in them; the browser has to sort settings to include these in the right order.

Figure 27-1
Working
with CSS

Affordable Lunar Travel is Within

Although modern technology offers clearly insurmountable barriers to present moment, our motto, currently under legal review, is, "Ad Asper Ignorance).

Heading 1 (H1) in its default browser style viewed in the GoLive Layout Editor...

Affordable Lunar Travel is Within

Although modern technology offers clearly insurmountable barriers to present moment, our motto, currently under legal review, is, "Ad Asper Ignorance).

...and looking fetchingly identical in a browser.

GoLive has particular ideas about the underlying formatting of H1 stored in the Browser Profiles tab of Web Settings. In this case, we're viewing the formatting for Windows Netscape 6.

But, of course, we can use the CSS Editor to redefine H1...

...and preview the results in GoLive.

- Any user preferences for fonts override (in most cases) the browser's defaults and CSS styles.

- The browser is now ready to actually display the tag on the page: it has calculated all the parameters that go into that single instance.

You can see the horsepower devoted to just dealing with one tag. Imagine how much more processing is involved when floating boxes with separate repeating backgrounds occur over and over again.

Previewing in GoLive

The giddy thrill of creating style sheets can give way to a bit of regret if you haven't done a thorough job of reviewing which properties and features work in standard browsers, or haven't tested your style sheets with extensive previewing. So before we show you the GoLive approach to CSS, allow us to offer a few words on planning and previewing your work.

Despite GoLive's generally excellent preview simulations of browsers, there's no reliable way to tell how a feature—especially a CSS property—works in an actual browser. In this regard, GoLive's failing is in being too good. All browsers are "broken" in some regard. A programming mistake or design choice makes combinations of tags work inconsistently. Tables are a notable example of broken behavior, in which small, insignificant changes in tags can cause a table to work or not.

GoLive implements all its previewing features consistently, using a structured framework, so a feature that works inconsistently in the actual browser shows up correctly in GoLive. (We don't want to be the ones to ask the GoLive engineers to purposely break their software; do you?)

Targeting Browsers

Before you ever design a style sheet, you must make hard decisions about which browsers you plan to support with your site. You face three primary options.

- Support all browsers and use no advanced features. In this case, you can exit this chapter (and especially this part of the book), since many CSS features, JavaScript, and even frames require you to abandon some part of the audience, even if it's a small percentage of users.

- Support all browsers by providing alternatives to advanced features. You can code CSS into a site that uses all tag selectors (explained later in this chapter) so a browser lacking CSS support falls back to using normal HTML tags, like H1, to display headings and body copy.

- Support only newer, CSS-capable browsers. The vast majority of users on the Net browse with either Netscape or Internet Explorer 4.0 or later, or use other browsers, such as Opera, that support virtually all CSS1 and CSS2 specifications. You're cutting out just a tiny part of your audience, and those folks can't visit many Web sites comfortably, anyway. Unless you have a particular segment of old-browser users, this is a perfectly reasonable option.

Previewing in GoLive

GoLive can preview an enormous number of the CSS properties it allows you to set. It also previews some features that you have to hand code.

Layout View Palette

GoLive's Layout View palette offers a number of different variables for determining how CSS styles will appear within a document window. Select View from the Window menu to bring the View palette into, well, view. The following options specifically affect CSS previewing.

Profile menu. You can simulate different browsers by selecting them from the Profile popup menu of the View palette. These simulations combine the defaults GoLive has encoded for each of the browser versions. (This is called Browser Profile in the contextual menu's View submenu.)

Tip: Default Assumptions

If you want to examine GoLive's assumptions about browser defaults, select Web Settings from the Edit menu and click the Browser Profiles tab. Select one of the browsers in the list, and bring up the Root Style Sheet Inspector. Though you can't edit any of the settings, clicking the Source tab shows you each default that GoLive has set for each tag. This approach lets Adobe easily add new browsers' defaults without recoding the whole program. (For more information, see Chapter 28, *Controlling Web Settings.*)

(A tip within a tip: choosing one of the CSS formatting options in the Global tab of the Web Settings window sets the readability of the items in the Source tab of the Root Style Sheet Inspector.)

Allow Overlapping Paragraphs. Checking Allow Overlapping Paragraphs in the View palette causes GoLive to preview negative margin values, so blocks that may cross each other are correctly displayed.

States menu. Selecting Normal Link, Active Link, Visited Link, Hover, or Focus from the View palette's States menu previews the look of links as you interact with them. This is nominally a CSS issue because you can also set all five of these properties through the Body tag or special selectors.

Highlight Palette

The Highlight palette can be used to call out items tagged with CSS class selectors (which are named definitions that can be attached to any range or object). It can also identify HTML tags by region or selection, which is handy when you're using CSS to redefine the appearance of a tag.

Previewing in Real Browsers

You know you have to do it, but many designers resist: preview your pages in multiple browsers to ensure that the CSS specifications are doing what you hoped and not flowing text off the screen, compressing it beyond legibility, or otherwise impairing the page.

We recommend testing every page of a site on the Macintosh (5 to 25 percent of traffic to most sites) and under Windows in multiple browsers. From our testing, it doesn't seem to matter what version of Windows (95 through present) or Mac OS (version 8 through present) you're running.

The minimally acceptable test bed at this writing includes Windows and Mac machines with few fonts installed (just the defaults, if possible, for best previewing effect) running the last or latest release of:

- Windows Internet Explorer 5.5 and 6; Netscape 4.8, 6.2; Opera 5

- Macintosh Internet Explorer 5 and 5.1; Netscape 4.8, 6.2; Opera 5

Tip: Full Compliance

Macintosh Internet Explorer 5 is fully compliant with all current CSS specifications (CSS1 and CSS2); Eric Meyer's Master List of compatibility at Web Review confirms this. If you want to test styles in the most ideal of all possible circumstances, use that version on that platform.

Netscape 6 (both platforms) and Internet Explorer 6 for Windows all meet practically all specifications, too, so a neat compact test suite would be Internet Explorer 5.1 (Mac OS 9/X), Netscape 6 (OS 9/X, Windows XP), and Internet Explorer 6 (Windows XP).

Creating Style Sheets

CSS has two distinct parts: creation and management of the styles themselves, and application of those styles to text or HTML ranges. We address the first part in this section, and the second in "Applying Style Sheets," later in this chapter.

Chapter 4, *Text and Fonts*, and Chapter 6, *Color* cover how to specifically use CSS to define text styles and color options.

GoLive Tools

It's easy to create CSS specifications in GoLive, as the program puts a friendly interface on top of a truly enormous number of choices and specifications. It's not quite an interactive editor, but it's structured just like you'd define a style sheet in a desktop publishing program. You work primarily with two tools: the CSS Editor and the CSS Style Inspector.

Tip: Styles versus Selectors

The formal name for these definitions are selectors, not styles. The term style isn't inaccurate; it's just more descriptive than precise. Adobe used to mix the term style and selector, and now seems to have come down firmly on consistency with a friendlier term that reminds graphic designers of the DTP world of style sheets.

Tip: Live CSS Preview

Create a new, blank page, and enter some sample text on it that's representative of what you'll be using the styles for. Create new empty CSS styles and name them. Where necessary, apply the styles to the text on the page (with classes and IDs; see "Applying Style Sheets," later in this chapter).

As you edit the style's specifications in the CSS Style Inspector, the type on your test page immediately displays the effects of the changes (see Figure 27-2).

GoLive previews changes in the CSS Style Inspector live on the page, such as changing a font.

CSS Editor

Click the Cascading Style Sheets button—the ziggurat-like stairstepped icon at the top right of the Layout Editor to open the CSS Editor, which handles style sheets just for that page.

You can also create a standalone set of style sheets in its own file that can be referenced from one or more HTML files on your site and edited via the CSS Editor; select Cascading Style Sheet from the New Special submenu of the File menu. This is a convenient way to create a site-wide, intranet-wide, or Internet-wide set of shared formatting.

Viewing styles. Styles are shown in the CSS Editor in pseudo-folders first by class, element, and ID; and then in the order they were added to the document or in which they appear in the source code.

Viewing options can be set in the View palette, or the contextual menu's View submenu. By default, the Folder for Sections and Show Prefixes options are checked. Unchecking Folder for Sections removes the artificial folder display that separates internal and external style sheets.

Folder for Styles adds faux folders to enclose tags, classes, and IDs; collapse their display and make items in the CSS Editor easier to sift through.

Prefixes removes the "#" or "." before IDs and classes, since they're already identified by the type of icon appearing before each style.

The Sort Statements option found in the CSS Editor's popup menu and the contextual menu is subtler than it appears. It takes the items in the CSS Editor and sorts them alphabetically. But in the nature of CSS, the order in which items appear reflects the order of precedence in which the browser interprets their settings: multiple selectors can redefine the same text or tag.

The up and down arrows at the bottom of the CSS Editor allow you to reorder selectors. See "Cascading," later in this chapter, for the full scoop on precedence.

Tip: CSS Editors

The difference between the CSS Editor that you use with editing styles located inside an HTML page and the editor that handles external style sheet files is twofold. The name in their respective title bars is different—the page-specific editor has the file name plus ":CSS Editor," while the standalone document displays only its file name—and the page-specific editor has a folder for Internal and External style sheets (see Figure 27-3). Using external style sheets is discussed under "Cascading," later in this chapter. In all other ways, they work identically.

Figure 27-3
Internal and external folders and the CSS Editor

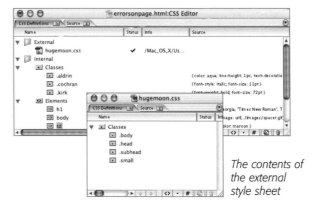

The contents of the external style sheet

Adding styles. You add styles based on their type (see "Style Sheet Selectors," below) by clicking the New Element Style, New ID Style, and New Class Style buttons at the bottom of the CSS Editor (see Figure 27-4). You can also add selector options using the contextual menu or the popout menu.

Figure 27-4
Adding styles

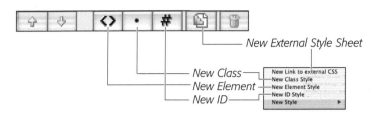

New External Style Sheet

New Class
New Element
New ID

New Link to external CSS
New Class Style
New Element Style
New ID Style
New Style

Creating a new style brings up the CSS Style Inspector. New tags, IDs, and class selectors are named "element", "#id", and ".class", by default. When you click the buttons repeatedly, new items are created with numbers following the default name, which then increment, like ".class1", ".class2", etc.

Importing styles. You can also import the entire contents of external style sheets. This is different from linking to an external style sheet, which merely references another file. The external style sheet stays intact and separate, and can be linked from many files. Importing style sheets copies the entire contents of a CSS style sheet as local styles.

From the File menu's Import submenu, select External Style Sheet. It's also available from the contextual menu and popout menu.

Tip: When to Import

Although you could use the Import External Style Sheet option to set the styles for each page you're working on, it's far more efficient (and less labor-intensive) to reference an external style sheet. Importing CSS is best for building a master style sheet from several different documents, or as a quick way to apply style sheets in one or two pages.

Naming styles. Styles can be named anything alphanumeric; that is, any name containing just letters and numbers. Be sure not to include any spaces or other characters, even though the CSS specification seems to allow some punctuation. It's better to avoid the complications. IDs must be preceded by a pound sign, and classes with a period (see Table 27-1).

Tip: Converting Styles

You can change one kind of selector to another by adding or removing their preceding symbol: remove a period in front of a class selector and it turns into a tag, and so on.

These changes appear in the selector's icon in the CSS Style Inspector when you click somewhere else in the editor to deselect the current selector. The

Table 27-1 Naming conventions	Selector	CSS Editor convention	CSS Style Inspector example	Example in HTML
	Tag	No brackets	H1	H1 { bold }
	Class	Leading period	fridges	.fridges { font-style: italic }
	ID	Leading pound-sign	#aquaman	{ border-top: 1pt dotted aqua }

change shows up immediately in the CSS Editor. To sort these chimerical selectors in their appropriate folders, use the View palette to turn off Folder for Styles and then back on.

If you're truly obsessed, switch to the Source tab of the CSS Editor to directly edit the names of selectors. When you return to the CSS Definitions tab, GoLive correctly re-interprets the names and resorts the items.

Duplicating existing styles. Select a style in the CSS Editor and select Duplicate from the Edit menu or contextual menu to create an exact copy of that existing style. This method is far preferable to making a similar style from scratch.

Deleting styles. Select the style you want to delete and press the Delete key, or select Clear or Delete from the Edit menu or contextual menu.

Tip: Undoable Delete

Undo is quite powerful; you can even undo the deletion of a style sheet. This feature is especially important because GoLive doesn't prompt you to confirm deletions. You can also use the History palette to step backwards through deletions.

Creating non-supported selectors. GoLive allows you to name styles that contain extended selections as described in "Style Sheet Selectors" and "Advanced CSS," later in this chapter. Generally, these kinds of selectors start with a tag, so create a new tag and, in the Name field of the CSS Style Inspector, enter the entire selector. (For instance, "H1.extended UL LI" is perfectly legal in GoLive, even though the program can't preview its effect.)

Linking external style sheets. Click the New Link to External CSS button, which looks like the stairstepped CSS icon overlaying a document. You can also select it from the contextual or popout menus. Either action adds an icon to the External folder of the CSS Editor and brings up the External Style Sheet Inspector, which lets you choose a file to link to (see Figure 27-5).

Figure 27-5
Adding
external style
sheets

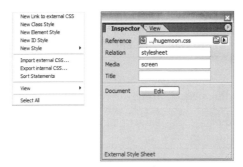

In the Files tab of the Site window, you can select one or more files and then use the CSS palette to link in external style sheets to multiple documents. Use the URL Getter at the bottom of the palette to specify a style sheet file, then click the Add button (see Figure 27-6).

Figure 27-6
Linking
external style
sheets to
multiple files

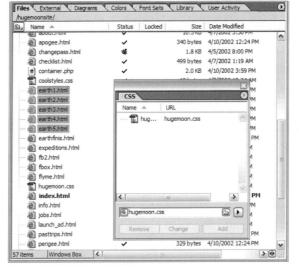

Selecting one or more files and then adding the style sheet through the CSS palette links that style sheet to the whole selection at once.

Relation, although you can edit it, should remain set to the default "stylesheet". Media is a simple reference which might someday be used by software that's customized depending on what device you're using. The default is "screen," but "wireless device" and other options might be appropriate in the future. Title can be anything you want, but it's not a required field. Clicking Edit opens the external style sheet in a CSS Editor.

If you link more than one external style sheet, you can change their order—and thereby the precedence of the properties of style sheets embedded in the external file—by selecting the file or files to re-arrange and clicking the up and down arrows in the CSS Editor. The closer to the top of the list the external style sheet appears, the lower its precedence. (For more on this subject, see "Cascading," later in this chapter.)

Exporting style sheets. You can export your local styles to an external style sheet by selecting Internal Style Sheet from the File menu's Export submenu; or, by selecting Export Internal CSS from the contextual or popout menus in the CSS Editor.

Editing external style sheets. Although you can use the CSS Editor combined with the CSS Style Inspector to edit individual styles, GoLive also offers the Source tab in the CSS Editor. This lets you edit the code directly as if you were viewing the style sheet as a text file (see Figure 27-7). You can also edit it via the Source Code palette (see Figure 27-8).

Figure 27-7
CSS Editor's
Source tab

Figure 27-8
Editing via the
Source Code
palette

CSS Style Inspector

Creating a new selector through the CSS Editor and selecting it activates the CSS Style Inspector, your window into the vast specification arena for CSS.

The first tab of this Inspector—varyingly called Basic or Basics, depending on platform—allows you to name your selector. It also provides a preview of how the actual code of the definition will appear in your HTML code or external CSS file. A full breakout of each tab of the CSS Style Inspector is explained in "Style Sheet Specifications," later in this chapter.

Style Sheet Selectors

CSS categorizes styles by how they get applied to HTML. GoLive and the CSS spec breaks these into three categories: element, class, and ID. Each of these types is a selector, the method by which text in the document is "selected."

You can name these selectors anything that contains just letters (including non-English Unicode-based characters) and numbers. Spaces and punctuation have specific, reserved meanings in selectors.

Element. Element selectors apply to specific HTML tags, whether they're real, like a Heading 3 (H3) or teletype (TT) tag, or invented, like <SPAGHETTI-NI> or <RAVIOLI>. The element selector modifies the element's default appearance if one is built into the browser that's displaying the page.

Tip: Inventing Elements

Invented elements generally work, as most browsers ignore tags they don't understand. But it makes more sense to use classes to define your own categories, unless you have specific reasons to roll your own.

Using elements is the most conservative course, since the few older browsers that don't support CSS use the browser's defaults for the tag; those that support CSS show the style sheets' specifications. Omit the < and > in an element's name when entering the text.

Class. Classes are like the French Club in high school: anyone can join the group whether they're a freshman, sophomore, junior, or senior. After defining a class, you can plug the class into any kind of tag and the text selected by that tag inherits the properties of that class.

Classes are preceded by a period (such as ".mynewfriend"). You can combine tags and classes, and have a class that only applies to a given tag. This can be useful for creating a style sheet that still works with an old non-CSS browser; you can use H2, for instance, for similar levels of information, while using the class to format some H2s differently than others.

Tip: Contextual Selectors

CSS supports selectors that use nested tags and classes, so you can define something as particular as "an unnumbered list element beneath another unnumbered list element in a list that belongs to class 'f1.'" This would be written simply as "UL.f1 UL LI"; pretty elegant, eh? GoLive previews some kinds of behavior like this; the ones it doesn't, it just leaves alone (and you can preview in a browser). This subject is discussed in greater depth in "Advanced CSS," later in this chapter.

New in 6: Better Previews

This is a bit self-referential, but the tip above in previous editions of the book had to explain why GoLive couldn't preview a few levels deep. GoLive 6 has improved its ability to parse more complex selectors and display them onscreen. This is a true boon while designing style sheets.

ID. IDs are uniquely numbered and can be used only once in a document. GoLive currently only lets you define IDs; you have to edit the HTML to apply them. When you define an ID, precede its name with a pound sign (#). (If you delete the pound sign, GoLive changes the selector to a tag selector.)

IDs are often used to define unique areas on a page, such as a region you want to manipulate via DHTML—that's right, floating boxes are nothing more than ranges of HTML tied together with an ID selector.

Tip: Action ID

Several new Actions in GoLive 6 allow you to swap or insert text in an area defined with a unique ID. See Chapter 26, *Applying Actions*.

Tip: Uniquely External

If you use external style sheets, everything in every document is uniquely numbered to avoid erratic behavior. (It's possible that some browsers would let you use the same ID for items on different pages, but not guaranteed.)

Style Sheet Specifications

Of the more than 50 CSS properties you can apply to text selections and blocks, GoLive lets you set almost all of them through popup menus or field values. However, GoLive can't preview all the choices it offers for selection or specification, although it's added more to its box of tricks from version to version.

Tip: Preview in Browsers for Best Results

GoLive previews many effects, but we recommend that you use GoLive just for coding style sheets. Rely on actual browsers to determine whether the effects or styles you're applying actually look the way you want them to.

As mentioned earlier in the chapter, Eric Meyer's Master List at styles. webreview.com is your best resource for determining which features to use to achieve maximum compatibility with the platforms and browsers expected to display your pages.

CSS Model

The CSS specification has a view of the world in which HTML is divided into two categories: inline definitions that control just text, and block definitions that control text and spacing around a selection. These categories correspond very closely to character and paragraph styles in programs like Adobe InDesign, QuarkXPress, or even Microsoft Word. This parallel is helpful to keep in mind if you've used those programs.

Character styles can be applied to any range of text, and typically include just font formatting, like size, typeface, or color. Paragraph styles include leading (the vertical space from one line of type to the next), rules (borders around the text), background shades, margins, and vertical space above and below the paragraph (see Figure 27-9). CSS differentiates between inline elements and block elements. Here's the critical distinction:

Figure 27-9
Paragraph and character styles

An inline element is one that doesn't have a line break before and after it, such as the B (bold) tag. It refers to properties that can affect ranges of HTML without affecting surrounding formatting.

- A block element creates a break in sequence with the HTML above and below it, such as the P (paragraph) tag.

HTML offers ways to create inline and block elements when using selectors that aren't based on the type of element you want to apply. The Span tag creates an inline range of text; the Div tag creates a super-block of text that can encompass one or more paragraphs (see Figure 27-10).

Because properties like line spacing, margins, or typeface by their nature apply to inline or block elements (or both), you can often write a single style that works for both inline and block elements; the block properties are ignored when the style is used with an inline selector.

CSS Specifications

GoLive lets you set most CSS specifications directly through the CSS Style Inspector. Many of the specs are self-explanatory, such as type size or weight.

The CSS Style Inspector has six kinds of settings:

- **Measurement.** For font size or line spacing, enter a number with a measurement (such as "1 px" for one pixel). You can also just enter a number, and then select a measurement unit from the popup menu next to the field. To reset the field value to empty, select Unchanged from the popup menu. (See the sidebar, "Units," for the in-depth story on measurement.)

Figure 27-10 Span versus Div

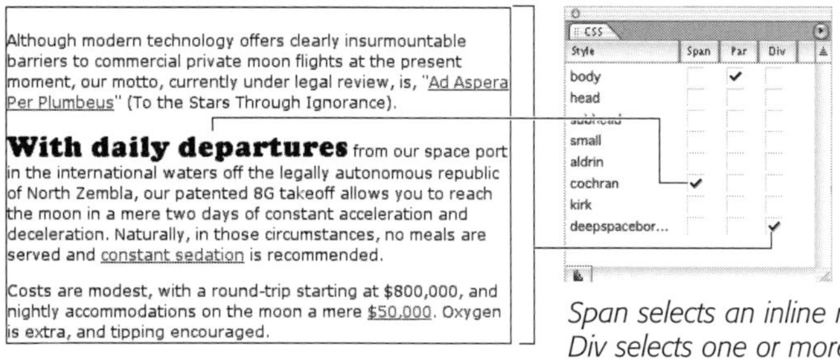
Although modern technology offers clearly insurmountable barriers to commercial private moon flights at the present moment, our motto, currently under legal review, is, "Ad Aspera Per Plumbeus" (To the Stars Through Ignorance).
With daily departures from our space port in the international waters off the legally autonomous republic of North Zembla, our patented 8G takeoff allows you to reach the moon in a mere two days of constant acceleration and deceleration. Naturally, in those circumstances, no meals are served and constant sedation is recommended.
Costs are modest, with a round-trip starting at $800,000, and nightly accommodations on the moon a mere $50,000. Oxygen is extra, and tipping encouraged.
CSS
Style
Span
Par
Div
body
head
small
aldrin
cochran
kirk
deepspacebor...

Span selects an inline range of text; Div selects one or more paragraphs.

- **Color.** Select a standard color from the popup menu or use the Color palette to drag in a swatch.
- **Popup selection.** Some options list only a few defined choices in a popup menu next to the specification's name. For instance, Float can only be set to Left, Right, or None.
- **Image reference.** A background for the area selected by this style or a list background can be chosen via the URL Getter. The CSS Editor displays the status of any links in a style sheet, showing a green bug for bad links and a checkmark if all the files exist. (See Chapter 19, *Managing Files, Folders, and Links* for a complete explanation of these icons.)
- **Font tab.** The Decoration checkboxes and Font Family list don't conform to the rest of the interface. Clicking New adds items to the Font Family list; the arrows rearrange order; pressing Delete with one or more items selected removes the fonts. The checkboxes under Decoration set the style of type.
- **Other properties.** You can add properties that aren't part of GoLive's repertoire by using the Other Properties list in the List and Others tab. If you've defined properties like this, they show up in this tab for editing. The Other Properties list also allows GoLive to open style sheets created in other programs or by hand without causing errors.

  We break down the kinds of specs into major categories for ease of reference.

Tip: Meaning

For more information about each of these specifications, it's best to refer to one of our CSS resources, as we could devote 100 pages to how the specifications work.

Tip: What a Tease

GoLive shows the definition of the style sheet as it gets written in the Basic or Basics tab; it includes any hand tweaking you've done in the Source Code Editor. Although you can't edit or copy the text in this preview, it's nice to see all the parameters in one place (see Figure 27-11, page 787).

Units

CSS uses several standard units for measuring items; GoLive supports all these through appropriate popup menus in the CSS Style Inspector.

Point, pica, inch, cm, and mm. These five units are absolutes. Traditionally, as well as in the CSS specification, there are 12 points to a pica, and six picas to the inch; therefore a point is $\frac{1}{12}$-inch and a pica is $\frac{1}{6}$-inch. Inches are inches all over the world. A centimeter (cm) is 10 times as large as a millimeter (mm); there are 2.54 centimeters to an inch.

Absolute units appear limited to two decimal places to the right of the decimal point, which in any unit is more precise than is even possible to display without an electron-scanning microscope to measure it. GoLive used to truncate additional digits; now it rounds them up (anything above .005 becomes an additional .01, more or less).

Tip: Rounding

Although GoLive 6 now rounds up precision (number of digits to the right of the decimal point) to two, it doesn't preview this effort. If you enter "0.249999 in", for instance, GoLive happily allows it. Switch to the Source tab in the CSS Editor, and you see in the definition that the program has already changed it to "0.25 in"! Switch back to CSS Definitions, and the rounding has occurred.

Point, pica, and inch are abbreviated "pt", "pc", and "in" in any measurement field.

Tip: Unit Conversions

If you select point, pica, pixel, inch, cm, or mm as your measurement unit and enter a value, you can then select a different unit from the popup menu and GoLive automatically converts one unit into terms of another. GoLive somehow stores extra digits for each number at least temporarily, as you can freely convert back and forth without encountering rounding or changes in the original value.

Tip: Inches Aren't Always Inches

Note that selecting these absolute units doesn't guarantee absolute results. Since Web pages are viewed on thousands of different computer and monitor configurations, an inch viewed at one resolution is different than an inch viewed at another resolution. At best, these measurements are relative guides.

Pixel. You can specify items in absolute pixels, abbreviated as "px" in a measurement field, which is the unit that can be used most reliably on a computer screen, since screens are measured in pixels.

Tip: Ideal Pixels

The CSS specification notes that browser developers should consider implementing the pixel measurement using a standard reference pixel so that the same measurement on different monitors would have the same pixel height regardless of the monitor's pitch, or the number of pixels per inch on screen. Most monitors display between 80 and 90 pixels per inch.

Tip: Higher DPI (Mac only)

Internet Explorer for Macintosh 5.x allows you to adjust the default ppi in its Preferences under Languages & Fonts. The default for this version is 96 dpi (really ppi), which freaked out a lot of Mac users, as it made the screen display much larger for a lot of sites. However, it's just the default. If you use CSS at all, it overrides Internet Explorer's dpi setting.

Figure 27-11
Text Selector

Em and ex. An em and an ex are relative measurements based on the height of the capital letter M (for em) and the lower-case x (for ex) in the font, style, and type size defined or inherited in the style sheet.

Tip: Not Your Auntie's Em

The em measurement in CSS may confuse typographers and desktop publishers who are used to the traditional definition of an em that dates back to the last century, if not longer: the width, not height, of a capital letter M. The typographer's name for the CSS em unit would be "cap height," while the ex would be "x-height."

Percentage. If you specify percentage, the question becomes, "Percentage of what?" The percentage is always in terms of another defined unit in the same style sheet, or of an inherited default. Each property that allows percentage as a unit also defines what property the percentage is based on.

In the case of line height, for instance, percentage is based on the text size. If you define H1 as using a font size of 24 points, you can define a line height of 125 percent, which a CSS-compliant browser calculates as 30 points (24 multiplied by 1.25).

Other relative measures (100, XX-Large, Larger, Lighter, Bolder, etc.). CSS uses several relative measures for font size, line thickness, and other specifications that rely heavily on the browser to figure out what's meant. For instance, you can set a font's size to XX-Large, but a browser has to figure out what the current size is and what's relatively extra-extra large by comparison.

Different browsers map these relative measurements to different aspects, so you're counting on testing and luck to get what you want if you use these kinds of measurements.

Auto. Selecting this option, where available, rescales the given specification to fit the space in question. So, a border set to Auto causes the border to be displayed and to span the width of whatever block it's applied to.

Normal. Where Normal is available as an option, CSS defaults to a standard specification. This option is more typically used to reset a value in a cascade. So if the style sheet that has more precedence in a cascade says that the line height should be 100 points, selecting Normal resets the item to the default without requiring you to enter an exact number.

Tip: Hand Editing

You can, in fact, edit the source code in the Source tab of the CSS Editor, in the Split Source pane of the Layout Editor, or in the Source Code palette. After making changes, click on the page or flip tabs in the CSS Editor to make GoLive update its display of the properties.

Typography. CSS lets you define characteristics of type, including character-specific attributes (font name, color, and size) and paragraph- and range-based settings (line spacing, spacing between letters, and vertical and horizontal alignment). GoLive splits the categories into the CSS Style Inspector's Font and Text tabs.

Font characteristics are, by their nature, inline properties, while some of the items found in the Text tab have an effect on blocks, like alignment. The Font Family list requires a little extra explanation.

The Font Family specifications work just like the Font tag's Face attribute discussed in Chapter 4, *Text and Fonts*. Clicking the New Font button adds a blank entry. You can type a font name from scratch, select a system font (i.e., one installed on your machine) from the popup menu to the right of the text field, or select a font set from the New Font Family popup menu next to the New Font button (see Figure 27-12). If you select a font set, GoLive inserts each member of the font set in order into the Font Family list.

Tip: Rearranging Fonts

The arrow buttons allow you to rearrange the items in the Font Family list into a new cascade. Select a font in the list, and click the up or down arrow repeatedly to move it to the correct order.

Tip: Making Type the Same on All Platforms

The same typeface with the same defaults in the same browsers display at varying sizes on different browsers. You can use an absolute pixel measurement to set type to a real size that will always use the same number of pixels, regardless of platform. Set the Size property to a pixel value in the Font tab.

For the world's best explanation of this problem and other solutions, see Geoff Duncan's TidBITS article, "Why Windows Web Pages Have Tiny Text" at db.tidbits.com/getbits.acgi?tbart=05284.

Borders, fills, and spacing. CSS offers substantial control over the borders and spaces surrounding a block. The CSS model breaks down a block into several areas, each of which has its own control in the Block and Border tabs of the CSS Style Inspector (see Figure 27-13). Select the bottom-most item (a four-sided

Figure 27-12
Choosing a
font or font set

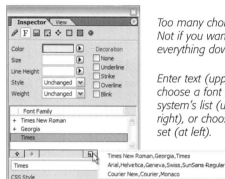

*Too many choices?
Not if you want to nail
everything down.*

*Enter text (upper left),
choose a font from the
system's list (upper
right), or choose a font
set (at left).*

Figure 27-13
CSS model
and GoLive
controls

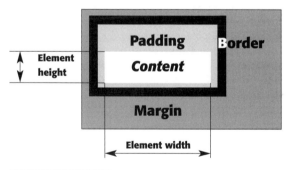

*The CSS model puts **content** in
the middle (with element width
and height measurements corresponding to the Block values in the
CSS Style Inspector). Padding
separates content from the border;
the border is separated from
adjoining elements by margin.*

box) for Margin and Padding in the Block tab to set the specifications identically for all four sides of that part of the object model (see Figure 27-14).

Two controls are particularly useful for controlling text flow: Float and Clear. Float allows you to set a block as a run-around element, so text flows around it to the right or left. Clear modifies a floating block so that text to the right or left starts flowing only at the vertical bottom of the box.

The Position tab has two additional block-display features: Overflow and Visibility. The Overflow options set how a block behaves when its contents overflow its container. Visibility allows a block's contents to be hidden or displayed. Both features are part of CSS2, and the level of support among the oldest browsers varies.

Figure 27-14
Setting all
four sides

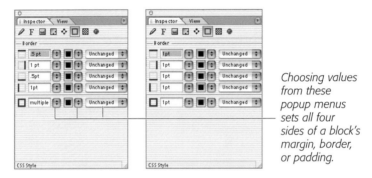

Choosing values
from these
popup menus
sets all four
sides of a block's
margin, border,
or padding.

Tip: Float and Clear

Float and Clear are equivalent to the Align attribute for the Img tag, and the Clear attribute for the P and BR tags. Because all items related to formatting have been steamrolled out of HTML proper, CSS takes the place of a lot of attributes in current HTML tags.

Positioning. With CSS, you can specify an exact position on a page relative to the upper-left corner of the browser window. Many of the controls in the Position tab are identical, or nearly so, to those in the Floating Box Inspector. The Z-Index field, for instance, corresponds to the Floating Box Inspector's Layer field.

Clipping. Clipping, found in the Position tab, is part of the CSS2 specification and controls how much overlap appears between adjacent, conflicting blocks.

Background tab. You can control the background of a block or entire page, including offsetting elements from the upper left. CSS lets you set a repeating image via the URL Getter, just like the Background attribute of the HTML Body tag, but you can also use images and colors to set the background of blocks.

A very cool CSS addition to background is the Attach feature: you can set a background image to be Fixed so that as you scroll down a page, the background is static in the window.

Lists. If you're tired of boring list element bullets, use list specifications in the List and Others tab to perk up the display, providing better control over the formatting; you can even choose a custom bullet image via the URL Getter, or set it to square, disc, or circle, overriding the list defaults.

If you're creating numbered lists, you can control the style of number applied (Roman numerals, Arabic numerals, and so on).

Other Specifications. GoLive supports adding properties that it currently doesn't offer through its List and Others tab. Click the New button, then enter the property name and its value. This feature doesn't work for properties without values, as it insists on putting a colon at the end of the property name, even when the value is empty.

This is a simple way to add CSS2 properties, as appropriate, without having to code by hand. It's also a way for GoLive to display properties it doesn't have specific menus or fields for.

Cascading

The rules of cascading define how conflicts between selectors that affect the same ranges of text or same tags are resolved based on the order in which they appear. The order can be overridden in some cases by other rules or by user preferences.

For instance, let's say you have an external style sheet with an H1 element selector that defines all Heading 1s as dark blue, 36-point Helvetica; an internal style sheet that defines H1 as 24-point (but has nothing to say about color font face); and another internal style sheet called H1.nimby that defines a 1-pt. border. For HTML that looks like:

```
<H1 class="nimby">Not In My Bike's Yoke</H1>
```

CSS's cascade rules would take the color and font face from the external style sheet, let the internal H1 selector override the size (setting it to 24 points), and put a 1-pt. border around it.

CSS has two distinct kinds of cascades:

- A general-to-specific set of rules which controls how the properties of one selector override those of another selector, preferring the more specific.

- A set of rules about precedence that resolves which specifications apply to or override properties in identical selectors or selectors that include the same HTML ranges based on a clearly defined hierarchy of style sheets in internal, external, and browser-based style sheets.

General to specific. CSS defines selectors in terms of how specific they are; there's even a little formula, with more technical detail than you may ever need to know, that you can use to calculate specificity (see the sidebar, "The Specificity Formula").

Typically, a more specific selector overrides properties in a more general selector. So you might define some characteristics for EM, but any properties in EM UL LI (a list element in an unnumbered list set inside an EM tag) override those in EM because they are more specific. For example, if you define a typeface as Bodoni Poster in the EM selector, and Bembo Book in the EM UL LI selector, the nested text would be set to Bembo Book.

Classes are always more specific than tags, and IDs are the most specific of all. Combining classes, tags, and IDs can create a complex set of overrides. If you start to develop style sheets that require this level of control, we suggest you learn the spec inside and out, especially the specificity formula.

Precedence. More commonly, you encounter issues of precedence and hierarchy in how rules get interpreted. In the CSS model, a browser has built-in style sheets that reflect the browser developer's assumptions. For instance, all the heading styles may be defined using certain fonts that are always found on an operating system.

The browser's styles are overridden by a user's browser preferences (also called the reader's preferences), which represent the next level up in the hierarchy. A user might choose, for instance, to use a font on their system, like Garamond, to display body copy. However, an author's styles—the author being the designer or the person who wrote the CSS style sheets that appear in or apply to a Web page—override a user's styles except in special cases.

External style sheets have lower precedence than ones embedded in a Web page, and the order in which external style sheets are listed controls their precedence: the earlier a style sheet appears (or higher in the HTML document), the lower the precedence.

You can adjust this precedence in the External folder in the CSS Editor by selecting an external reference and using the arrows to re-order its position up or down. External style sheets linked via the import command can also be re-arranged in this manner.

All external style sheets linked using the GoLive method or the Link tag are lower in precedence than any file linked via the import method.

! important. There's one way to assure precedence, which is to use the "! important" override, which GoLive doesn't support or preview. If you insert "! important" after any property's value, that value overrides all other values for that property based on the cascade.

For instance,

```
H1 { color: olive ! important }
```

in an external style sheet overrides

```
H1 { color: aqua }
```

in an internal style sheet. If more than one conflicting style uses "! important" for the same property, the general-to-specific and precedence cascade rules determine which "! important" is more important.

Tip: In CSS, Readers Come First

CSS2 uses the "! important" tag to let a reader or user override an author's definitions, the converse of the current version. This lets readers really have their way when they want it.

The Specificity Formula

We expect you won't need this information except for complex sets of interlocked documents or style sheets; nonetheless, we're here to serve you, so here goes. Specificity is like a contest with points assigned for degree of specificity.

An ID is worth 100 points. Classes are worth 10 points each. Tag selectors count as a single point each. The higher the number, the higher the precedence of the selector or the more likely it is to "win." Any conflict in a winning selector overrides anything with lower precedence.

Here are the examples modified from the CSS1 specification:

Tag	ID	Class	Tag	Specificity
LI	0	0	1	1
UL LI	0	0	2	2
UL OL LI	0	0	3	3
LI.red	0	1	1	11
UL OL LI.red	0	1	3	13
#x34y	1	0	0	100

Applying Style Sheets

So far, it may seem as if setting up style sheets is a chore…and sometimes it can be. But the reward comes when it's time to apply them to text on your page, which is a breeze.

You can only apply classes to ranges of text. IDs must be inserted by hand. Element selectors correspond directly to tags, so text defined by tags is automatically updated in the Layout Editor to reflect the style definitions.

Tip: Eyeball the Style

Chapter 4, *Text and Fonts,* gives you the designer-eye view of applying styles to text on a page. This section offers the coder-eye perspective.

Applying Classes

GoLive applies classes to text via the CSS palette. The palette either displays three categories corresponding to ranges of text or object selection, or a contextual column head based on a currently selected HTML element. Each class occupies a row with a checkbox below any available columns (see Figure 27-15).

Figure 27-15
Applying class styles

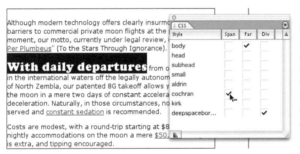

With text selected, clicking the box in the Span column next to a class applies it. Once applied, hovering over the checkmark adds a red minus sign to the cursor.

Hovering over a checkbox adds a green plus sign to the cursor; clicking puts a checkmark in the box. To remove the setting, hover over the box again, and notice that the cursor has a red minus sign; click to remove the checkmark.

You can apply multiple settings to the same text, checking one or more of the element categories. If you select text that has different settings applied, the checkboxes display a hyphen or dash to indicate multiple settings; hovering shows an equals sign.

Tag name. Where the CSS palette shows a given tag (such as <LI> when a list element is selected on the page), the underlying code inserts the class selector statement as an attribute into that tag.

To bring up a specific tag in the header, select the text carefully or use the Split Source view of the Layout Editor to select the whole tag range (see Figure 27-16). You can also click the tag name in the bottom line of the Layout Editor (see Figure 27-17).

Figure 27-16
Selecting tag range

Selecting a form text field changes the CSS palette's column head to read the tag name.

Figure 27-17
Using the markup bar

`<html> <body> <table> <tr> <td> <table> <tr> <td> <p>`

Selecting the <p> tag selects that in the column header in the CSS palette.

Span. Span corresponds exactly to inline elements; it's a special tag used to single out a range of text. Because the Span tag has no other purpose, it won't cause any other changes to the HTML.

To apply an inline element, select a range of text before checking the box corresponding to Span (see Figure 27-15, above).

Tip: Block That Class!

If you apply a class with block properties set using the Span setting, the CSS spec says that those properties are supposed to be ignored by the browser. However, as with all CSS properties and principles, each browser may have its own ideas.

Par. The Par element corresponds to the P, or paragraph, HTML tag. You can either place your insertion point anywhere in a paragraph, or select multiple paragraphs before checking the Par box for a class. If you select an entire paragraph, the header turns into just a <P>; see Figure 27-17, above.

Each paragraph in the selection becomes its own separate block (see Figure 27-18). This could work well for vertical spacing and other paragraph-specific attributes that affect type flow.

Figure 27-18
Par and Div
styles

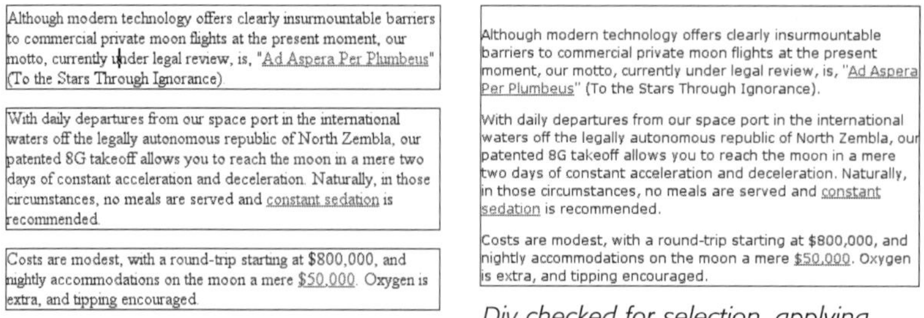

Par checked for selection, applying
block style to each paragraph

Div checked for selection, applying
block style around entire selection

Div. Unlike the Par element, the Div, or division, element creates just one set of Div tags around the entire set of selected paragraphs or other block units.

This creates one large block, and block properties, like borders and margins, get applied around the entire division (also see Figure 27-18, above).

Tip: Div Selection

You can select an entire Div unit using the selection techniques discussed under "Tag Name," above.

Applying IDs

Applying IDs is fairly easy, even though it has to be done by hand. GoLive neither tracks nor allows you to apply them directly, but it does appropriately preview any element with an ID applied.

Tip: Floating Boxes Took Over My Style!

GoLive is awfully possessive about absolute positioning. If you try to create an ID with both absolute positioning and Visibility set to Visible (an obvious choice), GoLive turns that ID selector into a floating box the next to you switch views from Layout Editor to Source Code Editor or close and open the file. Fortunately, starting in GoLive 6, you can continue to edit that selector in the CSS Editor.

1. Select the text or block to apply an ID to.

2. Switch to the Source Code Editor, or use the Split Source view in the Layout Editor or even the Source Code palette.

3. Omitting the leading pound sign (#) in the name of the ID, apply the ID to the text in one of three ways:

a. If the text you want is entirely surrounded by opening and closing HTML tags, insert the ID into the opening tag.

```
<H1 ID="flooby">Town of Flooby Nooby</H1>
```

b. If the text is a range inside a paragraph, use a set of Span tags.

```
The first time I heard of <SPAN ID="flooby">the Town of
Flooby Nooby</SPAN>, I was in the Caspian Sea.
```

c. If you want to create a block covering more than one set of block tags (like P or UL), surround the range with a set of Div tags.

```
<DIV ID="flooby">Lots of paraphenalia<P>here to
think<P>about.<P></DIV>
```

4. Switch back to the Layout Editor to preview your IDs.

> **New in 6: Editing Floating Boxes**
>
> Floating boxes are really just ID selectors with a limited number of choices available via the Floating Box Inspector. GoLive 6 adds the ability to change properties in a floating box by listing its ID in the CSS Editor.

Advanced CSS

There are two kinds of features we lump into "Advanced CSS": those that require more detail in the selector part of the CSS (the part that defines which tags, classes, IDs, or other characters a style sheet gets applied to), and those that are part of the style sheet definition itself.

Complex Selectors

CSS offers even more specificity and complexity in selectors than are available for preview and full support in GoLive. You can enter all these selectors in the Name field of the CSS Style Inspector, even though GoLive doesn't preview every instance of them.

Specificity. Selectors can be nested fairly deeply, so you can specify, for instance, that bold type in a list element of an unnumbered list inside a particular class has such-and-such properties. You'd write that as:

```
UL.classname LI B
```

That selector (which GoLive can preview) won't affect italic formatting in the same nested location. This specificity has a complex set of rules that affects which properties override others; this is explained in "Cascading," earlier in the chapter.

Mix-and-match. You can mix tags, selectors, and IDs with amazing aplomb. So, for instance, you can define a selector that affects only the ID #Z27 inside an H1. This would be distinct from ID #Z27 by itself, or ID #Z27 for an unnumbered list element:

```
H1#Z27
#Z27
UL LI#Z27
```

Multiple selectors. All the properties of a selector don't have to appear in the same, single definition, so you can set multiple selectors to have the same property by separating them with commas, and then applying specifics after that.

```
H1, P.barge, EM UL LI LI { font-size: 13 px }
H1 { color: fuchsia }
```

Pseudo-Selectors

The CSS spec provides for what it calls "pseudo-selectors": items that don't really fit the selector mode, but rather directly modify parts of the browser display. This allows the spec to be a little more flexible about certain aspects of the browser interface.

Tip: Adding Pseudo-Selectors

In the CSS Editor, you can select one of several anchor-related pseudo-selectors from the Apply CSS Style submenu of the contextual menu.

Anchor-related. A special class of selectors work with the A or anchor tag: active, link, visited, and hover. These selectors allow you to override the built-in browser behaviors, which typically display a link while being clicked on (active) as purple, a plain link on a page as blue, a visited address as red, and a link being hovered over as a sort of brown.

You can use these effects by combining "A" plus a colon plus one of the four magic words (active, link, visited, or hover). For instance, the following would make all links on a page display in italic regardless of other properties:

```
A:link { font-style: italic }
```

The a:hover selector is particularly nifty, because you can punch up links when a user hovers over them. It's a simple rollover, hidden inside HTML.

Paragraph-related. CSS defines a few DTP-like characteristics that allow you to provide special treatment on the first character of a paragraph (a drop cap) and the first line of a paragraph.

Use first-letter to select the first character, and first-line to—surprise!—select the first line. You have to append a colon and the pseudo-selector to a paragraph or a class. For instance,

```
P:first-letter { font-size: 36pt }
```

sets all paragraphs in a document to have a first letter that's 36 points large. Better, suppose you want to use a class selector with first-letter attached:

```
.bigstart:first-letter { font-size: 36pt }
```

This lets you set specific paragraphs in which the class has been applied to appear with a big first letter. The class is applied just with the class name, not with the pseudo-selector tacked on, as in:

```
<p class="test">
```

Extra Properties

These two properties added in CSS2 can't be set within GoLive as properties directly, but you can add them via the List and Other tab's Properties area. They only work inside Internet Explorer 5 or later and Netscape 6 or later. (Netscape 4 specifically had an incompatible way of hiding and displaying.)

Display. The display property has a very interesting set of options that controls formatting and can let you plop blocks inside inline text and vice-versa. But

Simple Click-Open Menus

With JavaScript and display:none, you can build a relatively simple set of instructions that combine to make a click open menus. Clicking a triangle, for instance, toggles whether the text below that item gets displayed or not.

You can create a hide/show trigger in the simplest manner possible; go for baroque later.

1. Create the item you want to not display, such as a block of text below a question in a list. Put Div tags around it and give it a unique ID by inserting id="box" into the Div tag. Each block must have a unique name.

2. Create a link that toggles the display of the text or item, such as a drop-down triangle.

3. In that link, add a simple onClick trigger:

```
<a href="#" onclick="box.style.
display = (box.style.display ==
'none') ? '' : 'none'">Your Image
Here</a>
```

If you want to make this more complicated, you can create a JavaScript function that toggles the setting:

```
function togglebox (boxName) {
document.all('boxName').style.
display = (all('boxName').style.
display == 'none') ? '' : 'none'; }
```

You can call this from each occurrence as

```
<a href="#" onclick="togglebox
('box')">Your Image Here</a>
```

we're not getting into the esoterica here, and it's pretty esoteric. Read www.w3.org/TR/REC-CSS2/visuren.html#display-prop if you want the gory details.

No, for our purposes, there's only one value for this property that we want to use: none. By setting display to none (via the List and Others tab), you can remove text from a page. Unlike the Visibility property which hides or shows the contents of a block, display:none actually removes it from the browser's rendering purview.

Practical use? See the sidebar, "Simple Click-Open Menus."

Cursor. The cursor property changes the shape of the cursor into a specified value when the cursor passes over the item that has the property attached to it. The possible values are quite extensive: hand (the little, um, "famous mouse" hand), crosshair, default (normal cursor), move (four direction cursor), text (the I-beam), wait (watch or hourglass), and help.

There is also a set of "resize" cursors (e-resize, ne-resize, nw-resize, n-resize, se-resize, sw-resize, s-resize, and w-resize) that corresponds to the compass point being used for resizing.

Tip: Hand in Glove

This property can be used neatly with the display:none option. Use a cursor to indicate that a block, once displayed, can be hidden again.

Designing with Style

Repetition is tedious. Repetition is tedious. Repetition is…okay, you get the point. We like using style sheets to avoid tedious repetition of repetitive tedium. It lets us not only control the look of our pages with more specificity, but with remarkably little work as well. And it gives us more cool toys to play with that can improve a site's usability and appearance with disproportionate ease.

For designers working on a Web site in teams, the ability to set central styles that work over an internal network or the Internet can provide a sense of continuity and consistency that many Web sites lack or spend an enormous amount of effort keeping track of.

Controlling Web Settings

Web Settings is GoLive's unsung hero. It stores all the program's assumptions about how tags work to create an accurate preview as you build pages visually. When you switch to the Layout Preview, the options listed in the Layout View Controller are all based on Web Settings for each browser.

GoLive uses Web Settings to store the rules governing tags in markup languages, including how they are written into a page (their syntax), how they interact with other tags, which browsers they work on, and how they display in the Source Code Editor and other GoLive markup editors.

By opening up the behind-the-scenes processes, GoLive gives you the ability to customize how it writes and displays markup code and to add new tags and languages as the range of the Web expands. You're not beholden to a product's update cycle to add some of the compatibility you need.

Web Settings can also be used:

- To reset some of GoLive's code writing defaults
- To define new defaults for some HTML objects that GoLive creates on pages
- As a markup language and character encoding reference
- To add browser-dependent, proprietary, or non-standard tags
- To add new special characters or "entities"
- To view examples of special characters
- To control what applications open which files in the Files and Designs tabs of Site windows

Web Settings Doesn't...

GoLive limits the kinds of changes to program behavior you can make by altering elements in Web Settings. You cannot change or add interface items to menus, Inspector palettes, or the Objects palette. (You can use the Software Developer's Kit or SDK for some of that. Consult Adobe's online help.) If you add an attribute to an existing tag, you won't have access to it through the Inspector palette. However, the new tag or attribute will appear as an option in the Outline Editor or other markup languages' editors (see Figure 28-1).

Specific to HTML, any new tags or special characters added to Web Settings aren't previewable by GoLive, either in the Layout Editor or the Layout Preview. Also, GoLive can't automatically detect the browser compatibility of new tags added to Web Settings; so if you want GoLive to be able to display warnings for the new tags using the Check Syntax feature and the Highlight palette, you must gather and set compatibility information yourself.

Figure 28-1
New attributes available in the Outline Editor

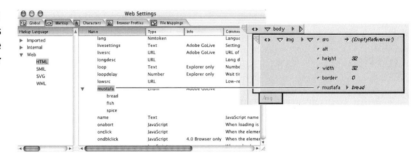

What's New in 6

Web Settings has always been GoLive's junk drawer, in which developers throw anything structured and anything that affects how markup languages write their code in pages via GoLive's visual approach. It also stows almost everything related to checking for code errors or deviations via the Check Syntax feature.

The CSS tab was renamed to the more accurate Browser Profiles tab, while the CSS formatting preferences were moved to a separate area on the Global tab.

The Version tab of the Web Settings Element Inspector now has much more limited functionality. HTML specs were removed; they're now part of Check Syntax.

The HTML tab has been recast as the Markup tab, which folds in various coding languages like HTML, WML, SMIL, and SVG. It also organizes a variety of GoLive internal structures.

Meanwhile, in an organizational issue just for this book, we've moved coverage of the File Mappings tab where it belongs: at the end of this chapter, instead of in the simpler Pages part of the book, where it bewildered our readers.

Tip: Previewing Output

Open the Source Code palette to preview the effects of changes you make to formatting specifications in the Global tab's settings by observing a sample bit of HTML (see Figure 28-2). You can edit this preview either by pasting in your own text, or editing material that's already there.

The Global tab affects all the preview (and HTML writing) of all tags and attributes; its CSS section controls just the CSS definitions in the Head section of the HTML and the preview in the Root Style Sheet Inspector's Source tab.

Global Tab

When you first open Web Settings, GoLive shows the Global tab, where most of its HTML-writing preferences appear regardless of whether they're single HTML pages or part of a site (see Figure 28-2). These settings affect the way GoLive writes source HTML code, not how the browser displays the page.

Figure 28-2
Previewing formatting in the Global tab

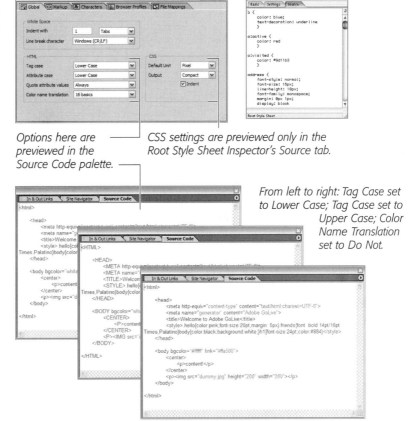

Options here are previewed in the Source Code palette.

CSS settings are previewed only in the Root Style Sheet Inspector's Source tab.

From left to right: Tag Case set to Lower Case; Tag Case set to Upper Case; Color Name Translation set to Do Not.

Tip: Global Post Facto

The Global tab's settings aren't retroactive to existing pages in a site, or open pages. After you change Global tab values, your existing pages remain with the old code. You can select individual pages and choose Rewrite Source Code from the Edit menu, but that's quite a tedious process.

HTML Formatting

The Global tab's settings affect only the appearance of underlying HTML code (such as you'd view in the Source Code Editor), to make reading and editing the code easier. GoLive groups these options into White Space, HTML, and CSS. White Space affects all HTML; HTML settings affect HTML tags; and CSS controls the formatting of CSS in the Head section of a page and on external style sheets.

Indent With. GoLive "nests" HTML, using tabs or spaces to make it more readable by applying a structure based on the blocks and elements. Table rows, for instance, are nested inside Table tags; cells are nested inside rows. You can turn off this function by setting the value to 0 (zero), or have GoLive use spaces instead of tabs.

Line Break Character. The line break character is the symbol or symbols that each of the three major platforms—Macintosh, Windows, and Unix—considers a signal for the end of a line. Don't ask why each platform decided on a

A Word of Warning

While it's commendable that GoLive offers access to its inner workings, this power doesn't come without grave responsibility. Before you dive into Web Settings and begin changing settings with wild abandon, be forewarned that the existing tag settings closely conform to currently ratified markup language standards. If you alter the tags, their attributes, enumerations, or compatibility settings, GoLive may create non-standard code that displays incorrectly in browsers, cell phones, and other viewers.

Also, GoLive uses Web Settings for some aspects of the Check Syntax feature. If the tags have been changed to non-standard settings, the Syntax Checker accepts them as correct and may fail to display important warnings.

However, you can revert to factory defaults if you've made changes that don't work out. Any modified tags are marked in the User column in various Web Settings tabs. The list of techniques has grown in GoLive 6, and it's thoroughly, exhaustively documented in GoLive's online help. Search for "restoring Web settings," and follow the elaborate instructions.

different symbol; line-break envy? GoLive tells you which platform corresponds to which signal as part of the popup values. Using Macintosh line endings puts in a carriage return, or ASCII 13; Unix uses a line feed, ASCII 10, to signal the end; and Windows is gluttonous and uses both.

Tip: Targeting Platform Endings

If you're creating pages in GoLive for Web serving or editing on another platform—often the case—choosing the line-ending style for that platform can prevent line break characters from becoming visible or uneditable in the local text editor; it can also prevent them from being ignored, thereby turning the entire page into a single, way-too-long-to-edit line of text. (FTP programs should convert line breaks to the destination platform, so this problem may only occur when copying files on a network or onto disks, or emailing them elsewhere.)

Tag Case, Attribute Case. The tag and attribute case affect capitalization. There's no technical reason to set them any specific way, as browsers ignore capitalization in tags and attributes. For example, some people prefer tags to appear in all caps, for example, to distinguish them from the rest of the text.

Tip: Oversensitive

Older browsers were less forgiving, which used to cause minor problems. Tag case sensitivity is really a pre-1996 browser issue, though. Future versions of HTML may require tags to be all lower case, unlikely as that now seems.

Quote Attribute Values. This setting adds quotation marks around values like image height and width. For the highest level of compatibility, set this option to Always.

Color Name Translation. GoLive can turn the hexadecimal values used to specify colors into sensible names like "red" and "white." Some browsers recognize only 16 common names, while Netscape has named many more. Although this option makes it easier to identify a color in the HTML code if it's named, you're likely to avoid compatibility snafus if you set this to Do Not.

Default Unit. The Default Unit setting controls which units are displayed when you define CSS styles. The CSS Style Inspector uses this default choice for all unit-based properties.

Output. The Output menu controls the display of all CSS output (see Figure 28-3). As with all HTML, white space is optional in most cases.

Figure 28-3
CSS formatting
in HTML

Compressed

```
.newclass{color:olive;font-weight:bold;font-size:11px;font-
family:Arial,Geneva;text-align:center}
```

Compact

```
.newclass { color: olive; font-weight: bold; font-size: 11px;
font-family: Arial, Geneva; text-align: center }
```

Pretty 1 & 2 (vertical space varies)

```
.newclass {
  color: olive;
  font-weight: bold;
  font-size: 11px;
  font-family: Arial, Geneva;
  text-align: center }
```

```
Compressed
Compact

Pretty 1
Pretty 2
✓ Pretty 3

Nice
```

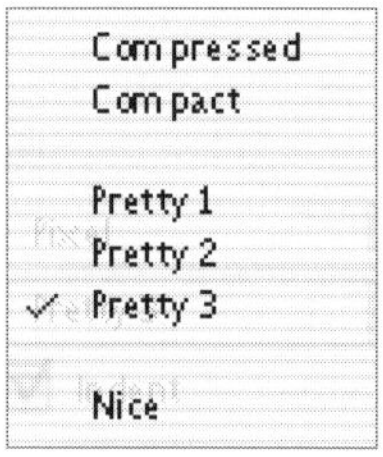

Pretty 3

```
.newclass {
  color: olive;
  font-weight: bold;
  font-size: 11px;
  font-family: Arial, Geneva;
  text-align: center
  }
```

Nice

```
.newclass {
  color:       olive;
  font-weight: bold;
  font-size:   11px;
  font-family: Arial, Geneva;
  text-align:  center }
```

Tip: No Preview in Palette

The Source Code palette appears to have a bug in previewing the Global tab: as you change Output options, the CSS in its Head section remains the same.

The first two Output options, Compressed and Compact, are two variations on tight packing. Compressed removes all extraneous spaces; Compact leaves in a few to keep it legible.

Pretty 1, Pretty 2, and Pretty 3 are variations on vertical spacing, indents, and whether the closing bracket appears on a line by itself. Nice is yet another variation on this theme that uses a little less vertical space.

If you uncheck the Indent box, all indents for the Output menu style are measured from a flush left start.

Tip: No Rewrite

If you change Output options after creating style sheets in a document and then use Rewrite Source Code for that page, the CSS formatting remains the same. However, all new style sheet definitions use the new CSS formatting regardless of whether you rewrite the source code.

Markup Tab

The Markup tab organizes all of GoLive's assumptions, preferences, defaults, and compatibility settings for tags—and their legal attributes and attribute values—in one convenient, easy-to-browse location. The tab structures details for the four Web standard tagging languages GoLive supports for authoring pages with graphical previews (HTML, SMIL, SVG, and WML).

The Markup tab is also a storage area for several of GoLive's internal features, such as Site Reports. The information is stored in XML format, and the Markup tab and Inspector palettes are views into these default settings. You almost certainly will never edit these internal settings, nor do their contents make much sense to the average user.

You can use the Markup tab in four primary ways:

- As a reference to the properties and syntax of existing tags

- To add new tags that Adobe hasn't yet added to GoLive or that the designers chose to exclude to increase compatibility

- To modify some of GoLive's defaults when creating certain new objects

- To import your own DTDs (Document Type Definitions) that define your own custom markup languages. (If you use GoLive to work with XML-based systems, it's a good way to be consistent when collaborating.)

Examining Tags

The Markup tab is divided vertically into languages at left and the contents of those languages at right. Expand the Web heading, for instance, and you see entries for HTML, SMIL, SVG, and WML. Select HTML, and its tags appear alphabetically at right.

Tip: Tab Ahead

Pressing the Tab key advances through the list of tags even when you've expanded the values beneath a tag.

The Markup tab uses several Inspector palettes to view and edit tags and associated values. To understand the Inspectors, we quickly need to cover the structure of structured tags, whether in GoLive or in the markup specifications.

Markup Syntax and Web Settings Inspectors

A structured tag has a name, like H1 or Card. Each property in a tag, like the height in pixels of an image, is an attribute. Each attribute may have enumerations, each of which is a legal or accepted (in other words, understood by a browser) value for that particular attribute. For instance, an enumerated attribute for Table is align; it can take the values center, char, decimal, justify, left, and right. Most attributes do not have specific enumerations, but can take a required value type, like a color value, number in some unit (pixels, inches, percentage, etc.), or URL (see Figure 28-4).

Figure 28-4
Tag structure

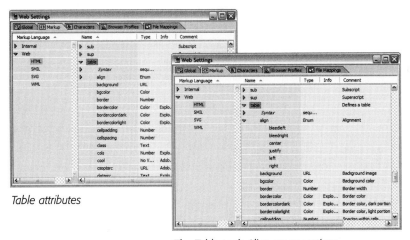

Table attributes

The Table tag's Align enumerations

Expanding the view under a tag shows its attributes; expanding enumerations under attributes shows the attribute's legal enumerations, when they exist. Using the Inspectors, you can view substantial detail about a tag's preview in GoLive, its nature and function in HTML, and how the tag gets structured and interpreted by GoLive.

The Syntax setting is unique no matter where it appears; there's no corresponding Inspector palette, nor can it be edited. Syntax items define the order and frequency of markup containers, such as the TD (table cell) and TH (table header) tags inside the TR (table row) container.

Web Settings Element Inspector. Selecting a tag from the Markup tab brings up the Web Settings Element Inspector, which includes naming and structure, output preview, and compatibility tabs (see Figure 28-5).

Web Settings Attribute Inspector. Selecting any tag's attribute brings up the Web Settings Attribute Inspector, through which the attribute's values are defined, as well as its compatibility and necessity; many attributes are optional (see Figure 28-6).

Web Settings Enum Inspector. If the attribute has only one set of allowed values—an enumerated list—you can drill down another level and select any enumeration to see the Web Settings Enum Inspector, which merely shows its name and compatibility (see Figure 28-7).

Figure 28-5
Web Settings
Element
Inspector

Figure 28-6
Web Settings
Attribute
Inspector

Figure 28-7
Web Settings
Enum
Inspector

Basic Inspector Settings

The Web Settings Inspectors' Basic tabs access the most general characteristics of tags, attributes, and enumerations.

Basic tab basics. The Basic tab for each Web Settings Inspector contains the name of the item and whether it's a tag, attribute, or enumeration. Generally, the Comment field is only filled in for tags, and contains a brief description of the tag's function.

The Can Be Stripped checkbox identifies an element or attribute as a GoLive-specific item which is removed from your markup page if you select the option to strip GoLive code on upload, export, or publish.

The Tag and Attribute Inspectors offer additional options in their Basic tabs; the Enumeration Inspector has just the Name and Comment fields.

Web Settings Element Inspector. This Inspector's Basic tab has several additional items: Structure, Content, and End Tag menus; and the Can Have Any Attribute checkbox.

The Structure menu defines a tag's nature in terms of its contents. (See Chapter 27, *Defining Cascading Style Sheets*, page 784, for more on block and inline elements.)

- **Block:** any tag that spans paragraphs or other block elements.

- **Inline Visible:** applies to tags that a browser interprets in order to insert content in their place, like the HL (horizontal line) tag.

- **Inline Invisible:** tags that affect their contents, like the H1 (heading 1) tag.

- **Inline Container:** can both insert content in their place and contain formatted text or other details. The Applet tag for inserting Java applets is an example of this mixed element.

- **Inline Killer:** used only with the BR tag. The BR (line break) tag is a special case, whether in HTML or in CSS, as it "kills" or ends a line.

The Content menu defines whether GoLive should remove what it considers extraneous information in a tag. Set to Normal, GoLive cleans up the tag and its contents (if a container) per standard rules.

- The Get All Spaces option preserves extra white space, which is needed in the Pre (preformatted) tag, primarily.

- Core Text leaves the tag and its contents alone to prevent any changes to the syntax of unusual tags. The Noedit tag, for instance, is set to Core Text to prevent GoLive from even attempting to rewrite its HTML.

The End Tag menu corresponds to whether the tag is a container, which requires both an opening and closing tag. Set to None, GoLive doesn't write an end tag; set to Required, it always does.

The two Optional menu items are a matter of fine distinction. Some tags don't require an end tag, but it's useful to insert one for consistency or for some specific browser support.

If the End Tag is set to "Optional (Do Not Write)", it means that the person who defined the tag wanted to note it could have an end tag, even though GoLive doesn't write it. "Optional (Write)" is identical to Required in function; this may also avoid errors in HTML validation. (The Attribute option is left as an exercise for the reader, as it is not explained in documentation or through testing.)

The Can Have Any Attribute checkbox suppresses error messages in the syntax checker if attributes exist for a tag that aren't defined in the Markup tab. This is useful for hand-coded HTML that contains nonstandard attributes necessary for particular Web sites or Web server applications.

A very few tags also have extra settings, such as the Font tag. These settings appear in a special outline at the bottom of the Basic tab. These cannot be added manually but are coded into the underlying structural documents that GoLive uses to create the Web Settings display.

Web Settings Attribute Inspector. This Inspector's Basic tab features three additional items. The Attribute Is menu has four values that fit into two categories. The Required and Optional settings control whether GoLive writes the tag or not, and whether the Syntax Checker marks an error if a required attribute is missing. The third option, Alternate, allows an attribute to be missing in raw HTML and not tagged as an error, although GoLive writes the attribute if you create the tag through its interface. Fixed, the fourth option, makes the value included and static.

Value Type defines the legal contents of an attribute. Some of the options are self-explanatory; see GoLive's online help for more details (search for "Editing an attribute"). If Enumeration is selected, GoLive has a set of finite possible values for an attribute. Other options, like NMToken, correspond to specific GoLive features or properties.

Create This Attribute provides a default value for GoLive to use when inserting the attribute, such as a default border of 1 (one) for tables.

Output Tab

The Output tab appears only in the Web Settings Element Inspector, and controls how GoLive previews a tag in the Source Code Editor. The tab displays a greeked preview of the HTML formatting.

Both the Inside and Outside settings are active if the tag is defined as requiring an end tag. Inside formats the space between the opening and closing tags; Outside formats the space before and after the set of tags.

Setting Inside and Outside to Small provides the simplest formatting, ensuring that each tag is on a line by itself with minimal space before and after. Setting both (or just Inside for standalone tags) to None runs the tags solid in the HTML without any line breaks.

Checking Indent Content indents the tag's contents. For nested blocks of HTML tags, indentation can help aid legibility if the HTML needs to be viewed in its raw state.

The Color setting allows you to choose a preview color for tags when viewing source code in any of the myriad places in GoLive where you can choose to color markup languages.

Version Tab

In previous releases of GoLive, the Version tab was directly tied in with syntax checking. Checking one or more of the browsers (and, formerly, HTML specifications) in the Version tab caused version-specific errors when you were testing a page against, for instance, IE versions 2 to 4.

In GoLive 6, however, the Version tab serves a much more limited purpose. Newer browsers than the several listed here use DTDs to define their legal tags and attributes, making the Version tab a vestige of a previous time.

The Version tab corresponds with the Source pane's Browser Sets settings in Preferences. You can create browser sets that comprise one or more of the browsers listed in this tab. Then, in Check Syntax, one of your options at the bottom of a long list, is to check for well-formed HTML that matches any of these browser sets.

It makes much more sense to check for conformity to one of the major HTML 4.0 standards these days.

Adding Markup Tags

Although you can add HTML, there's no good reason to know that HTML specifications have settled down. Conformance to these specifications makes much more sense than messing around with Web Settings's control over tags.

If you import DTDs, however, which are XML-related descriptions of markup languages that may be entirely data structured (that is, not tied to any particular output device, but used with a database), you may need to edit tags.

Importing a DTD

Use the contextual menu in the left pane of the Markup tab and select Import XML-DTD. Navigate to a valid DTD and open it; GoLive interprets the DTD and maps it to a hierarchical set of tags that it lumps under the new Import folder on the left pane. The name it lists the DTD by is the file's name with the extension removed.

Creating New Items

The Web Settings toolbar provides the necessary buttons for inserting new items, and offers contextual choices depending on what you have selected. The contextual menu offers the same (appropriately contextual) choices.

Once you add any of the items discussed in this section, the appropriate Web Settings Inspector allows you to modify any of the settings from the defaults.

New Element. Clicking the New Element button or selecting it from the contextual menu creates an untitled tag.

New Attribute. With a tag selected, clicking the New Attribute button or selecting it from the contextual menu adds an untitled attribute. You can click this button as many times as you want to create more attributes.

New Enumeration. If you set Value Type in the Web Settings Attribute Inspector to Enumeration, the New Enumeration button activates and the contextual menu's New Enum item appears. You can add as many enumerations as you need by selecting the menu item or clicking the button.

New Character. The New Character button (titled New Enumeration under Windows, but sharing the ampersand (&) symbol) works only when you're in the Web Settings Characters tab, and defines the ISO codes and other information for new characters (see "Characters Tab" later in this chapter).

Duplicate. The Duplicate button (also the same as selecting Duplicate from the Edit menu) creates an exact copy of any tag, attribute, or enumeration.

Characters Tab

Most markup languages can handle a limited set of characters and punctuation, even if you're using a Unicode-friendly operating system. Anything outside this set of characters is encoded as an entity, or a character given a name that is a mnemonic for its content. This also frees markup languages from relying on the character encoding of a specific platform; no two platforms use the same character code to generate an E with a grave accent over it (è), for example.

A browser interprets the entity and replaces it onscreen with the appropriate character from its local character set. An entity is signaled by an initial ampersand and terminated by a semicolon; for example, "©" is the code for ©, the copyright symbol in HTML.

The Characters tab groups all entities into three categories: Basics, Characters, and General Punctuation, redundantly enough (see Figure 28-8). The Characters heading includes everything but punctuation and a few common items, which are given their own headings. Characters includes most everything in the ISO 8859-1 character set, also known as ISOLatin1 to desktop publishers. The ISO standard reflects standard Roman character sets represented by American and European languages. You can see a list of all entities, ISO 8859-1 and HTML 3.2, at www.w3.org/TR/REC-html32.html.

GoLive also includes a few special characters defined as entities as part of the HTML 3.2 specification, like the greater-than sign (>) and less-than sign (<). It groups these under Basics. These are so-called reserved characters; they have a meaning in the syntax of HTML, so if you want to use the actual character, you have to use an entity that represents it.

View palette. GoLive can organize the tab by the character's name (Flat view) or into the three categories (Structured view): Basics, Characters, and General Punctuation.

Character details. The Characters tab shows several details about each entity: its name, the character produced, its Mac and ISO 8859-1 character code, and a comment that describes the entity.

Figure 28-8
Characters tab

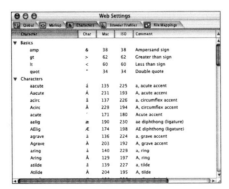

Character	Char	Mac	ISO	Comment
▼ Basics				
amp	&	38	38	Ampersand sign
gt	>	62	62	Greater than sign
lt	<	60	60	Less than sign
quot	"	34	34	Double quote
▼ Characters				
aacute	á	135	225	a, acute accent
Aacute	Á	231	193	A, acute accent
acirc	â	137	226	a, circumflex accent
Acirc	Â	229	194	A, circumflex accent
acute	´	171	180	Acute accent
aelig	æ	190	230	ae diphthong (ligature)
AElig	Æ	174	198	AE diphthong (ligature)
agrave	à	136	224	a, grave accent
Agrave	À	203	192	A, grave accent
aring	å	140	229	a, ring
Aring	Å	129	197	A, ring
atilde	ã	139	227	a, tilde
Atilde	Ã	204	195	A, tilde

Web Settings Entity Inspector. This Inspector includes all the information in the general list and provides the hexadecimal values for the ISO and Mac character codes. It also shows a preview of the character that the entity represents. Making the Inspector larger creates a larger preview (see Figure 28-9).

Figure 28-9
Web Settings
Entity
Inspector

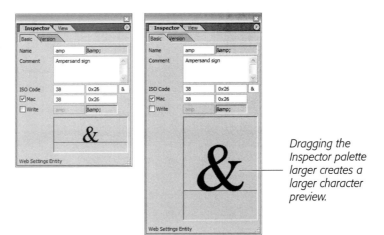

Dragging the Inspector palette larger creates a larger character preview.

Adding Characters

It's hard to imagine why and when you might need to add characters to this tab, but here goes. Click New Character in the Web Settings toolbar or select New Entity from the contextual menu.

Define the character by providing its entity name, which GoLive assumes is the name that gets inserted inside HTML. If you want to name the character differently from its entity value, enter the name in the Name field, and then check the Write box. Enter the entity value in that field, and the preview appears to its right.

Macintosh display. Both Windows and Mac versions of GoLive show the ISO character code for most entities, so the Macintosh version of GoLive must also have an entry for Macintosh character code in order to display it correctly.

Adding sections. If you add new kinds of characters, you might also want to create a new section under which to organize them. Click the New Section button on the Web Settings toolbar, then use the Web Settings Section Inspector to name it and add a comment describing it.

Browser Profiles Tab

The Browser Profiles tab reveals the settings that enables Layout Preview to simulate a variety of appearances based on major browsers and devices. GoLive creates previews of pages based on the selection in the Profile popup menu in the Layout 's View palette.

GoLive lists, by browser/platform pairs, the sets of assumptions that GoLive's designers encoded about how the browsers display specific tags differently than a GoLive-defined baseline. Expand the view under any profile to see the list of CSS definitions. GoLive uses CSS style sheets to express these specific differences; see Chapter 27, *Defining Cascading Style Sheets*, for more on CSS.

> **Tip: GL Phone Home**
>
> We cover coding for phones in Chapter 16, *Languages and Scripting*.

GoLive has 22 sets of built-in browser profiles:

- Adobe GoLive: the standard GoLive preview
- Internet Explorer 3, 4, and 5 for Windows and Mac (six sets)
- Navigator 3, 4, and 6 for Windows and Mac (six sets)
- A variety of DoCoMo telephones (eight sets)
- The Nokia XHTML phone (one set)

You can change the default for what the Layout View palette shows as its Profile selection by clicking the Root radio button next to your preferred browser (see Figure 28-10). Adobe GoLive is the default Root setting.

Figure 28-10
Setting default root browser set

The Root radio button controls the default browser set in the Layout View palette's Profile menu.

Settings

Selecting any browser set brings up the Root Style Sheet Inspector (see Figure 28-2, earlier in the chapter). For built-in styles, you can view, but not edit, settings. The Lock icon provides a visual reminder for these sets; new sets you create have a pencil next to them, showing they're "writable."

Basic tab. The Basic tab displays a browser set's name, operating system, and any comments. These items are all for reference and do not have any bearing on how GoLive creates a preview.

Settings tab. Each browser and platform includes a built-in idea of what the screen density or pixels per inch are. It uses this information to create appropriate sizes of text; we discuss this in depth under "Units" in Chapter 27, *Defining Cascading Style Sheets*. Windows monitors are typically set to 96 dpi, while Mac monitors are set to 72 dpi.

Gamma controls the relative darkness curve, which is dependent on the platform you're on. Windows generally displays images with a higher gamma, which makes darker colors even darker than on the Macintosh. The Can Handle Stylesheets checkbox toggles between whether a browser supports style sheets or not. Can Handle Images is checked for all default browsers; a browser like the Unix "lynx" would be an example of one which can't, as it is a terminal-based, text-only browser.

The six checkboxes labeled Does Create Virtual Body Element, Can Handle Inline Border, Inline Applies Inline Properties to Block, Inline Applies Block Properties to Block, Block Applies Inline Properties to Table, Body Applies Inline Properties to Table describe pretty accurately the level and consistency of CSS support for various properties taken as a whole.

Source tab. The Source tab lists all the style differences and their properties as they would be inserted into the Head section of an HTML page. This list cannot be edited directly.

Tip: Source Settings

The Global tab's CSS formatting settings control how the preview in the Source tab appears.

Adding New Sets

GoLive offers the flexibility to create new sets as new browsers and browser versions become available.

To create a new browser set, select any existing browser set and choose Duplicate from the Edit or contextual menu. You can't create a new, empty set.

After duplicating a set, use the CSS Style Sheet Inspector to manipulate any of the set-related preferences. To edit individual tags in the set, expand the set's view and select any tag. The familiar CSS Style Inspector appears, and all the standard options explained in Chapter 27, *Defining Cascading Style Sheets*, are available.

If you need to add new tags, you have to duplicate existing ones. Select a tag and choose Duplicate from the Edit or contextual menu. To delete tags, select the tag and press the Delete key, or choose Clear from the Edit menu.

File Mappings

Most kinds of documents can be viewed or edited by more than one application. GoLive maintains a list of document types and the programs that can handle working with them in its File Mappings tab, so you can open files directly by double clicking them inside GoLive just as you could from the Windows Desktop or Macintosh Finder (see Figure 28-11).

File Mappings exposes the defaults that Adobe built into the program, including the notion that GoLive itself can open a whole variety of files for editing. For instance, because GoLive can handle QuickTime files, GoLive "knows" it can open and edit AIFF sound files, QuickTime ".mov" (movie) files, and other video and sound formats.

GoLive relies on the bit at the end of a file following a dot—the extension—the same way Windows does. For instance, a PDF file is named "folderol.pdf" while an HTML file could be named "snooker.html" or "scrabble.htm" (either .html or .htm).

To make it easier to work with, the file mappings are broken into MIME groups like application, audio, and video. Click the triangle to the left of a heading to view its mappings settings.

Figure 28-11
File Mappings
tab

Tip: A MIME We Like

MIME (Multipurpose Internet Mail Extensions) were designed to add attachments to mail documents. They have since expanded to work with and describe virtually all manner of documents transferred over all manner of protocols.

Click a column's title to sort the list according to that heading. To hide or show a column, bring up the contextual menu while your cursor is on a column title, then select a column name from the list (see Figure 28-5). You can also opt to show or hide all columns.

Tip: Many Openings

File Mappings affects opening files in the Site window's Files tab; see Chapter 19, *Managing Files, Folders, and Links,* where it's more contextually appropriate.

Tip: Internet Control Panel (Mac OS 9 only)

At the top of the File Mappings tab, you can spot Use Internet Control Panel and a tiny logo of that item at the upper right. The Internet control panel is a small Mac OS 9 program that, among other things, maintains a list of file types and programs associated with them for use in programs like GoLive. (OS X did away with this part of the configuration.) If you check Use Internet Control Panel, any preferences you've changed in GoLive are overwritten. For more on using the Internet control panel, see Appendix A, *Macintosh Issues & Extras.*

Suffix. The Suffix column lists the file type's extension.

MIME Type. MIME defines the kind of data a given file type contains. This information is necessary for feeding out content over the Internet.

Kind. Kind is a text description created by Adobe to identify the variety of content.

Basic. Basic describes the type of file, to give GoLive an idea of how it's structured: unknown, Binary file, Text, HTML, XML, SGML, or XHTML.

Transfer. Transfer specifies how the data should be carried across the Internet: as bin (binary) or as text.

Application. Application lists the application that should open the file when it's double-clicked. The Default setting means that GoLive relies on its mappings or information stored in the file, but you can change Default to a specific program to override this.

Type and Creator. Under Mac OS 9 and X, these two columns appear and specify the Mac-specific Type and Creator codes. Mac OS 9 uses these attributes to identify which applications can open the file; OS X can use them as well, although Apple has been moving developers and users to rely on just the extension, like Windows! Windows users can display these columns through the View palette.

User. When you add a new file mapping to the list, a bullet or "x" appears in the User column to indicate that the file isn't part of GoLive's built-in library of mappings.

Modifying Settings

File Mappings allows all of its settings to be changed by clicking the line containing the settings and entering new values in the File Info Extension Inspector. For instance, if you want to map PDF files to be opened in Adobe Acrobat, you'd click the line starting pdf, and find Adobe Acrobat using the Application field's Browse button in the Inspector.

New Items

You might find it necessary to add extensions for files you regularly work with that GoLive doesn't currently list or that aren't available. Adding extensions is extremely simple. Click the New Extension button on the Toolbar, or select Add Suffix from the contextual menu. Enter the extension, choose an application to open the file, enter the MIME type (if you know it), choose an option from the Basic popup menu, select a Transfer type, and then type a description in the Kind field. Deselect the item to apply the changes.

Run Screaming into the Night

By giving users access to some of the "guts" of the application, GoLive opens the door to creative and useful customization unavailable in any other programs. Of course, freedom brings responsibility, as abusing Web Settings can backfire on you and cause GoLive to create bad code without you necessarily realizing it. But don't be afraid to get under the hood and tinker; you can always revert to factory settings even after disassembling the machine.

Appendices
and Index

Macintosh Issues & Extras

Even though GoLive appeared first on the Macintosh (as GoLive CyberStudio, the product's long ago name), Adobe has done a fairly seamless job of making sure the Mac and Windows versions of the product are in parity. GoLive 5 brought dangling feature differences into sync across platforms, making it hard to tell which machine you were on without examining the scrollbars or other minor interface elements. GoLive 6 continues the trend by snipping some unnecessary Mac features and adding more options to Windows.

Tip: Cross-Platform A-Go-Go

Starting with GoLive 5, Mac and Windows site files have been entirely compatible, which means you can exchange them across platforms and open them on either without requiring any conversion. You can share sites on a networked drive that both Macs and PCs can access, and use just a single site file to manage the site.

Better still, use the Workgroup Server to avoid any file conversion whatsoever: Mac and Windows machines can work interchangeably with the same files, and the server handles the rest.

Most of the Macintosh-only features in GoLive relate to operating system details, not functionality in the program itself. That is, GoLive taps into some items that the Mac OS already has built into it or that you extend the Mac OS to support; GoLive for Macintosh does not contain some kind of feature not found on Windows.

- **File details.** The Mac OS stores extra information with each file, such as the program that created it and a label in the Finder (on the Desktop in OS 9 only) that GoLive maps to a Windows-compatible setting.

- **Keychain.** Passwords for connecting to sites using the Workgroup Server, FTP, and WebDAV can be stored in the Mac OS Keychain, a secure storage location that GoLive can access to automatically connect to external servers.

- **Internet control panel.** GoLive 4 and 5 supported a few special features for file navigation and interface display found in Mac OS 8.5 to 9.2. These options, formerly set in GoLive's Preferences dialog box under the General pane in the Interface pane, are no longer present in GoLive 6. The only remaining special supported extra for Mac OS 9 is the Internet control panel, which centralizes file mapping, proxies, and account management.

- **Mac OS X and later.** GoLive doesn't take advantage of any extras in Mac OS X—in fact, the new operating system boasts fewer options in terms of what is offered by the Internet control panel and the Appearance Manager under Mac OS 9.

- **ColorSync.** Apple offers a system-level color management system called ColorSync in both Mac OS 9 and X that, ideally, lets you scan, edit, view, and output images in a variety of programs, on a variety of machines, with some semblance of color consistency and tonality.

- **AppleScript.** The Mac OS has a built-in scripting language that lets you control many functions of the Finder and various AppleScript-savvy programs. GoLive supports AppleScript in its Source Code Editor view; you can use AppleScript to automate certain tasks.

Tip: Version Support

GoLive 6 works under Mac OS 9.1 or later and OS X 10.1 or later only. When we refer to OS 9 or X below, we may mention 9 or X generically when talking about features that first appeared in those system releases.

File Features

GoLive inserts Macintosh-specific differences in a few of the Inspector palettes used to examine files.

Finder Label

The Finder label can be set up on the Macintosh Desktop in OS 9. From the Finder's Edit menu, select the Labels tab of the Preferences dialog box (see Figure A-1). (Mac OS X eliminated Finder Labels, but GoLive can still assign them to files internally, as it does with Windows.)

Figure A-1
Setting Label
color and text

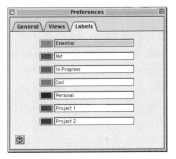

You have seven possible labels preset to generic names like "Essential" and "Project 1". These can be renamed (which we recommend) to something meaningful. Clicking the color swatch next to the name also changes the color. The order in which the items appear in the Labels tab affects the sorting order in the Finder when you sort the view by Label.

Labels may be assigned in the Finder by selecting one or more items and selecting a label from the Label item in the popup contextual menu or in the Label submenu of the File menu (see Figure A-2).

Figure A-2
Label
contextual
menu

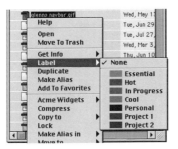

In GoLive, Label information is displayed in the Status popup menu in the File Inspector's File tab. For Windows and OS X, GoLive includes the standard default set of Mac OS 9 labels; you can also define new ones on a site-by-site basis. These are set in the Site pane of GoLive's Preferences or individual site settings.

Type and Creator

When you create or import HTML files from many sources, you can wind up with funky icons on the Macintosh Desktop and in the Site window's Files tab. Worse, double-clicking the file opens it in Microsoft Word, BBEdit, TextEdit, or SimpleText. GoLive provides a simple way to fix this problem.

The Macintosh stores two pieces of information with every file: its creator and its type. The creator and type are four-character codes that correspond to the program that created the file and the type of file it is. Each application on the Macintosh has a unique creator code so that every file knows exactly to which program it belongs. Each application can define any number of its own types so that the application knows what kind of file it's looking at—TIFF, GIF, or JPEG for an image-editing program, for example.

Select a file in the Files tab in the Site window and bring up the File Inspector's File tab if it's not automatically displayed. To change an HTML file so that it thinks it was created by GoLive, make sure the Type field is set to "TEXT" and the Creator field is set to "GoMk" (case is important). As soon as you press Return or switch to another field, the icon in the Files tab changes immediately to the GoLive icon (see Figure A-3).

Figure A-3
Changing
Creator code
to fix program
association

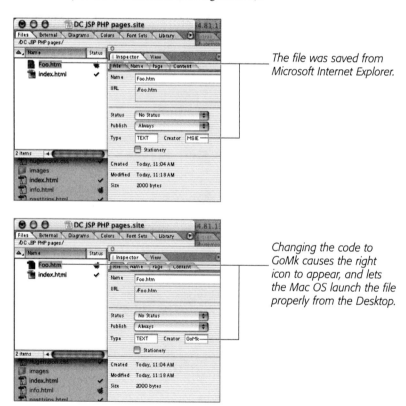

The file was saved from
Microsoft Internet Explorer.

Changing the code to
GoMk causes the right
icon to appear, and lets
the Mac OS launch the file
properly from the Desktop.

> **Tip: Batch Process Files (OS 9 only)**
>
> CTC (change-creator-type) is a freeware program that lets you batch process a set of files to change their creator or type to something else. You can download it from www.imagemontage.com/Docs/CTC.html

Keychain

The Mac OS Keychain allows you to store commonly used passwords in a single managed interface that is only accessible after you type in a master passphrase to unlock it (see Figure A-4). (In OS X, logging in unlocks the Keychain.) Instead of storing passwords in lots of insecure locations that someone could, potentially, snag from your machine, passwords are stored centrally in an encrypted format and only accessed as needed by programs.

You can use the Keychain quite simply. In GoLive's Preferences dialog box's Network pane, make sure Use System Keychain for Passwords is checked. You can choose to automatically add passwords to the Keychain by unchecking the Ask Before Adding Passwords box below the main preference.

To modify passwords stored in the Keychain, select the Keychain Access control panel in OS 9 or, under OS X, launch the Keychain Access program in the Applications folder's Utilities folder. GoLive passwords appear with a GoLive icon next to them, but Apple lists them just as "Internet passwords" under the Kind column. You can also delete and edit passwords here.

Extensions and OS X

While OS X supports file type and creator information, Apple has been firmly urging developers to use only file extensions like those used in Windows (like ".doc" for Windows documents). Apple explicitly hides the extensions in the Finder and in Open and Save dialog boxes. Fortunately, HTML and other Web files typically already have an extension.

However, the problem with this scheme is that many programs share file name extensions, leaving it up to the operating system to play Extension Cop. If you want to make sure every file ending in ".html" opens in GoLive when you double-click it in the Finder, you need to inform OS X of your preference.

Select an HTML file in the Finder and choose Show Info from the File menu. From the popup menu in the info window, choose Open with application, where you can see which program is already assigned. Click the program icon's popup menu to view a list of applications that support the HTML file format and choose GoLive (if GoLive isn't listed, choose Other and navigate to the GoLive application). To make the change stick for all HTML files, click the Change All button.

Figure A-4
Keychain
access

Internet Control Panel

The Internet control panel found in OS 9 began its life as Internet Config, a helpful Internet settings utility written and given away by Peter N. Lewis and Quinn "the Eskimo" to the Internet community. Their goal was to standardize the location and nature of Internet preferences—for email addresses, mail servers, etc.—and file mappings.

It worked; most programs adopted its settings, then Apple took over the public domain software lock, stock, and barrel by turning it into the Internet control panel. Many thanks are owed to Peter and Quinn for their selfless act.

Tip: OS X Sank Internet Controls

Unfortunately, Apple betrayed this mission in OS X, turning the Internet preference pane into a shadow of its former self. Proxy settings aren't even stored there, now being grouped with individual network configurations in the Network pane of System Preferences.

The Internet control panel from OS 9 gets used in two ways in GoLive: to supplement and manage file mappings for opening files directly from GoLive and to set up proxy server settings for environments (see Figure A-5).

Figure A-5
Internet
control panel's
File Mapping
settings in
Mac OS 9

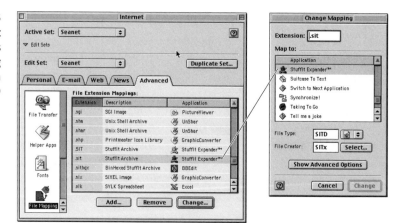

File Mappings

In Chapter 28, *Controlling Web Settings*, we talk about File Mapping: GoLive's built-in ability to know which applications should open which files when you double-click them in the Files tab, or select and open them directly from a page.

GoLive for Mac offers an additional feature: you can tie in a list of file extensions, MIME types, and programs associated with them from the Internet control panel.

Most Internet files have their type determined in part by their file extension: a three- or four-letter code after a period or dot at the end of their name. The Mac, however, can map files with the same kind of content to multiple programs, like one TIFF image launching Photoshop and another opening GraphicConverter.

Tip: Reaching Advanced Features

The default view of the Internet control panel is designed not to frighten small children and dogs, and therefore hides the file mappings. From the Edit menu, select User Mode, then choose Advanced or Administration from the resulting dialog box; the latter allows you to lock settings and protect them with a password. Click OK, and an Advanced tab appears; one of the panes at left is File Mapping.

In the File Mappings tab of Web Settings (available under the Edit menu), checking Use Internet Control Panel instantly imports all the Internet settings (see Figure A-6). In fact, it instantly overwrites any customized settings you might have applied, so beware. (You can apply settings via the Internet control panel itself and then, when you import, those settings are brought in as well.)

If, for some reason, you think you made a mistake by using the Internet control panel settings, uncheck Use Internet Control Panel and GoLive reverts to its default settings.

Figure A-6
GoLive File
Mappings tab

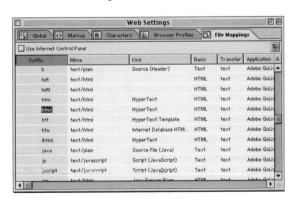

Tip: Extensive Mapping

The Internet control panel specifies default programs for lots of extensions that you've probably never heard of. It also lists programs you certainly don't have installed on your machine. But these settings are only invoked if a file with the appropriate extension is encountered. Even then, if you don't have the application, GoLive prompts you or tries to open it with the most likely application depending on what other software you have installed.

Proxy Servers

GoLive also relies on the Internet control panel in OS 9 and the Network system preference pane in OS X as an option for linking to a proxy server. If you don't know what a proxy server is and you've never had anything to do with one, you can ignore this section entirely.

But if you work in an institution or corporation, your Web requests may have to pass indirectly to the outside world. A proxy server generally sits on your local or corporate network; it receives requests from browsers or FTP clients inside the network, goes out on the Internet to retrieve the requests pages or items, then sends them back to the machine that requested them.

GoLive for Macintosh can import your proxy settings: in the Network pane of GoLive's Preferences, click Import Now to bring in the current settings (see Figure A-7). Checking Use Always keeps the settings current whenever you

Figure A-7
Proxy settings

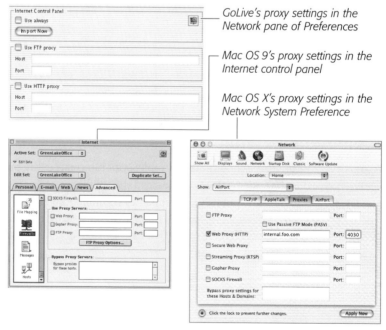

GoLive's proxy settings in the Network pane of Preferences

Mac OS 9's proxy settings in the Internet control panel

Mac OS X's proxy settings in the Network System Preference

change them in the Internet control panel and then launch GoLive. You can click the Internet control panel icon to set your proxy addresses and features and then return to GoLive to see them applied in OS 9.

In OS X, bring up System Preferences from the Apple menu, click the Network pane, and then review the Proxies tab's settings for each networking method you use.

ColorSync

ColorSync, as noted early in the chapter, tries to provide consistent color across machines, programs, devices (scanners, monitors, and printers), and platforms. It eliminates the variables and differences between systems and devices so that you're looking at the closest approximation to a standard image as possible.

Because Apple has long contended it would extend ColorSync onto Windows (even though years and years have passed without this happening), and because Microsoft built ColorSync support into the Macintosh version of Internet Explorer starting way back in version 4.5, we've opted to write about ColorSync in Chapter 5, *Images.*

We believed future updates of GoLive and Windows would make Color-Sync either an integral part or a simple add-on; but after years of waiting, we haven't seen results. In any case, we aren't gung-ho about its use on the Web, either, but see Chapter 5 for more on this subject, including updating and installing ColorSync in GoLive for Macintosh.

AppleScript

Apple offers a simple scripting language that most Macintosh users barely notice. It's an easy-to-learn programming language, but it *is* programming, and it's not for every user. However, for automating behavior that requires some flexibility or conditionality, AppleScript can create entire publishing and production systems that wildly extend the abilities of ordinary programs. For example, many publishing companies combine AppleScript and QuarkXPress to create a system that allows them to automate workflow from word-processing files through to final laid-out pages.

GoLive offers control only over items in the Source Code Editor, but it does provide tools to allow you to select, insert, and format text according to HTML specifications, as well as create and name documents.

The reference provided by Adobe in the GoLive manual is extensive and specific enough to avoid repetition here. You can also find much of the same detail built into GoLive's internal AppleScript dictionary definitions. Find the program called Script Editor that should have been installed along with your system. (If it's not on your hard drive, you need to go back and reinstall Apple-Script from your Mac OS disk or download it from www.applescript.com.)

Run Script Editor and select Open Dictionary from the File menu. Then select the GoLive application itself, and Script Editor displays the reference of events that GoLive knows how to work with (see Figure A-8).

Figure A-8
GoLive
AppleScript
dictionary

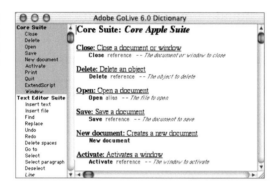

It's too bad Adobe hasn't taken the last few years to expand AppleScript support—and its Windows counterpart, VBScript—to allow full control of the program, as it has done with its new flagship page-layout program, InDesign. We can't recommend using AppleScript in conjunction with GoLive 6, as it would end in frustration and tears.

Core Apple

GoLive has shed most of its Macintosh origins by synchronizing features between the Mac and Windows versions. These improvements make it easier to work back and forth between platforms, and allow teams of people that might be using different operating systems to function more seamlessly with the same application and the same files.

APPENDIX B

Windows Issues & Extras

In the first edition of this book, this appendix didn't exist. In the second, we merely noted that Windows had no extras. Finally, in this exciting third edition, we have a few bits of information to report.

GoLive 6 works with Windows systems running Windows 98 or newer, including XP and 2000. We have found in our testing that feature for feature, GoLive running under every version of Windows and the two supported versions of Mac are virtually identical.

However, Adobe did include some special software for Windows users for previewing and debugging code.

On the GoLive update or install disc, when you run the installer program, you may notice that three options at the bottom of the screen refer to Nokia and i-Mode phone previews. These programs allow you to preview the effects of content developed in GoLive in a simulator of the actual phone, making it possible to fully test your pages before deploying them over the airwaves.

On the Workgroup Server disc, found bound in the back of the Adobe Web Workgroup Server manual, if you drill down into the Extras folder, an item labeled Zend contains the Zend Debugger, a handy tool for testing the syntax and operations of PHP scripts.

Wait, is that it? Yes, that's it. Adobe has trimmed many of its Mac-specific features over time, so if you consult Appendix A, you can see that the Windows and Mac versions are now even closer relatives, not just kissing cousins.

SECRET APPENDIX C

Last-Minute Tips

Congratulations! You've discovered our *double secret appendix*—remember that movie? hint: it was filmed in Glenn's home town—added at the last moment when we found ourselves with a few extra tips and a few empty pages to fill. Our buckets always overflow with tips, and there isn't always enough room in the book to fit. Plus, sometimes you learn things, well, a little too late: pages are laid out, figures are done, what can you do?

Herewith are a few items of interest.

Tip: Master Tab (Diagramming and Mapping)

The Master tab contains items which repeat on every page in a diagram. Although we explain how to lock items to the master page in a design diagram, we failed to break out the explanation when walking through the tabs in the design window.

Tip: Irritating Recurring Open Dialog Box (General)

A bug in GoLive 6.0 can cause you mental anguish: every time you try to save a file that's part of a site, GoLive presents you with one or a succession of Open dialog boxes. This problem is caused when any folder name in the path from the top of your hard drive down to where the item is stored contains a special character, like an ampersand (&) or the folder symbol often used on a Mac (ƒ). Changing the name of the offending folder or folders eliminates the problem, which we assume will be fixed in a future release.

Tip: Closing the Extend Script Debugger (Actions)

The problem just above, we've found, can be especially irritating when you install Extend Scripts, such as Adobe or third-party GoLive Actions. We have not only seen the extra Open dialog, but also a debugger screen full of JavaScript that doesn't have an obvious close box at the top. This is the software tool that Action developers use to troubleshoot their programs, and it can be closed by pressing Command-W on the Mac or Control-W under Windows even though the window looks impassive.

Tip: Opening GoLive 4 Site Files with GoLive 6 (Opening)

Short answer: you can't. If you have any remaining site files created in GoLive 4, you have to open them first with GoLive 5, and then with GoLive 6. This is a good reason to keep that old copy of GoLive 5 installed and handy just in case.

Tip: Remote Server Flakiness (FTP, WebDAV, Publish Servers)

As we were finishing up the book, we heard from many early users of 6.0 that the program was losing FTP settings. Older sites, when converted, sometimes lost the FTP values encoded in the site file. New files seem to lose the selected value for FTP, WebDAV, or Publish Server (with workgroup sites) each time they're closed, requiring you to reselect them.

Hopefully, Adobe will fix these problems in an interim release. Watch our Web site for details.

Tip: Mandatory Database Fields (Dynamic Content)

One user discovered that when they set up their MySQL database to work with Dynamic Content, they accidentally set some fields to require values. When they submitted forms using Dynamic Content controls, if any field was left empty, the form submission would fail. If you encounter this problem, make sure your database either automatically fills empty fields with a default value on creation, or those fields don't require a value.

Tip: Opening Older Revisions (Workgroup Server)

Somehow on page 647, we forgot to mention two options associated with the Revision List: the Open and Make Current buttons. When viewing a list of revisions of a file, you can select any one of them, click Open, and up pops that version named distinctly to avoid replacing an existing file. Likewise, select any revision and click Make Current to replace the current live file with the older revision.

Tip: Hidden Elements Disturb Table Measurements (Tables)

If your table cells contain any invisible elements—a Hidden form element, a comment tag, an imagemap, a floating box, or any other GoLive placeholder which the program previews with a tiny icon onscreen but isn't shown in a browser page—the table's measurements may be off. GoLive includes those invisible items as part of its calculations for a table's legal size.

The simple (incredibly simple) but non-obvious solution: select Hide Invisible Items from the View menu. By default, all of these placeholders are categorized as Invisible Items, and are swept off the screen but remain in the code. To change the set of Invisible Items or create a new set for just this purpose, see page 78.

Tip: Offsite Graphics (Images)

Many Web sites offer affiliate or click-through links that include graphics. Instead of providing you with a graphic itself, they offer up a small bundle of HTML they tell you to insert in your page. It's confused at least one reader that after pasting this HTML successfully, the image doesn't load.

GoLive only previews local content in the Layout Editor. To view the image that the Web site provided to you in the HTML, which is actually stored on their site or a partner's, preview the page in a browser. The browser should successfully retrieve the image over the Internet. If it doesn't, check that you pasted the HTML correctly.

Tip: Where's the XML Editor (Markup)

We weren't sure if we emphasized strongly enough that the XML editing functions found in GoLive 5 disappeared in GoLive 6. You're not missing them; they're just not there any more. Of course, simultaneously, GoLive 6 uses XML to store a number of its internal settings. Go figure.

Tip: Levels of SQL Access (Dynamic Content)

We've already discovered that GoLive 6 users have bumped into a permission issue with MySQL databases and GoLive's Dynamic Content feature. Each user of a MySQL (or any SQL) database is assigned certain privileges. A user can be assigned read-only access to a given database or even a single table in a database, which allows them to create dynamic pages, but not to create, delete, or modify records. If you're using the record changing features in GoLive 6 to update or add records in a database, make sure you have these permissions from the database administrator before you go nuts troubleshooting the problem from the GoLive side.

Index

Page numbers in **bold** refer to tips.

G

P

<P> tag, 109–110, **364–365**
padding images, 139–140, **140**
page breaks in diagrams, 470, 487, 509
page counts, 82–83
page elements, adding to pages, 5
Page icon
   changing page background color, **194**
   displaying Page Inspector, 73
   frames and frame sets, **270**
   overview, 67
   for pages with frames, **70**
Page Inspector. *See also* Diagram Page and Object Inspectors
   ColorSync tab, 76
   creating Components, 562–563
   displaying, 67, 73
   HTML tab, 75–76
   margin settings, 75
   Page tab, 74–75
page layout. *See* layout
Page tab
   diagram Page Inspectors, 468–469
   File Inspector, 529–530
   Page Inspector, 74–75
page titles
   default page title problem, **67, 74**
   editing, **529**
   search engines and, **74**
Page Up, Page Down keys, **99**
pages. *See also* files
   adding page elements, 5
   adding to mapped sites, 505–506, **506**
   changing background color, **194**
   converting HTML to scripting languages, 386–387
   creating, 4
   creating based on Template regions, 303–304, **304**

   creating for Dynamic Content, 385–386
   creating thumbnails, 536–547
   detaching Templates from pages, 306–307
   in diagrams (*See* pages in diagrams)
   entering and formatting text, 4–5
   generator meta tag, 29
   GoLive page management, 546
   Head section, 60
   loading automatically, 90
   page title, editing, **529**
   redirecting, 90, 540–541, 729–730, 743
pages in diagrams. *See also* diagrams
   adding to diagrams, 464–467
   converting to sections, 474
   Create From option, 469
   default directory for new items, 468, **469**
   links between items, 473
   master items, **461**, 467, 487
   Page Inspectors (*See* Diagram Page and Object Inspectors)
   relationships between items, **457**, 465, 466, **466**
Pages with Inaccurate Titles option, Site Reports tab, **67**
palettes. *See also names of specific palettes*
   docking and undocking, 13, 15
   hiding and showing, 14
   popout menus, 15
   reordering in groups, **13**
   resizing, 15
   super palette, **14**
Palettes palette, 198
panning in site maps, 463
Panorama pane, 464, 486, 504
Par tag, 103, 795
paragraph breaks, 96–97
paragraph formatting
   address format, 110

   aligning images, 142–145, **143, 144–145**
   block indents, 112
   carrying between paragraphs, **117**
   heading levels, 110
   HTML styles, 126
   lists, 114–115
   paragraph-related CSS selectors, 798–799
   paragraph styles, 125, **126**, 127, 129
   preformatted text, 110
   spaces between paragraphs, 109–110
   table alignment, **221**
   text alignment, 111–112
paragraph regions, 301
paragraph-related CSS selectors, 798–799
paragraph styles, 125, **126**, 127, 129
_parent frame target, 286
parent objects, diagrams, **457**
parentheses in regular expressions, 663
Password Action, 748
password fields, 333, **333**, 401, 736
password generator, 748
passwords. *See also* security
   Caps Lock key and, **641**
   FTP or WebDAV servers, 46, 591, **592**
   Keychain feature, **592**, 827
   Password Action, 748
   password fields, 333, **333**, 401, 736
   password generator, 748
   PDF files, **530**
   saving, **592**
pasting. *See* copying and pasting
Path icon, 518
paths
   displaying, 518, **518**
   Path icon, 518
   specifying in URL Getter, 72–73

U

V

Keep in Touch!

We improve our books by listening to readers, so stay in touch! Your feedback is valuable, and as you read through this book, you'll see many mentions of questions from readers that we answer in this edition, or suggestions provided by you all that we try to incorporate. We try to answer all the email we get, although a prompt answer isn't always possible.

We'd also recommend you hop on our moderated email list, which you can subscribe to via http://realworldgolive.com. This list is full of sophisticated GoLive users who share their questions and solutions for using the program to create their designs. The same is true of the Adobe Forums, where tech support and fellow users help out (http://www.adobe.com/support/forums/main.html).

Here's how to reach us:

Snail mail:
7300 E. Green Lake Dr. N., Suite 200
Seattle, WA 98115-5304
Fax (206) 528-2999

Email
authors@realworldgolive.com

—*Jeff Carlson, Never Enough Coffee creations, http://necoffee.com
& Glenn Fleishman, Unsolicited Pundit, http://glennf.com*